RECORDS OF THE
BOROUGH OF LEICESTER

RECORDS
OF THE BOROUGH
OF LEICESTER

Volume VI

THE CHAMBERLAINS' ACCOUNTS 1688–1835

Edited by

G. A. CHINNERY

KEEPER OF ARCHIVES, LEICESTER MUSEUMS

Published under the Authority of the
Leicester City Council

LEICESTER UNIVERSITY PRESS
1967

Printed at The Broadwater Press
Welwyn Garden City, Herts
for the
Leicester University Press

7185 1069 0

© LEICESTER CORPORATION 1967

CONTENTS

Note: The abbreviation R.B.L. indicates "Records of the Borough of Leicester, volume V", with reference to the appropriate item.

INTRODUCTION

The Chamberlains and their accounts

A N explanation of the preservation and publication of the Borough Records of Leicester and of their use by scholars was given in the Introduction to Volume V of this series (pp. xi–xii, xvi). The present volume is the second devoted to the period between 1688 and 1835. The first dealt with the decisions of the Town's governing bodies; the meetings of the Aldermen and Common Councilmen in Common Hall as they are recorded in the Hall Books and Papers. They gave a picture of the general working of the Borough and of specific pieces of business. The present volume deals with the financial records of the Borough during the same period.

Practically the only financial records which survive are those of the Borough's Chamberlains. The origin of the office of the Borough Chamberlains in Leicester is dealt with in Mrs A. M. Woodcock's article "Mr. Treasurer, Leicester, before 1835", printed in *Local Government Finance*, September 1954. In 1376 the first Chamberlains were appointed just after the Town obtained a lease of the bailiwick. This extended the Town's financial activity considerably and the task was too extensive for the Mayor to continue carrying it out alone. The question of confidence and trust may also have arisen, for one Chamberlain was ostensibly appointed for the Town and one for the Mayor.

The activities and responsibilities of the Chamberlains steadily increased and when, in 1601, the parchment roll on which they kept their accounts had grown to a length of about 12 feet the medieval format was changed to a series of paper sheets (10″ × 15″) filed, exchequer style, across their heads. This style continued until 1773, after which they were entered in ordinary paper books (13½″ × 10″). At present, the pre-1773 accounts are bound up in groups of, usually, four years each; after 1773 each year has a separate book. The changes in format did not, however, involve any changes either in the method of keeping the accounts or of their auditing. The Chamberlains' job was an unpopular one, for expenses had to be met out of the Chamberlains' own resources until the rents and other revenues could be collected. A small float from the former Chamberlains helped, but as the office was for one year only there was no chance to accumulate a reserve either of cash or of expertise. As a result the office was generally laid on the most junior and inexperienced members of the Corporation. They naturally followed as exactly as possible the precedents set by their predecessors and the system was virtually unchanged from the fourteenth century, a simple charge and discharge. The audit was similarly traditional. Each year, usually in March–May, a group of about twenty-four auditors (it varied slightly), chosen almost equally from the two companies of Aldermen and Common Councilmen, was appointed to audit the accounts of the preceding year. Quite often the auditing would spread over a long period, and it might be well over a year, sometimes several years, before the Chamberlains were finally relieved of their responsibilities. As only at that late date was the final balance determined the Chamberlains were reluctant to hand over a float to their successors which might subsequently have to be recalled to balance the books. The successors, therefore, had to start their term of office using their own resources. Only in 1782 was it ordered that the outgoing Chamberlains should hand over £100 as an advance. Naturally, this primitive system, in which the only continuity was in the hands of the permanant officials, principally the Town Clerk, led to abuses. Even the appointment of a professional Land Steward in 1794 only relieved the Chamberlains of the new business which was created, first, by changes in leasing the South Fields, and later, by their enclosure. The Chamberlains seem to have done their best, but the growing complexities of their job during the period, combined with its amateur status, its short duration, and their junior position in the Corporation, led to a chaotic situation. By 1835 it is very doubtful whether the Chamberlains' accounts represent anything like a full picture of the Corporation's financial activity, its resources, or its indebtedness. Indeed, the alleged mismanagement, and the use of Charity funds (principally Sir Thomas White's loan charity) and corporate moneys to influence parliamentary elections, particularly in 1826, all helped the radical arguments which led up to the passing of the Corporate Funds Act in 1832. The Report of the Commissioners on Municipal Corporations states: "as administrators of the public funds it is impossible to speak of the corporate authorities except in terms of unqualified censure". The Corporation did not share the Commissioners' viewpoint or their conception of its rights and duties, but even if they had, it would have been impossible for the Chamberlains to realize them. By 1835 the financial system was a shell and its frailty amply justified its reform by the New Corporation. A system designed to deal with simple responsibilities in a population of two or three thousand, which had survived into an age when too much was expected of it in a population of over forty thousand, was swept away and replaced by a recognizably modern system of finance committee, committee responsibility, and double-entry book-keeping.

The Corporation's Revenues

Most of the revenues the Chamberlains received were the rents from properties owned by the Corporation. There seems to have been no regular raising of a rate by the Corporation for general purposes, though occasionally a special-purpose rate was levied. In 1759, a by-law allowed two Pump Reeves to levy a rate for the upkeep of the town pumps "as often as need shall require" (R.B.L. no. 842). However, no assessments or levy returns survive. The Borough Justices, composed normally of the Mayor and four last past mayors, levied a Borough Rate for matters connected with the Gaol and House of Correction, the prosecution and apprehension of felons, the Coroners' Inquests, salaries of prison chaplains, and like matters, appointing a Borough Treasurer for administering the money (according to 12 G. II c. 29 and 13 G. II c. 18) from about 1769, though no accounts have survived. The rate was levied by the Justices demanding orally a certain proportion of each parish's Poor Levy which was handed over to the Treasurer by the Overseers. "It was not made by the Borough Justices at their Sessions, only by verbal order or warrant to the Chief Constable out of Sessions." Under pressure of public opinion the Justices began to announce in the newspapers a general statement of the money and its application from about 1817 onwards, usually once a year, but not every year. Expenditure varied but was normally around £2,000 per annum. This money was applied to the preservation of law and order only and made no contribution to the town's general administrative expenses. The whole of its ordinary running costs hinged, therefore, on the ownership of property. Earlier periods had seen considerable accessions to this, particularly the property granted under the 1589 Charter much of which had been owned by the suppressed religious houses in the town.

The Corporation owned, from antiquity, some property scattered in various parts of the town and South Fields, and this was massively increased when they acquired by the 1589 Charter many of the properties, chief rents, fee farm rents, tithes, and obits belonging to the dissolved College of the Annunciation of St Mary in the Newarke, St Margaret's Guild, the College of St Mary de Castro, and the Corpus Christi Guild. In the early seventeenth century there were several additions; in 1606 more of the St Mary de Castro land was bought, in 1613 Leicester Grange, in 1624 land from Lord Spencer, in 1625 Freake's Grounds, and in 1635 Castle Mills. In 1614 the incorporation of the Newarke Hospital in the name of the Mayor, Bailiffs, and Burgesses brought a desired, if dubiously acquired, property under their control. After 1635 there were few acquisitions and none of major importance. Most of the improvements in revenue in the eighteenth century came from raising rents or from rearrangement of existing property. In 1777 land in the South Fields was rearranged, the larger farms being let at as much as £2 10s. 0d. per acre per year. In 1804 the South Fields were eventually enclosed, and from then on the Corporation sold off plots for building at enhanced prices, though most were sold to members of the Corporation and it is doubtful if they paid the full market value.

Other sources of revenue were from the admission fines for freemen and from the letting of stalls and shops. Though the entry fine for a freeman who had served his apprenticeship was low (usually 10s. 0d.), strangers would pay £30 or more (R.B.L. no. 525), and these strangers' fines made a significant contribution to the revenues in some years.

By ancient right the Corporation owned the Market Places and charged rent for the stalls and shops therein. They occasionally leased the whole of the Shambles to a contractor who could sub-let (1702, 1727), although they still controlled the rent levels for the sub-tenants (R.B.L. no. 443).

The very fixity of its sources of income gave the Corporation little room to manœuvre to meet any exceptional circumstance. Fortunately in the early part of the period exceptional circumstances were rare, and it is only towards the end of the eighteenth century, with the price rises associated with the war with France, that the system really comes under severe strain. Its inadequacy to meet changing conditions forced the Corporation into expedients such as mortgaging all its lands for £10,000 in 1829, largely to meet the cost of the election of 1826, and this reinforced the political objections to the Corporation's close and self-perpetuating hold on the town's affairs. The Corporation could, by the 1830s, be held to be not only corrupt but inept as well.

The South Fields' Accounts

There were a number of attempts to enclose the open fields of St Mary's parish, known as the South Fields, from 1708 onwards (R.B.L. no. 191), but although the Corporation managed to have the area let as large farms it was not until 1803 (R.B.L. no. 1285) that they applied for the Act which was passed in 1804. The enclosure took place in practice between 1805 and 1807, under the superintendence of a Committee appointed on 25 December 1804. The account book of their activity survives and, as the enclosure so greatly altered the finances of the Corporation and the physical development of the town, it seemed appropriate to print it in full.

Presentation

It will be clear that the decision to attempt publication of accounts over a period of 150 years presents great difficulties. Indeed, it has not been attempted on this scale for any comparable series of borough accounts. With no precedents for such publication a number of experiments were tried and discarded, some on grounds of principle, some on grounds of practicability. The basic problem was to present them without importing so high a degree of subjectivity as to falsify them. Two extreme approaches might be typified: by selecting a few items from every year, or by reducing the whole to an historically analysed set of trends and conclusions. Both of these simple solutions appeared inappropriate where the aim was as far as possible to let the accounts speak for themselves. It was also quite impossible to publish all the accounts in full. The procedure finally decided on was to print certain years in full, and to provide a fairly detailed statistical summary of all the accounts year by year. A twenty-year gap between the years printed in full appeared reasonable, giving the first and last years of the period and six intermediate staging points. To these are added the separate accounts for the enclosure expenses of the South Fields incurred in 1805–7 (R.B.L. nos. 1314, 1317, 1616). This part of the task was relatively straightforward. The summaries, forming the second part of the book, though briefer, have occupied far more time and labour. A full account of the method of compression and presentation chosen precedes the tables of summaries on pp. 445–9. Briefly, however, each section into which the Chamberlains divided their accounts has been allocated a code number, and the total of receipts or expenditure under each section is given. As continuity rather than change is the keynote, the changes only are indicated, with a brief explanation of the causes of the change in the notes. Because compression has had to be so great, readers are advised to pay very careful attention to the full explanations before using the summaries.

The Chamberlains, keeping their accounts rigidly to a precedent, divided them first into sections dealing with the Receipts, the Payments, and the Supers. For the first part of the period a separate section dealt with the charities on a receipt and payment basis, though after 1729 these were drawn in to the main body of the accounts. The Supers were sums, usually rents, which were admitted to be due to the Corporation but, for one reason or another, were not collected that year, the debtors having the amount remitted. They were apparently entered to check the fidelity of the Chamberlains and to record the acknowledgement of indebtedness.

The whole volume represents an attempt to make eighteenth- and early nineteenth-century town accounts available in a full and systematic form, and it is hoped that it will encourage other authorities and boroughs to follow and improve on this piece of pioneering.

Conventions

In the years printed in full the following conventions have been used. As far as possible the transcripts are made without alterations either of spelling, punctuation, or capitalization. However, contractions have been extended and names given in full where they are known. Letters on the half line have been dropped for ease of printing so that 2nd becomes 2nd and so forth. The contractions y^e, y^t, y^m, are expanded as "the", "that", "them", and wch as "which".

Editorial notes are included in square brackets, and the extent of text to which they refer is indicated by asterisks; thus [*Item struck out in original] shows that in the original all the matter between the two foregoing asterisks has been deleted. An asterisk which occurs in the original has been indicated by a double dagger ‡.

Matter which in the original is out of the main body in the margins has been brought in with angle brackets; thus ⟨These two items received by the Mayor⟩ indicates that the comment is in the margin in the original. Items between daggers † are bracketed together in the original.

For easy reference the code numbers, used in the summaries to identify each section, and described in the "Explanations of the Summaries and the Code Numbers", pp. 445–9, have been placed in the running heads and carried in bold type into the text of the accounts printed in full.

Acknowledgements

As this volume is the second in the series it represents a continuing effort on the part of the Museums, Libraries, and Publicity Committee of the City Council. The General Purposes Committee have continued to allocate the money required for publication in spite of severe financial pressure on their resources. Mrs B. H. Waters, who played so large a part in typing and proof-reading the earlier volume, did even more for this in preparing the financial tables and transcribing entries. Much of the detailed work in the book is hers, though she left the Museum for another post before it actually went to press. Her place, as assistant to the editor, was taken by Miss M. M. Parry, who has retyped, helped to read proofs, and compiled the index. Mr T. A. Walden, M.SC., F.M.A., and Professor Jack Simmons have again given valuable help and encouragement. A book is a co-operative effort, but errors and imperfections are bound to remain. They must be my responsibility.

G. A. C.

THE CHAMBERLAINS' ACCOUNTS
1688–1835

CHAMBERLAINS' ACCOUNTS
1688/9

The accompt of Mr Thomas Simpson and Mr Joseph Roberts Chamberlaines of the Burrough of Leicester in the yeare of the Mayoralty of Mr William Bentley (vizt) from the Feast day of St Michael the Archangell 1688 untill the Feast day St Michaell the Archangell next Following (vizt) for one whole yeare.

1   Rents of Assize and Rents at will within the
                 Burrough of Leicester aforesaid.

Mr George Beckett and Mr John Goodall for one yeares Rent for the Sheep pens in their occupacion by Lease per annum	24	0	0
Mr William Thomas head Schoolmaster for one yeares Rent for the Schoolehouse payable at Michaelmas onely per annum			6
The heires or Executors of John Harrison Felmonger for certaine Lands in the Northgates now or late in the tenure or occupacion of Robert Tyler heretofore one Gaddesbies land due and payable at the Feast day of St Michael the Archangell yearely		1	9
Mr John Burdett for the Chamber over the East gates .		10	0
The heires of Robert Blunt deceased for the Butclose sold heretofore to Mr Thomas Blunt in Fee farme in the occupacion of John Loseby per annum		10	0
A Messuage or Tenement now divided at the neither end of Belgrave gate heretofore the land of Thomas Headley and now of Arthur Noone per annum	1	0	0
The heires or Executors of Thomas Norrice and Andrew Wheatecraft for a garden or peice of ground in the Senvy gate lately built upon in their occupacion per annum		2	6
Mr John Newton Vicar of St Martin Leicester for a chamber belonging to the Towne hall and now used with the vicaridg house adjoyncing to the Liberary with a doore comeing out at the topp of the house of office stares at will per annum		2	6

3

The Right Honorable the Earle of Devon for a Close of pasture ground whereupon lately stood a Messuage or Tenement lyeing in the Northgates late the Land of George Tatam per annum   13   4

The said Earle for a peice or parcell of ground adjoyneing to the backside of a Messuage or Tenement late William Fletchers heretofore sold to John Tatam in Fee farme per annum   4

The heires or Executors of the said William Fletcher for a messuage or Tenement and backside late in the occupacion of John Moore heretofore sold to the said John Tatam in Fee Farme per annum   1   8

The heires or Executors of John Erp for a peice of ground in the parish of St Nicholas now built upon late in the occupacion of William Adcock heretofore sold to his graund Father in Fee Farme per annum   6   8

Thomas Wallin for a Tenement in the Northgate late the land of Robert Freer per Annum   1   0   0

Mr Edmund Johnson Dyer for a peice of ground called the water laggs heretofore in the Occupacion of John Kirk & Richard Turner per annum   6   8

The heires or Executors of Thomas Cartwright for a peice of ground at the south end of But Close per annum   4

2   Rents in the Country

John or Roger palmer for lands meadowes & pastures in Gilmorton heretofore the land of John Sprigg and now or late of one Edward Whetehead per annum   3   4

Mr Carrington for lands in Much Ashby alias greate Ashby heretofore the Land of the said John Sprigg per annum   6

The heires of Mr Robert pawley late of South Croston for certaine lands and Tenements in Scraptoft once Mr Masons land & heretofore Simpkins and Taylers of Whetstone and now or late in the Occupacion of Mathew Hubbard per annum   6

3   Rents of the Graunges with the appurtenances and the four yard Land whereof Two yard Land is called Weightmans Land, the Towne purchased in Fee Simple and the other Twoyard Land is called Archers land and the halfe yard Land was purchased by the Corporacion of the Lord Spencers in Fee Simple as Followeth

	£	s	d
Mr Edmund Sutton for parte of the Newark Graunge and four yard Land in his occupacion per annum ⟨Q.x⟩	29	0	0
Of him more for the Graunge Barne and the yards thereunto belonging, and the moyety or one halfe part of three yard Land late in the occupacion of Francis Coultman per annum ⟨Q.x⟩	13	0	0
Henry Coulson for the other moyety or halfe part with thappurtenances of the said three yard Land lyeing in the Southfeilds etc. per annum	10	0	0
Mr philipp Abney for four yard Land per Annum . .	26	13	4
John pratt for Three yard land there per annum . . ⟨—out of Mr Pratts 3 yard Land is paid the Erle of Devons guift of £6 per annum⟩	14	0	0
Mr John Wilkins for three yard Land and an halfe per annum	23	0	0
Mr Thomas Ward for three yard Land per annum . .	20	0	0
Mr Joseph Cradock for the Newarke water corne mills & the windemill thereto belonging by Lease for one and Twenty yeares per annum ⟨£1 paid more by him this yeare & for the residue of 21tie yeares—£16 per annum⟩	15	0	0
Mr Richard Townsend For Gosling Close per annum .	13	6	8

5   Beadhouse Meadowes

	£	s	d
Mr Thomas Hartshorne for a meadow ground near the Newark mills per annum ⟨Md. £5 hereof to charitable uses being the guift of Mr John & William Standley⟩	5	0	0
John Mason the elder for another meadow ground there per annum	13	0	0

B

10 Other Rents for lands & Tenements which the Maior Bayliffs & Burgesses hold in fee Farme to them & their Successors belonging to the Hospitall of St John & St Leanard in the Burrough of Leicester heretofore belonging to the Colledg of the Newark of Leicester

10a   In the North gates

The Messuage or Tenement late in the occupacion of William palmer Cobler at will per annum	13	4
The heires or Executors of Mrs Anne Boadman for the north mills per annum	20 0	0
Anne Morrice for a Tenement there per annum . .	4	0

10b   In Senvy gate

Jane Hunt for a Tenement there at will per annum . .	3	4
John Stevenson for another Tenement there per annum .	3	4
Mr William Ward for a Messuage or Tenement there late William Cookes in Fee farme per annum	5	0
Widdow Wale for a Messuage or Tenement neare the north gates in her occupacion		10
The heires or Executors of William Biggs for a Messuage or Tenement there per annum	1	0
John Atwood for a Tenement scituate in the Soare Lane late Granham's land		2
The heires or Executors of Mrs Twickton & Thomas Gorton for a peice of Ground sometimes a Dunghill now built upon heretofore in the occupacion of William Rudyard scituate in the said Soare Lane in feefarme per annum	2	0

10d   Within the Northgates

The Overseers of the poore of the parish of All Saints for a house with the appurtenances late in the occupacion of Jane Jennard Joyce Tafts & Francis Tayler at will per annum	6	0
The heires of Mr Robert Hickling for a Messuage or Tenement one the South side of All Saints Church late Mr Hicklings land in the occupacion of Jacob Bothomley in Fee farme per annum	1 10	0

	£	s
Mary Dyer widow for a Messuage or Tenement late widow Kimberleyes in fee Farme per annum	6	0
The heires or executors of William Stevenson for a Messuage or Tenement in the high Street now or late in the occupacion of John Coleman per annum	5	0
The heires or Executors of Thomas Drake for a shopp and garden in the high Street heretofore in the occupacion of William Ludlam & now or late in the occupacion of Thomas Hopkins in Fee farme per annum	4	0
A house and Garden late in the occupacion of William Graunger & heretofore of one Henry Trowell per annum	4	6
Another Tenement heretofore in the occupacion of William Ludlam Chaffer dresser & heretofore sold to the said William Ludlam	2	10
Thomas Newton for certaine Leyes in the horse faire per annum	1 0	0

10e   In the Southgates

	£ s	d
Thomas Morton for a house heretofore Thomas Warners now in the said Thomas Mortons occupacion per annum	1 0	0
John Hardy for a Messuage or Tenement at the Corner end of Hangman Lane late in the occupacion of Mrs Elizabeth Chamberlaine widow per annum	16	0

10f   In Burges meadow

	s	d
The heires or Executors of Mr George Abney for a peice of meadow ground called the shield late Mr Mortons Land in feefarme per annum	16	0
Of them more for two acres of Meadow ground heretofore Mr Mortons Land per annum	13	4

10g   In Swines markett

	s	d
The heires or Executors of John Humphries or John Warbertons heretofore called the kings head heretofore Agnes Ortons Land in fee farme per annum	18	0

10h   In Parchment Lane

	s	d
The heires or Executors of Thomas Redley for a Tenement heretofore in the occupacion of Thomas pestell in feefarme per annum	13	4

10i In Saturday Markett

Mr Richard Mansfeild for a messuage or Tenement now divided into Two Tenements in the occupacions of Mr Robert Hobson & the Executors of Nicholas Sherwin in fee farme per annum	1	3	4
Robert Stevenson for a house & shop in the occupacion of John Cornewall in fee farme per annum			8

10j In Loaseby Lane

Mr William Orton Mercer for a Tenement or garden late Mr Folzers Land heretofore sold to Richard piercivall in Fee farme per annum		10	0
The heires of Mr Edward Palmer for a Tenement in the Swines Markett late Mr Benningtons Land in the Occupacion of Michael Bonshaw in Fee farme per annum		6	0
Mr William Southwell for Two houses and a garden heretofore sold to John Birley in Fee Farme per annum	1	6	0
Mr Jackson for a Tenement late widow Harlowes heretofore James Seeles in fee farme per annum		12	0
More of him for a little peice of ground adjoyneing to the said garden at Midsumer onely		A damask Rose	
Richard Yates for a Tenement and backside late in Richard Dawsons occupacion at will per annum	1	0	0
John Dallaway for a Tenement and yard heretofore in the occupacion of Valentine Davie at will per annum		10	0
John Davy for a messuage or Tenement late new built in his occupacion in fee farme per annum		10	0

10k In Gallowtree gate

Widow Dyson for a house late in the occupacion of Samuel Cooper late Mr John Wadlands Land in Fee farme per annum		8	0
More for a Messuage or Tenement comonly called the white horse in the occupacion of John Mason junior in Fee farme per annum	1	0	0
The heires or Executors of Mr Edward Palmer for one yard Land lyeing in St Margaretts feild late alsoe the Land of Mr John Wadland & enjoyed with the said messuage or Tenement in Fee farme per annum		15	0

10l In Gallowtree gate on the west side

Randolph Butler for a Messuage or Tenement neare the Roundhill heretofore the Land of Mr Edmund Cradock heretofore sold to John Beresford now in the occupacion of Thomas Lawrence in Fee farme per annum ⎫ 10 0

John Pollard for a Messuage or Tenement heretofore sold to Mr Edmund Cradock late the Land of Michael Pawley adioyneing to the northside of the angell now in the occupacion of the said John Pollard in Fee farme per annum ⎫ 4 0

The heires or Executors of Mr Edward Palmer for a messuage or Tenement in Fee farme per annum ⎫ 1 0 0

10m In Belgrave gate

Mr Thomas Palmer for a garden at the neither end of Belgrave gate in his occupacion in Fee farme per annum ⎫ 12 0

Mr William Ward for a Messuage or Tenement in the same streete late in the occupacion of Richard Yates Tayler in Fee farme per annum ⎫ 13 4

The heires or Executors of Thomas Glister for a Tenement late Robert Fletchers in fee farme per annum ⎫ 1 0 0

Thomas Ward Cordwayner for a Tenement late Ralph Simpsons adioyneing to the unicorne on the North side thereof in Fee Farme per Annum ⎫ 15 0

James Annis for a Messuage or Tenement on the east side of the same late the Land of Richard Ward Baker in Fee farme per annum ⎫ 18 0

The Churchwardens of the parish of St Margarett Leicester for a peice of ground lyeinge in the Cow pasture there in Fee farme per annum ⎫ 8 0

10n In the Countrey

James Winstanley Esquire for a Close lands leyes and pasture grounds in Braunston in the County of Leicester now or late in the occupacion of Joseph Roberts per annum ⎫ 12 8

Nathaniel Ball for a Croft or Close & one yard Land in Hinckley with thappurtenances in his occupacion in Fee Farme per Annum ⎫ 15 0

Mr Peter Overin for a certaine parcell of Lands or Leyes called Kimpton hill and one yard Land sold to one Mr Anthony Culverwell lyein in the Lordshipp of Belgrave in the County of Leicester in Fee farme per annum		9	0
The heires or Executors of Sir Thomas Noell Baronet for a Messuage or Tenement and one yard Land in Kirby Mallery in Fee farme per annum		6	8
*The heires or Executors of Mr Edward Palmer for a Messuage or Tenement late Mr Beningtons Land in the occupacion of John Hewett per annum	1	0	0*
[*Item struck out in original.]			
Thomas Storer of Thurshington for one yard Land there in his occupacion in Fee farme per annum		6	8
William Tompson of houghton for a certaine parcell of Land or meadow ground late William Hubbards in Fee Farme per annum		1	8
Anne Farmer of (blank) widow for certaine Lands in Houghton in the occupacion of Francis Walton in Fee farme per annum		5	0
Thomas Chamberlaine of Rearesby for a Messuage or Tenement there in his occupacion in Fee farme per annum		17	0
William Holding of Seagrave for a Close & Croft there in his occupacion late the Land of William Hubbard in Fee Farme per annum		2	0
George James of Barkby for certaine Lands there in his occupacion per annum		8	0
The heires or Executors of Thomas Dannett Esquire for severall Lands leyes and hades in the west feilds of Leicester with thappurtenances in the occupacion of Mr Joseph Cradock in Fee farme per annum		4	0
George Ashby of Quenby Esquire for a Messuage or Tenement in Hungerton now or late in the occupacion of Elias Marshall heretofore sold to Sir Thomas Cave Knight in Fee farme per annum	1	10	0
The heires of George Sheifeild of Siston for the mills there called Siston Mills and a house in Siston with thappurtenances heretofore in the occupacion of Robert Burbage & heretofore sold to the said Thomas Cave in Fee farme per annum	3	6	8

11a Other Rents for lands & Tenements parcell of the Towne obiit Lands St Margaretts Guild & parcell of the Fee farme Rents heretofore demised by Queene Elizabeth to Mr Hawke & Bates

Mr Marmion Gee for the ground heretofore belonging to the house of Mr Nurse Mr Watts William Hall & Francis Cole ruined in the late wars the ground being since sold to Mr Dannett Abney in Fee farme per annum ⟨Md. 40s of the whole rent is paid to charitable uses⟩	13	4
The heires or assignes of Mr Edward Barwell Clerk for a house with thappurtenances neare the Newarkgates in the occupacion of Richard Mawson in fee farme per annum	10	0
Mrs Martha Coates for a Messuage or Tenement called the white Lyon heretofore Mr Ives Land now in the occupacion of Edward Wagstaffe in fee farme per annum	10	0
Thomas Hartshorne senior for a Messuage or Tenement late William Campions and James Fox and late the Land of Robert Hartshorne in Fee Farme per annum	1 0	0
The heires of Mr George Abney for the ground belonging to Two Tenements late Paul Abneyes gentleman and the ground late belonging to a Messuage or Tenement knowne by the name of the Signe of the Bull ruined in the rebellious warrs and now built upon now in the occupacion of Mrs Clay widdow & others in Fee Farme per annum	1 6	8
The said Thomas Hartshorne for the ground lately belonging to the Grey hound and another late in the tenure of Henry Thorp heretofore Mr James Andrewes Land ruined in the said late warrs & now built upon in Fee Farme per annum	1 0	0

11b In the Swines Markett

Mr William Deane for a Messuage or Tenement late Mr Murfins Land in the occupacion of Richard Springthorp & others in fee farme per annum	1 0	4

11c In or neare Belgrave gate

Mr William Deane for a Tenement with the appurtenances next the corner of Humberstone gate now divided into two Tenements heretofore sold to William Hunt in Fee Farme per annum	1 1	0

The heires or Executors of Robert Martin of Thurmaston
for six tenements lat Mr Tatams in the occupacion of } 12 0
Richard Heyford & others in Fee Farme per annum

James Cartwright for a Tenement called the Lamb and
one Close or Backside thereunto adjoyneing late the Land
of Mr Thomas Blunt heretofore Sold to George Coates } 1 6 8
now in the occupacion of the said James Cartwright and
John Wellinger in Fee Farme per annum

The heires or Executors of Edward Smith Carpinter for a
Messuage or Tenement in Fee farme per annum } 1 0 0

Robert Burbage Carpinter for a house with the appurtenances in his occupacion in fee farme per annum } 12 0

Thomes Woolleston for a Tenement called the Cock in his
occupacion in fee farme per annum } 6 8

Richard Moseby for a Messuage or Tenement belonging
to the Corporacion at will pcr annum } 1 10 0

The Executors of Hellen Denshire for a Messuage or
Tenement & another in the occupacion of (blank) in Fee } 13 4
farme per annum

11d   In Senvy gate

The heires of William Ball for a Tenement heretofore sold
to Robert Roberts formerly in Tymothy Arnolds occupa- } 5 0
cion in Fee Farme per annum

Richard Scarborrow for a Tenement late in the occupacion of Henry Mugg and John Meacheam per Lease per } 1 0 0
annum in fee farme per annum

William Gamble for a Tenement heretofore in the occupacion of Richard Shilton in Fee farme per annum } 12 0

11e   In Canckstreete

George Steeres for a Tenement in the occupacion of
Thomas Ayres hosier in Fee Farme per annum } 13 4

11f   In St Nicholas and St Maries parish

The heires or Executors of Roger Lewin for a Messuage or
Tenement late John Attons Land now in the occupacion } 13 0
of Widdow Lewin in Fee Farme per Annum

Mr Thomas Palmer at the Crane for a Tenement neare
the west bridge in the occupacion of Robert Wilkins in Fee } 1 0 0
farme per annum

12 Other Rents for Lands & Tenements parcell of the Towne & Mannors of Leicester which were lately (amongst other things) given to the Maior Bayliffes and Burgesses & their Successors in Fee farme per annum for ever

Thomas Farlow for a Messuage or Tenement & peice of ground in St Margaretts Church gate late in the occupacion of Christopher Lewick per Lease per annum	I	o	o
Susannah Palmer widow for a peice of ground now built upon in the occupacion of her & John Palmer her son late Mr Tatams Land in Fee Farme per annum		2	6
The heires or Executors of Mr Thomas Wadland for a house & garden thereto belonging called the Armitage neare St James Chappell Close late in the occupacion of George Wadland in Fee farme per annum		I	o
The heires of Mr Edward Palmer for a Tenement with the appurtenances late the Land of William Ing Esquire once Smalleyes Land in fee farme per annum		8	o
The heires or Executors of Mr Samuel Robinson for parte of a peice of ground called the Lyon yard whereupon a house lately stood in fee farme per annum		2	6
Widow Stafford for a Messuage or Tenement & the other parte of the said yard called the Lyon yard in Fee Farme per annum		2	6
The heires or Executors of Mr James Palmer for a peice of ground in the parish of All Saints called the Vineyard in Fee farme per annum		4	o
Mr William Orton Mercer for a Messuage or Tenement & Barne called Senvyes Land Scituate in the Saturday Markett late William Michells Clerk in his & others occupacions in Fee farme per annum	2	o	o
John Maior Esquire for a Close or Croft neare the farme in Fee Farme per annum			6
Daniel ~~George~~ Carr for a peice of ground extending from the senvy gate to the Common Oven in the north gates whereupon a house was built now in his or William Taylors occupacion in Fee Farme per annum		2	6
Ralph Winfeild for a peice of ground neare Frogmire bridg in the north gates now built upon heretofore in the occupacion of Thomas Carr potter in Fee farme per annum		I	o

Richard Hill for a Messuage or Tenement a Corner house in the high Streete heretofore knowne by the name of the flying horse in fee farme per Annum	1	10	0
Thomas Beamount & John Groce for a garden or peice of ground in Deadmans Lane late Mr Tyrringhams Land in fee farme per annum		1	0

13   Other Rents part of Corpus Christi Guild in Leicester heretofore in Mr Archers Collection & now parcell of the Lands & Tenements which the Maior Bayliffs & Burgesses purchased of Queene Elizabeth to them & their Successors

The heires or Executors of Mr Edward Browne for a Messuage or Tenement in the Swines Markett heretofore knowne by the name or Signe of the Crowne in the occupacion of Mr John Cracroft in Fee farme per annum	1	1	8
The heires or Executors of Kenelme Shuttlewood for a Messuage or Tenement in the Swines Markett in the occupacion of Susannah Cooper in fee farme per annum		13	4
John Wildbore for a Messuage or Tenement in Gallowtree gate late in the occupacion of John Kirby in Fee Farme per Annum	1	6	8
The Executors of Thomas Brickhead for a house & peice of ground neare the Frogmire Bridge Leased to Robert Cozens deceased for 41 yeares from Michaelmas 1659 now in the occupacion of Robert Withers per Annum		10	0
George Steeres for a Messuage or Tenement late Thomas Brookesbys in Gallowtreegate in the occupacion of Alice Newton widow & others in fee farme per annum		13	4
Daniell Simpson for a house in his occupacion scituate in the Saturday Markett late the Land of Mr Hugh Watts in Fee Farme per Annum	1	0	0
John Mason junior Baker for another house thereunto adjoyneing late the Land of John Hall Baker & Mr Hugh Watts parte of the said Land in Fee farme per annum	1	0	0
The heires or Executors of Mr Samuel Wanley for a Messuage or Tenement in Holyrood Lane neare St Martins Church late in the occupacion of John Thurman in Fee farme per Annum		6	8

Mr Joseph Cradock for a Messuage or Tenement late Gabriel Caters land Scituate in parchment Lane in the occupacion of Abstinence Pougher in Fee Farme per annum } 16 0

Robert Hutchins of Loughburrough or Mr Clerk of the same for certaine Lands Meadowes & pastures with thappurtenances called Sadlers Land & now or late in the occupacion of Richard Sutton Miller in fee farme per annum } 10 0

Mr(s) John Blunt for a Messuage or Tenement neare the Eastgates late the Land of Mr Robert Blunt her former husband now in the occupacion of Mr Walter Hood in Fee Farme per Annum } 12 0

The heires or Executors of Mr George Rayson for a Chamber & a shop neare the Eastgates heretofore sold to Mr Davy & late the land of Mr Wigley now in the occupacion of Mr Joseph Cradock in Fee farme per annum } 12 0

The heires or Executors of Mr James Palmer for a peice of ground heretofore a Garden now built upon over against the Towne hall heretofore the Land of one Fitch and Coles in the occupacion of Lawrance Cooper in Fee Farme per Annum } 1 0

Mr John Goodall for a Tenement in parchment Lane late Mr William Springthorpes & heretofore in the occupacion of William Bliss in Fee Farme per Annum } 6 8

Thomas Potchen junior of Barkby gentleman for ¾ of a yard Land in Barkby late the Land of Thomas Seele in Fee Farme per Annum } 6 0

George James of Barkby aforesaid for a Croft and ½ yard Land there late Thomas Gibsons Land in Fee farme per Annum } 6 8

Mrs Sarah Bennington for a Messuage or Tenement & Garden in the Swines Markett late Mr Thomas Benningtons Land now in the occupacion of Mr John Goodall in Fee Farme per Annum } 6 0

A house & Garden in St Martins Churchyard in the occupacion of Widdow Wilcocks & others in fee farme per Annum } 13 4

Madam Franks for a Meadow ground in Aylston way late the Land of John Sherman gentleman deceased and heretofore Mr Henry Palmers Land in her occupacion in Fee farme per Annum } 4 0

Mr Perkins of Grantham for certaine Lands & Leyes in Gunnerby late in the occupacion of Thomas Kenelme in fee farme — 6 8

The heires or Executors of Mrs Katherine Henshaw deceased for a Close neare the Cowdrift late Mr Robert Eyricks Land in Fee Farme per annum — 10 0

John Fawsitt Sadler for a shop and other buildings on the Roundhill on the East side thereof in his & widow Wagstaffs occupacion in Fee Farme per Annum — 1 0 0

The heires or Executors of Samuel Marshall for a house & Backside in Applegate Streete heretofore in one Harvies occupacion & once Mr Bennetts Land now in the occupacion of Simon Thorp in Fee Farme per Annum — 1 0

14a Other Rents parcell of the possessions of the Guild called St Margaretts Guild & parcell of the Towne obiit Lands heretofore collected by Arthur Tatam (vizt)

Joseph Birstall Butcher for a Messuage or Tenement in Applegate Street late Henry Coates Land in Fee Farme per Annum — 1 0 0

The heires of Mr Hugh Watts for a Messuage or Tenement in Applegate Streete aforesaid heretofore in the occupacion of Anthony Biggs Baker in Fee farme per Annum — 9 0

Robert Moore for a Corner house in the said Streete late in the occupacion of one James Kirk heretofore in the occupacion of John Witherborne shoemaker in Fee farme per Annum — 6 8

William Storer of Stanton under Bardon for a house with the appurtenances late Mr Southwells Land and now in the occupacion of Robert Heyrick tobaccopipemaker in Fee farme per annum — 10 0

John Cooper Gardiner for a house in the occupacion of (blank) in Feefarme per Annum — 8 0

The heires or Executors of Robert Holcott for a house late John Silbies in the occupacion of Henry Meacham in Fee farme per Annum — 7 0

John Springthorp for a peice of ground now built upon lyeing neare unto a place heretofore called the Maiors old hall neare St Nicholas Church in the occupacion of the said J. Springthorp in fee farme per annum — 3 4

Elizabeth Bruce for a Messuage or Tenement heretofore in the occupacion of James Fletcher and now in the occupacion of widdow Browne in Fee farme per Annum — 14 0

14b In the Southgates

The heires of Mr Barwell Clerk for a house neare the Newarkgates in the occupacion of Richard Mawson in Fee farme per annum — 10 0

The heires or Executors of Robert Hartshone the late Cryer for the ground belonging to Two Messuages ruined in the late warrs sold in fee farme — 10 0

The heires of Mr Thomas Aston or Madam Franks for the ground belonging to Two Messuages one called the Swan with a Barne thereunto belonging both ruined in the late wars in Fee farme per Annum — 1 5 0

Thomas Hartshorne for the ground belonging to the house heretofore in the occupacion of Thomas Palmer Button maker in fccfarme per annum — 10 0

William Storer of Stanton under Bardon for another Tenement late Mr Southwells Land in the occupacion of Robert Heyrick pipemaker in Fee Farme per annum — 10 0

14c In Gallowtree gate

John Vain for a Messuage or Tenement called the Queenes head heretofore Freers Land now in his occupacion in Fee Farme per Annum — 1 6 8

Elizabeth Deakein widow for a Messuage or Tenement knowne by the signe of the Sincque foile in Fee farme per Annum — 2 0 0

Robert Lord for a Messuage or Tenement knowne by the signe of the Bucks head late the land of Bartholomew Hawkeins heretofore sold to widow Alsop in Fee Farme per Annum — 5 0

14d In Humberston gate

The heires or Executors of Mr John Day for a garden with thappurtenances sold to Michael Wulton of Bushby in Fee Farme per Annum — 2 0

14e In Belgrave gate

Thomas Taylor Baker for a Messuage or Tenement in his occupacion in Fee Farme per Annum — 16 0

The heires or Executors of Mr William Browne for a Messuage or Tenement late Johnsons Land in Fee Farme per Annum — 13 4

Mr Walter Hood for a little peice of ground in St Margaretts Parish late in the occupacion of Joseph Wright & Thomas Padman per Lease — 6 8

William Storer of Stanton under Bardon for a Messuage or Tenement late Mr Southwells Land in the occupacion of widow Awmey per Annum — 10 0

Mr Thomas Palmer at the Crane For a Messuage or Tenement late Robert Gambles in Fee Farme per Annum — 18 0

John Fawsitt sadler for another shop and Chamber scituate on the Round Hill in Fee farme per Annum — 1 0 0

Richard Garratt for a Messuage or Tenement late Stevensons Land in Fee farme per Annum — 12 0

The Executors of John Pratt or widow Awmey for two Messuages in their or some of their occupacions in Fee farme per Annum — 1 2 0
    Mr Thomas Ludlam payes 14s

William Mabison for a Messuage or Tenement in his occupacion in Fee Farm per Annum — 6 0

Francis Annis For an Orchard or Garden heretofore sold to George Bluntington in Fee Farme per Annum — 6 0

Richard Garratt for a Messuage or Tenement heretofore sold to John Norrice Butcher in Fee Farme per Annum — 8 0

The heires or Executors of Thomas Chapman Esquire for the ground whereupon lately stood an house called St Johns ruined in the late time of warrs in Fee Farme per Annum — 2 0 2

Parte of the house late Margarett Fletchers in Fee Farme per annum — 5 0
Edward Malson Baker purchased the other parte being 20s per annum

The heires or Executors of Mr Edward Palmer for an Orchard late Mr Ings and heretofore Mr Smallyes land in Fee farm per annum — 2 0

Of them more for a house late Mr Ings now in the occupacion of John Russell in Fee Farme per Annum — 5 0

14f   In Senvy gate

The heires or Executors of William Chamberlaine for a Messuage or Tenement late the land of John Newbold heretofore sold to William Inge now in widow Chamberlaines occupacion in Fee Farme per Annum — 1 0 0

The heires or Executors of Thomas Glister for a house and Garden late Christopher Pratts in the occupacion of John Walker in Fee Farme per annum — 8 0

Widow Tayler for a house being the Townes Land at will per annum — 6 8

Richard Palmer for a house & backeside being the Townes Land at will per annum — 13 4

The heires or Executors of James Palmer for a sponge of ground heretofore belonging to the house now in the occupacion of Richard Palmer per Lease — 8 0

The heires or Executors of Mr John Warberton for a Close called Sallowes Close in Fee Farme per Annum — 5 0

14g   Neare St Margaretts Church

David Deakeins for a peice of ground comonly called St Margaretts bedd late the land of Jane Biggs widow now in his occupacion in Fee Farme per Annum — 6

14h   Other Rents of Mr Wildes Lease

Mr Robert Heyrick for a Close neare the Cowdrift now or late Mr Chamberlaines land in the occupacion of William Page in Fee farme per annum — 13 4

14i   Other Rents parcell of Mr Wilds second Lease

The heires or Executors of Humphry Marshall for a house and garden in Soare Lane neare Redd Cross streete in the occupacion of Thomas Lyquorish in Fee Farme per annum — 6 0

Sir Nathaniell Curson Baronet for a Tenement Orchard garden or peice of ground in the said lane late Brittaines heretofore sold to Hugh Marshall late in the occupacion of Joseph Travell in feefarme per Annum — 2 0

William Higgs of Thurcaston for a house and garden in Belgravegate — 8 0

Mr John Pares for a Close in Archdeacon Lane in St Margaretts parish heretofore sold to John Mabbs in Fee Farme per Annum — 6 8

William Kirk of humberston for a house with thappurten- ances in Humberston aforesaid late the land of Tobias Garthorne in his occupacion in fee farme per Annum — 5 0

Thomas Hastwell Mason for a Messuage or Tenement scituate in Senvygate sold to him and Jane Ward widow in Fee Farme per annum — 1 6 8

The poor people of the Trinity Hospitall for a garden or Orchard neare the Butclose in the occupacion of Robert Renolds in fee farme per Annum — 2 0

Mr Edmund Sutton for a Tenement and Backside there- unto belonging scituate in Belgravegate late the Land of Francis Coates in the occupacion of (blank) in Fee Farme per Annum — 3 4

Thomas Cartwright for a Messuage or Tenement in the Church gate in Fee Farme per Annum — 8 0

Henry Kilby for a house with thappurtenances in Senvy gate heretofore the Land of Thomas Clay in Fee Farme per Annum — 10 0

The heires or Executors of Mr John Warberton for a house in the said street late the land of Thomas Chettleton in Fee farme per Annum — 6 8

The heires or Executors of Mr Edward Palmer for a Close neare Humberston gate heretofore sold to John Rowe & his wife in Fee Farme per Annum — 12 0

15a A Rentall of all the Lands and possessions belonging to the late Colledge of the Blessed Virgin Mary over against the Castle of Leicester & heretofore demised by our Sovereigne Lady Queene Elizabeth to Edward Holt Esquire for 21tie yeares expired at Michaelmas 1606 & by her Majestie graunted to the Major Bay- liffs and Burgesses of Leicester and their successors (amongst other things in Fee farme per annum

The heires or Executors of Thomas Bellamy for a Mes- suage or Tenement in the Swines Markett in Fee Farme per Annum — 6 8

John Winter Felmonger for parte of the Tenement late in the occupacion of widow Linsey and now in the occu- pacion of Martin Beeby in Fee Farme per Annum — 2 0

The heires or Executors of Mrs Katherine Henshaw for a Close lyeing neare Aylston way late the Land of Mr Robert Eyrick in the occupacion of (blank) in Fee Farme per Annum   5   0

The heires or Executors of Thomas Stavely Esquire for a Garden lyeing on the backside of A Messuage or Tenement heretofore knowne by the signe of the Talbott late the land of Mr Hugh Watts now in the occupacion of Mr Thomas Gery in Fee Farme per annum   1   0

Thomas Jackson Clerk for a Tenement in the Soare Lane late land of Mr Edward Wanley in the occupacion of George Bates in Fee Farme per Annum   10   0

Mr William Ward for Two Tenements in Soare lane aforesaid heretofore sold to John Underwood in Fee Farme per Annum   5   0

Mr Gabriell Hill for a Messuage or Tenement in Redcrosse streete and a garden in Chaff lane adjoyneing to the said Tenement late the Land of John folzer heretofore sold to Richard Redley now in the occupacion of Mary Fisher widow in Fee Farme per annum   1   0   0

William Biggs labourer for a Tenement and garden in Soare lane aforesaid heretofore sold to John Lawnder now in the occupacion of widow Smith in Fee Farme per Annum   12   0

The heires or Executors of Robert Atton or David Price for a Tenement and Garden in Fee Farme per Annum   1   6   8

A Garden in Soare lane in the occupacion of John Antill at will per annum   8

Francis Annis for the ground lately belonging to a Tenement in the Southgates ruined in the time of warr & for a Croft sold in fee Farme per annum   16   0

A peice of ground or garden neare Milson lane late in the occupacion of John Burbage heretofore sold to one Cadman in Fee Farme per Annum   4

Mr John Wilkins for the Herbage of St Maryes Churchyard by Lease for one and Twenty yeares from Michaelmas 1689 per Annum   10   0

Mr Marmion Gee for a Close neare the Cowdrift late the land of Mr Sherman heretofore in the occupacion of Edward Hawkes and heretofore sold to Henry Palmer in Fee Farme per Annum   1   0   0

C

Mr George Beckett for the Tith hay of Burgess meadow St Mary Meadow Southfeilds and tithable Meadowes beyond the Newark Mills per Lease per Annum } 5 0 0

Madam Frankes for St James Chappell Close and yard at the neither end thereof neare the Southgate Townsend late the land of the said Mr Sherman heretofore sold to one Mr Simpson in fee farme per Annum } 1 6 8

George Wilkinson for a house and garden in Soare lane late in the occupacion of (blank) Clayton in Fee Farm per Annum ⟨Q.⟩ } 12 0

Elizabeth Browne widow For a house and garden and backside in the parish of St Nicholas per Lease For 21tie yeares per Annum } 2 0 0

John Denshire for a house and garden in the same parish heretofore the Land of Anthony Biggs Baker sold in Fee farme per annum } 1 0 0

George Sackeverell Esquire for the tiths and vicariall Tents & other Dutes belonging to Dannetts Hall whelch Hall Mary Mills and Holms by Lease for 21tie yeares from Michaelmas 1669 per annum } 5 0 0

The heires or Executors of Mr John Heyrick for Tith & vicariall Tents of all those grounds heretofore belonging to Dannetts Hall by Lease as aforesaid per Annum } 2 0 0

William Rudings Esquire for all the vicariall Tents herbages and other duties belonging to the said colledg payable out of all the Lands ground, Meadowes Pastures and parcell of Land belonging to the westcoates by lease as aforesaid per annum } 5 0 0

The heires or Executors of Nathaniel Syms for a garden in Senvy gate late woodfords land in Fee Farme per Annum } 1 0

Mr Mathew Symonds for a peice or parcell of ground or garden place sometimes a wellyard on the backside of an house late Robert Griffins in Fee Farme per Annum } 1 4

Mr Thomas Palmer at the Crane for a Close neare St Margretts Cowpasture heretofore Mr Bennetts Land in Fee Farm per Annum } 3 4

The Heires or Executors of Mr Edmund Townsend for a parcell of ground late Mr Lawes of Wigston lyeing in or neare silver street at will per Annum } 2 0

The heires or Executors of Mrs Katherine Henshaw for parte of a Close late Mr Eyricks land neare Cowdrift in the parish of St Maryes Leicester in Fee Farme per Annum   4   0

The poore people of the Hospitall of the Holy Trinity in the Newark of Leicester for parte of the dovehouse close beyond the west bridge late the Land of Mr Hallam and Mr Ellis in the Tenure of Mary Adkinson widow in Fee Farme per Annum   1   6

John Carr or James Hassell for a Rood of Land there late Roger Rowes heretofore Richard Midgleyes in Fee Farme per Annum   6

The heires of Thomas Dannett Esquire or Thomas Charleston Esquire for certaine lands Leyes and pasture with thappurtenances in the west Feild of Leicester in Fee Farme per Annum   2   6

The poore people of the Hospitall of the Holy Trinity aforesaid for an acre of meadow in Burgess meadow called lady acre in Fee Farme per annum   3   4

William Rudings Esquire for a Close in Braunston gate sold to Mr Hunt in Fee Farme per Annum   5   0

Josiah Brickhead for a Colledg house and Garden called St Maryes Close heretofore sold to Job Lawnder in Fee Farme per Annum   1 10   0

Mr Fox Vicar of St Maries Leicester for the Ester Booke & dueties of the said Parish, Christenings, Mortuaries, Tith Piggs etc happening in the said Parish as the same has beene paid by the Vicar of the same Parish Tenants thereof   3   4

Anthony Abell and William Lyon for a garden in hotgate streete heretofore Theophilus Pares in Fee Farme per Annum   5   0

A garden in Soare Lane heretofore in the occupacion of George King & Thomas Birstall & late in the occupacion of James Bruce at will per Annum   13   4

The heires or Executors of Mr Edward Palmer for a peice of ground or Garden now built upon heretofore in the occupacion of Robert Ludlam Locksmith in Fee Farme per Annum   1   2

Of them more for a shopp in Swines Markett heretofore sold to Christopher Needham heretofore in the occupacion of William Tompson   2   6

15b   Rents payable at the Annunciacion of the Blessed Virgin
            Mary belonging to the Newark of Leicester

The heires or Executors of Mr Hugh Watts for a Messuage or Tenement heretofore in the occupacion of Doctor Chippingdale and Mr Walker in the Newark of Leicester in Fee Farme per Annum	1	6	8
Madam Palmer widow for a house there late in Mr Walkers occupacion in Fee Farme per Annum		13	4
The heires or Executors of Thomas Coltman for a Messuage or Tenement there late the land of Mr Hollingworth in Fee farme per annum	1	6	8
Mr Richard Ing of Knighton for Two parts of Chamberlains land there in Fee Farme per Annum		12	4
The heires of Geoffery Palmer Esquire For lands in Charleton Curlue in Fee Farme per Annum		1	8
James Cort of Bowden magna for lands there now in the occupacion of John Correll in Fee Farme per Annum		1	0
Godfrey Barodalle for land in Silby in Fee Farme per Annum			6
Mary Steedman of Glenfeild for land their late John Sheares in Fee Farme per Annum			3

17   Other Rents of the Towne and Mannor of Leicester and parcell of
         the Lands and possessions of the Dutchy of Lancaster parte of
         them Lyeing in the County of Leicester

William Higgs Mercer for a Messuage or Tenement in the occupacion of Mr John Brooksby heretofore sold to Mr Ellis in Fee Farme per Annum		16	8
The heires or Executors of Mr Edward Palmer for the Mault Mill in Swines Markett heretofore sold to Bartholomew Parnell in Fee Farme per Annum	1	13	4

18   Shambles and Drapery

Mr William Southwell and Mr William Deane for the Shambles & Drapery by Lease for 21tie yeares from Michaelmas 1682 per Annum	15	0	0

19   Other Rents received of new

Madam Frank for a peace of ground built upon the Towne
Wall in or neare the Freer lane late the land of Mr Samuel   2   6
Wanley in her occupacion in Fee Farme per Annum

Robert Langton for two peices of ground taken out of the
Comon Dunghill in a Lane neare the West Bridge per   10
Annum

The heires or Executors of William Blisse bone lace weav-
er for 2 Tenements in parchment lane heretofore the Land
of Mr John Heyrick & now in the occupacion of John Paul   3   4
and others in Fee Farme per Annum

*John Peabody for a shopp under Gaynsburrough per
Lease per Annum   10   0*
    [*Item struck out in original.]

20   Rents for certaine Lands purchased by the
                  Corporacion and other new Rents

The heires or Executors of Mr Robert Hartshone or Mr
John Roberts for a Close heretofore 2 Closes late the land
of Mr John Freak now lett to the said Mr Roberts paying
the Rent of £25 according to a former Lease to Mr Hart-   15   0   0
shorne dureing the terme thereby graunted and after-
wards £19 per Annum
    ⟨£10 of the £25 is paid to Charitable uses⟩

Mr John Buxton for the other closes parcell of the said
Freakes ground by Lease from Michaelmas 1689 per   19   4   0
Annum
    ⟨—paid more to charitable uses out of the said
    grounds £4 16s which makes the rent £24 per Annum
    Ex. Lease⟩

Mr Lawrance Carter for parte of the greate house by
Lease for 21tie yeares per Annum   8   10   0

Mr Henry Hargrave for the other parte of the house   .   1   0

Widow Seele pinmaker for one other parte of the said
house at will per Annum   2   13   4

Francis Annis for a little peice or spong of ground lyeing
at the Waterlaggs lately walled in by the said Francis
Annis by Lease for 21tie yeares from Michaelmas 1688   6   8
per Annum

William Savage the Elder for parte of the Messuage or Tenement being the Signe of the Swan scituate in the Satturday Markett in Fee Farme per Annum	2	0	0

22   Rents for shopps and stalls in Satturday markett

⟨Shoemakers stall⟩

Mr William Springthorp for a double shoemaker stall per annum	4	0
Thomas Ward for a stall per Annum	2	0
John Stretton for stall per Annum	2	0
George Boyer for a stall per Annum	2	0
Thomas Huffin for a stall per Annum	2	0
John Berridg for a stall per Annum	2	0
John Rayner For a stall late Henry Shewter per Annum .	3	0
John Rayner for another stalls per Annum . . .	2	0
Thomas Adcock senior for a stall	2	0
Richard Foxon for a stall per Annum	2	0
Henry Weston for a stall per Annum	1	0
Joseph Kilby for a stall per Annum	3	0
William Birstall for a stall per Annum	2	0

Mercers shops and other shopps

Mr Thomas Ludlam for a shop per Annum . . .		10	0
Mr Simon Thorp for the like per Annum . . .		10	0
Mr Thomas Lawrance for the like per Annum . .		5	0
Jonas Davy for the like per Annum		10	0
John Scampton for the like per Annum	1	10	0
George Steeres for a shop per Annum		2	0
William Devonport for a shopp per Annum . . .		8	0
More of Jonas Davy for his Freedom Markett dayes .		4	0
Richard Orton for a shopp per Annum		8	0

Chandlers shopps and other shopps and places

William Harris Chaundler for a shopp per Annum . .	2	0
Jane Biggs widow for the like per Annum . . .	2	0
John Worthington for the like per Annum . . .	2	0
Gilbert Fawsitt or (blank) for a shopp late John Ogden .	3	0
John Pebody for a shopp per Annum	10	0

Thomas Beamount for a shopp late John Browns per Annum	4	0
John Pollard for a shopp late William Robinsons per Annum	4	0
William Davy for a shopp per Annum	2	6
Elias Hartall for a shopp late John Ludlams per Annum .	4	0
Thomas Chapman for shopp per Annum . . .	11	0
John Mitchell for a shopp per Annum	2	6
Richard Linthwaite for a shopp per Annum . . .	5	0
Giles Coker for a Kitchin and Chamber lately built and alsoe the Barne and Stable upon a peice or parcell of ground where upon heretofore three shoemakers stalls lately stood	1 6	8
Richard Garton for a shopp at will per Annum . .	3	0
The Executors of John Mabbs for a shopp under Gaynsburrough now in the occupacion of Thomas Webster per Annum	6	0
The Executors of Mrs Ann Boadman or John Townsend for a mill Shopp per Annum	3	0

Glovers shopps

William Browne of Loughburrow senior for a shopp .	8	0
Samuel Sheffeild for the like	8	0
Samuel Holden for the like	8	0
William Browne for the like	8	0
Ralph Holden for the like	8	0
John Bennett for the like	8	0
George Holden for the like	8	0
Mary Browne widow for the like	8	0
Margarett Raphin for the like	8	0

25

Received this yeare for Tack of Beasts	9	2

26 ⟨Chapmans Guild⟩

Recieved of Nathaniel Wood apprentice with Robert Burbage Carpenter for his Freedome	10	0

Richard Wagstaffe apprentice with Edward wagstaff Vintner for his freedome		10	0
Richard Swingler apprentice with Daniel Pougher hosier for his freedome		10	0
Isaac Norrice Apprentice with Richard Lynthwaite Brasier made free		10	0
Richard Hood second son of William Hood Baker .		5	0
Robert Bingley Apprentice with Thomas Adcok Carpenter for his freedome		10	0
John Vaux in parte of Twenty pounds for his freedome .	10	0	0
Received of Robert Silby in parte of his freedome . .	1	0	0
Received of Isaac Harris in parte of his freedome . .	1	0	0
Received of Thomas Farley in part of his freedome . .	1	0	0
Received of John Dallaway in parte of his freedome . .	2	0	0

27   Received of the Severall Trades this yeare

The Company of the Carpenters		1	6
The Company of the Butchers	1	15	0

29 Cheife Rents belonging to the Hospitall of St John Baptist and St Leonard in or neare the Burrough of Leicester and are to be paid at Michaelmas onely for the use of the Maior Bayliffs and Burgesses of the said Burrough of Leicester

The Wardens of Wigston Hospitall in Leicester per Annum	1	4½
The heires or Executors of Mr Boone for A Messuage or Tenement in Gallowtreegate called the Black Lyon heretofore the Land of William Davy now in the occupacion of John Dawson per Annum		6
The Right Honorable the Earle of Stamford for Thurmaston Mills per Annum	6	8
The Heires or Executors of Sir Henry Beaumont Baronet Lands in Oadby late Mr Waldrons land per Annum	5	11½
Mr Smith vicar there for the vicaridge house per Annum .	1	0
William Devonport for certaine Lands in Oadeby late Marshalls Land per Annum		6
Thomas Tompson for a house in Senvy gate late John Tyrlingtons Land per Annum		9

30   Cheife Rents belonging to Corpus Christi Guild due at
Michaelmas onely

The heires or Executors of Mr Edmund Townsend for a messuage or Tenement in their occupacion per Annum	4	o
The heires or Executors of Mr William Palmer for 2 houses in the occupacion of widow Lustkin & Thomas Bull	3	o
John Pollard for the Messuage or Tenement late Edmund Astells	2	2
Mr Andrew Freeman For a messuage in Saturday Markett now divided in two houses in his & Mr Edmund Cradocks occupacion late Mr Robert Coates & Levitts Land per Annum	2	o
Mr Richard Mansfeild for a Messuage or Tenement in Saturday Markett now divided into two Tenements in the occupacion of Mr Robert Hobson & the Executors of Nicholas Sherwin heretofore the Land of one Pick per Annum	2	o
Robert Iliff of Oadeby for certaine Lands there in his occupacion late Blisses Land		10
The heires or Executors of Mr James Palmer for a peice of ground in parchment Lane late Mr Tobias Heyricks Land per Annum		3
The Right Honorable the Earle of Stamford for a Messuage or Tenement in Redd cross street heretofore one Simpsons land late the land of William Frank Esquire now in the occupacion of Geoffrey Hinman per Annum	1	o
Mr Mathew Simonds For a house in Reddcross streete heretofore Suffolks and Marshalls Land per Annum		8
Roger Fawsitt for a house there per Annum . . .		4
Mr John Hughs for a Messuage or Tenement neare St Nicholas Church late Mr Bickertons and late alsoe the land of Mr George Goodman and now in the occupacion of the said Mr Hughs per Annum	1	o
Samuel Wilson and Thomas Beamount for certaine Cottages in Deadmans Lane late Mr Teringhams land & Mr Cottons per Annum	1	o
Thomas Beamount for a garden neare the said lane per Annum	5	o

The heires or Executors of John Warberton for a Messuage or Tenement in the High Streete late Mr Becks land per Annum — 3 0

William Underwood for a garden in Deadmans Lane late William Slaters and Mr Mortons land per Annum — 6

Robert Spence For a Messuage or Tenement in high streete late Mr Wadlands land and late Mr Thorntons land per Annum — 1 0

A Messuage or Tenement in the Swines Markett in David Clayes occupacion late Mr Puseyes land and heretofore Mr Gilliotts per Annum — 14 0

The heires or Executors of Mr Edward Browne for a Messuage or Tenement lat the land of Elizabeth Eyrick lat Mr Palmer land per Annum — 9 6

The heircs or Executors of Mr Edward Palmer for a Messuage or Tenement in the Swincs Markett late Mr Benningtons land in the occupacion of Michael Bonshaw per Annum — 6

Joseph Bradley and Thomas Bosse of Lockinton for a Messuage or Tenement Scituate in the Swines Markett in the occupacion of John Gee & James Townesend late Mr Deuells land per Annum — 3 0

Widow Hooke for a Messuage or Tenement in the Swines Markett late James Coopers land in the occupacion of Thomas Adcock — 3 6

The poore people of the Hospitall of the Holy Trinity for a Barne called Clerkes Barne late the land of Mr James Ellis & by him given to the said poor people per annum — 6

Thomas Simpson Tayler for a house in Canck streete late Mr Pilkintons Land in his occupacion per Annum — 1 0

Richard Farrin for a house in the said streete heretofore the said Mr Pilkintons land per Annum — 8½

Mr William Deane for a house in Belgrave gate late fosters land — 3 0

William Mitchell Slater for the land late Thomas Mayes or Rothley per Annum — 10½

Sir John Watton Knight for a Close called sheire hall Close per Annum — 6

The heires or Executors of Mr William Rayson for a Messuage or Tenement late Burroughs Land per Annum	4	0
The heires or Executors of Mr George Rayson for a Messuage or Tenement called the Angell with thappurtenances in the occupacion of Joseph Cradock per Annum	2	0
John Davy Baker for a messuage or Tenement in Humberston gate late the land of Bartholomew Hunt per Annum	3	0
Mr John Goodall for a Messuage or Tenement neare the East gates late Websters land in the occupacion of Mr Samuell Woodland per Annum	1	0
The heires or Executors of Mr John Warberton for a messuage or Tenement neare the Freer lane called the George in the occupacion of Samuel Willcocks per Annum	4	0
William Heyrick for a Messuage or Tenement in the Swines Markett in the occupacion of Thomas Worrall per Annum	2	0
Of him more for a Messuage or Tenement in the same Street in the occupacion of *John Cooper Glasier* [*struck out] per Annum	2	0*
The heires or Executors of Mrs Katherine Henshaw for a messuage or Tenement in the same streete in the occupacion of Mr Wells late Ronders Land per annum	4	0
Mrs Mold widow for a Messuage or Tenement in Gallowtree gate late the land of John Mabbs and late Blackwins land per annum	7	6

31   Cheife Rents belonging to St Margaretts Guild

William Savage for a garden in Ironmonger lane in his occupacion late Mr Pilkintons land per Annum	1	0
Josuah Goodrich for a Messuage or Tenement in the high street neare Bakehouse lane late Mr Wadlands land per Annum	1	4
Sir John Whatton for a Close in Soare lane called the Mott orchard in the occupacion of (blank) Hitchcock per Annum	6	0
James Cartwright for a Messuage or Tenement in Belgrave gate late the land of Mr Robert Blunt per Annum		9
Mr Robert Coates for a house called the unicorne late the Land of Mr Gilliott per Annum ⟨Q.2d⟩		4½

Widow Tayler for a Tenement in Belgrave gate in her occupacion late the land of Robert Sutton per Annum		6
Edward Sutton for a Corner house in the said street late the said Robert Suttons Land per Annum		8
Robert Page for a Barne late the land of William Inge Esquire per Annum	I	$3\frac{1}{2}$
The Wardens of Wigston Hospitall for a peice of ground called the Normandy per Annum		6
Mr Edward Billers for a close neare the Spittlehouse sometimes called Bayliffs Close or the Learow per Annum	I	0
The heires or Executors of Thomas Fox for a Messuage or Tenement neare the Westbridg now or late in the occupacion of Peter Plumer per Annum	4	0
Thomas Brookes for a Messuage or Tenement in the Churchgate late Mr Manbyes Land		9
The heires or Executors of William Noone for a Messuage or Tenement neare All Saints Church per Annum	I	$1\frac{1}{2}$
More of James Cartwright for a Messuage or Tenement in Belgrave gate in his occupacion per Annum	3	4
Of him more for a messuage or Tenement in the said street knowne by the signe of the Lambe in the occupacion of John Wellinger per Annum		6
More of Robert Page for a little spong of ground taken out of the ground belonging to the Pinfold at the Corne wall leading to a Barne there per Annum		4

32   Cheife Rents for Cocks Capons and hens belonging to the late Colledge of St Mary Leicester over against the Castle of Leicester payable at Michaelmas onely

The heires or Executors of Mr Robert Hartshorne for a messuage or Tenement in the South gates heretofore called the Signe of the gray hound per Annum	4	0
The heires or Executors of Mr Dannett Abney for a Messuage or Tenement in the Southgates late Bennetts Land in fee farme per Annum		10
The poor people of the Hospitall of the holy Trinity in the Newark of Leicester for a house in the southgates called Fosters house scituate in the Southgates in thoccupacion of Richard Hames weaver and for a hen $3\frac{1}{2}$d in toto per Annum		$9\frac{1}{2}$

The heires or Executors of Mr Robert Hartshorne for a peice of ground in Burgesse meadow heretofore the Land of John Savage & Mr Mortons Land per Annum — 10 0

Mr John Wilkins for a Messuage or Tenement in the high street heretofore the Signe of the Crowne late Mr Dannett Abneys & late Duchams Land per Annum — $4\frac{1}{2}$

The heires or Executors of Mr Samuel Wanley for a Tenement in the North gates late Mr Mortons land and for 2 Capons per Annum — 1 2

The heires or Executors of Daniel Smith for a shopp in the South gates late Mr Mortons and Pippins Land per Annum — 5

The heires or Executors of Robert Atton for a Messuage or Tenement in the high street late John Attons land per Annum — 3 6

Robert Heyrick for a messuage or Tenement in high street late Mr Chettles land 15d & for 2 hens and a Cock 9d in toto per Annum — 2 0

John Stafford for a Close neare Braunston gate Bridge once Mr Cottons Land and late Mr Palmers land per Annum — 6

Mr William Bent for a Messuage or Tenement in the Swines Markett sometimes Mr Cottons late Mr Tyringhams land and Mr William Deanes 12d & for two hens & a cock 11d in toto per Annum — 1 11

The heires or Executors of Thomas Fox for a Messuage neare the westbridge late Mr Babingtons Land late in the occupacion of Peter Plumer per Annum — 9

Mr Pawley of Croston for a house in Applegate streete lat the land of Thomas Byrstall per Annum — 6

John Land of Birstall or his heires for a house there per Annum — 1 0

Mr Richard Mansfeild for a Messuage or Tenement in Saturday Markett now divided into two Tenements in the occupacion of Mr Robert Hobson & the Executors of Nicholas Sherwin per Annum — 6 8

Geoffery hynman for a house in Chaffelane near Redd crosse Streete sometimes the land of one Gulson & John Parker of Kibworth Hercourt 9d and for a hen $3\frac{1}{2}$d in toto per Annum — 1 $0\frac{1}{2}$

Robert Winfeild for land sometimes Rowell and Worthingtons land and late Mr Hugh Bothoms neare Soare lane & for three Capon & 2 hens	4	0
William Rudings Esquire for a Close in Branston gate sometimes new hospitall land per Annum		9
Mr William Billers for a garden in Hott gate Street 4d & for a hen 4½d and for another garden there late Balls heretofore a Swinsty per Annum	1	0½
Nicholas Smith for land in the high streete late Budworths land 6d & for 2 hens 8d for a shopp late in Thomas Hardimans occupacion per Annum	1	6
The heires of Mrs Alice Gilbert and William Browne for a Tenement over against All Saints Church in thoccupacion of Humphry Wright per annum	2	3
Mr Thomas Pawley for a house in Applegate street late Birstalls land now in the occupacion of Thomas Deakin 11d & for a cock and two hens 9d in toto per Annum	1	8
The heires or Executors of Mr Edward Palmer for a house in Swines Markett late Bestons Land per Annum		6
Thomas Cartwright senior for a house at the upper end of Belgravegate late Thomas Neales mercer	1	6
Thomas Padman for a Close neare Plankwell in all Saints Parish heretofore belonging to the same house & late Joseph wrights land per Annum	1	8
The heires or Executors of John Harrison for land in North gates once Boddimans land & Cadebies per Annum		6
Mary noone Spinster and widow derrey for 2 houses late Joseph Woodfords land and sometimes Lewicks 6½d and for two hens out of the same lands 6½d in toto	1	1
The heires or Executors of Mr Robert Hartshorne for land in the Southgates sometimes Mr Wilds, Owens and Messengers Land 2s & for two Capons 10d in toto	2	10
The heires or Executors of Mr Edward Palmer for a house in Swines Markett late Christopher Neadhams and John Byrelyes per Annum		4
The heires or Executors of William Rivett for a house and land in the Southgates late the land of one Mold and heyford per Annum	6	8

More of the heires or Executors of Mr Edward Palmer for a house in the Swines Markett heretofore Mr Manbies land and late Mr George Coopers next to the Horse mill per Annum   6

33 A Rentall of Lammas Tiths and Herbages due yearely to the Major Bayliffs and Burgesses of the Burrough of Leicester for diver land in St Maries parish late parcell of the Possessions of the late colledg of St Mary over against the Castle of Leicester
(vizt)

The heires or Executors of Mr Robert Hicking for a Close called Dovecoate Close neare Newark Lane late Mr Henry Palmers land   1   4

The heires of Mr Sherman or Madam Frank for lammas tithes of a Close called Archers Close neare St James Chappell late alsoe Mr Palmers land now in the occupacion of Mr Gee per Annum   1   0

Madam Frank for the tith of St James Chappell per Annum   1   0

More Mr Gee or the heires or Executors of Mr Sherman for the lammas Tithes of Benningtons Close neare Cowdrift in the occupacion of one Hawkins per Annum   1   0

Mr Marmion Gee for a Close neare the Cowdrift per Annum   1   0

The heires or Executors of Mr Robert Hickling for land next the grange once Birstalls land per Annum   1   0

John Stafford for a Close neare Braunston gate bridge once Mr Cottons land per Annum   6

The heires or Executors of Mr Hugh Watts for two Closes lyeing neare unto St James Chappell per Annum   1   8

More of the heires or Executors of Mr Robert Hickling for a Close neare unto St James Chappell per Annum   10

Of them more for a Close late Seth Kings land per Annum .   6

Of them more for a Close called the Paradice late Mr Manbies per annum   4

The heires or Executors of John Burbage or Madam Frank for parte of Cadmans Land late John Johnsons Land per Annum   10

The heires or Executors of Mr Hugh Watts or Mr William Ward for an Orchard one the backside of one Davy in the Southgates late in the occupacion of one Thomas Greene and late William Peters land per Annum		6
The heires or Executors of John Burbage or Madam Frank for a peice of ground called the Kilne yard late the said Johnsons Land and late in the occupacion of one white per Annum		4
Robert Heyrick or the heires or Executors of Mrs Henshaw for a Close neare Aylston way per Annum		8
Of him or them more for a Close neare the said way per Annum		4
Of him or them more for a Close late Archers land per Annum		10
The heires or Executors of Mr Robert Hickling for a peice of meadow ground neare St Maryes Mill called the Holme late Mr Manbies Land per Annum	1	8
William Chamberlaine for a Close neare Aylston way parte thereof is Colledge land heretofore in Mr Dethicks occupacion per Annum		10
Said William Chamberlaine for a Close heretofore in the said Mr Dethicks occupacion per Annum	1	0
William Rudings Esquire for a house in Braunston gate late Mr Hunts land per Annum		8
Robert Laughton for a Close late Brookes land per Annum .	2	2
William Rudings Esquire more for a Close there called Colledge Close late the said Hunts Land per Annum		4
Mr John Daintry for a Clos called Tippett in his occupacion per annum	13	4
Ralph Tompson for Booths land per Annum . . .		4
The heires or Executors of Mr William Rayson for certaine Closes lyeing neare the Dane Hills called Jelleyes Closes per annum	6	8
The Executors of William Charles and Richard Bruce for a Garden in Chafe late Mr Morton Land per Annum		10
The Executors of Mrs Boadman for the tith of the windmill per Annum	2	0
Thomas Hadden for a peice of ground or Garden in Millsone Lane late in Mr Henry Armstrongs occupacion per Annum		4

Francis Annis for the ground or Backside belonging to his house in the South gates per Annum		6
Mr Joseph Cradock for the tith of the Newark windmill .	2	0
Mr Edmund Sutton for the tith of the four yard Land in the Southfeilds his occupacion per Annum 〈supered〉	8	0
Of him more for the tith of the one halfe of three yard Land late in the occupacion of Thomas Coultman per Annum 〈supered〉	3	0
Mr Philipp Abney for the tith of four yard Land there per annum	8	0
Mr Thomas Ward for the tith of three yard Land there per Annum	6	0
Mr John Wilkins for the tith of three yard Land there .	6	0
John Prat for the tith of three yard Land there . .	6	0
Henry Coulson for the moyety or one halfe part of three yard Land there	3	0
Mr Joseph Cradock for the tith of the newark mills per Annum	16	0
Mr Richard Townsend for the tith of Goslinge Close .	2	0
William Tompson or Samuel Wilson for a house in Thorneton Lane per Annum		4

[End of Receipts]

[Payments start here]

1   Cheife Rents and other Rents paid this yeare

Paid this yeare to Mr Dyson for a broad arrowe for the but Close at the Auditt held at the Angell the 20th day of October last		1	0
For an acquittance for the same			6
Paid to the Bayliffe of the liberties of the Burrough of Leicester for one yeares rent for the Sheep penns there due and payable to their Majesties at Michaelmas last per Annum	4	0	0
To him more for Singletons Lease	2	12	8
To him more for shopps taken downe		11	6
Paid to him more for St Margaretts Guild . . .	1	13	5½
Paid to him more for Corpus Christy Guild alias Towne hall		7	9

D

Paid to him more for Luffkins Lease	2	0
Paid to him more for divers Cheife Rents for the Towne hall	7	8
Paid to him more for a Close neare the horse faire . .	3	4½
Paid to him more for a Close late websters Land . .	1	0
Paid to him more for Corpus Christy Guild . . .	11	9
Paid to him more for the great house or Lords place . .	4	2
Paid to him more for a Close called hollams . . .	1	0
Paid to him more for an acquittance for the same . .		4
Paid to the Bayliff of the Augmentacion for Lands due to Leicester Abby At the feast of St Michael Tarchangell last past & for an acquittance	7	4
Paid to the Bayliffe of Merton Colledge in Oxon for one cheife rent issueing & payable out of the hospitalls of St Johns & St Leanords in or neare the Burrough of Leicester aforesaid due at Michaelmas last past	1	3
Paid to James Readley one of the Serjeants at Mace for a cheife rent for a shopp under Gaynsburrough in the occupacion of John Scampton	2	6
To him more for a shopp in the occupacion of Richard Bayley Chaundler	1	0
Paid to the Company of the Taylers of the Burrough of Leicester for a Rent charge payable to them & their Successors from the Corporacion yearely for ever	1	8
Paid Henry Dyson gentleman their Majesties receiver at the Auditt held at the Angell in Leicester the (blank) day of October 1689 for one whole yeares rent due out of the Lands and Tenements belonging to the hospitall of St Johns and St Leonards in or neare the Burrough of Leicester heretofore in Harvies & Mr Tatams Colleccion in Countesthorp Humberston Siston Mills and the white Horse in Gallowtree gate for one whole yeares Rent due at St Michael tharchangell last past the Summe of	31 12	5
Paid to the said Receiver for Lands and Tenements belonging to the said late Guild called St Margaretts Guild in Leicester Towne obiit Lands & vicars Closes heretofore in the occupacion of Arthur Tatam for one whole yeares rent due at St Michael the Archangell last past the summe of	42 18	1

Paid to the said receiver for the Lands & Tenements parcell of the Lands and Possessions of the late Guild called
Corpus Christi Guild in Leicester for one whole yeares   14 12 6
rent due at the said feast day of St Michael the Archangell
last past the sume of

Paid to the said Receiver for the Lands and Tenements
cheife rents & Lammas Tithes parcell of the Possessions of
the said Colledge of the blessed virgin Mary over against   20 8 6
the Castle of Leicester for one whole yeares Rent due at St
Michael the Archangell last past the summe of

Paid to the said Receiver for certaine Tenements in the
Newark of Leicester collected by the Towne the Summe of   3 16 1

Paid to Mr Dyson for a receipt for the Same   .   .   .   2 6

Paid to the Doore Keeper 1 6

Paid more to Mr Dyson for portage & poundage of the
hundred & Thirteene pounds Thirteene shillings &   2 7 10
Eleaven pence farthing & for a receipt for the same

2 [No separate heading inserted]
⟨Castrum Leicester⟩

Paid to Mr Receiver Dyson at the Auditt held at the Angell
in Leicester for Two Tenements in the Swines Markett at
Leicester heretofore in the occupacion of Mr James Ellis   2 10 0
for one whole yeares rent due at the feast of St Michael the
Archangell last past in fee farme per Annum

Paid to the said Receiver for the Mault Mill in the Swines
Markett aforesaid heretofore in the occupacion of Bar-
tholomew Parnell & now in the occupacion of the heires or
Executors of Mr Edward Palmer heretofore the Land of   1 13 4
Sir Henry Hastings Knight for one whole yeares rent due at
St Michael the Archangell last past in fee farme per annum

Paid to the said Receiver at the same Auditt for the rent of
the Shambles & Drapery in Leicester aforesaid with
thappurtenances for one whole yeares Rent due at St   8 13 4
Michael the Archangell last past

Paid to the said Receiver at the same time for Gaynsburrough Chamber & all the shedds shopps & stalls in the
Saturday markett which the Major Bayliffs and Burgesses   4 8 8
purchased at Mr Bretton for one whole yeares rent due at
Michaelmas last past

Paid at the Angell in Leicester at the same time for an acquittance	2	o
Paid to the Doore Keeper		6
Paid at Lady day when wee Audited with Mr Dyson for 2 bottles of wine	2	o

4   Fees and wages and other payments this yeare

⟨Fees and wages⟩

Paid to Mr William Bentley maior for his yeares allowance according to an auncient custome	13	6	8
Paid to him more being the Rent of Gossling Close allowed by a Comon Hall	13	6	8
Paid to Nathan Wright Esquire Recorder for his yeares Sallary	10	o	o
Paid to the Towne Clerk for his yearely Sallery . .	1	6	8
Paid to him more as Clerk of the peace		6	8
Paid to him more for draughing & ingrosseing the Coroners Inquisicion	1	o	o
Paid to Mr Orton the macebearer for his halfe yearely sallery and Mr Higgs macebearer the other halfe yeare allowed them by a Comon Hall	2	13	4
Paid to them more for their yearely allowance in liew of a gowne but once in Three yeares	1	o	o
Paid to the Towne Clerk and Macebearer for an auncient allowance to them equally At Tow payments (vizt) upon All Saints day and white sunmunday allowed by a Common Hall	5	6	8
Paid Mr Orton the Macebearer more for his halfe yeares sallery allowed by a Common Hall	2	10	o
*Paid Mr Higgs macebearer for his halfe yeares Sallery .	1	18	2*
[*Item struck out in original.]			
Paid to Mr William Thomas headScholemaster of the free grammer Schoole in the Burrough of Leicester for his yearely Sallery being the Townes Free guift dureing Pleasure	16	o	o
Paid to the head Usher of the said Schoole being the Townes free guift dureing Pleasure	8	o	o

	£	s	d
Paid to the under Usher of the said Schoole for his yearely Sallary being the Townes free guift dureing pleasure	3	0	0
Paid to Mr John Newton present Lecturer of the said Burrough allowed by a Common Hall held on the Second day of february 1667 to be paid yearely dureing pleasure	30	0	0
Paid to Mr Fox vicar of St Mary Leicester being the Townes free guift dureing pleasure	10	0	0
Paid to Richard Linsey one of the Sergeants at mace for his yearely sallery		13	4
Paid to Isaace Brookes one other of the said Sergeants for his sallery		13	4
Paid to the four Serjeants at Mace to Keepe them from goeing abroad with their Christmas Box dureing Pleasure	1	6	8
Paid to Thomas Newton Cryer for his yearely Sallery .	1	6	8
Paid to him more for sweepeing Towne hall & Gaynsburrough		6	8
Paid to John Ogden Beadle for his yearely Sallery . .	2	0	0
Paid to the Cryer & Beadle to keep them from goeing abroad with their Christmas box dureing pleasure		4	0
Paid to William Higgs & Giles Coker liberary keepers .	3	0	0
Paid to John Hall senior for mending & repaireing the Conduit pipes & Sisterne	2	0	0
Paid to Widow Brookes for her yeares sallery for opening & shutting the Conduit doors dayley		15	0
Paid to the waites this yeare for their sallery . . .	6	13	4
Paid to Mr Major for two Sessions Dynners this yeare according to a former Allowance	3	0	0
Paid John Frankin for his yearely Sallery for keeping the house of Correccion	1	13	4
Paid to the Clerke of the Assizes for his fees . . .		13	4
Paid Thomas Newton and John Ogden for keeping the door the said Assizes		1	0
Paid Mr Henry Barwell for discharging two writts of habeas Corpus brought wrongfully against the Coroners to returne Inquisicions being all returned to the Clerke of the Assizes before		10	0
Paid for two paire of shoes for the Cryer & Beadle by Mr Majors order		8	0

Paid to Mr Francis Noble for five yards of broad red Cloth at nine shillings the yard to make the Cryer & Beadles Coates	2	5	0
To him more for nine yards of Green Bayes to line the said Coates at two shillings the yard		18	0
Paid to Mr Major for Triming for the said Coates as appeares by Bill		4	7
Paid for makeing the said Coates		6	8
Paid Mr Edmund Cradock for four yards of Blak broad Cloth at Ten Shillings the yard to make William Orton then Macebearer a Gowne	2	0	0
Paid to him more for six yards and an halfe of Blak Bayes at Two Shillings the yard to lyne the said Gowne as appears by bill		13	0
Paid for two yards of Colloured Fustian, silk, thread, & loope for the said Gowne		3	4
Paid to Mr George Bent junior for four yards of black broad Cloth at nine shillings the yard to make Richard Lynsey one of the Serjeants a Gowne	1	16	0
Paid to him more for Three yards of Greene Bayes at two shillings the yard to line the said Gowne as appeares by Bill		6	0
Paid to Mr Edmund Cradock for Fifteene yards & quarter of Redd broad Cloth at nine shillings the yard to make the waites Cloakes as appears by Bill	6	17	4½
Paid to Mr Maior for Sixteene yards of Silver Lace at Three Shillings & four pence the yarde to Lace the said Cloakes as appears by Bill	2	13	4
Paid to Mr Major for triming for the said Cloakes as appeares by Bill		5	0
For makeing the said Cloakes		16	0
Paid to the sexton of St Martin for ringing the Bell on St Mathew day		1	0
Paid the Towne Clerke for writeing the bill of payments .		2	6
Paid to the Graund Juries for Four Sessions dynners this yeare	2	8	0
Paid to the Constables for four Sessions dynners . .	1	4	0
Paid for bread Ale and Tobacco at the Viziting the schoole the Three and Twentieth day of October 1688		10	0

Paid the Sexton of St Maries for ringing when Mr Major was sworne at the Castle	2	6
Paid to the woman that Day that looks to the doors of the Castle	1	0
To Mr Dysons man the same day Mr Maiors order . .	2	0
Paid to the Waites for playing at Mr Maiors Feast by his order	10	0
Paid upon Christmas faire day for bread Ale and Tobacco when the schollers of the free schoole declaymed	11	0
Paid the Towne Clerke for Ingrossing the Commission .	3	4
Paid the macebearer for the seale thereof . . .	1	0
Paid to the Towne Clerke for writeing the Rent Roll . 2	0	0
Paid for a Ribbon for the Charter	1	8
Paid for a scuttle for the Cryer and askepp for the Beadle .	1	2
Paid Thomas Newton for bread Ale and straw for three prisoners committed to the Dungeon by the officers then in Towne		8
Paid Mr Orton then macebearer for the Badgg of his Gowne 1	0	0
Paid for the makeing the said Gowne	8	0
Paid the Towne Clerke for ingrossing of a letter of Attorney and the macebearer for the seale thereof	3	6
Paid the Waites for playing at the Feast the nine & Twentieth day of May by Mr Maiors order	10	0
Paid for bread Ale and tobacco at the Viziting the Schoole the sixteenth day of Aprill 1689	10	0
Paid to Twelve Halbert men that walked Mayday Faire .	12	0
Paid to Mr Hood for Candles this yeare and other things as appeares by bill	12	3
Paid William Harris Chaundler for Candles this yeare as appeares by bill 1	9	8
Paid John Peabody for Candles this yeare as appeares by bill	13	4
Paid Henry Andrewes for mending and scowreing the great mace by Mr Maior's order	6	8
Paid for Ale when Mr Maior and Aldermen staide in the Parlour for the Judges comeing	1	0

Paid William Spencer and John Denshire Butchers for a mutton and a veale presented to the Judg at summer Assizes	2	0	0
Paid Mr Hobson for Coales spent at the guard, & els where as appeares by bill	4	9	11
Paid for Forty hundred of Coales for the Townes use, & for bread & beere and carrying them in	1	3	11
Paid Mr Fox Vicar of St Maries Leicester for the tith of parte of the waterlaggs		2	0
Paid the Earle of Stamfords servants when Mr Maior and Aldermen were invited to dyne with his Honor at Broadgate by Mr Maiors order	1	0	0
Paid to the Waites when the Corporacion envited the Earle of Stamford to dynner to the Angell by Mr Majors order		10	0
Paid Mr Ward For a Colleccion of the Statutes bound up made in the time of King William and Queene		15	0
Paid Mr Francis Ward more for newes & other things this yeare as appeares by bill	2	8	8
Paid Mr Recorder for his advice and trouble this yeare by Mr Maiors order	3	0	0
Paid to the Receiver at Tutbury for portage and poundage and to the Auditors for a debenter, and two post letters to the Receiver	1	7	2
For Horse hyre and charges in fetching the Hundred marks from Tutbury	1	10	0
Paid Mr Thomas Hartshorne for gazetts this yeare & other newes as appeares by bill	1	17	11
Paid for two bottles of Wine when wee received the money due to the Hospitall of Mr Dyson upon Debenters that came from London		2	0
Gave to his man the same time			6
Paid at the Angell for Two bottles of sack when Mr Maior and some Aldermen mett to consider what to write to the King concerneing the Regulacion		4	0
Paid at the Angell for wine Ale and Tobacco at the Auditt held there by Mr Receiver Dyson		18	0
To the Cryer for a dozen of staffe beasomes . . .		2	6

Paid John Davie for him selfe and horse hyre for goeing to Derby to Sir Symon Degg with a Letter by Mr Maiors order } 7 6

Paid to John Wildboare for mending and fixing of Armes and other necessaries for three souldiers as appeares by bill } 14 2

Paid to Josuah Goodrich for mending and fixing of Armes & other things for three souldiers as appeares by bill } 8 0

Gave to a poore Traveller by Mr Maiors order . . 2

Paid to the sexton of St Maries for clensing the leaden spout at St Maries Chauncell twice } 1 0

Paid to seaven Trayne souldiers for Three daies pay and sixpence apiece for the muster master } 1 15 0

For a Redd Coate for Cooks son the Potter one of the Towne trayne souldiers } 15 0

For another Redd Coate for John Sheepy Roaper an other Trayne souldier for the Towne } 15 0

Paid to Mr Andrewes Tynman for a Lanthorne for the Townes use } 2 4

Paid to the Company of Taylers for their yearely Annuity . 1 8

For a new Redd Souldiers Coate fetcht by William Mabison Mr Joseph Cradocks servant for his masters use, and as hee said by Mr Maiors order ⟨Q.⟩ } 15 0
    [*Item struck out in original.]

Paid to John Nutter and seaven other men upon the request of the Right Honorable the Earle of Northampton and the Lord gray to Mr Maior to scout abroade severall waies upon the Roades about the Towne that night for their paines & horse hyre by Mr Majors order } 18 0

Paid to seaven and Twenty Trayne souldiers for keeping watch the one night & a day when her hignes the Princess Ann of Denmarke did lye in the Towne } 2 0 6

Paid to Mr John Cracroft for a Banquett presented to her Hignes the said Princess } 5 0 0

Paid at the same time for wine & bottles to Mr Joseph Cradock as appeares by bill } 7 12 6

Paid to Mr Cradock at the Feast at the Coronacion of King William and Queene Mary for ordinaries, Ale wine, Tobacco, and pipes and for Four Flasks of Clarett and Two bottles of sack as appeares by bill } 11 14 5

Paid more to him for wine as appeares by bill . . .	1	16	6
Paid more to him for wine when Mr Maior and severall Aldermen went to waite upon the Lord Commissioner Rawlinson as appeares by bill	2	17	6
Paid to him more for a Runlett of Canary sent to the Right Honorable the Earle of Stamford	4	0	0
Paid him more when the Corporacion entertained his Honor at a free feast; for ordinaries wine Ale and Tobacco as appeares by bill	19	15	0
Paid to Mr Thomas Palmer of the Crane for a hoggshead of Ale and tobacco the 29th of May last, & wine at severall times as appeares by bill	8	0	10
Paid John Nutter for drawing the Ale that day . .		1	0
Paid Mr Joseph Newton for wine and Ale at the Gaynsburrough as appeares by bill	4	4	6
Paid to Mr John Pare for Wine when the King and Queene were proclaymed as appeares by bill	2	12	0
Paid Mr Edward Wagstaffe for wine and Ale as appeares by bill	2	8	0
Paid to John Goddard Thomas Newton and John Ogdin for watching the night Princess Anne of Denmarke did lye in the Towne by Mr Maiors Order		3	0
Paid to John Ogden Beadle for sweeping the Pike at the uperend of Gallowtree gate		2	0
Paid the said Beadle for sweeping the west bridg . .			6
Paid for Buns and Ale when the Corporacion Treated the Lord Cullin and Mr Coke besides wine at the Towne hall		5	0
Paid John Beaumont for goeing to Northampton to bring intelligence concerneing the truth of the Irish marching this way & for his horse hyre & charges by Mr Majors order		8	0
Paid to six souldiers for fourteene dayes pay, at twice Trayneing	6	6	0
Paid to Samuel Holmes and John Davie for their charges, and Horses hyre goeing to Harborough to bring intelligence concerneing the march of the said Irish		12	0
Paid to Richard Wilkins for his charges and horse hyre goeing ascouting concerneing the said Irish, and to bring intelligence from Northampton & other places		5	0

Paid to Thomas Cartwright for setting up and removeing the Tables in the Towne Hall against Mr Maiors Feast	2	6
*Paid at Silbies for Bread and Ale for the Cryer & Beadle and other labourers for carrying the said Table to and fro [*Item has amount struck out in original.]	2	o*
Paid at Gaynsburrough when some officers were treated there by Mr Maior and severall Aldermen for Ale at that time	2	o
Paid Mr Woodland for a belt, a sett of bandaleers, and powder as appeares by bill	8	6
Paid John Goddard for Proclaymeing the day of Eleccion of Burgesse against the last Sessions of Parliament by Mr Maiors order	1	o
Paid to John Nutter for him selfe and Horse hyre when hee went towards Nottingham to bring intelligence of the Princess Anne of Denmarkes coming to the Towne and how neare shee was	2	o
Paid to severall souldiers travelling to their owne homes Mr Maior being then absent for some time when hee & Justices did sit to take Victuallers fines by the then Justices Order at the Gaynsburrough	1	4
Paid to six souldiers of the Towne when they were Commanded to Loughborough by their Lievetenant Robinson by Mr Maiors order	15	o
Paid John Cooke the younger a souldier for the Towne for Two daies pay hee had served—by Mr Maiors order	3	o
Paid to the sexton of St Maries for scowring the spowt twice more	1	o
Paid to a Quarter master on the behalfe of the Farmers to charge Teames in the Countrie for the carrying their Majesties Carriages by Mr Maiors order	1 10	o
Paid John Bass for goeing one Raineynight to stop the march of a Regiment that did lye at Upingham for comeing that night, by the officer in chiefe Command, the Towne being already over charged with souldiers	8	o
Paid to the Clerke of St Maries for brushing and clensing the inside of St Maries Channcell	2	o
Paid to Mr Maior for foureteene yards of Ribbon for Collours for seaven soldiers	7	o

Paid to the messenger that brought the Prince of Orange Circuletter for a Parliament by Mr Maiors order		2	6
Paid for four Proclamacions to the messenger that brought them		7	6
Paid for two pounds of bulletts for the souldiers when called to their Armes by Mr Maiors order			6
Paid Mr Maior for moneyes given to seamen souldiers and poore Travellers this yeare	6	4	6
Paid more to Josuah Goodrich for mending and fixing three Trayne souldiers Armes as appeares by Bill		4	8
Paid to John Goddard serjeant for Proclaymeing two Proclamacions and for other service as appeares by bill		5	0
Paid to Benjamin Garland for his charges and the Hyre of his horse to guyde a major and his companyes of dragoons to Nottingham as appeares by bill		4	0
Paid to Thomas Newton the Cryer for a Quarter of Charcoale this yeare		4	0
Paid to Samuell Heyford Baker for kidds to light the souldiere fires that kept Guard at the Towne Hall		1	3
Paid John Goddard for officiateing Mr Orton macebearer his place dureing his sicknes allowed by a Common Hall	1	0	0
Paid John Davie for his paynes and horse hyre for carrying a lame souldier to Glen by Mr Maiors order		1	0
Paid Mr William Stretton for Ale, brandy, bread, pipes and tobacco when Mr Maior and Aldermen waited for her highnes Princess Ann of Denmarke	2	2	6
The same night when the Towne Clerk, Chamlyns, and others were appoynted all night as a guard to waite for the Packett		11	6
Paid John Whipps Churchwarden of St Maries for the interest of Ten pounds for one yeare given to the use of the Poore of the said Parish by Mr Thomas Sherman		12	0
Paid to Mr John Burdett for halfe a pound of powder to severall souldiers to shoote when King William and Queene Mary was proclaymed			6
Paid Mr Bent for Bunns and Symnells at the Gaynsburrough when King William and Queene Mary were proclaymed		2	0

Paid the Waites for playing at the Coronacion of King William and Queene Mary by Mr Maiors order	10	0
Paid for the Horse Hyre of the Towne Clerk and Chamberlaine Roberts when they went to make Entrie of a meadow Ground at Botcheston Given by Mr Edward Palmer to the widowes of St Johns Hospitall and their charges	4	6
Paid for Ale tobacco and pipes when severall Aldermen treated Mr Carter at the Gaynsburrough	4	0
Paid John Davie and Goodfellow for four horses hyre and their charges for goeing Guides to Nottingham with two Dutch Regiments of Horse by Mr Maiors order	15	0
Paid John Davie more for goeing a Guide to Nottingham with the last dutch Regiment by Mr Maiors order	4	6
Paid to an officer for to march by the Towne with seaventy souldiers ordered to quarter that night in the Towne, the Towne being then full of souldiers, by Mr Maiors order	15	0
Paid John Davic more for Eight horses grass & hay for one night and four horses hyre to Burton upon Trent and bringing the rest of the horses back that were charged to carry severall officers and souldiers of Duke Schombergs Regiment thither	12	0
Paid more to John Davie for Guideing the last souldiers to Loughborough and for two horses hyre, and for his charges and horse hyre for two daies goeing to the Clerk of the Assizes at Lincolne for two habeas Corpus to remove two prisoners one to Nottingham and the other to Derby from our Gaole thither to be tryed	12	0
Paid to Mr John Norrice for his Constables staffe for Mr Thomas Hartshorne Constable of the ward late Mr Nobles Ward	5	0
Paid Mrs Orton for her husbands Gowne by order of a Common Hall	2 0	0
Paid John Wilde for maynteyning a sick souldier not able to march with the Regiment and for one to attend him by Mr Maiors order	6	0
Paid Mr George Crofts for Phizick for the said souldier by Mr Maiors order	2	8
Paid for Ale when the Aldermen staid at Gaynsburrough to waite upon the Earle of Stamford at his comeing from London	3	0

Paid to John Ogden Beadle for mending a forme, Cushin and other od things by Mr Maiors order	}	1	6
Paid to Mr Edward Wagstaffe towards buying a plate to be Run for in the Abbey meadowes by Mr Maiors order	}	2	0	0
Paid to Jaones and others for makeing a ditch from the old Conduit in the field to the poole there to drayne the water to mend the pipes according to agreement	}	6	0
Paid Mr Philipp Abney for interest and forty shillings principall to make up the summe for Dannett Abneyes porcion remayneing in the Corporacions hand upon stateing the account with Mr Philipp Abney as appeares by his receipt	}	3	0	0
Paid to John Silby Sexton of St Martins for lookeing to the Engions for one yeare	}	2	0
Paid John Wildbore for dressing Twelve Halberts . .		6	0
Paid John Nutter for drawing a hogshead of Ale when the Earle of Stamford dyned at the Angell	}	1	0
Paid Thomas Newton Cryer and John Ogden Beadle for their paynes in sumoning Carriages, and saddle Horses and the Constables severall daies & times to be ready upon their Majesties service allowed by a Common Hall	}	1	10	0
Paid Robert Page for carriage of and returneing into the Exchequer a Duplicate for the last Three monethes tax, and the other for the Poll by Mr Maiors order	}	10	0
Paid John Goddard for goeing to invite Mr Babington and Mr Palmer of oneleape to accompany the Earle of Stamford at the last feast held at the Angell, and proclaymeing two proclamacions	}	3	0
Paid for the Horse hyre of the Towne Clerke, Chamberlaines, and macebearer when Mr Maior and Aldermen were invited to the Earle of Stamfords to dynner	}	4	0
Paid to Mr Wood for Ale when the Aldermen met Mr Sutton about his Farme, and for Ale at severall times	}	8	8
Paid Thomas Newton for Cloves to sweten the Parler, for a sallow a pole to mend the barr for prisoners & severall other things as appeares by bill	}	2	9
Paid Mr Andrewes for mending John Goddars mace .		2	6
Paid Mr Maior for Tobacco, pipes, paper and other things as appeares by bill	}	1	5	6

Paid to the Earle of Stamfords Keeper for his fees for a Buck	10	0
Paid Mr Maior for Twelve Letters & one packett as appeares by bill	5	8
Paid to Thomas Huffin Constable of the ward late Mr Nobles ward for charges for the hyre of severall Horses to Ashby and Burton in Collonell Hastings and Richards Regiment to carry officers & soldiers & moneyes laid out besides his ordinary charges as Constable by Mr Majors order	7	0
Paid John Cotes for Thirty Kidds for a Burnefire upon proclaymeing King William and Queene Mary	7	6
For carriage thereof	1	0
Paid more for Thirty six Kidds for a Burnefire upon the Coronacion of the King and Queene and for Carriage thereof	10	0
Spent on the Tenant at Allexton when hee brought his Rent in Frost and snowe	1	0
Spent of othe Bayliffs that Brought Mr Poltneyes Ten pounds the same day		6

5 ⟨Repaires⟩

Paid James Redley for doeing some mending worke in the little roome in the Parlour where Mr Maior set his wine and Ale as appeares by bill	1	8
Paid more to Thomas Redley smith for mending a lock of the same Roome		4
Paid to John Browne mason for worke done at the Chappell well the Horse trough and pipes and for lime, sand, and workmanshipp	15	6
Paid John Wright Carpenter for Eleaven posts and four plancks and five dayes worke and allowance beere at the Gallow tree Cawsey	19	2
Paid Thomas Hastwell for worke done, stone, and gravell in the little lane comeing out of the Northgates into the Cow pasture	10	10
To Clay the smith for hanging the North gates . .	2	0
Paid to Robert Wright Carpenter for seaven new posts in Fryer Lane and one daies work and allowance Ale	7	4

Paid Mr Deane for two loades of stone and for two Loades to Hastwell and for sixteene dayes worke done at Dunns Corner and other places, and for allowance drink as appeares by bill ⟨Q.⟩	1	17	8
Paid Richard Heyford for carriage of gravell and stone to Dunns Corner the Cawsey at the neither end of Belgrave gate and the spittle bridg and other places as appeares by bill	2	8	0
For scowreing the ditch from one end to the other along Gallow tree Casway	1	15	0
For Ale to the workmen by Mr Maiors order . . .			6
Payd for carrying the earth to and from the ditch throwne up at the gates next the Lane leadeing to Swans mill ordered by Collonell Lyster for stopping the passage into the Newarke	1	6	0
Paid to Thomas Hastwell mason for paveing worke done betweene the bridges in the North gates, and senvy gate, and at the Northgates		9	6
Paid for three loades of stone for the said worke and for carrige thereof and for allowance Ale		12	0
Paid to Thomas Hastwell and his two sonns for worke done at the spittle house Cawsey, and neither end of Belgrave gate and for one Loade of stones and for allowance drinke as appeares by bill	1	4	4
Paid to two men for three daies worke apiece and allowance drink for scoureing the Pasture ditch		7	0
Paid Mr Beckett for two Loades of stone used at the neither end of Belgrave gate		5	0
Paid the neitheard for scowreing the horsepoole . .		4	4
Paid John Pebody and his son for worke done at Mr Hargraves house, and widow Seeles house as appeares by bill	2	19	8
Paid more for allowance beere to them		5	6
Paid John Mitchell, his son and Labourers for Eight and Thirty daies worke done at the Towne Gaole as appeares by Bill	1	16	8
More to him for slates slate pinns, gutter stones, lyme, bricks Ridg tiles, sand plaster, wood, carriage, and one dayes worke of John Noone, & more for lyme and allowance beere as appeares by bill	1	19	2

Paid Thomas Beaumont for worke done at the Towne Hall as appeares by Bill	1	18	8
For allowance beere to the said workemen . . .		4	0
Paid to Graunt mason for five dayes worke of him selfe and his man for paveing the Cawsey at the But close Lane end and grownselling of certaine glovers stalls		10	0
For two loades of stone for the said worke and carriage .		7	0
For two loades of gravell		5	0
For allowance drink		1	8
Paid William Harris for worke done at the glovers stalls, and for lyme sand slates and haire as appeares by bill		13	4
Paid for allowance beere		1	4
Paid to widow Hammond for one loade of stone for the Townes use		2	6
Paid Mr John Page for lathes & nailes for the glovers stalls, and a pad lock for Gaynsburrough as appeares by bill		5	7
Paid William Hall for glaseing worke done at the Towne Gaole as appeares by bill ⟨Q.⟩		14	1
More for new leade for mending the Conduit pipes as appeares by bill ⟨Q.⟩	1	9	6
More to him for glaseing worke done at the Towne Hall as appeares by bill		8	4
More to him for mending a gutter at the Lords place as appeares by bill		2	6
For glaseing worke at St Maries Chauncell as appeares by bill		2	4
Paid Mr John Dan for worke done for the Townes use as appeares by bill	1	5	0
Paid to Francis Page Smith for worke done for severall things for the Townes use as appeares by Bill	1	1	8
Paid to John Beaumont for worke done for the Townes use at severall times as appeares by Bill	1	0	1
Paid Mr John Burdett for lathes and Nailes used at the Lords place as appeares by bill		11	3
Paid to Robert Wright for worke done at the Towne hall as appeares by bill		6	2

E

Paid William Heyford for two loades of gravell for covering the Conduit pipes and one loade of Clay used about the Glovers stalls as appeares by bill	6	0
Paid Mr John Overing for severall things for the Townes use as appeares by bill	17	1
Paid Graunt the mason for repayreing the well in widdow Seeles yard as agreed upon for workman shipp onely	2 17	6
Paid for Two loades of stone for the said worke and carriage thereof	7	0
Paid John Wright for two Curbs for the bottome and the Topp of the said well and for use of severall pieces of wood and workman shipp as appeares by bill	19	6
For Lyme and sand for the said worke	3	6
For carrying the rubbage away	1	6
Paid for Allowance Ale for the said worke . . .	4	0
Paid Richard Heyford for two Loades of Gravell . .	5	0
Paid him more for carriage of two loade of stones . .	2	0
Paid widowe Gee for Gunpowder for the souldiers as appeares by bill	5	5
Paid Mr John Abney for casting the Cryers bell and for under weight as appeares by bill	6	1½

9 ⟨Taxes⟩

Paid to Mr Smith High Constable of Goodluxton hundred for a militia tax for the south field	5	6
Paid to Mr William Bent for the great house for Drumes & Collours		4
Paid Mr Capp high Constable of westgoscott hundred for a militia tax for freakes grounds	1	9
Paid Thomas Topp and James Ludlam Collectors for Two taxes for the poore of St Martin for Gaynsburrough ⟨Q.⟩	3	1
Paid Thomas Huffin Constable of the ward late Mr Nobles for amalitia tax for Gaynsburrough Shambles & sheepens	1	8
Paid Joseph Wilkins Churchwardens of St Martins parish for a Tax for the Church	1	6
Paid to the Constable of Braunston gate for two levies for Towne Lands in Brunkingsthorp for Constables charges	3	6

Paid Richard Yates for a tax for the repaire of the well neare the Towne Hall		1	0
Paid to John Roberts junior for two Three monethes taxes for Freaks grounds	1	9	2
Paid William Chettle Collector for the forrest grounds for two three moneths tax for the Towne Land there		15	5
Paid David Deakeins junior Collector for two Three monethes for the Southfields	4	14	6
Paid William Mitchell for a two three monethes tax for Towne hall		4	0
Paid to Symon Thorp for a Three monethes Tax for severall houses for the fee farmes thereof in the occupacion of Richard Hill		1	8
Paid John Stafford Collector for Two Three monethes taxes for the vicariall Tithes of Brunkingsthorp	1	0	0
Paid William Bunney for a Three monethes tax for the Swans mills the meadow in the occupacion of John Mason and the other meadow late in Mr Newtons occupacion		15	8
Paid to him more for a Three monethes tax for the Swans mill, & the meadowes beyond the mill and that parte of the Graunge yard in the occupacion of Mr Sutton	1	4	0
Paid Mr Thomas Hartshorne for a Two Three monethes tax for Gaynsburrough Sheepe pens and shambles	2	5	4
Paid Richard Foxon Collector for two three monethes taxes for the Greathouse and the Tenement in widow Seeles occupacion		11	0
Paid John Wood Roper for two three monethes taxes for the Farme Orchard		1	8
Paid Henry Colson Collector for one Three monethes tax for the Towne Gaole and parte of the backside of the great house & for theother Three monethes tax for the Towne Gaole oneley		4	0
Paid Mr David Cooke for Two Three monethes taxes for the North mills	1	0	0
Paid Richard Turner Constable of Brunkingsthorp for Constables charges for the vicariall tithes there		3	6
Paid Mr Churchman for Two Three monethes taxes for the weeke day Shambles		2	8

Paid Mr Thomas Weightman Collector for the hearth money within the said Burrough for the Chymneys in the Towne Hall and Gaynsburrough · · · · 8 · 0

Paid Mr George Beckett for the Tith of Burgesse meadow & the piece of meadow belonging to St Marie Mill · · 10 · 0

To Mr Richard Townsend for Two Three monethes taxes for Gosling Close · · · · · 9 · 4

Paid to Mr Thomas Hartshorne senior for severall fee farme Rents payable out of his house & backside in the South gates · · · · · 2 · 4

Paid Morton the shepheard for a two three monethes tax for the fee farme Rent of his house · · · · 8

Mr William Deane for Two three monethes tax for some feefarme rents · · · · · 1 · 4

Paid William Savage for Two three monethes tax for a feefarme Rent of his house · · · · 1 · 4

Paid Daniel Simpson for the said Taxes for his feefarme Rent · · · · · · 8

Paid the miller of Siston Mills for the Two Three monethes tax · · · · · 2 · 0

Mr William Southwell for two three monethes taxes for the feefarme of his house · · · · 8

Paid Scarburrow for the fee farme of the Cottage hee lives in · · · · · · 8

John Fawset sadler for the feefarme of his houses   .   .   2 · 0

Richard Moseby for the fee farme of his house   .   .   1 · 0

Francis Annis for severall feefarme rents   .   .   .   8

Richard Bruce for the feefarme of his house   .   .   .   4

Widow Fisher for the feefarme of her house   .   .   .   8

Mr Marmion Gee senior for his Fee farme Rents   .   .   2 · 0

Mrs Warburton widow for her feefarme Rents   .   .   1 · 4

Madam Frank for her feefarme Rents   8

Mr Heyrick for his feefarme Rents   .   .   .   .   1 · 4

Mr King for Mr Wattes his house for the feefarme thereof .   1 · 4

Mr Watts for the Two threemonethes tax for that parte of the great House hee lives in · · · · 5 · 4

Glister for their taxes   8

Richard Garrett for his taxes   8

Paid John Mason the younger for fee Farme Rents for his house in the Satturday markett and the white Horse hee now dwells in   1   4

10 [No separate heading inserted]

Paid to the Towne Clerk for drawing & ingrosseing the Accompt this yeare   3   6   8

Paid to him more for Fewell this yeare   5   0

Paid to him more for Ink and paper this yeare . .   6   8

Paid to the Chamberlaines for their paines & charges in Collecting the Towne Rents without Setting over any decay or debts other then what shalbe allowed them by the Auditors and at the Comon Hall   6   13   4

Paid to them more for the Auditors Dynners . . .   6   8

Paid to them more for the loss of Coales this yeare . .   13   4

[End of payments]

[Pious and Charitable Uses start here]

1   Receipts this yeare for pious and Charitable guifts

Received of their Majesties Receiver of the Honor of Leicester parcell of his Highnes Dutchy of Lancaster given by Queene Elizabeth to the Maior Bayliffs and Burgesses of the Burrough of Leicester towards the mainteynance of the Head usher of the Free Grammer schoole of the said Burrough one yeares annuity ending at Michaelmas last   10   0   0

Sir Richard Nudigate for one yeares Annuity due and payable out of the mannor of Thedingworth being the Guift of Sir Ralph Rowlett towards the mainteynance of the under Usher of the said Schoole   3   6   8

Mr John Norrice for one yeares Annuity out of a Close in the Abby gate called the Abby gate Close towards the mainteynance of the head usher of the said schoole   3   6   8

The heires or Executors of Mr Thomas Clerk for one Annuity issueing and payable out of a peice of ground called the water laggs given by him towards the mainteynance of the under Usher of the said Schoole   1   0   0

The Corporacion for one Annuity issueing and payable yearely out of certaine Closes in Willowby waterleyes in the County of Leicester lately conveyed to them by henry late Earle of Stamford upon the inclosure thereof being the guift of Mr John Norrice once one of the Aldermen of the said Burrough to Charitable uses for one yeares rente ending at Michaelmas last — 8 0 0

One yeares Rent out of a peice of meadow ground called Burgesse meadow which the Towne purchased with an hundred pounds given by Mr Thomas Gilbert and moneyes taken out of the Towne to and for charitable uses according to his Guift for one yeares Rent ending at Michaelmas last now sett to Mr Joseph Cradock for 21tie yeares from the (blank) day of June 1676 — 4 13 4

Henry Hitchcock Gardiner for an orchyard in his occupacion scituate in the parish of all Saints heretofore purchased of Mr William Ive by the money given by the First Countess of Devonshire for the use of the poore of Leicester and St Leanards — 3 1 8

Thomas Foreman of Whetston for a Messuage or Tenement and one yard Land there heretofore purchased of John Baker with the summe of Two hundred Marke given by Christopher Tamworth Esquire for divine service to be Celebrated in the parish Church of St Martin Leicester evening and Morneing every workday in the week — 7 3 4

Mr Joseph Cradock for the fourty acres in the Forrest of Leicester given by his sacred Majestie Kinge Charles the First (of ever blessed memory) upon the disaforresting of the forrest to the use of the poore of the Corporacion — 12 0 0

Mr John Wilkins for a meadow or pasture ground lyeing next to the Newark mills purchased of Mr Ive of Mr Nurse and by him given to Charitable uses to the poore of the Corporacion for one yeares Rent — 4 15 0

John Mason senior for another meadow ground lyeing there bought by the said Mr Ive of Mr Nurse and by him give to Charitable uses — 6 0 0

Mr John Wilkins or Mr Gee for a Barne yard whereupon heretofore stood a dwelling house being alsoe bought by the said Mr Ive of Mr Nurse which was Ruined in the late warrs & given to Charitable uses — 2 0 0

Mr Papillon for a house and Close in Hangman Lane which the Towne purchased of Mr Speechley and was afterwards demised to Mr David Papillon for 51tie yeares from Lady day 1639 payable on St Andrew day yearly given to Charitable uses & now is in the occupacion of Benjamen Stanley — 7 0 0

The heires or Executors of John Poultney Esquire issueing and payable yearely out of the mannor of Cotes divill given by his last will and Testament to the use of the poore of this Corporacion per Annum — 10 0 0

Mr St John Devonport of Bushby for lands and Closes there purchased by the Corporacion with the money given by Mr Nidd to the use of the poore of mountsorrell — 32 0 0

The heires or Executors of Mr Acham for one yeares Annuity to and for the use of the poore of the Corporacion per annum — 9 0 0

Mr Thomas Hartshorne for the ground lately belonging to two Tenements heretofore in the occupacion of Owen and Messenger in the Southgates being the guift of Margarett Hobby widow to the uses following (vizt) to the under usher of the gramer Schoole in Leicester 12s to the poore people of the Hospitall of the holy Trinity in the Newarke of Leicester 2s 6d to widowes of St Johns 6d to the poore of St Martins Leicester 4s 6d and to the poore of Wigston Hospitall Leicester 2s in toto per Annum — 1 1 6

Barton Overand of Belton in the County of Rutland for certaine Closes in the Towne and lordshipp of Allexton in the County of Leicester being the guift of Mr Thomas Hayne to severall Charitable uses (vizt) to the Schoole Master of Thrusington £6 to 2 schoolers in Lincolne Colledge in Oxon yeare £6 for preaching a sermon for the Kingdoms deliverance in 89 £1 to the poore of the Corporacion £6 and for three bibles to be disposed of by Mr Maior &c in toto — 19 0 0

Nathan Wright Esquire for one annuity issueing and Payable yearely out of a Messuage or Tenement called or knowne by the signe of the Parratt being the guift of Mr Hugh Bothom to & for the use of the poore of the Parishes of St Martin St Margarett & St Maryes per Annum — 2 0 0

Mr John Roberts senior for one Annuity issueing and payable yearely out of the ground called Freakes ground which he holds of the Corporacion being the guift of the Right honorable the Earle of Huntingdon for the better mainteynance of the head schoole master of the Free-grammer Schoole in Leicester per Annum   10 0 0

John Buxton for one other Close called freakes ground for one Annuity issueing and payable out of the same yearely to the poore of the Corporacion to be distributed in wheaten bread being the guift of Sir William Curteene & Gentlemen of the Lottery per Annum   4 16 0

The guift of the first Earle of Devon to 20 poore Freemen of the said Burrough yearely each of them 6s apeice to buy them Coles   6 0 0

Mr Thomas Hartshorne for a peice of meadow ground he holds for the Corporacion being the guift of Mr John & William Stanley   5 0 0

2   Payments this yeare for pyous and charitable guifts

	£	s	d
Paid to the head usher being Queene Elizabeths guift of	10	0	0
Paid Sir Ralph Rowletts guift of	3	6	8
Paid Mr Norrices guift of	3	6	8
Paid Mr Clerkes guift of	1	0	0
Paid Mr Norrices guift out of Willowby Lands of	8	0	0
Paid Mr John & Mr William Stanleyes guift of	5	0	0
Paid the Earle of Devon guift of	6	0	0
Paid the Countess of Devon guift of	3	0	0
Paid the guift of Christopher Tamworth Esquire	7	3	4
Paid the guift of King Charles the first	12	0	0
Paid the guift of Mr Ive	15	0	0
Paid the guift of Mr Elkington	5	0	0
Paid the guift of John Poultney Esquire	10	0	0
Paid the guift of Mr William Nidd	32	0	0
Paid the guift of Mr Acham	9	0	0
Paid the guift of Mr Hayne	19	0	0
Paid the guift of Mr Hugh Bothom	2	0	0
Paid the guift of the Earle of Huntingdon	10	0	0
Paid the guift of Sir William Curtin Mr Evington & the gentlemen of the Lottery	4	16	0
Paid the guift of Mrs Dorothy Baker	1	0	0
Paid the Guift of Mr Ward and Mr Bennett	1	0	0

Paid the guift of Mr Julius Billers	5	12	0
Paid more his guift		10	0
Paid the guift of Widow Ossiter	6	0	0
Paid the benevolence money	5	0	0
Paid the guift of Mr Thomas Hesleridg	1	4	0
Paid the guift of Mr Gilberte	5	0	0
Paid the guift of Mr Hitch		3	0
Paid the guift of Margarett Hobby widdow . . .	1	1	0

CHAMBERLAINS' ACCOUNTS
1708/9

Burg' Leic. The Accompt of Edward Palmer and Francis Coltman Chamberlaines of the Burrough of Leicester in the Mayoralty of James Annis Esquire being for one full year from Michaelmas 1708 to Michaelmas 1709

1 [No separate heading inserted]

	£	s	d
Mr Robert Lord for one yeares Rent of the Sheep pens by Lease for seven yeares payable at Lady day and Michaelmas	14	0	0
Mr William Thomas Head Schoolmaster for the School house due at Michaelmas onely			6
The heires or Executors of Mr John Harrison in Rents of Assize due yearly out of certaine Lands at the Northgate in the occupacion of Robert Tyler called Gadsby Land per Annum at Michaelmas only		1	9
Joseph Ashwell for the Chamber over the East gate per Annum	2	15	0
Mr John Blunt for the Butt Close heretofore sold to Mr Thomas Blunt now in the Occupacion of Susanna Freeman and late of John Loasby in Fee Farm per Annum		10	0
Mr Samuel Cart vicar of St Martins in Leicester for a Chamber belonging to the Corporacion being part of the Town Hall with a Door or Door place at the topp of the Staires goeing to the house of Office now used with the vicaridge house per Annum		2	6
Mr Arthur Noone for a Messuage or tenement at the nether end of Belgrave gate heretofore the Land of Thomas Headley now divided into severall tenements in Fee simple per Annum	1	0	0
The heires and Executors of Charles Stafford and Alice Brown for a Garden or peice of ground in the Senvy Gate now built upon in the occupacion of Brown and Norrice in Fee simple per Annum		2	6

His Grace the Duke of Devonshire for a Close or peice of ground in the Northgate whereupon stood one messuage or tenement heretofore the Land of George Tatam Tanner in Fee Farm per Annum — 13 4

The said Duke for a parcell of ground lying in the said Close late Fletchers land in Fee farm per Annum — 4

The heires or Executors of William Fletcher alias Thomas Alsopp for a peice of ground lying on the Backside of a messuage or tenement in the Northgate heretofore sold to John Tatam in Fee simple per Annum — 1 8

Widdow Earpe for a Messuage or tenement and peice of ground thereunto belonging in the Parish of St Nicholas heretofore the Land of William Adcocke in Fee Farme per Annum — 6 8

Thomas Wagstaffe for a tenement in the Northgate late the Land of Robert Freer being the Signe of the Sun per Annum — 1 0 0

Yates or Paul Smith for a peice of ground called the Waterlaggs late in the Occupacion of Mr Edmund Johnson deceased in Fee Farm per Annum — 6 8

Thomas Cartwright Joyner for a peice of ground at the south end of the Butt Close in Fee Farm per Annum — 4

Roger Palmer of Gilmorton for Land Meadow and pasture heretofore the Land of John Sprigg and now or late of Edward Whitehead per Annum — 3 4

Anthony Inglesby Esquire for lands in Great Ashby late the lands of Ralph Brookesby Gentleman heretofore the Lands of Nicholas Moreton in Fee Farm per Annum — 6

The heires or Executors of Robert Pawley Esquire for certain lands and tenements in Scraptoft late the land of Mr John Mason heretofore the Land of Thomas Simpkin and Tayler of Whetstone and now or late in the occupacion of Matthew Hubbard in Fee Farme per Annum — 6

3   Receipts of the whole Granges with thappurtenances and the four yard Land and two yard Land thereof known by the name of Weightmans Land called Archers land And a half yard land the Town purchased of the Lord Spencer in Fee Simple as followeth

Mr William Southwell for part of the Newarke grange & four yard Land in the South feild of Leicester and the Grange Barne and part of the yard by Lease per Annum — 29 14 4

Henry Colson for three yard land there by Lease per Annum	19	14	0
Of him more for the Grange yard and Barne per Annum .	3	0	0
Mr John Abney for four yard Land there and part of the Grange yard by Lease per Annum	25	16	9
Mr John Pratt for three yard land there by Lease per Annum	19	7	5
Mr John Wilkins for 3 yard Land & an halfe there per Lease per Annum	23	0	0
Edward Broughton for four Acres of land out of their Severall Farms to dig Clay to make brick per Lease per Annum	5	0	0
Thomas Ward for three yard Land there per Lease per Annum	20	0	0
William Bryers for the Newarke mills and Windmill there-to belonging per lease per Annum	26	0	0
Mr Richard Townsend for Gosling Close per lease per Annum	16	0	0
More of Mr Thomas Hartshorne for three Acres of Land lying and being in the Southfeilds of the said Burrough lately purchased of Simon Barwell Gentleman & late Mr Cottons Land & now in the possession of the said Mr Hartshorne per Annum	2	0	0

5   Bead house Meadow

Mr William Wells & Henry Coates for a meadow late in the possession of Mr Thomas Hartshorne per Annum	13	10	0
The said William Wells and Onesiphorus Raworth for the other meadowes there late in the possession of William Page and David Deakins by Lease per Annum	16	0	0

10a   In the North Gate

James Peter for a tenement late in the occupacion of William Palmer Cobler at will per Annum		13	4
Thomas Wall Milwright for the Northmills by Mr Bourmans Assignment of the Lease to him per Annum	26	0	0
Anne Morrice Widdow per Annum		4	0
Mr Pilgrim for the Shambles &c by Lease per Annum .	70	0	0

10b In Senvey Gate

William Stevenson for a tenement at will per Annum .	3	4
John Stevenson for another tenement thereunto adjoining at will per Annum	3	4
Mr James Annis for another tenement late William Cookes in the occupacion of Francis Moor & now John Reynors by Lease per Annum	5	0
Widdow Wate for a tenement near the Northgates per Annum		10
Mr Cradocke for a tenement near the Northgates . .		2
The heires or Executors of William Biggs for a tenement near the Northgates in Fee Farm per Annum	1	0

10c In Soar Lane or Walker Lane

The heires or Executors of Mr Twickden & Thomas Gorton for a peice of ground some time a dunghill now built upon heretofore in the occupacion of Mr William Rudyard in Fee Farm per Annum	2	0
The Overseers of the Poor of the Parish of All Saints for a house with thappurtenances late Jane Jennards late in the occupacion of Joyce Tofts & Francis Taylor per Annum	6	0

10d Within the Northgates

The heires or Executors of Robert Hycklyn for a messuage or tenement on the South Side of All Saints Church yard in the occupacion of John Orton in Fee farm per Annum	1	10	0
Mary Dyer for one Messuage or tenement late Kimberly's Land in Fee farm per Annum		6	0
Mr Windsor for a tenement in the high street now in the occupacion of John Duckett in Fee Farm per Annum		5	0
The heires or Executors of Thomas Drake for a house and Garden in the high street heretofore in the Occupacion of William Ludlam now in the occupacion of Joshua Goodrich in Fee Farm per Annum		4	0
For a house and Garden in the occupacion of William Granger heretofore in the occupacion of Worrall 4s 6d And for a house heretofore in the occupacion of Thomas Smith which was heretofore sold to William Ludlam and now used in two tenements		7	4

Robert Page now William Newton for severall Leyes in the horse Fair by Lease from the Corporacion per Annum — 1 0 0

10e   In the South Gates

Thomas Moreton for a house late in the occupacion of Lawrence Warner per Annum — 1 0 0

John Hardey for a messuage or tenement in the Corner end of Hangmans lane late the land of Elizabeth Chamberlyn in Fee Farm per Annum — 16 0

10f   In Burgess Meadow

The heires of Mr George Abney or William Palmer Esquire for a peice of Meadow Ground in St Mary's Meadowes called the sheild late Mr Moretons Land in the possession of Mr Hartshorne in Fee Farm per Annum — 16 0

Of them or one of them more for two Acres of Meadow there late also Mr Moretons land in the possession of Mr Hartshorne in Fee Farm per Annum — 13 4

10g   In Swines Markett

Widdow Warburton now Mr Smalley's for a tenement heretofore called the Kings Head late John Humfres land late alsoe Agnes Ortons Land in the occupacion of William Belgrave in Fee Farm per Annum — 18 0

Mr Thomas Palmer Atturney at Law for a Messuage or tenement late Mr Berringtons Land in the Occupacion of Michael Benshaw in Fee Farm per Annum — 6 0

10i   In Saturday Markett

Mr Richard Mansfeild for a messuage or tenement now divided into tenements in the occupacion of Mrs Hobson & Mr Buckerfeild in Fee Farm per Annum — 1 3 4

William Higginson for a tenement and shop there in Fee Farm per Annum — 8

10j   In Loseby Lane

Mr William Orton Mercer for a tenement late John Felzers land heretofore sold to John Parnell now in the Occupacion of John Moor in Fee Farm per Annum — 10 0

Mr William Southwell for the houses and Garden heretofore sold to John Bryerly in Fee Farm per Annum — 1 6 0

	£	s
John Underwood for a house late James Seetes in the occupacion of Mr Johnson in Fee Farm per Annum	12	0
Of him more for a little peice of ground adjoining to the said house paying yearly at Midsummer	A damask Rose	
John Dallaway for a house and backside being a parcell of a tenement heretofore in Vollentine Davies occupacion at will per Annum	10	0
Peter Davie Hosier for a messuage or tenement late built in Fee Farm per Annum	10	0
Richard Yates for a house and backside at will per Annum .	1 0	0

10k   In Gallow Tree Gate

	£	s
Mr Ayres for a house late in the tenure of Samuel Cooper and now in Thomas Reynolds occupacion in Fee Farm per Annum	8	0
Mr Ayres for a messuage or tenement commonly called or known by the name or Sign of the White horse in the Occupacion of Mr Ayres in Fee Farm per Annum	1 0	0
The heires or Executors of Mr Henry Palmer for one yard land in St Margaretts feilds lately purchased of Mr John Woodland in the Occupacion of Mr Mason in Fee Farm per Annum now sold to Mr Annis	15	0

10l   In Gallow Tree Gate on the West side

	£	s
Randolph Butler for a messuage or tenement over against the Roundhill sold to John Woodford late in the occupacion of John Hose now in the occupacion of Thomas Olive in Fee farm per Annum	10	0
Thomas Bennett for a Messuage or tenement adjoining to the north side of the Angell heretofore Edmund Astells and John Pollards Land in Fee Farm per Annum	4	0
The heires or Executors of Mr Henry Palmer for a messuage or tenement in Thomas Richards Occupacion in Fee Farm per Annum	1 0	0

10m   In Belgrave Gate

	£	s
Henry Hitchcock for a Garden at the nether end of the said Gate in his occupacion in Fee Farm per Annum	12	0
Thomas Redley for a tenement late in the occupacion of Richard Yates Taylor in Fee farm per Annum	13	4

The Executors of Thomas Elister for a house late Robert Fletchers per Annum now William Astwells	1 0 0
Ralph Ward Cordwainer for a tenement with thappurtenances heretofore Ralph Simpsons adjoining to the unicorne on the North side thereof per Annum in Fee Farm	15 0
Mr Edward Noone for a tenement on the East side of the same street late the land of Richard Ward in Fee Farm per Annum	18 0
The Churchwardens of St Margaretts Parish for a peice of Ground in the Cowpasture thereof in Fee Farm per Annum	8 0

10n   In the Country

James Winstanley Esquire for certain Lands Closes and Leyes and Pasture grounds in the Lordshipp of Braunston in the County of Leicester now or late in the occupacion of Joseph Roberts in Fee farm per Annum	12 8
Thomas Sanson for a Close and Croft and one yard Land with thappurtenances in Hinckly in his Occupacion in Fee Farm per Annum	15 0
The heires or Executors of Thomas Worrall for a parcell of land in Belgrave called Campton hill Leyes and one yard Land heretofore sold to one Mr Anthony Calverton lying in a Close of Pasture ground there near unto Belgrave bridge and late Mr Overings Land in fee farm per Annum	9 0
Sir Clobrey Noell Barronet for one messuage or tenement and one yard Land with thappurtenances in Kirby Mallory in Fee Farm per Annum	6 8
Thomas Chamberlyn of Rearsby for a messuage or tenement there in his occupacion in fee farm per Annum	17 0
William Kinston of Seagrave for a Close and Croft there late the Land of William Hubbard in Fee Farm per Annum	2 0
Thomas Storer of Thrussington for one yard Land there in his occupacion in Fee Farm per Annum	6 8
William Tompson of Houghton super monte for a parcell of land there in his occupacion or William Hubbards occupacion in Fee Farm per Annum	1 8
William Buckley of Thornton for another parcell of land thereto belonging in the Occupacion of Thomas Walton of Houghton in Fee Farm per Annum	5 0

Robert James for certain Lands in Barkby in the occupacion of Richard Iliffe in Fee farm per Annum	8	0	
John Wats for certain Lands Leyes and Hades in the west feilds of Leicester in the occupacion of William Rudeing Esquire in Fee Farm per Annum	4	0	
George Ashby Esquire or his mother for a Messuage or tenement in Hungerton now or late in the occupacion of Elias Marshall heretofore sold to Sir Thomas Cave Knight in Fee Farm per Annum	1	10	0
Thomas Burbage or the heires or Executors of George Sheffeild of Syseton for the Mill there called Syseton Mill and a house in Syseton heretofore Sold to Sir Thomas Cave in fee farm per Annum	3	6	8

11a Other Rents of Lands or tenements parcell of the Town Obiit Lands of St Margaretts Guild and parcell of the Fee Farm Rents heretofore demised by Queen Elizabeth to Mr Hacocks and Batesby's Indenture expired

In the South Gates

Marmion Gee for the Ground heretofore belonging to severall houses heretofore Mr Nurses William Hills and Francis Coates ruined in the late warrs heretofore sold to Mr Daniel Abney in Fee Farm per Annum	2	13	4
The heires or Executors of Edward Barwell Clerk for a house with the appurtenances near the Newarke gate late in the occupacion of Mr Richard Mawson in Fee Farm per Annum		10	0
Mr Thomas Hall for a messuage or tenement with thappurtenances commonly called or known by the name of the White Lyon in the occupacion of the said Thomas Hall in Fee Farm per Annum		10	0
Mr Thomas Hartshorne senior for a messuage or tenement in the occupacion of William Champion and James Fox in Fee Farm per Annum	1	0	0
Mr Lee for the ground lately belonging to two tenements late in the tenure of Paul Abney deceased belonging to a messuage or tenement known by the name of the Signe of the Bull ruined in the late warrs since built upon in Fee Farm per Annum	1	6	8

F

Mr Thomas Hartshorne for a messuage or tenement called the Grey Hound ruined in the late warr and since built upon in the farm per Annum — 1 0 0

11b   In the Swines Markett

Mrs Susannah Deane for a Messuage or tenement in Silver Street over against the Well late Daniell Murfins Land in Fee Farm per Annum now Mr Smalley pays 8s 4d and Thomas Hewson 4s — 1 0 4

11c   In or near Belgrave Gate

Mr John Newton for a Messuage or tenement at the Corner of Humberston Gate divided into severall tenements in the occupacion of Samuel Hunt & others in Fee Farm per Annum — 1 1 0

The heires of Robert Martin late of Thrumaston for land there late Mr Tatams in the Occupacion of Richard Hefford & others in Fee Farm per Annum — 12 0

Benjamin Cartwright Joiner for a tenement called the Lamb lately in John Wellingers occupacion and for one other messuage or tenement & a Close with thappurtenances heretofore sold to George Coates & late the land of Mr Thomas Blunt deceased now in the said Benjamin Cartwrights occupacion in Fee Farm per Annum — 1 6 8

Widdow Wagstaffe for a house there in her occupacion in Fee Farm per Annum — 1 0 0

The heires or Executors of Robert Burbage Carpenter for a house in William Headly's occupacion in Fee Farm per Annum — 12 0

Ralph Miles or Richard Hill for a house called the Cock in Fee Farm per Annum — 6 8

William Tayler for a Messuage or tenement in the occupacion of William Moseby in fee farm per Annum — 16 0

A Messuage or tenement in the Occupacion of Ellen Denshier & for one other part called the Cock in Fee Farm per Annum — 13 4
    Ellen Denshier   .   .   . 10s per Annum
    Widdow Freer or William Freer are to pay 3s 4d

Elizabeth Ball for a tenement heretofore sold to Robert Roberts late in one Gennards occupacion in Fee Farm per Annum — 5 0

	£	s	d
John Roberts Junior for a tenement late in the occupacion of William Gamble now of John Dennes per Lease per Annum		15	0
Richard Scarborow for a tenement in the occupacion late of John Meacham in Lease per Annum	1	5	0

11e   In Canck Street

	£	s	d
John Paine for a tenement there late in the occupacion of Thomas Ayres in fee farm per Annum		13	4

11f   In St Nicholas and St Mary's Parishes

	£	s	d
Widdow Lewin for a messuage or tenement late John Attons Land in Fee Farm per Annum		13	0
Mr Coates for a messuage or tenement at the West bridge called the Mitre heretofore sold to John Palmer Fel-monger now in the occupacion of Robert Wilkins in Fee Farm per Annum	1	0	0
Richard Hill for one messuage or tenement in the high street heretofore called or known by the name of the Flying horse heretofore the Land of Thomas Overing in fee farm per Annum	1	10	0

12   Other Rents of Lands or tenements parcell of the Town and Mannour of Leicester heretofore amongst other things given & Granted to the Mayor Bayliffes & Burgesses and their Successors in Fee Farm for ever

	£	s	d
Thomas Poiner for a house and peice of ground in or near St Margaretts Churchgate per Lease per Annum	2	0	0
Edward Palmer Slater for a peice of ground now built upon heretofore the Land of Mr Tatam in fee farm per Annum		2	6
William Earpe for a house or peice of ground called the Armitage near St Jame Chappell Close		1	0
The heires or Executors of Mr Thomas Carter Attorney at Law for a tenement with the appurtenances late the Land of William Ing Esquire late Smalley's Land in Fee Farm per Annum		8	0
The heires or Executors of James Palmer for a peice of ground in All Saints Parish called the vine yard in William Hitchcocks possession in Fee Farm per Annum		4	0

Mr Thomas Bradley for part of a peice of ground called the Lyon yard late the Land of Samuel Robinson deceased lying in St Martins Parish in Fee Farm per Annum   2   6

Widdow Stafford for one other part of the said Lyon yard & a messuage or tenement in her Occupacion in Fee Farm per Annum   2   6

Mr William Orton Mercer for a house and Barne with thappurtenances called Senby's Land scituate in Saturday Markett late the land of William Mitchell Clerke in the occupacion of the said William Orton & others in Fee Farm per Annum   2   0   0

John Coates for a peice of ground now Daniell Carrs extending from the Senvey gate to the Comon Oven whereupon a dwelling house was built by William Carr in Fee Farm per Annum   2   6

The Executors of John Major Esquire for a Close or Croft near St Margaretts Church yard near the Farm where a house formerly stood called the Farm house in Fee Farm per Annum   6

Ralph Winfeild for a peice of ground near Frogmore bridge now built upon in his or Anthony Groces possession in Fee Farm per Annum   1   0

Thomas Beaumont or John Groce or both of them for a peice of ground in Deadmans lane in Fee Farm per Annum   1   0

13 Of the Rents of Corpus Christi Guild in Leicester heretofore in Mr Archers Colleccion and now parcell of the Lands and tenements which the said Mayor Bayliffes & Burgesses purchased of Queen Elizabeth to them and their Successors for ever

Robert Bingley or the heires or Executors of (blank) Shuttlewood for a messuage or tenement with the appurtenances in the Swines Markett late in the occupacion of Susannah Cooper in Fee Farm per Annum   13   4

The heires or Executors of Mr Edward Brown for a messuage or tenement in the Swines Markett aforesaid heretofore known by the Sign of the Crown in the occupacion of Mr (blank) in Fee Farm per Annum   1   1   8

John Wildboar or Mr Robert Lord for a messuage or tenement in his occupacion in Fee Farm per Annum   1   6   8

George Couzin for a tenement near the Little Bridge in the North gate heretofore Leased to Robert Couzins for one and forty yeares & now leased to the said George Couzins for one & forty yeares — 15 0

The heires or Executors of George Steeres for a messuage or tenement in Gallow tree Gate now divided into two tenements in the occupacion of Alice Newton in Fee Farm per Annum — 13 4

Mr Daniel Simpson for a messuage or tenement in the Saturday Markett newly built in fee Farm per Annum — 1 0 0

Anthony Palmer or the heires or Executors of Mr George Becket for another messuage or tenement thereunto adjoining in the Occupacion of John Coates Baker in Fee Farm per Annum — 1 0 0

The heires or Executors of Mr Wanly for a messuage or tenement near St Martins Church in the occupacion of Widdow Tuft in Fee Farm per Annum — 6 8

Mr Abstinence Pougher for a messuage or tenement in Parchment Lane in his occupacion in Fee farm per Annum — 16 0

Mr Clarke or Robert Hutchins of Loughborow for certain Lands Meadowes & Pasture grounds in Loughborow aforesaid called Sadlers Land now or late in the occupacion of Richard Sutton in Fee Farm per Annum — 10 0

The Overseers of the Poor of the Parish of St Mary for a Chamber over the West Gates — 10 0

Mr Elsmere or Mr John Pratt for a Chamber or shop over the East Gates heretofore sold to Mr Davie and late the Land of Wigley in Fee Farm per Annum — 12 0

Mr John Blunt for a messuage or tenement on the East side of the East Gates in the Occupacion of the Executors of Mr Edward Hood in Fee Farm per Annum — 12 0

The Executors of Mr James Palmer for a peice of ground heretofore a garden over against the Town Hall now built upon late Fletchers Land now in the occupacion of Lawrance Cooper in Fee Farm per Annum — 1 0

Mr John Goodall for a tenement in Parchment Lane heretofore a stable sometimes Mr Herricks Land in Fee Farm per Annum — 6 8

Mr Thomas Putchin of Walton for 3 Quarter of a yard Land in Barkby late the land of Thomas Steel in Fee Farm per Annum	6	0
Robert James of Barkby for a Croft & half a yard Land in Barkby late Thomas Gibsons in Fee Farm per Annum	6	8
Mrs Elizabeth Palmer for a messuage or tenement in the Swines Markett late in the occupacion of Kenelme Robinson & now in Thomas Topps possession in Fee Farm per Annum	6	0
A house and garden in St Martins Churchyard in the occupacion of (blank) paid by the Overseers of St Martins in Fee Farm per Annum	13	4
William Frankes Esquire for a parcell of Land lying in the nether end of St James Chappell Close where a house formerly stood late the land of Mr William Sherman in his occupacion in Fee Farm per Annum	4	0
Mr Parkins of Grantham for certain Lands & Leyes lying in the Town feilds & territories of Gunnerly in the County of Lincoln heretofore in the occupacion of one Kenelme in Fee Farm per Annum	6	8
Mr Ralph Wells for a Close in or near Cowdrift late Mr Eyricks Land & heretofore Mr Hastings Land in Fee Farm per Annum	10	0

Widdow Wagstaffe for a shop and other buildings on the East side of the Round hill in her occupacion in Fee Farm per Annum	1	0	0
Mr Samual Marshall for a house and backside in Shambles lane heretofore one Harris's land and late Mr Bennetts in Fee Farm per Annum		1	0

14a Other Rents part of the possession of the late Guild in Leicester parcell of the Town obiit Land heretofore collected by Mr Arthur Tatham

Samuel Wilson or Joseph Burstall for a messuage or tenement in Apple gate street in the occupacion of the said Joseph Burstall late Henry Coates Land in Fee Farm per Annum	1	0	0
Thomas Cave for a messuage or tenement in the said street or of Samuel Wilson late being in the occupacion of John Wilson in Fee Farm per Annum		9	0

Robert Moor for a Corner house in the same street heretofore one William Clarks Mat maker and late James Kirks now in the said Moors occupacion in Fee Farm per Annum	6	8
Ralph Ward for a house in the same street late in the occupacion of Robert Eyrick pipemaker in Fee Farm per Annum	10	0
John Cooper in his occupacion in Fee Farm per Annum .	8	0
The heires or Executors of Robert Holcott for a house late John Silby in the occupacion of Henry Meacham in Fee Farm per Annum	7	0
John Bound for a tenement and Garden in the occupacion of William Savage of the White Swan in Fee Farm per Annum	14	0
Mary Hiles for a peice of ground now in the possession of Joseph Simpkin late Ellenor Bennetts Land heretofore Ralph Ortons near the house lately built where the house lately stood called the Mayors old hall and near St Nicholas Church in the occupacion of Robert Hewish in Fee Farm per Annum	3	4

14b   In the South Gates

The heires or Executors of Mr Richard Barwell for a house and Garden near the South Gates in the occupacion of Richard Mawson in Fee Farm per Annum	10	0
Widdow Gray or her daughter for a peice of ground belonging to the houses ruined in the late warrs sold to Robert Hartshorne or his Father in the occupacion of John Butlin in Fee Farm per Annum	10	0
Mr Thomas Hartshorne for the ground lately belonging to the house heretofore in the occupacion of John Palmer in Fee Farm per Annum	10	0
The heires of Doctor Coleman or Thomas Aston for ground belonging to two tenements late in the occupacion of John Turlington and Henry Charler called the Swan with a Barne thereunto belonging ruined in the late warrs since built upon by Mr Hugh Aston in the Occupacion of Mr Moor in Fee Farm per Annum	1 5	0
Ralph Ward Cordwainer for a tenement late Mr Southwells land in the occupacion of Widdow Ireland in Fee Farm per Annum	10	0

14c   In Gallow Tree Gate

Henry Vollentine for a messuage or tenement late John
Fryers late Mr Samual Woodlands now known by the   1 6 8
name of the Queens Head in Fee Farm per Annum

Doctor Hartopp for a messuage or tenement known by the
name of the Cinque Foyle in the occupacion of George   2 0 0
Broome in Fee Farm per Annum

Mr Robert Lord for a messuage or tenement heretofore
known by the Signe of the Bucks head in his occupacion   5 0
in Fee Farm per Annum

14d   In Humbaston Gate

John Major Esquire his Executors for a Garden place
heretofore sold to Michael Walton in Bushby in Fee Farm   2 0
per Annum

14e   In Belgrave Gate

Robert Brewin Baker for a tenement in his occupacion in   16 0
Fee Farm per Annum

Mrs Elizabeth Brown Widdow for a messuage or tenement late the Lands of Robert Johnson now in the occupacion of John Wellinger Blacksmith in Fee Farm per   13 4
Annum

John Bass for a messuage or tenement late the Land of
Robert Gamble in his occupacion in Fee Farm per Annum   18 0

Widdow Wagstaffe for a shop and Chamber scituate on
the Roundhill in Fee Farm per Annum   1   0 0

Richard Garrett for a messuage or tenement late Stephen-
sons Land in Fee Farm per Annum   12 0

Mr John Ludlam 14s & Elias Wallin 8s for two tenements
late in the occupacion of George Chamberlyn & Widdow   1   2 0
Aymey in Fee Farm per Annum

Henry Garrett for a house and Garden late the Land of
William Mabbinson in the occupacion of Thomas Newton   6 0
in Fee Farm per Annum

Richard Garrett for a messuage or tenement in his occupacion heretofore sold to George Norris in Fee Farm per   8 0
Annum

The heires of Robert Annis for an Orchard or Garden
heretofore sold to George Bluntington in Fee Farm per   6 0
Annum

The Heires or Executors of Thomas Chapman Esquire for an orchard or peice of ground whereupon stood a house called St Johns in the occupacion of Mr Pare senior in Fee Farm per Annum — 2 0 2

For part of Margarett Fletchers Land now or late in the occupacion of Nathaniel Gennard in Fee Farm per Annum — 5 0

Mr Thomas Palmer for an orchard once Mr Ings Land late Smalley's in Fee Farm per Annum — 2 0

Mr Thomas Palmer for a house and Garden late alsoe Mr Ings Land heretofore in the occupacion of John Russell in Fee Farm per Annum — 5 0

14f   In Senvey Gate

William Chamberlyn for a messuage or tenement late John Newbalds Land in his occupacion in Fee Farm per Annum — 1 0 0

Richard Kirke for a house and Garden now or late in the occupacion of Robert Harrison in Fee Farm per Annum — 8 0

Widdow Taylor for a house belonging to the Corporacion per Annum — 6 8

Madam Francis Palmer the Widdow or Relict of Mr James Palmer for a spunge of ground heretofore belonging to the abovesaid James Palmers house now William Goadby Junior per Annum — 8 0

Mr David Deakins and William Wells for a peice of Ground called Sallow Close in Fee Farm per Annum — 5 0

Richard Palmer for a house at will per Annum   . .   13 4

14g   Near St Margaretts Church

Thomas Deakins's widdow for a peice of ground called St Margaretts Bed lying in a close there late the Land of Jane Biggs in Fee Farm per Annum — 6

14h   Other Rents part of Mr Wilds Rents

Mr John Farmer for a Close near Cowdrift late in the occupacion of William Page Innholder now in the occupacion of Mr Marmion Gee senior in Fee Farm per Annum — 13 4

14i   Other Rents part of Mr Wilds Second Lease

The heires of Elister Stockden late of Glenn Magna Clerk for a house in Soar Lane near Redcross street in the Occupacion of Robert Liquorish in Fee Farm per Annum — 6 0

Sir Nathaniel Curson Barronet for a messuage or tene-
ment and peice of ground in the said Soar Lane late
Brittons Land in the occupacion of Mr Norris in Fee
Farm per Annum   2   0

John Worth Senior for a house and Garden in Belgrave
Gate late Higgs Land now or late in Richard Hawkins   8   0
occupacion in Fee Farm per Annum

Mr John Pare for a Close in Archdeacons Lane heretofore
sold to John Webbs in Fee Farm per Annum   6   8

William Kirke of Humberston for a house or Land
there now or late in Kirks Occupacion in Fee Farm per   5   0
Annum

Thomas Hastwell for a Messuage or tenement heretofore
two tenements sold to him and Jane Ward in Fee Farm   1   6   8
per Annum

The Poor People of the hospitall of the holy Trinity in the
Newarke of Leicester for a Garden or peice of ground
near the Butt Close now or late in the occupacion of   2   0
Robert Reignolds in Fee Farm per Annum

James or Thomas Cartwright for a house or backside near
St Margaretts Churchyard in the occupacion of Samuel   8   0
Brown in Fee Farm per Annum

Robert Cook for a house and Garden in Belgrave Gate
late the Land of Mr Edmund Sutton and heretofore the   3   4
Land of francis Coates in Fee Farm per Annum

Henry Gunnell for a tenement with thappurtenances in
Senvey Gate heretofore in Thomas Cay's occupacion now
in the occupacion of the said Henry Gunnell in Fee Farm   10   0
per Annum

David Deakins for a messuage or tenement heretofore
Thomas Chettles Land now or late in the occupacion of   6   8
Richard Harcourt in Fee Farm per Annum

Mr Thomas Palmer Attorney at Law for a Close near
Humberston gate formerly sold to John Row in Fee Farm   12   0
per Annum

15a A Rentall of the Lands and possessions belonging to the late
Colledge of the blessed Virgin Mary over against the Castle of
Leicester heretofore demised by Queen Elizabeth to Edward

Holt Esquire and by her Majestie granted to the Mayor Bayliffes
and Burgesses & their Successors amongst other things in Fee
Farm

Widow Bellamy for a Messuage or tenement in the Swines Market in Fee Farm per Annum	6	8
Robert Langton for part of a tenement now or late in the occupacion of Martin Beeby in Fee Farm per Annum	2	0
Mr Ralph Wells for a Close near Ayleston highway late the land of Mr Robert Herrick in Fee Farm per Annum	5	0
Elias Wallin for a Garden or peice of ground or the backside of a messuage or tenement near the Southgates heretofore the Lands of Mr Hugh Watts in Fee Farm per Annum	1	0
Thomas Jackson Clerk for a tenement in Soar Lane near Red Cross street late in the Occupacion of John Colson and now in the occupacion of Thomas Kitchin in Fee Farm per Annum	10	0
Samuel Dewick and Mrs Windsor 2s 6d a peice for a tenement in Soar Lane near Red Cross Street heretofore sold to John Underwood in Fee Farm per Annum	5	0
Edward Smith or William Dawson for a house or Garden in the same Lane heretofore Robert Stevensons in Fee Farm per Annum	12	0

The heires of Mr Gabriel Hill for a messuage or tenement in Redcross street and a Garden in Chaff Lane adjoining to the said house now in the occupacion of John Savage being the Signe of the Bird in the hand in Fee Farm per Annum	1	0	0
The heires or Executors of Robert Atton Butcher for a messuage or tenement in Soar Lane in Fee Farm per Annum	1	6	8

Robert Wrinkmore for a tenement or Garden in Soar Lane abovesaid heretofore sold to John Launder in Fee Farm per Annum	12	0
Mr Hill or Robert Fawsett For a Garden in Soar Lane in Thomas Trantams occupacion in Fee Farm per Annum		8
Mr John Abney for a peice of Ground lately belonging to a tenement in the South Gates ruined in the time of Warr & for a Croft in Fee Farm per Annum	16	0

William Franks Esquire for a peice of ground adjoining to Freers Lane heretofore in Mr William Collis occupacion lately in the occupacion of Mr John Burbage in fee farm per Annum	4		
Mr John Wilkins for the herbage of St Mary's Church yard by Lease per Annum		10	0
Mr John Farmer for a Close near Cowdrift Lane the Land of Mr John Herman in Feefarm per Annum	1	0	0
Mr Barwell for the tyth hay in Burgess Meadow Southfeild and tythable meadows beyond the Mills in Fee Farm per Annum	5	0	0
William Franks Esquire for St James Chappell yard and Close at the nether end of the Southgates heretofore sold to one Mr Simpson late Mr John Shermans Land in Fee Farm per Annum	1	6	8
Richard Brown for a house and Garden or backside in the Parish St Nicholas per Lease per Annum	3	0	0
John Denshire for a house and Garden in the said Parish late the Lands of Daniell Murfin Butcher in Fee Farm per Annum	1	0	0
Mr Watts Mrs Lucy Fawns for the Tyths vicariall tenths herbage and other dues belonging to Dannetts Hall Mary Mills the holmes by Lease for 21ty yeares per Annum	5	0	0
Mr Samuell Herricke for the tyths and tenths of all those grounds sometimes parcell of Dannetts hall per Lease of the same date	2	0	0
William Rudeing Esquire for all the tyths vicarially tenths herbage and other dutys belonging to the same payable out of all those grounds & parcells of Land belonging to the West Coates per Lease of the aforesaid date per Annum	5	0	0
The Executors of Nathaniel Sims for a Garden in Senvey gate late Woodfords Land in occupacion of Henry Sands in Fee Farm per Annum		1	0
Matthew Simonds Esquire for a garden or peice of ground sometimes a well yard heretofore the Land of Thomas Chetleton late Robert Griffins in the occupacion of Hugh Jordane in Fee Farm per Annum		1	4

The Executors of Mr Edmund Townsend for an orchard & garden in Silver Street at will per Annum	2	o
Mr Ralph Wells for the third part of a Close near Cowdrift in Fee Farm per Annum	4	o
The Poor of the hospitali of the holy Trinity in the Newarke of Leicester for part of Dove house Close beyond the West bridge in the occupacion of John Winter in Fee Farm per Annum	1	6
Richard Hassell for a Rood of meadow ground in Glenfeild late in the occupacion of John Carr in Fee Farm per Annum		6
Mr Thomas Hemsley for a Close lying near St Margaretts Cowpasture heretofore Bennetts Lands in Fee Farm per Annum	3	4
Mr Watts for certain Lands and Leyes in the west feilds of Leicester heretofore the Land of Thomas Dannett Esquire in Fee Farm per Annum	2	6
The Poor of Trinity hospitall for a peice of Meadow ground in Burgess Meadow called Lady Acre in Fee Farm per Annum	3	4
William Rudeing Esquire for a Close in Braunston Gate late Mr Hunts Lands in Fee Farm per Annum	5	o
Mr Robert Hobson for the house and Close called Close in the occupacion of John Holmes in Fee Farm per Annum	1 10	o
Mr Fox vicar of St Mary's Leicester for the Easter Booke and other duty's of the said Parish	3	4
For a Garden and tenement in Soar Lane near Redcross street heretofore in the occupacion of George King and lately of Richard Bruce at will per Annum	13	4
Anthony Abell and William Lyon for a Garden in Hott Gate Street alias Thornton Lane late the Land of Thomas Pare Butcher in Fee Farm per Annum	5	o
Mr Thomas Palmer Attorney at Law for a Garden in the Swines Markett lately built upon heretofore in the occupacion of Thomas Ludlam Locksmith in his occupacion in Fee Farm per Annum	1	2
Of him more for a shop heretofore sold to Christopher Needham late in William Tompsons occupacion in Fee Farm per Annum	2	6

15b Rents payable at the Annuncacion of the Blessed Virgin Mary
belonging to the Newarke of Leicester

The heires or Executors of Mr Hugh Watts for a Messuage or tenement heretofore Doctor Chippingdales and Mr Walkers Scituate in the Newarke of Leicester in the occupacion of Mr Bayley in fee Farm per Annum	1	6	8
Madam Francis Palmer Widdow for a house there late the said Doctor Walkers in the said William Halls occupacion in Fee Farm per Annum		13	4
Matthew Judd for a house in the Newarke late Mr Hollingworths in the occupacion of Francis Hall in Fee Farm per Annum		13	4
Richard Ing of Knighton for two parts of Mr Chamberlains Lands in Fee Farm per Annum		12	4
Jeffrey Palmer of Charlton Curlue Esquire for certain Lands there in Fee Farm per Annum		1	8
The heires or Executors of James Carr of Bowden Magna for Land there now or late in the occupacion of John Carroll in Fee Farm per Annum		1	0
The heires or Executors of Mr Godfry Barrodale for certain Lands in Syleby per Annum			6
William Steedman of Glenfeild for certain Lands there in Fee Farm per Annum			3

17 Of the Rents of the Town and Mannour of Leicester and parcell
of the Lands and possessions of the Dutchy of Lancaster part
thereof lying and being in the County of Leicester

The Executors of William Higgs mercer for a messuage or tencment heretofore the Land of Mr Ellis in the occupacion of Mr John Brookesby in Fee Farm per Annum		16	8
Mr Thomas Palmer Attorney for the horse Malt Mill in the Swines Markett aforesaid to Bartholomew Parnell in Fee Farm per Annum	1	13	4

19   Other Rents Received of New

William Franks Esquire for a peice of ground being part of The Town Wall scituate near Freer Lane late Mr Wanly's Land in Fee Farm per Annum		2	6

Robert Langton for two peices of Land taken off the Common dunghill in the Lane near the West bridge in Fee Farm per Annum	10	
Abstinence Pougher for two tenements in Parchment Lane late the Land of Mr John Herrick in the occupacion of Paul and others in Fee Farm per Annum	3	4
Mrs Alsopp for a shopp under the Gainsborough per Lease per Annum	10	0

20   Other Rents for certain Lands purchased by the Corporacion and other new Rents

Mr Richard Roberts for a Close of pasture ground late in two Closes and late the Land of Mr Frank per Lease per Annum	24	0	0
Mr Cooke for one other Close there commonly called Freakes ground per Lease per Annum	20	0	0
Augustine Hefford for a Cottage or tenement scituate near unto the horse fair in his occupacion per Annum	1	0	0
Thomas Garrett for another tenement to the said Cottage or tenement belonging & thereunto adjoining per Lease per Annum	1	0	0
Mr David Deakins for the waterlaggs		6	8
William Savidge for part of the house he dwells in being known by the Sign of the White Swann at will per Annum	2	0	0
Robert Annis for a little peice or spang of ground part of the ground belonging to a place called the waterlaggs by him walled out for a Felmongers yard per Lease per Annum		10	0

21   Rents given to School and other Charitable uses

Of her Majesties Generall Receiver Given by Queen Elizabeth out of the honour of Leicester for the better maintenance of the Free Grammer School of the Burrough of Leicester per Annum	10	0	0
One Annuity or Rent Charge payable yearly by Sir Richard Newdigate out of the Mannour of Theddington being the gift of Sir Ralph Rawlett for the better maintenance of the under Usher of the said school per Annum	3	6	8

Mr John Norris for one Annuity or Rent Charge payable yearly out of a Close in the Abby Gate called the Abby Gate Close for the better maintenance of the said Usher in the occupacion of William Rice } 3 6 8

Paul Smith for one Annuity payable yearly out of a peice of ground called the water Laggs to the Under Usher of the said School being the gift of Mr Thomas Clarke per Annum } 1 0 0

John Bryers for certain Lands lying in the Lordshipp of Willoughby Waterless being the Guift of Mr John Norris deceased for charitable uses per Annum } 8 0 0

Henry Hitchcock for an Orchard or Garden purchased with £50 given by the first Countess of Devon for and to-wards the Releif of the Poor of the Burrough & Parish of St Leonards per Annum } 3 1 8

Thomas Foreman of Whetstone for a messuage and Close and one yard there bought of John Baker Gentleman by the Corporacion with the mony given by Christopher Tamworth Esquire for celebrating divine service weekly in Lease per Annum } 7 3 4

Mr George Bent Junior for the forty Acres of ground in the Forest of Leicester given by King Charles the first of ever blessed memory to the use of the Poor of this Bur-rough per Annum } 14 0 0

Mr John Wilkins for a Close or meadow ground lying next the Newarke mills purchased of Mr Nurse and by him given to Charitable uses per Annum } 4 15 0

Thomas Richards for Burgess Meadow per Lease per Annum payable the 28th day of September in one pay-ment per Annum } 5 0 0

Mr Richard Townsend for a house and Close in or near Hangmans Lane which the Corporacion purchased of Mr Speechly per Annum } 8 0 0

The heires or Executors of John Poultney Esquire payable yearly out of the Mannour of Coates Devill and given by him to Charitable uses } 10 0 0

John Davenport of Bushby for Lands there being the guift of Mr Nidd toward the maintenance of the Poor of Mountsorrell per Annum } 32 0 0

The heires or Executors of Anthony Acham Gentleman being the gift of the Poor of the Corporacion payable out of the Mannour of Assersby alias Asterby in the County of Lincoln per Annum ⎫ 9 0 0

Mr Thomas Hartshorne for a certain ground in the South-gates belonging to two tenement heretofore in the occu-pacion of Messinger and Owen being the gift of Margarett Hobby for charitable uses per Annum ⎫ 1 1 8

Sir Nathan Wright for Rent Charge Issuing and payable yearly out of a house called or known by the Sign of the Parrott being the gift of Hugh Botham Gentleman to Charitable uses per Annum ⎫ 2 0 0

The Executors of Edward Claypool of Alexton for severall grounds & Closes there being the gift of Mr Haines for Charitable uses per Annum ⎫ 19 0 0

22   Receipts for Shops and Stalls in Saturday Markett

Shoemakers Stalls

Thomas Miles a double Stall	4	0
Robert Awmey	3	0
Mr Richard Foxton for his own and Joseph Kilby's . .	5	0
George Hartshorne	2	0
John Berridge	2	0
John Stretton	2	0
John Townsend	1	0
Thomas Huffin	2	0
William Burstall	2	0
Ralph Ward	2	0
Robert Warburton	2	0
Isaac Harris for his new house	4	0

Mercers Shopps

Mr Ludlam		10	0
Mr Simon Thorps Shopp		10	0
Jonas Davies lett to Richard Fawsett		10	0
More his Freedome upon Markett days		4	0
Mr Plummer of Glenn	1	10	0
Thomas Lawrence		5	0
Mr David Clay for a Shop under the Gainsborough .	1	10	0

G

Chandlers Shops

Mr William Harris	4	o
Jane Biggs Widdow	2	o
John Worthington	2	o
John Newton for John Bollards shopp	4	o
Gilbert Fawsett	3	o
Joseph Denshier for a shopp late Mr Davies . . .	2	6
Elias Hartall	4	o
John Adcock	11	o
John Mitchell	2	6
John Townsend for a Mill Shopp	3	o

John Ravenscreft for his Kitchin	1	6	8

Simon Ritchford for a shopp in Thomas Websters occupacion	10	o
The Executors of Mr John Dann for a Shopp . . .	8	o
Robert Low for a Shop	4	o
Mr Arthur Noone	3	o
Mr John Abney	13	4
The Executors of George Steers	2	o

Glovers Stalls or Shops

John Brown	8	o
Samuel or Bartholomew holding	8	o
Thomas Blower	8	o
George Holding	10	o
John Bennett or his Executors	8	o
Ralph Holding or Isaac Burbidge	8	o
Joseph Earpe	8	o
John Buckerfeild	10	o
Richard Kirke	8	o

29   Cheif Rents

Cheif Rents belonging to the hospitall of St John's & St Leonards and are to be paid at Michaelmas to the use of the Mayor Bayliffes and Burgesses of the Burrough of Leicester

The Warden of the new hospitall of Leicester called Wigstons hospitall	1	4½
The heires or Executors of Mr Boon for one Messuage or tenement in Gallow tree gate known by the Sign of the Black Lyon in the occupacion of John Dawson		6
The Earl of Stamford for Thrumaston mills . . .	6	8

Sir William Rawlinson for certain Lands in Oadby late Sir Henry Beaumonts Land and late Mr Waldrams Land per Annum — 5 11½

For the vicaridge house of Oadby .   .   .   .   . — 1 0½

William Davenport of Oadby for certain lands there late Marshalls Land — 6

Samuell Winterton for a house in Senvey Gate John Turlingtons Land — 9

30 Cheif Rents belonging to Corpus Christi Guild due at Christmas only

Mr Edmund Townsends Executors for a tenement in their possession — 4 0

Mr Freer for two houses late in the occupacion of Widdow Luskin & Thomas Ball per Annum — 3 0

Thomas Bennett for a messuage or tenement in his occupacion — 2 2

Mr Edmund Cradock for a messuage or tenement in Saturday Markett in his occupacion and Mr Thomas Hemsley's late Freemans Land — 2 0

Mr Richard Mansfeild for a Messuage or tenement in the occupacion of Mr Robert Hobson and Mr Buckerfeild — 2 0

Simon Iliffe of Oadby for certain Lands there late Mr Blisses Land per Annum — 10

Mr James Palmer for a peice of Ground in Parchment Lane late the Land of Tobias Herricke — 3

The Earl of Stamford for a Messuage or tenement in Red-Cross Street in the occupacion of Jeffery Hinman per Annum — 1 0

Matthew Simonds Esquire for certain houses in the said Street late the Land of Brittain and Suffolk per Annum — 8

Mr John Hughs for a Messuage or tenement near St Nicholas Church late Mr Buckertons Land in his occupacion per Annum — 1 0

Margarett Flavell Widdow for a Garden in Deadmans Lane per Annum — 5 0

Jonathan Gee for a Messuage or tencment in the high street late Mr Moretons in the Occupacion of Thomas Towers per Annum — 3 0

Thomas Beaumont John Groce and Samuell Wilson for their Cottages in Deadmans Lane late Mr Tyrringams Land   1   0

Roger Fawsitt Carpenter for a house near Red Cross Street in his occupacion per Annum   4

William Underwood for a Garden in deadmans Lane heretofore Mr Moretons Land per Annum   6

Mr Robert Spencer or Mr Thorpe for a tenement in the high street late Mr Woodlands Land heretofore Mr Thorntons per Annum   1   0

David Clay for a Messuage or tenement in the Swines Markett late Mr Pufiers Land in his occupacion per Annum   14   0

The Executors of Mr Edward Brown for a Messuage or tenement in the occupacion of Bartholomew King per Annum   9   6

The Executors of Mr Edward Palmer for a tenement in the same street late in the occupacion of Mitchell Benshaw and now in John Harrisons occupacion per Annum   6

Joseph Bradley or Thomas Ross of Lockington for a tenement now divided into two tenements in the Swines Markett in the occupacion of George Townsend or John Gray per Annum   3   0

John Welden for a tenement in the occupacion of Thomas Adcock lately Manbys Land per Annum   3   6

The Poor of the Old hospitall for a Barne called Clarks Barne given to the said hospitall   6

Mr Thomas Simpson Baker for a tenement in Church Street in his occupacion late Mr Pilkingtons Land per Annum   1   0

Robert Gamble for a house in Belgrave gate late the Land of Robert Foster per Annum   3   0

The Executors of Richard Farrian for a house late Mr Pilkingtons Land in Mr Danns possession per Annum   8½

William Mitchell Slater per Annum for Land late Mr Thomas May's of Rotherby   10½

Sir John Whatton Knight for a Close called Shire hall Close in the occupacion of Lewett of Loughborow per Annum   6

John Davie Baker for a Messuage or tenement in Humberston gate late in Bartholomew Hunts occupacion per Annum	3	0
Mr John Pratt for a Messuage or tenement known by the Sign of the Angell in Mr Elsmere occupacion per Annum	2	0
Mr John Goodall for a Messuage or tenement near the East Gates in his occupacion per Annum	1	0
The heires or Executors of Mr John Warburton for a Messuage or tenement at the Corner end of the Frier Lane known by the Sign of the George in the occupacion of John Oswin per Annum	4	0
Mrs Worrall for a tenement in the Swines Markett the Land of William Chamberlyn in her occupacion per Annum	2	0
For another tenement there the Land of the said William Chamberlyn late in Francis Lewins tenure now in the occupacion of Mr Gray and Rowland Marler per Annum	2	0
Ralph Wells for a Messuage or tenement there late Mr Henshaws Land in the occupacion of Francis Coltman per Annum	4	0
Mr Mould for a Messuage or tenement in Gallow tree Gate late Blackwells Land in the occupacion of Henry Hefford per Annum	7	6

31   Cheif Rents belonging to St Margaretts Guild

William Savidge for a Garden in Ironmonger Lane in his occupacion late Mr Pilkingtons Land per Annum	1	0
Joshua Goodrich for a messuage or tenement in the high Street being the Corner house of back house Lane late the Land of Mr Woodland in his occupacion per Annum	1	4
Sir John Whatton Knight for a peice of ground in Soar Lane near the Northgates called the Mott orchard in the occupacion of Thomas Hitchcock per Annum	6	0
James Cartwright for a house in Belgrave gate In his occupacion late Manby's Land per Annum		9
Mr Robert Coates for a Messuage or tenement in the said Street called the Unicorne in the occupacion of John Beaumont per Annum		4½

Widdow Taylor for a tenement late Robert Suttons Land in his occupacion per Annum		6
Widdow Wagstaffe for a tenement there being the Corner house late the Land of Robert Sutton and Edmund Sutton in Thomas Wards occupacion		6
Robert Page for a Barne the Land of William Ing Esquire .	1	3½
Mr Edward Billers for a Close near the Spittle house called Bailies Close per Annum	1	0
Mr Edmund Johnson for a Messuage near the West Bridge per Annum	4	0
The Warden of Wigstons hospitall for a peice of ground called the Normandy per Annum		6
John Brookes or Thomas Chapman for a house in the Church gate late Mr Manby Land per Annum		9
Mr John Pratt for a Messuage in all Saints Parish in the occupacion of Edward Bracebridge Senior per Annum	1	1½
James Cartwright for a Messuage or tenement in his occupacion	3	4
James Cartwright for a Messuage or tenement late in the Occupacion of John Wellinger per Annum		6
Robert Page or his Executors for a peice of ground taken out of the Pinfold per Annum		4
Mr Thomas Hartshorne for a Messuage or tenement in the Southgates heretofore known by the Sign of the Grey Hound per Annum	4	0
Mr Marmion Gee Senior for a house in the Southgates late Bennetts Land late Mr Dannett Abney's Land in the occupacion of Nathaniel Gee per Annum		10
The Poor of the Old hospitall for a house in the South Gates late Fosters Land in Thorps occupacion per Annum		9½
Mr Thomas Hartshorne for a peice of Ground in Burgess Meadow late the Land of John Savage per Annum	10	0
Mr John Wilkins for a Messuage in his occupacion late the Land of Mr Dannett Abney called the Crown per Annum		4½
The heires or Executors of Mr Samuell Wanly for a Close or tenement in the North gate and for two Capons in the occupacion of John Harcourt per Annum	1	2
The heires or Executors of Daniel Smith for a shop in the Southgates once Moretons Land and late Mr Pippins		5

	s	d
Henry Colson Junior for a house in the high Street late John Attons Land per Annum	3	6
Mr William Topp for a house in the high Street in his occupacion late the land of Ralph Cheatle per Annum	2	0
Benjamin Garland for a Close at Braunston Gate Bridge late Cottons Land per Annum		6
Mr William Bents Executors for a house in the Swines Markett late Mr Tyrringhams Land 1s And for 2 Hens and a Cock	1	11
Mr Johnson for a house near the West bridge late Mr Babingtons Land		9
The heires of Mr Pawley late of Croston for a Messuage or tenement in Applegate Street late in Thomas Deacons occupacion per Annum		6
Simon Ward for a house in Burstall late the Land of William Coates now John Reynars in Simon Wards occupacion per Annum	1	0
Richard Mansfeild for a Messuage or tenement in the Saturday Markett in the occupacion of Mr Hobson and Mr Ewell per Annum	6	8
Jeffrey Hinman for a house in Chaff Lane near Red Cross Street once Gulstons Land 9d & for a hen 3½d per Annum	1	0½
Mr Robert Winfeild for Land late Mr Bothams near Soar Lane & for 3 Capons & two hens per Annum	4	0
William Rudeing Esquire for a Close in Braunston gate per Annum		9
Mr William Billers for a Garden in Hott gate Street or Thornton Lane 3d and for a hen 3½d and for a Garden there late Balls sometimes a Swine Sty	1	0½
John Tyler near the Southgates for Land in the high-street late Budworths Land 5d And for two Hens 7d And for a shop near the Southgates now or late in John Tylers occupacion per Annum	1	6
Elizabeth Winter for a tenement over against All Saints Church late Mr William Rudiards late in Humphry Wrights occupacion per Annum	2	3
The heires or Executors of Mr Peuzey for a house in Apple gate Street one Burstalls Land late in the occupacion of Thomas Deaken 10d and two hens and a Cock 10d	1	8

	£	s
The heires or Executors of Mr Edward Palmer for a house in the Swines Markett late Breesons Land per Annum		6
Mr Thomas Chapman for a Messuage or tenement at the upper end of Belgrave gate late Neales Land per Annum	1	6
Thomas Palmer or Edward Daws for a Close in all Saints Parish near Planck well late the said Neales Land per Annum	1	8
Robert Tyler for a house and Land in the North gate late Boddimans Land & John Harrisons Felmonger per Annum		6
Robert Withers and Widdow Derry for certain houses late Woodfords Land near the North gate per Annum	1	1
Mr Thomas Hartshorne for Land in Southgate late Owen and Messingers Land in his occupacion & for Capons 10d per Annum	2	10
The heires of Mr Edward Palmer for a house in the Swines Markett late Christopher Needhams and Bryerly's Land per Annum		4
John Coleman for a house in the South Gates late Heffords Molds & Rivetts Land per Annum	6	8
The heires or Executors of Mr Edward Palmer for a house in the Swines Markett near the horse Mill late Mambres Land in the occupacion of John More per Annum		6

33 A Rentall of Lammas Tythes and herbage due yearly to the Mayor etc. And for diverse grounds in St Margaretts Parish in the possession of the late Colledge of St Mary over against the Castle of Leicester (vizt)

	£	s
The heires or Executors of Mr Robert Hycklyn for Dove house Close near the Newarke of Leicester late the Land of Henry Palmer per Annum	1	4
William Francks Esquire for a Close called Archers Close near St James Chappell Close and once alsoe Palmers Land per Annum	1	0
Of him more for the Tyth of St James Chappell Close per Annum	1	0
Mr Marmion Gee for Lammas Tyths for Benington Close near the Cowdrift per Annum	1	0
Benjamin Garland for a Close near Braunston Bridge per Annum		6

The heires of Mr Hugh Wats for one Close late two Closes over against St James Chappell in Mr Robert Lords occupacion per Annum	1	8
The heires or Executors of Mr Robert Hycklyn for Land near the Grange once Burstalls Land per Annum		10
Of them more for a Close late Mr Martins Land near St James Chappell per Annum		10
Of them more late Seth Kings Land per Annum .		6
For a Close called the Paradice late Mr Manby's Land per Annum		4
William Franks Esquire for Cadmans Land per Annum .		10
Of him more for a peice of ground called the Kilne and heretofore the Land of Cadmans & Johnsons per Annum		4
Mr Joseph Wilkins for an Orchard on the backside of a house of one Davies in the Southgates late the Land of Mr Hugh Watts & late Porters Land per Annum		6
Mr Ralph Wells for a Close near Ayleston Highway late Mr Herricks Land per Annum		8
Of them more for a close in the high way per Annum .		4
Of him more for a Close near Archers Land per Annum .		10
Mr Weston for a peice of Meadow ground near St Mary Mills called the holmes late Mr Manby's Land per Annum	1	8
Mr John Farmer for a Close near Ayleston way in the occupacion of William Page per Annum		10
Of him more for a Close in the said Mr Gees occupacion per Annum	1	0
William Rudeing Esquire for a Close in Braunston Gate late Mr Hunts Land per Annum		8
Of them more for a Close there called the Colledge Close late Mr Hunts Land per Annum		4
Robert Langton for a Close late Mr Brookes Land now Robert Langtons per Annum	2	2
The Heires or Executors of Mr John Daintry or of Mr John Cracroft for a Close called the Tippett per Annum	13	4
Mr Joseph Cradock for the Tyth of the Newarke Windmills per Annum	2	0
John Hinman for a Garden in Chaff Lane . . .		10
John Wall for the Tyth of Gallow Windmill per Annum .	2	0

Thomas Hadden for a Garden or peice of Ground in Millstone Lane late Henry Armstrongs Land per Annum	4	
The heires or Executors of Franck Annis for a backside belonging to his house in South gates per Annum	6	
Mr John Abney for the Tyth of his four yard Land . .	8	o
Mr Thomas Ward for the Tyth of his three yard Land .	6	o
Samuell Wilson for a house in Thornton Lane late in William Tompsons occupacion per Annum	4	
Thomas Tompson for Booths Land	4	
For the Tyth of Mr Southwells four yard Land . .	8	o
Mr John Wilkins for the Tyth of three yard Land and an half per Annum	6	o
Henry Colson for the Tyth of three yard Land . .	6	o
Mr John Pratt for the Tyth of Three yard Land . .	6	o
William Bryers for the Tyth of the Newarke Water Corne Mills	16	o
Mr Richard Townsend for the Tyth of Gosling Close .	2	o

36   Fines and Accidentall Receipts

Thomas third son of Henry Hitchcock Gardiner made Free & paid for his fine		10	o
Charles Melross of Slawston Apprentice to Mr Richard Foxton Cordwainer made Free & paid		10	o
Benjamin 2nd son of Isaac Harris Feltmaker made Free & paid		5	o
John Bakewell Apprentice to Josiah Coleman made Free & paid		10	o
William Bellamy Apprentice to Mr Thomas Bradley vintner made Free & paid		10	o
William Third son of Henry Dawson of Belgrave made Free & paid		10	o
Thomas Bradsworth a Stranger made Free & paid . .	20	o	o
Of the Butchers for fines		10	o
Daniel Queniborow Apprentice to John Cooke Butcher made Free & paid		10	o
Henry Hawkins Apprentice to Thomas Vallentine Woolcomber made Free & paid		10	o

John 2nd son of Roger Fawsitt Carpenter made Free & paid	5	0
Samuel Tuckwell of the Bishopps Fee a stranger made Free & paid	20 0	0
Joel Shuttlewood Apprentice to William Pollard made Free & paid	10	0
Thomas Farmer Apprentice to Edward Bracebridge made Free & paid	10	0
Abraham Hawkins Apprentice to Edward Nickelson made Free & paid	10	0
John Turvill Apprentice to Edward Springthorpe made Free & paid	10	0
William Swann Apprentice to Abstinence Pougher made Free & paid	10	0
John Duckett Apprentice to John Smalley made Free & paid	10	0
John Tuffley Apprentice to John Townsend made Free & paid	10	0
John 2nd son of John Warburton made Free & paid .	5	0

34   Deduccions for taxes

Mr William Thomas head Schoolmaster . . .	2	16	0
Mr Fox	2	0	0
Mr Hardy	1	12	0
Mr Ludlam		12	0
John Wilson for Stones			9
The treasurer of the County for worke don at St Sundays bridg		2	9
Mr Lee for damag'd Lime & bricks		4	0
Mr Page for paveing		7	0
Mr Manning for carriage		6	0

[End of Receipts]

[Payments start here]

1   Cheif Rents and other Rents paid this year

Paid to Mr Dyson at the Auditt of the Broad Arrow .		1	0
For an Acquittance for the same			6
Paid to Mr Thomas Palmer Bayliffe of the Burrough for one yeares Rent due for the Sheep pens at Michaelmas	4	0	0

Paid him more for Singletons Lease	2	12	8
For Shopps taken down		11	6
To him more for St Margaretts Guild	1	13	5½
To him more for Corpus Christi Guild alias Town Hall .		7	9
To him more for Luskins Lease		2	0
Paid him for diverse Cheif Rents from the Town . .		7	8
Paid him more for a Close near the horse fair . . .		3	4½
Paid him more for a close late Websters Land . . .		1	0
Paid him more for Corpus Christi Guild . . .		11	9
Paid him more for a Close late Hallams		1	0
Paid him for an acquittance for the said money . .			4
Paid to the Bayliffe of the Augmentacions for land due to Leicester Abby at the Feast of St Michael and for an Acquittance for the same		7	4
Paid to Mr Thomas Palmer for a Cheif Rent of a shopp under the Gainsborough in the occupacion of Mr Plummer		2	6
Paid the Bayliffe of Mereton Colledge Oxon for one Cheif Rent Issuing and payable out of the hospitall of St John and St Leonard in or near the Burrough of Leicester at Michaelmas last		1	3
Paid to him for a Shopp In Richard Bayliffes occupacion .		1	0
Paid to the Wardens of the Company of Taylors an Annual Rent payable to them etc		1	8
Paid to Mr Palmer for the Lords place		4	2
Paid to Mr Dyson her Majesties Receiver for one whole yeares Rent due out of the Lands & tenements belonging to the hospitall of St John's & St Leonards in or near the Burrough of Leicester, heretofore Mr Harvey and Mr Tatams Leases and in Countesthorpe and Humberston Syseton Mills & the White Horse in Gallow tree gate for one whole year at Michaelmas	31	12	5
Paid to the said Receiver for the Lands and tenements belonging to the said late Guild called St Margaretts Guild in Leicester Town Obiit Lands & vicars Closes heretofore in the occupacion of Arthur Tatam for a yeares Rent due at Michaelmas last	42	18	1
Paid him for the Lands Parcell of the Lands in the possession of the late Guild called the Corpus Christi Guild for one yeares Rent due at Michaelmas last	14	12	6

Paid to the said Receiver for certain Lands & tenements Cheif Rents & Lammas Tyth's parcell of the possessions of the Colledge of the Blessed Virgin Mary over against the Castle of Leicester for a years Rent due at Michaelmas last	20	8	6
Paid to the said receiver for certain tenements in the Newarke of Leicester collected by the town.	3	16	1
†Paid him more for the Portage and Poundage of £113 13s 11½d And for an Acquittance 1s 6d	2	7	10
Spent at the said Auditt		12	0
To the Door Keeper		1	0†

⟨This not allow'd noe debenture or any of these Fees yet paid⟩

3   At the Auditt held by Mr Loggins at the horse & Trumpett in Leicester

†Paid to the Queens Receiver for a tenement in the Swines Markett in the occupacion of (blank) due at Michaelmas last	2	10	0
Paid him more for the Malt mills in the Swines Markett in the occupacion of Mr Thomas Palmer	1	13	4†

⟨This not allow'd not being paid⟩

†Paid him more for the Rent of the Shambles & Drapery in Leicester due at Michaelmas last	8	13	4
Paid him more for the Gainsborow Chambers & all the Shopps and Shedds & for Saturday Markett which the Mayor Bayliffe & Burgesses purchased of Mr Brittain due for a years Rent at Michaelmas last	4	8	8
Paid him for 3 debentures & a quietus		8	0
Paid him for the portage & Poundage of one hundred Marks & for an Acquittance	1	18	6†

⟨This not being paid is not allowed⟩

4   Fees and other payments this year

Paid to Mr James Annis Mayor for his Sallary according to antient Custom	13	6	8
Paid him more the Rent of Gosling Close allowed him by an Order of Common hall	13	6	8

Paid him more as being Master of the hospitall of the holy Trinity	13	6	8
Paid to Lawrence Carter Esquire Recorder of this Burrough for his yeares Sallary	10	0	0
Paid the Town Clerke for taking the Coroners Inquest .	1	0	0
Paid him more for his Sessions Fee due at Michaelmas only		6	8
Paid him for the Booke of Payments		4	6
Paid Mr Thomas the head schoolmaster being the Towns Free gift during pleasure	16	0	0
Paid the head Usher of the said School his Sallary . .	8	0	0
Paid the under Usher of the said School being the Towns Free Gift during pleasure	3	0	0
Paid Mr Cart for his yeares allowance as Lecturer of the Burrough during pleasure	20	0	0
Paid Mr Fox vicar of St Mary's being the Towns free gift during pleasure	10	0	0
Paid the Town Clerke for his years Sallary . . .	1	6	8
Paid him more being the Towns free gift . . .	2	13	4
Paid for the Rentall	2	0	0
Paid him for proclaiming the Faires & Marketts . .		14	0
Paid him for the Commission this year		7	8
Paid the Macebearer for his yeares Sallary Gown mony & Pipes	6	9	8
Paid him more for 5 seales		5	0
Paid Edward Sutton and the other Serjeant . . .	1	6	8
Paid the four Serjeants to keep them from going about with their Christmas Box	1	6	8
Paid John Ogden and Joseph Abell for their years Sallary Sweeping the Town Hall & Gainsborough	1	13	4
Paid Thomas Olliver & George Beson their Sallary for Sweeping & Gates & weeding the Town Hall yard	2	0	0
Paid to them to keep them from going about with their Christmas Box		4	0
Paid Mr Kilby for keeping the Library	3	0	0
Paid the Waites for their years Sallary	6	13	4
Paid Mr Handy for keeping the house of Correction .	1	13	4
Paid the Sexton of St Martins for Ringing the Bell on Michaelmas day		1	0

Paid the halbert men for walking the fair on Michaelmas day		9	0
Paid the Clerke of the Assizes for two Assizes . .	1	6	8
Paid George Broom for hunting on Easter day . .		10	0
Paid the Cryer for keeping the Barr two Assizes . .		2	0
Paid for forty five hundred & an halfe of Coales for Mr Mayor & Carrying in	1	8	5¾
Paid the Grand Jury two Sessions And allowed by an Order of Hall £1	3	8	0
Paid the Constables two double Sessions . . .	1	4	0
Paid the Ringers at St Mary's when Mr Mayor was Sworn at the Castle		2	6
Paid Mr Dysons man John Hoyes and the Castle Keeper 1s each		3	0
Paid Mosely 1s per Week for a year	2	12	0
Paid Mr Palmer in the New hospitall 2s per week for a year	5	4	0
Paid James Watson for Burning Pipes & Pipes bought of him		5	9
Paid James Mason for 6 Besoms		1	0
Paid for a Ribbon for the Charter		2	0
Paid for a Quarter of Charcoal		4	0
For Bunns & Ale Tobacco & Pipes & Christmas Fair .		11	0
Paid Thomas Olliver for Sweeping the West bridge . .			6
Paid for Holly Ivy & Nails			6
Paid Walter Wyer for throwing the snow off the Town Chancell		1	6
Paid Mr Pare for a Hogshead of Ale on the day of Thanksgiving	4	0	0
Paid for drawing the Ale and Carrying it to the Gainsborough at night		2	0
Paid the Drums at the Burnfire		3	0
Paid for 10 Gallons of Ale at Mr Ayres . . .		11	8
Paid for 10 Gallons of Ale at John Dawsons . .		11	8
Paid for 12 Gallons of Ale at George Halls . . .		14	0
Paid for 20 Kidds for the Burnfire & fetching . . .		5	4
Paid for 7 Gentlemens Ordinarys		7	0
Paid for 15 Servants Ordinarys		10	0
Paid for Cleansing the East gates of the Ice . . .			6
Paid for fetching the Kidds to the Quick Sand at Belgrave gate end		1	2
Paid Sarah Parker for cleansing the Horsetrough . .		2	0

Paid for Biscuit to treat the Judge		1 6
For two Penny Loafes		2
Paid for peas Stray to Law upon the Kidds at the Belgrave gate cnd		9
Paid the Town Clerk for a Letter of Attorney . .		4 6
Paid for going to Loughborow & Horsehire to Meet the Commissioners		16 3
Paid the Town Clerk for his Jorney to Loughborow .		6 8
Paid him Lewin his Charges for going over to Loughborow about the Tax of Freaks grounds		3 0
Paid for Bunns Ale Pipes & Tobacco when the school was visited		11 0
Paid Susanna Ogden as by Order of Hall . . .		10 0
Paid the Old Beadle as by Order of Hall . . .	1	0 0
Paid George Townsend for the Beadles Staff . . .		1 6
Paid for Biscuit Pipes Tobacco & Ale to treat the Bishopp .		5 9
Paid Joseph Smith for makeing a handle to the Bell mans Bell		2
Paid for a Table for the Town Clerks Chamber . .		12 0
Paid Mr Lee to Ballance his Accompt		10 1½
Paid for Biscuits for the Judge		1 6
For Ale for the Servants & Tobacco		2 3
Paid Dr Hartopp for a years Interest of twenty Pound .	1	0 0
Paid the Duke of Rutlands Keeper for his Fee for a Buck .		10 9
A mans Charges & lying out all night		5 8
Paid Mr Foxton for two pair of Shoes for the Beadle & Cryer		8 0
For a Hogshead of Ale at the venison Feast at Mr Pares .	4	0 0
For 15 Gentlemens Dinners then		15 0
For 15 Servants at the same time		10 0
Paid the man for drawing the Ale		1 0
Paid Mr Noone for his Fee Farm rent out of Raisons Land due to him when Chamberlin		6 8
Paid Thomas Hall for Mending the Town Lanthorn .		6
Paid Mrs Coy being part of the purchase money And for the Fine & Writeings	14	0 0
And for 10 Months Interest		12 0
Paid John Ward & James Mason as being Well Reeves for the Well near the Town hall		2 0
Paid for taking upp and setting down the posts by Mr Nobles		6
Paid for setting down 6 posts at the Gallow Causeway .		1 2

Paid the Recorder for Advise upon the Tithe of Houghton Land & other business	2	3	0
Paid the Lottery to putt out Stevensons Boy of the Parish of St Martins Apprentice	6	0	0
Paid Mr Fox as by Order of Hall		13	4
Paid for a Letter from Mr Noble			3½
Paid Mr Lewin Mr Headly & Mr Denshier for the presents to the Judge 2 Assizes	4	5	0
Paid Mr Lee for the Town Plate	2	0	0
Paid the Town Clerk for Drawing and Ingrossing an Address to the Queen		10	0
Paid him for makeing the Chamberlains Accounts . .	3	6	8
Paid him for Coales allowed him		6	3
Paid the Chamberlins this year for their pains & Charges in Collecting the Town Rents without setting of any debts or decay's other than what are allowed by the Town	6	13	4
Paid them for the Auditors Dinners		6	8
Allowed them for wast of Coales		13	4
Paid Mr Smalley as per bill	2	1	9½
Paid Mr Caulton as per bill		18	7
Paid Mr Ludlam as per bill	1	15	8½
Paid William Wood for making a table etc as per bill .		18	0
Paid Mr Bunney as per bill	1	2	10
Paid Mr Gambles Bill		7	0
Paid Mr Wards Bill		13	6
Paid Mr Westons bill		17	6
Paid Mr Lees bill	11	15	8
Paid Mr Martins bill	7	11	6
Paid David Gee		3	4
Paid Mr Cradocks bill	12	2	0
Paid Mr Elsmere as per bill	10	15	10
And for Interest of £130	6	10	0
Paid Mr Nobles bill	3	6	2
Paid Mr Woodlands bill		15	10½
Paid Mr Noble for Debentures	(blank)		
Paid Mr Fox out of the waterlaggs		2	0
Paid Mr Berwells man for 2 Acquittances . . .			8
Paid Mr Lee as per another bill	3	2	0
Benjamin Garland as per bill	1	4	0
Joseph Ashwell per bill	1	0	4
George Lickerish per bill		7	6
Twiggs Pilgrim per bill		5	0

H

Augustine Hefford per bill	1	16	1½
Mr Goodrich per bill	2	0	0

This by new bills since the Auditt

5   For Repairs this year

Paid Nathaniel Hughs for 3 Load of Stones . . .		6	0
Paid Roger Dawson for one Load of stones . . .		2	0
Paid Joseph Leggitt for a Load of Stones . . .		2	0
Paid Ludlam & Shrewsbury for 6 days work & Bear. .		5	0
Paid Goodman Johnson for a Load of Stones . . .		2	0
For spreading the stones		1	0
Paid Rowland Marler for a Load of Stones . . .		2	0
Paid Shrewsbury for 4 days worke & Bear . . .		3	6
Paid Bassett & Ludlam for spreading the Rubbish . .		2	4
Paid Mr Dormer	1	1	6
Paid Benjamin Hunt for a Tubb		2	6
Paid the Carver	2	0	0
Paid Mr Hood for Ropes		3	9
Paid for fetching 5 Freestones		1	0
Paid Mr Abney for 6 Load of Sand & Carridge . .		15	0
Paid for 3 Stones from the Bear back gate and Carridge .		8	0
Paid Mr Rudings bill for Stones & Carridge . . .	1	3	0
Paid Mr Watts for 3 Ketton Stones		5	0
Paid Mr Manning as per bill	14	7	6½
Paid Henry Beaumonts bill	2	8	0
Paid Mr Willows Bill	10	6	4
Paid Mr Pratts bill	2	18	6
Paid Mr Broughton	5	1	11
Paid Robert Headley's bill	1	3	10
Paid Thomas Hewsons bill		7	7
Paid Mr Thomas Topp as per bill		17	0
Paid Augustine Heffords Bill	14	12	2
Paid Mr Joshua Goodrich his bill	3	0	10
Paid Mr Wilkins's bill	1	5	0
Paid Richard Skelsons bill		13	8
Paid Twigges Pilgrims bill	15	0	0
Paid William Staples bill	34	8	9½
Paid Edward Palmers bill	9	19	7
Paid Robert Halls bill		6	3
Paid Mr Low for Stones		1	3
Paid John Gutheridge's bill		14	0
Paid Mr Manning as per bill	1	1	2

	£	s	d
Paid Benjamin Garland as per bill	7	2	0
Paid the Cryer & Beadle for watching the Conduit . .		5	0
Paid George Liquorish as per bill	14	13	0
Paid for Stones from the Old Hospitall		5	0
Paid for Stones from the Abbey		18	0
Paid for 3 Stones at Mr Braces		2	3
Paid Henry Hind		8	6
Paid Mr Lee for Stones to pave with		(blank)	

9   Taxes allowed this year

	£	s	d
For the Stalls & Sheep pens	5	0	0
The window Tax for the Bridewell		6	0
The Queens Tax for the same		14	0
Paid Mr Noone the Cheif Constable		5	6
Paid Mr Perkins of Loughborow for Freaks ground .		2	3
Mr Abney for his Southfeild and Forest Close . .	8	6	0
Mr Southwell for the Southfeild & Grange and for his Close	8	10	8
Mr Pratt for the Southfeild Forrest Close & Wards . .	6	5	6
Thomas Wards years tax for the Southfeilds . .	5	15	6
Henry Colson years Tax for the Southfeild Grange & Forest Close	6	11	5
Mr John Wilkins the Southfeild & his Forest Close . .	6	1	9
Allowed him more out of Mr Southwells . . .	1	0	0
William Page & Mr Deakins for his Meadow behind the Mill	1	10	0
William Bryers for the Swans Mills	3	0	0
Thomas Wall for the North Mill & Shopp . . .	3	14	0
Mr Newton		4	0
Mr Hill		6	0
Robert Warburton		6	0
Edward Burley		4	0
Mr Bayley		4	0
Mr Orme		4	0
Mrs Hobson		4	0
Mr Hammond		8	0
Mr Hewett		4	0
William Astwell		4	0
Mrs Mansfeild		4	0
William Orton		8	0
Mrs Lee		4	0
Mr Treen		4	0

Mary Moreton	4	0
Mrs Coates	4	0
John Denshire	4	0
Mrs Wilson	4	0
Mr Hartshorne	1 4	0
Mr Noon	4	0
John Coates	4	0
Mr Simpson	4	0
Mrs Hill	4	0
Widow Chamberlyn	4	0
Mr Southwell	5	0
Matthew Sheffeild	12	0
Richard Roberts	3 4	4
William Hastwell	4	0
Richard Yates	4	0
Mr Farmer	12	0
Mr Rudeing	1 13	4
Ralph Ward	4	0
Mr Ayres	4	0
Mr Richards	4	0
William Newton	4	0
Mr Townsend	1 4	0
Mr Mawson	4	0
Mr Wells	4	0
John Cartwright	4	0
Mr Watts & Bellamy	1 13	4
Mrs Cooke	3 1	1
Mr Franks	6	0
John Savage	8	0
Widow Garratt	4	0
Widow Wagstaff	12	0
Augustine Hefford	4	0
Mr Johnson for Tyth	8	0
More for his Meadowes	1 10	0
Henry Vollentine	4	0
Mr Barwell	1 12	0
Mr Smalley	3	6
Mr Judd	4	0
Mr Pare	8	0
Mr Pilgrim	8 9	0
Mr Palmer	4	0
John Ashwell	8	0
George Broom	8	0

Samuell Ball	4	0
Attons Land	4	0

[End of Payments]

[Pious and Charitable Uses start here]

1   Receipts this year for pious and Charitable uses

Her Majesties Receiver of the honour of Leicester parcell
of her Majesties Dutchy of Lancaster given by Queen
Elizabeth of ever blessed Memory to the Mayor Bayliffes
& Burgesses of Leicester towards the maintenance of the   10 0 0
head Master of the Free Grammer School in Leicester
for one year at Michaelmas

Sir Richard Newdigate for one years Annuity payable out
of the Manor of Theddingworth being the Gift of Sir
Ralph Rawlett towards the maintenance of the Head   3 6 8
Usher per Annum

Mr John Norrice for one Annuity payable out of a Close
in the Abby Gate called the Abby Gate Close for the
better maintenance of the head usher of the said School   3 6 8
per Annum

The Corporacion for one Annuity payable out of certain
Lands in Willoughby Waterless Conveyed to the Corporacion by Henry Earl of Stamford upon the Inclosure   8 0 0
being the Gift of Mr John Norris one of the Aldermen of
the said Burrough to Charitable uses per Annum

Thomas Richards for a peice of ground called Burgess
Meadow which the Town purchased with the hundred
Pounds given by Mr Thomas Gilbert to Charitable uses   4 10 0
with other mony out of the Chamber of the Town per
Lease for 21ty yeares

Henry Hitchcock Gardiner for one orchard in his occupacion Scituate in the Parish of All Saints purchased by
Mr William Ives with the money given by the first   3 1 8
Countess of Devon for the use of the Poor of Leicester
and Parish of St Leonard

Thomas Freeman of Whetstone for a Messuage or tenement & one yard Land heretofore purchased by John
Baker with the 200 Marks given by Christopher Tam-
worth Esquire for divine Service to be celebrated in the   9 3 4
Parish Church of St Martin in Leicester every weekday
morning and evening per Annum

Mr George Bent for the forty Acres of Inclosed ground in the Forest of Leicester given by King Charles the first (of ever blessed Memory) for the use of the poor of this Corporacion to buy wood for twenty Poor People per Annum   14 0 0

Mr John Wilkins for a Meadow ground near the Newarke Mills purchased by Mr Ive of Mr Norris & by him given to Charitable uses per Annum   4 15 0

Mr Wilkins or Mr Gee for a Barn yard whereupon heretofore stood a dwelling house bought of Mr Ive of Mr Hunt and given to Charitable uses per Annum   2 0 0

Mr Richard Townsend for a Messuage Close and backside Scituate near a Lane called Hangmans Lane which the Town purchased of Mr Speechly & given to Charitable uses now held by Lease per Annum   8 0 0

The heires or Executors of Mr John Poultney for one Annuity by him to be paid out of the Mannour of Coates Devill towards the Releif of the Poor of this Corporacion   10 0 0

John Davenport of Bushby for severall enclosed grounds there purchased by the Corporacion by the gift of Mr Nidd for the use and benefitt of the Poor of Mountsorrell County of Leicester And now in the possession of the said Davenport per Lease per Annum   32 0 0

Mr Thomas Hartshorne for the ground late belonging to two tenements heretofore in the occupacion of John Owen and Messinger being the gift of Margarett Hobby to the uses following (vizt) to the under Usher of the Free School 12s to the Poor of the old hospitall 2s 6d to the Poor of the New hospitall 2s to the Widdowes of St Johns hospitall 6d And to the Poor of St Martins and St Mary's Parish 2s apeice   1 1 6

The Executors of Edward Claypole of Alexton County of Leicester for certain Closes there being the gift of Mr Thomas Haines to Certain Charitable uses (vizt) to the scholers of Thrussington £6 to two scholers in Oxford £6 for preaching a Sermon for the deliverance of the Kingdome from the Spanish Armado £1 to the Poor of the Corporacion £5 & for 3 bibles in all   19 0 0

Sir Nathan Wright for one Annuity or yearly Rent Issuing and payable yearly out of a Messuage or tenement called the Parrott being the gift of Mr Hugh Botham to the Poor of St Martins and St Margaretts   2 0 0

Mr John Roberts senior & Mr John Roberts Junior for certain grounds they held of the Corporacion being part of the Closes called Freakes grounds being an Annuity given by the Right honorable the Earl of Huntingdon to and for the Maintenance of the head Master of the Free-Grammer School per Annum — 10 0 0

John Buxton for another Close called Freakes ground being the gift of Mr Courteen & the Gentlemen of the Lottery to the Poor of the Corporacion to be distributed Wheaten bread and other Charitable use in Leicester — 4 16 0

The Earl of Devon Gift to twenty Poor People of this Burrough Six Shillings apeice to buy them Coales per Annum — 6 0 0

Mr Thomas Hartshorne for a peice of ground he holds of the Corporacion out of which Rent there is paid yearly one Annuity given by Mr John & Mr William Stanley for Charitable uses — 5 0 0

2   Charitable Gifts paid this year

	£	s	d
Paid to the Head usher being Queen Elizabeths gift	10	0	0
Paid the gift of Mr Ralph Rawlett	3	6	8
Paid the gift of Mr Norris	3	6	8
Paid the gift of Mr Clarke	1	0	0
Paid the gift of Mr Norris out of Willoughby Land	8	0	0
Paid the gift of Mr John & Mr William Stanley	5	0	0
Paid the gift of the Earl of Devon	6	0	0
Paid the gift of Christopher Tamworth Esquire	7	3	4
Paid the gift of King Charles the first	14	0	0
Paid the gift of Mr William Ives	15	0	0
Paid the gift of Mr Elkington	5	0	0
Paid the gift of Mr John Poultney	10	0	0
Paid the gift of Mr Nidd	32	0	0
Paid Mr Achams gift	9	0	0
Paid the gift of Mr Haines	19	0	0
Paid the gift of Mr Botham	2	0	0
Paid the gift of the Earl of Huntingdon	10	0	0
Paid the gift of Sir William Courteen & the Gentlemen of the Lottery	4	16	0
Paid the gift of Mr Baker	1	0	0
Paid the gift of Mr Ward & Mr Bennett	1	0	0
Paid the gift of Julius Billers	5	12	0

Paid the gift of Widow Orsiter	6	0	0
Paid the gift of Mr Gilbert	5	0	0
Paid the gift of William Hitch		3	0
Paid the gift of Margarett Hobby	1	1	0
Paid the gift of the Countess of Devon	3	0	0
Paid the gift of Mr Hesleridge	1	1	6

[End of Pious and Charitable Uses]

[Supers start here]

Supers

Mr Perkins of Grantham for certain Lands & Leases in Gunnerby	6	8
Sir William Rawlinson for Lands in Oadby . . .	5	$11\frac{1}{2}$
William Burstall for a stall now down	2	0
For a house in Deadmans Lane	1	0
The Earl of Stamford for Thrumaston Mills . . .	6	8
For a Cottage late Ralph Tompsons	1	0
One Empty Glovers Shopp for a year	11	0
Robert Spencer for the Tyth of the Newark Windmills & Watermills ⟨Q.⟩	18	0
Townsends Mill Shopp	3	0
Haddons house now Lewin	(blank)	
Queen Elizabeth Gift paid & not Received . . .	10	0	0

CHAMBERLAINS' ACCOUNTS
1729/30

Burg' Leicr. The Account of John Cartwright & Robert Winfield Chamberlins of the Burrough of Leicester in the Mayoralty of Richard Roberts Esquire for one whole Year from Michaelmas 1729 To Michaelmas 1730

1 [No separate heading inserted]

Augustine Heaford for one Years Rent of the Sheep pens with Cokers Kitchen By Lease payable att Lammas and Candlemas	20	0	0
Mr Clayton Headschoolmaster for the School house due att Michaelmas only			6
The Heires or Executors of Mr John Harrison for Rents of Assizc due Yearly out of Certaine Lands att the North Gates in Occupation of Thomas Turvile Called Gadsby Land att Michaelmas only per Annum		1	9
Josiah Ashwell for a Chamber over the East Gates and for a Shop and Chamber adjoyneing to them lately purchased of him by the Corporation	4	15	0
Mr John Blunt for Butt Close heretofore sold to Mr Thomas Blunt now in the Occupacion of Robert Roulston late Freeman late of John Loseby In Fee Farme per Annum		10	0
Mr Samuell Carte Vicar of St Martins in Leicester for a Chamber Belonging to the Corporacion being part of the Town hall with a Door or Door place att the Top of the Staires goeing to the house of Office now used with the Vicarage house per Annum		2	6
Mr John Noone for a messuage or Tenement att the neather End of Belgrave Gate heretofore the Land of Thomas Headley now Divided into Severall Tenements in Fee Farme per Annum and now in his occupation	1	0	0
The Heires or Executors of Charles Stafford and Alice Brown for a Garden or peice of Ground in the Sanvy Gate in the Occupacion of Brown and Norrise in Fee Farme per Annum		2	6

His Grace the Duke of Devonshire for a Close or peice of Ground in the North Gates whereupon Stood a messuage or Tenement heretofore the Land of George Tatam Tanner In Fee Farme per Annum — 13 4

The said Duke for a parcell of Ground Lyeing in the said Close Late Fletchers Land In Fee Farme per Annum — 4

The Heires or Executors of Thomas Fletcher alias Thomas Alsopp for a peice of Ground Lyeing on the Backside of a messuage or Tenement in the North Gates Sold to John Tatam In fee Simple per Annum paid by William Spencer Hosier — 1 8

John Erpe for a messuage or Tenement and peice of Ground thereunto belonging in the parish of St Nicholas heretofore the Land of William Adcock in fee farm per Annum — 6 8

John Turvile late Mr Barwell for a Tenement near the North Gates the Land of Robert Freer late being the Signe of the Taylors Armes — 1 0 0

John Earpe for a peice of Ground called the water Laggs late in the Occupation of Mr Edmund Johnson Deceased In fee farme per Annum paid by the said John Earpe — 6 8

Thomas Cartwright Joyner for a peice of Ground att the South End of the Butt Close In fee Farme per Annum — 4

Roger Palmer of Gilmorton for Land meadow and pasture heretofore the Land of John Sprigg and now or late of Edward Whitehead paid by William Burditt of Gilmorton — 3 4

Anthony Ingoldsby Esquire for Lands in Great Ashby late the Land of Ralph Brookeby Gentleman heretofore the Land of Nicholas Norton in Fee Farme per Annum — 6

The Heires or Executors of Robert Pawley Esquire for Certaine Lands and Tenements in Scraptoft the Land of Mr John Mason heretofore the Land of Thomas Simpkin and (blank) Tayler of Whetstone and now or late in the Occupation of Matthew Hubbartt paid now by Mr Noell of Scraptoft — 6

3   Receipts of the whole Grange with the Appurtenances and the four Yard Land and the two Yard Land Called Archers Land and

Known by the Name of Weightmans Land, and half Yard Land
the Town Purchased of the Lord Spencer as Followeth

Mr Thomas Willows for part of the Newarke Grange and four Yard Land in the South field of Leicester and the Grange Barne and part of the Yard by Lease per Annum	48	12	6
Mr Thomas Hall for three Yard Land there by Lease per Annum Of him more for the Grange Yard and Barne	37	17	6
Mr George Bent for 4 Yard Land there & parte of the Grange Yard per Lease per Annum	47	0	0
Mr John Pratt for 3 Yard Land there by Lease per Annum Allowed 20s otherwise would be £36 now Bonner	35	0	0
Mr Joseph Johnson for three yard Land and a halfe .	41	0	0
Thomas Foulds for 4 Acres of Land out of the Severall Farmes to Digg Clay to make Brick and for a parcell of Land lying up to the Swanns Windmill next the Cause way Leading up to the Pinfold towards Wiggstone along the Hedge Side and for five Lands Lyeing by the Hedge-Side against Mr Carters windmill to Digg Clay to make Brick per Lease per Annum	8	10	0
Mr Thomas Ward for three Yard Land per Lease per Annum	36	0	0
Michaell Peace for the Newark mills & windmills thereto belonging by Lease per Annum	26	0	0
Mr Richard Goodall and Mr William Brushfield for Goslin Close per Lease per Annum Mr Goodall pays £10 15s 0d and Mr Brushfield £13 5s 0d	24	0	0
Mr Thomas Hartshorne for 3 Acres of Land Lyeing & being in the South fields of the said Burrough late Purchased of Simon Barwell Gentleman late Mr Collins Land now in the possession of the said Mr Hartshorne paid by John Mason	2	0	0

5   Beadhouse Meadow

Mr Thomas Marshall for a meadow late in the possession of Mr Thomas Hartshorne per Lease per Annum	13	10	0
Mr Thomas Marshall for the other meadow late in the possession of Mr Edmund Johnson and Joseph How per Lease per Annum	16	0	0

Mr Edmund Johnson for an Acre and half of Land where- ⎫
upon stands a windmill near the Highway Comeing up ⎬   7   6
from the Horse Faire Close   ⎭

10a   In the North Gates

James Peters for a Tenement late in the Occupation of ⎫   1   0   0
William Palmer Cobler att Will per Annum   ⎭

Mr Edmund Johnson Dyer for the North mill per Annum .   26 0   0

Richard Lawerence per Annum for a Tenement in the ⎫   4   5   0
North Gates att will   ⎭

Mr Thomas Johnson for the Shambles per Annum .   .   85 0   0

The said Mr Edmund Johnson for a windmill lately pur- ⎫   5   0   0
chased by the Corporacion of Josiah Wall   ⎭

10b   In the Sanvey Gate

William Stevenson for a Tenement per Lease per Annum .   15 0

John Stevenson for another Tenement thereto adjoyning ⎫   15 0
per Lease per Annum   ⎭

The Executors of Mr James Annis for another Tenement ⎫
late William Cookes in the Occupation of William Moore ⎬ 5   0
Late John Raysons Land by Lease per Annum   ⎭

Mr Wilkes for a Tenement near the North Gates per ⎫   10
Annum   ⎭

Of him more for a Tenement near the North Gates .   .   2

The Heires or Executors of William Biggs for a Tenement ⎫
near the North Gates paid by Mr Henry Smith Baker in ⎬   1   0
fee farme per Annum   ⎭

10c   In the Soar Lane or Walker Lane   .

William Twickden or Thomas Gorton for a peice of ⎫
Ground sometime a Dunghill now Built upon heretofore ⎬
in the Occupation of Mr William Rudyard and now paid ⎥ 2   0
by Christopher Law in fee farme per Annum   ⎭

William Cave for a house with the Appurtenances late ⎫
Jane Jenards late in the Occupation of Widow Bingham ⎬ 5   10 0
per Annum   ⎭

10d   Within the North Gates

The Heires or Executors of Robert Hickling for a mes- ⎫
suage or Tenement on the South Side of All Saints ⎬   1   10 0
Churchyard in the Occupation of Robert Warburton in ⎥
fee farm per Annum   ⎭

Mary Dyer for a messuage or Tenement late Kimberlains Land in fee farm per Annum · 6 0

Mrs Windsor for a Tenement in the High Street in the Occupation of Joseph Waggett In fee farme per Annum · 5 0

Mr Thomas Carter for a house and Garden in the high Street att the Corner of Bakehouse Lane heretofore in the Occupation of William Ludlam now of Michaell Heard In fee farme per Annum · 4 0

A House and Garden in the Occupation of William Granger heretofore in the Occupation of Widow Worrell 4s 6d For a house in the Occupation of Thomas Smith which was heretofore in the occupation of Robert Grew now used in two Tenements 2s 10d · 7 4

William Newton for the house and Barne lately purchased and Severall Leyes in the horse faire next the house att Will per Annum · 5 0 0

John Willowes for the Ley of Ground on which the Tenters Stand per Lease per Annum · 10 0

Mr George Bent Junior and Mr William Cooke for Severall Leyes which the Corporation Sett them in Consideration they would make publick walkes att their own Expence · 1 0

10e   In the South Gates

Thomas Morton for a house in the occupation of Lawerence Warner per Annum · 1 0 0

Thomas Wall late John Hardy for a messuage or Tenement att the Corner End of Hangman lane late the Land of Elizabeth Chamberlaine in fee farme per Annum · 16 0

Mr Chapman and Mr Gamble for a messuage or Tenement call'd the Swann near the South Gates in the Occupation of Thomas Bradsworth in fee farme per Annum · 13 4

10f   In Burgess's Meadow

The Heirs or Executors of Mr George Abney or William Palmer Esquire for a peice of meadow Ground in Saint Marys meadow called the Shield late Mr Mortons Land in the possession of Mr Hartshorne in fee farme per Annum · 16 0

Of them or one of them more for two Acres of meadow late also Mr Mortons Lands In the possession of Mr Hartshorne In fee farme per Annum · 13 4

10g   In the Swines Markett

Mr Thomas Palmer Attorney att Law for a messuage or
Tenement late Mr Benningtons Land in the Occupation
of Michaell Benshaw now Mr Cromwell in fee farm per   6   0
Annum

Widow Warburton now Mr Smalley for a Tenement heretofore called the Kingshead late John Humpherys late   18   0
also Agnes Ortons Land now paid by John Throseby

10i   In the Saturday Markett

Mr William Cooke for a messuage or Tenement now
Divided into two Tenements in his Occupation and Mr   1   3   4
William Noones in fee farm per Annum

William Higginson for a messuage or Tenement there in
his Occupation in fee farm per Annum   8

10j   In Loseby Lane

Mr William Orton mercer for a messuage or Tenement
late John Felzers Land heretofore Sold to John Parnell
late in the occupation of John Moore now Palmer Cobler   10   0
In fee farme per Annum

Mr Jonathan Buckerfield and John Needham late Mr
Southwell for the houses and Gardens in fee farme per   1   6   0
Annum

Samuell Coates for a house called the Red Cow the Land
of Jackson in the Occupation of him In fee farme per   12   0
Annum

Of him more for a peice of Ground adjoyning to the said   A Damask
house paying yearly att midsummer   Rose

John Dallaway for a house and Backside being parcell of a
Tenement late in Vallintine Dallaways Occupation Since
new Built now in the Occupation of Jacob Bothomley per   4   0   0
Lease per Annum

Richard Garle Junior Hosier for a messuage or Tenement
lately Built in fee Farme per Annum   10   0

Edward Caulton for a house and Backside late Richard
Dawsons Since new Built per Lease per Annum   6   0   0

10k   In the Gallow tree Gate

Mr Thomas Ayre for a house late in the Tenure of Samuell
Cooper and now of Thomas Reynolds or Loftus Page in   8   0
fee farme per Annum

Mr Thomas Ayre for a messuage or Tenement commonly called or Known by the name of the white horse in the Occupation of William Peters in fee farme per Annum — 1 0 0

The Heires or Executors of Mr James Palmer for one Yard Land Sold to Mr James Annis paid by John Mason or Mr Smalley in fee farme per Annum — 15 0

10l   In the Gallow tree Gate on the west side

Randolph Butler for a messuage or Tenement over against the Roundhill Sold to John Woodford now Mr Lambert In fee Farme per Annum — 10 0

John Hose and Edward Beasely for a messuage or Tenement Adjoyning to the North Side of the Angell heretofore Edmund Astills Land in fee Farme per Annum — 4 0

The Heires or Executors of Mr Henry Palmer for a messuage or Tenement in Robert Graves Occupation In fee Farme per Annum — 1 0 0

10m   In the Belgrave Gate

Henry Hitchcock for a Garden at the neather End of the Belgrave Gate late in his Occupation in fee farm per Annum now Thomas Drake — 12 0

Thomas Redley for a Tenement in the Occupation of Robert Yates Tayler in fee farm per Annum — 13 4

The Executors of Thomas Glister for a house now Joseph Astill in fee farme per Annum — 1 0 0
⟨Q. if not at will⟩

Ralph Ward Cordwayner for a Tenement with the Appurtenances heretofore Ralph Simpsons Adjoyning to the Unicorn on the North Side thereof In fee farme per Annum — 15 0

Edward Noone for a Tenement on the East Side of the Said Street late the Land of Richard Ward In fee farme per Annum — 18 0

The Churchwardens of Saint Margaretts parish for a peice of Ground in the Cow pasture there in fee farm per Annum — 8 0

10n   In the Country

James Winstanley Esquire for Certaine Lands Closes Leyes and pasture Ground in the Lordshipp of Branston in the County of Leicester now or Late in the Occupation of William Burton in fee Farme per Annum — 12 8

Thomas Sansome for a Close and Croft and one Yard Land with the Appurtenances in Hinkley in his Occupation In fee farme per Annum   15 0

The Heires or Executors of Mr Thomas Worrall for a parcell of Land in Belgrave called Kimpton hill Leys and one Yard Land heretofore sold to Anthony Culverton Lyeing in a Close of pasture Ground there near to Belgrave Bridge and late Mr Overings Land paid by widow Cartwright of Oadby In fee farme per Annum   9 0

Sir Clobery Noell Baronet for one messuage or Tenement and one Yard Land with the Appurtenances In Kirkby Mallery in fee farm per Annum   6 8

Mr Richard Benskin of Rearsby for a messuage or Tenement there in his occupation In fee farme per Annum   17 0

William Knifton of Segrave for a Close and Croft there late the Land of William Hubbart In fee farme per Annum   2 0

Mr Benjamin Storer of Thrusington for one Yard Land there in his occupation in fee farm per Annum   6 8

Richard Hackett of Claybrook for the Foss Close & meadow in Frolesworth   16 0 0

Isaac Townesend George Walton Thomas Sutton and Edward Marshall for the Land att Burbage lately purchased of Mr Barnwell and others   29 0 0

More of the Said Townesend Walton and Sutton for Cheife Rent   13 2

William Tompson of Houghton Super Monten for a peice of Land in his Occupation or William Hubbarts occupation in fee farme per Annum   1 8

William Buckley of Thornton for another parcell of Land thereto belonging in the Occupation of Thomas Redley of Houghton in fee farme per Annum   5 0

Robert James for Certaine Lands in Barkby in the occupation of Thomas Redley in Fee farme per Annum   8 0

Mr John Watts for Certaine Lands Leyes & Hades in the west fields of Leicester in the Occupation of Walter Rudings Esquire in fee farme per Annum   4 0

George Ashby Esquire for a messuage or Tenement in Hungerton now or late in the Occupation of Elias Marshall heretofore Sold to Sir Thomas Cave Knight in fee farme per Annum   1 10 0

Thomas Burbage or the Heires or Executors of George Sheffield for the Mill there Called Siston Mill and a house in Siston heretofore Sold to Sir Thomas Cave Knight In fee farme per Annum	3	6	8

11a Other Rents of Lands or Tenements parcell of the Town Obiit Lands of Saint Margaretts Guild and parcell of the Fee Farme Rents heretofore Demised by Queen Elizabeth to Mr Hawkins and Mr Bates by Indenture Expired

Mr William Ive for the Ground heretofore belonging to Severall houses heretofore Mr Nurses William Hills and Francis Coles Ruined in the late wares heretofore Sold to Mr Dannett Abney In fee farme per Annum now paid by Mr Farmer	2	13	4
The Heires of Mr John Ludlam for a messuage or Tenement with the Appurtenances commonly called or Known by the name of the white Lyon late in the occupation of Thomas Hall now in the Occupation of John Veasey In fee farme per Annum		10	0
Mr Thomas Harteshorne for a messuage or Tenement in the Occupation of William Campion and James Fox In fee farme per Annum paid by Charles Tuffley Baker	1	0	0
Robert Bonner for the Ground lately belonging to two Tenements late in the Tenure of Paul Abney Deceased belonging to a messuage Known by the name of the Bull Ruin'd in the late wares Since Built upon and now paid by the Said Robert Bonner In fee farme per Annum	1	6	8
Mr Thomas Harteshorne for a messuage or Tenement called the Grayhound Ruin'd in the late wares Since Built upon and paid by Mr Chapman In fee farme per Annum	1	0	0

11b   In the Swines Markett

Mr Samuell Judd for a messuage or Tenement in Silver Street over against the pump late Daniel Murfines Land In fee farme per Annum	1	0	4

11c   In or near Belgrave Gate

Mr John Newton for a messuage or Tenement att the Corner of Humberston Gate Divided into Severall Tenements in the Occupation of Samuell Hunt and others In fee farm per Annum	1	1	0

I

Mr Thomas Ayres for Land late Mr Tatams in the Occupation of Richard Heaford and others In fee farme per Annum now Mr Thomas Pares   12   0

Benjamin Cartwright Joyner for a Tenement called the Lamb late in the Occupation of John Wellingar and for one other messuage or Tenement and Close with the Appurtenances heretofore Sold to George Coates and late the Land of Mr George Blunt in the Occupation of the said Benjamin Cartwright paid by John Cartwright in fee farme per Annum   1   6   8

John Noone for a house there in the Occupation of (blank) Noone widow in fee farm per Annum   1   0   0

Mr Cooper out of Rawletts Close the Gift of Mr Twickeen .   2   0   0

Mr Alcock of Enderby for Land there the gift of Mr John Bent to St Johns Hospitall   30   0   0

Mr Simpson for the Tippetts   13   4

Mr Rudings for the Duck Holmes   3   0   0

The Heires or Executors of Robert Burbage Carpenter for a house late in William Headleys Occupation now in Charles Houghtons occupation and Others in fee Farme per Annum   12   0

Augustine Heaford for a house called the Cock In fee farme per Annum Mr Edward Noones pays 1s 8d Thomas Worth pays 5s near the Cannon   6   8

William Taylor for a messuage or Tenement in the Occupation of William Moseby in fee farme per Annum now Theophilus Cramp   16   0

A messuage or Tenement in the Occupation of Ellenor Denshire and for another part call'd the Cock In fee farme per Annum Ellen Denshire per Annum 10s widow Freer or William Freer 3s 4d now paid by Mr Thomas Willowes   13   4

Elizabeth Bale for a Tenement heretofore Sold to Robert Roberts in Job Withers occupation In fee farme per Annum now William Harris Hatter   5   0

John Roberts Junior for a messuage or Tenement late in the Occupation of William Gamble late in John Dennis's Occupation and now of Thomas Adcock given him by the Town dureing pleasure per Annum   1   0

Richard Scarborow for a Tenement in the Occupation of
John Meachem in Lease per Annum In the Occupation of
Scarborow now Addition of Building for which he is ad- } 3 0 0
vanced Rent after £5 per Cent the Charge of which was
£75 now Thomas Adcock
   ⟨now Sett att £3 per annum for 3 years⟩

11e   In Canke Street

John Payne or Thomas Phipps for a Tenement late in the }
Occupation of Thomas Ayres In fee farme per Annum   13 4

11f   Saint Nicholas and St Maryes Parish

Widow Lewin for a messuage or Tenement late John }
Attons Land in Fee Farm per Annum   13 0

Oliver Grace for a messuage or Tenement att the west }
Bridge called the Mytre and Key in his Occupation In fee } 1 0 0
Farme per Annum

Mr John Cooper for a messuage or Tenement in the High }
Street heretofore called the Flying horse heretofore the } 1 10 0
Land of Thomas Overing In fee farme per Annum

12 Other Rents of Lands or Tenements parcell of the Town and
manner of Leicester heretofore among other things given and
Granted to the Mayor Bayliffes and Burgesses and their Successors in fee farme per Annum

Thomas Poyner for a house and peice of Ground in or }
near Saint Margaretts Church Gate per Lease per Annum } 2 0 0

Edward Palmer Slater for a peice of Ground now Built }
upon heretofore the Land of Mr Tatam In fee farme per } 2 6
Annum paid by Mr John Noon

Mr Thomas Palmer Attorney att Law for a Tenement }
with the Appurtenances late the Land of William Inge } 8 0
Esquire late Smalleys Land In fee farme per Annum

William Erpe or Charles Johnson for a house and peice of }
Ground called the Hermitage near Saint James Chappell } 1 0
Close per Annum

George Rayson Pratt for a peice of Ground in All Saints }
Parish called the Vine Yard in his own Occupation In fee } 4 0
farme per Annum

Mr Thomas Bradley for part of a peice of Ground called Lyon Yard late the Land of Samuell Robinson Deceased lyeing in St Martins parish In fee farme per Annum	2	6
Of him more for one other part of the Said Lyon Yard and a messuage or Tenement in his Occupation In fee farme per Annum now paid by John Weightman	2	6
Mr William Orton mercer for a house and Barne called Sansby Land Scituate in the Satterday markett late the Land of William Mitchell Clerk in the Occupation of the said William Orton In fee farme per Annum	2 0	0
John Coates for apeice of Ground now Daniell Carres Extending from the Sanvey Gate to the Common Oven whereupon a house was built by William Carr In fee farme per Annum	2	6
William Cromwell late John Major Esquire for a peice of Ground near St Margaretts Church Yard where a house formerly Stood called the farme house In fee farme per Annum		6
Thomas Turvile for a peice of Ground near Froggmore Bridge now Built upon in the Occupation of William Jarvise In fee farme per Annum	1	0
Francis Richards Thomas Beaumont or John Groce or one of them for a peice of Ground In Deadman Lane In fee farme per Annum	1	0

13 Of the Rents Christi Guild in Leicester heretofore Mr Archers Collection and now parcell of the Lands and Tenements which the said Mayor Bayliffes and Burgesses Purchased of Queen Elizabeth to them and their Successors Forever

Thomas Tayler Baker for a messuage or Tenement with the Appurtenances in the Swines markett late in the Occupation of Susannah Cooper in fee farme per Annum	13	4
The Heires or Executors of Mr Edward Browne for a messuage or Tenement in the Swines markett heretofore Known by the Signe of the Crown in the Occupation of Mr Hammond In fee farme per Annum	1 1	8
John Wildbore or Robert Lord for a messuage or Tenement In his Occupation In fee farme per Annum	1 6	8

George Barwell for a Tenement near the Little Bridge in the North Gates heretofore Leased to Robert Cousens for one and Forty Years and now Leased to George Cousens for one and Forty Years — 15 0

The Heires or Executors of Mr George Steers for a messuage or Tenement in the Gallowtree Gate now Divided into two Tenements in the Occupation of John Scoffield and David Hennell now Mr Smalley In fee farme per Annum — 13 4

Mr John Simpson for a messuage or Tenement in the Saterday markett newly Built in the Occupation of Mr Benjamin Lewis in fee farme per Annum — 1 0 0

Mr Anthony Palmer or the Heires or Executors of Mr George Beckett for another messuage or Tenement thereunto adjoyning in the Occupation of John Coates Baker in Fee Farm per Annum — 1 0 0

The Heirs or Executors of Mr John Ludlam late Mr Wanley for a messuage or Tenement near Saint Martins Church in the Occupation of Edward Scarborow In fee farme per Annum — 6 8

Mr Abstinence Pougher for a messuage or Tenement In Parchmine Lane in his Occupation In fee farme per Annum — 16 0

Robert Clarke or Robert Hutchins of Loughborough for Certaine Land and pasture Ground in Loughborough aforesaid called Sadlers Land now or late in the Occupation of John Boss of Loughborough In fee farme per Annum paid by the Trustees of Barrow Hospitall — 10 0

The Overseers of the poor of St Nicholas parish for a Chamber over the west Gates per Annum — 10 0

Edward Goode or Mr John Smalley for a Shopp near the East Gates heretofore Sold to Mr Davie late the Land of (blank) Wiggley in fee farme per Annum — 12 0

Mr Blunt for a messuage or Tenement on the East Side of East Gates in Mr Hoods Occupation In Fee Farme per Annum — 12 0

The Executors of Mr James Palmer for a peice of Ground heretofore a Garden over against the Townhall now Built upon late Fletchers Land now in the Occupation of William Cooke In Fee Farme per Annum — 1 0

Mr Richard Goodall for a Tenement in Parchmine Lane
heretofore a Stable Sometime Mr Herricks Land In Fee
Farme per Annum
}   6 8

Mr Thomas Pochin of Barkby for three Quarters of a
Yard Land in Barkby late the Land of Thomas Seale In
Fee Farme per Annum
}   6 0

Robert James of Barkby for a Croft & half Yard Land late
Thomas Gibsons In Fee Farm per Annum
}   6 8

Mrs Phillippa Palmer for a messuage or Tenement in the
Swines markett in the Occupation of Keneline Robinson
and now of Mr Thomas Halford in fee farme per Annum
}   6 0

William Franke Esquire for a parcell of Land Lyeing in
the neather End of St James Chappell Close where a house
formerly Stood late the Land of William Boman in his
occupation In fee farm per Annum
}   4 0

A house and Garden in Saint Martins Church Yard in
the occupation of (blank) Ougden paid by the Overseers
of St Martins parish In fee farme per Annum
}   13 4

Mr Perkins of Grantham for Certaine Lands and Leyes in
the Town Field and Territoryes of Gunnerby in County
of Lincoln heretofore in the Occupation of one Keneline
In Fee Farme per Annum
}   6 8

Mr Ralph Wells for a Close in or near the Cow Drift late
Mr Herricks Land & heretofore Hasteings Land In Fee
Farme per Annum
}   10 0

John Cooper for a Shopp and other Buildings on the East
Side of the Roundhill in the Occupation of Andrew Birstall Barber In fee farm per Annum
} 1 0 0

Samuell Marshall for a house and Backside in Shambles
lane heretofore Mr Harris's In fee farme per Annum
}   1 0

14a Other Rents part of the possession of the late Guild in Leicester
parcell of the Town Obiit heretofore Collected by Mr Arthur
Tatam

Henry Browne Hosier for a messuage or Tenement in
Apple Gate Street late in the Occupation of Joseph Birstall
late Henry Coates Land In fee farme per Annum now
John Wilsons Land
} 1 0 0

Thomas Cave for a messuage or Tenement in the Said
Street late being in the Occupation of Benjamin Hurst
Baker In fee farme per Annum
}   9 0

William Higginson for a Corner house in the Same Street heretofore one William Clarkes matt maker & late James Kirks late in one Silvesters occupation in fee farme per Annum — 6 8

Ralph Ward in the Same Street a messuage or Tenement heretofore in the occupation of Robert Herrick pipe maker In fee farme per Annum — 10 0

William Higginson for the weekday Shambles per Lease annum — 2 0 0

John Cooper Carpenter for a messuage or Tenement in his Occupation per Annum — 8 0

The Heires or Executors of Mr Robert Winfield for a house late John Silbys in the Occupation of John Foxon In fee farme per Annum now David Winfields — 7 0

John Bound for a messuage or Tenement and Garden in the Occupation of William Savidge att the white Swann In fee farme per Annum — 14 0

Mr Henry Smith for a peice of Ground in the possession of John Bull called the Mayors old hall and near Saint Nicholas's Church — 3 4

14b   In the South Gates

The Heires or Executors of Mr Richard Barwell for a house and Garden near the South Gates In the Occupation of Mr John Newton by Lease per Annum — 2 0 0

Widow Gray or her Daughter for a peice of Ground belonging to the house Ruined in the late wars Sold to Robert Hartshorne or his Father in the Occupation of John Bullin in fee farme per Annum paid by Thomas Lacey Brickmaker — 10 0

Mr Thomas Hartshornes Executors for the Ground lately belonging to two Tenements in the Occupation of John Palmer In fee farme per Annum Mr Chapman pays 6s & Charles Tuffley 4s — 10 0

The Heirs of Dr Coleman or Thomas Aston for the Ground belonging to two Tenements late in the Occupation of John Turlington and Henry Charles called the Swann with a Barne thereto belonging Ruined in the late wares Since Built upon by Hugh Aston in the Occupation of Joseph Treen In fee farme — 1 5 0

Ralph Ward Cordwayner for a Tenement late Mr South-wells Land in the Occupation of Widow Ireland In Fee Farme per Annum	10	0

14c   In the Gallow tree Gate

Henry Vallintine or Mr Hennell for a messuage or Tenement Late John Fryers late Mr Samuell Woodlands late in Henry Vallintines Occupation Known by the name of the Queens head now new Built In fee farme per Annum	1	6	8
The Heires or Executors of Dr Harthopp for a messuage or Tenement Known by the name of the Cinque Foyle late in the Occupation of George Broom per Annum Since new Built	2	0	0
Mr Robert Lord for a messuage or Tenement heretofore Known by the name of the Bucks head and now in the Occupation of John Mason In fee farme per Annum		5	0

14d   In Humberstone Gate

The Executors of John Major Esquire for a Garden here-tofore Sold to Michaell Walton of Bushby In fee farme per Annum paid by Mrs Goadby	2	0

14e   In Belgrave Gate

Joseph Tayler for a messuage or Tenement in the Occupation of Arthur Astlin In fee farme per Annum		16	0
John Wellingar for a messuage or Tenement late the land of Robert Johnson in the Occupation of George Redley per Annum		13	4
John Bass for a messuage or Tenement late the Land of Robert Gamble in his Occupation in fee farme per Annum		18	0
John Cooper for a Shopp and Chamber Scituate on the Roundhill In fee farme per Annum	1	0	0
The Heirs of Richard Garratt for a messuage or Tenement Called the Cannon late Stevensons Land In fee farme per Annum		12	0
The Heires or Executors of Mr John Ludlam 14s and Thomas Walton 8s for 2 Tenements late in the Occupation of George Chamberlaine and Widow Almey In fee farme per Annum	1	2	0
Thomas Gregory for a house and Garden late the Land of Henry Garratt in the Occupation of the said Thomas Gregory In fee farme per Annum		6	0

Of him more for a house late Garratts now in the occupation of Edward Payne In fee farm per Annum — 8 0

The Heirs of Robert Annis for an Orchard or Garden heretofore Sold to George Bluntington paid by Robert Yates In fee farme per Annum — 6 0

The Heirs of Dr Harthopp for an Orchard or peice of Ground whereupon Stood a house called Saint Johns now in James Peters Occupation — 2 0 2

For part of Margarett Fletchers Land now or late in the Occupation of Nathaniell Jennard In fee farme per Annum paid by Job Withers — 5 0

Mr Thomas Palmer for a house and Garden late Mr Inges heretofore in the Occupation of John Russell In fee farme per Annum — 5 0

Mr Thomas Palmer for an Orchard once Mr Inges Land late Mr Smalleys In fee farme per Annum — 2 0

14f   In Sanvey Gate

William Chamberlaine for a messuage of Tenement late John Newbolds Land in his Occupation In fee farme per Annum — 1 0 0

Richard Kirke for a house and Garden in the Occupation of Robert Harrison in fee farm per Annum — 8 0

Mr John Smalley for a peice of Ground in the Sanvey Gate belonging to the Corporation whereupon he built a house in Consideration whereof he had a Lease for one & Forty years in the Occupation of Throne and Shipman per Annum — 6 8

David Deakin and William Wells for a peice of Ground Called Sallow Close In fee farm per Annum — 5 0

Daniell Newbury Gardener for two new Erected houses in the Sanvey Gate att will with the Sponge of Ground belonging to the house — 6 10 0
    ⟨next year to charge £5 Thomas Crosby⟩

14g   Near St Margaretts Church

Thomas Deakin's widow for a peice of Ground called Margaretts Bed Lyeing in a Close there late the Land of James Biggs paid by Mr Thomas Pares In fee farme per Annum — 6

14h   Other Rents Part of Mr Wilds Rent

Mr John Farmer for a Close near the Cow Drift late in the Occupation of William Page now in the Occupation of Marmion Jee In fee farme per Annum	13	4

14i   Other part of Mr Wilds Second Lease

The Heires or Executors of (blank) Stockden of Glenn magna for a house in Soar Lane near Red Cross Street in the Occupation of Robert Liquerish In fee farme per Annum		6	0
Sir Nathaniell Curson for a messuage or Tenement and peice of Ground in the Soar Lane late Brittons Land now in the Occupation of Joseph Goodwin In fee farme per Annum		2	0
John Worth Senior for a house and Garden in Belgrave Gate late Higgs Land now or late in the Occupation of Richard Hawkins In fee farme per Annum		8	0
Mr John Pares for a Close in Arch Deacon Lane heretofore Sold to John Mabbs In fee farme per Annum		6	8
William Kirke of Humberston for a house and Land there now or late in Kirks Occupation in fee farme per Annum		5	0
Thomas Hastwell for a messuage or Tenement heretofore Sold to him and Jane Ward In fee farme per Annum	1	6	8
The poor of the Hospitall of the Holy Trinity in the Newarke of Leicester for a Garden and a peice of Ground near the Butt Close now or late in the Occupation of Thomas Hitchcock In fee farme per Annum		2	0
James or Thomas Cartwright for a house or Backside near Saint Margaretts Church Yard In the Occupation of Samuell Browne In fee farme per Annum		8	0
Robert Cooke for a house and Garden in Belgrave Gate late the Land of Edmund Sutton heretofore the Land of Francis Coates paid by Joseph Abell In fee farme per Annum		3	4
Henry Gunnell or Richard Seale for a Tenement with the Appurtenances In the Sanvey Gate heretofore in Thomas Coyes Occupation now in the Occupation of Henry Gunnell In Fee Farme per Annum		10	0
Mr William Wells for a messuage or Tenement heretofore Thomas Chettles Land now or late in the Occupation of Richard Hercourt In fee Farme per Annum		6	8

The Heirs or Executors of Mr Thomas Palmer attorney att Law Deceased for a Close near Humberston Gate Formerly Sold to John Rowe In fee Farme per Annum — 12 0

15 A Rentall of the Lands and possessions belonging to the late Colledge of the Blessed Virgin Mary over against the Castle of Leicester heretofore Demised by Queen Elizabeth to Edmund Holt Esquire and by her Majesty Granted to the Mayor Bayliffes and Burgesses and their Successors amongst other things In Fee Farme

Mr Hill attorney att Law for a messuage or Tenement in the Swines markett in fee farm per Annum — 6 8

Robert Langton for part of a Tenement in the Occupation of Martin Beeby In fee farme per Annum — 2 0

Mr Ralph Wells for a Close near Ayleston highway late the land of Robert Herrick In fee farm per Annum — 5 0

Elias Wallin for a Garden or peice of Ground on the Backside of a messuage or Tenement near the South Gates heretofore the Land of Hugh Watts In fee farme per Annum — 1 0

Richard Bacon of Markfield for a Tenement in Soar Lane near Red Cross Street late the Land of John Coulson now in the Occupation of Thomas Kitchen paid by Nathaniell Johnson In fee farme per Annum — 10 0

Samuell Dewick or Mrs Windsors Executors 2s 6d apeice for a Tenement in Soar Lane near Red Cross Street Sold to John Underwood In fee farme per Annum — 5 0

Edward Smith or William Dawson for a house or Garden in the Same Lane heretofore Robert Stevensons In fee farme per Annum — 12 0

Mr John Cooper for a messuage or Tenement in Red Cross Street and a Garden in Chaffe Lane adjoyneing to the Said house now in the Occupation of William Andrews formerly the Signe of the Bird in hand now Called the Old Mytree in fee farme per Annum — 1 0 0

The Heirs or Executors of Robert Atton Butcher for a messuage or Tenement in Soar Lane In fee farme per Annum of which George Kellett pays 15s 1d & William Baines pays 11s 7d — 1 6 8

Robert Ringmore for a Tenement or Garden in Soar Lane heretofore Sold to John Lander In fee farme per Annum		12	0
Mr Hill or Robert Fawsett for a Garden in the Soar Lane in the Occupation of Thomas Trantham in fee farme per Annum			8
Mr Thomas Ward for a peice of Ground belonging to a Tenement in the South Gates Ruined in the Late Wares and for a Croft In fee farme per Annum		16	0
Dr Cheshire and John Hunt for a peice of Ground adjoyneing to Fryer lane heretofore in the Occupation of Mr William Callis lately in the Occupation of John Burbage per Annum			4
Mr Fox Clerk for the Herbage of Saint Maryes Church Yard att will per Annum		10	0
Mr John Farmer for a Close near Cow Drift Lane the Land of Mr John Sherman In fee farm per Annum	1	0	0
Mr Barwell for the Tythe Hay in Burgess's Meadow, South Fields & Tythable meadows Beyond the Mill per Annum	9	0	0
William Franke Esquire for Saint James Chappell Yard and Close att the neather End of the South Gates heretofore Sold to one Mr Simpson & late John Shermans Land In fee farm per Annum	1	6	8
Richard Brown and Hannah Griffin for a house and Garden or Backside in the parish of Saint Nicholas per Lease per Annum	3	0	0
John Denshire for a house and Garden in the Said parish late the Land of Daniell Murfin In fee farme per Annum	1	0	0
Mr Samuell Herrick Clerk for the Tythes and Tenths of all those Grounds Sometimes parcell of Dannetts hall per Lease per Annum	3	0	0
Walter Rudings Esquire for all the Tythes Vicariall Tenths Herbage and other Dutys Belonging to the Same payable out of those Grounds and parcells of Land belonging to the west Coates per Lease per Annum	11	16	6
Mr Muxloe of Desford for all the Tythes Tenths Herbage and other Dutyes belonging to the Same payable out of that Close commonly called by the name of the house field and being parcell of the Ground belonging to the Estate or Farme Called Dennetts hall and welch hall per Lease per Annum	1	10	0

John Watts Gentleman for the Tythe and that part of Vicariall Tenths & Harbage and other Dues belonging to Dennetts hall being that part he hath Bought	4	0	0
John Moore for part of Mr Fawnes being part of Dennetts hall Mary Mill etc.	2	0	0
Walter Rudings Esquire for the Like	2	0	0
The Executors of Nathaniell Simms now Mr Smalley for a Garden in Sanvey Gate late Woodfords Land in the Occupation of Henry Sands In fee farme per Annum		1	0
Mr Richard Jordaine for a Gardaine or peice of Ground Sometime a well Yard heretofore the Land of Thomas Chettleton late Robert Griffins in his Occupation in fee farme per Annum		1	4
The Executors of Mr Edmund Townesend for an Orchard & Garden in the Silver Street att will per Annum		2	0
Mr Ralph Wells for the third part of a Close near Cow Drift In fee farm per Annum		4	0
The poor of the Hospitall of the holy Trinity in the newark of Leicester for part of the Dovehouse Close beyond the west bridge In the Occupation of John Winter In fee farm per Annum		1	6
Richard Hassell for a peice of meadow Ground in Glenfield late in the Occupation of John Carre In fee farme per Annum			6
Mr Terringham Palmer for a Close lyeing near Saint Margaretts Cow pasture heretofore Bennetts Land in the Occupation of Widow Sands In fee farme per Annum paid by Thomas Bass		3	4
Mr John Watts for certain Lands and Leyes in the South fields of Leicester heretofore the Land of Thomas Dannett Esquire In fee farme per Annum		2	6
The poor people of Trinity Hospitall for a peice of meadow Ground in Burgesses Meadow called the Lady Acre In fee farme per Annum		3	4
Walter Rudings Esquire for a Close in Branston Gate late Mr Hunts Land In fee farm per Annum		5	0
Robert Hobsons Executors for a house & Close in the Occupation of John Holmes In fee farm per Annum	1	10	0
Mr Fox Vicar of St Marys Church in Leicester for the Easter and other Dutyes of the Said parish		3	4

A Garden & Tenement in Soar Lane near Red Cross Street heretofore in the Occupation of George King lately Richard Bruce att will per Annum	13	4
Mr Robert Palmer for a Garden in the Swines Markett lately Built upon heretofore in the occupation of Thomas Ludlam Locksmith in his Occupation In fee farme per Annum	1	2
Of him more for a Shopp heretofore Sold to Christopher Needham late in William Tompsons Occupation In fee farm per Annum	2	6
Anthony Abell or William Lyon for a Garden in Hott Gate Street alias Thornton Lane late the Land of Mr Thomas Pare Butcher In fee farm per Annum	5	0
John Mason for a messuage or Tenement heretofore Dr Chippingdales and Mr Walkers in the Newarke of Leicester in the Occupation of Mr Bayley In fee farme per Annum	1 6	8
Of him more for a house there late Dr Walkers in William Halls Occupation In fee farme per Annum	13	4
Mr William Inge of Knighton for 2 parts of Mr Chamberlaines Land In Fee farme per Annum	12	4
Sir Jeffery Palmer of Carleton Curlieu Baronet for Land there in fee farme per Annum	1	8
The Heirs or Executors of James Carr of Bowden Magna for Land there now or late in the Occupation of John Carrall In fee farme per Annum It is three peices of meadow in hay meadow called Leicester Land	1	0
Mr John Herrick of Beaumont Leyes for Certaine Lands in Sileby per Annum		6
William Steedman of Glenfield for Lands there In fee farm per Annum		3

17 Of the Rents of the Town and Manner of Leicester parcell of the Land and possession of the Dutchy of Lancaster part thereof Lyeing in the County of Leicester

The Executors of William Heggs for a messuage or Tenement heretofore the Land of Mr Ellis late in the Occupation of Mr John Brooksby now Mr Hood In fee farme per Annum	16	8

Mr Robert Palmer for the Horse Malt Mill in the Swines Markett aforesaid Sold to Bartholomew Parnell In fee farme per Annum now Mr Ford	1	13	4
The Heirs or Executors of Mr John Ludlam for the use of the Chamber over the high Cross		5	0
John Armston for the Town Goale by order of Hall .	3	0	0

19   Other Rents Received of New

William Franke Esquire for a peice of Ground being part of the Town Wall Scituate near the Fryer Lane late Mr Maneby's Land In fee farme per Annum		2	6
Robert Langton for two peices of Land taken off the Common Dunghill in the Lane near the Westbridge In fee farme per Annum			10
Mr Abstinence Pougher for two Tenements in Parchmine Lane late the Land of Mr John Herrick in the Occupation of the Said Mr Pougher in fee farme per Annum		3	4

20   Other Rents for Certaine Lands purchased by the
                Corporation & other new Rents

Mr Richard Roberts for a Close of pasture Ground late in two Closes and late Mr Freekes per Lease per Annum ⟨Next year £36 he alowing half 3 years⟩	24	0	0
Mr Nutt & Mr Pares for one Close there commonly called Freekes Ground per Lease per annum and is £30 when Graized ⟨the standing Rent 26 years from Michaelmas 1730 (?) 36⟩	30	0	0
Augustine Heaford for a Cottage or Tenement Scituate near unto the horse Faire in his Occupation per Lease per Annum	1	5	0
Thomas Garratt for another Tenement to the said Cottage or Tenement belonging & thereunto adjoyning per Lease per Annum	1	5	0
David Deakin or William Wells for the Water Laggs .		6	8
Joseph Savidge for part of the house he now Lives in being the Signe of the white Swann per Annum	2	0	0

Robert Annis for a Little peice or Spunge of Ground part of the Ground belonging to the Ground or place called the water Laggs by him walled out for a fellmongers Yard paid by Mrs Wells In Lease per Annum   10   0

21   Rents given to the Schoole and other Charitable Uses

His Majestys Generall Receiver given by Queen Elizabeth out of the Honour of Leicester for the better maintaineing the Usher of the Free Grammer Schoole of the Burrough of Leicester   10   0   0

One Annuity or Rent Charge payable Yearly by Sir Richard Newdigate out of the mannor of Thedingworth being the Gift of Sir Ralph Rawlett for the better maintaineing of the Under Usher of the Said Schoole per Annum now paid by Dr Davise of Brimingham   3   6   8

Mr John Norrise for one Annuity payable Yearly out of a Close in the Abby Gate called the Abby Gate Close for the better maintaineing the said Usher in the Occupation of Mr Alderman Pares per Annum   3   6   8

Paul Smith for one Annuity payable yearly out of a peice of ground called the Water Laggs to the Under Usher of the said Schoole being the Gift of Mr Thomas Clarke per Annum   1   0   0

Mr Gamble for Certaine Lands in the Lordship of Willowby Warterless being the Gift of Mr John Norris Deceased for Charitable uses per Annum   8   0   0

Mr Ayre for an Orchard or Garden Purchased with Fifty pounds given by the first Countiss of Devonshire for & Towards the reliefe of the poor of this Burrough & the Parish of St Lenords for the payment of Three pounds per Annum   6   10   0

Daniel Pratt of Whetstone for a messuage Close and One Yard Land Bought of John Baker Gentleman by the Corporation with the money given by Christopher Tamworth Esquire for Celebrating Divine Service weekly In Lease per Annum   9   0   0
        ⟨next year £7 15s⟩

Mr Thomas Hall for Forty Acres of Land in the Forrest of Leicester Given by King Charles the first of ever Blessed memory to the use of the poor of this Burrough per Annum   19   0   0

Michaell Peace for a Close or meadow Ground Lyeing next the Newarke Mills by Mr Ives Purchased of Mr Nurse and by him given to Charitable uses per Annum	4	15	0
Mr Alderman Martin for Burgesses meadow per Lease per Annum	6	0	0
Mr Richard Stephens for a house and Close in or near Hangman Lane which the Corporation Bought of Mr Speechley per Annum	12	0	0
The Heirs or Executors of John Poultney Esquire payable yearly out of the mannor of Coates Devill and given by him to Charitable uses per Annum	10	0	0
John Devonport of Bushby or George Plummer of Eveington for Lands in Bushby being the Gift of Mr Nidd to the Poor of Mountsorrell	32	0	0
The Heirs or Executors of Anthony Acham Gentleman being the Gift to the poor of this Corporacion out of the mannor of Astfordby alias Asterby in the County of Lincoln per Annum	9	0	0
Mr Thomas Hartshorne for a Certaine Ground in the South Gates belonging to Two Tenements heretofore in the Occupation of Messingar and Owen being the Gift of Margarett Hobby to Charitable Uses per Annum paid by Samuell Ball	1	1	8
Mr Joseph Cradock for a Rent Charge Issueing out of a house called or Known by the Signe of the Parriott being the Gift of Mr Hugh Botham by half yearly payments (vizt) on the Fryday before Christmas and the Fryday before Easter per Annum	2	0	0
The Executors of Mr Claypole of Alexton for Severall Grounds and Closes there being the Gift of Mr Haynes for Charitable Uses now in the Tenure of Andrew Cattwell per Annum	19	0	0
The Parish Officers of St Martins for a years Interest of £130 Lent by the Corporation Due in January	6	10	0

22	Shopps in the Saturday Markett Payable att Lady day and Michaelmas				
John Fox	No 1	.	.	1	12	6
Mr Nutt	No 2	.	.	1	0	0
John Tyler or George Hartshorne .	No 3	.	.	1	0	0

K

Francis Smith	No 4	. .	1	0	0
Francis Brewin	No 5	. .	1	0	0
William Mitchell . . .	No 6	. .	1	0	0
Joseph Mitchell	No 7	. .	1	0	0

⟨To be 10s only his shop being pulled down⟩

Robert Aumey	No 9	. .	1	0	0
Clement Stretton . . .	No 10	. .	1	7	6
John Willowes	No 11	. .	1	12	6
Arthur Astley	No 12	. .	1	5	0
John Hose	No 13	. .	1	5	0
Richard Griffin	No 14	. .	1	5	0
Thomas Tayler	No 15	. .	1	5	0
Late Mr Charles Tuffley . .	No 16	. .	1	5	0
John Johnson of Siston . .	No 17	. .	1	5	0
John Wilson	No 18	. .	1	5	0
William Chamberlaine of Ansty .	No 19	. .	1	5	0
Mr John Pares	No 20	. .	1	12	6
Humphery Wastall for a house marked }	No 34	. .		4	0
Augustine Heaford for a Stable .	No 36	. .	1	5	0
Cockers Kitchen Added to Mr Heafords Lease }	No 37	. .		(blank)	
Thomas Hewson for a Shop under the Gainsborow }	No 38	. .	1	0	0
Mr William Spencer a Shopp there }	No 39	. .	1	10	0
Mr Billars a Shopp there . .	No 40	. .	1	10	0
John Hose a Shopp there . .	No 41	. .	1	10	0
Samuell Brown a Shopp there .	No 42	. .		15	0

Stalls and Standings in the Saturday Markett

Thomas Bates of Earle Shillton .	No 1	. .	1	0	0
(Stall apparently un-let.)	No 2				
(Stall apparently un-let.)	No 3				
John Townesend of Ayleston Miller }	No 4	. .		15	0
(Stall apparently un-let.)	No 5				
(Stall apparently un-let.)	No 6				
John Shippey Miller . . .	No 7	. .		15	0
(Stall apparently un-let.)	No 8				
Mr Thomas Willowes . .	No 9	. .	1	0	0

	£	s	d
John Hickling of Loughborough for a Stall 6 foot Long per Annum		10	0
Noell Hickling of Loughborough Glover for the like paid by Vincent Wing		10	0
Thomas Shippey per Annum		10	0
Willowes Edingburgh per Annum		10	0
James Darbyshire per Annum		10	0
John Derry per Annum		10	0
Thomas Goode per Annum		10	0
Michaell Abbott per Annum		10	0
Thomas Chamberlaine per Annum		10	0
Joseph Sanderson per Annum		10	0
Samuell Basford per Annum		10	0
Daniell Newbury per Annum		10	0
Dr Harthopp for the Ground lately built upon taken from the Sheep penns		5	0
Mr Lord for the Ground lately built upon taken from the Sheep penns	1	0	0
Mr Smallcy for the like paid by Mr Hennell		10	0
Mr Hennell for the Ground lately Built upon	1	0	0
John Hitchcock for a Stall		10	0
William Chapman for a Stall		10	0
James Wattson for a Stall		10	0
William Brabston Baker for a Stall		10	0
Robert Coultman for a Stall		10	0
Humphery Wastall for a Stall		10	0

⟨next year Widow Cobley a Stall 10s Elizabeth Newton 10s⟩

29 Chiefe Rents belonging to Saint Johns and St Lenords and are
to be paid att Michaelmas to the use of the Mayor Bayliffes and
Burgesses of the Burrough of Leicester

	£	s	d
The Wardens of the new Hospitall called Wiggston Hospitall	1	4½	
The Heires or Executors of Mr Boone for one Messuage or Tenement in the Gallowtree Gate Known by the Signe of the Black Lyon in the Occupation of Robert Page lately purchased by Mr Terryingham Palmer		6	
The Earle of Stamford for Thurmaston Mill		6	8
Sir William Rawlingson for Certaine Lands in Oadby late Sir Henry Beaumonts Land & late Mr Wildrams Lands now Mr Wrights per Annum		5	11½

For the Vicaridge house of Oadby Mr Frankes payes .   1   0½

William Davenport of Oadby for Certaine Lands there Called Marshalls Land   6

Widow Hammont for a house in Sanvy Gate late John Turlingtons Land   9

30   Chiefe Rents belonging to Corpus Christi Guild

Samuell Belton late Mr Edmund Townesends Executors for a Tenement in his own Occupation   4   0

Mr Freer for the house late in the Occupation of Mr Norton per Annum   3   0

John Hose for a messuage or Tenement in his Occupation .   2   2

Mr Edmund Cradock for a messuage or Tenement in the Saturday markett in his Occupation   2   0

Mr Helmsley late Freemans Land . . . .   (blank)

Mr William Cooke for a messuage or Tenement in the Occupation of Mr Noone   2   0

Simon Iliffe of Oadby for Certaine Lands there late Mr Blisses Land per Annum   10

Mrs Jane Palmer for a peice of Ground in Parchmine Lane late the Land of Tobias Herrick in the Occupation of John Farrin paid by Mr Roberts   3

The Earle of Stamford for a messuage or Tenement in the Red Cross Street in the Occupation of John Hunt Junior   1   0

Widow Simpkin late John Simons Esquire for Certaine houses in the said Street late the Land of Britton and Suffolk per Annum   8

The Executors of Mr John Groocock for a messuage or Tenement near St Nicholas's Church late Mr Brittons Land in his Occupation   1   0

William Slater for a Garden in Deadmans Lane per Annum   5   0

Jonathan Jee for a messuage or Tenement in the high Street late Mr Mortons Land in the Occupation of Thomas Jee   3   0

Thomas Beaumont John Groce and Samuell Wilson for his Cottage in Deadmans Lane late Mr Terryinghams per Annum   1   0

George Deane Framesmith for a house near Red Cross Street in his occupation per Annum } 4

William Underwood for a Garden in Deadmans Lane heretofore Mr Mortons Land per Annum } 6

Robert Spencer or Mr Thorpe for a Tenement in the high Street late Mr Woodlands Land per Annum } 1　0

David Clay or Mr Hallen for a messuage or Tenement in the Swines Markett Late Mr Poughers Land in the Occupation of Thomas Bennett and others per Annum } 14　0

George Heggs for a messuage or Tenement in his Occupation per Annum } 9　6

The Executors of Mr Edward Palmer for a Tenement in the Same Street late in the Occupation of Michaell Benshaw now of Mr Clay per Annum } 6

Joseph Bradley or Thomas Boss for a Tenement now Divided into two Tenements in the Swines markett in the Occupation of George Townesend and Thomas Jee per Annum } 3　0

John Walden for a Tenement in the Occupation of Thomas Adcock late Manebys Land per Annum } 3　6

The poor of the old Hospitall for a Barne called Clarkes Barne given to the said Hospitall } 6

Mr Samuell Simpson Broaker for a Tenement in the Cank Street in his occupation late Mr Pilkingtons Land per Annum } 1　0

Robert Bonner for a house in the Belgrave Gate late the Land of Robert Foster per Annum } 3　0

The Executors of Richard Farraine for a house late Mr Pilkingtons Land in Edward Bates Possession per Annum } 8½

Sir John Whatton Knight for a Close called Shirehall Close in the Occupation of John Lewett per Annum } 6

Thomas Huffen late William Mitchell Slater for Land Late Mr Thomas Mays of Rotherby } 10½

Edward Davise for a messuage or Tenement in Humberstone Gate late in Mr Bartholomew Hunts Occupation per Annum } 3　0

Mr John Smalley for a messuage or Tenement Known by the Signe of the Angell in the Occupation of Thomas Barnshaw per Annum } 2　0

Mr Richard Goodall for a messuage or Tenement in his Occupation near the East Gates per Annum	1	0
Mr Noble for a messuage or Tenement att the Corner of Fryer lane known by the Signe of the George in the Occupation of John Oswin and Mr Samuell Carte per Annum	4	0
Mrs Worrall for a Tenement in the Swines markett in her Occupation per Annum	2	0
One other Tenement there the Land of William Chamberlaine late in Mr Francis Lewins Tenure now in the Occupation of Job Stevenson and John Astell per Annum	2	0
Mr Ralph Wells for a messuage or Tenement there late Mr Henshaws Land in the Occupation of Mr Francis Coultman per Annum	4	0
Mr Mould for a messuage or Tenement in the Gallow Tree Gate late Blackwells Land in the Occupation of Theophelus Cramp per Annum	7	6

31   Chiefe Rents belonging to Saint Margaretts Guild

Mr Bent for a Garden in Ironmongers Lane in his Occupation late Mr Pilkingtons Land per Annum paid by Widow Padman	1	0
Mr Joshua Goodrich for a messuage or Tenement in the high Street being the Corner of Bakehouse lane late Mr Woodlands Land in his Occupation per Annum	1	4
Mr Noble for a peice of Ground in Soar Lane near the North Gates called the Mott Yard late in the Occupation of Thomas Hitchcock per Annum	6	0
Benjamin Cartwright for a house in the Belgrave Gate in his Occupation late Manebys Land per Annum		9
Mr Edward Hood for a messuage or Tenement in the Said Street called the Unicorne in the Occupation of John Beaumont per Annum		4½
Widow Tayler for a Tenement late Mr Suttons Land in her Occupation per Annum Paid by John Astill		6
Robert Yates & Thomas Worth for a Tenement now being the Corner house late the Land of Robert Sutton in Thomas Wards Occupation per Annum		6
Mr Thomas Pares for a Barne the Land of William Inge Esquire	1	3½

The Heirs or Executors of Mr John Ludlam for a Close near the Spittle house Called the Bayliffes Close per Annum	1	0
Mr Joseph Johnson for a messuage near the West Bridge .	4	0
The Wardens of Wiggston Hospitall for a peice of Ground called the Normandy per Annum		6
John Brookes or Thomas Chapman for a house in the Church Gate late manebys Land per Annum		9
Mr George Rayson Pratt for a messuage in All Saints Parish in his Occupation	1	1½
John Cartwright for a messuage or Tenement in the Occupation of John Wellinger per Annum		6
Benjamin Cartwright for a messuage or Tenement or John Brookes in the Occupation of George Bassett	3	4
Robert Page or his Executors for a peice of Ground taken out of the Pinfold		4
Mr Humphery Chapman late Mr Thomas Hartshorne for a messuage or Tenement in the South Gates heretofore Known by the Signe of the Grey hound per Annum	4	0
Mr Farmer for a messuage or Tenement in the South Gates late Bennetts Land in the Occupation of Nathaniell Jee per Annum		10
The poor of the Old Hospitall for a house in the South Gates late Fosters Land in Thorps Occupation per Annum		9½
Mr Thomas Hartshorne for a peice of ground in Burgess meadow late the Land of John Savidge per Annum	10	0
Mr John Wilkins for a messuage or Tenement in his Occupation late the Land of Dannett Abney called the Crown per Annum now Mr Foster		4½
The Heires or Executors of Mr Wanley for a Close or Tenement in the North Gates and for two Capons in the Occupation of John Hercourt per Annum	1	2
The Heires or Executors of Mr Daniell Smith for a Shopp in the South Gates once Mortons Land		5
Henry Coulson Junior for a house in the high Street late John Attons Land now Richard Ougden	3	6
Mr William Topp for a house in the high Street in his Occupation late the Land of Ralph Chettle per Annum	2	0

William Slater late Benjamin Garland for a Close att Branston Gate Bridge late Cottons Land per Annum	6
Mr Richard Turvile for a house in the Swines Markett in the Occupation of Mr Thomas Carter late Terryinghams 11d and for two hens and a Cock 1s per Annum	1 11
Mrs Elizabeth Johnson for a house near the west Bridge late Mr Babbingtons Land	9
The Heires of Mr Pawley of Croston of a messuage or Tenement in the Apple Gate Street now in Mr Henry Smith Occupation per Annum	6
Simon Ward for a house in Birstall late the Land of William Coates now John Raynors in Simon Wards Occupation per Annum now Thomas Green	1 0
Mr William Cooke for a messuage or Tenement in the Saturday markett in the Occupation of Mr Cooke and Mr Noone per Annum	6 8
Elizabeth Hebb for a house in Chaffe Lane near Redcross Street once Gulsons Land 9d and for a hen 3½d per Annum paid by Thomas Wellingar	1 0½
The Heirs or Executors of Mr Robert Winfield for Land late Mr Bothams near Soar Lane and for three Capons and two hens	4 0
Walter Rudings Esquire for a Close in Branston Gate per Annum	9
Mr John Billars for a Garden in hott Gate Street alias Thornton lane 3d and for a hen 3½d and for a Garden late Bells Sometimes a Swine Stye 6d	1 0½
John Tyler near the South Gates for Land In the High Street late Budworths Land 9d and for two hens 7d and for a Shop near the South Gates 6d now or late in John Tylers Occupation per Annum	1 10
John Winter for a Tenement over against All Saints Church Yard late Mr Rudyards and Late in David Deakins Occupation per Annum	2 3
The Executors of Mr Edward Palmer now Mr Robert Palmer for a house in the Swines Markett late Beesons Land per Annum	6
The Heires or Executors of Mr Pawley for a house in Apple Gate Street once Birstalls in the Occupation of Mr Henry Smith 10d and for two hens and a Cock 10d	1 8

Mr Thomas Chapman for a messuage or Tenement att the Upper End of Belgrave Gate late Neals Land per Annum	1 6
Thomas Palmer or Edward Dawse for a Close in All Saints Parish near Plank well late Walls now Mr Annis's Land per Annum	1 8
Thomas Turvile for a house and Land in the North Gates late the Land of Bodyman and Robert Harrison per Annum	6
Samuell Turlington and John Derry for a Certaine house late Woodfords now Mr Hodgkins of Glenn near the North Gates per Annum	1 1
Mr Edward Davise for Land in the South Gates late Owens and Messingars Land in his Occupation and for a Capon 10d per Annum	2 10
The Heires or Executors of Mr Edward Palmer for a house in the Swines markett late Christopher Needhams and Byerleys Land per Annum	4
Mr Chapman for a house in the South Gates late Heafords Molds and Revitts Land	6 8
The Heirs or Executors of Mr Edward Palmer for a house in the Swines markett near the horse mill late Mr Manebeys Land in the Occupation of John Moore per Annum	6

33 A Rentall of Lammas Tythes and Herbage due Yearly to the Mayor etc for Divers Grounds in St Marys Parish in the possession of the late Colledge of Saint Marys over against the Castle of Leicester (Vizt)

Mr Richard Westons Executors for Dovehouse Close near the Newarke of Leicester late Mr Hicklings Land per Annum	1 4
William Franke Esquire for a Close called Archers Close once Palmers near Saint James Chappell Close per Annum	1 0
Of him more for the Tythe of Saint James Chappell Close per Annum	1 0
Mr John Farmer for the Lammas Tythes for Benningtons Close near the Cow Drift per Annum	1 0
William Slater late Benjamin Garland for a Close near Branston Gate Bridge per Annum	6

John Mason for a Close late two Closes over against St James Chappell Close in his Occupation per Annum	1	8
The Heires or Executors of Mr Robert Hickling for Land near the Grange once Birstalls Land per Annum paid by Mrs Weston		10
Of them for a Close late Mr Martens Land near St James Chappell Close per Annum		10
Of them more for Seth Kings Land		6
A Close called the Paradice late Manebeys Land per Annum		4
William Franke Esquire for Cadmans Land per Annum .		10
Of him more for a peice of Ground called the Kilne & heretofore the Land of Cadman & Johnson per Annum		4
Mr Joseph Wilkins for an Orchard on the Backside of a house once Davys in the South Gates late the Land of Mr Hugh Watts per Annum John Lacey payes		6
Mr Ralph Wells for a Close near Aylestone Highway late Mr Herricks Land per Annum		8
Of him more for a Close near the Highway . . .		4
Of him more for a Close near Archers Land . . .		10
The Executors of Mr Richard Weston for a peice of Meadow Ground near Saint Marys Mill Called the holme late Manebys Land per Annum	1	8
Mr John Farmer for a Close near Ayleston Highway in the Occupation of Augustine Heaford per Annum		10
Of him more for a Close in the Occupation of Mr Jee per Annum	1	0
Walter Rudings Esquire for a Close in Branston Gate late Mr Hunts Land per Annum		8
Of him more for a Close called Colledge Close late Mr Hunts Land per Annum		4
Mr Robert Langton for a Close late Mr Brookes Land per Annum now Mr Cooper	2	2
Mr John Simpson for a Close called the Tippitts per Annum	13	4
Michaell Peace for the Tythes of the Newarke Windmill per Annum	2	0

Thomas Haddon or John Lewin for a Garden or peice of Ground in Millstone Lane late Henry Armstrongs Land per Annum	4	
William Anderson for a Garden in Chaffe Lane . .	10	
The Heirs or Executors of Francis Annis for a backside belonging to his house in the South Gates per Annum	6	
Mr George Bent for the Tythe of four yard Land . .	8	0
Mr Thomas Ward for three Yard Land	6	0
Samuell Wilson now Mr Joseph Newton for a house in Thornton Lane late William Tompsons	4	
Thomas Tompson for Booths Land	4	
The Tythe of Mr Southwells four Yard Land . .	8	0
Mr Joseph Johnson for the Tythe of Three Yard Land .	6	0
Mr Thomas Hall for the Tythe of Three Yard Land .	6	0
Mr John Pratt for the Tythe of Three Yard Land . .	6	0
Michaell Peace for the Tythe of the Newarke Corne mills	16	0
Mr Goodall and Mr Brushfield for the Tythe of Gosling Close	2	0
Mr Edmund Johnson for the Tythe of the windmill .	2	0
Marmion Jee Junior Dyer for Laying of planks and Setting of posts in the River Soar Dureing Pleasure	6	

The End of the Rentalls

34   Deduction of Taxes

Mr Clayton head Schoolmaster	1	15	0
Mr Fox	1	5	0
Mr Elley	1	0	0
Mr Adcock		6	0
Mr Lucas for the Gainsborow	1	1	0

36   Fines & Accidentall Receipts

George Davye for his Freedome		5	0
William Underwood of Melton Mowbray for Scott & Lott		16	0
John Norman of Oadby for the same		8	0
The Butchers Fines		10	0
John Brewin for his Freedome		10	0
John Guyer for his Freedome		10	0
Richard Roberts for his Freedome		5	0
John Hall a Stranger for his Freedome	20	0	0
Twiggs Pilgrim for his Freedome		10	0

	£	s	d
Joseph Goodwin a Stranger for his Freedome . . .	20	0	0
John Vice of Blaby for Scott & Lott		10	0
Henry Mason for his Freedome		10	0
Joseph Gregory for the like		10	0
Francis Muxloe for the like		10	0
Ralph Watts of Thurmaston for Scott & Lott . . .		4	0
James Innocent for his Freedome		10	0
Ballance of the late Chamberlins accounts . . .	311	0	7¼

[End of Receipts]

[Payments start here]

1   Chiefe Rents and other Rents paid this Year

	£	s	d
Paid Mr Harte att the Auditt of Broad Arrow . . .		1	0
For Acquittance for the Same			6
Paid Mr Harte Receiver for one Years Rent of due for the Sheep penns att Michaelmas	4	0	0
Paid him more for Singletons Lease	2	12	8
For Shopps taken Down		11	6
To him more for Saint Margaretts Guild . . .	1	13	5½
To him more for Corpus Christi Guild alias Town hall .		7	9
To him more for Lufkins Lease		2	0
Paid him more for Diverse Chiefe Rents from the Town .		7	8
Paid him more for a Close near the horse Faire . .		3	4½
Paid him more for a Close late Websters Land . .		1	0
Paid him more for Corpus Christi Guild . . .		11	9
Paid him more for a Close late Hallams		1	0
Paid for Acquittance for the Said money's . . .			4
Paid to the Bayliffes of the Augmentations for Lands due to Leicester Abby att the Feast of Saint Michaell and for Acquittance		7	4
Paid to Mr Harte for a Chiefe Rent for Shopps under the Gainsborow		2	6
Paid to the Bayliffe of Merton Colledge in Oxford for one Chiefe Rent Issueing and Payable out of the Hospitall of Saint John and Saint Lenoard in or near the Borough of Leicester att Michaelmas Last		1	3
Paid for a Shopp in Richard Waggstaffes Occupation .		1	0
Paid to the Wardens of the Company of Taylers the Annuall Rent Due to them etc		1	8

Paid Mr Hart his Majestyes Receiver for one Whole Years Rent due out of the Lands and Tenements belonging to Saint John and Saint Leonards in or Near the Borough of Leicester heretofore Mr Harveys and Mr Tatams Leases and in Countisthorpe and Humberstone Mills and the White horse in the Gallow tree Gate for one whole Year Att Michaelmas	31	12	5
Paid to the Receiver for Lands and Tenements belonging to the late Guild called St Margaretts Guild in Leicester Town Obiit Land and Vicars Closes heretofore in the Occupation of Arthur Tatam for a years Rent due att Michaelmas Last	42	18	1
Paid him for Parcell of the Land in the Possession of the late Guild Called Corpus Christi Guild for one Year due att Michaelmas last past	14	12	6
Paid to the Said Receiver for Certaine Lands and Tenements Chiefe Rent and Lammas Tythes Parcell of the Possession of the Colledge of the Blessed Virgin Mary over against the Castle of Leicester for a Years Rent Due att Michaellmas last	20	8	6
Paid to the Said Receiver for a Certaine Tenement in the Newarke of Leicester	3	16	1

3   Att the Auditt held by Mr Harte att the horse and Trumpett

Paid the Kings Receiver for 2 Tenements in the Swines markett in the Occupation of (blank) Due att Michaelmas last	2	10	0
Paid him more for the Malt Mills in the Swines Markett in the Occupation of Mr Thomas Palmer	1	13	4
Paid him more for the Shambles and Drapery in Leicester due att Michaelmas Last	8	13	4
Paid him more for the Gainesborow Chambers and Other Shopps and Sheds and for the Saturday Markett which the Mayor Bayliffes and Burgesses Purchased of Mr Britton Due for one Year att Michaelmas Last	4	8	8

4   Fees and other Payments this Year

Paid to Richard Roberts Esquire Mayor his Sallary According to Antient Custome	13	6	8

	£	s	d
Paid to him more out of the Rent of Gosling Close allowed by order of a Common hall	13	6	8
Paid to him more being the Additionall Annuall Sallary to the Mayor made in the Year 1712/13	20	0	0
Paid William Wrighte Esquire Recorder of this Borough his Years Sallary	10	0	0
Paid the Town Clarke for takeing the Coroners Inquest .	1	0	0
Paid him more for the Book of Payments . . .		4	6
Paid him more for his Sessions Fees Due att Michaelmas only		6	8
Paid Mr Clayton the headschoolmaster being the Towns free Gift Dureing pleasure	16	0	0
Paid the head usher of the Said Schoole his Sallary Dureing Pleasure	8	0	0
Paid the Under Usher being the Towns free Gift Dureing Pleasure	3	0	0
Paid him more being the Towns free Gift Dureing Pleasure	5	0	0
Paid Mr Carte his Years Sallary as Lecturer of the Borough Dureing Pleasure	20	0	0
Paid him more by an Order of Common hall . . .	10	0	0
Paid Mr Fox Vicar of Saint Marys being the Towns free Gift dureing Pleasure	10	0	0
Paid Mr Kilby for the Like	10	0	0
Paid Mr Clayton the Like	10	0	0
Paid Mr Hackett the Like	10	0	0
Paid to the Town Clarke his Years Sallary . . .	5	0	0
Paid him more being the Towns free Gift . . .	2	13	4
Paid for the Rentall	2	0	0
Paid for Proclaimeing the Faires and Marketts . .		14	0
Paid for the Commission of this Year		9	10
Paid the Macebearer his Years Sallery and for Pipes Burning	5	9	8
John Armstone as Keeper of the Bridewell . . .	1	13	4
Paid the Mace bearer for 2 Seale		2	0
Paid the 4 Serjants their Years Sallary by an Order of hall att 15s per Quarter	12	0	0
Paid Joseph Abell the Cryer for Sweeping the Town hall and Gainsborow	1	13	4
Paid the Bidle his Years Sallary for Sweeping the Gates and weeding the Town hall Yard	6	0	0

Paid the Bidle and Cryer to Keep them from Goeing about with their Christmas Box						4	0
Paid Josiah Payne for Keeping the Liberary	.	.	.		3	0	0
Paid the Waites their Years Sallary	.	.	.	.	6	13	4

6　　Accidentall Payments

Paid the Halbert men for walking the Faire	.	.	.			9	0
Ringing the Bill that day	.	.	.	.	.	1	0
Paid for 4 Sessions dinners	.	.	.	.	2	8	0
Paid the Constables the like	.	.	.	.	1	4	0
For wood & Coale & Makeing the Bonefire Kings Coronation						6	8
For Bunns & ale Visiting the Schoole 3 times	.	.	.	1	10	0
Paid for 2 Basses for the Town	.	.	.	.			6
For wood & Coale & Makeing the Fire Kings Birthday	.				6	10
For 6 Leather Chaires for the Town Hall	.	.	.		12	0
Paid the Bidle for cleanscing the West Bridge twice	.	.		1	0
Paid the Ringers at St Marys	.	.	.	.		2	6
To the Keeper of the Castle & Mr Rudings man 1s each	.			2	0
Paid for a Ribbon for the Charter	.	.	.	.		2	0
Spent at the Goale upon Sealing Hanfords Mortgage	.			1	0
Sweeping the Snow off St Marys Chancell	.	.	.		1	0
Paid for 32 Loads of Stones at 3s per Load	.	.	.	4	16	0
For 6 Strike of Lime for Spittlehouse Causeway	.	.		5	3
Paid Chamberlin for Gravell & Astlyn for Stone	.	.		3	4
Paid for wood & Coale for the Bonefire the Queens Birthday & Makeing						7	6
Paid towards the repaires of the well by the Town Hall	.			1	0
Paid the Clerk of Assize his Fees for both Assizes	.	.	1	6	8
Paid Bidle & Cryer for both assizes	.	.	.	.		2	0
Paid for ale then	.	.	.	.	.		4	0
Paid for washing St Marys Chancell	.	.	.	.		2	6
Paid the Huntsman Easter Monday	.	.	.	.		10	0
Paid for playing the Ingines 4 times & attending them at the River					1	1	0
Paid a Serjeant for Serveing processes	.	.	.	.		2	6
Paid Mr Hall for Carriage of Muck from the 3 Crowns	.			11	0
Expences of Mr Mayor & others at Burbage when they Sett the Land						10	6
Paid John Erpe for Ale for a Troop of Soldiers	.	.	1	0	0
Wood Coale & Makeing the Fire the 29th of May	.	.		5	11

Paid John Kirk for 6 Quarries & 4 bricks at the Free Schoole		2	1
Paid to the new Scavenger for a Cart by order of Hall .	9	15	0
Wood Coale & Makcing the Fire the 11th June . .		5	11
Paid for ale at the Gainesborow the Recorder being there .		2	6
Paid John Webster bricklayer for work at the Town Goale .		5	0
Paid the Clerk of Assize for the transport . . .	1	1	0
For 40 cwt of Coales for the Town Hall & Gainsborough .	1	8	4
Paid Beswick for writeing an account the Town Pavement & a Ball of pack thread		2	9
Paid the Fees for a Brace of Bucks at the Venizon Feast .	1	1	0
Paid the Grecian Princes by order of Hall . . .	10	10	0
Paid for their Charges at the Crane	2	11	3
Paid for their Charges goeing to Coventry with them .	2	13	1
Paid to Horse Race Town plate by order of Hall . .	5	0	0
Paid a man to prepare Carriages 4 times . . .		6	0
Paid Craxtall for Potts & Muggs for the Gainsborow .			11
Paid Mr Clayton for Tythe for the Waterlaggs ⟨Q.⟩ . .		2	0
Paid Mrs Gutheridge for a Cock for the Conduit . .		5	0
Paid for drawing the waters		2	0
Paid Townsend for Measureing the Stones at the Mills .		5	0
Paid Mr Lucas for the Rent of the Gainsborough . .	7	6	4
Spent at the audit more than allowed in the Hospitall account		6	6
Paid Mr Noble for a Debenture	1	12	6
Paid for Cleansing the Horse Trough		2	0
Paid the Lottery Money to St Nicholas	5	0	0
Paid for 2 Fines sett upon the Corporation at the assizes .		12	0
Paid Mr Edmund Ludlam for a years Interest of £300 .	15	0	0
Paid Mr Newton for a years Interest of £250 (the Interest of £150 he receives from the Toll Gate	12	10	0
Allowed Robert Bonner out of Broughtons Land . .		8	0
Paid Mr Mayor for Travellers	1	10	0
Paid the Judges presents both assizes	4	5	0
Paid the Cryer for Weighing the Coales in & out of the Town Hall		10	0
Paid for the loss of Coales & Lowering price . . .	2	10	0
Paid the Lords Rent for the Land at Burbage . . .		13	2
Paid the Town Clerk for Penns Ink & paper . . .		10	0
Paid him for allowance of Coales		6	8
More for makeing up the Chamberlins accounts . .	3	6	8
Allowed the Chamberlins for Collecting the Town Rents & for the Auditors dinners by order of Hall	12	0	0

For a Letter of Attorney		5	6
Paid for the Bidle & Cryers Shoes		9	0
Paid for a peece of parchment			6
Paid Mr Watts a year of Lord Huntingtons Gift to the Hospitall	10	0	0
Paid For 4 quarters taxes for the Week day Shambles		3	9
The like for the Shopps & Stalls in Saturday Markett	1	8	2
Paid for 2 quarters for Griffins House 3s 5d 2 for Scarborows 1s 6d		4	11
Paid for 4 quarters for Caves House 4s 4d & 4 for Newberys 6s 4d		10	8
Spent goeing to Litchfield for the Tilbury money		10	0
Paid for dischargeing the presentments in the Church Gate & Grange Lane £1 8s 4d each	2	16	8
Paid Mr Marten a Shop Bill	6	2	6
Paid him another Bill for Ale etc	10	17	8
Paid John Cartwrights Bill	6	18	1
Paid John Hardstaffs Bill	5	2	3
Paid Thomas Cartwrights Bill	6	5	4
Paid Joseph Goodrichs Bill	3	14	2
Paid Alderman Goodrichs Bill	1	10	7
Paid William Higginsons Bill	13	6	7
Paid Samuel Browns Bill	2	15	6½
Paid Thomas Hewsons Bill		7	1
Paid Mr Cooks Bill	10	13	2½
Paid Samuel Broadhursts Bill	1	1	8
Paid William Hardys Bill	11	15	8
Paid Benjamin Roberts Bill	8	7	6
Paid Richard Bruces Bills	9	18	10
Paid John Liquorishes Bills	2	10	5
Paid Thomas Bass's Bill	4	13	10
Paid Mr Bents Bill	8	18	6
Paid John Veaseys Bill	19	17	4
Paid Mr Brothers Bill	6	15	10
Paid Robert Smiths Bill	3	14	9
Paid the Town Clerks Bill £11 9s & one other for Mr Duckett Mrs Coltman etc £2 17s 2d	14	6	2
Paid Mr Nobles Bill	41	18	4

9   Allowance of Taxes one half at 3s the other at 2s per Pound

Allowed Richard Roberts		1	17	6
Allowed Richard Hackett for Frolesworth Land		1	12	6

L

Thomas Hall for the Forrest Closes	2	8	6
Thomas Sutton & Zachariah Parker for Burbage Land .	1	12	6
Mr Herrick for the Tythe		7	6
Mr Nutt & Mr Pares	2	10	0
Mr Ashby		3	9
Richard Hanford		2	6
John Coates		2	6
Mr Cooper Apothecary		2	6
Alderman John Newton		2	6
Mr Cooper Glazier		5	0
James Peters		2	6
Mr John Simpson		2	6
Alderman Hammond		2	6
Robert Warburton		3	9
John Turvile		2	6
Jonathan Buckerfield		2	6
Mr Rudings	1	10	0
Mr Joseph Treen		3	2
Mr Hennell		3	4
Mr Alderman Cooper		7	6
Joseph Astell		2	6
Mr Hartopp		10	0
William Higginson		3	9
Mrs Hobson		3	9
Mr Ford		3	9
Mr Stephens	1	13	0
Charles Tuffley		2	6
Alderman Ayre		2	6
Mathew Sheffield Siston Mills		7	6
Samuell Ball		2	6
Mr Cooke		3	9
Mary Moor		2	6
Thomas Denshire		2	6
Thomas Poyner		5	0
Mr Watts		10	0
More for Muxloes		3	9
Mr Alderman Chapman		3	9
John Noon		5	0
Mr Farmer		8	9
Henry Brown		2	6
Alderman Pares		5	0
John Cartwright		3	4
Edmund Johnson	2	13	9

Widow Ward		2	6
John Armston		6	8
Thomas Johnson for the Shambles	5	0	0
John Mason		5	0
Robert Greaves		2	6
Mr Orton		5	0
Thomas Hastwell		2	6
Robert Bonner		3	4
George Wildboare		3	4
Jacob Bothomley		5	2
Edward Coulton		7	6
Mrs Hartshorn		4	3
Joseph Savage		5	0
Oliver Grace		2	6
Mr Bass and Mr Marshall	1	16	3
Mrs Judd		2	6
Mr Franke		3	4
William Newton		7	6
Josiah Ashwell		7	6
Francis Smith		2	6
Michaell Peace for the Mills	2	10	0

11 [No separate heading inserted]

Paid the Gift of Queen Elizabeth to the head usher . .	10	0	0
Paid the Gift of Ralph Rawlett	3	6	8
Paid the Gift of Mr Norrise	3	6	8
Paid the Gift of Mr Clarke	1	0	0
Paid the Gift of Mr Norrise out of Willowby Lands .	8	0	0
Paid the Gift of Mr John and Mr William Stanley . .	5	0	0
Paid the Gift of the Earle of Devonshire . . .	6	0	0
Paid the Gift of Christopher Tamworth Esquire . .	9	0	0
Paid the Gift of King Charles the first	19	0	0
Paid the Gift of Mr William Ive	15	0	0
Paid the Gift of Mr Elkington	5	0	0
Paid the Gift of Mr Poultney	10	0	0
Paid the Gift of Mr Nidd	32	0	0
Paid the Gift of Mr Acham	9	0	0
Paid the Gift of Mr Hayne	19	0	0
Paid the Gift of Mr Botham	2	0	0
Paid the Gift of the Earle of Huntington . . .	10	0	0
Paid the Gift of Mr Curteen and the Gentlemen of the Lottery	4	16	0

	£	s	d
Paid the Gift of Mr Baker	1	0	0
Paid the Gift of Mr Billars	5	12	0
Paid the Gift of Mr Ward and Mr Bennett . . .	1	0	0
Paid the Gift of Widow Ositor	6	0	0
Paid the Gift of Mr Gilbert	5	0	0
Paid the Gift of Mr Hitch		3	0
Paid the Gift of Margarett Hobby	1	1	8
Paid the Gift of the Countiss of Devonshire . . .	3	0	0
Paid the Gift of Mr Haselrigg	1	1	0
Paid the Gift of Mr Thomas Ayre	1	0	0
Paid the Gift of John Ludlam	2	10	0
Paid the Gift of Mr Weightman		5	0

[End of Payments]

[Supers start here]

Supers

	£	s	d
Perkyns of Grantham for Gunnerby Lands . . .		6	8
Mr Wrighte for Land at Oadby		5	$11\frac{1}{2}$
Earle of Stamford for Tythe of Thurmaston Mills . .		6	8
For a house in Deadmans Lane		1	0
Paradise			4
Mr Fox by order of Hall		13	4
The Tythe of the Newark Mills		18	0
William Stephenson for a House in Senvey Gate . .		15	0
Anthony Ingoldsby Esquire for Land at Great Ashby .			6
The Executors of Francis Annis for a Cheife Rent . .			6
Mr Herrick for Land at Sileby			6
William Cave a whole year	5	10	0
Daniel Newbury part of his House	2	0	0
Widow Griffins House	3	0	0
Lost in Setting Whetston Lands		12	6
Scarborows House half a year	1	10	0
Francis Smith a Shop No. 4 Empty	1	0	0
Mr Billers Shop allowed Mr Noon	1	10	0
John Hitchcock a Stall		10	0
Richard Griffins Shop Empty	1	5	0
Paid Mr Watts for 2 receipts 8d & a Letter from Mr Lucas 4d }		1	0
Allowed the Burbage Tenant for Quicking by order of Hall }	10	0	0

[End of Supers]

[Summary]

Receipts	1363	14	1¼
Payments & Supers	957	5	11½
Ballance due to the Corporacion	406	8	1¾
To which add received of Dunnerly towards Mr Nobles Bill	1	18	8
Of Widow Cobley for a stall		10	0
By William Newtons taxes		7	6
	409	4	3¾
Out of which deduct paid Mr Bradley 31 weekes . .	7	15	0
Overcharged in Joseph Michells Shop		10	0
Mr Lees Bill		9	8
Mr Halls Bill	2	16	6
Mr Newtons Bill	1	0	0
Paid Mr Noon which he omitted in his account paid to Mr Ward		6	0
Thomas Drakes Bill for Stones		2	0
Francis Smiths taxes		3	0
Joseph Ashwells taxes		12	0
More for Cheife Rent		2	0
	13	16	2
Ballance due to the Corporation	395	8	1¾
To which add to ballance the Hospitall account for which See the Hospitall Book	3	9	6
More upon account to the Town in fol. 1 & 2 [these numbers refer to entries in the original which form part of Payments, Headings 1 and 3, above] charged to Mr Hart as paid £141 16s 9d whereas he should receive of Mr Hart only the sum of £139 0s 7½d So the Chamberlin is debtor £2 16s 2d	2	16	2
	401	13	9¾
Added being Lord Huntingtons Gift charged Twice fol. 8 & 14 [these numbers refer to entries in the original which form part only of Payments, Headings 6 and 11, above]	10	0	0
Ballance due to the Corporation	411	13	9¾

The Kings Receiver pays	139	0	$7\frac{1}{2}$
Sir Philip Pells Tutbury money	66	13	4
	205	13	$11\frac{1}{2}$

Memorandum that upon inspecting these accounts there was overcharged in the Gowns	7	0	0

Which was paid to Mr Birstall in money	5	0	0
By order of Hall in John Veaseys Bill for ale	2	0	0
	7	0	0

CHAMBERLAINS' ACCOUNTS
1750/1

Borough of Leicester to wit }	The Account of Clement Stretton and Joseph Chambers Chamberlains of the Borough of Leicester in the Mayoralty of Thomas Marten Esquire for one whole Year (to wit) from Michaelmas 1750 to Michaelmas 1751.

1 [No separate heading inserted]

Augustine Heaford for a Years rent of the Sheep pens with Cokers Kitchen by Lease payable at Lammas and Candlemas — 9 0 0

The Heirs or Executors of Mr John Harrison for Rents of Assize due yearly out of certain Lands at the North Gates late in the occupation of Thomas Turvile called Gaddesbys Land at Michaelmas only late Thomas Noble Esquire deceased now Rogers Ruding Esquire — 1 9

Samuell Brown for a Chamber over the East Gates & for a Shop & Chamber adjoyning to them in his occupation & late of one Josiah Ashwell per Annum — 5 0 0

Mr John Blunt for Butt Close heretofore sold to Mr Thomas Blunt late in the occupation of Mr Robert Roulson late Freemans late also John Loseby & now or late of Mr Alderman Hood in Fee Farm per Annum — 10 0

The Reverend Mr Gustavus Broughton Viccar of Saint Martins in Leicester for a Chamber belonging to the Corporation being part of the Town Hall with a door place at the top of the stairs going to the house of Office now used with the Viccaridge house per Annum — 2 6

Mr John Weightman late Edward Noone for a Messuage or Tenement at the neather end of Belgrave Gate heretofore the Land of Thomas Headly now divided into several Tenements in Fee Farm per Annum late in the occupation of Edward Noone & now of William Yates — 1 0 0

The Heirs or Executors of Charles Stafford & Alice Brown for a garden or piece of ground in the Senvey Gate in the occupation of John Jee & George Webb in Fee Farm per Annum paid by John Elliott 2 6

His Grace the Duke of Devonshire now Lord William Manners for a piece of ground in the North Gates whereupon stood a Messuage or Tenement heretofore the Land of George Tatham in Fee Farm per Annum 13 4

The said Duke for a parcell of ground in the said Close late Fletchers Land in Fee Farm per Annum 4

The Heirs or Executors of Thomas Fletcher alias Thomas Alsop for a piece of ground lying on the backside of a Messuage or Tenement in the North Gates sold to John Tatham in Fee Farm per annum paid by William Spence Hosier now Daniel Lambert 1 8

John Erpe now Widow Bassett for a Messuage or Tenement & piece of ground thereunto belonging in the Parish of St Nicholas heretofore the Land of William Adcock in Fee Farm per Annum 6 8

John Turvile late Mr Barwell for a Tenement in the North Gate the Land of Mr Robert Freer heretofore the Sign of the Sun in the occupation of Rowland Watts per Annum 1 0 0

John Erpe for a piece of ground called the Water Laggs late in the occupation of Mr Edmund Johnson in Fee Farm per Annum sold by John Erpe to Robert Cook 6 8

John Campion for a piece of ground at the South end of Butt Close in Fee Farm per Annum 4

Roger Palmer of Gilmorton for Land Meadow & pasture ground heretofore the Land of John Sprigge & now or late of Edward Whitehead paid by William Burdett of Gilmorton or Mr Gamble of Willoughby now (blank) Chandler 3 4

Anthony Ingoldsby Esquire for Lands in Great Ashby late the Land of Ralph Brookesby Gentleman heretofore the Land of Nicholas Norton per Annum 6

The Heires or Executors of Robert Pawley Esquire for certain Lands & Tenements in Scraptoft the Land of John Mason heretofore the Land of Thomas Simpkin & (blank) Taylor of Whetstone & now or late in the tenure of Mathew Hubbard paid now by Mr Wigley of Scraptoft aforesaid Esquire 6

3 Receipts of the whole Grange with the appurtenances & 4 Yard
Land & the 2 Yard Land called Archers Land & known by the
name of Weightmans Land & a halfe Yard Land which the Corporation purchased of the Lord Spencer as followeth

	£	s	d
Thomas Willowes for part of the Newark Grange & 4 yard Land in the South fields of Leicester & the Grange Barn & part of the Yard by Lease per Annum	48	12	6
Walter Hall for 3 yard land & for the Grange Barn & yard by Lease per Annum	37	17	6
Thomas Stanley for 4 yard Land there & part of the Grange yard by Lease per Annum	47	0	0
Mr Robert Bonner for 3 yard land there by Lease allowed 20s otherwise would be £36 per Annum	35	0	0
Mr Stanley more for 3 Yard Land & halfe there . .	40	0	0
Henry Volentine late Foulds for 4 acres of Land out of the several Farms to dig Clay to make Bricks & for a parcell of Land lying upon the Swanns Wind Mill next the Cause-way leading up to the Pinfold towards Wigstone along the Hedge side & for 5 Lands lying against the Hedge side of Mr Carters Wind Mill to dig Clay to make Bricks per Annum	8	10	0
Thomas Ward for 3 yard land per Annum . . .	36	0	0
John Guilford for the Newark Mills & Wind Mill & Meadows thereto belonging by Lease per Annum 〈—£4 15s 0d Mr Ives gift is payable out of these Meadows〉	25	0	0
Mr Goodall & Mr Brushfield for Gosling Close by Lease per Annum Mr Goodall pays £10 15s 0d & Mr Brushfield £13 5s 0d	24	0	0
Mr Thomas Hartshorne for 3 acres of Land lying in the Southfields of the said Borough late purchased of Simon Barwell Gentleman late Mr Collins Land now in the occupation of Thomas Mason & paid by him	2	0	0

5 Beadhouse Meadows

	£	s	d
Mr Thomas Marshalls Executors for a Meadow in the Possession of Mr William Pagett by Lease per Annum	13	10	0
Mr Mathew Daniel for another Meadow late in the possession of Mr Alderman Bass by Lease per Annum	16	0	0

10a   In the North Gate

	£	s	d
James Peters for a Tenement in the North Gate in the occupation of William Palmer Cobler at will per Annum	1	0	0
John Brookes for the North Mill, Brookes's whole rent was £31 7s 6d but in consideration of his making a Bolting Mill at his own expence it was Leased to him for 20 Years per Annum	20	0	0
Richard Lawrence for a Tenement in the North Gate at will per Annum	6	0	0
Mr Thomas Johnson for the Shambles per Annum . .	120	0	0

10b   In Senvey Gate

	£	s	d
William Stephenson for a Tenement by Lease per Annum .		15	0
Mr Jordaine for another Tenement thereto adjoyning by Lease per Annum		15	0
The Executors of Mr James Annis for another Tenement late William Cookes in the occupation of Mr William Moore late John Raysons Land by Lease per Annum now paid by Edward Goodis		5	0
Mr Thomas Penford for a Tenement near the North Gates in Fee Farm per Annum			10
The Heirs or Executors of William Biggs for a Tenement near the North Gates paid by Mr William Smith Clerke in Fee Farm per Annum		1	0
Mr Thomas Penford for a Tenement near the North Gates late George Webb			2
According to the Old Rentall this should be 2s			

10c   In Soar Lane or Walker Lane

	£	s	d
William Twickden or Thomas Gorton for a piece of ground sometimes a Dunghill now built upon heretofore in the occupation of William Rudyard now paid by Joseph Smith in Fee Farm per Annum		2	0
William Cave for a house with the appurtenances late James Jennards late in the occupation of William Bingham per Annum now Benjamin Harris	4	0	0

10d   Within the North Gates

	£	s	d
The Heirs or Executors of Robert Hickling for a Messuage or Tenement on the South side of All Saints Church yard in the occupation of William Warburton in Fee Farm per Annum	1	10	0

Mary Hewson late Dyer for a Messuage or Tenement late Kimberlains Land in Fee Farm per Annum	6	0
Mrs Windsor for a Tenement in the High Street late in the occupation of Joseph Waggatt & now of Mrs Bamford per Annum	5	0
Mr Thomas Carter for a house & garden in the High street at the Corner of Bakehouse Lane heretofore in the occupation of William Ludlam & now of John Fisher	4	0
A House & garden in the occupation of William Grainger heretofore in the occupation of Widow Worrall 4s 6d & for a house in the occupation of Thomas (blank) heretofore in the occupation of Robert Grew used in 2 Tenements 2s 10d per Annum	7	4
Mr Alderman Howkins & Mr Alderman Newton for the house lately built & Barn lately purchased & several Levys in the Horse Fair next the house	24 0	0

10e   In the South Gates

Thomas Morton for a house in the occupation of Mary Moore per Annum	1 0	0
Thomas Whall late John Hardy for a Messuage or Tenement at the Corner of Hangman Lane late the Land of Elizabeth Chamberlain in Fee Farm per Annum	16	0
Mr Chapman & Mr Gamble for a Messuage or Tenement called the Swann near the South Gates in the occupation of Joseph Whoton in Fee Farm per Annum	13	4

10f   In Burgess Meadow

The Heirs or Executors of Mr George Abney or William Palmer Esquire for a piece of Meadow ground in St Marys Meadow called the Shield late Mortons Land in the occupation of Mr Oliver in Fee Farm per Annum	16	0
Of them or one of them more for two acres of Meadow late also Mr Mortons Land in the occupation of the said Mr Oliver & paid by him in Fee Farm per Annum	13	4

10g   In the Swines Markett

The Heirs of Mr Thomas Palmer Attorney at Law for a Messuage or Tenement late Mr Benningtons Land in the occupation of Michael Benshaw now Mr John Willows in Fee Farm per Annum	6	0

Widow Warburton now Mr Smalley for a Tenement heretofore called the Kings Head late John Humphrys late also Agnes Ortons Land now paid By William Throseby of Elston — 18 o

10i   In the Saturday Markett

Mr William Cooke for a Messuage or Tenement now divided into 2 parts or Tenements in the occupation of Elizabeth Dyson in Fee Farm per Annum — 1 3 4

Thomas Slater now Samuel Brown for a Messuage or Tenement late in the occupation of John Hackett in Fee Farm per Annum — 8

10j   In Loseby Lane

The Heirs or Executors of William Orton Mercer for a Messuage or Tenement late John Felziers Land heretofore sold to John Parnell late in the occupation of John Moore & now paid by Mrs Hood in Fee Farme per Annum — 10 o

Mr Jonathan Buckerfield Senior & Mr John Needham late Southwell for a house & garden in Fee Farme per Annum — 1 6 o

Samuell Coates for a house called the Red Cow late the Land of (blank) Jackson in the occupation of William Millward in Fee Farm per Annum — 12 o

Of him more for a piece of ground adjoyning to the said house paying Yearly a Damask Rose at Midsomer

Widow Bothomley for a house & backside being parcell of a Tenement late in Valentine Dallaways occupation since new built — 4 o o

Mr Richard Garle for a Messuage or Tenement lately built in Fee Farm per Annum — 10 o

Mr Richard Garle for a house & backside late Richard Dawsons since new built late in the occupation of Edward Caulton by Lease per Annum — 6 o o

10k   In the Gallowtree Gate

Mr Thomas Ayre for a Messuage or Tenement late in the tenure of Samuel Cooper & Thomas Reynolds or Loftus Page & now of Widow Batchelder in Fee Farm per Annum — 8 o

The said Mr Ayre for a Messuage or Tenement commonly called or known by the Sign of the White Horse late in the occupation of Backhous Ayre in Fee Farm per Annum — 1 o o

The Heirs or Executors of Mr James Palmer for one yard Land sold to Mr James Annis in the occupation of Mr Thomas Mason paid by Mr Joseph Cradock } 15 0

10l   In the Gallowtree Gate on the West side

Randolph Butler for a Messuage or Tenement over against the Round Hill sold to John Woodford now Mr Alderman Lambert in Fee Farm per Annum } 10 0

Mr Orme & Mrs Fish for a Messuage or Tenement adjoyning to the North side of the Angell heretofore Edmund Astwells Land in Fee Farm per Annum } 4 0

The Heirs or Executors of Mr Henry Palmer for a Messuage or Tenement in Widow Bassetts occupation in Fee Farm per Annum } 1 0 0

10m   In the Belgrave Gate

Thomas Drake for a garden at the neather end of Belgrave Gate late in his occupation paid by Mr Joseph Cradock in Fee Farm per Annum } 12 0

William Yates late Thomas Roadley for a Tenement in his occupation in Fee Farm per Annum } 13 4

The Executors of Thomas Glister now Widow Astwell in Fee Farm per Annum now Richard Bellamy } 1 0 0

John Ward Cordwainer for a Tenement heretofore Simpsons adjoyning to the Unicorne on the West side thereof in Fee Farm per Annum } 15 0

Edward Noone for a Tenement on the East side of the said street late the Land of Richard Ward in Fee Farme per Annum } 18 0

The Church Wardens of St Margarets Parish for a piece of ground called the Cow pasture there in Fee Farm per annum } 8 0

10n   In the Country

James Winstanley Esquire for certain Lands Leys & pasture grounds in the Lordship of Braunstone in the County of Leicester now or late in the occupation of William Burton in Fee Farm per Annum } 12 8

Mrs Hurst late William Warner for a Close & Croft & one yard land with the appurtenances in Hinckley in the County of Leicester in his occupation in Fee Farm per Annum } 15 0

The Heirs or Executors of Mr Thomas Worrall for a piece of ground in Belgrave called Knipton Hill leys & one yard Land heretofore sold to Anthony Culverwell being a Close of pasture heretofore called Belgrave Bridge late Mr Overings Land paid by Mathew Cartwright of Oadby   9 0

Sir Edward Noel Baronet for a Messuage or Tenement & one yard Land with the appurtenances in Kirkby Mallory in Fee Farm per Annum   6 8

Thomas Boothby of Tooley Esquire for a Messuage or Tenement in Rearsby in his occupation in Fee Farme per Annum   17 0

William Knifton of Seagrave for a Close & Croft there the Land of William Hubbard paid now John Heggs in Fee Farm per Annum   2 0

Mr Benjamin Storer of Thrussington for one yard Land there in his occupation in Fee Farm per Annum   6 8

William Whale of Frolesworth for the Foss Close & Meadow per Annum   16 0 0

Mr William Tompson of Houghton super Montem for a piece of Land in his occupation or William Hubbards in Fee Farme per Annum   1 8

William Buckley of Thornton for another parcell of Land thereto belonging in the occupation of Thomas Readley now Moses Cotton of Houghton aforesaid in Fee Farm per Annum   5 0

Widow Ryley late Robert James of Barkby for certain Lands there in the occupation of Thomas Readley in Fee Farme per Annum   8 0

John Watts Esquire for certain Lands Leys & hades in the West field of Leicester in the occupation of William Ruding Esquire in Fee Farm per Annum   4 0

Wareing Ashby Esquire for a Messuage or Tenement in Hungerton now or late in the occupation of Elias Marshall heretofore sold to Sir Thomas Cave Knight in Fee Farm per annum   1 10 0

Thomas Burbidge or the Heirs or Executors of George Sheffield for the Mill there called Syston Mill & a house heretofore sold to Sir Thomas Cave Knight in Fee Farm per Annum   3 6 8

11a Other Rents of Lands or Tenements parcell of the Town Obiit Lands of Saint Margaretts Guild & parcell of the Fee Farm rents heretofore Demised by Queen Elizabeth to Mr Howkins & Mr Bates by Indentures expired

The Heirs of Mr William Ive for the ground heretofore belonging to several houses heretofore Mr Nurses William Hills & Francis Coles ruin'd by the late Warrs heretofore sold to Mr Dannett Abney in Fee Farm per Annum paid by Robert Bonner & Sarah Dafforn (to wit) Mr Bonner 13s 4d, Mrs Dafforn £2	2	13	4
The Heirs of Mr John Ludlam for a Messuage or Tenement with the appurtenances commonly called or known by the name of the White Lyon in the occupation of John Price in Fee Farm per Annum		10	0
Mr Thomas Hartshorn for a Messuage or Tenement in the occupation of William Campion & John Fox in Fee Farm per Annum paid by Charles Tuffley Baker	1	0	0
Robert Bonner for the ground lately belonging to 2 Tenements late in the tenure of Paul Abney deceased belonging to a Messuage known by the name of the Bull ruin'd in the late Warrs since built upon & now Paid by the said Robert Bonner in Fee Farm per Annum	1	6	8
The Heirs of Mr Thomas Hartshorn for a Messuage or Tenement called the Grey Hound ruin'd in the late Warrs since built upon paid by Mr Thomas Chapman in Fee Farm per Annum	1	0	0

11b In the Swines Markett

Harpur Judd for a Messuage or Tenement in the silver street over against the Pump late David Murfins Land in Fee Farm per Annum paid by Mr James Sismey	1	0	4

11c In or near Belgrave Gate

Mr John Newton for a Messuage or Tenement at the corner of Humberstone Gate divided into several Tenements heretofore in the occupation of Samuel Hunt & others in Fee Farm per Annum	1	1	0
Mr Thomas Pares for Land late Mr Tathams in the occupation of Richard Heaford & others in Fee Farm per Annum Mr Pares pays 6s John Wilbourne 2s 6d Widow Stokes 3s 6d		12	0

Benjamin Cartwright Joyner for a Tenement called the Lamb in the occupation of John Wellinger & for one other Messuage or Tenement & Close with the appurtenances heretofore sold to George Coates & late the Land of George Blunt late in the occupation of the said Benjamin Cartwright now paid by Mrs Farmer widow	1	6	8
John Noone for a house late in the occupation of Widow Noone & now of Henry Sands in Fee Farme per Annum	1	0	0
Mr Cooper now Mr Heyrick out of Rawletts Close the gift of Mr Twickden	2	0	0
Mr Edmund & Mr Thomas Johnson for Land in Enderby Lordship the gift of Mr John Bent to St Johns Hospitall	26	0	0
Mr Simpson for the Tippetts	3	0	0
Mr Ruding for the Duck Holmes Mr Wards gift . .	3	0	0
Mr Edmund Ludlam out of the Leyroe Mr Billers gift .	12	0	0
*To the Poor of the Old Hospitall at 2 equal payments .	5	16	0
More by 2s weekly for 2 Almswomen 12d to each which makes the Hospitall weekly pay £2 15s 8d	5	4	0
More for a Gown	1	0	0*

[*These payments account for Mr Billers gift above]

The Heirs or Executors of Robert Burbidge Carpenter for a house late in William Headleys occupation & now of John Brookes Baker in Fee Farm per Annum		12	0
Augustine Heaford for a house called the Cock in Fee Farm per Annum Mr Edward Noone pays 1s 8d Thomas Worth 5s near the Cannon		6	8
William Taylor for a Messuage or Tenement in the occupation of William Moseby in Fee Farm per annum now paid by Theophilus Cramp		16	0
A Messuage or Tenement in the occupation of Ellen Denshire & for another part called the Cock in Fee Farm per Annum now sold to John Biggs		13	4
Elias Bates for a Tenement heretofore sold to Robert Roberts in the occupation of Job Withers in Fee Farm per Annum now Mrs Harris Widow		5	0
Samuel Turlington for a Messuage or Tenement in his occupation given by the Town during pleasure		1	0

Samuel Turlington for a Messuage or Tenement late in the occupation of John Meacham in Lease to Richard Scarborow per Annum	2	5	0
Bartholomew Godfory for a Messuage or Tenement in his occupation per Annum	2	15	0
Michael Shaw for a Messuage or Tenement in his occupation per Annum	2	10	0

11e   In Cank Street

John Payne or Mr Thomas Phipps for a Messuage or Tenement in the occupation of Mr William Noone per Annum	13	4

11f   St Nicholas & St Marys Parish

Widow Lewin for a Messuage or Tenement late John Attons Land in Fee Farm per Annum	13	0
The Executors of Mrs Grace for a Messuage or Tenement at the West Bridge called the Miter & Keys in the occupation of Thomas Towers in Fee Farm per Annum	1 0	0
Nicholas Throseby for a Messuage or Tenement in the High street heretofore called the Flying horse heretofore the Land of Thomas Overing in Fee Farm per Annum	1 10	0

12 The Rents of Lands & Tenements parcell of the Town & Mannour of Leicester heretofore amongst other things Given and Granted to the Mayor Bayliffs & Burgesses & their Successors in Fee Farm per Annum

Mr Alderman Marten for a piece of ground in or near Saint Margaretts Church Gate whereon a Messuage or Tenement lately stood in the Possession of George Stearsmore	1	10	0
Edward Palmer Slater for a piece of ground built upon heretofore the Land of Mr Tatham in Fee Farm per Annum paid by Mr Francis Powers		2	6
The Executors of Mr Thomas Palmer Attorney at Law for a Tenement with the appurtenances late the Land of William Inge late also Smalleys Land now paid by Mr Alderman Cartwright		8	0
William Erpe or Charles Johnson for a house or piece of ground near Saint James's Chappell Close called the Hermitage per Annum paid by Thomas Davy Scrivener		1	0

M

George Rayson Pratt for a piece of ground in All Saints Parish called the Vine yard in his occupation in Fee Farm per Annum   4   0

The Heirs of Mr Thomas Bradley for part of a piece of ground called Lyon yard late the Land of Samuel Robinson deceased lying in Saint Martins Parish per Annum now paid by Joseph Spence Tayler   2   6

More for another part of the said Lyon yard & a Messuage or Tenement in the occupation of (blank) in Fee Farm per Annum paid by Mr Weightman   2   6

The Heirs or Executors of Mr William Orton Mercer for a house & barn called Sansbys Land scituate in the Saturday Markett late the Land of William Mitchell & aliarum in the occupation of Mr William Brushfield & John Linthwaite, Mr Brushfield pays 30s. John Linthwaite 10s   2   0   0

Mr Joseph Newton for a piece of ground once Daniel Carrs extending from Senvey Gate to the Common Oven whereupon a house was built by William Carr in Fee Farm per Annum in the occupation of Mr Watts Baker paid by Mr Watchorn   2   6

William Cromwell late John Major Esquire for a piece of ground near Saint Margarets Church yard where a house formerly stood called the Farm House in Fee Farme per Annum paid by Mr Joseph Cradock   6

Thomas Turvile for a piece of ground near Frogmire Bridge now built upon in the occupation of Widow Jarvis per Annum   1   0
     ⟨the Old Rentall at Will⟩

Francis Richards, Thomas Beaumont & John Groce or one of them for a piece of ground in Deadmans Lane in Fee Farm per Annum   1   0

13   Other Rents of Corpus Christi Guild Hall in Leicester heretofore Mr Archers Collection & now parcell of the Lands & Tenements which the said Mayor Bayliffs & Burgesses purchased of Queen Elizabeth to them & their Successors for ever

Thomas Taylor Baker for a Messuage or Tenement with the appurtenances in the Swines Markett in Fee Farm per Annum   13   4

The Heirs or Executors of Mr Edward Brown for a Messuage or Tenement in the Swines Markett heretofore known by the Sign of the Crown in the occupation of Mr John Hammond in Fee Farm per Annum   1 1 8

John Wilebore or Robert Lord for a Tenement in his occupation in Fee Farm per Annum   1 6 8

George Barwell for a Tenement near the Little Bridge in the North Gates heretofore Leased to Robert Cousins for 41 Years & since Leased to Joseph Fossett for 41 Years   15 0

The Heirs or Executors of Mr George Steers for a Messuage or Tenement in the Gallowtree Gate now divided into 2 Tenements in the occupation of Daniel Oldham Paid by Mr William Hall in Fee Farm per Annum   13 4

Mr Nathaniel Simpson now Joseph Simpson for a Messuage or Tenement in the Saturday Markett new built in the occupation of Mr Thomas Jee in Fee Farm per Annum   1 0 0

Mr Anthony Palmer or the Heirs or Executors of Mr George Berkhead for One Messuage or Tenement thereunto adjoyning in the occupation of Thomas Ascough Baker in Fee Farm per Annum   1 0 0

The Heirs or Executors of Mr John Ludlam late Mr Wanley for a Messuage or Tenement near Saint Martins Church in the occupation of William Scarborow in Fee Farm per Annum   6 8

The Executors of Mr Abstinence Pougher for a Messuage or Tenement in Parchment Lane late in his occupation & now of Thomas Pougher in Fee Farme per Annum   16 0

Robert Clarke or Robert Hutchings of Loughborow for certain Lands & pasture ground in Loughborow aforesaid called Sadlers Land now or late in the occupation of John Boss of Loughborow in Fee Farm per Annum paid by the Trustees of Barrow Hospitall   10 0

The Overseers of the Poor of the Parish of Saint Nicholas for a Chamber over the West Gates per Annum   10 0

Mr Bernard Smalley for a Shop near the East Gates heretofore sold to Mr Davis late the Land of (blank) Wigley in Fee Farm per Annum   12 0

Mr Blunt for a Messuage or Tenement on the East side of the East Gates late in Mr Alderman Howkins occupation in Fee Farm per Annum   12 0

The Heirs or Executors of Mr James Palmer for a piece of ground heretofore a garden over against the Town Hall now built upon heretofore Fletchers Land & now in occupation of Thomas Astle Baker } 1 0

Mr Richard Goodall for a Tenement in Parchment Lane heretofore a stable sometime Mr Herricks Land in Fee Farm per Annum } 6 8

Robert James of Houghton for a Croft & halfe yard Land late Thomas Illsons in Fee Farm per Annum paid by Thomas Illson } 6 8

Thomas Pochin of Barkby Esquire for 3 quarters of a yard Land there late the Land of Thomas Seale in Fee Farm per Annum } 6 0

Mrs Philippa Palmer for a Messuage or Tenement in the Swines Markett in the occupation of Kenelm Robinson & late of William Cooper Hosier in Fee Farm per Annum } 6 0

William Franke Esquire for a piece of ground lying on the neather end of Saint James's Chappell Close where a house formerly stood late the land of William Bowman late in the occupation of Mr Pocklington & now of Henry Hitchcock in Fee Farm per Annum } 4 0

A house & Garden in St Martins Churchyard in the occupation of Mrs Hood & paid by her in Fee Farm per Annum } 13 4

Mr Perkins of Grantham for certain Lands & Leys in the Town fields of Gunnerby in the County of Lincoln (heretofore in the occupation of one Kenelme) in Fee Farm per Annum } 6 8

The Executors of Mr Ralph Wells for a Close in or near the Cow drift late Mr Herricks Land heretofore Hastings Land & now (blank) in Fee Farm per Annum } 10 0

The Heirs or Executors of Mr John Cooper for a Shop & other buildings on the East side of the Round Hill in the occupation of Edward Jennings & aliorum in Fee Farm per Annum paid by Mr Bass } 1 0 0

The said Mr Bass more being an Acknowledgement for erecting 4 Columns upon the Corporation ground belonging to the aforesaid building } 1 0

Samuel Marshall for a house & backside in Shambles Lane heretofore Mr Harrisons in Fee Farme per Annum } 1 0

14a Other Rents of the Possession of the late Guild in Leicester Parcell of the Town Obiit heretofore collected by Mr Tatham

Henry Brown Hosier for a Messuage or Tenement in Applegate street late in the occupation of Joseph Birstall late Henry Coates Land now (blank) Wilsons in Fee Farme per Annum — 1 0 0

Thomas Cave for a Messuage or Tenement in the said Street in the occupation of Benjamin Hurst Baker in Fee Farm per Annum — 9 0

William Higginson for a Corner house in the said Street heretofore one William Clarkes Mattmaker & late James Kirkes now Thomas Slater in Fee Farm per annum — 6 8

Ralph Ward for a house in the same street heretofore in the occupation of Robert Herrick Pipemaker & now Edward Guy & John Coates in Fee Farm per Annum — 10 0

William Higginson for the Week days Shambles by Lease per Annum — 2 0 0

John Cooper Carpenter now William Denshire for a Messuage or Tenement late in his occupation in Fee Farm per Annum paid by Phillip Allchurch — 8 0

The Heirs or Executors of Mr Robert Winfield for a house late John Silbys in the occupation of John Foxon in Fee Farm per Annum late David Winfield paid by Mrs Roberts — 7 0

John Bound for a Messuage or Tenement & garden late in the occupation of Joseph Savidge at the Swan in Fee Farm per Annum now William Blackwell paid by Widow Burley & Mr John Watchorn Burley pays 10s Mr Watchorne 4s — 14 0

The Heirs or Executors of Mr Henry Smith deceased for a piece of ground in the possession of Edward Mortimer called the Mayors Old Hall near St Nicholas Church — 3 4

14b In the South Gates

The Heirs or Executors of Mr Richard Barwell for a house & garden near the South Gates in the occupation of John Newton by Lease per Annum — 2 0 0

Widow Gray or her Daughter for a piece of ground belonging to the house ruin'd in the late Warrs sold to Mr Robert Hartshorn or his father late in the occupation of Conyers White & now of Joseph Cox paid by Benjamin Hitchcock in Fee Farm per Annum — 10 0

The Executors of Mr Thomas Hartshorn for the ground lately belonging to 2 Tenements in the occupation of John Palmer in Fee Farm per Annum Mr Chapman pays 6s Charles Tuffley 4s	10	0
The Heirs or Executors of Doctor Coleman or Thomas Aston for the ground lately belonging to 2 Tenements late in the occupation of John Turlington & Henry Charles called the Swan with a Barn thereto belonging ruin'd in the late Warrs since built upon by Hugh Orton in the occupation of Joseph Treen in Fee Farm per Annum	1 5	0
Ralph Ward Cordwainer for a Tenement late Mr Southwells Land in the occupation of Widow Ireland in Fee Farm per Annum paid by Edward Guy	10	0

14c   In the Gallowtree Gate

Mr David Hennell for a Messuage or Tenement late John Freers late also Samuel Woodlands late in Henry Valentines occupation formerly known by the Sign of the Queens Head now new built in the occupation of the said Mr Hennell in Fee Farm per Annum	1 6	8
The Heirs or Executors of Doctor Hartopp for a Messuage or Tenement known by the Sign of the Cinque Foyle late in the occupation of George Broome since new built now in the occupation of John Hackett & Mr Robert Lee in Fee Farm per Annum paid by Mr Alderman Lee	2 0	0
Mr Lord for a Messuage or Tenement heretofore known by the name of the Bucks head & now or late in the occupation of James Mason in Fee Farm per Annum	5	0

14d   In the Swines Markett

The Executors of John Major Esquire for a garden heretofore sold to Michael Walton of Bushby in Fee Farm per Annum late Mr Goadby now Mr John Watchorne	2	0

14e   In the Belgrave Gate

Mr Joseph Taylor for a Messuage or Tenement in the occupation of Arthur Astle in Fee Farm per Annum	16	0
The Executors of Mr John Farmer Attorney at Law for a Messuage or Tenement late the Land of Robert Johnsons in the occupation of Thomas Taylor in Fee Farm per Annum	13	4

Of them more for a Messuage or Tenement late the Land of Robert Gamble in the occupation of (blank) Pepper in Fee Farm per Annum		18	0
Mr John Bass late John Cooper for a Shop & Chamber scituate on the Round Hill in Fee Farm per Annum	1	0	0
The Heirs or Executors of Richard Garratt for a Messuage or Tenement called the Cannon late Stevensons Land late in the occupation of Edward Davis & now of Thomas Flude in Fee Farm per Annum paid by Mrs Jordaine & John Ward		12	0
The Heirs or Executors of Mr John Ludlam 14s & John Yates Wool Comber 8s for 2 Tenements late in the occupation of George Chamberlain & Widow Almey in Fee Farm per Annum the whole is now paid by the said John Yates	1	2	0
The Executors of the said Richard Garratt for a house & garden in the occupation of John Wright in Fee Farme per Annum now paid by the said Mrs Jordaine		6	0
The Heirs of the said Richard Garratt for a house late in the occupation of Thomas Marshall now paid by Robert Johnson in Fee Farme per Annum		8	0
The Heirs of Robert Annis for an Orchard or garden heretofore sold to George Bluntington paid by Anthony Ward late in the occupation of William Chapman Comber & now of John Hunt Worrall in Fee Farm per Annum		6	0
The Heirs of Doctor Hartopp now Mr Alderman Lee for an Orchard or piece of ground whereupon stood a house called St Johns in James Peters occupation per Annum	2	0	2
Part of Margarett Fletchers Land now or late in the occupation of Nathaniel Jennard in Fee Farm per Annum		5	0
The Heirs of Mr Thomas Palmer for a house & garden late Mr Inges heretofore in the occupation of John Russell in Fee Farm per Annum		5	0
Of them more for an Orchard once Mr Inges Land late Mr Smalleys in Fee Farm per Annum		2	0

⟨N.B.⟩ The 2 last Rents & the Rent of 8s late Inges Land folio 17 [see Heading 12 above] are paid thus

Mr Alderman Cartwright to pay . . .	8	9
Francis Hollis	1	3
Jacob Brookes	1	3
David Deakin	1	3

Henry Johnson	I	3
John Squire		7½
Widow Miles		7½
	15	0

14f   In Senvey Gate

William Chamberlain for a Messuage or Tenement late John Newbolds Land late in his occupation in Fee Farm per Annum now in the occupation of Thomas Biggs ⎫ — I 0 0

Richard Kirke for a house & garden in the occupation of Widow Harrison in Fee Farm per Annum paid by Joseph Fossett ⎫ — 8 0

Mr John Smalley for a piece of ground in Senvey Gate belonging to the Corporacion whereupon he built a house in consideration whereof he had a Lease for 41 Years in the occupation of William Froane & (blank) Shipman paid by Mrs Ann Smalley per Annum ⎫ — 6 8

David Deakins & William Wells for a piece of ground called Sallow Close in Fee Farm per Annum paid by the Overseers of St Margarets Parish ⎫ — 5 0

Thomas Throseby for 2 more Tenements new erected in the Senvey Gate at Will with a Spong of ground belonging to the house ⎫ — 5 0 0

14g   Near St Margarets Church

William Deakin for a piece of ground called Margarets Bed lying in the Close late the Land of James Biggs in Fee Farm per Annum paid by Mr Thomas Pares ⎫ — 6

14h   Other Rents part of Mr Wildes Rents

Mr John Farmers Executors for a Close near the Cow drift late in the occupation of William Page & now of Augustine Heaford & paid by James Stockdale in Fee Farm per Annum ⎫ — 13 4

14i   Other part of Mr Wildes 2nd Lease

The Heirs or Executors of Mr Stockden of Glenn Magna for a house in Soar Lane near Red Cross street in the occupation of John Baxter per Annum paid by him ⎫ — 6 0

Sir Nathaniel Curzon Baronet for a house & piece of ground in the said Soar Lane late Brittons Land now in the occupation of Jonah Fossett in Fee Farm per Annum ⎫ — 2 0

John Worth the Elder for a house & garden in Belgrave Gate late Heggs's Land in the occupation of Richard Hawkins now John Yates in Fee Farm per Annum		8	0
The Executors of Mr John Pares for a Close in Arch Deacon Lane heretofore sold to John Mebbs in Fee Farm per Annum sold to Mr Thomas Pares		6	8
William Kirke of Humberstone for a house & Land there in his occupation in Fee Farm per Annum		5	0
Thomas Hastwell for a Messuage or Tenement heretofore sold to him and Jane Ward per Annum	1	6	8
The Poor of the Hospitall of the Holy Trinity in the Newark of Leicester for a garden & piece of ground near the Butt Close now or late in the occupation of Henry Hitchcock in Fee Farm per Annum		2	0
James or Thomas Cartwright for a house & backside near St Margarets Church in the occupation of Samuel Brown in Fee Farm per Annum paid by Mr Chapman of London		8	0
Robert Cook for a house & garden in Belgrave Gate late the Land of Edmund Sutton heretofore the Land of Francis Coates in Fee Farm per Annum paid by William Orton		3	4
Henry Gunnell or Richard Seale for a Tenement with the appurtenances in the Senvey Gate heretofore in the occupation of Thomas Coye & late of Henry Gunnell & now of Nathaniel Hunt in Fee Farm per Annum		10	0
William Wells for a Messuage or Tenement heretofore Thomas Chettles Land now or late in the occupation of Richard Harcourt in Fee Farm per Annum lately paid by John Armstone & now by the said William Wells		6	8
The Heirs or Executors of Mr Thomas Palmer Attorney deceased for a Close near Humberstone Gate formerly sold to John Roe now Mr Thomas Halford in Fee Farm per Annum		12	0

15 A Rentall of the Lands and Possessions belonging to the College of the Blessed Virgin Mary over against the Castle of Leicester heretofore Demised by Queen Elizabeth to Edmund Holt Esquire and by her Majesty Granted to the Mayor Bayliffs and Burgesses & their Successors amongst other things in Fee Farm

Mr Hill Attorney at Law for a Messuage or Tenement in the Swines Markett in Fee Farm per Annum	6	8

	s.	d.
Hannell Langton for part of a Messuage or Tenement in the occupation of Martin Beeby in Fee Farm per Annum	2	0
The Executors of Mr Ralph Wells for a Close near Ayleston Highway late the Land of Robert Herrick in Fee Farm per Annum Paid now by Mrs Leadman	5	0
Elias Wallin for a garden or Piece of ground on the backside of a Messuage or Tenement near the South Gates heretofore the Land of Hugh Watts Esquire in Fee Farm per Annum Paid by Widow Wallin	1	0
Richard Bacon of Markfield for a Tenement in Soar Lane near Red Cross street late the Land of John Coulson now in the occupation of Thomas Kitchen Paid by Mr Norrice Cradock in Fee Farm per Annum	10	0
Thomas Dewick & Mrs Ward 2s 6d each for a Tenement in Soar Lane near Red Cross street sold to John Underwood in Fee Farm per Annum paid by Robert Whiteing 1s 3d Mr Ward 2s 6d Mary Dawson 1s 3d	5	0
Edmund Smith or William Dawson for a house & garden in the Soar Lane heretofore Robert Stevenson in Fee Farm per Annum paid by John Armstones Executors & now by (blank) Foreman of Kirby	12	0

		s.	d.
Mr William Cooper Apothecary for a Messuage or Tenement in Red Cross street & garden in Chaffe Lane adjoyning to the said house in the occupation of Robert Bruce formerly the sign of the bird in hand now called the Old Miter in Fee Farm per Annum	1	0	0
The Heirs or Executors of Robert Allen Butcher for a Messuage or Tenement in Soar Lane in Fee Farm per Annum of which (blank) White 15s 1d (blank) Foulds 11s 7d now paid by Mrs Ludlam	1	6	8

	s.	d.
The Heirs of Robert Ringmore for a Tenement or garden in Soar Lane heretofore sold to John Launder in Fee Farm per Annum paid by Elizabeth Raworth	12	0
Mr Hill or Robert Fossett for a garden in Soar Lane in the occupation of Thomas Trantham in Fee Farm per Annum <At will>		8
Thomas Ward for a piece of ground belonging to a Messuage or Tenement in the South Gates ruin'd in the late warrs & for a Croft in Fee Farm per Annum	16	0

Doctor Cheshire for a piece of ground adjoyning to the Fryer Lane heretofore in the occupation of Mr William Callis lately in the occupation of William Burbage per Annum		4	
John Tyler for the Herbage of St Marys Church Yard at Will per Annum	2	0	0
William Wrighte Esquire late Mr John Farmer late also Sharman for a Close near Cow drift Lane per Annum	1	0	0
Mr Barwell for the Tythe Hay in Burgess's meadow South fields & Tythable meadows beyond the Mill now paid by the Farmers of the South fields per Annum	7	0	0
William Franke Esquire for Saint James's Chappell Close at the neather end of the South Gates heretofore sold to Mr Simpson & late John Sharmans Land in Fee Farm	1	6	8
Jonathan Hunt for a house & garden or backside in the Parish of St Nicholas by Lease per Annum	2	0	0
Mr Nathaniel Heyrick Clerk for the Tythe & Tenths of all those grounds sometime parcell of Dannetts Hall by Lease per Annum	3	0	0
John Denshire for a house & garden in the said Parish late the Land of Daniel Murfin in Fee Farm per Annum paid by Mr Richard Denshire	1	0	0
Walter Ruding Esquire for all the Viccarial Tenths Herbage & other Dutys belonging to the same payable out of the ground & parcell of the Land belonging to West Coates by Lease per Annum	11	16	6
Mr Muxloe of Desford for all the Tythes Tenths Herbage & other Dutys belonging to the same payable out of the Close called or known by the name of the South fields & being parcell of the ground belonging to the Estate or Farm called Dannetts Hall & Welch Hall by Lease per Annum now paid by Mr Watts	1	10	0
The said Mr Watts for the Tythe & part of the Viccarial Tenths Herbage & other Dutys belonging to Dannetts Hall being that part he hath bought	4	0	0
Walter Ruding Esquire for part of Fawnes being part of Dannetts Hall Mary Mill etc.	2	0	0
The said Walter Ruding Esquire for the like . . .	2	0	0
The Executors of Nathaniel Simms now Mr John Smalley for a garden in the Senvey Gate late Woodfords Land in the occupation of Henry Sands in Fee Farm per Annum		1	0

Mr Richard Jordaine for a garden or Piece of ground sometime a Well Yard heretofore the Land of Thomas Chettleton late Robert Griffins in his occupation in Fee Farm per Annum paid by Mr Thomas Pares — 1 4

The Executors of Mr Edmund Townsend for an Orchard & garden in Silver street at Will per Annum now paid by Thomas Slater — 2 0

Mr Ralph Wells's Executors for the third part of a Close near Cow drift in Fee Farm per Annum — 4 0

The Poor of the Hospitall of the Holy Trinity in the Newark of Leicester for part of Dovecoat Close beyond the West Bridge late in the occupation of John Moore & now of John Jervis in Fee Farm per Annum — 1 6

Richard Hassold for a piece of Meadow ground in Glenfield late in the occupation of John Carr in Fee Farme per Annum — 6

Mr Tyrringham Palmer for a Close near Saint Marys Cow pasture heretofore Bennetts Land in the occupation of (blank) in Fee Farm per Annum paid by Mr Joseph Cradock — 3 4

John Watts Gentleman for certain Lands & Leys in the West fields of Leicester heretofore the Land of Thomas Dannett Esquire in Fee Farm per Annum — 2 6

The Poor of the Hospitall of the Holy Trinity for a piece of Meadow ground in Burgesses Meadow called the Lady acre in Fee Farm per Annum — 3 4

Walter Ruding Esquire for a Close in Braunstone Gate late Mr Hunts Land in Fee Farm per Annum — 5 0

Robert Hobsons Executors for a house & Close late in the occupation of John Holmes now John Flower in Fee Farm per Annum now paid by Mr Thomas Pares — 1 10 0

Mr Pocklington Viccar of Saint Marys Church for the Easter & other Dutys in the said Parish — 3 4

A certain Tenement & Garden in Soar Lane near Red Cross street heretofore in the occupation of George King now Joseph Bruce at Will per Annum — 2 0 0

The Heirs of Mr Robert Palmer for a garden in Swines Markett lately built upon heretofore in the occupation of Thomas Ludlam Locksmith late in his occupation paid by Mr Thomas Halford in Fee Farm per Annum — 1 2

		£	s	d
Of them more for a shop heretofore sold to Christopher Needham late in William Tomsons occupation in Fee Farm per Annum paid by the said Mr Halford			2	6
Anthony Abell or William Lyon for a garden in Hottgate street alias Thornton Lane late the Land of Mr Thomas Pares Butcher in Fee Farm per Annum			5	0
William Mason for a Messuage or Tenement heretofore Doctor Chippingdales & Mr Walkers in the Newark of Leicester late in the occupation of (blank) Bailey in Fee Farm per Annum		1	6	8
Of them more for a house there late Doctor Walkers in William Halls occupation in Fee Farm per Annum			13	4
William Inge of Knighton Gentleman for 2 parts of Chamberlains Land now Mr Joseph Cradock in Fee Farm per Annum			12	4
The Heirs or Executors of James Carr of Bowden Magna for Land there now or late in the occupation of John Carrall in Fee Farm per Annum it is 3 pieces of Hay meadow called Leicester Land paid by John Tibbott			1	0
Mr John Herrick of Beaumont Leys for certain Lands in Sileby per Annum				6
William Stedman of Glenfield for Lands there in Fee Farm per Annum paid by Mr John Penford				3

17   Other Rents of the Town & Mannour of Leicester parcell of the Lands & possessions of the Dutchy of Lancaster part thereof being in the County of Leicester.

		£	s	d
The Executors of William Heggs for a Messuage or Tenement heretofore the Land of Mr Ellis late the Land of John Brookesby late Mr Hood now John Cartwright & John Slater in Fee Farm per Annum			16	8
Elizabeth Dyson late Mr Robert Palmer for the Horse Malt Mill in the Swines Markett sold to Bartholomew Parnell in Fee Farme per Annum		1	13	4
The Heirs or Executors of Mr Ludlam for the use of the Chamber over the High Cross			5	0
Charles Coulson for the Town Goal by order of Common Hall		3	0	0

19   Other Rents received of New

William Franke Esquire for a piece of ground being part of the Town Wall scituate near the Freyer Lane late Mr Manebys Land in Fee Farm per Annum	2	6
Hannell Langton for 2 pieces of Land taken off the Common Dunghill in the Lane near the West Bridge in Fee Farm per Annum		10
Mr Abstinence Poughfer for 2 Tenements in Parchment Lane late the Land of Mr John Herrick in Thomas Poughfers occupation in Fee Farm per Annum	3	4

20   Other Rents for certain Lands purchased by the
                        Corporation & other Rents

Mr Samuell Belton for a Close of Pasture ground late in 2 Closes late Mr Freakes Land by Lease per Annum	24	0	0
The Executors of Mr John Pares for one Close called Freakes ground by Lease per Annum & is £30 when Grazed	30	0	0
Augustine Heaford for a Cottage or Tenement scituate near the Horse Fair in his occupation by Lease per Annum	1	5	0
John Garratt for another Tenement to the said Cottage or Tenement adjoyning & thereto belonging by Lease per Annum	1	5	0
David Deakin or William Wells for the Water Laggs paid by Michael Cooke		6	8
William Blackwell for part of the House called the White Swann in the Saturday Markett per Annum	2	0	0
Robert Annis for a piece or Spong of ground part of the ground belonging to the ground or place called the Water Laggs by him walled out for a Felmongers Yard in Lease per Annum		(blank)	

⟨Sold to Robert Cook 10s⟩

21   Rents given to the School & other Charitable uses

His Majestys General Receiver given by Queen Elizabeth out of the Honour of Leicester for the better maintaining the Usher of the Grammar School of Leicester	10	0	0

One Annuity or Rent charge payable Yearly by Sir
Richard Newdigate out of the Mannour of Theddingworth being the Gift of Sir Ralph Rawlett for the maintaining the Under Usher of the said School paid now by   3 6 8
Sir Thomas Cave Baronet & heretofore by Doctor Davis
of Birmingham now His Honour Spencer & paid by Mr
Farrer of Harborow

Mr John Norris for One Annuity Payable yearly out of a
Close in the Abby Gate called the Abby Gate Close for the
better maintaining the Head Usher in the occupation of   3 6 8
Mr John Hammond per Annum

Paul Smith for One Annuity Payable yearly out of a piece
of ground called the Water Laggs to the Under Usher of
the said School being the gift of Mr Thomas Clarke per   1 0 0
Annum paid by Francis Smith

Mr Gamble for certain Lands in the Lordship of Willoughby Warterless being the gift of Mr John Norris   8 0 0
deceased for charitable uses

Mr Thomas Ayre for an Orchard or garden purchased
with £50 given by the first Countess of Devonshire for
and towards the reliefe of the Poor of this Borough & the   5 0 0
Parish of Saint Leonards for the Payment of three Pounds
per Annum paid by John Farrin in his occupation

David Pratt of Whetstone for a Messuage a Close & one
yard Land bought of John Baker Gentleman by the Corporation with the money given by Christopher Tamworth   7 15 0
Esquire for celebrateing Divine service Weekly in Lease
per Annum

John Bruin for 40 acres of Land in the Forrest of Leicester
given by King Charles the first of ever Blessed Memory to   18 0 0
the use of the Poor of this Borough per Annum

Joseph Horton for Burgess's Meadow per Annum   .   .   5 10 0

The Executors of Mr Richard Stephens for a house Close
& Barn thereto belonging in or near Hangman Lane which   12 0 0
the Corporation purchased of Mr Speechley per Annum

The Heirs or Executors of John Poultney Esquire payable
yearly out of the Mannour of Coats Devil & given by him   10 0 0
to Charitable uses per Annum now Mr Shuckburgh Ashby

George Plummer of Evington for Land in Bushby being
the Gift of Mr Nidd to the Poor of Mountsorrell per   32 0 0
Annum

The Heirs or Executors of Anthony Acham Gentleman being the Gift to the Poor of the Corporation out of the Mannour of Asfordby alias Asterby in the County of Lincoln per Annum & now paid by Edward Southwell Esquire of Wisbeach } 9 0 0

Mr Thomas Hartshorne for a certain ground in the South Gates belonging to 2 Tenements heretofore in the occupation of Messenger & Owen being the Gift of Margarett Hobby paid by Samuel Ball now John Curtis } 1 1 8

Mr Joseph Cradock for a Rent charge issuing out of a house heretofore called or known by the Sign of the Parrott being the Gift of Mr Hugh Botham by halfe yearly payments (vizt) the friday before Christmas & the friday before Easter per Annum } 2 0 0

The Executors of Mr Claypole of Allexton for several grounds & Closes there being the gift of Mr Haynes for charitable uses now in the occupation of Andrew Catwall per Annum } 19 0 0

The Parish Officers of St Martins for a Years Interest of £300 at £4 per Cent lent upon Bond by the Corporacion from Lady day 1741 to Lady day 1742 } 12 0 0

23 [No separate heading inserted]

Mr Alderman Lee for the ground lately built upon taken from the sheep pens } 5 0

Mr John Bass for the like late Mr Lord 1 0 0

Mr Smalley for the like paid by Mr Hennell .   .   . 10 0

Mr Hennell more for the like 1 0 0

29   Chiefe Rents belonging to St Johns & St Leonards to be paid at Michaelmas for the Use of the Mayor Bayliffs & Burgesses of the Borough of Leicester

The Warden of the New Hospitall called Wigstons Hospitall } 1 4½

The Heirs or Executors of Mr Boon for one Messuage or Tenement in the Gallowtree Gate lately known by the Sign of the Black Lyon in the occupation of John Gamble lately purchased by Mr Tyrringham Palmer } 6

The Right Honourable the Earl of Stamford for Thurmaston Mills } 6 8

Sir William Rawlinson for certain Lands in Oadby late Sir Henry Beaumonts Baronet & late John Waldrams Land now George Wrighte Esquire per Annum	5	11½
For the Viccaridge House at Oadby Mr Liptrot pays .	1	0½
William Tebbs of Oadby for certain Lands there called Marshalls Land		6
Widow Hammond for a House in Senvey Gate late John Turlingtons Land now Mathew Webster		9

30 Chiefe Rents belonging to Corpus Christi Guild

Mr Samuell Belton late Mr Edmund Townsends Executors for a Tenement in his occupation	4	0
Mrs Kinsborow for a house in the occupation of Mr Edward Tilly	3	0
Mr Orme for a Messuage or Tenement late John Hose's Land now Mr Ormes in his occupation per Annum	2	2
Mr Joseph Cradock late Freemans Land or of Edmund Cradock Esquire for a Messuage or Tenement in the occupation of Mr Pocklington per Annum	2	0
Mr William Cooke for a Messuage or Tenement in Elizabeth Dysons occupation	2	0
Simeon Iliffe of Oadby for certain Lands there late Bliss Land		10
Mrs Jane Palmer for a piece of ground in Parchment Lane late the Land of Tobias Herrick in the occupation of John Farren paid by Mr Richard Roberts		3
The Right Honourable The Earl of Stamford for a Messuage or Tenement in the Red Cross street in the occupation of William Goodrich per Annum	1	0
Widow Simpkin late John Simons Esquire for a certain house in the said Street late the Land of Britton & Suffolk per Annum		8
The Executors of Mr John Groocock for a Messuage or Tenement near St Nicholas's Church late Mr Brittons Land in the occupation of John Lewin paid by Mr Nathaniel Simpson per Annum	1	0
Samuel Brown for a garden in Deadmans Lane per Annum	5	0

N

Jonathan Jee for a Messuage or Tenement in the High street late Mr Mortons Land in the occupation of Thomas Jee paid by Mrs Farmer Widow } 3 0

Thomas Beaumont John Goode & Samuel Wilson for a Cottage in Deadmans Lane late Mr Tyrringham Palmers Land per Annum } 1 0

John Dean for a house in Red Cross street in his occupation per Annum } 4

William Underwood for a garden in Deadmans Lane heretofore Mr Mortons Land per Annum paid by Mrs Coltman } 6

Robert Spencer or Mr Thorpe for a Tenement in the High street late Mr Woods Land in the occupation of William Clarke per Annum } 1 0

David Clay or Mr Hallon for a Messuage or Tenement in the Swines Markett late Mr Poughers Land late in the occupation of Thomas Bennett & aliorum paid by Mr Westley per Annum } 14 0

William Timpson for a Tenement in the Swines Markett in his occupation late the Land of George Heggs per Annum } 9 6

The Executors of Mr Edward Palmer for a Tenement in the said Street late in the occupation of Mr John Willows } 6

Joseph Bradbury or Thomas Boss for a Tenement now divided into 2 Tenements in the Swines Markett in the occupation of John Townsend & Thomas Jee per Annum } 3 0

John Weltden for a Tenement in the occupation of Thomas Adcock late Manebys Land per Annum } 3 6

The Poor of the Old Hospitall for a Barn called Clarkes Barn per Annum } 6

Mr Samuel Simpson for a Tenement in Cank street late in his occupation late Billingtons Land per Annum } 1 0

Robert Bonner for a certain house in Belgrave Gate late the Land of Robert Foster in the occupation of John Westton Hosier per Annum } 3 0

The Executors of Richard Farrin for a house late Mr Pilkingtons in the occupation of Mr Alderman Bates per Annum } 8½

Sir John Whatton Knight for a Close called Shire Hall Close late in the occupation of John Lewett Gardener now Mr Thomas Herrick per Annum	6
Thomas Huffin late William Mitchell Slater for Land late Mr Mays of Rotherby	10½
George Davis for a Messuage or Tenement in Humberstone Gate late in John Davies occupation & now of John Barwell per Annum	3 0
Mr Bernard Smalley for a Messuage or Tenement in the Gallowtree Gate known by the Sign of the Angell in the occupation of William Mason per Annum	2 0
Mr Richard Goodall now James Croxall for a Messuage or Tenement near the East Gates in his occupation per Annum	1 0
The Executors of Thomas Noble Esquire for a Messuage or Tenement at the corner of Fryer Lane known by the Sign of the George in the occupation of John Fenton per Annum	4 0
James Bates for a Messuage or Tenement in the Swines Markett in his occupation per Annum	2 0
For another Tenement there late the Land of William Chamberlaine late in Mr Francis Lewins occupation & now of Mark Volentine & Robert Smith per Annum	2 0
The Executors of Mr Ralph Wells for a Messuage or Tenement late in his occupation & now of William Ashby Esquire late Mr Henshaws Land per Annum	4 0
Mr Mould now Mr Gilbert for a Messuage or Tenement in the Gallowtree Gate late Blackwells Land in the occupation of Theophilus Cramp per Annum	7 6

31   Chiefe Rents belonging to Saint Margarets Guild

The Executors of Mr Bent for a garden in Ironmonger Lane late in his occupation late Mr Pilkingtons Land per Annum paid by Mr Thomas Herrick	1 0
Mr Joshua Goodrich for a Messuage or Tenement in the High street being the corner of Bakehouse Lane in his occupation late Woodlands Land per Annum	1 4
The Executors of Thomas Noble Esquire for a piece of ground in Soar Lane near the North Gates called the Mott yard late in the occupation of Phillip Hackett per Annum	6 0

The Executors of Mr John Farmer Attorney at Law for a house in the Belgrave Gate late in his occupation late Manebys Land per Annum   9

Mr Alderman Hoods Executors for a Messuage or Tenement in Belgrave Gate called the Unicorn in the occupation of John Litherland per Annum   4½

Widow Tayler for a Tenement late Suttons Land in his occupation per Annum paid by Widow Astwell   6

Robert Bonner or Thomas Worth for a Tenement now being the Corner house late the Land of Robert Sutton in Thomas Wards occupation per Annum   6

Mr Thomas Pares for a Barn late the Land of William Inge Esquire   1 3½

The Heirs or Executors of Mr John Ludlam for a Close near the Spittle house called the Bailiffs Close per Annum   1 0

Mr Joseph Johnson for a Messuage or Tenement near the West Bridge in his occupation per Annum   4 0

The Wardens of Wigstons Hospitall for a piece of ground called the Normandy per Annum   6

John Brookes or Mr Thomas Chapman now John Harrison for a house in Church Gate late Manebys Land per Annum   9

Mr George Rayson Pratt for a Messuage or Tenement in All Saints Parish in the occupation of John Pratt salter now paid by him   1 1½

John Cartwright for a Messuage or Tenement late in the occupation of John Wellinger now paid by Mrs Farmer Widow   6

The Executors of Mr John Farmer for a Messuage or Tenement late in the occupation of George Bassett per Annum   3 4

The Executors of Robert Page for a piece of ground taken out of the Pinfold per Annum paid now by Widow Page or Richard Iliffe   4

Mr Thomas Chapman late Mr Hartshorne for a Messuage or Tenement in the South Gates heretofore known by the Sign of the Greyhound per Annum   4 0

Robert Bonner for a Messuage or Tenement in the South Gates late Mr Bennetts Land late in the occupation of Nathaniel Jee per Annum   10

The Poor of the Hospitall of the Holy Trinity for a house in the south Gates late Fosters Land in the occupation of (blank) Thorpe per Annum ⟩ 9½

Mr Oliver for a piece of ground in Burgess meadow late the Land of John Savidge per Annum ⟩ 10 0

John Wilkins for a Messuage or Tenement late in his occupation late the Land of Dannett Abney now Mr Foster paid by him ⟩ 4½

The Heirs or Executors of Mr Wanley now William Davey for a Tenement in the North Gate & for 2 Tenements in the occupation of John Harcourt paid by the said William Davey per Annum ⟩ 1 2

Mr Robert Iliffe for a Shop near the South Gates once Mortons Land per Annum ⟩ 5

Mr Richard Ogden for a house in the High street once Attons Land per Annum ⟩ 3 6

Mr William Topp for a house in the High street in the occupation of John Stephens late the Land of Robert Chettle per Annum ⟩ 2 0

William Slater late Benjamin Garland for a Close at Braunstone Gate Bridge late Cottons Land per Annum paid by Robert Iliffe ⟩ 6

Mr Richard Turvile for a house in the Swines Markett late in the occupation of Mr Gabriel Newton late Tyrringhams Land 11d & for 2 Hens & a Capon 1s ⟩ 1 11

Mr Joseph Johnson for a house near the West Bridge late Babingtons Land ⟩ 9

The Heirs of Mr Pawley of Croxton alias Croson for a Messuage or Tenement in Applegate street now in the occupation of Hamblet Clarke Baker paid by William Smith Clerk ⟩ 6

Simon Ward for a house in Birstall late the Land of William Cole now John Rayner in the occupation of Giles Tuffley paid by (blank) Dormer of Birstall ⟩ 1 0

Mr William Cooke Apothecary for a Messuage or Tenement in the Saturday Markett in the [occupation] of the said Mr Cooke & Elizabeth Dyson Widow ⟩ 6 8

Elizabeth Hebb for a house in Chaffe Lane near Red Cross street once Gulsons Land 9d & for a Henn 3½d per Annum paid by John Wells ⟩ 1 0½

The Heirs or Executors of Mr Robert Winfield for Land late Mr Bothams near Soar Lane & for 3 Capons & 2 Hens — 4 0

Walter Ruding Esquire for a Close in Braunstone Gate per Annum — 9

Mr John Billers for a house in Hott gate street alias Thornton Lane 3d & for a hen 3½d & for a garden late a Swine stye 6d paid by Mr Bentley 6d — 1 0½

John Tyler near the South Gates in the High street late Budworths Land 9d & for 2 Hens 7d & for a Shop near the South Gates 6d now or late in the said John Tylers occupation per Annum — 1 10

John Winter for a Tenement over against All Saints Church yard late Mr Rudyards land late in David Deakins occupation per Annum — 2 3

The Executors of Mr Edward Palmer late Mr Robert Palmer for a house in the Swines Markett late Mr Bonsars Land now Mr Thomas Halford Attorney at Law — 6

The Heirs or Executors of Mr Pawley for a house in Applegate street once Birstalls in the occupation of Hamblet Clarke 10d & 2 Hens & a Cock 10d — 1 8

Mr Thomas Chapman for a Messuage or Tenement at the upper end of Belgrave Gate late Neals Land per Annum in the occupation of Mr Samuel Simpson — 1 6

Mr Thomas Palmer or Edward Daws for a Close in All Saints Parish near Plankwell late Wells's now Mr Joseph Cradocks Land per Annum — 1 8

Thomas Turvile for a house & Land in the North Gates late Bodymans & Robert Harrisons per Annum now Widow Carnall — 6

Samuel Turlington & (blank) for a certain house in the North Gates late Woodfords now Mr Green Hodgkins of Great Glenn per Annum — 1 1

Edward Davis now Charles Tuffley for Land in the South Gates late Owens & Messengers Land in his occupation 2s & for a Capon 10d — 2 10

The Heirs or Executors of Mr Edward Palmer for a house in the Swines Markett late Christopher Needhams & Baylys Land now Mr Halford — 4

Mr Thomas Chapman for a house in the South Gates late Heafords Moulds & Rivetts now Mr Joseph Tayler — 6 8

The Heirs or Executors of Mr Edward Palmer now Mr Halford for a house in the Swines Markett near the Horse Malt Mill late Mr Manebys Land in the occupation of William Leadbeater per Annum ... 6

33 A Rentall of Lammas Tythe & Herbage due yearly to the Mayor Bayliffs & Burgesses for diverse grounds in St Marys Parish in possession of the late College of Saint Marys over against the Castle of St Marys Leicester

	£	s
Mr Richard Westons Executors for Dovehouse Close near the Newark of Leicester late Mr Hicklings Land per Annum	1	4
William Franke Esquire for a Close called Archers Close now Palmers near St James's Chappell Close per Annum	1	0
Of him more for the Tythe of St James's Chappell Close per Annum	1	0
The Executors of Mr John Farmer Attorney for the Tythes of Benningtons Close near the Cow drift per Annum	1	0
William Slater late Benjamin Garland for a Close near Braunstone Gate Bridge per Annum now Mr Iliffe		6
Mr John Mason for a Close late 2 Closes over against St James's Chappell Close now William Wrighte Esquire Recorder in his occupation per Annum	1	8
The Heirs or Executors of Robert Hickling for Land near the Grange once Birstalls Land per Annum now the Heirs of Mr Thomas Weston	1	0
Of them more for a Close late Mr Mortons Land near St James's Chappell Close per Annum		10
Of them more for Seth Kings Land		6
The Heirs or Executors of Mrs Brown now Mr Iliffe for a Close near the Paradice		4
William Franke Esquire for Cadmans Land per Annum .		10
Of him more for a piece of ground called the Kilne heretofore the Land of Cadman & Johnson per Annum		4
Mr Joseph Wilkins for an Orchard on the backside of a house once Davys in the South Gate late the Land of Hugh Watts Esquire paid by John Lacey per Annum		6

The Executors of Mr Ralph Wells for a Close near Ayleston Highway late Mr Herricks Land now (blank)		8
Of them more for another Close near the said Highway .		4
Of them more for a Close near Archers Land .　.　.		10
The Executors of Mr Richard Weston for a piece of ground near St Marys Mill called the Holme late Manebys Land per Annum	1	8
The Executors of Mr John Farmer Attorney for a Close near Ayleston Highway late in the occupation of Augustine Heaford per Annum now William Wrighte Esquire		10
Of him more for a Close in the occupation of Mr Jee per Annum	1	0
Walter Ruding Esquire for a Close in Braunstone Gate late Mr Hunts Land per Annum		8
Of him more for a Close called College Close late Mr Hunts Land per Annum		4
Hannell Langton for a Close late Mr Brookes Land per Annum	2	2
Mr Nathaniel Simpson for a Close called the Tippett per Annum	13	4
John Guilford for the Tythe of the Newark Mills per Annum	2	0
Thomas Haddon or John Lewin for a garden or piece of ground in the Milstone Lane late Armstones Land per Annum		4
Widow Anderson for Land in Chaffe Lane now Mr Robert Hall		10
The Heirs or Executors of Francis Annis for a backside belonging to his house in the South Gates now in the occupation of Thomas Ward per Annum		6
Mr Thomas Stanley for the Tythe of 4 Yard Land .　.	8	0
Thomas Ward for 3 Yard Land .　.　.　.　.	6	0
Mr Joseph Newton for a house in Thornton Lane late William Tomsons		4
Thomas Tompson for Booths Land now Benjamin Hurst .		4
Thomas Willows for the Tythe of Mr Southwells 4 yard Land	8	0
Mr Thomas Stanley more for the Tythe of 3 Yard Land .	6	0

Walter Hall for the Tythe of 3 Yard Land . . .	6	0
Robert Bonner for the Tythe of 3 Yard Land . . .	6	0
John Guilford for the Tythe of the Newark Mills . .	16	0
Mr Richard Goodall & Mr William Brushfield for the Tythe of the Gosling Closes	2	0
John Brookes for the Tythe of the North Wind Mill .	2	0
Marmion Jee for laying Planks & setting Posts in the River Soar during Pleasure		6
James Derbyshire for the Tythe of a Piece in the Marys Meadows	6	0
Mr William Pagett for the Tythe of the Beadhouse Meadows	13	6
Mathew Daniel for the like	16	0
Mr Thomas Hartshorne for the Tythe of a Piece in the Mary Meadows	(blank)	
⟨Q. What the rent of Mr Hartshornes Land is⟩		
John Guilford for the Tythe of the Meadows belonging to the Mill	(blank)	
⟨Q. Whether the Miller ought to pay Tithe for the grass ground⟩		

The End of the Rentalls

36   Fines & Accidental Receipts

Thomas Thorpe of Gaddesby for Scott & Lott . .		10	0
Thomas Spawton for his freedom		10	0
John Lewin for the like		10	0
Thomas Judd for the like		10	0
John Fletcher for the like		10	0
John Brown for the like		10	0
Robert Bryan of Little Stretton for Scot & Lott . .		4	0
Francis Bates for his Freedom		10	0
Thomas Clarke for the like		10	0
Samuel Birch a Stranger for his Freedom as by order of Hall	20	0	0
William Sands for his Freedom		10	0
Benjamin Hurst a Stranger for his Freedom as by order of Hall	20	0	0
William Underwood of Melton for Scott & Lott . .		6	0
Received the Ballance of the late Chamberlains accounts .	328	16	1

Received for breaking of ground in St Marys Chancell .   6 8

Received for an old Tree blown down at the North Mill .   4 0

Received for Wood sold from off the Estate at Allexton of
Mr Bagnall   30 0 0

Received of Mr Thomas Ayre Junior as a Fine or Income
for the house Close & other the Premises near the Horse
Fair late in the possession of Mr Stephens   70 0 0

[End of Receipts]

[Payments start here]

1 [No separate heading inserted]

Paid Mr Hart at the Audit of broad Arrow   .   .   .   1 0

Acquittance for the same   6

Paid Mr Hart Receiver for one years rent of the sheep
pens due Michaelmas last   4 0 0

Paid him more for Singletons Lease   .   .   .   2 12 8

For shops taken down 11 6

Paid him more for St Margarets Guild .   .   .   1 13 $5\frac{1}{2}$

To him more for Corpus Christi Guild alias Town Hall .   7 9

To him more for Luskins Lease 2 0

To him more for diverse chiefe rents of the Town .   7 8

Paid him more for a Close late Websters Land   .   1 0

Paid him more for a Close near the Horse Fair   .   3 $4\frac{1}{2}$

Paid him more for Corpus Christi Guild   .   .   11 9

Paid him more for a Close late Hallams .   .   .   1 0

Paid him more for an acquittance for the said money   .   4

Paid him more for a chiefe rent for the Shops under the
Gainsborow   2 6

Paid him more for a shop in Richard Wagstaffes occupation   1 0

Paid Mr Hart his Majestys Receiver for one whole years
rent due out of the Lands & Tenements belonging to
Saint Johns & St Leonards in or near the Borough of
Leicester heretofore Mr Harveys & Mr Tathams Leases
& in Countesthorpe & Humberstone Syston Mills & the
White Horse for one years rent at Michaelmas last   31 12 5

Paid to the Receiver for Lands & Tenements belonging
to the late Guild called St Margarets Guild Hall in
Leicester Town Obiit Lands & Viccars Closes heretofore
in the occupation of Arthur Tatham for a Years rent due
at Michaelmas last   42 18 1

Paid him more for a parcell of Land in the possession of the late Guild called Corpus Christi Guild for one years rent due at Michaelmas last	14	12	6
Paid to the said Receiver for certain Lands & Tenements chiefe rents & Lammas Tythes parcell of the possession of the College of the Blessed Virgin Mary over against the Castle in Leicester for a Years rent due at Michaelmas last	20	8	6
Paid to the said Receiver for certain Tenements in the Newark of Leicester	3	16	1

3   At the Audit held by Mr Harte at the Horse & Trumpet

Paid the Kings Receiver for 2 Tenements in the Swines Markett in the occupation of (blank) due at Michaelmas last	2	10	0
Paid him more for the Malt Mills in the Swines Markett in the occupation of Mrs Carter paid by John Dyson	1	13	4
Paid him more for the Shambles & Drapery in Leicester due at Michaelmas last	8	13	4
Paid him more for the Gainsborow, Chamber, Shop & sheds & for the Saturday Markett which the Mayor Bayliffes & Burgesses Purchased of Mr Britton for one Year due at Michaelmas last	4	8	8

4   Fines & other Payments this Year

Paid Thomas Marten Esquire Mayor his Sallary according to an Antient custom	13	6	8
Paid him more out of the Rent of Gosling Closes allowed by order of Common Hall	13	6	8
Paid him more being the Additional Annual Sallary to the Mayor in the year 1712/3	20	0	0
Paid him more by order of Hall made in the year 1736 .	40	0	0
Paid William Wrighte Esquire Recorder of the said Borough for his Years Sallary	10	0	0
Paid to the Town Clerke for taking the Coroners Inquest.	1	0	0
Paid him more for the book of Payments . . .		4	6
Paid him more for the Sessions due at Michaelmas last only		6	8

Paid Mr Andrews Head School Master being the Towns free gift during pleasure	16	0	0
Paid the Head Usher during pleasure	8	0	0
Paid the Under Usher being the Towns free gift during pleasure	3	0	0
Paid him more being the Towns free gift during pleasure.	5	0	0
Paid Mr Broughton his Years sallary as Lecturer for the said Borough during pleasure	20	0	0
Paid him more by order of Common Hall during pleasure.	10	0	0
Paid Mr Pocklington Viccar of Saint Marys being the Towns free gift during pleasure	10	0	0
Paid Mr Haynes the like	10	0	0
Paid Mr Burneby the like	10	0	0
Paid Mr Andrews the like	10	0	0
Paid the Town Clerke his Years Sallary	5	0	0
Paid him more being the Towns free gift . . .	2	13	4
Paid for the Rentall	2	0	0
Paid for proclaiming the Fairs & Marketts . . .		14	0
Paid for the Commission for this Year		9	10
Paid the Macebearer his Years Sallary & for burning of Pipes	7	9	8
Paid the Macebearer for 2 Seals		2	0
Paid the 4 Serjeants their Years Sallary by order of Hall per Quarter £1	16	0	0
Paid the Cryer for his Wages & sweeping the Town Hall & Gainsborow	1	13	4
Paid the Beadle his Years sallary & for sweeping the Gates & weeding the Town Hall Yard	6	0	0
Paid the Beadle & Cryer to keep them from going about with their Christmas box		4	0
Paid John Veasey for keeping the Library . . .	3	0	0
Paid the Waits their Years Sallary	6	13	4
Paid Charles Coulson keeper of the Bridewell . . .	1	13	4
Paid the Bailiff of the Augmentation for Lands due to Leicester Abby at the Feast of Saint Michael & acquittance		7	4
To the Bailiff of Merton College in Oxford for one chiefe rent issuing & payable out of Saint Johns & St Leonards in or near the Borough of Leicester		1	3

	£	s	d
Paid the Warden of the Company of Taylors the Annual Rent of		1	8
Paid the Halbert Men for walking the Fair cleansing the Armour & tolling the Bell on Michaelmas day		11	0
Paid for attendance & weights at the Cheese fair . .	2	15	0
Paid for carrying out Warrants to Impress Carriage for Soldiers Baggage		3	0
Paid Mr Lucas for a chiefe rent out of the Gainsborow .	6	1	0
Paid for Bunns & Ale at visiting the school 3 times . .	1	10	0
Paid St Marys Ringers & Mr Rudings Men on the Feast day		4	6
Paid the Clerke of Assizes Fees for both Assizes . .	1	6	8
Paid for Biscuits Wine & Ale (blank) & the Beadle & Cryer 2s	1	7	0
Paid for 40 cwt of Coales used at the Gainsborow & Town Hall	2	6	8
Paid for Holly & Ivy used at the Town Hall & Gainsborow		2	6
Paid the Clerke of St Marys for washing the Chancell .		2	6
Paid the Grand Jury for 4 quarter Sessions dinners . .	6	0	0
Paid the Constables for the like	1	4	0
Paid Mr Winstanleys Huntsman on Easter Monday .		10	0
Paid Men for playing the Engines 2 times . . .	1	4	0
Paid towards repairs of the Well by the Town Hall for useing water there		1	0
Paid for sweeping the Streets for the whole year . .	6	4	10
Paid towards the Horse Race Town purse . . .	10	10	0
Paid the Fees at the Venizon Feast	1	1	0
Paid drawing drink then		1	0
Paid Mr Pare for acquittance for the Earl of Huntingtons gift			8
Paid Mr Smalley a Chiefe rent		2	0
Paid the Cryer for taking & weighing the Coals in & out of the Town Hall		10	0
Paid the late Mr Page 26 weeks at 5s a week . . .	6	10	0
Paid James Wileboare 52 weeks at 2s 6d per week . .	6	10	0
Paid for 2 pair of Shoes for the Beadle & Cryer . .		9	0
Paid the Lottery money to All Saints Parish Officers .	5	0	0
Paid the Judges presents	4	15	0

Paid Robert Johnson for keeping the Pavement in repair before the Meeting house	1	0	0
Paid Mr Bonner for allowance for loss of Clay ground .		8	0
Paid taking the Engines to and from Taylors fire . .		5	0
Paid John Coe for a Nett for taking the fish out of the Stew		2	0
Paid for 2 several times sweeping the Chimneys at the Town Hall		5	0
Allowed the Chamberlains for the Auditors Dinners . .	12	0	0
Paid the Town Clerke for making up the Accounts . .	3	6	8
Parchment for the same			6
Paid for a Ribbon for the Charter		2	0
Paid for paper & pens		10	0
Allowance of Coals		6	8
Paid for the Letter of Attorney		5	6
Allowed the Farmers for damage done by the Horse Race	6	6	0
Allowance by loss of Coals	12	8	4
Paid Doctor Heighington Organist of St Martins . .	10	0	0
Paid for Stones		5	0
Paid for Cleansing the Horse Trough		2	0
Paid (blank) Goddard for prosecuting Lewitt . . .		3	0
Paid for a Buckett at the Town Goal pump . . .		2	0
Paid the expences in prosecuting John Caunt . . .		9	0
Paid the Expences in searching for Lady Moyers Will .		10	0
Paid James Wileboare for mending 17 Bucketts & putting new Handles to them		7	0
Paid William Ward & (blank) Iliff for their trouble in going to settle the Mears between the South Fields & Knighton field		1	0
Paid for repairs at the Wall by the Horse fair . . .		3	8
Paid for removing the Engines out of the Guard house .		1	0
Paid for Lime used at one of the houses in Senvey Gate .		2	6
Paid Chapman for keeping the Channell clean in Belgrave Gate & carrying away the Dirt		18	0
Paid for 3 Kidds used at the Town Hall . . .			8
Paid for getting Gravell & mending the Road to the Cow Pasture	1	12	0
Paid the Clerke of Assizes for his Fees for transporting Caunt	1	1	0

7   Tradesmens Bills paid as follows

Paid Mr Alderman Ogden	5	1	7
Paid William Clarke	10	2	6

Paid Robert Johnson	9	7	0
Paid him one other Bill	1	7	0
Paid John Westley	8	12	7¾
Paid John Webster	29	3	6
Paid him one other Bill		17	6
Paid Joseph Bruce	21	5	5
Paid Cornelius Norton		3	3½
Paid Mr Henry Gutheridge		15	6
Paid Mr Joseph Chambers	17	11	3½
Paid Mr Alderman Marten	10	3	6
Paid John Wigley	4	14	6
Paid William Hunt		6	0
Paid Augustine Billing		8	7¾
Paid John Volentine	1	18	3
Paid Thomas Wootton		14	8
Paid Mr Alderman Brushfield	1	19	9
Paid Thomas Elliott	5	18	0
Paid John Brown		9	0
Paid Tyrringham Palmer		12	0
Paid George Townsend	1	5	7
Paid Mr Oliver	13	11	3
Paid Thomas Hewson		15	1
Paid Mr Alderman Ludlam	1	8	9
Paid Mr Samuel Brown	3	4	9
Paid Mr Alderman Lee	1	4	0
Paid Mr Alderman Cartwright		13	4
Paid William Higginson	1	10	11
Paid Nicholas Throseby	1	1	4½
Paid Widow Hall	8	11	0
Paid for a quarter of Charcoal		6	0
Paid John Cartwright		4	1
Paid William Hose		3	6

9   Allowance of Taxes at 3s per pound

Samuell Brown Junior		4	6
Mr Alderman Ayre		3	0
Widow Astwell		3	0
Wareing Ashby Esquire		4	6
Mr Pagett & Mr Daniel	2	3	0
Mr Buckerfield		3	0
Widow Bothomley		6	0
Widow Bassett		3	0

	£	s	d
Robert Bonner		4	6
Henry Brown		3	0
Thomas Biggs		3	0
The several Farmers for their Tythes	1	4	0
Mr Cooke		4	6
John Garle		9	0
Mr Thomas Chapman		3	0
Mr Samuel Heyrick		6	0
Mr William Cooper		3	0
Mr John Bass		6	0
Mr Richard Denshire		3	0
John Farrin		3	9
Elizabeth Dyson Widow		4	6
Mrs Farmer		3	0
Mrs Franke		3	0
Mrs Grace		3	0
Augustine Heaford	1	1	0
(blank) Whall	1	19	0
Mr Hammond		12	0
Mr Alderman Howkins & Mr Alderman Newton	1	4	0
Bartholomew Godfary		3	0
John Hurst		3	0
Benjamin Harris		5	3
Mr Hannell		3	0
Mr Alderman Lee		6	0
Thomas Hastwell		3	0
Mr Samuel Heyrick		9	0
John Brewin for the Forrest Closes	1	19	0
John Brooks for the North Mill	2	8	0
John Guilford for the Swans Mill	2	6	0
Mr Johnson	6	0	0
Richard Lawrence		6	0
William Mason		4	6
Jonathan Hunt		6	0
Thomas Mason now Mr Stretton		4	6
Widow Moore		3	0
Mr John Newton		9	0
Mrs Orton		4	6
Mr Alderman Lee		6	0
Mr Alderman Martin		3	0
Mrs Pares	3	0	0
Swanns Mill shop		3	0
Walter Ruding Esquire	1	16	0

Mr Alderman Belton	2	5	0
Syston Mills		9	0
William Higginson		4	6
Mr Joseph Simpson		3	0
William Blackwell		6	0
Mr Ayre		18	0
Francis Smith		3	0
Shops & stalls	1	14	0
Rowland Watts		3	0
Charles Tuffley		3	0
Joseph Treen		3	9
Thomas Throseby		7	6
John Wilbore		3	0
Mr Watts		16	6
Widow Ward		3	0
William Warburton		4	6
Mr Oliver		4	0
Mr Thomas Pares		4	6
John Brooks a Mill shop		3	0
Joseph Bruce		6	0
More by Mrs Dafforn		6	6
Mr James Sismey		3	0
Henry Sands		3	0
Nicholas Throseby		4	0

11   Charitable Gifts

Paid the Gift of Queen Elizabeth to the Head Usher	10	0	0
Paid the Gift of Sir Ralph Rawlett	3	6	8
Paid the Gift of Mr Norris	3	6	8
Paid the Gift of Mr Clarke	1	0	0
Paid the Gift of Mr Norris out of Willoughby Lands	8	0	0
Paid the Gift of Mr John & Mr William Stanley	5	0	0
Paid the Gift of the Earl of Devonshire	6	0	0
Paid the Gift of Christopher Tamworth Esquire	7	15	0
Paid the Gift of King Charles the first of ever Blessed Memory	18	0	0
Paid the Gift of Mr William Ive	15	0	0
Paid the Gift of Mr Elkington	5	0	0
Paid the Gift of Mr William Poultney	10	0	0
Paid the Gift of Mr Nidd	32	0	0
Paid the Gift of Mr Acham	9	0	0
Paid the Gift of Mr Haines	19	0	0

O

Paid the Gift of Mr Botham	2	0	0
Paid the Gift of The Earl of Huntington . . .	10	0	0
Paid the Gift of Sir William Courteen & Gentlemen of the Lottery	4	16	0
Paid the Gift of Mrs Dorothy Baker	1	0	0
Paid the Gift of Mr Julius Billers	5	12	0
Paid the Gift of Mr Ward & Bennett	1	0	0
Paid the Gift of Mrs Ossiter Widow	6	0	0
Paid the Gift of Mr Gilbert	5	0	0
Paid the Gift of Mr Hitch		3	0
Paid the Gift of Mrs Margaret Hobby	1	1	8
Paid the Gift of the Countess of Devonshire . . .	3	0	0
Paid the Gift of Mr Hesilrige	1	1	6
Paid the Gift of Mr Thomas Ayre	1	0	0
Paid the Gift of Mr John Ludlam	2	10	0
Paid the Gift of Mr Thomas Weightman . . .		5	0
Paid the Gift of Mr John Roberts	1	0	0
Paid the Gift of Mr Robert Hall		10	0
Paid the Gift of Mr George Bent		5	0
Paid the Gift of Mr William Sutton being the Interest of £70 at £4 per Cent given to the Poor of the Hospitall of St Johns alias St Jones's	2	16	0
Paid more being his Gift the Interest of £20 to the Poor of the Old Hospitall		16	0
Paid the Gift of Benjamin Garland to the Parish of St Martins		5	0
Paid the Gift of Mr Topp to the Poor of the Old Hospitall .	1	0	0
Paid more his Gift to St Johns Hospitall . . .		10	0
Paid the Gift of Mr Alderman Thomas Ludlam being the Interest of £300 which he left to Charitable uses	12	0	0

[End of Payments]

[Supers start here]

Supers

(blank) Perkins for Gunnerby Land	6	8
George Wrighte Esquire for Land at Oadby . . .	5	11½
The Earl of Stamford for the Tythe of Thurmaston Mills .	6	8
For the Easter & other Dues for the Viccar of St Marys .	3	4
Anthony Ingoldsby Esquire for Land at Ashby . .		6
For the Tythe of the Swanns Mill	18	0
Mr John Herrick for Land at Sileby		6

Mr Wrightes Taxes	3	0
Mrs Sutton	1	0
Mr Farmer Chiefe rent	1	9
Mr Wrightes Chiefe rent	1	0

[End of Supers]

[Summary]

Total of the Receipts	1433	15	9
Total of the Payments	944	7	0
Ballance due to the Corporation	489	8	9
More being the Ballance of the Hospitall account . .	5	0	2
Ballance now due to the Corporacion	494	8	11

From which Deduct which Mr Mayor paid to Vagrants etc. .	5	12	5		
More which he paid to Mr Bents Hospitall according to an order of Hall made 17th October 1750 that whatever should happen to be wanting should be paid by the Chamberlains which appears to be . .	2	8	0	Deduct	8 1 11
More for Letters . . .	1	6			
	8	1	11		

Ballance now due to the Corporacion	486	7	0
From which deduct being paid to Richard Godfrey for himselfe Horsehire & Expences in going over to Allexton & dischargeing the Tenant from holding the Land out 2 days	1	1	0
Ballance now due to the Corporation	485	6	0

From which Deduct as appears by Bill paid to Thomas Linsey for Lime	1	8	8½
More to Jonathan Hunt as by Bill	1	2	6
More to Mr Johnson as by order of Hall . . .	4	4	0
	6	15	2½
Ballance now due to the Corporation	478	10	9½

CHAMBERLAINS' ACCOUNTS
1771/2

Borough of Leicester to wit } The Accounts of William Taylor and Thomas Barwell Chamberlains of the Borough of Leicester in the Mayoralty of John Cartwright Esquire for one whole year to wit from Michaelmas 1771 to Michaelmas 1772

1 [No separate heading inserted]
⟨Imprimis in the Rental 1652⟩
No.

1	Augustine Heafford for a years rent of the Sheep pens with Cokers Kitchen by lease payable at Lammas and Candlemas	9	0	0
3	Rogers Ruding Esquire late Thomas Noble Esquire and heretofore Mr John Harrison for rents of Assize due yearly out of the Lands at the North Gates late in the occupation of Thomas Turvile call'd Gadesby's land at Michaelmas only paid by Mr Garle in the North		1	9
4‡	William Wills heretofore Josiah Ashwell and late of Mr John Poynton for a Chamber over the East Gates and for a Shop and Chamber adjoining to them in his occupation & late of Josiah Ashwell	5	0	0
7	Lady Greasley late Mr Alderman Hood and heretofore John Blunt for Butt Close formerly sold to Mr Thomas Blunt late in the occupation of Mr Robert Roulson late Freeman's late also John Loseby's		10	0
9	Mr John Wightman late Edward Noon for a messuage or tenement at the nether end of Belgrave Gate heretofore the Land of Thomas Headley now divided into several tenements in fee farm per Annum late in the occupation of Edward Noon & now of Mr John Yates		1	0	0
12	Mr Plumber of Evington & Francis Stafford 1s 3d each late John Elliott late also Charles Stafford & Alice Brown for a Garden or a piece of Ground in the Senvey Gate in the occupation of John Jee and George Webb		2	6

16 Lord William Manners late the Duke of Devonshire
for a piece of Ground (being a Close) in the North
Gates whereon stood a messuage or tenement here-
tofore the Land of George Tatham in fee farm per   13   4
Annum paid by John Simpson Esquire for Lord
Manners

The said Lord William Manners late the said Duke
for a parcel of Ground being part in the said Close
late Fletchers land in fee farm per Annum paid by   4
the said Mr Simpson for Lord Manners

John Lambert late the heirs or Executors of Thomas
Fletcher alias Thomas Alsop for a piece of Ground
lying on the backside of a Messuage or tenement in   1   8
the North Gates sold to John Tatham in fee farm per
Annum paid by Samuel Daws the tenant

14 John Halford late John Erpe for a messuage or tenement and piece of Ground thereunto belonging in the
Applegate Street & in the Parish of Saint Nicholas   6   8
heretofore the Land of William Adcock in fee farm
per Annum

15 Rowland Watts late John Turvile late Mr Barwell for
a tenement in the North Gate late the land of Mr
Robert Freer heretofore the Sign of the Sun in the   1   0   0
occupation of Rowland Watts per Annum

22 Thomas Gardener late Robert Cook late also John
Erpe for a piece of Ground called the water Laggs in
the Parish of St Nicholas late in the occupation of Mr   6   8
Edmund Johnson in fee farm per Annum sold by
John Erpe to Robert Cook

24 John Campion for a piece of Ground at the South end
of Butt Close in fee farm per Annum   4

26 (blank) Chandler of Gilmorton late Mr Gamble of
Willoughby or William Burdett of Gilmorton late
also Robert Palmer of Gilmorton aforesaid for land
meadow and Pasture Ground at Gilmorton hereto-   3   4
fore the land of John Spriggs afterwards of Edward
Wighthead

27 Anthony Ingoldsby Esquire for lands in Great Ashby
in the County of Lincoln late the Land of Ralph
Brookesby Gentleman heretofore the land of Nicho-   6
las Norton per Annum

28 Mrs Wigley late James Wigley Esquire late Robert
Pawley Esquire for certain Lands and tenements in
Scraptoft late the Land of John Mason & heretofore
the Land of Thomas Simpkin and (blank) Taylor of
Whetstone and now or late in the tenure of Matthew
Hubbert

6

3   Receipts of the whole Grange with the appurtenances and four
yard land and the yard land called Archers land and known by the
name of Wightmans land & a half yard land which the Corporation purchased of Lord Spencer as followeth

‡Mr Thomas Chatwin late John Guildford for a years
rent of the Newark Mills and Wind Mill and Meadows thereto belonging by lease per Annum

30 0 0

‡Mr Johnson late John Wright for part of Gosling
Close by lease per Annum

16 5 0

‡Mr Jordan for other part of Gosling Close by lease
per Annum

15 0 0

5   Beadhouse Meadows

‡Mr Fisher, Mr James Cooper Mr Clement Stretton
& Mr Johnson £7 10s each late Mr Thomas Marshall
for Meadow Ground late in the possession of Mr
Pagett & Mr Daniell by lease per Annum

30 0 0

‡John Valentine for 4 acres of land to dig clay to make
bricks per Annum

4 0 0

‡Mr Backhouse Ayre late Mr Alderman Ayre for the
Rowdike field and Meadows thereto belonging as by
lease per Annum

92 11 0

‡Mr Thomas Phipps late Mr Alderman Phipps for the
Gallow field and meadow Ground thereto belonging
as by lease per Annum

97 2 0

‡Mr Alderman Oliver for the middle field and meadow
Ground thereto belonging as by lease per Annum

84 7 0

‡Mr Nutt and Mr Martin late Mr Alderman Chapman for the Forest Closes which had used to be
rented by the Farmers along with their livings in the
South Fields

9 0 0

10a   In the North Gate

	£	s	d
46‡Mrs Davie late James Peters for a tenement in the North Gate in his occupation by lease per Annum	1	0	0
‡Mr Fisher late John Brook's for the North Mill Brooks's whole rent was £31 7s 6d but in Consideration of his making a Bolting Mill at his expence it was leased to him for 20 years at £20 per Annum	20	0	0
‡Thomas Taylor for a tenement in the North Gate at will per Annum now Robert Phipps	6	6	0
Robert Smith for the Week days Shambles . .	110	0	0
‡Mr Topham for the North Mill holme . . .	6	10	0

10b   In Sanvy Gate

	£	s	d
52‡Mr William Taylor late William Stevenson for 3 tenements by lease per Annum	4	0	0
‡Mrs Goodess late Mr James Annis for another tenement heretofore William Cook's in the occupation of Mr William Moor late John Rayson's land by lease per Annum		5	0
Mrs Burgess of Oadby late Mr Burgess of Grooby Lodge heretofore Mr Thomas Penford late Mr Gulson for a tenement near the North Gates in fee farm per Annum			10
56 The Reverend Mr William Smith heretofore William Biggs for a tenement near the North Gates in fee farm per Annum paid by Mr Pares for Mr Smith		1	0
The said Mrs Burgess late (blank) Burgess of Grooby Lodge heretofore Mr Gulson & late Mr Woodland late also George Webb for a tenement near the North Gates According to the Old Rental this should be 2s			2

10c   In Soar Lane or Walker Lane

	£	s	d
57 Mrs Clough at Mr Samuel Taylors late Joseph Smith for a piece of Ground sometime a Dunghill now built upon heretofore in the tenure of William Rudyard per Annum		2	0
54‡Benjamin Harris late William Cave for a house with the appurtenances late in the occupation of William Bingham per Annum	4	0	0

10d　　　　　　　　　Within the North Gates

The heirs or Executors of Robert Hickling for a messuage or tenement on the South side of All Saints Church yard late in the occupation of Benjamin Warburton & now of Benjamin Hitchcock in fee farm per Annum　　　　　　　　　　　1　10　0

63　William Frisby late Mary Howson for a messuage or tenement in High Street late Kimberlains land in fee farm per Annum　　　　　　　　　　　　　　6　0

John Brown Framesmith late Mrs Windsor for a tenement in the High Street late in the occupation of Joseph Waggott & now of (blank) Ireland Gardener per Annum　　　　　　　　　　　　　　　5　0

64　Mrs Horton late Thomas Carter for a house and Garden in High Cross Street at the Corner of Bakehouse Lane in the occupation of Mrs Davie　　　　　4　0

65　For a house and Garden in Bakehouse lane in the occupation of Robert Grew heretofore in the occupation of Widow Worrall late of William Grainger 4s 6d & for a house in the occupation of the said Robert Grew in 2 tenements 2s 10d Nicholas Richmonds Executors pays 2s 10d and Mr Fisher 4s 6d　　7　4

‡William Burleton Esquire LLD Recorder for a house lately built & barn lately purchased and several leys in the horse fair next to the house　　　　40　0　0

10e　　　　　　　　　In the South Gates

72　Thomas Moreton for a house in the occupation of William Saunderson per Annum paid by John Moore　1　0　0

Mr Fisher and Mr Bankart late the land of Thomas Wall and heretofore of Elizabeth Chamberlain for a messuage or tenement at the Corner of Hangman lane in fee farm per Annum Mr Fisher pays 9s Mr Bankart 7s　　　　　　　　　　　　16　0

Mr Martin late Mr Alderman Chapman and Mr Gamble for a Messuage or tenement called the Swan near the South Gates late in the occupation of Joseph Whatton & now of the said Mr Martin in fee farm per Annum　　　　　　　　　　　　　　13　4

10f   In Burgesses Meadow

75 Mr John Heyrick late John Gilford & heretofore of
Mr George Abney or William Palmer Esquire for a
piece of meadow Ground in Saint Mary's meadow   16   0
called the Shield late Moreton's land in the occupation of Mr Samuel Jordan in fee farm per Annum

76 The said Mr John Heyrick more for 2 acres of meadow late also Mr Moreton's land now also in the
occupation of the said Mr Jordan in fee farm per   13   4
Annum

10g   In the Swines Market, now called the High Street

78 Mr John Willows late of The heirs of Mr Thomas
Palmer Attorney at Law for a messuage or tenement
late Mr Berrington's land late in the occupation of   6   0
Michael Benshaw & now of the said Mr Willows in
fee farm per Annum

77 Mrs Wilmore late Mrs Throsby late Mr Smalley &
heretofore Widow Warburton for a tenement hereto-   18   0
fore called the King's head late Agnes Ortons land

10i   In the Saturday Market

81 Mr Belgrave of North Kilworth late Mr William
Cook for a messuage or tenement now divided into
two parts or tenements in the several occupations of   1   3   4
Miss Ledbrookes and Mr Smith in fee farm per
Annum

Mr Alderman Brown late Thomas Slater for a mes-
suage or tenement late in the occupation of John
Hackett in fee farm per Annum & now of Mr John   8
Clark Milliner

10j   In Loseby Lane

Mr Alderman Chambers for Lady Greasley late
William Orton Mercer for a Messuage or tenement in   10   0
the occupation of John Moore in fee farm per Annum

84 Mr John Iliff late Mr John Buckerfield Senior & Mr
John Needham late Southwell's for a house & Garden   1   6   0
in fee farm per Annum

85 The heirs or Executors of Samuel Cotes for a house late called the Star & Ball & now the Crown and Thistle late the land of (blank) Jackson in the occupation of Alexander Forrester in fee farm per Annum	12	0
Of them more for a piece of Ground payable yearly a Damask Rose at Midsummer	(blank)	
‡Jacob Bothomley for a house and back side being parcel of a tenement late in Valentine Dalloway's occupation since new built	4 0	0
Mr Richard Garle for a Messuage or tenement lately built in fee farm per Annum	10	0
88‡Robert Smith heretofore Mr Garle late Robert Lee for a house and back side late Richard Dawson since new built	7 0	0

10k   In Gallowtree Gate

95 Mrs Towers late Mr Garle & Mr Jee late also Mr Thomas Ayres for a messuage or tenement heretofore in the occupation of Loftus Page & Widow Batcheldor late of Thomas Towers and Jee & now of (blank) Batcheldor in fee farm per Annum	8	0
96 Mrs Towers late Mr Garle & Mr Jee late also the said Mr Ayre for a messuage or tenement known by the Sign of the White horse late in the occupation of Thomas Towers & Jee & now of Samuel Bunney in fee farm per Annum	1 0	0
96 Mr James Bishop late Mr John Palmer for one yard land in Saint Margarets Field sold to James Annis in the occupation of the said James Bishop	15	0

10l   In the Gallowtree Gate on the West side

99 The Reverend Mr Lambert late Randolph Butler for a messuage or tenement against the Roundhill sold to John Woodford in the occupation of Mrs Martha Wallin in fee farm per Annum	10	0
98 Mr Lewin & Mr Nutt for a messuage or tenement adjoining to the North side of the Angel heretofore Edward Ashwells land in fee farm per Annum Nutt pays 1s 4½d Lewin 2s 7½d	4	0

97 The heirs or Executors of Henry Palmer for a messuage or tenement in the occupation of John Spittlehouse & paid by him in fee farm per Annum   1 0 0

10m   In Belgrave Gate

100 Roe or Foster for a Garden at the nether end of Belgrave Gate late in Thomas Drake's occupation late
paid by Mr Pares for Joseph Cradock Esquire of
Gumley in fee farm per Annum   12 0

101 Mr John Yates late Mr Thomas Yates late also
Thomas Readley for a house in his occupation in fee
farm per Annum   13 4

103 Thomas Sarson & Joseph Bruin for a house in the
tenure of Jonathan Cramp in fee farm per Annum
Sarson pays 10s Bruin 10s   1 0 0

104 Mrs Sarah Ward Widow for a tenement heretofore
Simpson's adjoining to the Unicorn on the West side
thereof in fee farm per Annum   15 0

Mr Alderman Coleman for a tenement on the North
side of the said Street late the land of Richard Ward
in fee farm per Annum   18 0

107 The Churchwardens of St Margarets Parish for a
piece of Ground called the Cowpasture in fee farm
per Annum   8 0

10n   In the Country

108 Clement Winstanley Esquire for certain Lands leys
and pasture Grounds in the Lordship of Braunston
in the County of Leicester now or late in the occupation of William Burton in fee farm per Annum paid
by Thomas Bennett   12 8

109 Mrs Hurst of Hinkley late William Warner for a
Close and Croft and one yard land with the appurtenances in Hinkley in the County of Leicester in her
occupation in fee farm per Annum   15 0

111 Matthew Cartwright of Oadby late Mr Thomas
Worrall for a piece of Ground in Belgrave called
Knipton hill leys and one yard land heretofore sold to
one Culverwell being a Close of pasture heretofore
called Belgrave Bridge late Mr Overing's land   9 0
        M. Cartwright pays 5s 9d
        Mr Cartwright   3s 3d

110 Lord Wentworth for a messuage or tenement & one yard land with the appurtenances in Kirkby Mallory in fee farm per Annum — 6 8

114 William Pochin Esquire late Thomas Roddle late Mr Boothby of Tooley for a messuage or tenement in Rearsby in his occupation in fee farm per Annum — 17 0

George Chamberlain late William Knifton of Seagrave for a Close and Croft there the land of William Hubbert late paid by John Heggs in fee farm per Annum — 2 0

115 (blank) Barsby late Mr Benjamin Storer of Thrussington for one yard land there in fee farm per Annum — 6 8

113‡Robert Campion late William Whale of Frolesworth for the Foss Close and Meadow — 27 0 0

116 Mr William Thompson of Houghton on the Hill for a piece of Ground in his occupation or William Hubberts in fee farm per Annum — 1 8

116 Moses Cotten of Houghton late Buckley & Ward for another parcel of Land thereto belonging late in the occupation of Thomas Readley in fee farm per Annum — 5 0

117 John Whattoff Cleaver of Syston heretofore Widow Ryley & late of Robert James ⟨Q. Kilby⟩ of Barkby for certain Lands there late in the occupation of Thomas Readley in fee farm per Annum — 8 0

118 Mrs Watts for certain Lands leys and hades in the West field of Leicester in the occupation of Rogers Ruding Esquire in fee farm per Annum Mrs Watts pays 3s & Mr Buckley 1s — 4 0

120 Shuckburg Ashby Esquire late Sir Thomas Cave for a certain messuage or tenement in Hungarton late in the tenure or occupation of Elias Marshall in fee farm per Annum & now in the tenure of Thomas Walton & paid by him — 1 10 0

George Sheffield of Syston for the Mill there called Syston Mill & an house heretofore sold to Sir Thomas Cave Knight in fee farm per Annum — 3 6 8

11a Other rents of Lands or tenements parcel of the Town Objit Lands of St Margarets Guild and parcel of the Fee farm Rents

heretofore demised by Queen Elizabeth to Mr Howkins and Mr
Bates by Indentures expired

122 Of the heirs of Mr William Ive for Ground late belonging to several houses in South Gates heretofore
Mr Nurses William Hill's & Francis Coles ruin'd by
the late Wars heretofore sold to Mr Dannett Abney   2 13 4
in fee farm per Annum paid as follows to wit
    Mr Wildboar pays .   .   .   6 8
    Mr Townsend   .   .   .   6 8
    Mr Mackaig 2 0 0

123 Mr Armston late Mrs Morton late Mr John Ludlam
for a messuage or tenement with the appurtenances
commonly called or known by the name of the White   10 0
Lyon late in the occupation of John Wright & now of
Joseph Haseldine in fee farm per Annum

125 Mr Tuffley Baker, late Mr Thomas Hartshorn for a
messuage or tenement in the occupation of William   1 0 0
Campion & James Fox in fee farm per Annum

126 Joseph Johnson for the Ground lately belonging to 2
tenements late in the tenure of Paul Abney deceased
belonging to a messuage known by the name of the   1 6 8
Bull ruin'd by the late Wars since built upon & now
paid by him in fee farm per Annum

127 Mr Bankart late Mr Alderman Chapman for a messuage or tenement in South Gate Street formerly
called the Greyhound ruin'd in the late Wars since   1 0 0
built upon in his own occupation in fee farm per
Annum

11b   In the Swines Market now called High Street

Mr Sismey for a messuage or tenement in the Silver
Street over against the Pump late in the occupation   1 0 4
of Joseph Eburne and now of Robert Dowley in fee
farm per Annum

11c   In or near Belgrave Gate

130 Mr Cramant late the Executors of Mr John Newton
for a tenement at the Corner of Humberstone Gate
divided into several tenements heretofore in the   1 1 0
occupation of Samuel Hunt & others & now of Mr
Cramant in fee farm per Annum

132 For Land late Mr Pares late also Mr Tatham's late in the occupation of Richard Heafford & others in fee farm per Annum, Mr Chamberlain pays 6s John Wilmore 2s 6d & Sarah Noon 3s 6d   12 0

139 Mr John Lewin Merchant for a tenement heretofore called the Lamb late in the occupation of John Wellinger & for one other messuage or tenement & Close with the appurtenances heretofore sold to George Coates and late the land of George Blunt late in the occupation of Benjamin Cartwright & now of Mr Coleman   1 6 8

138 John Billings for a house late in the occupation of Widow Noon & now of Henry Sands in fee farm per Annum Billings pays 10s Sands 5s & Joshua Kirke 5s   1 0 0

Mr Andrews out of Rawletts Close the Gift of Mrs Twickden   2 0 0

Mr George Roe for Lands in Enderby Lordship being the Gift of Mr John Bent to Saint John's Hospital   45 2 0

Mr Simpson for the Tippetts in Saint Mary's Parish .   3 0 0

Rogers Ruding Esquire for the Duck holmes in St Mary's Parish Mr Wards Gift   3 0 0

Mr Alderman Ludlam out of the Leyroes in St Margarets Parish Mr Billows's Gift paid by Mr Andrews   12 0 0

*To the poor of the Old Hospital at 2 equal payments .   5 16 0

More by 2s weekly to 2 Alms women 12d each which makes the Hospitall weekly pay £2 15s 8d   5 4 0

More for a Gown 1 0 0*

     [*These payments account for Mr Billows's Gift above]

140 Mrs Bassett late of the heirs or Executors of Robert Burbage Carpenter for a house in Redcross Street late in William Headley's occupation in fee farm per Annum   12 0

143 Mr John Yates late Austin Heafford for a house call'd the Cock in fee farm per Annum near the Cannon   6 8

144 William Taylor for a Messuage or tenement in the Gallowtree Gate in the occupation of Widow Moseby in fee farm late paid by Theophilus Cramp paid by Widow Simpkin — 16 0

For a Messuage or tenement in the occupation of Ellen Denshire & for another part called the Cock in Fee farm per Annum sold to John Biggs, Mr John Yates pays 10s and John Biggs Junior 3s 4d — 13 4

146 Elias Bates for a tenement in Belgrave Gate heretofore sold to Robert Roberts in the occupation of Job Withers in fee farm per Annum late Mrs Harris Widow paid by Mr John Clark Baker — 5 0

‡(blank) Vesie late Francis Norman late Bartholomew Godfary for a Messuage or tenement in Senvy Gate in his occupation per Annum — 2 15 0

147‡(blank) Maslin late Samuel Turlington for a Messuage or tenement in the Senvy Gate late in the Occupation of John Meachamp in lease to Richard Scarborough per Annum — 2 5 0

148 Of him more for a tenement in his occupation given by the town during pleasure now Mr Bickerstaffs — 1 0

‡(blank) Tilby late Michael Shaw for a messuage in his occupation per Annum heretofore Joseph Gulson — 2 10 0

11e In Cank Street

149 Mr William Sutton for a Messuage or tenement late in the occupation of John Cart afterwards of Mr Robert Brewin and now of Mr Armston per Annum — 13 4

11f Saint Nicholas and Mary's Parishes

152 William Lewin for a messuage or tenement late John Orton's Land afterwards William Lewin's in fee farm per Annum Mr Pyne pays 7s William Spencer 6s — 13 0

153 Mr Palmer Carpenter late the Executors of Mrs Grace for a messuage or tenement in Applegate Street near the West bridge called the Mitre & Keys in the occupation of Widow Watts — 1 0 0

154 Mr Alderman Throsby for a Messuage or tenement in the High Street heretofore called the Flying horse late the land of Thomas Overing in fee farm per Annum — 1 10 0

12 Other Rents of Lands and tenements parcel of the town and Manor of Leicester heretofore amongst other things given and granted to the Mayor Bailiffs and Burgesses and their Successors in fee farm per Annum

155‡	Mr William Simpson late Mr Alderman Sismey for a piece of Ground in the Church Gate whereon a messuage or tenement lately stood in possession of George Staresmore	1 10 0	
156	Mr John Bracebridge late Mr Edward Powers late Mr Edward Palmer, Slater for a piece of Ground in Church Gate built upon heretofore the Land of William Tatham in fee farm per Annum	2	6
	Mr Alderman Cartwright late Mr Thomas Palmer Attorney at Law for a tenement with the appurtenances in the Church Gate late the Land of William Inge late also Smalleys land, paid as directed on folio 25 [see Heading 14e]	8	0
	(blank) Snapes Widow late John Snapes & heretofore William Erpe or Charles Johnson for a house or piece of Ground near St James Chapel Close called the Hermitage per Annum	1	0
160	Thomas Cobley for a piece of Ground in All Saints Parish call'd the Vineyard in his occupation in fee farm per Annum	4	0
163	John Coates heretofore Thomas Bradley & late of John Coates for part of a piece of Ground called Lyon Yard late the Land of Samuel Robinson deceased lying in Saint Martins Parish	2	6
163	Mr Alderman Gamble for another part of the said Lyon Yard & a messuage or tenement in the occupation of the said Mr Gamble in fee farm per Annum	2	6
164	Mr Oldershaw & Mr Haines for a house & barn called Sanby's land situate in the Saturday market in the occupation of Mr Oldershaw & Mr Cave. Mr Oldershaw pays 30s and Mr Haines 10s	2 0 0	
166	Mr John Clarke late Mr Joseph Newton for a piece of Ground once Daniel Carrs in North Gate Street extending from Senvy Gate to the Common Oven whereon a house was built by William Carr in fee farm per Annum in the occupation of John Clark	2	6

165 Mr Samuel Miles late William Cromwell for a piece of Ground near Saint Margarets Church yard where a house formerly stood called the Farm house in fee farm per Annum — 6

167 Mr Robert Hartshorn late Thomas Turvile for a piece of Ground near Frogmire Bridge now built upon in the occupation of (blank) Hartshorn late Moore per Annum — 1 0

168 Mr Johnson & Mr Kertins late Francis Richards Thomas Beaumont & John Grace or one of them for a piece of Ground in Deadman's Lane in fee farm per Annum Mr Johnson pays 10d & Mr Kertins 2d — 1 0

13 Other Rents of Corpus Christi Guild in Leicester heretofore Mr Archer's Collection and now parcel of the Lands and tenements which the said Mayor etc purchased of Queen Elizabeth to them and their Successors forever

172 Mr Taylor Baker, late Thomas Turvile Baker for a messuage or tenement with the appurtenances in the Swines market (now High Street) in fee farm per Annum — 13 4

173 William Watson late Joseph Johnson heretofore Mr Edward Brown for a Messuage or tenement in the Swines market (now High Street) heretofore known by the Sign of the Crown in fee farm per Annum — 1 1 8

174 John Wildbore of Loseby for a tenement in the Gallowtree Gate in the occupation of Mr William Marston & others in fee farm per Annum — 1 6 8

169‡ William Loseby late Joseph Fossett for a tenement (between the bridges) near the Frogmire bridge in the North Gates in his occupation — 15 0

177 Mr James Oldham late George Steirs for a messuage or tenement in Gallowtree Gate now divided into two tenements in the occupation of the said James Oldham in fee farm per Annum — 13 4

179 Joseph Simpson late Mr Nathaniel Simpson for a Messuage or tenement in the Saturday market (new built) in the occupation of Matthew Reid in fee farm per Annum — 1 0 0

P

180 (blank) Cumbrey late Mr George Birkhead for a Messuage or tenement & (blank) thereto adjoining in the occupation of Andrew Larratt Baker & paid by him for Cumbrey in fee farm per Annum — 1 0 0

182 Mr John Mason late Mr Alderman Ludlam for a Messuage or tenement in Town hall lane near Saint Martin's Church in the occupation of the said John Mason in fee farm per Annum — 6 8

186 Mr Thomas Poughfer for a messuage or tenement in Parchment lane (now Swines market) in his own occupation in fee farm per Annum — 16 0

185 Mr Foster of Loughborough (paid by Mr John Palmer for him) late Robert Clark or Robert Hutchins of Loughborough aforesaid for certain Lands and pasture Grounds in Loughborough aforesaid called Sadlers Land now or late in the occupation of John Bass of Loughborough in fee farm per Annum paid by the Trustees of Barrow Hospital — 10 0

Mr Joseph Neal late John Brown for a Chamber over the West Gates — 19 0

189 Mr Barwell 6d Mr Cobley 3s Mr Lambert 2s Mr Oldham 4s & Mr Walker 2s 6d late Bernard Smalley for a Shop formerly near the East Gates now converted into several tenements heretofore sold to Mr Davis late the Land of (blank) Wigley in fee farm — 12 0

190 Mr Hextall for a messuage or tenement on the East side of East Gates in his own occupation late Mr Hoods — 12 0

191 Mr Thomas Astle late Mr John Palmer for a piece of Ground heretofore a Garden in the Town hall lane over against the Town hall now built upon heretofore Fletchers land late in the occupation of Abraham Sapcote & now of Mr Chamberlain — 1 0

192 John Slater late Mr Goodall for a tenement in Parchment lane now called Swines market heretofore a Stable sometime Mr Heyrick's land in fee farm per Annum — 6 8

192 (blank) Cook of Barkby late Robert James of Houghton for a Croft & half yard land in Barkby late Thomas Ilston's in fee farm per Annum — 6 8

194 William Pochin Esquire of Barkby, for three quarters of a yard land there late the land of Thomas Seal in fee farm per Annum	6	0
193 Samuel Brookes late Mrs Philippa Palmer for a Messuage or tenement in the Swines Market now High Street late in the occupation of Joseph Eburne & now of the said Samuel Brookes in fee farm per Annum	6	0
196 Mr Edward Davie late Joseph Bunney Esquire for a piece of Ground lying on the nether side of Saint James's Chapel Close where a house formerly stood late the land of William Bowman late in the occupation of Henry Hitchcock in fee farm per Annum	4	0
198 For a house & Garden in St Martins Church yard late in the occupation of Mrs Newton & now empty paid by Lady Greasley in fee farm per Annum	13	4
195 Mr Perkins of Grantham for certain Lands & leys in the Town field of Gunnerby in the County of Lincoln in fee farm per Annum	6	8
201 Mr Samuel Gamble for a Close near the Cowdrift late Mr Heyricks land in fee farm per Annum	10	0
203 Mr Oliver for a Shop & other buildings on the East side of the Roundhill known by the name of the Roundhill in fee farm per Annum	1 0	0
The said Mr Oliver more being an acknowledgement for erecting 4 Columns on the Corporation Ground belonging to the aforesaid building	1	0
Thomas Marshall for a house & backside in Shambles lane heretofore Mr Harrisons in fee farm per Annum	1	0

14a Other Rents of the possession of the late Guild in Leicester parcel of the Town Obiit Lands heretofore collected by Mr Tatham

207 Mr Goode late Mr Wilcox and heretofore John Coates for a messuage or tenement in Applegate Street late Henry Cote's land in fee farm per Annum	1 0	0
208 Mr Thomas Carr for a messuage or tenement in the said Street late in the occupation of John Paling late paid by Thomas Hurst Baker & now by Mr Alexander Hurst of Leicester Forest in fee farm per Annum	9	0
209 Mary Hubbard late Mr Alderman Higginson for a house in the said Street late Slater & now Mary Hubbards in fee farm per Annum	6	8

210 John Coates late Ralph Ward for a house in the said
Street now in the occupation of (blank) late John
Coates & now of (blank) Cumberland in fee farm per
Annum   10   0

‡Mrs Higginson Junior late Mr Alderman Higginson
for the Week days Shambles by lease per Annum   2   0   0

215 Widow Bassett late Mr Denshire & John Cooper
Carpenter for a messuage or tenement in Applegate
Street in the occupation of (blank) in fee farm per
Annum   8   0

212 Mrs Lee for a house in Applegate Street late David
Winfields in the occupation of Mr Chamberlain in
fee farm per Annum   7   0

114 For a messuage or tenement and Garden in Applegate Street late in the occupation of Joseph Savidge
at the Swan in fee farm per Annum heretofore Widow
Blackwells & late John Bounds paid as follows vizt.   14   0
Widow Burley pays 10s Roddle in Leicester Forest 4s

215 Mr Goode late the heirs or Executors of Mr Henry
Smith deceased for a piece of Ground in possession of
Edward Goodess called the Mayors Old hall in   3   4
Shambles lane near St Nicholas's Church

14b   In the South Gates

217‡Mrs Higginson late Mr Alderman Higginson & heretofore Mr Richard Barwell for a house and Garden   5 10   0
near the South Gates

219 Mr Benjamin Hitchcock heretofore Mr Robert Hartshorn or his father & late of Widow Gray or her
Daughter for a piece of Ground situate in the South
Gate Street belonging to the house ruin'd in the late   10   0
Wars sold to the said Mr Hartshorn late in the occupation of Conyers White & now of (blank) in fee farm
per Annum

220 For the Ground lately belonging to 2 tenements
situate in the same Street in the occupation of John
Palmer late Mr Thomas Hartshorn's in fee farm per   10   0
Annum Mr Tuffley pays 4s & Mr Bankart 6s

221 Mr John Wood for the Ground lately belonging to 2
tenements lately in the occupation of Thomas
Throsby & himself ruin'd in the late Wars since built   1   5   0
upon in fee farm per Annum

John Coates for a house in South Gate Street heretofore Mr Southworth's land late in the occupation of
Widow Ireland in fee farm per Annum ⎬ 10 0

14c   In Gallowtree Gate

222 Mr Cramant late David Hennell for a Messuage or
tenement on the Cornwall formerly known by the
Sign of the Queens head now new built in the occupation of Mrs Burgess in fee farm per Annum ⎬ 1 6 8

223 Mr John Lee for a messuage or tenement on the
Cornwall heretofore known by the Sign of the Cinque
foil late in the occupation of George Broome since
new built late in the occupation of the Reverend Mr
Smith & now of Mr Silvester ⎬ 2 0 0

224 John Clark late Mr Tunney for a Messuage or tenement heretofore known by the name of the Buck's
head & late in the occupation of James Mason in fee
farm per Annum ⎬ 5 0

14d   In the Swines Market

226 John Richards late John Major Esquire for a certain
Garden heretofore sold to Michael Walton of Bushby
in fee farm per annum ⎬ 2 0

14e   In the Belgrave Gate

227 Mr Thomas Astle for a messuage or tenement in his
own occupation in fee farm per Annum ⎬ 16 0

229 Mr Richard Barry for a messuage or tenement known
by the Sign of the Star in the occupation of Joseph
Grocock in fee farm per Annum ⎬ 13 4

230 Dr Burrell for a messuage or tenement late the Land
of Robert Gamble in the occupation of Mr Coleman
in fee farm per Annum paid by Mr John Moore for
Mr J. Lewin ⎬ 18 0

225 Mr Alderman Oliver for a Shop & Chamber situate
on the Round hill in fee farm per Annum ⎬ 1 0 0

234 John Wright late Richard Garratt for a Messuage or
tenement late called the Cannon now the Crown &
Cushion late in the occupation of Arthur Rickards &
now of the said John Wright in fee farm per Annum ⎬ 12 0

239 Mr John Yates and others for 2 tenements late in the occupation of George Chamberlain & Widow Abney in fee farm per Annum, Mr John Yates pays £1 & Mr Cook 2s   1 2 0

240 Mrs Jordaine for a house and Garden in the Belgrave Gate in the occupation of John White in fee farm per Annum   6 0

242 Mr Edward Davie for a house in the same Street in the occupation of Thomas Marshall in fee farm per Annum   8 0

241 Mr John Langdon late Anthony Ward for an orchard or Garden in the same Street heretofore sold to George Blintingdon now in the occupation of John Langdon in fee farm per Annum   6 0

245 The Reverend Mr Lee for an Orchard or piece of Ground whereon stood a house called St John's late in Samuel Jarvis's occupation per Annum now of Mr Lambert   2 0 2

237 For part of Margaret Fletchers land in the Belgrave Gate now or late in the occupation of Nathaniel Hennard in fee farm per Annum paid by Mr John Yates   5 0

247 The heirs of Mr Thomas Palmer for a house and Garden in the Church Gate late Mr Inge's heretofore in the occupation of John Russell & now of Mr Alderman Cartwright in fee farm per Annum paid as directed by next Item   5 0

246 Of them more for an orchard in Church Gate once Mr Inge's land late Mr Smalley's in fee farm per Annum, now Mr Alderman Cartwright   2 0

N.B. The last two rents and the rent of 8s folio 17 [see Heading 12] are paid thus.

Mr Alderman Cartwright pays	.	.			8	9
Widow Foulds	.	.	.	.	1	3
Samuel Brookes	.	.	.	.	1	3
William Goodfellow	.	.	.	.	1	3
William Cooke	.	.	.	.	1	3
Thomas Alsop	.	.	.	.		$7\frac{1}{2}$
Richard Sturgis	.	.	.	.		$7\frac{1}{2}$

15 0

14f   In Sanvy Gate

248 Mr William Cook Maltster for a messuage or tenement late William Chamberlain's land in his occupation in fee farm per Annum   1   0   0

249 Widow White for a house and Garden in the occupation of Widow Harris in fee farm per Annum   8   0

250‡Mr Hamlet Clarke & Mr Fisher heretofore Mr
Smalley for a piece of Ground in Senvy Gate belonging to the Corporation whereon he built a house in   1 15   0
Consideration whereof he had a lease for 41 years by
lease per Annum

233 Mr Matthew Johnson late Mr Barwell Maltster late
David Hennell and William Wells heretofore John
Farren for a piece of Ground called Saller Close, in   5   0
fee farm per Annum

252‡Late of Edward Newberry now of Francis Levis for
2 more tenements new erected in the Senvy Gate at
Will with a Spong of Ground belonging to the house   6   0   0
per Annum

14g   Near St Margarets Church

256 Mr Cooper Apothecary for a piece of Ground called
Margarets Bed lying in the Close late the Land of   6
James Biggs in fee farm per Annum

14h   Other Rents part of Wilders Rents

258 Richard Walker Esquire for a Close near the Cowdrift in his own occupation in fee farm per Annum   13   4

14i   Other part of Wilders 2nd Lease

259 John Baxter Baker late the heirs or Executors of Mr
Stockden of Great Glen for a house in Soar Lane
near Redcross Street in the occupation of John Baxter   6   0
Baker

260 Lord Scarsdale for a house & piece of Ground in the
said Soar Lane late Briton's land now in the occupation of Joseph Wheatley late of Thomas Jones in fee   2   0
farm per Annum & paid by the said Joseph Wheatley

262 Mr Edward Davie late John Worth the Elder for a
house and Garden in Belgrave Gate late Hegg's land   8   0
in the occupation of Mr Dalby in fee farm per Annum

263 Mr Thomas Pares for a Close in Archdeacon lane heretofore sold to John Mobbs in fee farm per Annum — 6 8

266 William Kirk of Humberstone for a house and land there in his occupation in fee farm per Annum paid by Dennis Kirke — 5 0

267 Thomas Hastwell for a messuage or tenement in Sanvy Gate heretofore sold to him and Jane Ward per Annum — 1 6 8

268 The Poor of the Hospital of the Holy Trinity in the Newark of Leicester for a Garden and piece of Ground near the Butt Close now or late in the tenure of (blank) in fee farm per Annum — 2 0

269 Mr John Harrison late James & Thomas Cartwright for a house and backside near St Margarets Church in the occupation of Mr Brown in fee farm per Annum — 8 0

272 Mr John Yates late Robert Cook for a house & Garden in Belgrave Gate late the Land of Edmund Sutton late in the occupation of John Coe & now of (blank) in fee farm per Annum — 3 4

273 Mr Thomas Barwell for a tenement with the appurtenances in Senvy Gate heretofore in the occupation of Henry Gunnell and now of Nathaniel Hunt in fee farm per Annum — 10 0

274 John Davie late William Wells for a messuage or tenement in Sanvy Gate heretofore Thomas Chettle's Land now or late in the occupation of Richard Hercourt in fee farm per Annum lately paid by John Armston — 6 8

276 Sir Charles Halford late the heirs of Mr Thomas Palmer Attorney deceased for a Close near Humberstone Gate formerly sold to John Roe in fee farm per Annum — 12 0

15 A Rentall of the Lands & possessions belonging to the College of the Blessed Virgin Mary over against the Castle of Leicester heretofore demised by Queen Elizabeth to Edmund Holt and by her Majesty granted to the Mayor etc. and their Successors (amongst other things) in fee farm

277 William Hill Esquire late Mr Hill Attorney at Law for a messuage or tenement in the Swines market (now High street) in fee farm per Annum — 6 8

280 Mr Hudson late Hanell Langton for part of a messuage or tenement near the West bridge in the occupation of the said Mr Hudson in fee farm per Annum   2 0

282 Mr Samuel Gamble late Ralph Wells for a Close near Ayleston highway late the land of Robert Heyrick in fee farm per Annum   5 0

Mrs Sharpe late Widow Wallin for a Garden or piece of Ground on the backside of a messuage or tenement near the South Gates heretofore the land of Hugh Watts in fee farm per Annum   1 0

284 Mr Thomas Bruce late Richard Bacon for a messuage or tenement in Soar Lane near Redcross Street late the Land of John Coulson in fee farm per Annum and now in the occupation of the said Thomas Bruce   10 0

285 For a tenement in Soar lane near Redcross Street sold to John Underwood and late Thomas Dewicks and Mrs Ward's and now paid as follows vizt. Mrs Pochin pays 1s 3d Mr Lambert 1s 3d Ward 2s 6d   5 0

286 Mrs Bassett heretofore Edmund Smith or William Dawson & late Mr Forman of Kirby for a house and Garden in the Soar lane near Redcross Street heretofore Robert Stevenson's in fee farm per Annum   12 0

290 Mr William Cooper Apothecary for a messuage or tenement in Redcross Street & Garden in Chaff Lane adjoining to the said house in the occupation of John Wikes called the Old Mitre in fee farm per Annum   1 0 0

293 For a Messuage or tenement (late Robert Allen's) in Soar Lane near Redcross Street in fee farm per Annum paid as follows vizt. Mr Ludlam pays 11s 7d Thomas White 15s 1d   1 6 8

295 Onesiphorus Bonner late Robert Dingmore for a tenement or Garden in Soar Lane near Redcross Street heretofore sold to John Bonner in fee farm per Annum   12 0

296 At will of (blank) Tompson of Glenfield late Mr Hill or Robert Fossett for a Garden in Soar Lane in the occupation of Thomas Trentham in fee farm per Annum   8

298 Widow Hall late Thomas Ward for a Piece of Ground belonging to a messuage or tenement in the South Gates ruin'd in the late wars and for a Croft in fee farm per Annum — 16 0

300 Mr Dabbs late Mr Henry Mason & heretofore Dr Cheshire for a piece of Ground adjoining to the Freer Lane heretofore in the occupation of Mr William Callis late in the occupation of Mr Burbage & now of the said Mr Dabbs — 4

‡John Nutt for the herbage of St Mary's Church yard per Annum — 3 5 0

303 Nathan Wright Esquire late William Wright Esquire heretofore Mr John Farmer for a Close called Sand Pit Close near Cowdrift lane per Annum paid by Mr Coleman — 1 0 0

306 The Governors of the Leicester Infirmary late Richard Walker Esquire for St James Chapel Close at the nether end of the South Gates heretofore sold to Mr Simpson & late John Sharman's land in fee farm per Annum — 1 6 8

308‡Mr Denshire for a house or Garden or backside in the said Parish of Saint Nicholas & near to the Talbot by lease per Annum in the occupation of John Smith — 2 0 0

Joseph Cradock Esquire heretofore Mr Nathaniel Heyricks & now Mr Joseph Cradock's for the tythes and tenths of all the Grounds sometime parcel of Dannetts Hall by lease per Annum — 3 0 0

309 Mr Denshire for a house and Garden in the said Parish near the Applegate Street late the Land of Murfin in fee farm per Annum — 1 0 0

312 Rogers Ruding Esquire for all the Vicarial tythes tenths herbage & other Duties payable out of the Ground & parcel of the Land belonging to West Coates by lease per Annum — 11 16 6

310 Mr Watts late Mr Muxloe of Desford for all the tythes tenths herbage & other Duties belonging to the same payable out of the Close called or known by the name of the South field & being parcel of the Ground belonging to the Estate or Farm called Dannetts hall & Welch hall by lease per Annum — 1 10 0

No.	Description	£	s	d
310	The tythe & part of the Vicarial tenths herbage & other Duties belonging to Dannetts hall being that Part Mr Watts lately bought. Mr Hunt Pays 8s Mr Wightman £1 18s od & Mr Cradock £1 14s od	4	0	0
310	Rogers Ruding Esquire for part of Mr Fawne's being Part of Dannetts Hall, Mary Mills etc.	2	0	0
	The said Rogers Ruding Esquire for the other Part of Dannetts Hall	2	0	0
	N.B. Mr Lewin now receives the tythes in kind.			
313	Mrs Ashby late Mr Smalley for a Garden in Senvy Gate in the occupation of William Sands in fee farm per Annum		1	0
317	Jonathan Chettle for a Piece of Ground or Garden sometime a Well yard in High Street (heretofore the Land of Mr Thomas Pares) in his occupation in fee farm per Annum		1	4
319	Mr Alderman Belton late Edward Townsend for an Orchard and Garden in Silver Street at Will per Annum		2	0
321	Mr Samuel Gamble for a third part of a Close near Cowdrift in fee farm per Annum		4	0
322	The Poor of the Hospital of the Holy Trinity in the Newark of Leicester part of dovecote Close beyond the West bridge in the occupation of (blank) in fee farm per Annum		1	6
323	Richard Hassold for a Piece of meadow Ground in Glenfield late in the occupation of John Carr in fee farm per Annum			6
318	John Bruin late Mr Tyrringham Palmer for a Close near Saint Margarets Cow Pasture heretofore Bennetts land in the occupation of Mr Cradock in fee farm per Annum		3	4
324	Joseph Cradock Esquire late Mr Watts for certain Lands and leys in the West Field of Leicester heretofore the Land of Thomas Dannett Esquire in fee farm late Mr Watts		2	6
327	The Poor of the Hospital of the Holy Trinity for a piece of meadow Ground in Burgesses meadow called the Lady acre in fee farm per Annum		3	4

325 Rogers Ruding Esquire for a Close in Braunston Gate late Mr Hunts land in fee farm — 5 0

328 Mr John Baxter Baker late Robert Hobson for a house and Close in Redcross Street late in the occupation of John Holmes now Widow Flower in fee farm per Annum — 1 10 0

329 Mr Simmonds Vicar of St Mary's Church for the Easter & other Duties in the said Parish — 3 4

330‡ Joseph Bruce for a certain tenement and Garden in Soar Lane near Redcross Street heretofore in the occupation of George King and now of the said Joseph Bruce by lease per Annum — 2 0 0

332 Sir Charles Halford Baronet late Mr Thomas Palmer for a Garden in Swines market now High Street lately built upon heretofore in the occupation of Thomas Ludlam Locksmith & now of (blank) — 1 2

326 The said Sir Charles Halford for a house in the same Street heretofore sold to Christopher Needham in the occupation of William Tompson in fee farm per Annum — 2 6

331 Anthony Abell or William Lyon for a Garden in Hot Gate Street otherwise Thornton Lane late the land of Mr Thomas Pares Butcher in fee farm per Annum paid as follows vizt. — 5 0
         Hubbard 1 8
         Mr Edward Powers . . . 1 8
         William Ward at the Admiral . . 1 8

333 Mr Alderman Mason for a Messuage or tenement heretofore Mr Walker's in the Newark of Leicester late in the occupation of (blank) Bailey in fee farm per Annum — 1 6 8

334 Of him more for a house in the Newark late Dr Walkers in William Hall's occupation in fee farm per Annum — 13 4

336 Joseph Cradock Esquire of Leicester late William Inge Gentleman of Knighton for 2 parts of Chamberlains land at Knighton in fee farm per Annum — 12 4

339 Mr John Tebbutt late James Carr of Bowden magna for Land there now or late in the occupation of John Corrall in fee farm, it is 3 pieces of meadow called Leicester Land — 1 0

340 Mr Colton of Kettleby late Mr John Herrick of Beaumont leys for lands in Sileby per Annum — 6

341 Mr Gulson late Mr Stedman of Glenfield for lands there in fee farm per Annum — 3

17 Other Rents of the Town and Manor of Leicester parcel of the Lands and possessions of the Dutchy of Lancaster part thereof being in the County of Leicester

343 Mr Poynton & John Slater 8s 4d each late William Heggs for a messuage or tenement in High Street heretofore the land of John Brooksby late Mr Hood in fee farm per Annum — 16 8

344 Mr Cooper Hosier late Elizabeth Dyson late Mr Robert Palmer for the Horse Malt Mill in the Swines Market (now High Street) sold to Bartholomew Parnell in fee farm per Annum — 1 13 4

65‡Henry Coulson for the Town Goal by order of Common hall — 3 0 0

19   Other Rents received of new

347 Mr Alderman Ogden late Mr Franke for a Piece of Ground being part of the Town wall situate near the Fryer lane late Maneby's land in fee farm per Annum — 2 6

349 William Hudson late Hanell Langton for 2 Pieces of Land taken out of the common Dunghill in the Lane near the West bridge in fee farm per Annum — 10

350 Mr Thomas Poughfer late Abstinence Poughfer for 2 tenements in Parchment lane now called Swines market late the land of Mr John Heyrick in fee farm per Annum — 3 4

20   Other rents for certain Lands purchased by the Corporation and other rents

352‡Mr Alderman Belton for a Close of Pasture Ground late 2 Closes late Mr Freake's land near Leicester by lease per Annum — 26 0 0

353‡Mr Alderman Brown for one Close called Freake's Ground near Leicester by lease per Annum — 40 0 0

357‡Austin Heafford for a Cottage or tenement situate near the Horse fair in his occupation by lease per Annum ⎱ 1 5 0

357‡(blank) Tomlin late Mary Garratt Widow for another Cottage or tenement to the said Cottage or tenement adjoining or belonging by lease per Annum paid by Mr Stephen's ⎱ 1 5 0

David Deakins or William Wells for the Water Laggs heretofore paid by Michael Cook since by Thomas Walton & now by Thomas Gardener ⎱ 6 8

Thomas Johnson late Benjamin Boyer for part of the house called the White Swan in the Saturday market per Annum ⎱ 2 0 0

21   Rents given to the School and other charitable uses

His Majesty's General Receiver given by Queen Elizabeth out of the honor of Leicester for the better maintaining the Usher of the Grammer School of Leicester ⎱ 10 0 0

364 One Annuity or rent charge payable yearly out of the Manor of Theddingworth by Sir Richard Newdigate being the Gift of Sir Ralph Rawlett for maintaining the Under Usher of the said School now paid by Mr George Bosworth of Brampton near Harborough for Mr Shipton near Newport Pagnell late paid by his honor Spencer ⎱ 3 6 8

365‡Mr John Hammond of Whitwick late Mr John Morris for one Annuity payable yearly out of a Close in the Abbey Gate called the Abbey Gate Close for the better maintaining the Head Usher in the occupation of William Stubbs per Annum ⎱ 3 6 8

366 Mr Hudson for one annuity payable yearly out of a Piece of Ground called the Water Laggs to the Under Usher of the said School being the Gift of Thomas Clark per Annum ⎱ 1 0 0

Mr Edward Sutton late Thomas Hunt of Whetstone for certain Lands in the Lordship of Willoughby Waterless being the Gift of Mr John Norris deceased for charitable uses ⎱ 16 0 0

‡John Farren late Mr Thomas Ayre now Mr Thomas Mann for an orchard or Garden (in All Saints Parish) purchased with £50 given by the first Countess of Devonshire for & towards the relief of the poor of this Borough & the Parish of St Leonard for the payment of £3 per Annum — 6 0 0

‡Mr Alderman Fisher & Mr Joseph Johnson late David Pratt for a messuage Close & one yard land at Whetstone bought of John Baker Gentleman by the Corporation with the money bequeathed by Christopher Tamworth Esquire for celebrating divine Service in lease per Annum — 16 0 0

John Brewin for 40 acres of Land in the Forrest of Leicester given by King Charles the first of ever blessed memory to the use of the poor of this Borough — 35 0 0

‡Mr Samuel Jordan late Joseph Horton for part of Burgesses meadow per Annum — 4 10 0

Mr Thomas Smart late Mr Thomas Ayre Junior for a Close & Barn thereto belonging in or near Hangman Lane which the Corporation purchased of Mr Speechley in lease per Annum — 37 0 0

Mr Pares late Shuckburg Ashby Esquire heretofore John Poultney Esquire payable yearly out of the Manor of Coates Deveil and given by him to Charitable uses — 10 0 0

Epiphanius Goodrich late George Plummer of Evington for lands in Bushby being the Gift of Mr Nidd to the Poor of Mountsorrell per Annum — 51 0 0

13 Sir Philip Vasasor of Wisbeach late Anthony Acham Gentleman & also late Edward Southwell Esquire being the said Mr Acham's Gift to the Poor of the Corporation out of the Manor of Asfordby alias Asterby in the County of Lincoln per Annum — 9 0 0

For certain Grounds in the South Gates belonging to 2 tenements heretofore in the occupation of Messenger & Owen being the Gift of Mrs Margaret Hobby paid as follows vizt. — 1 1 8

Bassett pays	. . .	6 0
Thomas Gregory	. .	6 0
Hurst	. . .	2 6
Tilly	. . .	7 2

Mr Pares for a rent Charge issuing out of the house in his occupation heretofore called or known by the Sign of the Parrott being the Gift of Mr Hugh Botham by ½ yearly payments vizt. the Friday before Christmas & the Friday before Easter   2 0 0

(blank) Wighthead late the Executors of Mr Clayton of Allexton for several Closes & Grounds there being the Gift of Mr Haines for charitable uses late in the occupation of Andrew Catwell per Annum   24 0 0

23 [No separate heading inserted]

Mr Lee for the Ground lately taken from the Sheep pens   5 0

Mr Oliver (late John Bass Esquire) for the like .   .   1 0 0

Mr Smalley for the like paid by Mr Eames   .   .   10 0

Mr Hennell for the like paid by Mr Cramant .   .   1 0 0

Thomas Raworth for a piece of Ground adjoining to the West bridge per Annum   2 6

29 Chief rents belonging to St John's & St Leonards to be paid at Michaelmas for the use of the Mayor Bailiffs & Burgesses of Leicester Borough

1 The Wardens of the New Hospitall called Wigston's Hospital   1 4½

3 Mr Gregory late Mr William Stephens late also Mr Boons Executors for one Messuage or tenement in the Gallowtree Gate lately known by this Sign of the Black Lyon lately purchased by Mr Tyrringham Palmer & now in Mr Gregory's Occupation   6

4 The Right Honorable the Earl of Stamford for Thurmaston Mills   6 8

5 George Wright Esquire heretofore Sir William Rawlinsons late Sir Henry Beaumont Baronet for certain Lands in Oadby   5 11½

6 For the Vicarage house at Oadby late paid by Mr Cooper for Mr Liptrott   1 0½

(blank) Woodward of Oadby late Mr Tebbs of Oadby for certain Lands there called Marshalls land   6

9 Mr William Cook Maltster late William Hammond for a house in Senvy Gate late Webster's land   9

30   Chief rents belonging to Corpus Christi Guild

10 Mr Alderman Belton late Mr Edward Townsends Executors for a tenement in Silver street in his Occupation per Annum	4	0
11 Mr Capp for a house in Silverstreet in his own Occupation late Edward Daniell	3	0
12 Mr Nutt (late Mr Orme) for a Messuage or tenement in the Gallowtree Gate in his Occupation per Annum	2	2
13 Mr Cradock late Freeman's for a Messuage or tenement in the Occupation of Miss Ascough Milliner per Annum	2	0
14 Mr Belgrave of North Kilworth for a Messuage or tenement in Saturday Market in Miss Ledbrooke's Occupation per Annum	2	0
8 Simeon Iliff of Oadby for certain Lands late Bliss's land now Woodwards		10
18 John Freeman late Deakin for a piece of Ground in Parchment lane now called Swines Market lately the land of Tobias Heyrick late in the Occupation of John Farren & now of the said (blank) Freeman		3
19 The Right Honorable the Earl of Stamford for a Messuage or tenement in Red Cross street in the Occupation of William Goodrich per Annum	1	0
20 Mrs Treen late John Simons Esquire for a certain house in the said street late the land of Briton & Suffolk per Annum		8
22 Mr Goode Hosier for a Messuage or tenement near St Nicholas's Church late Mr Briton's land late in the Occupation of John Lewin and now of the said Mr Goode	1	0
24 Mr Alderman Brown for a Garden in Deadman's Lane	5	0
25 Mr Thomas Chapman late Jonathan Jee for a Messuage or tenement in the High street now called High Cross street in his own Occupation late Mr Moreton's land	3	0
23 Johnson 10d & Mr Thomas Kestin 2d for a Cottage in Deadman's lane late Mr Tyrringham's Palmer's land per Annum	1	0

Q

Mr William Watts for a house in Redcross street late in the Occupation of John Dean & now of (blank) per Annum	4	
28 Mr John Shipley late Widow Groce for a Garden in Deadman's lane		6
29 Widow Davie for a tenement in the Highstreet now called Highcross street late Mr Woodland late in the Occupation of William Clark & now of John Pratt per Annum	1	0
30 Mr William Oldham late Alderman Westley for a Messuage or tenement in the Swines Market now High Street per Annum	14	0
16 Edward Powers late William Timpson for a tenement in the Swines Market now High Street in the Occupation of the said Edward Powers late the land of George Heggs per Annum	9	6
17 Mr Willows late Mr Edward Palmer for a tenement in the said Street in the Occupation of the said Mr Willows		6
31 William Hill Esquire & Mr Wood for a tenement now divided into two tenements in the High street (heretofore call'd Swines market) in the several Occupations of the said (blank) Wood & Joseph Watson	3	0
33 John Weldon for a tenement in High street in the Occupation of Crowdall & Marshall	3	6
34 The poor of the Old Hospital for a barn called Clarks barn per Annum		6
37 Mr Alderman Simpson for a tenement in Cank Street late in his Occupation late Billington's land per Annum	1	0
39 Mr Joseph Johnson for a certain house in Belgrave Gate late the land of Robert Foster in the Occupation of John Weston Hosier per Annum	3	0
38 Mr Clement Stretton Junior for a house in Cank street late Mr Pilkington's late in Alderman Bate's Occupation		8½
41 Mr William Herrick late Sir John Whatton Knight for a Close called Shire hall Close in the Parish of All Saints late in the Occupation of John Lewitt Gardener & now of George Webb per Annum		6

40 Mr Edward Powers late Thomas Huffin for a Messuage in Loseby lane in the Occupation of Mrs Staws — 10½

44 Mr Thomas Barwell late George Davie for a Messuage or tenement in Humberston Gate late in John Davy's Occupation & now of the said Mr Thomas Barwell Baker per Annum — 3 0

43 The Reverend Mr Lambert for a Messuage or tenement in the Gallowtree Gate known by the Sign of the Angel in the Occupation of Robert Raven — 2 0

53 Mr William Simpson late Mr Richard Goodhall for a Messuage or tenement near the East Gates in his Occupation per Annum — 1 0

46 Rogers Ruding Esquire for a Messuage or tenement at the Corner of Fryer lane lately known by the Sign of the George in the Occupation of Mr John Pocklington per Annum — 4 0

47 Mrs Bates Widow for a Messuage or tenement in the Swines Market now Highstreet in her Occupation per Annum — 2 0

49 Miss Lettice (late Samuel Gamble Esquire) for a Messuage or tenement in the said street in her own Occupation late Mr Henshaws land — 4 0

51 Mr Alderman Oliver late Mr Gilbert for a Messuage or tenement in the Gallowtree Gate in the Occupation of Theophilus Cramp — 7 6

48 For a tenement in Highstreet abovementioned late William Chamberlains land late in Mr Francis Lewin's Occupation & now of Mark Valentine & Robert Smith & paid by them — 2 0

31   Chief rents belonging to Saint Margarets Guild

53 Mr William Herrick late Mr Bent for a Garden in Ironmonger lane near the Saracens head late Mr Pocklington's land per Annum — 1 0

54 Edward Harris for a Messuage or tenement in the High street now High Cross street at the Corner of Bakehouse lane in his Occupation — 1 4

56 Mr William Garle for a piece of Ground in Soar lane called the Maltyard in the Occupation of Thomas Jones per Annum now Pitts Ward — 6 0

58 Mr Alderman Oliver for Mr Oxley late Mr Alderman Hood's Executors for a Messuage or tenement in
the Belgrave Gate called the Unicorn late in the   4½
Occupation of John Litherland & now of Mr Alderman Mason

59 Mr Lewin for a house in Belgrave Gate late Maneby's
land in the Occupation of Mr Coleman per Annum   9

62 Thomas Sarson & Joseph Bruin for a tenement in the
same street late Sutton's land late paid by Widow   6
Ashwell

61 Mr William Herrick late Robert Bonner or Thomas
Worth for a tenement in Humberstone Gate called
the Fox and Goose now being the Corner house late   6
the land of Robert Sutton late in Thomas Wards
Occupation & now in John Hall's per Annum

64 Mr T. Pares for a barn in the Churchgate late William
Inge Esquire paid by Bass in the Church gate   I 3½

67 Mrs Andrews late Mr John Ludlam for a Close near
the Spittlehouse called the Bailiffs Close per Annum   I o

68 Mr Joseph Johnson for a Messuage or tenement near
the West bridge in his Occupation per Annum   4 o

66 The Wardens of Wigston's Hospital for a piece of
Ground called the Normandy per Annum paid by   6
Mr Pares

70 John Harrison late John Brookes or Mr Thomas
Chapman for a house in Church Gate late Maneby's
land in the Occupation of John Weston late Jeffry   9
William Spence

72 George Rayson Pratt for a Messuage or tenement in
All Saints parish late in the Occupation of John Pratt I 1½
now (blank) Fancote

74 Mr Barry late Mr Lewin & John Cartwright for a
Messuage or tenement in the Belgrave Gate called
the Star late in the Occupation of John Wellinger   6
late paid by Mrs Farmer Widow

73 Mr Lewin late the Executors of Mr John Farner
Attorney at Law for a Messuage or tenement in the
Belgrave Gate late in the Occupation of George   3 4
Bassett & now of Mr Henry Coleman per Annum

Mr Pares late Robert Page for a piece of Ground
taken out of the Pinfold per Annum   4

75 Mr Samuel Bankart late Mr Thomas Chapman for a tenement in the South Gates heretofore known by the Sign of the Greyhound	4	0
76 Mr Richard Denshire late Mrs Bonner of Aylestone for a Messuage or tenement in the South Gates late Mr Bennetts land in the Occupation of Nathaniel Jee per Annum		10
77 The Poor of the Hospital of the Holy Trinity a house in the South Gates late Fosters land in the Occupation of (blank) Thorpe per Annum		9½
79 Mr John Heyrick for a piece of Ground in Burgesses Meadow late the land of John Gilford	10	0
80 (blank) Harris late Samuel Cooper for a Messuage late in his Occupation late the land of Dannett Abney		4½
81 William Davis Widow late Mr Wanley for a tenement in the North Gatestreet and for two tenements in the Occupation of John Hercourt	1	2
83 Mr Samuel Tuffley late Robert Iliff for a Shop near the South Gates once Moreton's land per Annum		5
84 Mr Ogden for a house in the Highstreet once Orton's land per Annum	3	6
85 Miss Topp late Mr William Topp for a house in the Highstreet now called Highcross street in the Occupation of John Stephens late the land of Robert Chettle per Annum	2	0
89 Mr Alderman Sutton late Mr Wightman late Benjamin Garland for a Close at Braunston Gate late William Slaters		6
90 Mr Richard Turvile for a house in Swines Market now High street late in the Occupation of Mr Newton now William Scott 11d & for 2 hens & a Capon 1s	1	11
92 Mr Joseph Johnson for a house near the West bridge called Babington's Land per Annum		9
94 Mr Clark Baker late Mr Pawley of Croson for a Messuage or tenement in Applegate street now in the Occupation of (blank)		6
96 Ann Turlington late Simon Ward for a house in Birstall late the land of John Raynor now in the Occupation of Nathan Tuffley	1	0

97 Mr Belgrave late Mr Cook Apothecary for a Messuage or tenement in the Satturday Market in the several Occupations of Mr Smith Apothecary & Miss Ledbrookes	6	8
99 Mr Joseph Neal late John Wells & also late Elizabeth Hobbs for a house in Chaff lane near Redcross street once Gulsons land 9d & for a hen 3½d	1	0½
100 Mr Joseph Johnson for land late Mr Bothams near Soar lane & for 3 Capons & two hens	4	0
93 Rogers Ruding Esquire for a Close in Braunston Gate per Annum		9
98 Mr Joseph Coltman late Mr John Billers for a house in Hotgate street alias Thornton lane 3d & for a hen 3½d & for a Garden late a Swine Stye 6d	1	0½
101 Mr Stevenson late Mr Tyler for a house near the South Gates in the High Cross street late Rudworths land 9d & for 2 hens 7d & for a Shop near the South Gates 6d per Annum	1	10
103 Mr John Winter for a tenement over against All Saints Church yard late Mr Rudyard land and late in Jacob Brookes's Occupation	2	3
106 Sir Charles Halford Baronet late Mr Edward Palmer for a House in Swines market now Highstreet late Mr Bonsar's land		6
104 Mr Hamlet Clark late Mr Pawley for a house in Applegate street once Birstalls in the Occupation of (blank) 10d & for two hens & a Capon 10d	1	8
108 Mr Alderman Simpson late Mr Thomas Chapman for a Messuage or tenement at the Upper end of Belgrave Gate late Mr Neal's land per Annum	1	6
108 Mr Woodland late Thomas Palmer or Edward Davis for a Close in All Saints parish abutting upon Elbow lane near Plank well late Cradock's land per Annum	1	8
109 John Richard & Widow Carnell & heretofore Thomas Turvile for a house & land in the North Gates late Bodyman's & Robert Harrison's per Annum		6
110 Mr Green Hodgkin of Glenn late Woodford for a certain house in the North Gates per Annum	1	1
111 Thomas Tuffley late Edward Davis for Lands in the South Gates late Owens & Messengers in his Occupation 2s & for a Garden 10d	2	10

112 Sir Charles Halford Baronet for a house in Swines
Market (now High street) late Needham's & Bailey's   4
land

114 Mr Mortimer of Narborough for a house in the South
Gate street late Mr Thomas Chapmans   6   8

113 Sir Charles Halford for a house in the Swines Market
now Highstreet near the Horse Malt Mill late Mr
Maneby's in the Occupation of Samuel Hill per   6
Annum

33 A Rentall of Lammas tythe & Herbage due yearly to the Mayor
Bailiffs & Burgesses for divers Ground in St Mary's Parish in
Possession of the College of Saint Mary's over against the Castle
of Saint Mary's Leicester

115 Mrs Wood late Richard Weston for Dovehouse Close
near the Newark of Leicester late Mr Hicklings per   1   4
Annum

116 Mr Bunney or Mr Davie late William Franke Esquire
for a Close called Archer's Close near Saint James's   1   0
Chapel Close

116 The Governors of the Infirmary for the tithe of Saint
James's Chapel Close near the Cowdrift per Annum   1   0

118 Nathan Wright Esquire for the tithe of Bennington's
Close (part of Sandpit Close & meadow) near the   1   0
Cowdrift per Annum

121 Mr Alderman Sutton late (blank) Horton late
William Slater & Benjamin Garland for a Close near   6
Braunston Gate per Annum

125 Nathan Wright Esquire late James Mason for a Close
late two Closes called Sandpit Close & meadow over   1   8
against St James's Chapel Close per Annum

119 Mrs Wood late Mr Thomas Weston for land near the
Grange once Birstall's land per Annum   1   0

128 Mrs Wood for a Close near Saint James's Chapel
Close per Annum late Moreton's land   10

129 Of her more for Seth King's Land part of the above
Close   6

130 Mr Thomas Wightman late Mr Iliff for a Close near
the Paradise   4

136 Mr Edward Davie for Cadman's land near St James's Chapel Close per Annum   10

137 Mr Davie late Mr Bunney late William Franke Esquire for a piece of Ground called the Kiln (near St James's Chapel Close) heretofore the land of Cadman and Johnson per Annum   4

138 John Lacey late Joseph Wilkins for an Orchard on the backside of an house once Davy's in the South Gate's late the land of Hugh Watts Esquire   6

139 Mr Samuel Gamble late Mr Ralph Wells for a Close near Aylestone Highway late Mr Herrick's   8

140 Of him more for another Close near the said highway .   4

141 Of him more for a Close near Archers land in St Mary's Parish   10

142 Joseph Tisdale late William Pochin of Barkby Esquire late Mr Richard Weston for a piece of Ground near St Marys Mill call'd the Holme late Maneby's land per Annum   1 8

144 Nathan Wright Esquire late the heirs of Mr John Farmer Attorney for a Close near Ayleston highway called Sandpit Close late in the Occupation of Austin Heafford   10

145 Nathan Wright Esquire late William Wright Esquire for part of the said Close called Sandpit Close in the Occupation of Mr Jee per Annum   1 0

146 Rogers Ruding Esquire for a Close in Braunston Gate late Mr Hunts land per Annum   8

148 Of him more for a Close called College Close in St Mary's parish late Mr Hunt's land   4

149 Mr Cart at the Bull's head for a Close in Saint Mary's Parish late Mrs Brookes's land per Annum   2 2

150 Mr William Simpson for a Close called the Tippetts per Annum   13 4

153 Thomas Chatwin for the tithe of the Newark Mills per Annum   2 0

157 George Rayson Pratt for a Garden or piece of Ground in Millstone lane late Armston's land per Annum   4

155 Widow Anderson for land in Chaff lane late Mr Hall now Joseph Bruce   10

158 Thomas Hall late Francis Ward for a messuage or backside belonging to his house in the South Gates now or late in the Occupation of Thomas Ward per Annum — 6

Mr Thomas Newton for a house in Thornton lane late Mr Tompson's — 4

(blank) late Paling late also Joseph Tompson for Booths land in Shambles lane — 4

Thomas Chatwin for the tithe of the Newark Mills . — 16 0

Messrs Johnson & Jordan 1s each for the tithe of the Gosling Closes — 2 0

Mr Fisher for the tithe of the North Windmill . . — 2 0

Mr Jordan late James Darbyshire late Joseph Horton for the tythe of a piece of Grass Ground in the Mary Meadows — 6 0

Mr Joseph Johnson, Mr Fisher Mr Cooper Baker & Mr Stretton each 7s 4½d for the tithe of the Beadhouse Meadow — 1 9 6

Mr John Hartshorn for the tithe of a piece of Grass Ground in the Mary Meadows — (blank)

Thomas Chatwin for the tithe of a piece belonging to the Mill — (blank)

Mr Sutton for laying planks & setting Posts in the River Soar during pleasure — (blank)

36 Fines and Accidental Receipts

By George Hunt's freedom	10	0
By Isaac Hambleton Springthorpe's Do. . . .	5	0
By John Stone's Do.	10	0
By John Hall's Do.	5	0
By Henry Seagrave's Do.	10	0
By William Bassetts Do.	10	0
By William Chambelain's Do. . . .	10	0
By Robert Bruce's Do.	10	0
By Thomas Brooke's Do.	10	0
By Joseph Fletcher's Do.	10	0
By John Palmer's Do.	10	0
By Francis Chettle's Do.	10	0

By John Cave's Do.	5	0
By Thomas Topham's Do.	10	0
By Thomas Johnson's Do.	10	0
By Francis Burgess's Do.	10	0
By Thomas Fisher Cooper's Do.	10	0
By George Oram's Do.	10	0

By Richard Steines a Stranger made free by Order of Common Hall	20	0	0
By John Sly the like	20	0	0
By James Rose the like	20	0	0
By Thomas Irwin the like	20	0	0
By Joseph Stevenson the like	20	0	0
By Scot & Lot of John Arnold		8	0
By the like of John Freestone		8	0
By Cash of Mr Thomas Ayre, which the Corporation accepted as a Satisfaction for his breach of a Covenant contained in a lease to him of a Close & barn in the Hangman lane	10	10	0
By the Balance of Mr Clark and Mr Topps Chamberlains Accounts	175	15	$6\frac{3}{4}$
By Do. of Mr Cartwright which he receiv'd of George Roe for part of the rent of the Enderby land more than he paid to Saint John's Hospital	16	2	0

⟨Memorandum⟩ At a Common Hall held the 11th December 1772 It was ordered that for the (then) future the tenants to the Corporation Estates should pay their rents due at Lady day on or before the last Wednesday in May & the rents due at Michaelmas on or before the last Wednesday in October—In virtue of which order the following rents have been received

(The further Account of the said William Taylor and Thomas Barwell from Michaelmas 1772 to Lady day 1773.)

⟨1st part of the Rental⟩

Fo. 1‡William Wills for half a years rent of a Chamber over the East Gates & for a Shop and Chamber adjoining to them in his Occupation	2	10	0
4‡Mr Thomas Chatwin for half a year's rent of the Newark Mills & Windmill and Meadows thereto belonging	15	0	0

Mr Johnson for half a years rent of part of the Gosling Close	8	2	6
Mr Jordan the like of other part of the same Close .	7	10	0
Mr Fisher Mr James Cooper, Mr Clement Stretton & Mr Johnson £3 15s od each the like for Meadow Ground in Beadhouse meadows	15	0	0
John Valentine the like for 4 Acres of Land to dig Clay to make Bricks	2	0	0
Mr Backhouse Ayre the like for the Rowdike field & meadows thereto belonging	46	5	6
Mr Thomas Phipps the like for the Gallow field & meadow Ground thereto belonging	48	11	0
Mr Alderman Oliver the like for the Middlefield & Meadow Ground thereto belonging	42	3	6
Mr Alderman Chapman's Executors the like for the Forrest Closes which had used to be rented by the Farmers along with their livings in the Southfields	4	10	0
5‡Mrs Davy for a tenement in the North Gates (half a years rent)		10	0
Mr Fisher for half a Year's rent of the North Mill .	10	0	0
Mr Topham the like for the North Mill Holme .	3	5	0
6‡Mrs Goodess the like for a tenement in the Sanvy Gate		2	6
10‡Jacob Bothomley the like for a house & backside in Loseby lane		2	0	0
12‡Robert Campion the like for the Foss Close & meadow in Frolesworth	13	10	0
23‡Mrs Higginson the like for a house and Garden near the South Gates		2	15	0
26‡Mr Fisher & Mr Clark the like for a piece of Ground in Senvy Gate belonging to the Corporation whereon they built a house		17	6
Francis Levis for the like of 2 tenements in the Sanvy Gate with a Spong of Ground thereto belonging	3	0	0
31‡Mr John Nutt for the Herbage of Saint Mary's Churchyard (half a year)	1	12	6
32‡Mr Denshire for half a years rent of a house & Garden or backside in the said Parish of Saint Nicholas & near to the Talbott in the Occupation of John Smith	1	0	0

34‡Joseph Bruce the like for a certain tenement or Garden in Soar lane near Redcross street	1	0	0
37‡Mr Alderman Belton the like for a Close of Pasture Ground late two Closes near Leicester called Freak's land	13	0	0
Mr Alderman Brown for the like of one Close called Freakes's Ground	20	0	0
38‡William Stubbs for Mr John Hammond of Whitwick for one half year's Annuity payable out of a Close in the Abby Gate called the Abby Gate Close for the better maintaining the Head Usher	1	13	4
39‡Thomas Mann for an Orchard or Garden in All Saints parish purchased with £50 given by the first Countess of Devonshire for and towards the relief of the poor of this Borough and the Parish of Saint Leonard (half a years rent)	3	0	0
Mr Alderman Fisher & Mr Joseph Johnson for a Messuage Close & one yard Land at Whetstone bought of John Baker Gentleman by the Corporation with the money bequeathed by Christopher Tamworth Esquire for celebrating divine Service in lease (being half a years rent)	8	0	0
Mr Samuel Jordan for half a years rent of part of Burgesses Meadow	2	5	0
19‡Joseph Fossett the like for a tenement near Frogmire bridge		7	6
5‡Robert Phipps the like for a tenement in the North Gates at Will	3	3	0
6‡William Tayler the like for 3 tenements by lease .	2	0	0
Benjamin Harris the like for a house in Soar lane .	2	0	0
8‡William Burleton Esquire the like for the Bowling Green house etc.	20	0	0
10‡Robert Smith the like for a tenement in his Occupation	3	10	0
16‡(blank) Vesie for a Messuage in Sanvy Gate . .	1	7	6
(blank) Maslin for tenement in the same street . .	1	2	6
(blank) Tilby for a Messuage in the same street .	1	5	0
17‡Mr Simpson for a piece of Ground in the Churchgate		15	0

	£	s	d
22‡Mrs Higginson Junior for the Week days Shambles .	I	0	0
36‡Henry Coulson the like for the Town Goal . .	I	10	0
37‡Augustine Heafford for a Cottage situate in the Horsefair		12	6
Tomlin the like		12	6
39‡Mr Sutton for the Willoughby land . . .	8	0	0
John Brewin for the forrest Closes	17	10	0

[The folio numbers refer to the original.]

The End of the Rentalls

	£	s	d
Mr Ayre half a years rent due at Lady [day] 1772 for now Smarts	6	0	0
Mrs Andrews for the like of the Leyroes . . .	6	0	0

[End of Receipts]

[Payments start here]

I [No separate heading inserted]

	£	s	d
Paid Mr Harte at the Audit of the Broad Arrow . .		I	0
Acquittance for the same			6
Paid Mr Hart the receiver for one whole Years rent of the Sheep pens due at Michaelmas		4	0	0
Paid him more for Singleton's Lease	2	12	8
To Shops taken down		11	6
Paid him more for Saint Margarets Guild . . .	I	13	5½
To him more for Corpus Christi Guild		7	9
To him more for Luskin's Lease		2	0
To him more for divers chief rents of the Town . .		7	8
Paid him more for a Close late Webster's land . . .		I	0
Paid him more for a Close near the Horsefair . . .		3	4½
Paid him more for Corpus Christi Guild . . .		11	9
Paid him more for a Close late Allams		I	0
Paid him more for acquittance of the said money . .			4
Paid him more for a Chief rent for the shops under the Gainsborough		2	6
Paid him more for a Shop in Richard Wagstaffs Occupation		I	0

Paid Mr Harte his Majesty's receiver one whole years rent out of Lands & Tenements belonging to St John's & Saint Leonards in or near the Borough of Leicester heretofore Mr Harvey & Mr Tatham's lease and in Countesthorpe & Humberston Syston Mills & the White horse for one years rent due at Michaelmas last	31	12	5
Paid to the said receiver for Lands and tenements belonging to the late Guild called St Margarets Guild in Leicester Town Obiit Lands & Vicars Closes heretofore in the Occupation of Arthur Tatham for a years rent due at Michaelmas last	42	18	1
Paid him more for a parcel of Land in possession of the late Guild called Corpus Christi Guild for one years rent due at Michaelmas last	14	12	6
Paid him more for certain lands & tenements Chief & Lammas tithes parcels of the possession of the blessed Virgin Mary over against the Castle of Leicester for a years due at Michaelmas last	20	8	6
Paid to the Receiver for certain Tenements in the Newark of Leicester	3	16	1

3   At an Audit (formerly held at the Sign of the Horse & Trumpet by Mr Hart)

Paid to the Kings Receiver for two tenements in the Swines Market in the Occupation of (blank) due at Michaelmas last	2	10	0
Paid him more for the Malt Mills in the Swines Market in the Occupation of Mr Carter paid by John Dyson	1	13	4
Paid him more for the Shambles & Drapery in Leicester due at Michaelmas last	8	13	4
Paid him more for the Gainsborough Shop & sheds & for the Saturday Market which the Mayor Bailiffs & Burgesses purchased of Mr Britton for one whole year due at Michaelmas last	4	8	8

4   Fees and other Payments this Year

Paid John Cartwright Esquire Mayor for his year's Sallary according to ancient Custom	13	6	8
Paid him more out of the rents of the Gosling Closes allowed by Order of Common Hall	13	6	8

Paid him more being the Additional annual Sallary to the Mayor in the year 1713	20	0	0
Paid him more by Order of Hall in the year 1736 . .	40	0	0
Paid him more by Order of Hall in the Year 1769 . .	50	0	0
Paid William Burleton L.L.D. Recorder of the said Borough for his Years Sallary due at Michaelmas 1772	40	0	0
Paid him more for half a year due at Lady day 1773 .	20	0	0
Paid the Town Clerk for taking the Coroners Inquest .	1	0	0
Paid him more for the Sessions due at Michaelmas only .		6	8
Paid him more for the Book of Payments . . .		4	6
Paid Mr Pigott head Schoolmaster being the Towns free Gift during Pleasure	16	0	0
Paid the Under Usher being the Towns free Gift during pleasure	3	0	0
Paid him more being the Town's free Gift during Pleasure	5	0	0
Paid Mr Haines his Sallary as Lecturer for the said Borough during Pleasure	20	0	0
Paid him more by order of Common hall during Pleasure .	10	0	0
Paid Mr Simmonds Vicar of Saint Mary's being the Town's free gift during pleasure	10	0	0
Paid Mr Haines the like	10	0	0
Paid Mr Burnaby the like	10	0	0
Paid Mr Pigott the like	10	0	0
Paid the Town Clerk for his Years Sallary . . .	5	0	0
Paid him more being the Towns free Gift . . .	2	13	4
Paid for the Rentall	2	0	0
Paid for proclaiming Fairs & Marketts		14	0
Paid him for the Commission for the Year . . .		10	10
Paid the Macebearer his Years Sallary & for burning of Pipes	7	9	8
Paid the Macebearer for two Seals		2	0
Paid the four Serjeants their Years Salary by Order of Hall per Quarter	16	0	0
Paid the Cryer for his Wages & sweeping the Town hall & Gainsborough	1	13	4
Paid the Beadle his Years Sallary for sweeping the Gates & weeding the Town hall Yard	6	0	0

Paid the Beadle & Cryer to prevent them from going about with their Christmas box		4	0
Paid the Library Keeper	3	0	0
Paid the Waits their Years Sallary	6	13	4
Paid to the Bailiff of the Augmentation for lands due to (blank) at Leicester at the feast day of Michaelmas and Acquittance		7	4
To the Bailiffs of Merton College in Oxford for one Chief rent issuing and payable out of Saint Johns & St Leonard in or near the Borough of Leicester		1	3
Paid the Wardens of the Company of Taylors the annual rent of		1	8
Paid tolling the Bell on Michaelmas day . . .		1	0
Paid the Halbert men for walking the fair & cleaning the Armour on the fair day		10	0
Paid for attendance and weights on the Cheese fair at Michaelmas	1	10	0
Paid Mr Lucas a Chief rent out of the Gainsborough (taxes deducted) now William Morehead Esquire due the 10th day of October 1771	6	1	10
Paid Lady Fitzwilliams a years rent for the Southfield tithes due at Michaelmas 1770 (taxes Deducted)	4	10	2
Paid for Buns & Ale at visiting the School two times . .	1	2	0
Paid for Biscuits and Macaroons at Assizes & Sessions .	1	2	0
Paid for Coals used at the Town hall & Gainsborough .	2	19	6½
Paid for Holly & Ivy used at the Town hall . . .		2	6
Paid the Clerk of Saint Mary's for washing the Chancel .		2	6
Paid the Grand jury for Quarter Session's Dinners . .	6	6	0
Paid the Constables for the like	3	0	0
Paid the Huntsman on Easter Monday by Order of Mr Mayor	1	11	6
Paid Men for playing the Engines & drawing one of them to Mr Oldhams		14	6
Paid to Shuckburg Ashby Esquire for the tithe of Mr Recorder's house & land due at Michaelmas last	1	5	1½
Paid the Cryers Son for lighting fires at Change . .		10	6
Paid for lighting the Lamps at the Exchange for the whole year	1	13	6
Paid for mending the Netts		14	9

Paid for the Coals at the Guardhouse		1	4
Paid Jennings for tithe		1	8
Paid for Lime & Gravel getting 11s & for a load of Sand 3s .		14	0
Paid Cryer & Beadle for their attendance at the Assizes .		2	0
Paid for sweeping the Chimnies		3	0
Paid for sweeping the Street after the Fairs . . .		14	0
Paid towards the Horse Race Town Purse . . .	10 10		0
Paid the fees at the Venison feast £0 os od for fetching Venison 7s 6d		7	6
Paid drawing drink then		2	0
Paid Mr Pares for an Acquittance for the Earl of Huntingdon's Gift			8
Paid Mr Foster a Chief rent		5	2
Paid for the two pair of shoes for the Cryer & Beadle . .		12	0
Paid the Lottery money to Saint Mary's Parish Officers .	5	6	0
Paid Miss Greatorex the Organist for one year ending at May day	10	0	0
Paid for seales & attendance at May fair . . .	1	1	0
Paid for a Quarter of Charcoal		6	0
Paid for drawing the Waters of the River Soar for fishing .		9	0
Paid the Macebearer for carrying out 4 baggage Warrants .		4	0
Paid for cleaning under the East Gates twice . . .		5	0
Paid for thatching Mr Smiths Market house . . .		10	6
Paid a person for taking up the Kings Arms (blown off of the South Gates)			6
Paid (blank) Brown for Stones		10	6
Paid for whitewashing Vesie's house		6	0
Paid for getting Gravell		9	8
Paid for cleaning the Carpetts & Curtains . . .		5	6
Paid for a Post Letter 2s 4d — Candles 7d . . .		2	11
Paid for two Netts		5	6
Paid for Kidds		4	4½
Paid for Cleaning Churchgate		10	6
Allowed the Chamberlains for the Auditors Dinners . .	20	0	0
Paid the Town Clerk for making up the Accounts . .	3	6	8
Parchment for the same			6
Paid for a Ribbon for the Charter		2	0
Paid for paper and pens		13	4

R

Paid for the Letter of Attorney		7	6
Allowance for loss of Coals	14	12	6
Paid for the Duty of 600 Ounces of plate . . .	1	10	0
Paid Mr Cartwright late Mayor the money by him paid to Vagrants	3	10	0
Paid to the poor of the Hospital of the Holy Trinity the interest of £100 left by Mr Cradock	4	0	0
Paid the Macebearer as the Inspector of the Market for one year	2	12	0
Paid to the Poor of the said Hospital the interest of £5 left by Mr Andrews Will		5	0
Paid Mark Valentine's a free Gift during pleasure . .	5	4	0
By Loss in the rent of the West Gates		19	0
Paid the poor of Trinity Hospital a years rent for that part of the Recorders Garden which belongs to the Hospital	2	0	0
Paid a Years Interest of £100 due on bond from the Corporation to Miss Frances Babington	4	10	0
Paid a Chief rent for Nathaniel Palmer		1	3

7   Tradesmen's Bills

Paid John Webster's Bill	1	7	4
Paid Mr Denshires Do.	1	1	0
Paid Mr Elliott's Do.		14	0
Paid John Clark's Do.		8	9
Paid Mr Bankart's Do.	9	9	0
Paid Mr Smith's Do.		7	0
Paid John Hales's Do.		15	4
Paid John Dean's Do.		3	6
Paid Mr Firmadge's Do.		10	6
Paid Thomas Throsby's Do.	2	8	7
Paid Mr Wright's Do.		12	0
Paid Thomas Coleman's Do.		17	6
Paid Mr Alderman Ogden's Do.	2	7	7
Paid John Webster's Do.	8	4	5
Paid Mr Thomas Tuffley's Do.		10	6
Paid Mrs Higginson's Do.	5	2	2
Paid Henry Hitchcock's Do.	2	0	0
Paid Robert Smith's Do.		7	0
Paid John Brewin's Do.	3	14	1
Paid Edward Goodess's Do.	5	18	10
Paid Joseph Cooper's Do.		2	6

Paid Mr Gregory's Do.	12	2	6
Paid Joshua Kirks Do.		16	2
Paid Mr Bishop's Do.	1	1	0
Paid Mr Smarts Do.	12	15	5
Paid Mr Cristey's Do.	9	1	7
Paid Mrs Chamberlain's Do.	1	2	4
Richard Linsey's Do.		18	9
Paid John Valentine's Do.		18	0
Paid Mr Joseph Newbold's Do.		18	0
Paid Thomas Hall's bill	20	16	6
Paid Mr Alderman Palmer's Do.	7	11	0
Paid Mr Cart's Do.	2	12	6
Paid Mr Oldham's Do.	20	18	10
Paid Mr Alderman Throsby's Do.		10	0
Paid Mr Alderman Chamber's Do.	26	18	10
Paid Mr Harriss's Do.	3	17	3
Paid Mr Beale's Do.	5	18	2
Paid Mr Smart's Do.	13	4	11
Paid Mr Lewins Do.		16	8
Paid Joseph Cooper's Do. (Allowed by order of Hall towards the expence of building a Stable for Mr Recorder)	60	0	0
Paid Mr Price's bill		7	9
Paid Mr Lowdham's Do.	31	10	0
Paid Joseph Bowns's Do.	25	1	4
Paid Mr Wallin's Do.		4	4
Paid John Roe's Do.		17	11
Paid Mr Alderman Gutheridge's Do. . . .		10	6
Paid Mr Ward's Do.	4	0	10
Paid Mr Heyrick in part of his bill . . .	60	0	0
Paid Mr Valentine's Do.		18	0
Paid Mr Alderman Simpson's Do.		4	1
Paid Mr Wootton's Do.	1	8	2
Paid Mr Tilly's Do.	17	16	7
Paid Mr Cartwright's bill	26	14	4
Paid towards the expence of erecting an Organ in St Martin's Church by order of Hall	80	0	0

9   Allowance for Land tax at 3s 6d in the Pound

Mr Poynton	5	3
Mr Lee	3	6
Widow Hastwell	3	6
Shuckburg Ashby Esquire	5	3

Mr Iliff	.	3	6
Mr Bothomley	.	7	0
Widow Bassett	.	3	6
Mr Johnson	.	5	3
Henry Brown	.	3	6
Thomas Biggs	.	3	6
Mr Cook	.	3	6
Mr Robert Smith	.	10	6
Mr Chapman	.	3	6
Mrs Andrews late Mr Samuel Heyrick	.	7	0
William Cooper	.	3	6
Mr John Bass Oliver	.	7	0
Mr Denshire	.	3	6
Thomas Mann	.	5	3
Elizabeth Dyson	.	5	3
William Wright Esquire	.	3	6
The Infirmary	.	3	6
John Burton	.	3	6

Augustine Heafford	.	1	4	6
(blank) Campion	.	2	5	6
For the Bowling Green	.	1	10	4

Francis Norman	.	3	6
Widow Ascough	.	3	6
Benjamin Harris	.	6	1½
(blank) Cramant	.	3	6
Miss Lee	.	7	0
Thomas Hastwell	.	3	6
(blank) Cradock	.	10	6

Mr Fisher for North Mills	.	2	17	2
Thomas Chatwin for Swans Mill	.	2	13	4¼

Thomas Taylor now Phipps	.	5	8¼
William Mason	.	5	3
Mr Denshire	.	7	0
Widow Moore	.	3	6
Henry Smith	.	3	6
Mr Oldershaw	.	5	3
The Reverend Mr John Lee	.	7	0
Mr Alderman Sismey	.	3	6

Mr Alderman Brown	.	3	10	0
Rogers Ruding Esquire	.	2	2	0
Mr Alderman Belton	.	2	12	6

Syston Mills	.	10	6
Mr Higginson	.	5	3

Mr Joseph Simpson		3	6
Mr William Blackwell now Johnson		7	0
Mr Thomas Ayre	1	1	0
Shops & Stalls	2	3	9
Rowland Watts		3	6
Charles Tuffley		3	6
Hurst & Taylor		4	4½
Levies		8	9
(blank) Sykes of Loseby		3	6
Mrs Watts		19	3
(blank) Coates		3	6
Mr Warburton		5	3
Mr Alderman Oliver		4	8
Mr Pares		5	3
Joseph Bruce by Mr Dafforn		3	6
James Sismey Esquire now Mr William Simpson . .		3	6
Henry Sands		3	6
Alderman Throsby		5	3

Further Allowance of Land tax to those who
paid One year and an half's rent.

Mrs Chatwin	1	8	0
Mrs Davie		1	6
Mr Alderman Fisher		12	4
Jacob Bothomley		2	0
Mrs Higginson		7	6
Francis Levis		2	9½
Joseph Bruce		2	0
Mr Alderman Bolton	1	10	0
Mr Alderman Brown	1	10	0
Thomas Mann		3	0

11   Charitable Gifts

Paid the Gift of Queen Elizabeth to the Head Usher . .	10	0	0
Paid the Gift of Sir Ralph Rawlett	3	6	8
Paid the Gift of Mr Norris	3	6	8
Paid the Gift of Mr Clarke	1	0	0
Paid the Gift of Mr Norris out of the Willoughby lands .	8	0	0
Paid the Gift of Mr John & Mr William Stanley . .	5	0	0
Paid the Gift of the Earl of Devonshire	6	0	0
Paid the Gift of Christopher Tamworth Esquire . .	16	0	0
Paid the Gift of King Charles the 1st of ever blessed Memory	35	0	0

	£	s	d
Paid the Gift of Mr William Ive £14 & Mrs Ive £1 .	15	o	o
Paid the Gift of Mr William Elkington	5	o	o
Paid the Gift of William Poultney Esquire . . .	10	o	o
Paid the Gift of Mr Nidd	51	o	o
Paid the Gift of Mr Acham	9	o	o
Paid the Gift of Mr Haines	24	o	o
Paid the Gift of Mr Botham	2	o	o
Paid the Gift of the Earl of Huntingdon to Wigston's Hospital	10	o	o
Paid the Gift of Mr John Holmes to Trinity Hospital £45 & to St Johns & Mr Bents Hospital £6 10s 0d	51	10	o
Paid the Gift of Sir William Courteen & Gentlemen of the Lottery	4	16	o
Paid the Gift of Mrs Dorothy Baker	1	o	o
Paid the Gift of Mr Julius Billers	5	12	o
Paid the Gift of Mr Bennett & Mr Ward . . .	1	o	o
Paid the Gift of Mrs Ossiter Widow	6	o	o
Paid the Gift of Mr Gilbert	5	o	o
Paid the Gift of Mr Hitch		3	o
Paid the Gift of Mrs Margaret Hobby	1	1	o
Paid the Gift of the Countess of Devonshire . . .	3	o	o
Paid the Gift of Mr Hesilrige	1	1	6
Paid the Gift of Mr Thomas Ayre	1	o	o
Paid the Gift of Mr John Ludlam	2	10	o
Paid the Gift of Mr Thomas Wightman . . .		5	o
Paid the Gift of Mr John Roberts	1	o	o
Paid the Gift of Mr Robert Hall		10	o
Paid the Gift of Mr George Bent		5	o
Paid the Gift of Mr William Sutton being the interest of £70 at £4 per Cent given to the poor of the Hospital of Saint Jones	2	16	o
Paid more being the Interest of his Gift of £20 to the poor of the Old Hospital		16	o
Paid the Gift of Mr Topp to the poor of the Old Hospital .	1	o	o
Paid more his Gift to Saint John's Hospital . . .		10	o
Paid the Gift of Mr Alderman Thomas Ludlam being the Interest of £300 which he left to Charitable uses	12	o	o
Paid the Gift of Benjamin Garland to the Parish of Saint Martin		5	o

[End of Payments]

[Supers start here]

Supers

Perkins for Gunnerby land	6	8
George Wright Esquire for Land at Oadby . . .	5	11½
The Earl of Stamford for the tithe of Thurmaston Mills .	6	8
For the Easter and other Duties to the Vicar of Saint Mary .	(blank)	
Anthony Ingoldsby for Lands at Ashby		6
More for the tithe of the Swans Mill	16	0
Mr John Heyrick for Land at Sileby		6
Mr Wright's Taxes	3	0
Mr Sutton	1	0
Mr Farmer's chief rent	1	9
Mr Wrights Chief rent	1	0

To be super'd or deducted for the following Vicarial tithes & Lammas tithes which have none of them been received this year by the Chamberlain (the same having been agreed to be taken in kind)

Mr Cradock's—Mr Ruding, Mrs Watts } several Charges for Vicarial tithes	24	6	6
For Lammas tithes	4	12	6
	28	19	0
From which sum of £28 19s 1d is to be deducted for taxes allowed to the several persons paying the said Vicarial & Lammas tithes the sum of	2	19	1

[End of Supers]

25	19	11

[Summary]

By Cash being the balance of the Hospital Account . .	6	10	8½
To be deducted from Cristey's bill £1 11s 11d—from John Brewin's 12s 9d & from Cooper 2s 6d for work done at Trinity Hospital and which by Error are allowed in the Tradesmans bills	2	7	2
	4	3	6½

Total of the receipts	1779	9	2¾
Total of the payments	1508	9	7¾
Balance	£270	19	7

CHAMBERLAINS' ACCOUNTS
1792/3

The Accounts of
William Firmadge ⎱ Chamberlins
Samuel Towndrow ⎰
to
Joseph Burbidge Esquire
from
Michaelmas 1792 to Michaelmas 1793

1 [No separate heading inserted]

⟨Imprimis in the Rentall 1652 No. 1⟩

Alderman Palmer late Augustine Heafford for a Year's Rent of the Sheepens with Cocker's Kitchen by Lease per Annum at Lammas and Candlemas	20	0	0
Rogers Ruding Esquire late Thomas Noble Esquire heretofore Mr John Harrison for Rent of Assize due Yearly out of the Lands of the North Gates late in the Occupation of Thomas Turvile called Gadesby's Land at Michaelmas only paid by Cowdell		1	9
Sir Nigil Greasley (by Mr Alderman Chambers) late Mr Alderman Hood and heretofore John Blunt for Butt Close formerly sold to Mr Thomas Blunt late in the Occupation of Mr Robert Roulson late Freeman's, late also John Loseby's		10	0
Messrs Bellamy & Biggs (Executors of Mr John Yates) late Mr John Wightman and heretofore Edward Noon for a Messuage or Tenement at the Nether End of Belgrave Gate heretofore the Land of Thomas Headley now divided into several Tenements in fee farm per annum late in the Occupation of Edward Noon	1	0	0
Roberts for Mr Plummer of Evington & Mr Bollard 1s 3d each, late also Charles Stafford and Alice Brown for a Garden and peice of Ground in Sanvy Gate		2	6

John Manners Esquire, late the Duke of Devonshire, for a piece of Ground (being a Close) in the North Gates, whereon stood a Messuage or Tenement, heretofore the Land of George Tatham, in fee farm per annum	13	4
The said John Manners Esquire, late the said Duke, for a piece of Ground being part of the said Close, late Thomas Fletcher's Land, in fee farm per annum		4
Mr John Lambert late Mr Thomas Fletcher, late also Thomas Alsop, for a piece of Ground lying on the Backside of a Messuage in the North sold to John Tatham in fee farm per annum	1	8
Mr Joseph Boulton, heretofore Mr John Palmer, late John Stafford, late also John Erpe, for a Messuage or Tenement & piece of Ground in Applegate Street and in the parish of St Nicholas, heretofore the Land of William Adcock in fee farm per annum	6	8
Mr Cristey heretofore Rowland Watts, late John Turville, late Mr Barwell, for a Tenement in the North Gate Street, late the Land of Mr Robert Freer, heretofore the Sign of the Sun per annum	1 0	0
Alderman Gamble's Heir, late Robert Cook, for a piece of Ground called the Water Laggs now the Bath Gardens in the Occupation of John Emmerson	6	8
Wells & others of Loughborough, late Mr John Champion for a piece of Ground at the South end of the Butt Close in the occupation of Mr Johnson in fee farm per annum		4
Mr Chandler of Gilmorton, late Mr Gamble of Willoughby or William Burdett, late also Robert Palmer of Gilmorton, for Land, Meadow and pasture Ground at Gilmorton heretofore the Land of John Spriggs, afterwards of Edward Whitehead	3	4
Anthony Ingelasby Esquire for Land in Great Ashby in the County of Lincoln, late the Land of Ralph Brookesby Gentleman heretofore the Land of Nicholas Norton per annum		6
Mr Lowdham for Wigley Hartopp Esquire late James Wigley Esquire for certain Lands & Tenements in Scraptoft, late the Lands of John Mason & heretofore the Lands of Thomas Simpkin & (blank) Taylor of Whetstone & now or late in the Tenure of Matthias Hubbard		6

3   Receipts of the whole Grange with the Appurtenances & 4 Yard lands and the Land called Archer's Land & known by the Name of Wightman's Land & a half Yard land which the Corporation purchased of Lord Spencer, as follows

	£	s	d
Mr Thomas Chatwyn, late John Gilford, for a Year's rent of the Newark Mills & Windmill and Meadow thereto belonging (inclusive of a Meadow late Daft's) by Lease per annum	33	o	o
Mr Alderman Johnson, late John Wright, for part of Gosling Closes by Lease per Annum	16	5	o
Mrs Jordan for other part of Do. by Lease per annum .	15	o	o

5   Beadhouse Meadows

	£	s	d
Mr Fisher £11 5s, Mr Cooper £7 10s & Mr Johnson £11 5s for the Meadow Grownd late Mr Thomas Marshall's by Lease per annum	30	o	o
Woolston Wigston, late John Brewin of Leicester Forest, late Alderman Chapman, for the Forest Closes, which used to be rented by the Farmers along with their Livings in the South Fields	16	o	o

6   In the South Fields
(which are let on Lease to the following Tenants)

	£	s	d
Mr Thomas Mann a Year's Rent due at Lammas 1793 for Land in the Rowdike field	16	16	9
The Executors of Augustine Peters Do. for Land in Do. .	17	19	1
William Hardy Do. for Land in Do. . . .	13	8	9
Mr William Dabbs Do. for Land in Middlefield . .	29	12	5
Mr Richard Toon Do. for Do.	11	11	4
Mr William Watts Do. for Land in Gallow field . .	27	8	2
Mr Alderman Johnson Do. for Land in Gallowfield, & Rowdike Field The Farmer's Leas etc.	94	2	2
Mr Edward Sutton Do. for Land in Middle & Rowdike Fields	57	4	8
Thomas Bruce Do. for Land in Middle & Rowdike Fields .	68	11	11
Mr Chambers Do. for Land in Gallow & Rowdike Fields .	43	5	o
Thomas Pettifor Do. for Land in Gallow field. . .	22	9	o
Mr Oldham Do. for Land in Middle Field . .	43	4	7
Mr Henry Valentine Do. for Land in Gallow and Middle Fields	40	13	9

Mr Horner Do. for Land in Gallow Field   .   .   .   21 9 11

7   Saint Mary's Meadow
             (Which is set on Lease to the following Tenants)

Mr Alderman Cooper a Year's rent for Land in this ⎫
Meadow due at Michaelmas 1793   ⎭   3 12 6

Mr Alderman Burbidge Do. 6 0 0

Mr Cristey Do. 6 0 0

Mr Watts Do. 3 0 0

Mr Francis Hayes Do. 7 19 4

8   Far Meadow
             (Which is also set on Lease to the following Tenants)

Mr Alderman Chambers a Years Rent for Land in this ⎫
Meadow due at Michaelmas 1793   ⎭   4 2 10

Mr Bruce Do. 5 15 0

Mr Cristey Do. 2 15 1

Mr Bishop Do. 13 16 8

Mr Cristey a Year's Rent for one Acre of Land in St ⎫
Mary's Meadow, not included in his Lease, due at   ⎬   1 0 0
Michaelmas 1793   ⎭

9 [No separate heading inserted]

Mr Alderman Johnson for a Messuage Farm Yard & ⎫
Homestead call'd Hall's Grange, a Year's Rent, due ⎬   8 0 0
Michaelmas 1793   ⎭

Mr Frisby for two Meadows at Do. 6 0 0

Dorothy Daniel Widow for Do.—Year's rent due at Do. .   6 0 0

Mr Alderman Fisher for a Barn and Yard or Homestead ⎫
in Grange Lane, a Year's Rent due at Michaelmas 1793 ⎭   5 8 0

10a   In the North Gates

Mr John Clark for a Tenement in the North Gate in the ⎫
Occupation of (blank) Taylor by Lease per annum a Year's ⎬   2 0 0
Rent due at Michaelmas 1793   ⎭

Mr Alderman Fisher late John Brookes for the rent of the ⎫
North Mills—Brooke's whole Rent was £31 7s 6d, But in |
Consideration of the Alderman's making it a Bolting Mill ⎬   20 0 0
at his own Expence, it was leased to him from the 10th |
October 1786 for 20 Years at £20 per Annum   ⎭

	£	s	d
Mr E. Sutton late Robert Phipps for a Tenement in North Gate Street by Lease per annum	5	0	0
Mr George Luck late Robert Smith for the Weekday Shambles otherwise Saturday Market, paid quarterly— The whole Year's rent due at Michaelmas 1793	110	0	0
Mr William Abel late Mr Topham for the North Mill Holmes—Year's Rent due Michaelmas 1793	10	0	0

10b In Sanvey Gate

	£	s	d
Wood £3 10s Hubbard £2 10s & Davie £2 late Mr W. Taylor late W. Stevenson for 3 tenements at Will per annum due at Lady Day & Michaelmas	8	0	0
Mr Goodess, late Mr James Annis for another Tenement late John Rawson's Land, by Lease per annum a Year's Rent due at Michaelmas		5	0
Mr Joseph Wheatley late Robert Cowdall Hosier late Mrs Burgess of Oadby late Mr Thomas Penford for a Tenement near the North Gates, in Fee farm per annum			10
The said Joseph Wheatley late Robert Cowdall late the said Mrs Burgess late George Webb for a Tenement near the North Gates according to the Old Rentall, this should be 2s			2
(blank) Cave late Mr Alderman Oldham, for Mrs Smith, heretofore William Biggs, for a Tenement near the North Gate in Fee Farm per annum		1	0
Francis Holmes, late Benjamin Harris, late also William Cave, for a House with the Appurtenances due at Michaelmas per annum	4	0	0

10c In Soar's Lane or Walker's Lane

	£	s	d
Mr Clough, late Joseph Smith for a piece of Ground sometime since a Dunghill, now built upon, heretofore in the Occupation of William Rudyard per annum		2	0

10d Within the North Gates

	£	s	d
Mr Alexander Forrester late John Lovett late the Heirs or Executors of Robert Hicklington for a Messuage or Tenement on the South Side of All Saints' Church Yard now in the Occupation of (blank) Fox, in Fee Farm per annum	1	10	0
Thomas Darbyshire late Mary Hewson for a Messuage or Tenement in Highcross Street, late Kimberlain's Land in Fee Farm per Annum		6	0

Miss Browns the Heirs of the late John Brown Frame-smith late Mrs Windsor for a Tenement in High Street, late in the Occupation of Joseph Waggatt & now of the said Miss Browns per Annum		5	0
Mrs Orton late Thomas Carter for a House & Garden in High Cross Street at the Corner of Bakehouse Lane in the Occupation of (blank) late Mrs Davie		4	0
Mr Alderman Fisher 4s 6d, for a House & Garden in Bake-house Lane, late in the Occupation of Robert Green & of Thomas Johnson's Widow, late Bellamy 2s 10d for a House in two Tenements late in the Occupation of the said Thomas Green		7	4
Mr Alderman Chambers for the Bowling Green House & Garden thereto adjoining with the Appurtenances now in his Occupation by Lease per annum due at Michaelmas & Lady Day	50	0	0

10e   In the South Gates

Mr John Moore for a House in the Occupation of William Sanderson (late Thomas Moreton's) per Annum	1	0	0
Mr Alderman Fisher & Mr Bankart late the Land of Thomas Wall for a Messuage or Tenement at the Corner of Hangman Lane, in Fee Farm per annum Mr Daniel pays 9s Mr Bankart 7s		16	0
(blank) Sharpe (Taylor) for Thomas Martin late Mr Alderman Chapman & Mr Gamble for a Messuage or Tenement late the Swan, now or late in the Occupation of the said Thomas Martin & (blank) Sharpe in Fee Farm per Annum		13	4

10f [No separate heading inserted]

Mr John Heyrick late William Palmer Esquire for a piece of Meadow Ground called the Shield late Moreton's Land in Fee Farm per annum		16	0
The said John Heyrick more for two Acres of Meadow late also Mr Moreton's Land in Fee Farm per Annum		13	4

10g   In the Swine's Market, now call'd High Street

Mr John Willows for a Messuage or Tenement in his Occupation late Mr Bonnington's Land in Fee Farm per annum		6	0

Widow Burley of New Parkes, late Agnes Horton's Land, for a Tenement heretofore called the King's Head — 18 0

10i   In the Saturday Market

Mrs Higginson, Chandler, for a Messuage or Tenement now divided into 2 Tenements in the several Occupations of the said Mrs Higginson & Messrs Cape & Hodgkin — 1 3 4

Mr Stevens, Watchmaker, late Mr Alderman Watchorn, late Alderman Brown, for Messuage or Tenement in Mr Stevenson's own Occupation, in Fee Farm per annum — 8

10j   In the Loseby Lane

Mr Francis Burgess Thomas Pares Esquire late Mr Ingle, late Mr Tilly, late Lady Greasley, for a Messuage or Tenement, late in the Occupation of the said Mr Tilly & now of the said Mr Pares, in Fee Farm per annum — 10 0

Mr Forrester & Captain Perry, late Mr Thomas Ayre, late Mr Buckerfield, for a House late in the Occupation of John Ferryman, now rebuilt & in the Occupation of the said Captain Perry, in Fee Farm per annum — 1 6 0

Mr Alexander Forrester, late the Heirs of Samuel Coates, for a House lately called the Star & Bell & now the Crown & Thistle in the Occupation of Robert Hoe in Fee Farm per annum — 12 0

Of him more for a piece of Ground a Damask Rose payable at Midsummer — a Damask Rose

Thomas Bothamley late the Widow of Jacob Bothamley, for a House & Backside being parcel of Tenement late in the Valentine Dallaways Occupation since new built — 5 5 0

Mr Rawson late Mr Garle for a Messuage or Tenement now called the Crown & Thistle, in Fee Farm per annum — 10 0

George Luck, late Mr Garle, for a House & Backside due at Michaelmas & Lady Day — 7 0 0

10k   In the Gallowtree Gate

Mr Alderman Benjamin Gregory, late Mr Alderman Oliver, late Mr Alderman Thomas Ayre, for a Messuage or Tenement late in the Occupation of Loftus Page & now of Mr Cotchett in Fee Farm per annum — 8 0

Mr Alderman Mansfield, late Mr Alderman Oliver, late Mr Alderman Thomas Ayre, for a Messuage or Tenement known by the Sign of the White Horse now in the Occupation of John Taylor, in Fee Farm per annum	1	0	0
Mr Willey for one Yard land in St Margaret's Field, late Mr Alderman Bishop		15	0

10l
In Gallowtree Gate
on the West Side

Mr James Nutt late The Reverend Mr Lambert for a Messuage or Tenement near the Play House, in the Occupation of (blank) Hudson & William Freer, in Fee Farm per annum		10	0
The said James Nutt for a Messuage or Tenement heretofore Edward Ashwell's Land in his own Occupation		4	0
Mr Watts & Dixon for a Messuage or Tenement called the Magpye & Crown, late the Land of Henry Palmer in Fee Farm per Annum	1	0	0

10m
In Belgrave Gate

Dr Arnold for a Garden at the Nether End of Belgrave Gate heretofore in Thomas Drake's occupation late paid by Mrs Pares for Joseph Cradock Esquire of Gumley, & now paid by & in the Occupation of the said Dr Arnold		12	0
Mr Yates's Executors (Bellamy & Biggs) late Thomas Roadley for a House in his Occupation in Fee Farm per Annum		13	4
Thomas Withers for Thomas Sarson & Francis Foulgham 10s each, for a House in the Tenure of the said Thomas Withers, in Fee Farm per Annum	1	0	0
Mrs Holmes late Mrs Ward Widow for a Tenement heretofore Simpson's adjoining the Unicorn (which Unicorn is now Alderman Bishop's House) on the West Side thereof in Fee Farm per Annum		15	0
Mr Alderman Coleman for the House in his Occupation on the North Side of the said Street, late the Land of Richard Ward in fee farm per Annum		18	0
The Churchwardens of St Margarets for a Piece of Ground call'd the Cowpasture in Fee Farm per Annum		8	0

10n   In the Country

Clement Winstanley Esquire for certain Lands Leys and Pasture Grounds in the Lordship of Braunstone in the County of Leicester now or late in the Occupation of (blank) Burton, in Fee Farm per Annum	12	8
Mr Hurst of Hinckley late William Warner for a Close Croft & one Yard land with the appurtenances in Hinckley in the County of Leicester in the Occupation of (blank) in Fee Farm per Annum	15	0
Mr Robert Walker & Mrs Gossip, late Mr Thomas Worral for a piece of Ground in Belgrave, call'd Knipton Leys, & one Yard land heretofore sold to one (blank) Culverwell being a Close of Pasture heretofore called Belgrave Bridge Close, late Mr Overing's Land—Walker pays 5s 9d Gossip 3s 3d	9	0
Lord Wentworth for a Messuage or Tenement & one Yard land with the Appurtenances in Kirby Mallory, in Fee farm per Annum	6	8
(blank) Roddle of Rearsby, late Mr Boothby of Tooley for a Messuage or Tenement at Rearsby, in the Occupation of Mrs Roddle in Fee Farm per Annum	17	0
Mrs Monk of Seagrave, late Mr George Chamberlain of Seagrave for a Close & Croft there, the Land of William Hubbard, in Fee Farm per Annum	2	0
Barsby of Thrussington, late Mr Benjamin Storer, of Thrussington for one Yard land there in fee farm per Annum	6	8
Robert Campion late William Whale of Frolesworth, for a Foss Close & Meadow, by Lease per Annum due at Michaelmas & Lady Day	27 0	0
Mr William Tompson of Houghton on the Hill for a Piece of Ground in his Occupation or William Hubbard's, in fee farm per Annum	1	8
Mr William Ward of Houghton for another Parcel of Ground thereto belonging, late Thomas Readley in Fee Farm per Annum	5	0
The Reverend H. Woodcock late Mr Whatoff Cleaver of Syston, for certain Lands at Barkby, late in the Occupation of Thomas Readley, in Fee Farm per Annum	8	0

Mr Alderman Peach, late Mr Watts for certain Lands, Leys & Hades in the West Field of Leicester in Fee Farm per Annum ... 4 0

Mr George Henton, for Shuckburgh Ashby Esquire, late Sir Thomas Cave, for a Messuage or Tenement in Hungerton, now or late in the Tenure of Thomas Walton, in Fee Farm per Annum ... 1 10 0

George Sheffield of Syston, for Syston Mill, and a House heretofore sold to Sir Thomas Cave in Fee Farm per Annum ... 3 6 8

11a Other Rents of Lands & Tenements parcel of the Town obiit Lands of St Margaret's Guild & Parcel of the Fee Farm Rents heretofore demised by Queen Elizabeth to Mr Howkins & Mr Bates by Indentures expired

The Heirs of Mr William Ives, for Ground late belonging to several Houses in the Southgates, heretofore Mr Nurses & Mr Hills & Francis Coles ruin'd by the late Wars heretofore sold to Mr Dennett Abney, in Fee Farm per Annum Paid as follows, to wit, ... 2 13 4

    Mr Wildbore of Tilton pays . . . 6 8

    Mr Townsend of Ailestone . . . 6 8

    Mr Moore of Leicester 2 0 0

John Reynolds late Mr Armston, late Mr Norton, late also Mr John Ludlam, for a Messuage or Tenement with the Appurtenances commonly called or known by the Name of the White Lyon, now in the Occupation of the said John Reynolds in Fee Farm per Annum ... 10 0

Mr Tuffley Baker, late Mr Thomas Hartshorn, for a Messuage or Tenement in the Occupation of the said Mr Tuffley in Fee Farm per Annum ... 1 0 0

Mr Alderman Johnson for the Ground late belonging to two Tenements in the South Gate Street, late in the Tenure of Paul Abney deceased, since known by the Name of the Bull, ruin'd by the late Wars, and since then built upon, in Fee farm per Annum ... 1 6 8

Mr Bankart late Alderman Chapman, for a Messuage or Tenement in South Gate Street, formerly called the Grey Hound, ruin'd in the late Wars, since built upon in his Sons Occupation in Fee Farm per Annum ... 1 0 0

S

11b

In the Swine's Market
now called
High Street

Mr Fosbrooke, late Mr Sismey, for a Tenement in the Silver Street, near the Pump, late in the Occupation of Robert Dowley, now of the said Mr Fosbrooke, in Fee Farm per Annum — 1 0 4

11c   In or near Belgrave Gate

Mr Clay Hextall, late Mr Cramant, late Mr John Newton, for a Tenement at the Corner of Humberstone Gate, in his own Occupation in Fee Farm per Annum — 1 1 0

Land late Mr Pares's, now Mr Chamberlin's & others Mr Chamberlin pays 6s & Sarah Noon 6s in Fee Farm per Annum — 12 0

Mr Moore (for Lewins Heirs) for a Messuage or Tenement once called the Lamb & for one other Messuage or Tenement & Close with the Appurtenances late in the Occupation of Benjamin Cartwright and now of Mr Coleman — 1 6 8

Mr Foulgham 10s Mr Kirke 5s & George Door for Sands 5s for a House late in the Occupation of Widow Noon & now of George Door and (blank) in Fee Farm per Annum — 1 0 0

Mr Andrews out of Rowlett's Close, the Gift of Mr Twickden — 2 0 0

†Mr Oldham, late George Roe, for Lands in Enderby Lordship being the Gift of Mr Bent to St John's Hospital — 45 2 0

Mr Robert Brewin for Mr Simpson for the Tippetts in St Mary's Parish, paid by Robert Brewin — 3 0 0†

⟨These two Items are received by the Mayor⟩

Rogers Ruding Esquire for the Duck holmes in St Mary's Parish, Mrs Ward's Gift, paid by Walter Ruding Esquire — 3 0 0

The Proprietors of the Leicester Navigation late the Reverend Gerrard Andrews, out of the Learoes in St Mary's Parish, the Gift of Mr Billers — 12 0 0

Mr Moore (for Lewin's Heirs) out of a House in the Belgrave Gate 2 0 0
Mr Barry the like 2 0 0
Mr Francis Hayes—out of the Cranes . . 4 0 0
Reverend W. S. Lee out of the Crabtree Close 2 0 0
— 10 0 0

Mr Mansfield for Mr Lovell (the Heir of Mr Farmer) out of Houses in the Silver Street the Gift of Mr Bent to the Poor of St John's Hospital, payable the Sunday after St John	2 10	0
Mr Alexander Forrester, late Mr Benjamin Liquorish, late Mr Smith of Burbadge, for a House in the Belgrave Gate known by the Sign of the Joseph, in the Occupation of John Highton in Fee Farm per Annum	12	0
John Yates's Executors, late Augustin Heafford for a House call'd the Cock, in Fee Farm per Annum	6	8
Mr Hextall late Mr Taylor for a Messuage or Tenement late in the Occupation of Widow Moseley, in Fee Farm per Annum	16	0
Messrs Bellamy & Biggs (Executors of Yates) for a Messuage or Tenement late in the Occupation of Ellen Denshire, for another part calld the Cock, in Fee Farm per Annum—Sold to John Biggs	13	4
Mr John Clarke, late Mr Charles Bates, for a Tenement in the Occupation of Robert Withers, in Sanvy Gate, heretofore sold to Robert Roberts, in Fee Farm per Annum	5	0
Widow Vesie for a Messuage or Tenement in Sanvy Gate in her own Occupation per Annum due at Michaelmas	3 0	0
Widow Maslin, late Samuel Turlington, for a Messuage or Tenement in Sanvy Gate in Lease to Richard Scarboro' now in Maslin's Occupation per Annum due at Michaelmas	2 5	0
Thomas Armstrong late Ruding Vesie, for a Messuage in his own Occupation per Annum due at Michaelmas	2 10	0
Mr G. H. Vaughan for a Tenement in the Occupation of (blank) given to him by the Town during Pleasure	1	0

11e In Cank Street

Mr Stephen Dumelow, late Mr W. Sutton, for a Messuage or Tenement, late in the Occupation of Mr Armstrong & now of Mr Dumelow in fee farm per Annum	13	4

11f Saint Nicholas's & St Mary's Parishes

Alderman Sutton late Joseph Brown & William Spencer for Mary Spencer for a Tenement late John Orton's Land afterwards William Lewin's per Annum Alderman Sutton pays 7s and William Spencer 6s	13	0

George Carter's heirs for a Messuage or Tenement in Applegate Street, near the West Bridge called the Mytre & Key in the Occupation of Nutt in fee farm per Annum ⎫⎬⎭ 1 0 0

Mr John Throsby Parish Clerk, late Alderman Throsby, for a Messuage or Tenement in the High Street, heretofore called the Flying horse in Fee farm per Annum ⎫⎬⎭ 1 10 0

12 Other Rents of Lands and Tenements parcel of the Town and Manor of Leicester heretofore (amongst other things) given and granted unto the Mayor Bailiffs and Burgesses & their Successors in fee farm per Annum

Mr Slater, late Mr William Simpson, late Mr Alderman Sismey, for a piece of Ground in Church Gate, whereon a Messuage or Tenement lately stood in the Possession of George Stearesmore, by Lease per Annum due at Lady Day and Michaelmas ⎫⎪⎬⎪⎭ 3 13 6

Mr Edward Bracebridge for two Houses in Church Gate in the Occupation of the said Edward Bracebridge & Mr Brewin late a Piece of Ground in Fee Farm per Annum ⎫⎬⎭ 2 6

Mrs Kirke late Mr John Cartwright for a Tenement with the Appurtenances in Church Gate paid as directed on folio 25 [see Heading 14e] ⎫⎬⎭ 8 0

Widow Snapes, for a House or piece of Ground near St James's Chapel, called the Hermitage per Annum ⎫⎬ 1 0

Mr Cobley for a piece of Ground in All Saints' Parish called the Vineyard in his Occupation in fee farm per Annum ⎫⎬⎭ 4 0

Webster and Jordan, late Seal, for part of a piece of Ground calld the Lyon Yard, late the Land of Samuel Robinson deceased, in St Martin's Parish in Fee Farm per Annum ⎫⎪⎬⎪⎭ 2 6

Mr Samuel Bradley for Alderman Gamble for another part of the said Lyon Yard & a Messuage or Tenement in the Occupation of Mr Bradley in fee farm per Annum ⎫⎬⎭ 2 6

Mr Read 30s, Mr Cave 10s for a House & Barn call Sandby's Land, situate in the Saturday Market in their respective Occupations ⎫⎬⎭ 2 0 0

Mr John Clark for a piece of Ground in Sanvy Gate extending from thence to the Common Oven, whereon a house was built by William Carr, in fee farm per Annum ⎫⎬⎭ 2 6

Mr Samuel Miles for a piece of Ground near St Margaret's Church Yard where a house called the Farm house formerly stood, in Fee farm per Annum			6
Mr William Watts late Robert Hartshorn, for a House in Rice's Occupation near Frogmire Bridge, late a piece of Ground in Fee farm per Annum		1	0
Mr William Johnson 1od & Mr Oram, late Mr Kestin's 2d for a piece of Ground in Deadman's Lane in Fee farm per Annum		1	0

13 Other Rents of Corpus Christi Guild in Leicester, heretofore in Mr Archer's Collection & now Parcel of Lands and Tenements which Mayor etc purchased of Queen Elizabeth to them and their Successors for ever

Mr John Burrows Baker, late Taylor for a Messuage or Tenement with the Appurtenances in the High Street, in fee farm per Annum		13	4
William Moore late John Steers, for a Messuage or Tenement in High street heretofore known by the Sign of the Crown, in fee farm per Annum	1	1	8
Mr Thomas Phipps, late John Wildbore of Loseby, for a Tenement in Gallowtree Gate in the Occupation of (blank) & others in fee farm per Annum	1	6	8
Mr Edward Sutton late John Fossett for three Quarters of a Year's Rent of a Tenement near Frogmire Bridge on Lease per Annum	2	5	0
N.B. Mr Read received 5 Quarters of a Years rent instead of four ⟨Different next year⟩			
Mr Thomas Phipps, late David Oldham, for a Messuage or Tenement in Gallowtree Gate in his Occupation in fee farm per Annum		13	4
William Johnson, late Mr Marshall, late Parkinson, late Mr Burgess, late also Joseph Simpson for a Messuage or Tenement in Saturday Market, new built, in fee farm per Annum	1	0	0
James Wilby late Andrew Larratt for a Messuage or Tenement with the Appurtanences (Mr Cumbrey's) in fee farm per Annum	1	0	0

Mr Willey for a Messuage or Tenement in Town Hall Lane near St Martin's Church in the Occupation of Robert Pindar & William Brown in fee farm per Annum — 6 8

Mr Richards for a Messuage or Tenement in Parchment Lane now Swine's Market in the Occupation of (blank) and John Burgess in fee farm per Annum — 16 0

Josiah Wood (late Mrs Foster of Loughborough as Tenant of the Trust Estate of Joseph Clarke deceased) for certain Lands and Pasture Grounds in Loughborough aforesaid called Sadler's Lands—For the Trustees of the Hospital of Barrow upon Soar, in fee farm per Annum — 10 0

Mr Harris 6d Mr Cobley 3s Mr Lambert 2s Mr Haines (for Mr Iliff) 4s & Mr Nicholson 2s 6d for several Tenements near the East Gates (late Bernard Smalley for a Shop) in fee farm per Annum — 12 0

Mr John Reynolds, late Mr Hextall for a Messuage or Tenement on the East Side of East Gates, in his Occupation late Mr Hoods in fee farm per Annum — 12 0

(blank) Lomas for a piece of Ground heretofore a Garden in the Town Hall Lane over against the Town Hall now built upon heretofore Fletcher's Land now in the Occupation of John Ferryman in fee farm per Annum — 1 0

Mr John Slater, late Mr Goodhall for a Tenement in Parchment Lane, now called Swine's Market, heretofore a Stable, sometime since Mr Heyrick's Land, in Fee farm per Annum — 6 8

William Pochin Esquire late Mrs Cook of Barkby, late Robert James of Houghton for a Croft & Half Yardland at Barkby late Thomas Ilston — 6 8

William Pochin Esquire for three Quarters of a Yard land at Barkby, late the Land of Thomas Seal in fee farm per Annum — 6 0

Mr George Smith late Samuel Brookes, late Mr Philip Palmer, for a Messuage or Tenement in High Street in his own Occupation in fee farm per Annum — 6 0

Mr Inkersole late Mr Davie for a piece of Ground on the Nether Side of St James's Chapel Close where a House lately stood late the Land of William Boreman in Mr Davie's Occupation — 4 0

Mr Pares late Mr Ingle late Mr Tilly (for Lady Greasley) for a House & Garden in St Martin's Church Yard in his own Occupation in fee farm per Annum	13	4
Mr Perkins of Grantham for certain Lands & Leys in the Town fields of Gunnerby in the County of Lincoln in Fee Farm per Annum	6	8
(blank) Day late Samuel Gamble Esquire for a Close near the Cow Drift, late Mr Heyrick's Land in Fee Farm per Annum	10	0
Mr Hubbard late Mr James Nutt, late Mr Alderman Oliver for a Shop & other Buildings on the Eastside of Round Hill, now the Play House	1 0	0
The said Mr Hubbard, late Mr James Nutt, late the said Mr Oliver (being an Acknowledgment for erecting 4 Columns on the Corporation Ground belonging to the aforesaid Building)	1	0
Thomas Marshall for a House & Backside in Shamble's Lane heretofore Mr Harrison's in Fee farm per Annum	1	0

14a Other Rents of the Possession of the late Guild in Leicester, parcel of the Town Obiit Lands heretofore collected by Mr Tatham

Mr Rickards late Mr Goode late Mr Wilcox & heretofore Coates for a Messuage or Tenement in Applegate Street in fee farm per Annum	1 0	0
William Knight late William Johnson for a Messuage or Tenement in the said Street, late Hurst's in the Occupation of Mr Keightley and others	9	0
Mr Alderman Clarke late Mr Hubbard late Mr Higginson for a House in the said Street, late Slater's in fee farm per Annum	6	8
Mr Cobley for John Coates, late Randolph Ward, for a House in the said Street now or late in the Occupation of (blank) Cumberland	10	0
William Bassett late Mr Denshire & John Cooper for a Messuage or Tenement in Applegate Street in the Occupation of (blank) in Fee farm per Annum	8	0
Mr Cart for Mr Lee for a House in Applegate Street late David Winfields in the Occupation of Mr Chamberlin in Fee farm per Annum	7	0

	£	s	d
Widow Burley 10s & Mr Burley 4s for a Messuage or Tenement & Garden in Applegate Street formerly in the Occupation of Joseph Savage who kept the Swan in fee farm per Annum	14	0	
Mr Good late the Heirs or Executors of Mr Henry Smith deceased for a piece of Ground in the Occupation of Higginson called the Mayor's Old hall in Shamble's Lane	3	4	

14b   In the South Gates

	£	s	d
Mr Alderman H. Clarke, late Higginson, for a House & Garden near the South Gates in Lease per Annum	5	0	0
Mr John Springthorpe, late Mr Hitchcock, for a piece of Ground situate in the South Gate Street belonging to a House ruined in the late Wars, sold to Mr Hartshorn late in Conyers White's Occupation, now of John Gibson in fee farm per Annum		10	0
Mr Tuffley 4s Mr Bankart 6s for the Ground belonging to two Tenements situate in the same Street in Fee Farm per Annum		10	0
Mr Alexander Forrester late John Wood, for the Ground belonging to 2 Tenements now or late in the Occupation of (blank) Smith in Fee farm per Annum	1	5	0
Mr Thomas Cobley for Mr Farmer of London, for Tenements in Applegate Street, late John Coates, heretofore Mr Southworth's Land in the Occupation of (blank) in fee farm per Annum		10	0

14c   In the Gallowtree Gate

	£	s	d
Mr Burgess late David Hennell for a Messuage or Tenement on the Cornwall formerly known by the Sign of the Queen's Head now built upon in his Occupation in Fee farm per Annum	1	6	8
Mr Thomas Eames £1 & Mr W. Watts £1, late Mrs Lee, for a Messuage or Tenement on the Cornwall, heretofore known by the Sign of the Cinquefoil, in Mr Eames's & Mr Chamberlins Occupations	2	0	0
Widow Green, late John Clarke, late Mrs Timney, for a Messuage or Tenement heretofore known by the Name of the Buck's head in her own Occupation in Fee Farm per Annum		5	0

14d   In the Swine's Market

Mr Richards late John Major Esquire for a certain Garden heretofore sold to Michael Whatton of Bushby in Fee farm per Annum	2	0

14e   In the Belgrave Gate

Mr Bond for a Messuage or Tenement in his own Occupation late Mr Thomas Astle's Heirs in Fee farm per Annum — 16 0

The Widow of Joseph Grocock, for a House called the Star in her own Occupation late Richard Barry in Fee farm per Annum — 13 4

Henry Coleman Esquire late Mr John Lewin's Heirs for a Messuage or Tenement late the Land of Robert Gamble in the Occupation of the said Henry Coleman in Fee farm per Annum — 18 0

Mr Hubbard, late Mr Nutt, late Mr Oliver, for a Shop and Chamber situate on the Roundhill (now the Play House) in Fee Farm per Annum — 1 0 0

John Wright for a Messuage or Tenement now called the Crown & Cushion, late the Cannon in Fee farm per Annum — 12 0

Mr Yates's Executors 8s & of Mr Kell 14s for 2 Tenements late in the Occupation of George Chamberlin & Widow Abney & now of the said Mr Kell & Mr Copson in fee farm per Annum — 1 2 0

Mr Noble late Mrs Jordan for a House & Garden in Belgrave Gate in the Occupation of George White in Fee farm per Annum — 6 0

(blank) heretofore Mr Davie late Mr Alderman Dalby for a House in the same Street in (blank) Occupation in fee farm per Annum — 8 0

Mr Langdon late Mr Anthony Ward for an Orchard & Garden in the same Street now in Mr Langdon's Occupation in Fee farm per Annum — 6 0

Mr Alderman Burbidge late the Reverend W.S. Lee for an Orchard or Piece of Ground whereon stood a House called St John's late in Samuel Jarvas's Occupation since of Joseph Collett & now of (blank) Whittle in fee farm per Annum — 2 0 2

Messrs Bellamy & Biggs (Executors of John Yates) for part of Margaret Fletcher's Land in the Belgrave Gate, in fee farm per Annum	5	0
The Heirs of Mr Thomas Palmer for a House & Garden in the Church Gate late Mr Inge's in fee farm per Annum (paid as directed in the next Item)	5	0
Of them more for an Orchard in the Church Gate, once Mr Inge's Land, late Mr Smalley's in fee farm per Annum	2	0

The 2 last mentioned Rents & the Rent of 8s on folio 17 [see Heading 11f] paid thus

Mr Cartwright	8	9
Messrs Dalby & Deakin . . .	1	3
Mrs Bass	1	3
Do.	1	3
Thomas Barras for Miss Heard . .		7½
Frost		7½
Foulds	1	3
	15	0

14f   In Sanvy Gate

Mr Gutteridge for a Messuage or Tenement late in the Occupation of William Chamberlain in Fee farm per Annum	1	0	0
(blank) Dawson for (blank) White for a House & Garden in Fee farm per Annum		8	0
Mr Alderman H. Clark & Alderman Fisher heretofore Mr Smalley for a piece of Ground in Sanvy Gate belonging to the Corporation whereon was built a House in Consideration whereof a Lease was granted them for 41 Years	1	15	0
Matthew Johnson late Mr Barwell for a piece of Ground called Sadler's Close in Fee Farm per Annum		5	0
John Popplewell, late Levis, late Mr Edward Newberry for two more Tenements new erected in Sanvy Gate with a Spong of Ground belonging to the House by Lease per Annum due at Michaelmas	10	0	0

14g   Near St Margaret's Church

The Reverend Dr Walker late Mr Clayton Apothecary late Mr Cooper for a piece of Ground called St Margarets Bed lying in the Close late the Land of James Biggs in Fee farm per Annum	6

14h   Other part of Wilders's Rent

	£ s d

Mr Moore late Richard Walker Esquire for a Close near the Cow Drift in his own Occupation in Fee farm per Annum — 13 4

14i   Other Parts of Wilders's 2nd Lease

Mr John Baxter for a House in his Occupation in Soar Lane near Redcross Street late the Heirs of Mr Stockden of Great Glenn — 6 0

Mr Joseph Wheatley for Lord Scarsdale for a House & peice of Ground in the said Soar Lane late Briton's Land now in the Occupation of the said Joseph Wheatley in fee farm per Annum — 2 0

Late Mr Alderman Dalby for a House & Garden in Belgrave Gate in the occupation of (blank) late Heggs's Land — 8 0

Mr Pares for a Close in Archdeacon's Lane heretofore sold to John Mobbs in Fee farm per Annum — 6 8

Mr Henry King for Miss Warner of Humberstone for a House & Land there, in the Occupation of Denis Kirk in Fee farm per Annum — 5 0

Mr Taylor & Tompkin, late Thomas Ashwell for a Messuage or Tenement in Sanvy Gate heretofore sold to him & Jane Ward per Annum — 1 6 8

The Poor of Trinity Hospital for a Garden & piece of Ground near the Butt Close now built upon in the Tenure of Mr Samuel Clark & others in fee farm per Annum — 2 0

Mr Harrison late James & Thomas Cartwright for a House and Backside near St Margaret's Church in the Occupation of the said Mr Harrison in Fee farm per Annum — 8 0

Messrs Bellamy & Biggs (Executors of Yates) for a house & Garden in Belgravegate late the Land of Edmund Sutton, late in the Occupation of John Coe & now of (blank) Asher in fee farm per Annum — 3 4

Mr William Abell late Mr Barwell's Heir for a Tenement with the Appurtenances in Sanvy Gate now in the Tenure of Nathaniel Hunt in fee farm per Annum — 10 0

Mr John Clark for a Messuage or Tenement in Sanvy Gate heretofore Thomas Chettle's Land now or late in the Occupation of Richard Harcourt in fee farm per Annum — 6 8

Dr Vaughan late Sir Charles Halford for a Close near the
Humberstone Gate formerly sold to John Roe in Fee   }   12   0
farm per Annum

15 A Rentall of the Lands & Possessions of and belonging to the
College of the Blessed Virgin Mary over against the Castle of
Leicester heretofore demised by Queen Elizabeth to Edmund
Holt & by her Majesty granted to the Mayor etc & their Succes-
sors (amongst other things) in fee farm per Annum

William Hill Esquire heretofore Mr Hill Attorney at Law
for a Messuage or Tenement in Swine's Market now High   }   6   8
Street in Fee farm per Annum

Mr Hudson late Hannal Langton for part of a Messuage
or Tenement near the West Bridge in the Occupation of   }   2   0
the said Mr Hudson, in fee farm per Annum

Mr Day late Samuel Gamble Esquire late Ralph Wells for
a Close near Ailestone Highway, late the Land of Mr   }   5   0
Robert Heyrick in Fee farm per Annum

Mr Marshall late Mr Sharpe for a Garden or piece of
Ground on the Backside of a Messuage or Tenement near
the South Gates heretofore the Land of Hugh Watts, in   }   1   0
fee farm per Annum

Thomas Bruce for a Messuage or Tenement in Soar Lane
near Redcross Street in his own Occupation late the Land   }   10   0
of John Collinson, in fee farm per Annum

(blank) Pickard late Hudson Norton, late Pochin, 15d
Hunt for Mr Lambert 15d & Mr Bruce late Ward 2s 6d
for a Tenement in Soar Lane near Red cross Street sold to   }   5   0
John Underwood & late Thomas Derwick's & William
Wards

William Bassett late Mr Forman of Kirby for a House &
Garden in Soar Lane near Red Cross Street heretofore   }   12   0
Robert Stevenson's in fee farm per Annum

Mr Clayton, late Mr William Cooper Apothecary for a
Messuage or Tenement in Redcross Street & Garden in
Chaff lane adjoining to the said House in the Occupation   }   1   0   0
of Edward Daniel's Widow called the Old Mytre, in fee
farm per Annum

John Palmer 11s 7d & of the Widow of Brown of Desford 15s 1d for a Messuage or Tenement in Soar Lane near Redcross Street (late Robert Allen's) in fee farm per Annum	1	6	8
Mr Michael Payne for Onesiphorous Bonner late Robert Dingmore for a Messuage & Garden in Soar Lane near Redcross Street, heretofore sold to John Bonner, in fee farm per Annum		12	0
Mr Thomas Astell late William Tompson of Glenfield late Mr Hill for a Garden in Soar Lane otherwise Redcross Street in the Occupation of Thomas Frenham in fee farm per Annum			8
Mr Bankart for Mr Hall 5 4			
(blank) Dawson 5 4			
Mr Coltman (Slater) 5 4		16	0
For a piece of Ground late of Thomas Ward belonging to a Messuage or Tenement in the South Gates ruined in the late Wars & for a Croft in fee farm per Annum			
Mr Henry King late Mr Henry Mason heretofore Dr Cheshire for a piece of Ground adjoining to the Fryar Lane in Mr King's Occupation			4
The Churchwardens of St Mary for the Herbage of Saint Mary's Churchyard per Annum	3	5	0
Henry Callis for Nathan Wright Esquire for a Close called Sand Pit Close near Cow Drift Lane per Annum	1	0	0
The Governor's of Leicester Infirmary for St James's Chapel Close, in fee farm per Annum	1	6	8
Mr Alderman Sutton, late Joseph Bown, late Mr Denshire, for a House & Garden or Backside in the Parish of St Nicholas & near to the Talbott by Lease per Annum in the Occupation of (blank)	9	10	0
Joseph Cradock Esquire heretofore Mr Nathaniel Heyrick, for the Tythes & Tenths of all the Ground some time parcel of Dennet's Hall by Lease per Annum	3	0	0
Mr Denshire for a House & Garden in the said Parish of St Nicholas near the Applegate Street, late in the Occupation of Murfin in fee farm per Annum	1	0	0
Rogers Ruding Esquire for all the Vicarial Tythes, Tenths, Herbage & other Duties payable out of the Grounds & Parcel of the Lands belonging to the Westcotes by Lease per Annum	11	16	6

	£	s	d
Mrs Watts, Mr Unwin & Mr Peach for all the Tythes Tenths Herbage & other Dues belonging to the same payable out of the Close called or known by the Name of the South field & being Parcel of the Ground belonging to the Estate or Farm called Dennett's & Welch Hall by Lease per Annum	1	10	0
Mr Peach, Mr Hunt, Mr Unwin & Mr Cradock for the Tythes & part of Vicarial Tenths Herbage & other Duties belonging to Dennett's Hall being that which Mr Watt's bought	4	0	0
Rogers Ruding Esquire for part of Mr Fawnes being part of Dennett's Hall, Mary Mills etc	2	0	0
Rogers Ruding Esquire for other part of Dennett's Hall .	2	0	0
Mr William Lamb late Mrs Ashby's Heirs late Mrs Smalley for a Garden in Sanvy Gate in the Occupation of William Sands, in Fee farm per Annum		1	0
Joseph Hopwell (for the Heirs of Mrs Chettle) late William Willimott for a piece of Ground or Garden in the Occupation of the said Joseph Hopwell some time a Well Yard in High Street in fee farm per Annum		1	4
Mr Carrick for an Orchard or Garden in Silver Street at Will per Annum		2	0
Mr John Moore late Samuel Gamble Esquire for a Third part of a Close near Cowdrift in fee farm per Annum		4	0
The Poor of Trinity Hospital for part of Dovecoat Close beyond the West Bridge in the Occupation of (blank) in fee farm per Annum		1	6
Richard Hassold of Glenfield for a piece of Ground there late in the Occupation of John Carr, in fee farm per Annum			6
Mr Sutton (Coal Merchant) late John Brewin late Tyrringham Palmer for a Close near St Margaret's Cow Pasture heretofore Bennett's Land in the Occupation of (blank) in fee farm per Annum		3	4
Mr Goodman (for Joseph Cradock Esquire) late Mr Watts for certain Lands & Leys in the West Fields of Leicester heretofore the Land of Thomas Dennett Esquire in fee farm per Annum		2	6
The Poor of Trinity Hospital for a piece of Ground in the Burgesses Meadow called the Ladyacre, in fee farm per Annum		3	4

Rogers Ruding Esquire for a Close in Braunstone Gate late Mr Hunt's Land in fee farm per Annum	5	0
John Baxter, Baker, late Robert Hodson for a House & Close in Red cross Street	1 10	0
Thomas Bruce for a certain Tenement & Garden in Soar Lane near Red cross Street in his own Occupation by Lease per Annum	2 0	0
Dr Vaughan late Sir Charles Halford for a Garden in Swine's Market now Highstreet lately built upon in his own Occupation	1	2
Dr Vaughan late Sir Charles Halford for a Messuage in the same Street heretofore sold to Christopher Needham in his own Occupation	2	6
Mrs Bull for Sly 1s 8d Edmund Powers 1s 8d & Edward Webb 1s 8d for a Garden in Hotgate Street alias Thornton Lane late the Land of Mr Thomas Pares per Annum	5	0
Mr Alderman Watchorn late Alderman Peach late Alderman Mason for a Messuage or Tenement heretofore Mr Walker's in the Newarke of Leicester, late in the Occupation of (blank) Bayley in fee farm per Annum	1 6	8
Of him more for a House in the Newarke in his own Occupation late Dr Walker's in fee farm per Annum	13	4
Mr Goodman of Saddington (for Joseph Cradock Esquire) for two parts of Chamberlain's Land at Knighton in fee farm per Annum	12	4
Mr John Tebbutt of Bowden Magna for Land there, now or late in the Occupation of John Corrall in fee farm—It is three pieces of Hay Meadow called Leicester land	1	0
The Reverend George Coulton of Abkettleby late Mr John Herrick of Beaumont Leys for Lands in Sileby per Annum		6
Reverend Mr Lee late Mr Gulson late Mr Stedman of Glenfield for Land there, in fee farm per Annum		3

17 Other rent of the Town & Manor of Leicester Parcels of the Lands & Possessions of the Duchy of Lancaster part thereof being in the County of Leicester

Mr Poynton & Mr Slater 8s 4d each, late Mr Higgs for a Messuage or Tenement in Highstreet, heretofore of John Brookesby, late Mrs Hood, in fee farm per Annum	16	8

Mr Dyson for a Horse Malt Mill in Swines Market, now Highstreet, in fee farm per Annum	1	13	4
*William Loseby for the Town Gaol, by Order of Hall . [*Item struck out in original and "Gaol sold" written in margin]	3	0	0*

19   Other Rents received of new

Widow Groce late Widow Ogden late Mr Franks for a piece of Ground being part of the Town Wall situate near the Fryer Lane in fee farm per Annum	2	6
William Hudson late Hannell Langton, for two pieces of Land taken out of the Common Dunghill in the Lane near the Bridge, in fee farm per Annum		10
Mr Whittle late Abstinence Pougher for 2 Tenements in Parchment Lane now called Swine's Market late the Land of Mr John Herrick in fee farm per Annum	3	4

20   Other Rents for certain Lands purchased by the
                   Corporation & other Rents

Edward Sutton, late Mr Belton, for a Close of Pasture now two Closes late Mr Freake's Land near Leicester at Will per Annum	39	12	0
Mr John Mortimer, late Alderman Brown, for one Close called Freake's Ground near Leicester by Lease per Annum	43	10	0
Mr Alderman Beale late Augustine Heafford for a Cottage or Tenement situate near the Horse fair in his Occupation by Lease per Annum due at Michaelmas	2	5	0
Smart late Simeon Tomlinson for another Cottage or Tenement to the said Cottage or Tenement belonging by Lease per Annum	5	0	0
John Emmerson for Mr Alderman Gamble's Heir for the Water Lags now Vauxhall Garden, in fee farm per Annum		6	8
William Wood for part of a House called the White Swan in the Saturday Market now in the Occupation of the said Wood	2	0	0

21   Rents given to the School & other charitable Uses

His Majesty's Receiver General given by Queen Elizabeth out of the Honor of Leicester for the better maintaining the Head Usher of the Grammar School of Leicester	10	0	0

George Bosworth Esquire of Brampton one Annuity or Rent Charge payable out of the Manor of Theddingworth being the Gift of Sir Ralph Rowlett for maintaining the Under Usher of the said School late paid by Lord Althorpe	3	6	8
Mr John Iliff late Mr John Norris for one Annuity payable Yearly out of a Close in Abbey Gate call'd Abby Gate Close for the better maintaining the Head Usher in the Occupation of Mr Iliff per Annum	3	6	8
Mr Hudson for one Annuity payable yearly out of a piece of Ground called the Water Laggs to the Under Usher of the said School being the Gift of Thomas Clark per Annum	1	0	0
John Needham of Whetstone late Edward Sutton for certain Lands in the Lordship of Willoughby Waterless being Norris's Gift by Lease per Annum	12	0	0
Mr Mann for an Orchard or Garden in All Saint's Parish (purchased with £50 given by the first Countess of Devonshire for & towards the relief of the Poor of the Borough & the Poor of St Leonard for the Payment of £3 per Annum) by Lease per Annum	6	0	0
William Gillam for a Messuage & Close & one Yard land at Whetstone bought of John Baker Gentleman by the Corporation with the Money bequeathed by Christopher Tamworth Esquire for celebrating divine Service by Lease per Annum	44	5	0
Woolston Wigston late John Brewin for 40 acres of Land in the Forest of Leicester given by King Charles 1st of ever blessed Memory to the Poor of the Borough by Lease per Annum ⟨This is received by Mr Mayor⟩	35	0	0
Mrs Jordan, late Joseph Horton for part of the Burgesses Meadow per Annum	4	10	0
Mr Thomas Smart for a Close & Barn thereto belonging in Hangman Lane, which the Corporation purchased of Mr Speechley in Lease per Annum	37	0	0
Mr Pares payable yearly out of the Manor of Cotes Delville being the Gift of Mr Poultney to Charitable Uses	10	0	0
Mr Seal of Bushby late George Plummer of Evington for Lands in Bushby being the Gift of Mr Nidd to the Poor of Mountsorrel per Annum	42	0	0

T

Mr Stone for Sir Philip Vavasor being Mr Acham's Gift to the Poor of the Corporation out of the Manor of Asfordby alias Asterby in the County of Lincoln per Annum due at Michaelmas · · · · · · 9 0 0

Mr Thomas Coleman for himself & Tilley 13s 2d Thomas Gregory 6s & Joseph Hurst 2s 6d for certain Grounds in the South Gates belonging to two Tenements in the Occupation of (blank) being the Gift of Mr Hobby · · · 1 1 8

Mr Pares a Rent Charge issuing out of his House heretofore called the Parrot being the Gift of Mr Hugh Botham & paid on St Thomas's Day · · · · · · 2 0 0

Mr Whitehead of Belton in Rutlandshire for several Closes & Grounds there being the Gift of Mr Haines for charitable Uses late in Catwell's Occupation by Lease per Annum due at Michaelmas & Lady Day · · · 24 0 0

23 [No separate heading inserted]

Mr Thomas Eames late Mr Lee for Ground lately taken from the Sheeppens · · · · · · · 5 0

William Clarke late Mr Alderman Oliver for the like . 1 0 0

Mr Eames for the like, late (blank) Smalley . . . 10 0

Mr Burgess for the like, late Hannell, late paid by Mr Cramant · · · · · · · · 1 0 0

Mr Raworth for a piece of Ground adjoining to the West Bridge per Annum · · · · · · · 2 6

Total of the preceding folios & of this—£1565 2s 5d

29 Chief Rents belonging to St John & St Leonards to be paid at Michaelmas for the Use of the Mayor Bailiffs & Burgesses of the Borough of Leicester

The Wardens of Wigston's Hospital paid by Mr Pares . 1 4½

Mr Benjamin Gregory late Mr Stephens for a Messuage or Tenement in the Gallowtree Gate in his own Occupation late the Black Lyon · · · · · · · 6

The Right Honorable the Earl of Stamford for Thurmaston Mills · · · · · · · · 6 8

	£	s	d
George Wright Esquire heretofore Sir William Rawlinson, late Sir Henry Beaumont, for certain Lands at Oadby		5	11½
The Reverend Mr Rye for the Vicarage House in Oadby .		1	0½
(blank) Woodward of Oadby for certain Lands there calld Marshall's Lands			6
Mrs Gutteridge late William Cook for a House in Sanvy Gate late Webster's Land			9

30   Chief Rents belonging to Corpus Christi Guild

	£	s	d
Mr Carrick, late Mr Belton, late Mr Townsend's Executors for a Tenement in Silver Street in his Occupation per Annum		4	0
Mrs Daniel for a House in Silver Street in the Occupation of Vasier & Agar		3	0
Mr Nutt late Mr Orme for a Messuage or Tenement in Gallowtree Gate		2	2
Mr Fox's Executors, late Cradock Hartopp Esquire late Mr Cradock for a Messuage or Tenement in the Occupation of Miss Ascough & Mr Fox		2	0
Mr Higginson for a house in his Occupation & Messrs Cape & Hodgkin's per Annum		2	0
Mr Iliff, late Simon Iliff of Oadby for certain Lands late Bliss's Land			10
Manton Reynolds for a piece of Ground in Parchment Lane now called Swine's Market late the Land of Mr Tobias Heyrick in the Occupation of (blank) Walker			3
Lord Stamford for a Messuage or Tenement in the Red cross Street in the Occupation of William Goodrich & paid by him		1	0
Mr Bassett of Countesthorpe late Mrs Freer late John Simons Esquire for a certain House in the said Street late the land of Briton & Suffolk			8
Mr Goode, Hosier, for a Messuage or Tenement near St Nicholas's Church in his Occupation late Mr Briton's Land		1	0
Mr Neal, Pawnbroker, late Stubbs for Slater, late Mrs Brown for a Garden in Deadman's Lane		5	0
Mr Thomas Chapman for a Messuage or Tenement in Highcross Street calld the Peacock in the Occupation of John Springthorpe		3	0

William Johnson 10d & Mr Oram 2d for a Cottage in Deadman's Lane per Annum	1	0
Thomas Brothers, late William Watts for a house in Red cross Street late in the Occupation of John Dean & now of (blank) per Annum		4
Mr John Shipley late Widow Groce for a Garden in Deadman's Lane		6
Mr Joseph Springthorpe, late Widow Davie for a Tenement in Highcross Street late in the Occupation of John Pratt & now of George Smith per Annum	1	0
Mr Alderman Oldham for a Messuage or Tenement in High Street per Annum	14	0
Mr Willows for his House in the same Street . . .		6

⟨Next item should be before this⟩

(blank) Leeson late Edward Powers for his House in High Street late the Land of George Heggs per Annum	9	6
William Hill Esquire & James Wilson for a Tenement now divided into two Tenements in the High Street in the Occupation of the said Wilson & (blank) Weston	3	0
Mr Burton late Mr Cox for a Tenement in High Street in Mr Burton's Occupation	3	6
The Poor of Trinity Hospital for a Barn called Clarke's Barn		6
The Heirs of Alderman Simpson for a Tenement in Cank Street in Mr Corts Occupation per Annum	1	0
Mr Alderman Johnson for a House in Belgrave Gate in the Occupation of Edmund Wright per Annum	3	0
Mr Clement Stretton for a House in Cank Street late in Mr Alderman Bates's Occupation		$8\frac{1}{2}$
William Herrick Esquire late Sir John Whatton Knight for a Close called Shire Hall Orchard in All Saint's Parish in the Occupation of (blank) Orton		6
Mr Michael Payne for a Messuage or Tenement in the Loseby Lane in the Occupation of Mr Thomas Watchorn		$10\frac{1}{2}$
Mr Thomas Marston late Mr Barwell for a Messuage or Tenement in Humberstone Gate in his Occupation	3	0
Mrs Harris late the Reverend Mr Lambert for a Messuage or Tenement in Gallowtree Gate known by the sign of the Angel part of which is in the Occupation of Robert Haines	2	0

	£	s
Mr Cornish late Mr William Simpson for a Messuage or Tenement near the East Gates, in the Occupation of Mrs Stone per Annum	1	0
Mr Alderman Mansfield late Cooke Lovell, late Rogers Ruding Esquire for a Messuage at the Corner of Fryar Lane lately known by the Sign of the George in the Occupation of Mr Thomas Farmer per Annum	4	0
Mrs Bates for a Messuage in the High Street in her own Occupation per Annum	2	0
Mr Woodford for a Tenement there late Mark Valentine's	2	0
Mr Woodford late Arthur Hesilrige Esquire for a Messuage or Tenement in High Street in his Occupation late Henshaw's Land	4	0
Henry Callis late Alderman Oliver for a Tenement in Gallowtree Gate in his own Occupation	7	6

31   Chief Rents belonging to St Margaret's Guild

	£	s
Mr Alderman Oldham late William Herrick Esquire for a Garden in Ironmonger's Lane near the Saracen's Head late Bent's per Annum	1	0
Edward Harris for a Messuage or Tenement in Highcross Street at the Corner of Bakehouse Lane in his own Occupation	1	4
Mr Cowdall for Rogers Ruding Esquire for a piece of Ground in the Soar Lane call the Mott Yard per Annum	6	0
Mr J. B. Oliver for a Messuage or Tenement in Belgrave Gate called the Unicorn in his Occupation		4½
The Widow of H. Coleman Esquire late Mr J. Moore (for Lewin) for a House in Belgrave Gate in Mrs Coleman's Occupation per Annum		9
Thomas Withers late Sarson & Foulgham for a Tenement in the same Street, late Sutton's Land		6
Widow Bailey late William Herrick Esquire for a Tenement in the Humberstone Gate called the Fox & Goose in her occupation		6
Mr William Firmadge late Mr Bass for a Barn in the Church Gate, late W. Inge Esquire	1	3½

Mr Andrews late Ludlam for a Close near the Spittal house called the Bailiff's Close per Annum	1	0
Mr Johnson for a Messuage or Tenement near the West Bridge in the Occupation of Messrs Watchorn per Annum	4	0
The Wardens of Wigston's Hospital for a piece of Ground called the Normandy per Annum Paid by Mr Pares		6
Mr William Watts for a House in Church Gate called the Black Swann late Manley's Land in the Occupation of Samuel Wright's Widow		9
Alexander Forester late George Rayson Pratt for a Messuage in All Saint's Parish in the Occupation of (blank)	1	1½
The Widow of H. Coleman Esquire late Mr J. Moore for Mr Lewin for a Messuage or Tenement in Belgrave Gate in the Occupation of said Henry Coleman's Widow		6
Do. for Do. in Do. in the Occupation of Do. . . .	3	4
Mr Dowley formerly Joseph Wallin, late Mr Pares, late Robert Page for a Piece of Ground taken out of the Pinfold		4
Mr Bankert heretofore Alderman Thomas Chapman for a Tenement in the South Gates heretofore called the Grey Hound	4	0
Mr Richard Denshire late Mr Bonner of Ailestone for a Messuage or Tenement in the South Gates late Mr Bennett's Land in the Occupation of Mr Thomas Wood		10
The Poor of Trinity Hospital for a House in the South Gates in the Occupation of (blank) late Foster's Land		9½
Mr Heyrick for a piece of Ground in Burgesses Meadow late the Land of John Gilford	10	0
Mr William Harris late Samuel Cooper for a Messuage or Tenement in Harris's Occupation late the Land of Dennett Abney		4½
Mr John Clark for the Reverend Mr Franks late Mr Davie late Mr Wanley for a Tenement in North Gate Street & for 2 Tenements now or late in the Tenure of John Harcourt	1	2
Mr Wheatley late Mr Henry Clarke for a Shop now a House near the South Gates once Moreton's Land in his own Occupation per Annum		5
Mr Ogden for a House in High street once Olton's Land per Annum	3	6

Mr Stephens late Mr Topp for a House in Highcross Street in the Occupation of Mr Stephens late Robert Chettle per Annum — 2 0

Mr Alderman Sutton late Mr Wightman for a Close in Braunstone Gate — 6

William Scott (for Mr Turvill) for a House in Highstreet in his own Occupation 11d & for 2 Hens & a Capon 1s — 1 11

Mr Johnson for a House near the West Bridge called Babington's Land — 9

Mr Alderman Clark late Mr Pawley of Croxton for a Messuage or Tenement in Applegate Street now in his own Occupation — 6

Nathan Tuffley late Tebbs of Birstall late Turlington for a House in Birstall late the Land of John Reynolds now or late in the Occupation of the said Nathan Tuffley — 1 0

Mr Bassett late Wells for a House in Chaff Lane near Redcross Street once Gulson's Land 9d & for a Hen 3½d in the Occupation of Thomas Holyland — 1 0½

Mr Higginson for a Messuage in the Saturday Market in the several Occupations of the said Higginson & Messrs Cape & Hodgkin — 6 8

Mr Alderman Johnson for Land, late Botham's, near Soar Lane & for three Capons & two hens — 4 0

Rogers Ruding Esquire for a Close in Braunstone Gate . — 9

Mr Joseph Coltman late Billars for a House in Hotgate gate Street alias Thornton Lane 3d & for a Hen 3½d & for a Garden late a Swine's Stye — 1 0½

Joshua Howes late Wigston late Stevenson, for a House near the South Gates called the Blue Boar, late Rudworth's Land 9d for 2 hens 7d & for a Shop near the South Gates 6d — 1 10

William Burley late John Wrider for a Tenement over against All Saint's Church late Mr Rudyard's Land in the Occupation of (blank) — 2 3

Mrs Saintjohn late Sir Charles Halford for a Messuage in High Street late Mr Bonner's House — 6

Mr Alderman Clark late Pawley for a House in the Applegate Street once Birstall's in his own Occupation 10d & for 2 Hens & a Capon — 1 8

Mr Alderman Simpson's Heirs for a Messuage at the Upper End of the Belgrave Gate late Neal's Land per Annum	1	6
Mr Woodland for a Close in All Saints' Parish near Elbow Lane late Cradock's Land per Annum	1	8
John Richards for a House & Land in the Northgate Street late Bodyman's in the Occupation of (blank) per Annum		6
Mr Nicholson 3d Dorman & Turlington 10d for a certain House in Northgate Street late Woodford's per Annum	1	1
Mr Tuffley late Edward Davie for Lands in Southgates in his Occupation 2s & for a Garden 10d	2	10
Mrs Saintjohn late Sir Charles Halford for a House in High Street late Needham's & Bailey's Land		4
(blank) Smith late Mr Mortimer of Narborough for a House in South Gate Street, late Mr Alderman Joseph Taylor		6 8
Joseph Springthorpe late Joseph Watson's Widow late Sir Charles Halford for a House in Highstreet near the Horse Malt Mill		6

33 Rentall by Lammas Tythes due Yearly to the Mayor Bailiffs & Burgesses for divers Grounds in St Mary's Parish in Possession of the College of St Mary over against the Castle of Saint Mary Leicester

Thomas Coleman late Mrs Wood late Richard Weston for Dovehouse Close near the Newark of Leicester late Hickling per Annum	1	4
Mr Inkersole late Mr Davie late William Frank's Esquire for a Close near St James's Chapel Close called Archer's Close	1	0
The Governors of the Infirmary for St James Chapel Close Tythes	1	0
Nathan Wright Esquire for the Tythe of Bennington's Close called Sand Pit Close & Meadow per Annum	1	0
Mr Alderman Sutton for a Close near Braunstone Gate per Annum		6
Nathan Wright Esquire late James Mason for a Close late two Closes called Sandpit Close & Meadow over against St James's Chapel Close per Annum	1	8

Thomas Coleman late Mrs Wood late Weston, for Land near the Grange once Birstall's Land per Annum	1	0
Thomas Coleman late Mrs Wood for a Close near James's Chapel Close late Moreton's Land per Annum		10
Thomas Coleman late Mrs Wood for Seth King's Land part of the above Close		6
Mr Lowdham late Mr Astle for Miss Weightman's late Mr Iliff for a Close near the Paradise Close		4
Mr E. Davie late W. Franks Esquire for a piece of Ground called the Kiln late Cadmann's near St James's Chapel Close		4
Mr E. Davie for Cadmann's Land near St James's Chapel Close per Annum		10
Mr John Lacey late Joseph Wilkins for an Orchard on the Backside of a House late Davie's in the South Gates late the Land of Hugh Watts Esquire		6
(blank) Day late Samuel Gamble Esquire for a Close near Ailestone Highway late Mr Heyrick		8
Of him more for a Close near the same Highway . .		4
Of him more for another Close near Archer's Land in St Mary's Parish		10
(blank) late Joseph Fisdale, late William Pochin Esquire late Richard Weston for a piece of Ground near St Mary's Mill calld the Holmes late Manley's Land per Annum, late Simpson Hosier deceased	1	8
Nathan Wright Esquire late the Heirs of Mr John Palmer Attorney for a Close near Aileston Highway called Sand-pit Close in the Occupation of Henry Callis		10
Nathan Wright Esquire late William Wright Esquire for part of the said Close called Sand pit Close in the Occupation of Henry Callis per Annum	1	0
Rogers Ruding Esquire for a Close in Braunstone Gate late Hunt's Land		8
Of him more for a Close called College Close in St Mary's Parish late Mr Hunt's Land		4
Mr Edward Harrison late Cart at the Bull's Head for a Close late Brook's Land in St Mary's Parish late Bennett's called Duck Holmes per Annum	2	2
Mr W. Simpson for a Close called the Tippetts per Annum	13	4

	£	s	d
Thomas Chatwyn for the Tythe of the Newarke Mills per Annum		2	0
William Knight for a Garden or piece of Ground in Millstone Lane late Armston's Land per Annum			4
Joseph Bruce for Land in Chaff Lane late Halls . .			10
The Widow of Thomas Hall late Francis Ward for a Backside belonging to his House in South Gates now or late in the Occupation of the Widow of Thomas Ward per Annum			6
(blank) Foulds late Mr Newton for a House in Thornton Lane late Mr Thompson's			4
William Johnson late Paling for Booth's Land in Shamble's Lane			4
The Reverend Mr Pigott an Acknowledgement for the House adjoining the Freeschool 2s 6d or 3s varied annually		3	0
Mr Jackson an Acknowledgement for an Encroachment in putting out 2 Windows from his House on the Cornwall late in Mr Alderman Chambers's Occupation per Annum		1	0
Thomas Chatwyn for the Tythes of the Newark Mills .		16	0
Messrs Johnson & Jordan 1s each, for the Tythes of the Gosling Closes		2	0
Mr Alderman Fisher for the Tythes of the North wind Mill .		2	0
Mr Jordan late Darbyshire late Joseph Horton for the Tythe of a Piece of Grass Ground in the Mary Meadow		6	0
Mr Fisher, Mr Johnson, Mr Cooper, & Mr Stretton each 7s 4½d for the Tythe of the Beadhouse Meadow	1	9	6
John Hartshorn for the Tythe of a Piece of Grass Ground in the Mary Meadow	(blank)		
Thomas Chatwyn for the Tythe of a piece of Ground belonging to the Mill	(blank)		
Mrs Sutton for laying Planks & setting Posts in the river Soar during Pleasure	(blank)		

The End of the Rentalls

36   Fines and other accidental Receipts

	£	s	d
Samuel Knight for his Freedom		5	0
William Hardy for Do.		10	0
Benjamin Page for Scot & Lot		1	0
John Dudgeon for his Freedom		5	0

William Stevenson for his Freedom	20	0	0
Richard Glover for Do.	20	0	0
John Watts Do.	20	0	0
John Walker Do.	20	0	0
Richard Bates Do.	20	0	0
Robert Thompson Do.	20	0	0
Thomas Miller Do.	20	0	0
Henry Mansfield Do.	20	0	0
James Jones Do.		5	0
Messrs Read & Clark last preceding Chamberlains being Moneys ordered by Common Hall to be paid to the Chamberlains in each Year on the Commencement of their Office	100	0	0
Of Do. the balance of Accounts due from them over and above the said £100	295	1	$7\frac{1}{4}$
Arrears transferred by them exclusive of the said Balance .	175	7	7
Mr Mansfield one Year's Interest of £1100 3 per Cent Consolidated Bank Annuities due 5th July 1793	33	0	0
A part of Mr Haines's Gift to two Scholars of Lincoln College Oxford which has not been paid this Year—There being no Student to claim it—These Accountants must therefore give Credit for that part of it here, having been allowed the Payment of the whole £24 among the Charitable Gifts	6	0	0
Mr John Fox (by Order of Hall) being a Fine directed to be paid by him for refusing to serve the Office of Chamberlain	20	0	0

Total of the first Folios brought forward	1565	2	5
Total of the last Pages & of this . .	805	4	$8\frac{1}{4}$
Total Receipts	2370	7	$1\frac{1}{4}$

[End of Receipts]

[Payments start here]

1 [No separate heading inserted]

Paid Mr Hart at the Audit for a Broad Arrow . . .		1	0
Acquittance for the same			6
Paid Mr Hart, the Receiver, for one whole Year's Rent of the Sheeppens, due at Michaelmas	4	0	0

Paid him more for Singleton's Lease	2	12	8
To Shops taken down		11	6
Paid him more for St Margaret's Guild	1	13	5½
To him more for Corpus Christi Guild		7	9
To him more for Luskin's Lease		2	0
To him more for divers chief Rents of the Town . .		7	8
To him more for a Close late Webster's Land . .		1	0
To him more for a Close near the Horse Fair . . .		3	4½
To him more for Corpus Christi Guild		11	9
To him more for a Close late Hallam's		1	0
To him for an Acquittance of the said Money . . .			4

To him more for a Chief Rent for the Shops under the
Gainsborough } 2 6

To him more for a Shop in Richard Wagstaff's Occupation . 1 0

Paid Mr Hart, His Majesty's Receiver, for one whole
Year's Rent out of Lands & Tenements belonging to St
John & St Leonards in or near the Borough of Leicester,
heretofore Mr Harvey & Mr Tatham's Lease & in } 31 12 5
Countesthorpe & Humberstone Syston Mills etc & the
White Horse for one Year's rent due at Michaelmas last

Paid to the said Receiver for Lands & Tenements belonging to the late Guild called St Margaret's Guild in Leicester Town obiit Lands Vicars Close heretofore in the } 42 18 1
Occupation of Arthur Tatham for a Year's Rent due at
Michaelmas last

Paid him more for a Parcel of Land in Possession of the
late Guild called Corpus Christi Guild for one Year's } 14 12 6
Rent due at Michaelmas

Paid him more for certain Lands & Tenements chief &
Lammas Tythes parcels of the Possessions of the Blessed
Virgin Mary over against the Castle of Leicester for a } 20 8 6
year's rent due at Michaelmas last

Paid to the Receiver for certain Tenements in the Newarke
of Leicester } 3 16 1

3   At an Audit formerly held at the Sign of the
Horse & Trumpet by Mr Hart

Paid to the King's Receiver for two Tenements in the
Swine's Market in the Occupation of (blank) due at } 2 10 0
Michaelmas last

Paid him more for the Malt Mills in the Swine's Market in the Occupation of Mr Carter paid by John Dyson	1	13	4
Paid him more for the Shambles & Drapery in Leicester due at Michaelmas last	8	13	4
Paid him more for the Gainsborough Shop & Sheds & for the Saturday Market which the Mayor Bailiffs & Burgesses purchased of Mr Britton for one whole Year due at Michaelmas last	4	8	8

4   Fees and other Payments this year

Paid Joseph Burbidge Esquire his year's Salary according to ancient Custom	13	6	8
Paid him more out of the Rent of the Gosling Closes by Order of Common Hall	13	6	8
Paid him more being the Additional annual Salary to the Mayor 1713	20	0	0
Paid him more by Order of Common Hall in 1736 . .	40	0	0
Paid him more by Order of Common Hall in 1769 . .	50	0	0
Paid him more being Coal & Capon Money . . .	5	11	6
Paid Edmund Wigley Esquire, Recorder, his Year's Salary due at Michaelmas	40	0	0
Paid the Town Clerk for his Year's Salary . . .	5	0	0
More the Town's free Gift	2	13	4
For the Rental	2	0	0
For proclaiming Fairs & Markets		14	0
For the Commission for the Year		14	8
For taking the Coroner's Inquest	1	0	0
For the Sessions due at Michaelmas only . . .		6	8
For the Book of Payments		4	6
For making up the Accounts	3	7	2
For a Ribbon for the Charter		2	0
For the Letter of Attorney		11	4
For Pens & Paper		13	4
Paid Mr Pigott, Head Schoolmaster, the Town's free Gift during Pleasure	16	0	0
Paid the Reverend J. D. Ross, Head Usher, the Town's free Gift during Pleasure	8	0	0
Paid the Under Usher, the Town's free Gift during Pleasure	3	0	0

More the Town's free Gift during Pleasure . . .	5	0	0
More by Order of Hall in 1781 on Condition of his taking poor Children free of Entrance	5	0	0
Paid the Reverend J. Gregory his Year's Salary as Lecturer of the said Borough during Pleasure	20	0	0
More by Order of Common Hall as Vicar of St Martins Church during Pleasure	10	0	0
More as Vicar of All Saint's during Pleasure . . .	10	0	0
Paid the Reverend Thomas Robinson as Vicar of St Mary's during Pleasure	10	0	0
Paid the Reverend Robert Burnaby as Vicar of St Margaret's the like	10	0	0
Paid the Reverend John Anderson as Vicar of St Nicholas's the like	10	0	0
Paid the Macebearer his Year's Salary & for burning Pipes	7	9	8
Paid him more as Inspector of the Market for one Year .	2	12	0
More his Additional Salary	5	0	0
More his Additional Salary ordered by a Common Hall to be paid to him for rendering his Assistance to the Chamberlin's etc.	20	0	0
Paid him more for 3 Seals		3	0
Paid the 4 Serjeants at Mace their Salary . . .	32	0	0
Paid them a Year's Additional Salary	8	0	0
Paid the Cryer his Wages & for sweeping the Town Hall & Gainsborough	1	13	4
Paid him more for lighting Fires at the 'Change . .	1	1	0
Paid him more for cleaning the Carpets & Cushions . .		5	6
Paid the Beadle his Year's Salary for sweeping the Gates & Weeding the Town Hall Yard	6	0	0
Paid the Cryer & Beadle to prevent them going about with their Christmas Box		4	0
Paid the Cryer & Beadle for Attendance at the Assizes .		2	0
Paid for two Pairs of Shoes for the Cryer & Beadle . .		15	0
Paid the Library keeper her Salary	3	0	0
Paid the Waites their Salary, there being only three Waites for the three first Quarters & 4 the last . .	9	15	0

Paid Miss Greatorex the Organist her Salary ending at May day	10	0	0
Paid Miss Valentine the like	10	0	0
Paid the Subscription to the Infirmary	10	10	0
Paid towards the Horse Race Town Purse . . .	10	10	0
Paid Robotham his Salary for mending the 'Change Clock .	2	2	0
Allow'd the Chamberlins the Auditors Dinners . .	20	0	0
Paid the Bailiff of the Augmentation for Land due to (blank) at Michaelmas & Acquittance		7	4
Paid to the Bailiff of Merton College in Oxford for one chief Rent issuing & payable out of St John's & St Leonard's in or near the Borough of Leicester		1	3
Paid the Wardens of the Company of Taylors the Annual rent of		1	8
Paid for tolling the Bell on St Michael's Day . . .		1	0
Paid the Halbert Men for walking the Fair & cleaning the Armour on the Fair Day		10	0
Paid Mr Lucas a chief Rent out of the Gainsborough Taxes deducted now William Morehead Esquire due 10th October	5	18	6
Paid Lady Fitzwilliam a Year's Rent for the South Fields due at Michaelmas Taxes deducted	4	7	10
Paid for Holly & Ivy used at the Town Hall . . .		2	6
Paid the Clerk of St Mary's for washing the Chancel .		2	6
Do. when the Chancel was repaired		2	0
Paid Mrs Latham for the Tythes of the Bowling Green House	1	5	1½
Paid the Poor of Trinity Hospital a Year's Rent of that part of the Garden adjoining the Bowling Green House which belongs to the Hospital & which was given to it by Mr Hinman & rented by the Corporation	2	0	0
Paid for drawing Drink at the Venizon Feast . . .		2	0
Paid Mr Pares for an Acquittance for the Earl of Huntingdon's Gift			8
Paid the Lottery Money towards putting out a Boy Apprentice	5	0	0
Paid the Lamplighter his Christmas Box . . .		1	0

Paid the Clerk of Assize his Fee at two Assizes . .	1	6	8
Paid for cleaning the Fishhouse etc.		4	0
Paid Messrs Stevenson & Oliver next succeeding Chamberlains being Moneys ordered by Common Hall to be paid to the Chamberlins in each year on the Commencement of their Office	100	0	0
Paid for the Mayor's Newspaper	6	0	0
Paid for Coals & Kids used at the Town Hall & 'Change .	5	4	3
By Loss in Coals for the Poor	25	4	8½
Paid the Beadle for sweeping after the Fairs . . .	1	2	0
Paid for Playing the Engines twice	1	4	0
Paid for repairing Do. & Oil.		4	4
Paid for Wine Biscuits & Ale at the Assizes . . .	2	17	0
Paid for Ale at the Visitation of the Schoole . . .		6	0
Stamp Receipts for Bills of Tradesmen etc. . . .	(blank)		
Paid for sweeping Chimnies		12	6
Paid Clark for making & mending Fish Nets . . .	2	11	8
Paid Hartshorn for Do.		6	0
Paid Samuel Ward for clatting in the Pasture . . .		8	0
Paid for Attendance & Weights at the Cheese Fairs at Michaelmas & in May	2	12	0
Paid Joseph Burbidge Esquire for Postage of Letters in his Mayoralty	(blank)		
Paid the Grand Jury for 2 Quarter Session Dinners . .	10	10	0
Paid the Constables for the same	3	0	0
Paid the 2 Bellmen their Salary	10	10	0
Paid the Town Servants for their trouble at the Fairs the Sums collected by the Tolls this Year being not sufficient to pay them		7	0
Paid the Cryer for crying several times		5	6
Paid cleaning Snow from off the leads of St Mary's Chancel		4	0
Paid the Cryer etc for attendance at the 'Change to try Weights and Measures	1	0	0
Paid Do. for killing Dogs by Order of the Mayor . .	1	10	0
Paid Throsby his Salary for attendance as Macebearer .	25	14	6
Paid the Town Servants for driving the Beast from the Gallow tree Gate—two fair Days & 2 Market Days	3	4	0

Paid by Order of Hall the Corporations Subscription for the Relief of the Widows and Orphans of Soldiers — 52 10 0

Paid Mr Lewin, by Order of Hall 80 0 0

Paid Mrs Cammack's Legacy to the Poor of St John's Hospital which was laid out in erecting 2 Houses on their Land — 50 0 0

Paid Mr Pocklington by Order of Hall 21 0 0

Paid Mr Lowdham the Solicitor on account . . . 100 0 0

Paid Mr Read the late Chamberlain being the Salary allowed to the Bellmen which was omitted to be charged in his Accounts — 10 10 0

Paid Mr Heyrick's Bill for soliciting an Act for the Establishment of a House of Industry in Leicester—the Plan being abandoned after the Act was Drawn — 55 0 0

By Mr Hurst's arrear appearing on Inspection of his Receipts to be less than what was charged in the Books — 1 10 0

Paid the Cryer & Beadle on St Thomas's Day . . 5 0

7   Tradesmens Bills

No.		£	s.	d.
1	Mr Deakin	19	12	0
2	Mr Johnson	1	4	4
3	Mr Newcomb	1	18	2½
4	Mr Webster	2	12	6
5	Mr Lockwood	13	14	11
6	Mr Cook	6	18	6
7	Miss Coleman	1	10	1
8	Mr Firmadge	24	14	11
9	Mr Parsons	3	3	10½
10	Mr Bishop	50	15	8
11	Mr Hough	33	1	9
12	Mr Gregory	32	5	8
13	Mr Palmer	16	4	3
14	Mr Heyrick	23	6	1
15	Mr Parrott	31	8	8
16	Mr Reid	8	1	3
17	Mr Jackson	1	3	0
18	Mr Elliott	1	19	2½
19	Mr Read		10	6
20	Mr Raynes		16	1
21	Mr Burbidge		17	6
22	Mr Mallett	5	1	4

U

23	Mr Mark Oliver	. . . .	2	6
24	Mr Webster	. . . .	1 17	4
25	Mr Horner	. . . .	8 16	9
26	Mr Lewin	. . . .	1 17	6
27	Mr Turner	. . . .	9	0
28	Mr Hall	. . . .	16 10	7
29	Casual Bill	. . . .	5 4	0

8   Levies

Paid several Levies for the Highways Church & Poor Tythes of St Mary's Meadow }	1 16 0

9   Allowance for Land tax at 4s in the Pound

To Land tax at the Bowling Green House . . .	1 14	8
To Do. for Gainsboro' & Sheeppens	1 1	0
To Messrs Bellamy & Biggs	4	0
To Mr Cristey late Abney	4	0
To Mr Chatwyn	1 6	4
To Mr Alderman Fisher	1 4	6
To Mr William Abell	6	6
To Mr Alexander Forrester	6	0
To Mr John Moor	4	0
To Mr Higginson	4	0
To Mr Forrester & Johnson	5	0
To Thomas Bothomley	5	0
To George Luck	10	0
To Mr Mansfield, late Oliver, late Towers . . .	4	0
To Messrs Watts & Dixon	4	0
To Thomas Whithers	4	0
To Shuckburgh Ashby Esquire	6	0
To George Sheffield 13s	(blank)	
⟨Rent not paid⟩		
To Mr John Moor	8	0
To Mr Tuffley	4	0
To Mr Alderman Johnson	5	0
To Mr Bankart	4	0
To Mr Fosbrooke	4	0
To Mr Clay Hextall	4	0
To Mr John Moor	5	0
To Mr Foulgham, Billings etc.	4	0
To the Navigation Company late the Reverend Gerard Andrews }	8	0

To George Carter's Widow 4s . . . . . (blank)
   ⟨No rent paid⟩

	£	s	d
To Mr John Throsby		6	0
To Mrs Reid		6	0
To Mr Moor (late Steers)		4	0
To Mr Phipps late Wildbore		5	0
To Mr William Johnson		4	0
To Mr James Wilby		4	0
To Mr Richards.		4	0
To Mr Hubbard late Alderman Oliver		4	0
To Mr Forrester		5	0
To Mr John Burgess		5	0
To Mr Thomas Eames & Mr Watts		8	0
To Mr Hubbard, late Nutt, late Alderman Oliver . .		4	0
To Mr Alderman Burbidge, late the Reverend W. S. Lee .		8	0
To Mrs Gutteridge late Mr Cook		4	0
To Taylor & Tompkin		5	0
To Mr Clayton, late Mr Cooper		4	0
To Mr Callis, late Nathan Wright Esquire . . .		4	0
To the Governors of the Infirmary		5	0
To Mr Denshire		4	0
To Mr Baxter		6	0
To Mr T. Bruce		1	10
To Mr Alderman Watchorn, late Alderman Peach . .		5	0
To Mr Cave, late Dyson, late Cooper		6	6
To Mr John Mortimore	4	3	4
Mr Edward Sutton	3	0	0
Paid the Land tax for St Mary's Fields & Meadow . .	50	10	0
Paid Land-tax for Houses in Sanvy gate . . .		4	8

11   Charitable Gifts

	£	s	d
Paid the Gift of Queen Elizabeth to the Head Usher . .	10	0	0
Paid the Gift of Sir Ralph Rawlett	3	6	8
Paid the Gift of Mr Norris	3	6	8
Paid the Gift of Mr Clarke	1	0	0
Paid the Gift of Mr Norris out of Willoughby Lands .	10	0	0
Paid the Gift of Mr John & William Stanley . . .	5	0	0
Paid the Gift of the Earl of Devonshire	6	0	0
Paid the Gift of Christopher Tamworth Esquire . .	44	5	0
Paid the Gift of King Charles 1st of ever blessed Memory .	35	0	0
Paid the Gift of Mr William Ives £14 Mrs Ives £1 . .	15	0	0
Paid the Gift of Mr W. Elkington	5	0	0

Paid the Gift of (blank) Poultney Esquire . . .	10	0	0
Paid the Gift of Mr Nidd	42	0	0
Paid the Gift of Mr Acham	9	0	0
Paid the Gift of Mr Haines	24	0	0
Paid the Gift of Mr Botham	2	0	0
Paid the Gift of the Earl of Huntingdon to Wigston's Hospital	10	0	0
Paid the Gift of Mr John Holmes to Trinity Hospital £45 to St John's & Mr Bents £6 10s	51	10	0
Paid the Gift of Mrs Twigden	2	0	0
Paid the Gift of Mr John Bent	45	2	0
Paid the Gift of Mr Moreton out of the Tippetts paid by Mr Mayor	3	0	0
Paid the Gift of Mrs Ward	3	0	0
Paid the Gift of Mr Billers	12	0	0
Paid the Gift of Sir William Courteen & the Gentlemen of Lottery	4	16	0
Paid the Gift of Mrs Dorothy Baker	1	0	0
Paid the Gift of Julius Billers	5	12	0
Paid the Gift of Messrs Bennett & Ward . . .	1	0	0
Paid the Gift of Widow Ositer	6	0	0
Paid the Gift of Mrs Hitch		3	0
Paid the Gift of Mr Gilbert	5	0	0
Paid the Gift of Mrs Margaret Hobby	1	1	0
Paid the Gift of the Countess of Devonshire . . .	3	0	0
Paid the Gift of Mr Hesilrige	1	1	6
Paid the Gift of Mr Thomas Ayre	1	0	0
Paid the Gift of Mr John Ludlam	2	10	0
Paid the Gift of Thomas Weightman		5	0
Paid the Gift of Mr John Roberts	1	0	0
Paid the Gift of Mr Robert Hall		10	0
Paid the Gift of Mr George Bent		5	0
Paid the Gift of Mr William Sutton to the St John's Hospital	2	16	0
Paid more being the Interest of £20 due to the Poor of the Old Hospital		16	0
Paid the Gift of Mr Topp to the Poor of the Old Hospital .	1	0	0
Paid the Gift of Mr Topp to St John's Hospital . .		10	0
Paid the Gift of Benjamin Garland to St Martin's Parish .		5	0

Paid the Gift of Mr Alderman Thomas Ludlam . .	12	0	0
Paid the Gift of Mr Cradock to Trinity Hospital . .	4	0	0
Paid the Gift of Mr Andrews to Do.		5	0
Paid the Gift of Mr Blunt on St Thomas's Day . .	10	0	0
Paid the Gift of Mr Bent to St John's & Mr Bent's Hospital	2	10	0

[End of Payments]

[Supers start here]

Supers

Perkins for Gunnerby Lands	6	8
George Wright Esquire for Lands at Oadby . . .	5	11½
The Earl of Stamford for the Tythes of Thurmaston Mills .	6	8
Anthony Innglesby Esquire for Lands at Ashby . .		6
Mr John Heyrick for Lands at Sileby		6
Mr Farmer's Chief Rent	1	9

To be supered or deducted for the following Vicarial Tythes & Lammas Tythes none of which have been received this Year by the Chamberlins the same having been agreed to be taken in kind.

For Mr Cradock, Mr Ruding & Mr Watts several Charges of vicarial Tythes	24	6	6
For Lammas Tythes	4	12	6
	28	19	0

[End of Supers]

[Arrears start here]

Arrears
for particulars whereof refer to Messrs Swinfen & Parsons Accounts

Names of the Tenants	Amounts of Arrears transferred to Messrs. Firmadge & Towndrow & still due			Amount of Arrears in this Year	Total Amount of Arrears		
⟨Ground Rents⟩							
†Phipps (Stone cutter) . .	28	13	0		28	13	0
Higginson	1	5	0		1	5	0
Tomlin	5	17	6		5	17	6

	£	s	d	£	s	d	£	s	d
Widow Hall . . .	12	0	0				12	0	0
Mr Chatwyn . . .	1	10	0				1	10	0
William Simpson . .	7	10	0				7	10	0
Hall of Cosby . . .	7	0	0				7	0	0
Widow Levis . . .	15	0	0				15	0	0
Woolston Wigston . .	8	0	0				8	0	0
Jane Veasey . . .	4	10	0				4	10	0
(blank) Armstrong . .	2	10	0				2	10	0
(blank) Hubbard (½ years) .	1	5	0				1	5	0
Strange	2	0	0				2	0	0†

⟨Fee farm & Chief rents⟩

	£	s	d	£	s	d	£	s	d
†William Clarke . . .	23	0	0	1	0	0	24	0	0
J. Clarke or Porter . .	3	0	0		5	0	3	5	0
Wigston's Hospital . .		3	9		1	4½		5	1½
Late Samuel Gamble now Day }	9	10	0		10	0	10	0	0
Do. Do.	4	15	0		5	0	5	0	0
Do. Do.	3	16	0		4	0	4	0	0
Woodford or Hesilrige . .		4	0					4	0
Mr Barwell's Executors .		10	0					10	0
Do.		6	0					6	0
Late John Willmore . .		2	6					2	6
Late James Oldham . .		13	4					13	4
Warner now Iliff . . .		5	0					5	0
Tebbs now Tuffley . .		13	0		1	0		14	0
Widow Foulds . . .		2	6		1	3		3	9
Widow Green . . .		10	0		5	0		15	0
Joseph Cradock Esquire .		12	0					12	0
Edward Power . . .		1	8		1	8		3	4
William Abell . . .	10	0	0				10	0	0
Widow Bailey . . .						6			6
Daniel Woodland . .					1	8		1	8
Mrs Monk of Seagrave .					2	0		2	0
George Sheffield Syston .				3	6	8	3	6	8
Thomas Nutt (late Carter's heirs) }				1	0	0	1	0	0

| Assignees of the late Alder-
 man Dalby | 8 | 0 | | 8 | 0 | |
| Do. . . . . . | 8 | 0 | | 8 | 0† | |

[End of Arrears]

[Summary]

Total of Receipts—brought forward 2370 7 1¼

Total of the Payments etc. 2211 17 9½

Balance due to the Corporation exclusive of Arrears . . 158 9 3¾

The Arrears to be transferred to the next succeeding Chamberlains in addition to the above Balance amount (as appears by the
last Page on which they were allowed to the Credit of these
Accountants) to—£163 6s 4½d

CHAMBERLAINS' ACCOUNTS
1813/14

The Accounts
of

William Howcutt
and ⎱ Chamberlains
Richard Warner Wood ⎰
in the Mayoralty of
Sir William Walker
from
Michaelmas 1813 to Michaelmas 1814

1 [No separate heading inserted]

Mr Edward Parsons late Mr Henry Palmer late Mr Alderman Palmer late Augustine Hefford for a year's rent of the Sheep Pens with Cocker's Kitchen on lease expiring 28th February 1821 payable half yearly — 40 0 0

Mr Robert Hitchcock late Henry Hitchcock late Whetstone late Hulse, Baker late Roger Ruding Esquire late T. Noble Esquire heretofore Mr J. Harrison for rents of Assize due yearly out of the land at the North Gates late in the occupation of Thomas Turville called Gadsby's lands at Michaelmas only — 1 9

Sir Nigil Greasly (by Mr E. Parsons) late Mr Alderman Hood heretofore Mr John Blunt for the Butt Close formerly sold to Mr Thomas Blunt late in the occupation of Mr Robert Rolleston late Foreman's late Mr John Loseby's — (blank)
⟨Given to Saint Margaret's Charity School⟩

Mr Thomas Yates late Mr Bellamy (Executor of Mr John Yates) late Mr John Wightman and heretofore Edward Noon for a Messuage or tenement at the nether end of Belgrave Gate heretofore the land of Thomas Headley now divided into several tenements in the fee farm per annum late in the occupation of Edward Noon — 1 0 0

Mr Barnes late Roberts for Sykes and Mr Coates late Bollard 1s 3d each late Charles Stafford and Alice Brown for a Garden and piece of Ground in Sanvey Gate — 1 3
⟨Coates 1s 3d sold⟩

Sir William Manners late John Manners Esquire late the
Duke of Devonshire for a piece of Ground (being a close)
in the North Gate whereon stood a Messuage or tenement
heretofore the land of George Tatham in fee farm per
annum
   ⟨Sold⟩

Do. late the said John Manners Esquire late the said Duke
for a piece of Ground being part of the said close late
Thomas Fletcher's land in fee farm per annum
   ⟨Sold⟩

Mr Froane late Mr John Lambert late Thomas Fisher late
also Thomas Allsop for a piece of Ground lying on the
Backside of a Messuage in the North Gate Street sold to
Mr John Tatham in fee farm per annum   1 8

The Widow of Joseph Boulton heretofore Mr John Palmer
late John Stafford late also John Earpe for a Messuage or
tenement & piece of ground in Applegate Street in the
parish of Saint Nicholas heretofore the land of William
Adcock in fee farm per annum   6 8

Mrs Christey (by Mr William Moore) heretofore Rowland
Watts late John Turville late Mr Barwell for a tenement in
the North Gate Street late the land of Mr Robert Freer
heretofore the sign of the Sun per annum
   ⟨Sold⟩

Thomas Moxon late John Varley's Assignees late John
Throsby late Captain Gamble late the Widow of Mr
Alderman Gamble late Robert Cook for a piece of ground
called the Water Laggs now Bath Gardens late in the
occupation of (blank)
   ⟨Sold⟩

(blank) Johnson late Wells of Loughborough late Mr John
Champion for a piece of Ground at the South End of the
Butt Close in the occupation of William Johnson in fee   4
farm per annum

Mr Chandler of Gilmorton late Mr Gamble of Willoughby or William Burdett late also Robert Palmer of Gilmorton for land Meadow and pasture ground heretofore
the land of John Spriggs afterwards of Edward Whitehead
3s 4d
   ⟨Sold⟩

Anthony Ingoldsby Esquire for lands at Great Ashby in
the County of Leicester late the land of Ralph Brooksby
Gentleman heretofore the land of Nicholas Norton per
annum   6
    〈Supered〉

Mr Lowdham for Edward Wigley Hartopp Esquire late
James Wigley Esquire for certain lands & tenements in
Scraptoft late the lands of John Mason and heretofore the
lands of Thomas Simpkin and (blank) Taylor of Whetstone and now or late of Matthew Hubbard 6d
    〈Sold〉

3   Receipts of the old Grange with the appurtenances and four yard
     lands and the land called Archer's land and known by the name of
     Whiteman's lands and a half yard land which the Corporation
                    purchased of Lord Spencer, as follows

The widow of the late Mr Thomas Chatwyn late John
Guilford for a years rent of the Newark Mills (inclusive
of a Meadow late Dafts) by Lease per annum due 10th   50   0   0
October 1814 (inclusive of 2r 25p of Meadow taken from
Mr Dabbs)

4   Gosling Closes

Mr Alderman Joseph Johnson a year's rent of the Close
late in Alderman Watchorn's occupation with part of the   28 10   0
other Close laid to it

Mr Leach late Alderman Watchorn a year's rent of the
close late Johnson's from which a part was taken to the   12 12   0
other Close

5   Beadhouse Meadows

Thomas Martin late Alderman Eames a year's rent of two
plots in these Meadows due Michaelmas 1814   15 12   0

William Coltman late Cort for two more plots due same
time   18   3   0

John Bates late Swinfen for two more plots due same time .   16   6   0

Mrs Chatwyn for one plot due same time   .   .   .   3 15   2

Do. for part of plot No. (blank) late Dabbs due same time .   2   0   0

Abraham Walker for plot (blank) late Alderman Johnson
& the remainder of plot No. (blank) late Dabbs due same }   11 17 0
time

John Abbott for one plot due same time   .   .   .   17 6 0

Woolaston Wigston late John Brewin of Leicester Forest
for the Forest Closes on Lease due Michaelmas 1814 pay- }   31 0 0
able half yearly

No. on the **6**	In the South Fields which are now inclosed under			
plan made	the Act of 44 Geo. 3d. cap. and divided into small			
on the sub-	allotments (except the part over which the race			
division of	course now runs,) and are let to the following ten-			
the Fields	ants, upon leases from year to year commencing at			
	Lady Day 1806.			

No. 1 (Race Plot)	Joseph Taylor a year's rent due Michaelmas 1814	90	0	0
2 & 3	Alderman Bishop a year's rent due do. .	93	4	0
66	Do. do. .	22	10	0
4	Thomas Gilbert do.	16	0	0
5	William Spencer do.	16	0	0
6 & 22	John Jackson do. reduced by part being laid to the New Walk	21	10	0
8 & 11	William Hall (Blue Lion) do. . . .	34	1	0
7	Robert Clarke do.	16	16	0
9	Thomas Rider do.	16	16	6
10	Joseph Slater do.	18	2	0
12,13,14 & 15	Alderman Marston do.	47	17	0
16,17,18, 19 & 59	Thomas Clarke do.	61	16	6
20	John Colban late Highton do. . . .	24	10	0
21	Thomas Bown do.	19	11	6
23	Benjamin Jackson do. reduced by part being laid to the New Walk	10	8	0
24 & 25	Edward Parsons do.	29	3	0
26	Samuel Bankart do.	17	19	0
27	John Barratt Senior do.	20	17	0
28	George B. Hodges do.	22	17	0

	Alderman Marston a year's rent of the Wind-mill & the Mill Close due do.	25	0	0
	Thomas Neal for part of No. (blank) which lay exposed for sale—a year's rent due Michaelmas	8	7	0
	John Sarson a year's rent of part of the late Windmill Close due at the same time—the other part of what he had last year being exposed for sale the rent this year is reduced to	8	10	0
29	Edward Sanderson one year's rent due at Michaelmas 1814	10	14	6
30	Thomas Oliver do.	18	8	0
31	Francis Brown late William Harrison late George Everard do.	17	0	0
32	Thomas Warner do.	13	1	0
34	William Rice do.	15	0	0
35	Thomas Wright late Benjamin Sarson do. .	11	15	0
36	Robert Higginson do.	13	6	6
37	Isaac Barnes late Davenport do. . .	14	5	0
38	Alderman T. Peach do.	40	5	0
39	George Ireland do.	8	13	0
40	Joseph Illson do.	10	0	0
41	John Higginson do.	9	15	6
42	John Adams do.	13	10	6
43	Miss Eames late John Eames do. . .	15	0	0
44	Joshua Harrison late Joseph Fosbrey do. .	15	5	6
45	John Edwyn late Johnson late Valentine do.	21	10	0
46	John Sargeant late Alderman Wright do. .	18	6	0
52	James Bankart do.	10	18	6
47	Caleb Lowdham late Alderman S. Clarke do.	21	2	0
48	Alderman Gregory do. increased by a small part being added to it which was intended for the New Walk	18	9	0
49	M. & W. Gregory do.	17	16	0
50	Alderman Stevenson do.	18	3	0
51	John Wright do.	11	11	0
53	Joseph Farmer's Executors do. . . .	10	10	0

54	Alderman Burgess do. { reduced 10s by a small piece being taken off	10	0	0
56	Walter Hall a years rent of part of this Close part being cut through for a Street	11	10	0
67	Thomas Neal one year's rent due Michaelmas 1814	16	8	6
60	William Sultzer do.	15	9	0
61	Charles Coleman do.	15	19	0
62	Robert Kinton late Infirmary late Sanderson do.	16	16	6
63	Messrs Robys late Benjamin Sutton do. .	13	15	6
64	Thomas Higginson do.	13	10	6
65	Matthias Tillson do.	14	0	0
68	Jonathan Neal do.	16	9	0
69	Thomas Cook late William Heyrick late Reverend E. T. Vaughan do.	16	1	6
70	James Collison do.	16	0	6
71	Henry Wood late Barston do. . . .	19	1	6
72	John Higginson (High Street) do. . .	22	7	6
73	Alderman Robert Johnson do. . . .	22	7	6
74	James Cort do.	22	5	6
75	Alderman Swinfen's executors do. . .	23	2	0
76	Alderman Miles do.	21	1	6
77	William Heard do.	20	12	0
78 & 79	Edward Quilter do.	36	12	6
87	The Widow of William Mann do. . .	9	13	6
88	Alderman Joseph Johnson do. . . .	29	4	0
89	Henry Mansfield do.	29	8	6
90	T. Freer late William Godfrey do. . .	5	9	0

7 St Mary's Meadow

80	Alderman Marston one year's rent due Michaelmas 1814	24	15	0
81	William Whitehead do.	23	13	6
82	Edward Parsons late Richards do. . .	21	9	6
83	Alderman Marston late James Briggs do. .	15	12	0
84	Richard Spencer do.	14	13	0
85	Alderman Parsons do.	13	19	9
86	Edward Parsons do.	13	19	0

8   Far Meadow

91	Thomas Withers late John Jackson one year's rent due Michaelmas 1814		16 14 0
92	The Widow of William Mann do. . .		13 2 6
93	Thomas Hodson do.		11 10 0
94	Thomas Withers late Gibson do. . .		11 17 6
95	Thomas Lowe do.		11 7 0
96	Joseph Illson late Henry Mansfield do. .		12 12 6
97	Richard Willson do.		18 11 6

9 [No separate heading inserted]

Mr Alderman Joseph Johnson for a Messuage farm yard and homestead called Hall's Grange   ⎱ 10 0 0

William Frisby for two Meadows beyond the Swann's Mill at Will Per annum payable at Old Michaelmas and Lady Day   ⎱ 13 8 0

Mr William Frisby a year's rent for a barn yard and homestead and Grange Lane   ⎱ 12 0 0

10a   In the North Gates

Mrs Ann Clarke (Widow of the late Mr John Clarke) for a year's rent of a Tenement in North Gates in the occupation of (blank) Taylor
    ⟨Sold to Mr John Clifton⟩

Mr Robert Hitchcock late Henry Hitchcock late Mr Alderman Fisher late John Brooks for the North Mills with the house etc. adjoining & the Windmill now removed to the Freake's Grounds which before stood in South Fields—The Close in South Fields in which it stood being partly cut up for sale   ⎱ 70 0 0

Thomas Bramley late Whyley late Mr Terry late Richard Sutton of Kegworth (executor of Edward Sutton deceased) late Robert Phipps rent of a tenement in North Gate Street
    ⟨Now sold to Bramley⟩

George Luck late Robert Smith for the week day Shambles otherwise Saturday Market payable quarterly the whole year's rent due at Michaelmas 1814   ⎱ 110 0 0

Messrs Abell & Slater late William Abell a year's rent for the North Holmes on Lease } 15 0 0

10b   In the Sanvey Gate

Mr Cooper late Thomas Bromley late Mrs Goodis late James Annis for another tenement late John Rawson's land by lease per annum a year's rent
  ⟨sold⟩

Mr Joseph Wheatley late Robert Cowdall Hosier late William Burgess of Oadby late Mr Thomas Penford for a tenement near the North Gates in fee farm per annum 10d
  ⟨sold⟩

The said Joseph Wheatley late the said Cowdall late the said Mr Burgess late Mr George Webb for a tenement near the North Gates according to the old Rentals this should be 2s 2d
  ⟨sold⟩

William Cave late Alderman Oldham for Mr Smith heretofore William Biggs for a tenement near the North Gates in fee farm per annum } 1 0

William Johnson late Noble late Green late Francis Holmes late Benjamin Harris late William Cave for a year's rent of a tenement with the appurtenances at Will per annum payable half yearly
  ⟨Now sold to Henry Johnson Baker⟩
  N.B. This was under lease to Green which would have expired Michaelmas 1814 but Green failed some years ago upon which it was let to Noble and has since been let to Johnson and Green has surrendered the Lease.

10c   In the Soar Lane or Walker's lane

Mr Clough late Joseph Smith for a piece of ground sometime since a Dunghill now built upon heretofore in the occupation of William Rudyard per annum 2s
  ⟨Sold⟩

10d   Within the North Gates

Mr William Forrester late Alexander Forrester late John Lovett late the heirs or executors of Robert Hicklington for a Messuage or tenement on the South side of All Saints Church Yard now or late in the occupation of (blank) Fox in fee farm per annum } 1 10 0

Thomas Derbyshire late Mary Howson for a messuage or tenement in High Cross Street late Kemberton's lands in fee farm per annum   6 0

Mr Flude late Miss Browns (the heirs of the late John Brown) for a tenement in High Street late in the occupation of Joseph Waggott and now or late of the said Miss Browns per annum   5 0

Mr William Horton late Mrs Horton late Thomas Carter for a house & Garden in High Cross Street at the Corner of Bakehouse Lane in the occupation of (blank) late Mrs Davie   4 0

Mr James Valentine late Henry Fisher late Mr Alderman Fisher 4s 6d for a house & Garden in Bakehouse Lane late in the occupation of Richard Grew & Mr Thomas Bilson late John Atkins late of Thomas Johnson's Widow late Bellamy 2s 10d for a house & two tenements late in the occupation of the said Richard Grew & now of (blank)   2 10
⟨Valentine's 4s 6d sold⟩
N.B. The Bowling Green House is sold to Mr William Heyrick and the garden in lots to many different persons.

10e   In the South Gates

Mr John Moore for a house in the occupation of William Sanders late Thomas Moreton's per annum   1 0 0

Mr James Cooper late Alderman Fisher & Mrs Bankart late the land of Thomas Wall for a messuage or tenement at the Corner of Hangman's Lane in fee farm per annum Mr Cooper pays 9s Mrs Bankart pays 3s 6d and Thomas Bennett 3s 6d   7 0
⟨Cooper's 9s sold⟩

Thomas Martin's Widow late Mr Alderman Chapman and William Gamble for a messuage or tenement late the Swan now or late in the tenure or occupation of the said Thomas Martin and (blank) Sharp in fee farm per annum   13 4

10f   In the Burgesses Meadow

Mr John Heyrick late William Palmer for a piece of Meadow ground called the Shield late Moreton's land in fee farm per annum   16 0

The said John Heyrick more for two acres of Meadow late also Mr Moreton's land in fee farm per annum } 13 4

10g   In the Swines Market
                              now called
                           High Street

The Reverend Thomas Willows for a messuage or tenement in his own occupation late Mr Bonnington in fee farm per annum }
 ⟨Sold⟩

The Widow of Joseph Bruce late Thomas Burley of New Parks for a tenement late Agnes Orton's land heretofore called the King's Head } 18 0

10i   In the Saturday Market

Mr John Higginson (Chandler) for a messuage or tenement now divided into two tenements in the several occupations of the said Mr Higginson and Mr Spence in the fee farm per annum } 1 3 4

Mr Thomas Healey (Taylor) late Mr Stevens late Mr Alderman Watchorn late Mr Alderman Brown for a messuage in the said Healey's occupation in fee farm per annum } 8

10j   In the Loseby Lane

Mr Alderman Burgess late Thomas Pares Esquire late Mr Ingle late Lady Greasley for a messuage or tenement late in the occupation of the said Mr Ingle since of Mr Peach and now of Mr Burgess per annum 10s } (blank)

Mr Alexander Forrester late Mr Thomas Ayre late Mr Butchrufield for a house late in the occupation of John Ferryman late of Mr Peach and now of Mr R. Cook 1s 6d }
 ⟨Sold to Mr R. Cook the present owner of this house⟩

Thomas Kirk late the said Alexander Forrester late the heirs of Samuel Cotes for a house lately called the Star and Ball and now the Crown and Thistle late in the occupation of John Highton in fee farm per annum } 12 0

Of him more for a piece of ground a Damask Rose payable at Midsummer } A Damask Rose

v

Thomas Bothamley late Jacob Bothamley for a house and
backside being parcel of a tenement late in Valentine
Dallaway's occupation since new built at Will per annum
due at (blank)
  ⟨Now sold to Mr James Rawson⟩
Mr James Rawson late Mr Garle for a Messuage or tene-
ment lately called the Crown & Thistle in fee farm per
annum
  ⟨Sold⟩
George Luck late Mr Garle for a year's rent of a house &
backside due (blank)
  ⟨Sold⟩

10k   In the Gallowtree Gate

Mr Alderman Gregory late Alderman Oliver late Mr
Alderman T. Ayre for a Messuage or tenement late in the
occupation of Loftus Page since of Mr Cotchett and now
of (blank) in fee farm per annum 8s
  ⟨Sold⟩
Mr Alderman Mansfield late Mr Alderman Oliver late
Mr Alderman T. Ayre for a Messuage or tenement known
by the sign of the White Horse late in the occupation of   1   o   o
John Taylor and now of William Whitehead in fee farm
Per annum
(blank) late Mr James Willey for one yard land in St Margaret's field late Mr Alderman Bishop
  ⟨sold⟩

10l   In the Gallowtree Gate on the West side

Mr Richards late Isaac Cockshaw late Mr Nutt late Mr
Fosbrooke Grocer late Mr James Nutt late the Reverend
Mr Lambert for a Messuage or tenement near the Play-   10   o
house in the occupation of the said Isaac Cockshaw and
George Cowdell in fee farm per annum
Mr William Nutt late the said James Nutt for a messuage
or tenement heretofore Edward Ashwell's late in the
occupation of (blank) 4s
  ⟨sold⟩
Mr John Bailey late William Watts late Watts & Dixon
for a messuage or tenement called the Magpie and Crown
late the land of Henry Palmer Gentleman in fee farm per
annum £1
  ⟨sold⟩

10m   In the Belgrave Gate

Dr Arnold for a garden at the Nether End of Belgrave
Gate heretofore in Thomas Deake's occupation late paid
by Mr Pares for Joseph Cradock Esquire of Gumley now
paid by and in the occupation of Dr Arnold 12s
   ⟨sold⟩

Mr Thomas Yates late Mr John Yates late Thomas Rode-
ley for a house in the occupation of (blank) in fee farm per   13 4
annum

Mrs Foulgham (by Fewkes) late Thomas Withers for
Thomas Sarson & Francis Foulgham for a house in the   1   0   0
tenure of the said Withers in fee farm per annum

Joseph Chamberlain Esquire late Mrs Holmes late Mrs
Ward widow for a tenement heretofore Simpsons adjoin-
ing the Unicorn which Unicorn is now the late Alderman   15 0
Bishop's House on the West side thereof in fee farm per
annum

Mr John Bailey late Alderman Coleman for a house late in
the occupation of William Bell & now of Foster on the
North side of the said Street late Richard Ward in fee   18 0
farm per annum

The Churchwardens of St Margaret's for a piece of
ground called the Cowpasture in fee farm per annum   8 0

10n   In the Country

Clement Winstanley Esquire for certain lands leys &
pasture grounds in the Lordship of Braunstone in the
County of Leicester now or late in the occupation of
(blank) Burton in fee farm per annum 12s 8d
   ⟨sold⟩

Nicholas Hurst Esquire of Hinckley late Mr Warner for a
close croft & half yard land in Hinckley in the County of
Leicester in the occupation of (blank) in fee farm per   15 0
annum

Henry Walker of Thurmaston late Robert Walker of
Beaumont Leys & Mrs Gossip (by Mr Carter) late
Thomas Worroll for a piece of ground in Belgrave called
Knipton Hill leys and one yard land heretofore called   3 3
Belgrave Bridge close heretofore Overing's land Walker
pays 5s 9d Gossip 3s 3d
   ⟨5s 9d purchased by Walker⟩

Lord Viscount Wentworth for a messuage or tenement &
one yard land with the appurtenances in Kirby Mallory
in his occupation in fee farm per annum 6s 8d
   ⟨sold⟩

(blank) Wollerton late Mrs Rodwell of Rearsby late Mrs
Boothby of Tooley for a Messuage or tenement in Rearsby
in his occupation in fee farm per annum 17s
   ⟨sold⟩

Mr David Monk late Mrs Monk of Seagrave late Mr
George Chamberlain for a close & croft there late the land   2   0
of William Hubbard in fee farm per annum

(blank) Barsby of Thrussington late Mr Benjamin Storer
of Thrussington for one yard land there in fee farm per   6   8
annum

Mr John Campion late (blank) Wale of Frolesworth for a
year's rent of the Foss close & meadows due at Lady Day   46   0   0
1814 on lease from year to year

Mr William Tompson of Houghton on the Hill for a piece
of ground in his occupation or William Hubbard's in fee
farm per annum 1s 8d
   ⟨Now sold to G. A. L. Keck Esquire⟩

William Ward of Houghton for another piece of land
thereto belonging late Thomas Roadley's in fee farm per   5   0
annum

The Reverend Henry Woodcock late Mr Whattoffe
Clever of Syston for certain lands at Barkby in the occupa-
tion of Thomas Bradley in fee farm per annum 8s
   ⟨Sold⟩

Henry Peach Esquire late Mr Alderman Peach late
William Watts for certain land leys & hades in the West   4   0
Fields of Leicester in fee farm per annum

Mr George Henton for Sir Thomas Apriece late Shuck-
burghs Ashby Esquire late Sir Thomas Cave for a mes-
suage or tenement in Hungerton and now or late in the   1   10   0
tenure of Thomas Walton in fee farm per annum

George Sheffield of Syston for Syston Mills & a House
heretofore sold to Sir Thomas Cave in fee farm per   3   6   8
annum

11a Other rents of Lands & tenements parcel of the Town Obiit lands of St Margaret's Guild and parcel of the Fee farm rents heretofore demised by Queen Elizabeth to Mr Hawkes & Mr Bates by Indenture expired

The Heirs of Mr William Ives for ground late belonging to houses in the South Gates heretofore Mr Nurse William Hills & Francis Cole ruined by the late Wars or heretofore sold to Mr Dannett Abney paid as follows	2 6 8
Withers late Sheffield late Townsend of Aylestone 6 8	
Mr Moore of Leicester 2 0 0	

John Reynolds late Mr Armston late Mr Norton late also Mr John Ludlam for a messuage or tenement with the appurtenances commonly called or known by the name of the White Lion late in the occupation of John Messenger in fee farm per annum 10s
    ⟨Sold⟩

Messrs Mansfield & Miller late Hawkins late Tuffley late Hartshorn for a messuage or tenement in the occupation of (blank) £1
    ⟨Sold⟩

Mr Alderman Joseph Johnson for the ground late belonging to two tenements in the South Gate Street late in the tenure of Paul Abney deceased since known by the name of the Bull ruined by the late Wars and since built upon in fee farm per annum £1 6s 8d
    ⟨sold⟩

Mr Samuel Bankart late Mr Alderman Chapman for a messuage or tenement in South Gate Street formerly called the Greyhound ruined by the late Wars since built upon in his own occupation in fee farm per annum £1
    ⟨sold⟩

11b
In the Swines Market
now called
High Street

Mr Bradley Grocer late Mr Fosbrooke late Mr Sismey for a tenement in the Silver Street near the Pump late in the occupation of Mr Robert Dowley now of (blank) in fee farm per annum	1 0 4

11c   In or near Belgrave Gate

Mr Clay Hextall late Mr Cramant late Mr Newton for a
messuage or tenement at the Corner of Humberstone Gate
in his own occupation in fee farm per annum   1   1   0

Land late Mr Parsons's now Mr Joseph Chamberlains
and others Mr Chamberlain pays 6s and Sarah Noon 6s in
fee farm per annum   6   0
⟨6s sold to Noon⟩

Mr George Peake late Henry Coleman Esquire late
Lewin's Heir for a Messuage or tenement once called the
Lamb & for one other Messuage or tenement & close with
the appurtenances late in the occupation of Benjamin
Cartwright & now of Mr Peake £1 6s 8d
⟨Sold⟩

Mr Henry Sands late Foulgham (by Fewkes) for a house
late in the occupation of Widow Noon & now of George   1   0   0
Noon & (blank) in fee farm per annum

†The Reverend Mr Andrews out of Rawlett's close the
gift of Mr Twigden received of Mr Lowdham   2   0   0

Robert Marston of Enderby late Mr Oldham late George
Roe for a year's rent of land in Enderby Lordship being   77   0   0†
the gift of Mr Bent to Bent's Hospital on Lease expiring
⟨These two Items are received by the Mayor⟩

Walter Ruding Esquire late Mr Simpson out of the Tip-
pitts in St Mary's Parish being Mr Moreton's gift   3   0   0

Walter Ruding Esquire late Roger Ruding Esquire out of
the Duck Holmes in St Mary's parish Mr Ward's gift   3   0   0

The Leicester Navigation Company (by Messrs Carter &
Cardale) late the Reverend Gerrard Andrews out of the   12   0   0
Leroes in St Margaret's parish the gift of Mr Billers

Mr George Peake late Henry Coleman Esquire late Mr
Moore (for Lewin's heirs) out of the House in Belgrave
Gate   2   0   0
Dr Arnold late Mr Barry the like   .   .   . 2   0   0   10   0   0
Mr Peter Oliver late Hayes out of the Cranes .   4   0   0
Mr Harrison Gardener out of the Crab tree
close   2   0   0
⟨Blunt's Gift⟩

William Whetstone late Lovell (Heir of Farmer) out of a
House in the Silver Street the gift of Mr Bent to the Poor   2 10   0
of St John's Hospital payable the Sunday after St John

Mr Alexander Forrester late Benjamin Liquorish late Smith of Burbage for a house in Belgrave Gate late known by the Sign of the Joseph but now of the Nottingham Arms late in the occupation of John Highton & now of Benjamin Johnson's widow in fee farm per annum   12 0

Mr Thomas Yates late John Yates late Augustine Hefford for a house called the Cock in fee farm per annum   6 8

Mr Edward Hextall late Taylor for a Messuage or tenement late in the occupation of Widow Moseley in fee farm per annum
    ⟨sold⟩

Mr Thomas Yates late John Yates for a messuage late in the occupation of Ellis Denshire and of another part called the Cock in fee farm per annum sold to John Briggs   13 4

John Barlow late Mrs Clarke late John Clarke late Charles Bates for a tenement in the occupation of Thomas Withers heretofore sold to Robert Roberts in fee farm per annum   5 0

Benjamin Taylor for 3 Messuages in Sanvey Gate late in the occupation of Widow Veasey John Maslin & Thomas Armstrong on lease expiring 1815 payable half yearly   13 2 6

(blank) Barrowdell late Tailby late George Harley Vaughan half a year's rent due at (blank) for a tenement in his occupation formerly given to Mr Vaughan by the Town during pleasure
    ⟨sold to Barrowdell⟩

Widow Abell late the Reverend Mr Ross for a garden in Elbow Lane the rent of which is, by order of Hall, given to the Head Schoolmaster during pleasure   2 12 6

11e   In Cank Street

Mr Stephen Dumelow late Mr William Sutton for a messuage or tenement late in the occupation of John Armstrong and now of the said Stephen Dumelow in fee farm per annum 13s 4d
    ⟨Sold⟩

11f   St Nicholas & St Margaret's parishes

Benjamin Cave late Satchell late Brown late Alderman Sutton late Joseph Brown & (blank) Flude late William Spencer for Mary Spencer for a Messuage or tenement late John Orton's land afterwards Lewin's per annum Cave late Satchell pays 7s & Elizabeth Hall late Food pays 6s   13 0

Richard Poole late Thomas Nutt late George Carter's Heirs for a Messuage or tenement in Applegate Street near the West Bridge called the Mitre & Key in the occupation of the said Thomas Nutt in fee farm per annum — 1 0 0

Mr Joseph Boulton's Widow late John Throsby (parish Clerk) late Alderman Throsby for a Messuage or tenement in High Cross Street heretofore called the Flying Horse in fee farm per annum — 1 10 0

12 Other rents of lands & tenements parcel of the Town & Manor of Leicester heretofore (amongst other things) given and granted unto the said Mayor Bailiffs & Burgesses in fee farm per annum

Mr Alderman Burbidge late Mr John Slater late Mr William Simpson late Alderman Sismey for a piece of ground in the Church Gate whereon a Messuage or tenement late stood in the possession of George Stearsmore late on Lease
   ⟨This is now sold to Mr Alderman Burbidge⟩

Mr Edward Bracebridge for two Houses in the Church Gate in the occupation of the said Edward Bracebridge & late a piece of ground in fee farm per annum 2s 6d
   ⟨sold⟩

Mr Peter Heward late Holmes late of Mr Kirke late John Cartwright for a tenement with the appurtenances in the Church Gate paid as directed on folio 27 [see Heading 14e] — 8 0

Thomas Clark late Widow Snapes for a house or piece of ground near St James's Chapel called the Hermitage in fee farm per annum 1s
   ⟨Sold⟩

(blank) Loseby late (blank) Stubbs for Mr Lucas late Cobley for a piece of ground in All Saints parish called the Vine Yard in his occupation in fee farm per annum — 4 0

Webster & Jordan 1s 3d each late Seal for part of a piece of ground called the Lion Yard & a Messuage or tenement in the occupation of Mr Bradley in fee farm per annum — 1 3
   ⟨Webster's 1s 3d sold⟩

Joseph Nunneley late Mr S. Bradley late Alderman Gamble for another part of the said Lion Yard & a Messuage or tenement in the occupation of Mr Bradley in fee farm per annum — 2 6

Mr Fosbrooke late Reid 30s Mr A. K. Holmes late Mrs Reid late Lieutenant Edmonds late Mrs Cave 10s for a house & Barn late Sandy's land situate in the Saturday Market in their respective occupations   10   0
   ⟨30s sold to Fosbrooke⟩

John Barlow late John Clarke's Widow for a piece of ground in the Church Gate extending from thence to the Common Oven whereon a house was built by William Cave in fee farm per annum   2   6

Mr S. Miles for a piece of ground near St Margaret's Church Yard whereon a House called the Town House formerly stood in fee farm per annum 6s
   ⟨sold⟩

Mr William Watts late Robert Hartshorn for the house in Rice's occupation near Frog mire Bridge late a piece of ground in fee farm per annum   1   0
   ⟨Supered⟩

Mr William Waring late William Johnson (by Mr Carter) 10d & Mr Oram late Kestins 2d for a piece of ground in Deadman's lane   10
   ⟨Oram's 2d sold⟩

13   Other rents of Corpus Christi Guild in Leicester heretofore in Mr Archer's collection and now parcel of the Lands & tenements which the Mayor etc. purchased of Queen Elizabeth to them and their successors for ever.

John Burrows (Baker) late Neale of Billesdon late Taylor for a Messuage or tenement in High Street with the appurtenances in fee farm per annum   13   4

Mr Methuselah Moore late John Stears for a Messuage or tenement in High Street heretofore known by the sign of the Crown in fee farm per annum
   ⟨sold⟩

Mr Thomas Phipps (by Mr Lowdham) late John Wild-bore of Loseby for a tenement in Gallowtree Gate in the occupation of (blank) & others in fee farm per annum   1   6   8

Mr Robert Brewin late John Lomas late Sutton's execu-tors late Fossitt late West for rent of a piece of land formerly built upon near Frog mire bridge late on lease
   ⟨Sold to Brewin⟩

Mr Solomon Holmes late Thomas Phipps late Oldham for a Messuage or tenement in Gallowtree Gate in his own occupation in fee farm per annum 13s 4d
  〈Sold〉

William Johnson late Marshall late Parkinson late Burgess late also Joseph Simpson for a Messuage in Saturday Market new built in fee farm per annum   1   0   0

James Wilby late Larratt for a Messuage with the appurtenances (Mr Cramley's) in fee farm per annum   1   0   0

(blank) late Mr Alderman Willey for a Messuage or tenement in Town Hall lane near St Martin's Church in the occupation of Robert Pinder & William Brown in fee farm per annum 6s 8d
  〈Sold〉

Mr Richards for a Messuage in Parchment Lane now Swine's Market late in the occupation of John Burgess in fee farm per annum   16   0

Josiah Wood late Mr Ireland late Foster of Loughborough as tenant of the trust estate of Joseph Clarke Esquire for certain lands & pasture grounds in Loughborough aforesaid called Sadler's land for the Trustees of the Hospital of Barrow upon Soar in fee farm per annum   10   0

Mr Harris by Loseby 6d Cawood late Cobley 3s Lambert by Harris 2s Quilter late Harris for Iliffe 4s and Weston late Nicholson 2s 6d for several tenements near the East Gates late Smalley for a shop in fee farm per annum   4   0
  〈6d & 2s bought by Harris & 2s 6d by Weston also
  Cobleys 3s〉

Thomas King late Reynolds late Hextall for a messuage on the West side of the East Gates in his occupation late Hoods in fee farm per annum   12   0

Thomas Webster late Francis Lomas for a piece of ground heretofore a garden in the Town Hall Lane, over against the Town Hall, now built upon heretofore Fletcher's lands in the occupation of Thomas Webster Hatter in fee farm per annum   1   0

Mr John Slater late Goodhall for a tenement in Parchment Lane now called Swines Market heretofore a Stable some time since Mr Heyrick's land in fee farm per annum 6s 8d
  〈sold〉

Charles William Pochin Esquire of Barkby late Robert
James of Houghton for a croft & half yard land at Barkby   6   8
late Illson's in fee farm per annum

The said C. W. Pochin Esquire for three quarters of a yard
land at Barkby late the land of Thomas Seal in fee farm   6   0
per annum

Mr Samuel Brooks for a Messuage in High Street in the
occupation of (blank) Bass in fee farm per annum   6   0

Francis Brown late Robert Valentine late Inkersole late
Davie for a piece of ground at the nether side of St James's
Chapel Close where a house lately stood late the land of
Widow Boreman in the occupation of (blank) in fee farm
per annum
   ⟨Sold⟩

Mr Alderman Burgess late Pares late Ingle late Lady
Greasley for a house & yard in St Martin's Church yard in
his own occupation in fee farm per annum
   ⟨sold⟩

Mr Perkins of Grantham for certain lands and leys in the
Town Fields of Gummorley in the County of Lincoln in   6   8
fee farm per annum
   ⟨supered⟩

Mr Moore late Day late Samuel Gamble Esquire for a
close near the Cow Drift late Heyrick's land in fee farm   10   0
per annum

Mr Harding late Robert Hubbard Esquire late James
Nutt late Alderman Oliver for a shop and other buildings
on the East side of the Round Hill near the Old Playhouse
£1
   ⟨Now sold⟩

The said Harding late Robert Hubbard late the said James
Nutt late the said Mr Oliver being an acknowledgement
for erecting 4 Columns in the Corporation ground belonging to the aforesaid buildings 1s
   ⟨now sold⟩

(blank) Smith for Thomas Marshall for a house & backside in Shambles Lane heretofore Mr Harrison in fee farm
per annum 1s
   ⟨sold⟩

14a Other rents of the possession of the late guild in Leicester parcel of the Town obiit lands heretofore collected by Mr Tatham

Samuel Robinson late Messrs Mansfield & Miller late Thomas Richards late Goode late Wilcox & heretofore Coates for a messuage or tenement in Applegate Street in fee farm per annum	1	0	0
Thomas Knight late William Johnson for a messuage or tenement in the same Street late Hursts in the occupation of (blank) Knight & another		9	0
Alderman Clark late William Hubbard late Alderman Higginson for a house in the said Street late Slater's in fee farm per annum 6s 8d ⟨sold⟩			
(blank) Cooper of Syston late the Executors of the late Mr Cobley for John Coates late Randolph Ward for a house in the said Street now or late in the occupation of (blank) Cumberland in fee farm per annum 10s ⟨sold⟩			
(blank) Hunt (Combmaker) late Bassett late Denshire late Cooper for a Messuage in Applegate Street in the occupation of (blank) in fee farm per annum		8	0
The said Hunt late Cart for Lee for a house in Applegate Street late David Winfield in the occupation of (blank) Chamberlain in fee farm per annum		7	0
Mr William Hill late Widow Burley 10s and William Burley 4s for a messuage and garden in Applegate Street formerly in the tenure of (blank) Savage in fee farm per annum		14	0
(blank) Goude late the heirs or executors of Henry Smith for a piece of ground late in the occupation of William Astle & now of Mr Higginson called the Mayor's old Hall in Shambles Lane		3	4

14b   In the South Gates

Alderman Clark late Higginson for a house & garden in the South Gates now sold to the County Justices ⟨Sold⟩			
Thomas Edwin late Springthorpe's representatives late Hitchcock for a piece of Ground situate in South Gate Street belonging to a House ruined by the late Wars sold to Mr Hartshorn late in Conyer White's occupation & now of John Gibson in fee farm per annum		10	0

Messrs Mansfield & Miller late Hawkins late Tuffley 4s Bankart 6s for ground belonging to two tenements in the same Street in fee farm per Annum
  ⟨Mansfield & Miller's 4s sold—Bankart's sold also⟩

Mr Alexander Forrester late Wood for the ground belonging to two tenements now or late in the occupation of (blank) Smith in fee farm per Annum   1 5 0

Mr John Marshall late Coates of Stamford late the Executors of the late Cobley late Farmer of London for tenements in Applegate Street late Coates in fee farm per annum   10 0

Mr Stone late Burgess late David Hennell for a Messuage or tenement in the Cornwall formerly known by the sign of the Queens Head now built upon in Fee farm per annum   1 6 8

Mr John Peberdy late Barfoot late Thomas Eames £1 & Alderman Peach late Watts £1 for a Messuage in the Cornwall formerly known by the sign of the Cinque foil now new built upon in his own occupation in fee farm per Annum   2 0 0

Widow Green late John Clarke for a Messuage heretofore known by the sign of the Buck's head in her own occupation in fee farm per Annum   5 0
  ⟨Supered⟩

14d   In the Swine's Market

Mr James Dowley late John Richards late John Major Esquire for a certain Garden heretofore sold to Michael Whatton of Bushby in fee farm per Annum   2 0

14e   In the Belgrave Gate

Richard King late Mr D. Harris late Copson late Mrs Bond for a Messuage or tenement in his occupation late Astle's in fee farm per annum   16 0

Thomas Lowe late the Widow of Joseph Groocock for a House called the Star in his own occupation late Barrys in fee farm per annum   13 4

Mr George Peake late Henry Coleman Esquire late Lewin for a Messuage or tenement late the land of Robert Gamble late in the occupation of the said George Peake in fee farm per Annum 18s
  ⟨Sold⟩

Mr Harding late Robert Hubbard Esquire for a shop and Chamber situate in the Round Hill now or late the Playhouse in fee farm per Annum £1
  ⟨Now sold⟩

Mr Henry Harrison late Alderman Watts late Charles Duneclift late John Wright for a Messuage now called the Crown & Cushion late the Cannon in fee farm per Annum 12s
  ⟨Sold⟩

Thomas Yates late John Yates and others for two tenements late in the occupation of George Chamberlain & Widow Abney in fee farm per annum   8   o
    N.B. The tenements in the occupation of Hill & Copson were the property of the Corporation but have been since resold to Mr Alderman Willey

Mr Noble late Jordan for a tenement & Garden in Belgrave Gate in the occupation of George White in fee farm per annum   6   o

Mr Godfrey of Scraptoft late Alderman Dalby late Davie for a house in the same street now in the occupation of (blank) in fee farm per annum 8s
  ⟨Sold⟩

Mr Langdon late Anthony Ward for a house & Garden in the same Street now in Langdon's occupation in fee farm per Annum   6   o

Alderman Burbidge late Lee for an orchard or piece of ground whereon stood a house called St John's late in Samuel Jarvis's occupation since of Joseph Cotchett and now of (blank) Whittle in fee farm per Annum £2 os 2d
  ⟨Sold⟩

Thomas Yates late the executor of John Yates for part of Margaret Fletcher's land in Belgrave Gate in fee farm per annum   5   o

The heirs of Thomas Palmer for a house and garden in the Church Gate late Mr Inge's in fee farm per annum paid as directed in the next item   5   o

Of them more for an Orchard in the Church Gate once Mr Inge's land late Smalley's in fee farm per Annum   2   o
    The two last mentioned rents & the rents of 8s on folio 19 [see Heading 12] are paid thus
    Mr Holmes late Cartwright   .   .   .   8   9

Messrs Dalby & Deakin	1	3
Mrs Bass (now Bailey)	1	3
Do.	1	3
Widow Miles late Barrass for Miss Heard .		7½
Joseph Pegg late William Bucknall late Sturgess late Bailey for Frost		7½
Thomas Cartwright late Newbolds for Foulds	1	3

| | 15 | 0 |

14f   In the Sanvey Gate

Mr Robert Clarke late Mrs Gutheridge for a Messuage or tenement late in the occupation of William Chamberlain in fee farm per annum	1	0	0
Richard Dawson for (blank) White for a house and garden in the occupation of Dawson in fee farm per Annum		8	0
Mrs Noon for two tenements in Sanvey Gate built upon a piece of ground heretofore leased to Smalley but late to Mr Alderman Clark & Alderman Fisher at Will per Annum ⟨Sold to Noon⟩			
John Johnson late Matthew Johnson late Mrs Barwell for a piece of ground called Sadlers close in fee farm per annum		5	0
Richard Popplewell, Framework-knitter, late John Popplewell late Levi late Mr Edward Newberry for two more tenements now erected in Sanvey Gate with a spong of ground belonging to the house ⟨Now sold to Creswell⟩			

14g   Near Saint Margaret's Church

Mr Richard Rawson late Reverend Mr Walker late Mr Clayton Apothecary late Mr Cooper for a piece of ground called St Margarets bed being a close late the land of James Biggs in fee farm per Annum	6	

14h   Other part of Wilder's rent

Mr Moore late Richard Walker Esquire for a close near the Cow Drift in his own occupation in fee farm per annum	13	4

Mr John Baxter for a house in his occupation in Soar lane near Red Cross Street late the heirs of Mr Stockden of Great Glenn 6s
  〈Sold〉

Mr Joseph Wheatley for Lord Scarsdale for a house & piece of ground in the said Soar lane late Bretton's land now in the occupation of the said Joseph Wheatley in fee farm per Annum 2s
  〈Sold〉

Mr Thomas Godfrey of Scraptoft late Mr Alderman Dalby for a house & garden in Belgrave Gate late Higg's land 8s
  〈Sold〉

Mrs Pares for a close in Archdeacon lane heretofore sold to John Mobbs in fee farm per Annum 6s 8d
  〈Sold〉

Mr Joseph Iliffe late Mr Henry King for Miss Warner of Humberstone for a house & Land there in the occupation of Dennis Kirk in fee farm per Annum   5   0

Messrs Keen & Taylor late Taylor & Payne late Thomas Ashwell for a Messuage or tenement in Sanvey Gate here-tofore sold to him & Jane Ward in fee farm per Annum   1   6   8

The Poor of Trinity Hospital for a Garden and piece of ground near the Butt close now built upon late in the tenure of Mr Samuel Clarke & others in fee farm per Annum   2   0

Mr Harrison late James & Thomas Cartwright for a house & backside near St Margaret's Church in the occupation of the said Harrison in fee farm per annum 8s
  〈Sold〉

Mr Thomas Yates late the executors of John Yates for a house & garden in the Belgrave Gate late the land of Edward Sutton late in the occupation of John Coe and now of (blank) Asher in fee farm per Annum   3   4

Thomas Barsby Carpenter late William Abell late Mr Barwells heirs for a tenement with the appurtenances in Sanvey Gate now in the tenure of Nathan Hunt in fee farm per Annum   10   0

The Widow of John Clarke for a Messuage or tenement in Sanvey Gate heretofore Thomas Chettle's in the occu-pation of Richard Harcourt in fee farm per Annum   6   8

Dr Vaughan late Sir Charles Halford for a close near the
Humberstone Gate formerly sold to John Roe in fee farm
per annum 12s
  〈Sold〉

15 A Rentall of the lands and possessions of and belonging to the
College of the Blessed Virgin Mary over against the Castle of
Leicester heretofore demised by Queen Elizabeth to Edward
Holt Esquire and by her Majesty granted to the Mayor etc and
their successors (amongst other things) in fee farm per Annum

Mr Thomas Paget (Surgeon) late Mr Thomas Cotchett
late William Hill Esquire heretofore Mr Hill Attorney at
Law for a Messuage or tenement in Swines Market now
High Street in fee farm per Annum 6s 8d
  〈now sold〉

Francis Brown late Buxton late Hudson late Langton for
a part of messuage or tenement near the West bridge late
in the occupation of Coleman and others in fee farm per
Annum 2s
  〈Sold〉

Mr Moore late Mr Day late Samuel Gamble Esquire late
Ralph Wells for a close near Aylestone late the land of Mr   5 0
Robert Heyrick in fee farm per annum

Mr Marshall late Sharpe for a garden or piece of ground
near the backside of a messuage or tenement near the
South Gates heretofore the land of Hugh Watts in fee
farm per annum
  〈Sold〉

The Widow of Joseph Bruce for a messuage or tenement
in Soar Lane near Red Cross Street in her own occupa-   10 0
tion late the lands of John Collison in fee farm per annum

Thomas Alsop late Pickard late Hudson Norton late
Pochin 15d William Gill late Hunt for Lambert 15d and
Bruce late Ward 2s 6d for a tenement in Soar Lane near   5 0
Red Cross Street sold to John Underwood late Thomas
Derrick's & William Ward's

William Bassett late Foreman for a house and garden in
Soar Lane near Red Cross Street heretofore Robert
Stevenson's in fee farm per annum 12s
  〈Sold〉
W

William Barrar late Mr Clayton by Mr Carter late Cooper
for a messuage or tenement in Red Cross Street & a garden
in Chaff lane adjoining to the house in the occupation of
Timothy Atkins called the Old Mitre in fee farm per annum }   1   0   0

Lovett late John Satchell 11s 7d & of Christopher Bennett
late the Widow of John Brown of Desford 15s 1d for a
messuage in Soar Lane near Red Cross Street in fee farm
per annum late Robert Atkins }   1   6   8

Onesiphorus Coltman late Robert Dugmore for a messuage & garden in Soar Lane near Red Cross Street heretofore sold to John Bonner in fee farm per annum }   12   0

Thomas Astell late William Thompson late Mr Hill for a
garden in Soar Lane otherwise Red Cross Street in the
occupation of Thomas Trentham in fee farm per Annum 8d }
    ⟨Sold⟩

Widow Hall late Mrs Bankart for Mr Hall .	5	4
William Cook late Bankart Senior for Dawson	5	4
Coltman (Slater)	5	4
	16	0

for a piece of ground late Thomas Ward's belonging to a
Messuage or tenement in the South Gates ruined in the
late Wars and for a croft in fee farm per annum
    ⟨Cook's 5s 4d sold⟩ }   10   8

Mr Henry King for Mr Turner late Mason heretofore Dr
Cheshire for a piece of ground adjoining to the Friar Lane
in Turners occupation 4d
    ⟨Sold⟩

The Churchwarden's of St Mary's for the Herbage of
Saint Mary's Church Yard per Annum }   3   5   0

Mr Henry Wood late Henry Callis for Nathan Wright
Esquire for a Close called Sand pit close near the Cow
Drift lane per Annum £1
    ⟨Sold⟩

The Governors of the Leicester Infirmary for Saint
James's Chapel Close in fee farm per annum }   1   6   8

Alderman Clark late Mr Samuel Roberts late James
Rawson late Mr Brown late Joseph Brown for a year's
rent of a house and garden or backside in the parish of
Saint Nicholas due Michaelmas 1814 }   15   15   0

Hewens late Nixon late Mr Denshire for a house & Garden in the parish of Saint Nicholas near the Applegate Street called the Talbot in the occupation of George Taylor in fee farm per Annum   1   0   0

[15 resumed below]

16   Receipts for tythes on Estates in St Mary's

Walter Ruding Esquire for the tythes of his estate payable at Lady Day and Michaelmas   136   0   0

(blank) Usherwood Esquire (by Mr Joshua Willcox) for the tythes of his 3 Closes called the 1st 2nd and 3rd Limes in the occupation of Joshua Willcox at Will per Annum due Michaelmas 1814   2   4   9

William Ratcliffe Esquire late Ward of Nottingham for the tythes of his 4 Closes called Taylor's House close, South Close North Close & Meadow close in the occupation of Joseph Taylor   7   0   0

Thomas Pares Esquire late Joseph Cradock Esquire for the tythes of his estate due Lady Day and Michaelmas including also a part of the estate late Buxton's   25   0   0

Thomas Pares Esquire late Mrs Joan Watts for the tythes of his estate due Lady Day & Michaelmas   5   6   6

Henry Peach Esquire late Robert Peach Esquire for the tythes of the Dane Hill close and a Garden taken out of the Waste due Lady Day and Michaelmas   9   14   6

Dr Alexander for the tythe of part of the estate late Buxton's due Michaelmas   7   10   6

Messrs Bates late Sargeants for the tythes of other part of the same estate   3   0   0

Thomas Mitchell for other part thereof   1   11   0

Dr Alexander late Alderman Jeffcutt for other part   .   .   14   6

Samuel Kinton for other part   8   0

(blank) Baxter for Hall Meadow late Heyricks & sold by him to Buxton   12   0

Alderman Oldham for other part   2   6

Mr Kelly late Mr J. Heyrick for the Tythes of Bow Bridge Close   13   0

Clement Winstanley Esquire for the Tythes of the Estate late Ruding's   2   8   6

15 [resumed]

James Dowley late William Lamb late Mr Ashby's heirs late Mr Smalley for a garden in Sanvey Gate in the occupation of William Sands in fee farm per annum ⎫ 1 0

Thomas Thornelow's Widow late Joseph Hopwell (for the heirs of Mr Chettle) late William Willmots for a piece of ground or garden in the occupation of the said Joseph Hopwell some time since a Well yard in High Street in fee farm per annum

⟨This property is now purchased by the Corporation⟩

Mr Field late Carrick for an Orchard or Garden in Silver Street at Will per annum ⎫ 2 0

Mr John Moore late Samuel Gamble Esquire for the 3rd part of a close near the Cow Drift in fee farm per annum ⎫ 4 0

The Poor of Trinity Hospital for part of a Dove Coat close beyond the West Bridge in fee farm per annum ⎫ 1 6

Richard Hashold of Glenfield for a piece of ground there late in the occupation of John Carr in fee farm per annum 6d

⟨Sold⟩

Mr Sutton (Coal Merchant) late John Brewin late Tyrringham Palmer for a Close near St Margaret's Cow pasture heretofore Bennett's Land in the occupation of (blank) in fee farm per annum ⎫ 3 4

Joseph Cradock Esquire late Mr Watts for certain lands and leys in the West fields of Leicester heretofore the lands of Thomas Dennett Esquire in fee farm per annum 2s 6d

⟨Sold⟩

The Poor of Trinity Hospital for a piece of Meadow ground in the Burgesses Meadow called Lady acre in fee farm per annum ⎫ 3 4

W. Ruding Esquire for a Close in Braunstone Gate late Mr Hunt's land in fee farm per annum ⎫ 5 0

John Baxter, Baker, late Robert Hodgeson for a house and close in Red Cross Street

⟨Sold⟩

Joseph Bruce's Widow for a tenement & Garden Soar Lane near Red Cross Street in her own occupation on Lease expiring (blank) payable half yearly ⎫ (blank)

Dr Vaughan late Sir Charles Halford for a garden in Swine's Market now High Street late built upon in his own occupation — 1 2

The said Dr Vaughan late the said Sir C. Halford for a messuage in the same Street heretofore sold to Christian Needham in his own occupation — 2 6

(blank) Sly 3s 4d Benjamin Hames late Edward Powers 1s 8d for a garden in Hot gate Street alias Thornton lane late the land of Mr Thomas Pares per annum — 5 0

Thomas Paget Esquire late Watchorn late Peach late Mason for a messuage or tenement heretofore Mr Walkers in the Newarke of Leicester in the occupation of the said Mr Paget in fee farm per annum £1 6s 8d
    ⟨Sold⟩

Of him more for the same house in fee farm per annum 13s 4d
    ⟨Sold⟩

Joseph Cradock Esquire of Gumley late Goodman of Saddington for 2 parts of Chamberlain's land at Knighton in fee farm per annum 12s 4d
    ⟨Sold⟩

John Tebbutt of Bowden Magna for land there now or late in the occupation of John Corrall in fee farm per annum it is three pieces of Hay Meadow called Leicester land — 1 0

William Herrick Esquire of Beaumanor late the Reverend G. Coulton late Mr John Herrick of Beaumont Leys for lands in Sileby per annum — 6

The Reverend Mr W. S. Lee late Mr Gulstone late Mr Steadman of Glenfield for land there in fee farm per annum 3d
    ⟨Sold⟩

17   Other rents of the Town and Manor of Leicester parcel of the lands and possessions of the Duchy of Lancaster part thereof being in the County of Leicester

William Smith Cheesemonger late Mr Poynton & Mr Slater 8s 4d each late Mr Higgs for a messuage or tenement in the High Street heretofore of John Brooksby late Mr Hood in fee farm per annum — 8 4
    ⟨Mr Slater's 8s 4d sold⟩

Mrs Edmonds late Mr Dyston for a horse Malt Mill in Swines Market now High Street in fee farm per annum }   1 13 4

19   Other rents received of new

George Groce late William Ogden late Mr Franks for a piece of ground being part of the Town situate near the Friar lane in fee farm per annum 2s 6d }
    ⟨Sold⟩

Francis Brown Carpenter late Thomas Buxton Esquire late William Hudson late (blank) Langton for two pieces of ground taken out of the Common Dunghill in the lane near the West Bridge in fee farm per annum 10d }
    ⟨Sold⟩

Francis Lomas late Miss Whittle late Abstinence Pougher for 2 tenements in Parchment Lane called Swine's Market late the land of Mr John Heyrick in fee farm per annum }   3 4

20   Other rents for certain Lands purchased by the Corporation and other rents

Caleb Lowdham Esquire a year's rent of a Cottage or tenement (now a Stable) and Garden situate near the Horse fair (late Mr James Cort and before him Mr Alderman Neal) and of 2 cottages or tenements adjoining and also of a small part of Speechley's close adjoining thereto in Messrs Roby's occupation due Michaelmas }   13 15 0

Thomas Moxon late Varley's Assignees late Throsby late Captain Gamble for the Water Laggs now Vauxhall Gardens in fee farm per annum 6s 8d }
    ⟨Sold⟩

Messrs Mansfield and Miller late Mr Richards late the Widow of William Wood for part of a house called the White Swan in the Saturday's Market now or late in the occupation of William Mosedale in fee farm per annum £2 }
    ⟨Sold⟩

21   Rents given to the Schools & other charitable uses

His Majesty's Receiver General paid by Jonathan Foster Esquire given by Queen Elizabeth out of the honor of Leicester for the better maintaining the Under Usher of the Grammar School of Leicester }   10 0 0

Thomas Inkersole Esquire for Earl Spencer one Annuity or rent charge payable out of the Manor of Thedding-worth being the gift of Sir Ralph Rowlett for maintaining the Under Usher of the said School late by Lord Althorpe	3	6	8
Mr Simpson late Mr John Iliffe late Mr John Morris one Annuity payable yearly out of a Close in Abbey Gate called Abbey Gate close for the better maintaining the Head Usher in the occupation of Mr Iliffe per annum	3	6	8
Francis Brown, Carpenter, late Thomas Buxton Esquire late Mr Hudson for one annuity, payable yearly out of a piece of ground called the Water Laggs to the Under Usher of the same School being the Gift of Thomas Clarke per annum	1	0	0
(blank) Gimson late Thomas Shuttlewood late John Needham of Whetstone late Edward Sutton for Lands in the Lordship of Willoughby Waterless late Hall of Cosby (out of which Norris's gift is payable) by Lease expiring Lady Day 1816	20	0	0
The Widow of William Mann for an Orchard or Garden in All Saints parish purchased with £50 given by the first Countess of Devonshire for & towards the relief of the Poor of the Borough and the Parish of Saint Leonard for the payment of £3 per annum	16	0	0
Charles Mann a year's rent of the remainder of the said Orchard	6	0	0
William Gillam for half a year's rent of a messuage or tenement and close & one yard land at Whetstone bought of one John Baker Gentleman by the Corporation with the money bequeathed by Christopher Tamworth Esquire for celebrating divine service on Lease expiring Lady day 1814	22	2	6
Jonathan Gillam half a year's rent of the same Estate due Michaelmas 1814	39	0	0
Wollaston Wigston late John Brewin for a year's rent of 40 acres of land in the Forest of Leicester given by King Charles the 1st of ever blessed memory to the poor of the Borough due Michaelmas 1814 on Lease	52	0	0
Mr Roby late Mr Thomas Smart for a year's rent of a close & barn thereto belonging in Hangman lane which the Corporation purchased of Mr Speechley due Michaelmas 1814 (decreased £2 in consequence of a small part being let to Mr Lowdham)	40	0	0

Mr Pares payable yearly out of the Manor of Cotes Deval being the gift of Mr Poultney to charitable uses	10	0	0
Mr Seal of Bushby late George Plummer of Evington for a year's rent of Lands in Bushby being the gift of Mr Nidd to the poor of Mountsorrell on lease from year to year	70	0	0
Mr Stone for Sir Philip Vavasour being Mr Acham's gift to the Poor of the Corporation out of the Manor of Asfordby alias Asterby in the County of Lincoln per annum due at Michaelmas	9	0	0
Thomas Coleman for himself & Mr Tilley 13s 2d and William Bassett late Thomas Gregory 6s & John Hurst 2s 6d for certain grounds in the South gates belonging to 2 tenements in the occupation of (blank) being the gift of Mrs Hobbey 〈Gregory's 6s sold〉		15	8
Mr Alderman Burgess late Pares for a rent charge issuing out of his house late occupied by Mr Samuel Markland heretofore called the Parrot being the gift of Mr Hugh Botham and paid at St Thomas's day	2	0	0
(blank) Clarke late Whitehead of Allexton for several Closes & grounds there bing the gift of Mr Haines to charitable uses late in Catwell's occupation by Lease per annum	40	0	0

23 [No separate heading inserted]

Mr John Peberdy late Mr Thomas Eames late Mrs Lee for ground taken from the Sheep pens		5	0
William Clarke late Alderman Oliver for the like . . 〈Supered〉	1	0	0
Mr Solomon Holmes late Alderman Eames for the like late Smalley		10	0
Mr Burgess for do. late Hanwell paid by Cramant . .	1	0	0
Mr Raworth for a piece of ground adjoining to the West Bridge per annum		2	6
Mr Geary late Richard March late Mr William Proudman late Joseph Barrett for two tenements in Causeway Lane belonging to St John's Hospital built with the £50 given by Mr Cammock's Will and the £115 arising by the sale of the Hospital garden towards building the Town Gaol on Lease per annum due Lady Day & Michaelmus	17	17	0

John Edwyn, late J. M. Johnson, for the clay of 257,000 bricks at 2s 6d per 1,000 made upon the Plot No. (blank) from Michaelmas 1813 to Michaelmas 1814, payable in addition to his rent for the Land	32	2	6
Edward Rice for 181,870 bricks made on the plot No. (blank) from Michaelmas 1813 to 1814 at 2s per thousand	18	3	6
Do. for 20 Kilns of plaister on the same plot . . .	20	0	0
Do. for 34 cwts plaister Stone		8	0
Thomas Ryder for a small piece of Ground part of what was purchased of Mr William Heyrick a year's rent	3	3	0
Mr Joseph Slater late Henry Lenton for other part of the same ground	3	3	0
Joseph Smith late Thomas Kirk a year's rent of the tenement in the Market Place which used to be included in the Lease of the North Mills	9	0	0

24 Of the following persons for certain grounds near Leicester called Freake's grounds which were lately only 2 closes and in the occupation of Edward Sutton and John Mortimore but are now divided into small parcels and were let on Lease for 14 years from Lady Day 1796 but are now let on lease from year to year to the following tenants the rent payable half yearly

Elizabeth Johnson a years rent due Michaelmas 1813 .	17	8	0
William Forrester . . . do. due do. . .	17	7	0
James Orton's Executors . . do. due do. . .	16	9	0
Thomas Marston . . . do. due do. . .	20	17	0
William Adams . . . . do. due do. . .	17	8	0
John Mudford . . . . do. due do. . .	16	16	0
Alderman Clark . . . . do. due do. . .	17	4	0
Alderman Neal . . . . do. due do. . .	17	9	0
William Howcutt . . . do. due do. . .	16	2	0
William Tompson's Executors by Alderman Burgess .	19	10	0
Robert Hitchcock . . . do. due do. .	19	9	0
Thomas Cox . . . . do. due do. . .	17	14	0
Alderman Slater & John Abell late S. Clarke do. due do. .	27	7	0
John Priestman . . . . do. due do. . .	17	19	0

28 [No separate heading inserted]

Henry Mansfield a year's rent of the house known by the sign of the Nag's Head purchased by the Corporation of Mrs Elizabeth Thorneloe due Michaelmas 1814	50	0	0
(blank) Wollands a year's rent of a House in High Cross Street purchased of Mr William Hall due Michaelmas 1814	14	0	0
Alderman Jeffcutt late (blank) Highton a quarter of a year's rent of another House there purchased also of Mr William Hall due at the same time N.B. unoccupied ¾ year	4	0	0
Miss Hartell a year's rent of a House in the same Street purchased of Mr William Hardy due at the same time	20	0	0
Hosea Hafford a year's rent of another House purchased of Hardy	14	0	0
Rowland Austin a year's rent of a Stable etc part of the property purchased of the Duchy of Lancaster	10	0	0
Thomas Webster a year's rent of Shops etc purchased of the Duchy due Michaelmas 1814	8	0	0

29 Chief rents belonging to St John's and St Leonards to be paid at Michaelmas for the use of the Mayor Bailiffs and Burgesses of the Borough of Leicester

The Wardens of Wigston's Hospital paid by Mr Pares .	1	4½
Mr Alderman Gregory late Mr Stevens for a messuage or tenement in Gallowtree Gate in his own occupation late the Black Lion 6d ⟨Sold⟩		
The Right Honorable the Earl of Stamford for Thurmaston Mills ⟨supered⟩	6	8
George Wright Esquire heretofore Sir William Rawlinson late Sir Henry Beaumont for certain lands at Oadby ⟨supered⟩	5	11½
Mr Alderman Gregory late T. F. Cooper for the Reverend Mr Liptrott for the Vicarage House at Oadby	1	0½
(blank) Woodward of Oadby for certain lands there called Marshall's lands 6d ⟨sold⟩		

Mr Robert Clark Gutheridge late William Cook for a
house in Sanvey Gate late Webster's land   9

30   Chief Rents belonging to Corpus Christi Guild

Mr Field late Mr Carrick late Mr Belton late Mr Townsend's executors for a tenement in Silver Street in his   4   0
occupation per annum

Mr Thomas Hollier late John Bullock (by Mr Vaissier)
late Timothy Atkins late Mrs Daniel for a house in Silver
Street in the occupation of Vaissier & Agar
    ⟨sold⟩

Mr Nutt late Mrs Orme for a messuage or tenement in
Gallowtree Gate   2   2
    ⟨Supered⟩

Mr Fox's executors (by Mr Pares) late Cradock Hartopp
Esquire for a messuage or tenement late in the occupation
of Miss Ascough & Mr Fox per annum 2s
    ⟨sold⟩

Mr Higginson for a house in the occupation of himself &
Spence per annum   2   0

Mr Iliffe of Oadby late Simon Iliffe of Oadby for certain
lands late Bliss's land 1od
    ⟨Sold⟩

William Shelton late Mrs Walker late the Widow of
Manton Reynolds late Widow Kilsall for a piece of ground
in Parchment Lane now called Swines Market late the   3
land of Tobias Heyrick

Mr Goodrich late Lord Stamford for a messuage or tenement in Red Cross Street in the occupation of the said
Goodrich
    ⟨Sold⟩

Mr Goude Hosier for a messuage or tenement near St
Nicholas's Church in his occupation late Britton's land   1   0

John Simons Esquire for a certain House near Red Cross
Street late the land of Britton & Suffolk 8d
    ⟨Sold⟩

Mr Neale, Pawn Broker late Stubbs for Slater late Mr
Brown for a Garden in Deadman's Lane   5   0

Mr Thomas Chapman for a messuage or tenement in
High Cross Street Called the Peacock late in the occupa-
tion of William Smith 3s
   ⟨Sold⟩

(blank) of Shambles Lane 1od & Mr Oram 2d for a Cottage in Deadman's Lane per annum   10
   ⟨Supered Oram's 2d Bought⟩

Joshua Banner late Thomas Brothers late William Nutt
for a house in Red Cross Street late in the occupation of
John Dean & now of (blank) per annum 6d
   ⟨sold⟩

Mr Thomas Cotchett late John Shipley late Widow Groce   6
for a garden in Deadman's lane

Mr William Hardy late Joseph Springthorpe late William
Davis for a house in High Cross Street late in the occupa-   1   0
tion of John Pratt & now of George Smith per annum

Mr Alderman Oldham for a Messuage or tenement in   14   0
High Cross Street per annum

William Leeson late Edward Powers for his House in
High Street late the land of George Higgs per annum
   ⟨Sold⟩

Mr John Willows for his house in the said Street 6d.   .
   ⟨Sold⟩

Mr Cotchett late William Hill Esquire for a tenement now
divided into two tenements in the occupation of James   3   0
Willson & William Collison

William Stretton late William Burton late also William
Case for a tenement in High Street in Stretton's occupa-   3   6
tion

The Poor of the Trinity Hospital for a Barn called Clark's   6
Barn

Mr Cort late Miss Simpson's, Grocers, for a tenement in
Cank Street in Cooper's occupation per annum
   ⟨Sold⟩

Mr Alderman Joseph Johnson for a house in Belgrave
Gate in the occupation of Edmund Wright per annum 3s
   ⟨sold⟩

Mr Clement Stretton for a house in Cank Street late in   8½
Alderman Bates's occupation

The Reverend T. Burnaby late William Herrick Esquire late Sir John Whatton Knight for a close called Shire hall Orchard in All Saint's parish late in the occupation of James Orton 6

Mr Michael Payne for a Messuage or tenement in Loseby Lane late in the occupation of Mr Thomas Barry 10d
  ⟨sold⟩

Mr Edward Marston late Mr Barwell for a messuage or tenement in Humberston Gate in his own occupation 3 0

Mrs Harris (by Loseby) late the Reverend Mr Lambert for a messuage or tenement in Gallowtree Gate known by the sign of the Angel part of which is in the occupation of E. Quilter 2s
  ⟨sold⟩

Mr Cornish late Mr W. Simpson for a messuage or tenement near the East Gates in the occupation of (blank) Stone per annum 1s
  ⟨sold⟩

Mr James Barston late Mr Bishopp Surgeon late John Mansfield Esquire late Joseph Cooke Lovel late Roger Ruding Esquire for a tenement at the Corner of Friar lane lately known by the sign of the George late in the occupation of Thomas Farmer per annum 4 0

Mr Robert Green late Walker late Bates for a messuage or tenement in High Street in the occupation of (blank) per annum
  ⟨Sold⟩

Mr Woodford for a tenement there late Mark Valentines . 2 0

Do. late Arthur Haselridge Esquire for a messuage or tenement in High Street in the occupation of Mr Mason & others (late Henshaw's land) 4 0

Mr Henry Callis (by Gadsby) late Alderman Oliver for a tenement in Gallowtree Gate in his own occupation 7 6

31   Chief Rents belonging to St Margaret's Guild

The Subscribers to the Hotel (by Mr T. Freer) late Alderman Oldham late William Herrick Esquire for a garden in Ironmonger's Lane near the Saracen's Head late Bents per annum
  ⟨Sold⟩

Francis Brown late Edward Harris for a messuage or
tenement in High Cross Street at the Corner of Bakehouse
Lane 1s 4d
⟨sold⟩

Henry Hitchcock late Whetstone late Mrs Hulse (late
Cowdall) for Walter Ruding Esquire for a piece of ground   6   0
in Soar Lane called the Moat Yard per annum

Mr John Bass Oliver for a messuage or tenement in Belgrave Gate called the Unicorn in his occupation 4s 2d
⟨sold⟩

Mr George Peake late Henry Coleman Esquire late Mr
John Moore for Lewin for a house in Belgrave Gate in Mr
Peake's occupation 9d
⟨sold⟩

Miss Foulgham for a tenement in the same Street late   6
Sutton's land

(blank) Peet of Mountsorrel late Widow Bailey late
William Heyrick Esquire for a tenement in the Humber-   6
stone Gate

Mr Alderman Firmadge late Mr Bass for a Barn in the
Church Gate late William Inge Esquire 1s 3½d
⟨Sold⟩

Mr Cardale for the Leicester Navigation Company late
Mr Andrew late Mr Ludlam for a close near the Spittle-   1   0
house called the Bailiff's close per annum

Mr Joseph Johnson late Edward Johnson for a messuage
or tenement near the West Bridge late in the occupation of 4   0
Weldon Gibbs but now of (blank) & others per annum

The Warden of Wigston's Hospital for a piece of ground   6
called the Normandy per annum paid by Pares

Mr Henry Harrison late John Fancotes late Mr William
Watts for a house in the Church Gate called the Black
Swan late Manby's late in the occupation of Samuel
Wright's Widow & now of the said Fancote 9d
⟨Sold⟩

Mr William Forrester late Alexander Forrester late
George Rayson Pratt for a messuage or tenement in All   1   1½
Saints parish in the occupation of the said Forrester &
others

Mr George Peake late Henry Coleman Esquire for a messuage or tenement in Belgrave Gate in the occupation of Mr Peake 6d
   ⟨Sold⟩

Do. late do. in the occupation of do. 3s 4d . . .
   ⟨Sold⟩

Mr John Jackson late Dowley late Joseph Wallin late Mr Pares late Robert Page for a piece of ground taken out of the Pinfold   4

Mr Bankart heretofore Mr Alderman Thomas Chapman for a tenement in the South Gates heretofore called the Greyhound 4s
   ⟨Now sold⟩

Mr Joseph Johnson late Denshire late Nixon late Richard Denshire late Mr Bonner of Aylestone for a tenement in the South Gates Mr Bennett's land in the occupation of (blank) Gee 10d
   ⟨sold⟩

The Poor of Trinity Hospital for a house in the South Gates in the occupation of (blank) late Foster's land   9½

Mr Heyrick for a piece of ground in Burgesses Meadow late the land of John Guilford   10   0

Mr Joseph Harris late Samuel Cooper for a messuage or tenement in Harris's occupation late the land of Dannett Abney
   ⟨sold⟩

Samuel Howe late Widow Clarke for Franks late Mrs Davie Widow late Mr Stanley for a tenement in North Gate Street and for 2 tenements now or late in the tenure of John Harcourt   1   2
   ⟨Supered⟩

Mr Wheatley late Henry Clarke for a shop now a house near the South Gates once Moreton's land in the occupation of Freer per annum 3d
   ⟨sold⟩

Mr Alderman Peach late William Watts late William Ogden for a house in High Street once Otter's land per annum   3   6

Mr Stephens late Mr Topp for a house in High Cross Street in his occupation late Robert Chettle per annum 2s
   ⟨Sold⟩

Mr Alderman Sutton late Mr Whiteman for a close in Braunstone Gate 6d
  ⟨Sold⟩

Mr John Saywell's executors late William Scott (for Mr Turville) for a house in High Street in his own occupation 11d and for 2 hens and a Capon
  ⟨Sold⟩

Mr Joseph Johnson late Edward Johnson late Alderman Johnson for a house near the West Bridge called Babington's land in the occupation of (blank)   9

Mr Alderman Clark late Mr Pawley of Croxton for a tenement in Applegate Street now in his own occupation 6d
  ⟨sold⟩

(blank) Porter late Nathan Tuffley late Mr Tebbs of Birstall late Turlington for a house in Birstall late the land of John Rayner now or late in the occupation of the said Nathan Tuffley   1   0

Mr Christopher Bennett late John Gill late Bassett late Wells for a house in Chaff Lane near the Red Cross Street once Gillson's land 9d and for a Hen 3½d in the occupation of Thomas Holyland
  ⟨sold⟩

Mr Higginson for a messuage in the Saturday Market in the several occupations of said Higginson and Spence   6   8

Mr Edward Johnson late Alderman Johnson for land late Bothams near Soar Lane and for 3 Capons and two Hens 4s
  ⟨Sold⟩

Walter Ruding Esquire for a close in Braunstone Gate   .   9

Mr John Coltman late Billows for a House in Hot gate Street alias Thornton Lane
  ⟨sold⟩

William Harrison (Blue Boar) late Joshua Howes late Wigston late Stevenson for a house near the South Gates called the Blue Boar late Rudworth's land 9d for 2 Hens 7d and for a shop near the South Gates 5d   1   10

William Burley late John Rider for a tenement over against All Saints Church late Mr Rudyard's land in the occupation of (blank)   2   3

Mr Benjamin Sutton late Mrs St John late Sir Charles Halford for a messuage in High Street late Bonners House   6

Mr Alderman Clark late Pawley for a house in Applegate
Street once Birstall's in his own occupation 10d & for two
Hens & a Capon 10d 1s 8d
  ⟨sold⟩

John Adams late Miss Simpson late Alderman Simpson
for a messuage at the upper end of Belgrave Gate near
Neal's land per annum 1s 6d
  ⟨sold⟩

Mr Woodland for a Close in All Saints parish near Elbow
Lane Mr Cradock's land per annum 1s 8d
  ⟨sold⟩

Henry Johnson at the Orange tree late John Richards for
a house & land in the North Gate Street late Badyman's in
the occupation of (blank) per annum
  ⟨sold⟩

Nicholson 3d and Dorman 10d for a house in the North   10
Gate Street late Woodward's per annum
  ⟨3d sold to Mr Slater⟩

Messrs Mansfield & Miller late Hawkins late Mr Tuffley
late Edward Davie for lands in the South Gates in his own
occupation 2s and for a Garden 10d
  ⟨sold⟩

Mr Benjamin Sutton late Mrs St John late Sir Charles
Halford for a house in High Street late Needham &   4
Bailey's land

Edward Smith late Mr Mortimore of Narborough for a
house in South Gate Street late Alderman Joseph Taylor   6 8

Joseph Springthorpe late Joseph Watson late Sir Charles
Halford for a close in High Street near the Horse Malt Mill   6

33 A Rental of Lammas Tythes due yearly to the Mayor, Bailiffs and
Burgesses for divers gardens in St Mary's parish in the possession
of the College of Saint Mary over against the Castle of Saint Mary,
Leicester

†Mr Thomas Coleman late Mrs Wood late Richard Weston for Dovehouse Close near the Newarke of Leicester   1 4
late Hickling per annum

Mr Davis late William Franks Esquire for a Close near St
James's Chapel close called Archer's close   1 0

x

The Governors of the Infirmary for Saint James's chapel close tythe	1	0
Messrs H. & T. Wood late Nathan Wright Esquire for the tythe of Bonningtons Close called Sand pit close & Meadow per annum	1	0
Mr Alderman Sutton for a close near Braunstone Gate per annum		6
Mr H. Wood late Nathan Wright Esquire late James Mason for a close late 2 closes called Sand pit close and Meadow over against St James's chapel close per annum	1	8
Mr Thomas Coleman late Mr Wood late Weston for land near the Grange once Birstall's land per annum	1	0
Mr Thomas Coleman late Mrs Wood for a close near St James's Chapel close late Morton's land per annum		10
Do. late do. for Seth King's land part of the above close .		6
Mr Lowdham late Mr Astill for Miss Whitemans late Mr Iliffe for a close near Paradise close		4
Mr Edward Davie late William Franks Esquire for a piece of ground called the Kiln late Cadman's near St James's Chapel close per annum		4
Do. for Cadman's land near St James's Chapel close per annum		10
Mr John Lacy late Mr Joseph Wilkins for an Orchard on the backside of an House late Davis in the South Gates late the land of Hugh Watts Esquire		6
Mr John Moore late Samuel Gamble Esquire for a close near Aylestone Highway late Mr Heyrick's		8
Of him more for a close near the same Highway . .		4
Of him more for another close near Archer's land in St Mary's parish		10
(blank) late Joseph Tisdale late William Pochin Esquire late Richard Weston for a piece of ground near St Mary's Mill close called the Holmes late Mareby's land per annum late William Simpson Hosier deceased	1	8
Nathan Wright Esquire late the Heirs of Mr John Farmer Attorney for a close near Aylestone Highway called Sand pit close in the occupation of Henry Callis		10
Nathan Wright Esquire late William Wright Esquire for part of the said close called Sand pit Close in the occupation of Henry Callis per annum	1	0

Description	£	s	d
W. Ruding Esquire for a close in Braunstone Gate late Hunt's land			8
Of him more for a Close called college close in St Mary's parish late Hunt's land			4
Mr Edward Harrison late Cart of the Bull Head for a close late Brook's land in St Mary's parish late Bennett's called Duck Holmes per annum		2	2
Mr William Simpson for a Close called the Tippett's Per annum paid by Mr Brewin		13	4
Thomas Chatwyn for the tythes of the Newarke Mills per annum		2	0
William Knight for a garden or piece of ground in Millstone lane Armstrong's land per annum			4
Joseph Bruce for land in Chaff Lane late Hall's . .			10
The Widow of Thomas Hall late Francis Ward for a backside belonging to his house in the South Gate now or late in the occupation of Thomas Ward per annum			6
Foulds late Mr Newton for a house in Thornton lane late Mr Thompson's			4
William Johnson for Pailing for Booth's land in Shambles Lane			4†
⟨Supered⟩			
The Reverend Mr Bullen late the Reverend Mr Heyrick late Pigott for an acknowledgement for the house adjoining to the Free School 2s 6d or 2s varied annually due Midsummer 1814		2	0
†Mr John Jackson an acknowledgement for an encroachment for putting out 2 Windows from his house in the Cornwall late in Mr Alderman Chamber's occupation per annum		1	0
Mr Thomas Chatwyn for the tythe of the Newarke Mills .		16	0
Messrs Johnson & Jordan each one shilling for the tythes of the Gosling closes		2	0
Mr (blank) late Alderman Fisher for the tythes of the late North Wind Mill		2	0
Mr Jordan late Derbyshire late Joseph Orton for the tythes of a piece of grass ground in the Mary Meadow		6	0
Mr Jordan, Mr Cooper & Mr Stretton each 7s 4½d for the tythe of the Beadhouse Meadows	1	9	6†
⟨supered⟩			

Mr John Hartshorn for the tythes of a piece of ground in St Mary's Meadow	}	(blank)
Thomas Chatwyn for the tythes of a piece of ground belonging to the Mill	}	(blank)
Mrs Sutton for laying Planks & setting posts in the river Soar during pleasure	}	(blank)

37   Freedoms

[Precedes No. 36 this year]

	£	s	d
John Brown for his Freedom		10	0
James Morris for the like		10	0
William Hackett for the like	30	0	0
George Hughes for the like		10	0
Thomas Martin for the like	30	0	0
Henry Goddard for the like		5	0
Henry Peach for the like		5	0
William Brown for the like		5	0
George Bellairs for the like	30	0	0
William Kenworthey Walker for the like . . .	30	0	0
William Harrison Junior for the like	30	0	0
John Nokes for the like		5	0
John Goodman for the like		10	0
Joseph Pettifor for the like		10	0
William Pettifor for the like		5	0
William Tomlinson for the like		10	0
William Chamberlain for the like		5	0
Francis Moore for the like		10	0
John Hincks for the like	30	0	0
Solomon Bray for the like	30	0	0
Samuel Scott for the like	30	0	0
Isaac Jackson for the like	30	0	0
William Foster for the like	30	0	0
William Threlfall for the like	30	0	0
Benjamin Hackett for the like		10	0
Edward Webb for the like		10	0
William Stevenson for the like	30	0	0
Joseph Fowler Bloomar for the like	30	0	0
Joseph Jeyes, for the like	30	0	0
Thomas Butler for the like	30	0	0

36   Incidental Receipts

	£	s	d
Francis Rayns for Osiers	2	10	0

Messrs Rawson & Forrester late Chamberlains being monies ordered by Common Hall to be paid to the Chamberlains in each year on the commencement of their office   100 0 0

Of Do. more 100 0 0

Of Do. more 69 0 0

Of them more the balance of their Accounts .   .   .   804 18 11

By arrears transferred by them to these Accountants, exclusive of the said balance   53 11 8

[End of Receipts]

[Payments start here]

4 [No separate heading inserted]

Paid Sir William Walker Mayor his year's salary according to ancient custom   13 6 8

Paid him more out of the rent of the Gosling Closes allowed by order of Common Hall   13 6 8

Paid him more being the additional Salary to the Mayor in 1713   20 0 0

Paid him more by order of Common Hall 1736 .   .   40 0 0

Paid him more by order of Common Hall 1769 .   .   50 0 0

Paid him more by order of Common Hall in January 1797 .   50 0 0

Paid him more by order of Common Hall in 1806 .   .   50 0 0

Paid him more being Coal & Capon money .   .   .   5 11 6

Paid Mr Serjeant Vaughan, Recorder, his year's Salary due at Michaelmas (increased by order of Hall held in 1810)   105 0 0

Paid the Town Clerk his year's Salary (increased to £200 per annum by order of Hall on 8th April 1811)   200 0 0

Paid for Stamp & Paper for Commission for the year .   1 0 6

For Stamp & paper for the Letter of Attorney .   .   1 0 4

Paid the Reverend Mr Bullen (head Schoolmaster) the Towns free gift during pleasure   16 0 0

Paid do. more the Towns annual Free gift during pleasure .   8 0 0

Paid do. more the Town's annual Free gift during pleasure   3 0 0

Paid Do. more Do. .   .   .   Do. .   .   .   5 0 0

Paid Do. by order of Hall in 17— on condition of his taking boys free of entrance	5	o	o

N.B. The 5 foregoing gifts were formerly paid to the head Master & head & Under Ushers but by order of Hall in July 1797 were all directed to be paid to the Reverend Mr Heyrick on his being appointed sole Master and are now paid to Mr Bullen as his Successor.

Paid Do. more the Town's free gift during pleasure by order of Hall in July 1797	30	o	o
Paid do. more do. by the like order being the rent of a tenement in Sanvey Gate let to Barrowdale & a Garden let to Widow Abell in Elbow Lane	8	18	6
Paid the Reverend Mr Vaughan his year's Salary as Lecturer of this Borough during pleasure	20	o	o
Paid him more by order of Common Hall as Vicar of St Martins during pleasure	10	o	o
More as Vicar of All Saints during pleasure . .	10	o	o
Paid the Reverend Mr Mitchell as Vicar of St Mary's during pleasure	10	o	o
Paid the Reverend Mr Davies as Vicar of St Nicholas the like	10	o	o
Paid the Reverend Mr Burnaby as Vicar of St Margaret's the like	10	o	o
Paid Miss S. Valentine the Organist her Salary for playing at St Martins	10	o	o
Paid Miss Valentine her Salary for playing at St Margaret's	10	o	o
Paid the Steward his year's Salary . . .	100	o	o
Paid the Macebearer his year's Salary and for burning pipes	7	9	8
To him more as Inspector of the Corn Market for one year .	2	12	o
More his Salary the like	5	o	o
More his additional Salary ordered by a Common Hall to be paid for rendering his assistance to the Chamberlains	20	o	o
Paid him more for 2 Seals		2	o
Paid him more by order of Common Hall in lieu of Boarding with the Mayor	40	o	o

Paid him more additional Salary by order of Common Hall .	20	0	0
Paid the 4 Serjeants at Mace their Salaries at £20 each being increased to this sum by order of Hall in 1810	80	0	0
Paid the Cryer & Beadle their Salaries at £20 each, being also increased by the same order	40	0	0
Paid the 2 Bellmen their Salaries at £10 10s each being also increased by the like order	21	0	0
Paid the Waits their Salary £3 each (only 3 Waits this year)	9	0	0
Paid the Library Keeper her Salary	3	0	0
Paid the Cryer and Beadle to prevent their going round with their Christmas Box		4	0
Paid them on Saint Thomas's day what used to be paid by the parishes		5	0
Paid for a pair of shoes each for the Cryer & Beadle . .	1	2	0
Paid the Mole Catcher a year's salary	1	11	6
Allowed the Chamberlains for Auditors Dinners by order of Hall	10	10	0
Paid the Bailiffs to the Augmentation for land Tax to (blank) at Michaelmas & acquittance 7s 4d N.B. This 7s 4d of late has not been demanded.		(blank)	
Paid the Bailiff of Merton College, Oxford, for three year's chief rent issuing and payable out of St John's and Saint Leonard's in or near the Borough of Leicester at 1s 3d per annum		3	9
Paid the Wardens of the Company of Taylors the annual rent of 1s 8d		(blank)	
Paid for tolling the Bell on Michaelmas day . . .		1	0
Paid the Halbert Men for Walking the Fairs and cleaning the Armour on the Fair days		10	0
Paid Mr George late Pepys late Lucas a chief rent out of the Gainsborough, Property tax and Land tax deducted, now William Morehead Esquire due 10th October	5	8	6
Paid Lady FitzWilliams a year's rent of the South Fields due at Michaelmas Property tax & Land tax deducted	3	19	10
Paid the Cryer for Holly and Ivy used at the Town Hall and Change		6	0
Paid the Clerk of St Mary's for washing the Chancel . .		6	6

Paid Do. for Mop & brush		5	9
Paid Mr Pares for an acquittance for the Earl of Huntingdon's Gift		1	0
Paid a year's chief rent for the ground near the Marquis of Granby bought of Mr W. Heyrick 4s 9½d Not paid	(blank)		
Paid Thomas Gadsby for Winding up the Change Clock .	2	2	0
Paid him for cleaning & repairing it	1	1	0
Paid the Lottery money towards putting out a boy apprentice	5	0	0
Paid the Lamplighter his Christmas Box . . .	(blank)		
Paid the Clerk of Assize his fee at the Assizes . . .	1	6	8
Paid Messrs Higginson & Kinton succeeding Chamberlains being money ordered by Common Hall to be paid to the Chamberlains in each year on the commencement of their Office	100	0	0
Do. more by the like order	100	0	0
Do. more by the like order	100	0	0
Paid for the Mayors London newspaper . . .	9	5	6
Paid for the Nottingham Gazette	2	12	6
Paid the Beadle for sweeping after the Fairs . . .	1	12	0
Paid for sweeping chimnies at the Town Hall and Change .		7	0
Paid for mending the fish Nets	1	2	7
Paid for attendance & weights at the Cheese Fair in Michaelmas & May	2	2	0
Paid Sir William Walker for postage of Letters in his Mayoralty	8	0	0
Paid the Grand Jury for 3 Sessions Dinners at £5 15s 6d .	17	6	6
Paid Do. additional by order of Hall	10	10	0
Paid the Constables for Do.	2	18	0
Paid the Bellmen's Christmas Box.		3	0
Paid for Coals and Kidds used at the Town Hall and Change	9	2	9
Paid for playing the Engines four several times. . .	10	0	0
Paid for repairing Do.	1	5	6
Paid the annual subscription to the Infirmary . . .	10	10	0
Paid the annual subscription to the Horse Race . .	10	10	0

Paid the annual Allowance for expences of the rent days .	15	15	0
Paid the Cryer for attendance at rent days . . .		2	6
Paid for lighting Lamps at the Free school . . .	2	2	0
Paid for making Gowns for the Waits		13	6
Paid Lamplighter for trimming 'Change Lamps . .		10	0
Paid John Pratt one year's donation by order of Common Hall	20	0	0
Paid John Throsby 52 weeks allowance at 10s 6d per week .	27	6	0
Paid Michael Staples 52 weeks allowance at 10s per week by order of Hall	26	0	0
Paid the Town Servants for their trouble at the Fairs, the sums collected by the Tolls being insufficient to pay them	1	17	10
Paid the Cryer for crying several times		3	0
Paid Mr Joseph Brown's executors a year's rent of the Guardhouse & buildings bought of the Duchy due 10th October 1814—£20 15s 8d Deducting Propetry tax £2	18	15	8
Paid the Town Servants for their fees on two newly elected Aldermen & 3 Common Council men	1	13	6
Paid the Tax for the Corporation Steward to Michaelmas 1814	2	0	0
Paid a year's Property Tax on the 'Change & Guard house	6	0	0
Paid a year's Property Tax on the Rents. . . .	309	9	0
Paid Do. on the Osier beds		6	7
Paid Do. on the money received for Freedoms on the average of 3 last years	25	12	0
Paid Messrs Carbonell for a pipe of Wine . . .	147	1	0
Paid for the carriage thereof	5	11	0
Paid for receipt Stamps for the rents	4	1	3
Paid the extra expence of the Dinner on St Thomas's day .	28	0	8
Paid the Steward for work done in the South Fields and the Meadows, & at the occupation roads etc. as per Account produced by him	94	7	3
Paid for insurance of the houses in High Street in the Globe Insurance Office	2	3	6
Paid expences of Journey to Belvoir Castle to present an address to His Royal Highness the Prince Regent, Chaise hire etc. etc.	92	6	9

Paid for advertizing the Address & the Prince Regent's answer thereto etc. etc. in the London Papers	64	11	0
Do. in the Nottingham, Northampton, Stamford & Derby Papers	7	10	2
Paid the Corporation's Subscription to the German Sufferers by order of Common Hall	105	0	0
Paid the Corporation's Subscription to the Poor of Leicester by order of Common Hall of 25th April 1814	210	0	0
Paid by order of Hall 2s 6d to each of the Noncommissioned Officers & privates of the Leicester Militia who volunteered for Foreign Service, on their passing through Leicester 281 @ 2s 6d	35	2	6
Paid by order of Hall the expences of a public dinner at the 3 Crowns Inn to those Officers who were in the Town at the time a General Peace took place in 1814	46	0	3
Paid for a piece of Plate for Mr Heyrick, the late Town Clerk, by order of Hall	107	16	8
Paid for engraving Inscription, chest, carriage & insurance .	12	15	6
Paid the Silversmith at Leicester Commission of £5 per Cent for procuring it	5	8	0
Paid sundry expences at the illumination of the 'Change etc. on the General Peace taking place	27	8	6
Paid the Town Servants for attending on the Fair & Market days to keep the Cattle within the Streets & places allotted for them in order to prevent the more public Streets from being crowded by them	15	0	0
Paid William Welton, Constable, for guarding the Horsepool (since filled up) at the bottom of Horsepool Street		5	0
Paid to Henry Mansfield 3 year's Land-Tax to Lady day 1814 of the house in his occupation & the adjoining one	3	13	6

7   Tradesmen's Bills

No. 1	Thomas Jackson, Carpenter	.	.	.	.	108	6	2
2	Isaac Cockshaw, Printer .	.	.	.	.	26	17	9
3	William Sultzer, Draper .	.	.	.	.	24	6	5
4	Henry Berridge, Taylor .	.	.	.	.	4	9	6
5	J. G. Browne, Printer	.	.	.	.	75	12	3
6	M. Miles, Coachmaker	.	.	.	.	1	12	6

7	Thomas Sing, Potseller	10	11	0
8	Thomas Riley, Engraver	21	0	0
9	Higginson & Sons, Chandlers	10	14	10
10	Dowley Meller & Co., Hatters	16	14	0
11	J. Nichols, Grocer		17	8
12	J. Edwyn, Brickmaker	1	10	2
13	John Adams, Oilman	20	16	0
14	Joshua Harrison, Carpenter	8	12	10
15	J. Jackson & Sons		7	0
16	Thomas Webster, Whitesmith	24	8	11
17	John Forsell, Glassman	21	14	0
18	Bosworth & Parr, Drapers	18	4	2
19	R. Willson, Ironfounder		10	6
20	W. Howcutt, Ironmonger	132	0	0
21	W. Bishop, Inkeeper	10	6	8
22	John Rice, Printer	19	19	6
23	Thomas Cooper, Wheelwright	1	9	7
24	John Bailey, Matseller	9	3	0
25	William Butcher, Pumpwright	12	13	0
26	Lawrence Smith, Carpenter	18	17	10
27	James Caparn, Brazier	6	7	10
28	Isaac Lovell, Draper	15	9	6
29	T. Combe, Printer	11	7	6
30	Francis Jones, Bricklayer	12	4	9
31	Thomas Watkinson, Carpenter	30	10	1
32	William Higginson, Painter	43	4	1
33	Do. for work at St John's Hospital . . .	4	12	2
34	J. Fox, Grocer	30	8	9
35	B. S. Chamberlain, Printer	16	0	3
36	Richard Angrave, Glazier	15	19	0
37	Richard Swinfen, Do.	22	11	4
38	W. Firmadge	16	18	9
39	J. Watkinson, Carpenter		5	0
40	Corts & Barston, Ironmongers	41	18	8
41	J. Measures, Upholsterer	31	12	6
42	Proprietors of Leicester Chronicle . . .	14	7	0
43	Forsell & Caparn, Coppersmiths . . .	12	2	10
44	J. Fowler, Printer	1	5	0
45	F. Raynes, Basketmaker		8	0
46	William Wall, Bricklayer	5	10	3
47	Samuel Oliver, Wine-merchant	3	18	0
48	James Wale, Carpenter	2	10	11
49	G. Webb & Co., Lime dealers		19	0

			£	s	d
50	F. Browns Executors		1	6	4
51	John Gregory, Grocer		1	10	0
52	John Edwyn, Brickmaker		2	12	3
53	James Rouse, Blacksmith		2	15	10
	Town Clerk's General Bill		182	15	0
	Do. for copies of Charters, Conveyancing business etc.	}	191	12	8
	Paving Bills		79	19	0
	Casual Bill		51	17	10

8   Levies

	£	s	d
Paid several Levies of the Highway Church & Poor and for tythes of St Mary's Meadows }	(blank)		
Allowed St Mary's Churchwardens for tythes out of the rent of the Herbage in the Church Yard }	(blank)		
Paid for the Levies on Freakes ground	1	1	10
Paid poors Levies on the Willow Bedds		4	8

9   Allowance of Land tax at 4s in the Pound

	s	d
Mr Alexander Forrester	6	0
Mr John Moore	4	0
Mr Higginson	4	0
John Mansfield Esquire	4	0
Foulgham by Fewkes late Withers	4	0
Shuckburghs Ashby Esquire	6	0
Withers late Sheffield	13	0
Mr John Moore	8	0
Mr Bradley late Fosbrooke	4	0
Mr Clay Hextall	4	0
Mr Henry Sands late Foulgham	4	0
Mr Poole late Thomas Nutt	4	0
Mr Joseph Boulton	6	0
Mr Phipps late Wildbore	5	0
Mr William Johnson	4	0
Mr William Moore late Christy	4	0
Mr Robert Clarke	4	0
Burgess late Hanwell	4	0
Mr Andrews (on Twigden's Gift)	8	0

		£ s. d.
Mr Samuel Robinson		4 0
Mr James Wilby		4 0
Mr Forrester		5 0
Mr Stone late John Burgess		5 0
Mr Peberdy late Thomas Eames & Mr Watts . . .		8 0
Mrs Edmonds late Dyson		6 0
Keen & Taylor late Tompkin		5 0
William Barrar late Clayton		4 0
The Governors of the Leicester Infirmary . . .		5 0
Hewins late Nixon		4 0
A year's Land tax on the House in Miss Hartell's occupation }		9 6
Do. to Hosea Hafford		14 6
A years Land tax on the Houses in Horse fair (now pulled down) purchased by Brooks }		4 0

11   Charitable Gifts

		£ s. d.
Paid the Gift of Queen Elizabeth to the Head Usher .		10 0 0
Paid the Gift of Sir Ralph Rowlett to the Under Usher .		3 6 8
Paid the Gift of Mr Norris to the Head Usher . .		3 6 8
Paid the Gift of Mr Clarke to the Under Usher . .		1 0 0
Paid the Gift of Mr Norris out of the Willoughby lands vizt.		
To St Martin's parish . . .	1 14 4	
St Margaret's	1 14 4	
St Mary's	1 14 4	
All Saints'	1 7 6	10 0 0
St Nicholas'	19 6	
St Leonard's	10 0	
Trinity Hospital	1 13 4	
Saint John's	6 8	
Paid the Gift of Mr John Stanley vizt.		
To the Vicar of Saint Martin's . .	1 10 0	
Head Master	1 0 0	
Head Usher	13 4	4 0 0
Under Usher	6 8	
10 Widows or Maids . . .	10 0	
Paid the Gift of Mr William Stanley to the Poor of Trinity Hospital }		1 0 0
Paid the Gift of the Earl of Devonshire (part of the Wood and Coal Money) }		6 0 0

Paid the Gift of Christopher Tamworth Esquire to the Vicar of St Martin's			61	2	6
Paid the Gift of King Charles the first of ever blessed memory part of the Wood & Coal money			52	0	0

Paid the Gift of Mr William Ives (vizt.)

To Trinity Hospital . . .	5 12 0		
The New Hospital	8 0		
For 2dy bread for the parishes 13s 4d		14 0 0	
every Friday in Lent . . .	4 0 0		
For 8 Widows Gowns . . .	4 0 0		

Paid the Gift of Mrs Ives to Trinity Hospital . . .	1 0 0	

Paid the Gift of Mr Elkinton (vizt.)

To Saint Martins	2 0 0	
Lutterworth	2 10 0	5 0 0
The Town Clerk	10 0	

Paid the Gift of (blank) Poultney Esquire (vizt.)

To Saint Martin's parish . . .	2 4 0	
Saint Margaret's	2 4 0	
Saint Mary's	2 4 0	10 0 0
All Saints	1 3 0	
Saint Nicholas	16 0	
Land Tax	1 9 0	

Paid the Gift of Mr Nidd to the Poor of Mountsorrel (received & paid by the Mayor)		70 0 0
Paid the Gift of Mr Acham in Bread		9 0 0

Paid the Gift of Mr Haines (vizt.)

To the Schoolmaster at Thrussington .	6 0 0	
Two Scholars Lincoln College . .	6 0 0	
3 Bibles	1 0 0	24 0 0
For preaching a Sermon . . .	1 0 0	
Disposed of in Wood and Coal . .	10 0 0	

Paid the Gift of Mr Botham (vizt.)

To Saint Martin's parish . . .	13 4	
Saint Margaret's	13 4	2 0 0
Saint Mary's	13 4	

Paid the Gift of the Earl of Huntingdon to Wigston's

Hospital	10 0 0	9 0 0
Deducting property tax . . .	1 0 0	

Paid the Gift of Mr John Holmes to Trinity Hospital .	45 0 0	
To Saint John's & Bents	6 10 0	

Paid the Gift of Mrs Twigden (vizt.)
   For 3 Gowns to the Widows of Saint
   John's 1 10 0
   To Do. for Coals .   .   .   10 0   2 0 0

Paid the Gift of Mr John Bent to Bent's Hospital (received
& paid by the Mayor)   77 0 0

Paid the Gift of Mr Moreton out of the Tippetts (received
& paid by the Mayor) being disposed of with the Wood &
Coal money   3 0 0

Paid the Gift of Mrs Ward (vizt.)
   Three Widows of St John's to buy
   Gowns 1 10 0
   Do. for Coals 10 0
   To 2 Alms women in Trinity Hospital. 10 0   3 0 0
   To the Common Box there . .   10 0

Paid the Gift of Mr William Billers (vizt.)
   To the Widows in Trinity Hospital 1s
   each weekly 5 4 0
   To Trinity Hospital for Oatmeal .   5 16 0   12 0 0
   For a gown 1 0 0

Paid the Gift of Sir William Courteen & the Gentlemen of
the Lottery to the different parishes in 4dy bread   4 16 0

Paid the Gift of Mrs Dorothy Baker to the head and under
Ushers   1 0 0

Paid the Gift of Mr Julius Billers to Trinity Hospital .   5 12 0

Paid the Gift of Messrs Bennett & Ward (part of the Wood
& Coal money)   1 0 0

Paid the gift of Widow Ossiter Do.   .   .   .   6 0 0

Paid the gift of Mr Hitch to Trinity Hospital .   .   .   3 0

Paid the gift of Mr Thomas Gilbert (vizt.)
   To the head Schoolmaster   .   .   3 0 0
   The head Usher 1 10 0   5 0 0
   The Under Usher 10 0

Paid the Gift of Mrs Margaret Hobby (vizt.)
   To the Under Usher .   .   .   12 0
   the Old Hospital .   .   .   2 6
   the New Hospital .   .   .   2 0
   Saint John's   6   1 1 0
   the poor of St Martin's .   .   .   2 0
   Do. of St Mary's 2 0

Paid the Gift of the Countess of Devonshire (vizt.)
 To Saint Martin's parish .   .   .   9   0
 Saint Margaret's   9   0
 Saint Mary's   9   0   3   0   0
 All Saints   7   0
 Saint Nicholas   6   0
 Saint Leonards   1   0   0

Paid the gift of Mrs Haselridge (vizt.)
 To Trinity Hospital   .   .   .   12   0
 Saint John's   7   6   1   1   6
                                         2   0

Paid the gift of Mr William Cooper to Saint John's
Hospital   2   4   9

Paid the gift of Mr Thomas Ayre to St John's Hospital   .   1   0   0

Paid the gift of Mr John Ludlam to Do.   .   .   .   2 10   0

Paid the gift of Mr John Wightman to Trinity Hospital   .   5   0

Paid the gift of Mr John Roberts (vizt.)
 To Trinity Hospital   .   .   .   10   0
 Saint John's   10   0   1   0   0

Paid the Gift of Mr Robert Hall to 8 Widows of St John's
Hospital   10   0

Paid the Gift of George Bent to Trinity Hospital   .   .   5   0

Paid the Gift of Mr William Sutton to St John's Hospital.   2 16   0

Paid the Gift of Do. to Trinity Hospital being the interest
of £20   16   0

Paid the Gift of Mr Thomas Topp to Trinity Hospital   .   1   0   0

Paid the Gift of Do. to St John's   10   0

Paid the Gift of Mr Benjamin Garland to St Martin's
parish   5   0

Paid the Gift of Alderman Thomas Ludlam (vizt.)
 For apprenticing a Boy   .   .   .   8   0   0
 For preaching a Sermon for St John's.   1   0   0
 For the Nurse of St John's 1s per Week   2 12   0   12   0   0
 Remainder divided on Sunday after
 St John's   8   0

Paid the Gift of Mr Cradock to Trinity Hospital   .   .   4   0   0

Paid the Gift of Mr Andrews to Do.   5   0

Paid the Gift of Mr Blunt on St Thomas's day (vizt.)

For Shoes	6 10 0	
To be spent	10 0	
To Town Clerk & Macebearer 2s 6d each	5 0	
To 4 Serjeants at Mace 1s each . .	4 0	
Beadle & Cryer 6d each . . .	1 0	10 0 0
Minister of Walton Superwoulds .	18 0	
Vicar of St Margaret's . . .	1 0 0	
Clerk & Sexton	5 0	
The Mayor	5 0	
The Spittlehouse poor . . .	2 0	

Paid the Gift of Mr Bent to St John's & Bent's Hospital .	2 10 0
Gave to the Poor of Leicester in Coals	30 13 5
Paid the Poor of St John's Hospital the rent arising from the two tenements in Causeway lane now occupied by Parrott which were built with £50 given by Cammock's Will & £115 arising from the sale of the Hospital Gardens towards rebuilding the Town Gaol	17 17 0

[End of Payments]

[Supers start here]

Supers

Perkins for Gunnerby Land	6 8
George Wright Esquire for Land at Oadby . . .	5 11½
The Earl of Stamford for the tythes of the Thurmaston Mills	6 8
Anthony Ingoldsby for Land at Ashby	6
Lammas Tythes	4 12 6

Watts	1 0	
Green	5 0	
W. Clark	1 0 0	
Nutt	2 2	
Johnson	10	
Howe	1 2	
Jackson	1 0	
		1 11 2

[End of Supers]

Y

[Arrears start here]

Arrears

Names of Tenants	Amount of Arrears transferred by the last Chamberlains			Amount of Arrears accrued this year			Total Amount of Arrears		
Thomas Yates	2	0	0	1	0	0	3	0	0
James Gibson	11	7	6				11	7	6
(blank) Flude	2	0	0		5	0	2	5	0
Thomas Yates	2	0	0		13	4	2	13	4
Nicholas Hurst	10	10	0		15	0	11	5	0
David Monk		10	0		2	0		12	0
Thomas Yates	1	0	0		6	8	1	6	8
Do.	1	6	8		13	4	2	0	0
John Burrows	2	13	4		13	4	3	6	8
Thomas Yates	1	4	0		8	0	1	12	0
Do.		15	0		5	0	1	0	0
Do.		10	0		3	4		13	4
Widow Bruce					10	0		10	0
(blank) Bruce	1	0	0		2	6	1	2	6
William Herrick		4	6			6		5	0
Widow Bruce	2	0	0				2	0	0
Sir Philip Vavasor	9	0	0	9	0	0	18	0	0
(blank) Woodford	4	4	0		6	0	4	10	0

[End of arrears]

[Summary]

	£	s	d
Payments	5072	3	6½
Receipts	5058	1	11
Balance due to the Chamberlains	14	1	7½

Amount of Arrears to be transferred to the
next Chamberlains £67 9s 0d

CHAMBERLAINS' ACCOUNTS
1834/5

Accounts of Messrs
Bonnett & T. Rawson
in the Mayoralty of
Richard Rawson Esquire

[These accounts run from September 1834 to December 1835. No fresh Chamberlains were appointed for the last three months of the old Corporation's existence.]

1a Receipts of the Old Grange etc. vizth. South Fields Burgesses Meadows, Beadhouse Meadows, Gosling Closes etc. etc.

Mr George Hardstaff late Mr Thomas Chatwyn's Representatives late Alderman Chatwyn late John Guilford a year's rent of the Newarke Mills inclusive of one Beadhouse Meadow late Daft's marked on new Plan No. 105 and inclusive of 0 acres 2 rods 25 perches late Dabbs marked on new Plan No. 94 due 29th September 1835	134 5 0	

1b Gosling Closes

J. P. Stallard late Mr Alderman J. Johnson a year's rent of the close late in Alderman Watchorn's occupation with part of the other Close laid to it due Michaelmas 1835	24 0 0	
Mr William Parsons late Mr Alderman Wood late Mr Leach late Alderman Watchorn half a year's rent of the close late Johnson's from which a part was taken to the other close due Lady Day 1835	4 10 0	
Mr J. P. Stallard the other half year's rent due Michaelmas 1835	4 10 0	

1c Beadhouse Meadows

Tapscote late Thomas Stevenson late Gabriel Withers late Thomas Martin a year's rent of two plots in these meadows numbered on new Plan 109 & 110 — due Michaelmas 1835	11 0 0	

Joseph Morris late William Gamble late Gabriel Withers late William Coltman a year's rent of two more plots in these meadows numbered on new Plan 111 & 112 due Michaelmas 1835	11	0 0
James Gunn late Gabriel Withers late John Bates a years rent for two more plots numbered on new Plan 113 & 114 due Do.	12	0 0
George Hardstaff late Chatwyn a year's rent of two plots numbered on new Plan No. 100 due same time	3 15	0
George Hardstaff late Chatwyn for part of these meadows late Dabbs numbered on new Plan Nos. 95 & 96 due Michaelmas 1835	2	0 0
Harrold late Hunt late Collins late Abraham Walker a year's rent for two plots numbered on new plan Nos. 103 & 104 due Michaelmas 1835	10	0 0
James Gunn late the Executors of John Abbott a year's rent of Meadow numbered 115 due same time	10	0 0
William Hitchcock late Gabriel Withers late Rice late Black and before John Frisby a year's rent of two plots marked on new plan Nos. 107 & 108 due Michaelmas	9	0 0

⟨This item is inserted here as part of the Beadhouse Meadows instead of where it used to appear⟩

No. on the Plan made on the sub- division of the Fields

1d In the South Fields which are now inclosed under the Act of 44th Geo. 3rd Cap. (blank) and divided into small allotments (except the part over which the Race Course runs) and are let to the following Tenants upon Leases from year to year commencing at Lady Day

1 Race Plot	Joseph Taylor a years rent due Michaelmas 1834 as above stated	93 4	4
2	Joseph Taylor late Willoughby Bishop a years rent due same time	73 10	6
3	Joseph Taylor late W. Bishop a years rent of a close adjoining the Race Course due same time	11 14	0
4	John Higginson late Isaac Barnes late William Spencer late Gilbert a years rent due same time	12 10	0

5	William Johnson late Alderman George Ireland late Smith or Gilbert's executors one years rent as increased	17	0	0
6	Richard Rawson late John Jackson's executors a years rent	11	0	0
7	John Sarson late Robert Clarke a years rent .	14	5	10
8 & 11	William Hall's executors (Blue Lion) Do. .	27	10	0
9	Joseph Taylor late Mr W. Bishop late Rider Do.	16	16	6
10	John Hincks late Joseph Slater a years rent due Michaelmas (as increased)	19	0	0
12, 13, 14, 15,	Mr J. K. Holmes late Alderman Marston half a years rent due Lady Day 1835 (as increased)	30	0	0
	Of him half a years rent as reduced as part of his Land having been taken for the New Lunatic Asylum due Michaelmas 1835	22	0	0
16, 17	John Measures late Thomas Clarke a years rent of these plots due Michaelmas	32	0	0
18, 19	J. Briggs late Thomas Clarke half a years rent of these plots due Lady Day 1835	16	0	0
	(blank) Heggs half a years rent of Plot No. (blank) due Michaelmas 1835 The whole of Plot No. (blank) has been sold for the New Asylum	8	0	0
59	C. Musson late Thomas Clarke a years rent of this plot due Do.	16	0	0
20	Henry Dalby late John Colban late Highton Do. (as increased)	24	10	0
21	Edward Rawson late Thomas Bown's executors a years rent due Michaelmas (as increased)	20	0	0
22	Alderman Miller late Benjamin Jackson .	9	16	0
23	Do. late Benjamin Jackson . . .	10	8	0
24	Thomas Toone late Edward Parsons . .	14	17	0
25	Henry Highton late Do.	18	10	6
26	Samuel Bankart half a years rent of this plot due Lady Day 1835	8	19	6

	William Sturgess the other half years rent due Michaelmas (as reduced)	8	0	0
27	Mr Thomas Barratt late John Barratt Do. .	20	17	0
28	Edward Rice late G. B. Hodges Do. . .	22	17	0
	Laxton Boyall late (blank) Blood late Alderman Marston a years rent of the Wind Mill close due Michaelmas 1835	7	0	0
	Laxton Boyall a years rent of the other part on which the Wind Mill stands due Michaelmas 1835	5	0	0
29	Edward Sanderson one years rent due Michaelmas 1835	10	14	6
30	Simeon Morris late Thomas Oliver Do. .	18	8	0
31	Alderman Bankart late Brown late Harrison late Everard Do.	17	0	0
32	Thomas Warner Do.	13	1	0
34	Edward Rice Do.	15	0	0
35	Thomas Wright late Benjamin Sarson Do. .	11	15	0
36	Edward Rice late Robert Higginson Do. .	13	6	6
37	J. G. Brown late Barnes late Davenport Do. .	14	5	0
38	Mr John Bosworth late Alderman Peach a years rent due Michaelmas	60	0	0
41	(blank) Higginson a years rent due Michaelmas (sold to the Borough)			
43	Alderman James Rawson late Samuel Hunt late Miss Eames late John Eames a year's rent due Michaelmas. 25s deducted for a piece added to the new Street	15	0	0
44	Alderman J. Rawson late Samuel Hunt late Joshua Harrison late Fosbrey Do.	15	5	6
45	John Hincks late Samuel Hunt late Jones late Edwyn late Johnson late Valentine a year's rent due Michaelmas	12	0	0
46	John Sargeant's executors late Alderman Wright half a years rent due Lady Day 1835	9	3	0
	Mr Alderman James Rawson the other half years rent due Michaelmas 1835	9	3	0

47	Richard Hole late Caleb Lowdham late Alderman S. Clarke	21	2	0
48	James Rawson late Alderman Gregory . .	18	9	0
49	George Willey late Francis Moore late M. & W. Gregory — Do. as reduced	17	0	0
50	Mr John Marshall late Mr Dabbs late John Measures late Alderman Stevenson a years rent due Michaelmas 1835 (part of this close taken for sale)	12	0	0
	Simeon Morris for a year's rent of land on sale	(blank)		
67	Alderman Hodges late Thomas Neale a year's rent due Michaelmas 1835 (as increased)	16	10	0
60	William Sultzer Do.	15	9	0
61	Charles Coleman Do.	15	19	0
62	Kinton late Infirmary late Sanderson . .	16	16	6
66	Mr G. B. Hodges one years rent of close late Alderman Bishop due Michaelmas	22	10	0
63	John Oldacre late Robys late B. Sutton Do. .	13	15	6
64	Thomas Higginson one year's rent due Michaelmas 1835	13	10	6
65	William Howcutt late Bishop late Tillson Do.	14	0	0
68	G. B. Hodges late James Kirk's assignees late Henry Wood late Neale for a year's rent of this plot due Michaelmas	17	0	0
69	Thomas Cook late Heyrick late Vaughan Do.	16	1	6
70	Samuel Stretton late Alderman Burgess's Representatives late Collison a year's rent of this plot due Michaelmas	16	0	0
71	Mrs Withers late Thomas Berry late W. James Bishop late H. Wood late Barston's a year's rent of this plot due Michaelmas 1835 (as abated)	18	0	0
72	Alderman John Higginson a year's rent due Michaelmas	22	7	6

73	Alderman R. Johnson Do. . . .	22	7	6
74	James Cort Do.	22	5	6
75	B. Payne late R. B. Swinfen half a year's rent of this plot due Lady Day 1835	11	10	0
	Thomas Higginson the other half year's rent due Michaelmas 1835	11	10	0
76	(blank) Barrows late Mrs Miles late Alderman Miles a year's rent due Michaelmas 1835	21	0	0
77	Mr T. Miller late Decimus Cooke late Rawson late Heard a year's rent Do.	23	0	0
78 & 79	Mr T. Pettifor late Mrs Threlfall late Quilter a years rent due Michaelmas 1835	30	0	0

1e   Saint Mary's Meadow

80	Walter Hall late Alderman Marston one year's rent due Michaelmas 1835	24	15	0
81	Messrs Herberts late Thomas Kilbourn late William Chamberlayne late William Whitehead a years rent due Do.	24	0	0
82	Samuel Stretton late Edward Parsons late Richards Do.	21	9	6
83	Jerry Herbert late Alderman Marston late Briggs a year's rent due Michaelmas 1835 as reduced	14	0	0
84	Samuel Stretton late Alderman Wood late Thomas Kilbourn late Spencer a years rent due Michaelmas (as reduced)	13	0	0
85	Mr J. P. Stallard late Joshua Harrison late the Governors of the Infirmary late Reverend G. B. Mitchell a years rent due Michaelmas 1835	12	0	0
86	William Coleman late Edward Parsons Do. .	13	19	0
87	Thomas Withers late Widow Mann Do. .	9	13	6
88	Simeon Morris late J. Johnson a year's rent due Michaelmas 1835	30	0	0
89	Simeon Morris late Mansfield Do. . .	29	8	6
90	Simeon Morris late T. Freer late Godfrey Do.	5	9	0

1f Far Meadow

91	Thomas Withers late Jackson one year's rent due Michaelmas 1835	16	14	0
92	Robert Higginson late Mann Do. . .	13	2	6
93	Thomas Warner late Hodgson Do. . .	11	10	0
94	Thomas Withers late Gibson Do. . .	11	17	6
95	Matthew Green late Gird late Lowe do. .	11	7	0
96	Simeon Morris late Illston late Mansfield Do.	12	12	6
97	Do. late Metcalf late Wilson Do. . .	23	0	0

1g [No separate heading inserted]

Mr Alderman J. Johnson for a messuage Farm yard and Homestead called Hall's Grange	10	0	0
Gabriel Withers late Rice late Black late John Frisby for (blank)	(blank)		
⟨Inserted [previously] being part of Beadhouse Meadows⟩			
Mr Alderman J. Johnson late Thomas Frisby a year's rent for a Barn Yard and Homestead in Grange Lane due Michaelmas 1835	12	0	0
Mr Alderman James Rawson late Samuel Hunt for the clay of 353,580 Bricks made from the close late Harrison's at 2s 6d per thousand from Michaelmas 1833 to Michaelmas 1834 payable in addition to his rent for the land	44	3	4
Edward Rice for the clay of 447,251 Bricks made on the Plot No. (blank) from Michaelmas 1833 to Michaelmas 1834 at 2s 6d per thousand	55	18	0
Do. for (blank) Kilns of Plaister on the same Plot 20s . (No Plaister burn't this year)	(blank)		
Edward Rice for the Clay of 879,298 Bricks made on the Plot No. (blank) from Michaelmas 1834 to Michaelmas 1835 at 2s 6d per thousand	109	18	4
Mr Alderman James Rawson late Samuel Hunt for the clay of 569,000 Bricks made from the close late Harrisons at 2s 6d per thousand from Michaelmas 1834 to Michaelmas 1835 payable in addition to his rent for the land	71	2	6

1h Of the following persons for the rents of Gardens adjoining the New Walk (part of the South Fields)

No. 1	Mr Thomas Higginson late Foreman late Crammant a year's rent	4	11	4

Mr McAlpine late Gilbert Do. . . .	4	8	6
Harris Do.	3	14	10
Mr Coleman late Humphreys Do. . .	5	1	6
Richards Do.	8	0	0
Mrs Dalby late Graves Do. (4. 5. 2.) . .	2	3	0
Mr John Mortin late Winfield Do. . .	4	3	4
R. Rawson late Dalby Do. . . .	3	10	0
Pratt Do.	4	19	4
Horsepool late Alderman Burgess Do. .	3	7	0
Goddard Do.	3	5	6
Gray half years rent	2	1	7
Weston the other half year	2	1	7

No. 15 & Mr Ackland for a year's rent of 2 Gardens
16   formerly in the occupation of Staines and one
        Garden formerly in the possession of Free-   12 0 0
        man

Thorpe late Jolly late Everard a year's rent .   3 3 8
Freeman   Do. 3 15 8

Total of this & the preceding pages vizt.
Old Grange etc. £2160 18s 2d

2a   Premises passing under
                          Charters and Grants

(blank) late Mr F. Burgess late Mr Edward Parsons late
Mr Henry Palmer late Mr Alderman Palmer late Augus-
tine Hefford a year's rent of the Sheep Pens with Cocker's   (blank)
Kitchen on Lease payable half yearly

Henry Hitchcock late Robert Hitchcock late Henry
Hitchcock late Mr Alderman Fisher late John Brooks a
year's rent for the North Mills including new Dwelling-   175 0 0
house etc.

By the clear Receipts from the Saturday's Market (after
deducting expences) for the year ending Michaelmas 1835
as Per the Account produced by Mr Rawson the Treasurer, vizt.

Receipts—Quarterly 800 8 7
          Casual 267 18 3   626 6 8
                                  ——————————
                                  1068 6 10

Deduct payments and incidental ex-}
pences   442 0 2

Messrs John & Isaac Abell late William Abell a year's rent of the North Mill Holme on lease	15	0	0
Widow Abell late The Reverend Mr Ross for a Garden in Elbow Lane the rent of which is by order of Hall given to the Head Master during pleasure	2	12	6
The Churchwardens of St Mary's for the herbage of St Mary's Church Yard per annum £3 5s 0d	(blank)		

2b   Receipts for Tithes on Estates in St Mary's

Part of Ruding's Estate

John Mellor Senior (as reduced on account of Stone Quarry)	8	11	0
John Mellor Junior (Do.)	14	9	8
Thomas Barfoot Oliver Esquire	3	2	7
Joseph Harris	7	9	2
Thomas Saunderson	2	16	0
William Stretton	6	10	8
John Abell	7	12	4

Part of Mitchell's Tithe and Ruding's

Dr Noble late Mr Mellor	27	14	0
Late Mrs Kirshaw for part of Buxton, part Ruding and part Mitchell	27	10	3
Late Thomas Mitchell part of Rudings . . .	5	17	7
William Kelley's Executors part of Bates's tythes and Bow Bridge Close	1	19	3
Late Mrs Kirshaw for close late Baxter . . .		16	3

Part of Pares's Land

Mr Willis late Edmund Packe Esquire reduced on account of land being in grass	1	2	9
David Hefford	1	12	6

The Corporation of Leicester . .	4	1	6
	2	16	6
	6	18	0

Thomas Withers	6	15	8
John Pares Esquire	13	1	6
Thomas Paget Esquire (reduced on account of Railway) .	13	6	8

Thomas Freer Esquire	10	11	9
The Reverend C. Berry	1	10	0
(blank) Dexter late Highton	(blank)		
C. Winstanley Esquire—part Ruding part Pares and part Ratcliffe	47	8	7
John Clarke Esquire	10	10	3
The Executors of the late Henry Peach Esquire . .	9	16	0
Charles Meredith Esquire now Mr Samuel Harris . .	(blank)		
Mr Loseby all built over	(blank)		
Mr Harris (Bracemanufacturer) built over . . .	(blank)		
Mr Nokes late Joseph Smith's Executors late Thomas Kirk a year's rent of a tenement in the Market Place which used to be included in the Lease of the North Mills	12	12	0

Total under Charters
& Grants   £1061 15s 7d

3a   Purchases etc.

Mr John Campion late Wale of Frowlesworth for a year's rent of the Foss Close & Meadow due at Lady Day 1835 on Lease from year to year	46	0	0
Gabriel Sutton late Gimson late Thomas Shuttlewood late John Nedham of Whetstone late Edward Sutton for lands in the Lordship of Willoughby Warterless late Hall of Cosby (out of which Norrice's Gift of £10 per Annum is payable) due Lady Day 1835—as abated	20	0	0
Widow Mann a year's rent for an Orchard or Garden in All Saints Parish	16	0	0
Charles Mann a year's rent for the remainder of the said Orchard—as increased	16	0	0
(blank) Stafford late the widow of Thomas Ryder for a small piece of ground part of which was purchased of Mr William Heyrick a year's rent	3	3	0
Edward Blood late Reeve late Lee late Hafford late Slater late Henry Lenton for the other part of the same ground	3	3	0

3b Of the following Persons for certain Grounds near Leicester called Freake's Grounds which were formerly only two closes and in the occupation of Edward Sutton and John Mortimore but are now divided into smaller closes and are let on Lease from year to year to the following Tenants—the rent payable half yearly

Note—These closes have been intersected by the Rail-road and the rents and quantities are therefore varied.

John Musson late Elizabeth Johnson a years rent due Michaelmas 1835	17	10	0
Thomas Thompson late John Jervis late S. Kelly late William Forrester a years rent due same time	17	10	0
Henry Hitchcock late John Barlow do. due do. . .	16	0	0
Thomas Marston do. due do.	18	10	0
Mrs Abell late William Adams do. due do. . . .	10	0	0
John Mudford do. due do.	16	10	0
John Brown late Alderman Clarke do. due do. . .	20	0	0
John Slater late Joseph Bland late Alderman Neale do. due do.	12	10	0
John Higginson late William Howcutt do. due do. .	16	0	0
George Marston late Robinson late Thompson do. due do.	22	0	0
Henry Hitchcock do. due do.	31	0	0
John Slater late Thomas Cox do. due do. . .	18	0	0
Thomas Thompson late Abell for a piece divided by the Rail Road do. due do.	8	0	0
Nicholas Higginson late the executrix of the late John Priestman do. due do.	18	0	0

3c [No separate heading inserted]

Henry Mansfield a year's rent of the House known by the Sign of the Nag's Head purchased by the Corporation of Mrs Elizabeth Thornelow due Michaelmas 1835	50	0	0
(blank) Beadman late Petzold late Hewitt late Woollands a year's rent of a House in High Cross Street purchased of Mr William Hall due at the same time	14	0	0
Thomas Mitchell late Alderman Jeffcutt late Highton a year's rent of another House there purchased also of Mr William Hall due at the same time	14	0	0
Mr Aulesbrook late Samuel Grace late Miss Hartall a year's rent of a House in the same Street purchased of Mr William Hardy due at the same time	16	0	0

Thomas Mitchell late Hosea Hafford a year's rent of another House purchased of Hardy — 14 0 0

(blank) Gray late Thomas Sharpless late Webster a year's rent of Shops etc. held under Lease of the Duchy due Michaelmas 1835 — 12 0 0

Do. for a year's rent of Engine House due same time   .   3 0 0

(blank) Payne late Mrs Burkhill a year's rent of stables part of the property held under Lease of the Duchy due Do. — 10 0 0

(blank) Payne late Burkhill a year's rent of the Parlour to the Little Crown — 6 0 0

B. Ward late John Whitmore for a year's rent of the Bull's Head premises in the Market Place and a House at the back purchased of Mr Greasley due Michaelmas 1835 as reduced — 100 0 0

William Hester a year's rent of Stables etc. other part of the same property (due Do.) — (blank)
⟨Now part of the New Market House⟩

Mr Henry Dalby a year's rent of a Garden etc. other part of the same property (due Michaelmas 1835) — 10 10 0

The Reverend Mr Davies late The Reverend Mr Bullen late The Reverend Mr Heyrick late Pigott for an acknowledgement for the House adjoining the Free School due Midsummer 1835—2s 6d — (blank)

Alderman Parsons a year's rent of a Garden in Bowling Green Street purchased of him due Michaelmas 1835 — 6 0 0

The Trustees of the Harborough Road late Dand a year's rent of a Garden lately purchased of Mr Bosworth due Michaelmas — 10 0 0

Mr Parr a year's rent of part of the above Garden due Do. (reduced to £3 per annum) — 3 0 0

Mr Charles Mann late Hutchinson a year's rent of a Close in St Mary's Parish purchased of Mr Pares's Trustees due Michaelmas — 30 0 0

(blank) Illstone a year's rent due Michaelmas (reduced to) .   22 0 0

Charles Mann for a close purchased of Mr Pares late William Withers a year's rent due Michaelmas — 20 0 0

Mr Charles Mann late William Withers a year's rent of a Meadow purchased of Mr Ruding's Trustees due Michaelmas — 24 0 0

By the receipts from the Sheep Pens and the new Market
as superintended by Mr Yates and Mr Rawson, vizt.

By Receipts from Michaelmas 1834 to Michaelmas 1835	}	359	19	2
Deduct Incidental expences . . .		178	0	1

	181	19	1

Total of purchased property
£892 5s 1d

4   Receipts for the Schools and
Charitable Uses

The Reverend Dr Andrews out of Rowlett's Close near Braunstone Gate in the occupation of Henry Mansfield the Gift of Mrs Twigden received of Mrs Lowdham	2	0	0
John Clarke Esquire late Walter Ruding Esquire late Mr Simpson out of the Tippitts in Saint Mary's Parish being Mr Moreton's Gift	3	0	0
Mr Bates late Thomas Mitchell late said Walter Ruding Esquire out of the Duck Holmes in St Mary's Parish Mr Ward's Gift	3	0	0
The Leicester Navigation Company (by Mr Cardale) late The Reverend Gerard Andrews out of the Leroes in Saint Margarets parish the Gift of Mr William Billers	12	0	0

Mr Nedham late Mr Peake late Henry Coleman Esquire late Mr Moore for Lewin's Heirs out of the House in Belgrave Gate	2	0	0			
Mr Cooper late Dr Hill late Dr Arnold late Mr Barry—the like . . .	2	0	0	10	0	0
Mr Towndrow late Peter Oliver late Hayes out of the Cranes . . .	4	0	0			
Mr Cooper late Mr Harrison Gardener, out of the Crab Street . . .	2	0	0			

    ⟨Blunt's Gifts⟩

Mr Whetstone late Lovell heir of Farmer out of a House in Silver Street now called Town Hall Lane the Gift of Mr Bent to the poor of St John's Hospital payable on Sunday after St John	2	10	0
His Majesty's Receiver General of the Duchy by Mr Thomas Freer given by Queen Elizabeth out of the Honor of Leicester for the better maintaining the Under Usher of the Grammar School of Leicester	10	0	0

Messrs Goddard (Bankers) late Inkersole for Earl Spencer one moiety or Rent charge payable out of the Manor of Theddingworth being the gift of Sir Ralph Rowlett for maintaining the Under Usher of the said School lately Lord Althorpe   3   6   8

Mr Simpson late Mr John Iliffe late Mr John Morris one annuity payable yearly out of a close in Abbey Gate called Abbey Gate Close the Gift of Mr William Norrice (one of the Aldermen) for the better maintaining the Head Usher in the occupation of Mr Iliffe per annum   3   6   8

Joseph Hudson late Francis Brown, carpenter, late Thomas Buxton, Esquire late Mr Hudson for one annuity payable out of a piece of ground called the Water Laggs to the Under Usher of the same School being the Gift of Thomas Clarke per annum   1   0   0

William Hall late Jonathan Gillam for a years rent of a messuage or tenement and close and one yard land at Whetstone bought of one John Baker, Gentleman, by the Corporation with the money bequeathed by Christopher Tamworth Esquire for celebrating Divine service—on Lease expiring Lady Day (now reduced to)   60   0   0

W. K. Walker Esquire, late Samuel Brewin late Wollaston Wigston late John Brewin for a year's rent of 40 acres of land in the Forest of Leicester given by King Charles the 1st of ever blessed memory to the poor of the Borough due Michaelmas 1834   52   0   0

Mr Pares payable yearly out of the Manor of Cotes Deval being the Gift of Mr Poultney to Charitable Uses   10   0   0

Mr Richardson late Mr Seal of Bushby late George Plummer of Evington for a year's rent of lands in Bushby being the gift of Mr Nidd to the Poor of Mountsorrel on Lease from year to year   70   0   0

Mr Stone for Sir Philip Vavasour being Mr Acham's Gift to the Poor of the Corporation out of the Manor of Asfordby alias Asterby in the County of Lincoln per annum due at Michaelmas (now received from Mr John Calthorpe of West Ashby near Horncastle out of the estate of Sigismund Trafford Esquire at Asterby in Lincolnshire   9   0   0

Peter Colston late Mr Alderman Burgess late Pares for a rent charge out of his house late occupied by Mr Samuel Markland heretofore called the Parrott being the gift of Mr Hugh Botham and paid at Saint Thomas's Day   2   0   0

Ward late Clarke late Whitehead of Allexton for several
Closes of ground there being the gift of Mr Haines to
Charitable Uses late in Chatwell's occupation by Lease
per annum abated £3 }   32   0   0

Mr George Bradley late Richard March late Mr William
Proudman late Joseph Parrott for two tenements in Causeway Lane belonging to St John's Hospital built with the
£50 given by Mr Cammack's will and the £115 arising
by the sale of the Hospital Gardens towards building the
Town Gaol on Lease per annum due Lady Day and
Michaelmas }   18   0   0

Total of Charity Receipts
£303 3s 4d

5a   Fee Farm Rents and Chief Rents

Mr Robert Hitchcock late Henry Hitchcock late Whetstone late Hull, Baker, late Roger Ruding Esquire heretofore Mr J. Harrison for rents of Assize due yearly out of
the lands at the North Gates late in the occupation of
Thomas Turville called Gadsby's land at Michaelmas only }   1   9

Sir Nigil Greasley (by Mr E. Parsons) late Mr Alderman
Wood heretofore Mr John Blunt for the Butt Close for-
merly sold to Mr Thomas Blunt late in the occupation of
Mr Robert Rollestone late Foreman's land late Mr John
Loseby's }   (blank)
⟨Given to St Margaret's Charity School⟩

Mr (blank) late Thomas Yates late Mr Bellamy Executor
of Mr John Yates late Mr John Whiteman and heretofore
Edward Noon for a messuage or tenement at the Nether
end of Belgrave Gate heretofore the land of Thomas
Headley now divided into several tenements in fee farm
per annum late in the occupation of Edward Noon deducting 4s for Land Tax }   16   0

Mr Barnes late Roberts for Sykes and Mr Coates late Mr
Bolland 1s 3d each late Charles Stafford and Alice Brown
for a Garden and piece of ground in Sanvy Gate }   1   3
⟨Coates 1s 3d sold⟩

Mr Froane late Mr John Lambert late Thomas Fisher late
also Thomas Allsop for a piece of ground lying on the
backside of a messuage in the North Gate Street sold to
Mr John Tatham in fee farm per annum }   1   8

z

The Widow of Joseph Bolton heretofore Mr John Palmer late John Stafford late also John Earp for a messuage or tenement and piece of ground in Apple gate Street in the parish of St Nicholas heretofore the land of William Adcock in fee farm per Annum	6	8
Mrs Christie by Mr Moore heretofore Rowland Watts late John Turvile late Mr Barwell for a tenement in the North Gate late the land of Robert Freer heretofore the Sign of the Sun per annum deducting 4s for Land Tax	16	0
(blank) Johnson late Wells of Loughborough late Mr John Champion for a piece of ground at the South end of the Butt Close in the occupation of William Johnson in fee farm per annum	4	
Anthony Ingoldsby Esquire for lands at Great Ashby in the County of Leicester late the land of Ralph Brooksby Gentleman heretofore the land of Nicholas Norton per Annum ⟨Supered⟩	(blank)	
William Cave late Alderman Oldham for Mr Smith heretofore William Biggs for a tenement near the North Gates in fee farm per annum	1	0

5b   Within the North Gates

Mr William Forrester late Alexander Forrester late John Lovett late the heirs or executors of Robert Hicklington for a messuage or tenement on the South side of All Saints Church Yard now or late in the occupation of Fox in fee farm per Annum ⟨Sold⟩		
Susannah Browning late Thomas Derbyshire late Mary Howson for a messuage or tenement in High Cross Street late Humberstone's land in fee farm per annum	6	0
Mr Flude late Miss Browns the heirs of the late John Brown for a tenement in High Street late in the occupation of Joseph Waggot and now or late of the said Miss Browns per annum	5	0
Mr William Horton late Mrs Horton late Thomas Carter for a house and garden in High Cross Street at the corner of Bakehouse Lane in the occupation of (blank) late Mrs Davie	4	0

Mr Billson late John Atkins late of Thomas Johnson's Widow late Bellamy 2s 10d for a House and two tenements late in the occupation of Richard Grew & now of himself — 2 10

5c In the South Gates

Mr John Moore for a house in the occupation of William Sanders late Thomas Moreton's per annum—deducting 4s for Land Tax — 16 0

Mr James Cooper late Alderman Fisher and Mr Thomas Bankart late the land of Thomas Wall for a messuage or tenement at the corner of Hangman Lane in fee farm per annum Mr Cooper pays 9s Mr Bankart 3s 6d and Thomas Bonnett 3s 6d — 7 0
⟨Cooper's 9s sold⟩

Thomas Martin's widow late Mr Alderman Chapman and Mr William Gamble for a messuage or tenement late the Swan and now or late in the tenure or occupation of the said Thomas Martin and (blank) Sharpe in fee farm per annum — 13 4

5d In the Burgesses Meadow

Mr John Heyrick's executors late William Palmer for a piece of Meadow ground called the Shield late Moreton's land in fee farm per annum — 16 0

The said John Heyrick's executors more for two acres of Meadow late also Mr Moreton's land in fee farm per annum — 13 4

5e In the Swines Market
now called High Street

John Brewin late Joseph Bruce late Thomas Burley of New Parks for a tenement late Agnes Orton's land heretofore called the King's Head — 18 0

5f In the Saturday Market

Mr Brodribb late Bartram, Druggist for a messuage or tenement (now divided into two tenements) in the several occupations of the said Mr Brodribb and Mr Rogers in fee farm per annum deducting 4s for land Tax — 19 4

(blank) Cort late Thomas Healey late Mr Alderman Watchorn late Mr Alderman Brown for a messuage in the occupation of (blank) in fee farm per annum — 8

5g   In the Loseby Lane

Andrew Lawrence late Mr Hooke late Padmore late John
Smith late Thomas Kirk late Alexander Forrester late the
heirs of Samuel Coates for a House lately called the Star
and Ball and now the Crown and Thistle formerly in the
occupation of John Highton in fee farm per annum

12 0

Of him more for a piece of ground a Damask Rose payable
at Christmas

a Damask
Rose

5h   In the Gallowtree Gate

John Mansfield Esquire late Mr Alderman Oliver late Mr
Alderman T. Eyre for a messuage or tenement known by
the sign of the White Horse in the occupation of William
Whitehead in fee farm per annum deducting 4s for land
Tax

16 0

5i   In the Gallowtree Gate on the West side

Mrs Mansell late Mr Richards late Isaac Cockshaw late
Mrs Nutt late Mr Fosbrooke, Grocer, late Mr James Nutt
late The Reverend Mr Lambert for a messuage or tenement near the Playhouse in the occupation of George
Cowdall & John Thompson in fee farm per annum

10 0

5j   In the Belgrave Gate

Mr (blank) late Thomas Yates late Mr John Yates late
Thomas Rodley for a House in the occupation of (blank)
in fee farm per annum

13 4

Mr Brydone late Foulgham late Thomas Withers for
Thomas Sarson and Francis Foulgham for a House in the
tenure of the said Withers in fee farm per annum deducting 4s for Land Tax

16 0

The widow of the late Joseph Chamberlain Esquire late
Mrs Holmes late Mrs Ward widow for a tenement heretofore Simpson adjoining the Unicorn which Unicorn is the
late Alderman Bishop's House on the west side thereof in
fee farm per annum

15 0

(blank) Lister late John Bailey late Alderman Coleman for
a House late in the occupation of William Bell and now of
(blank) Forster on the North side of the said Street late
Richard Ward in fee farm per annum

18 0

The Churchwardens of St Margaret for a piece of ground
called the Cow Pasture in fee farm per annum

8 0

5k In the County

Henry Walker of Thurmaston late Robert Withers of Beaumont Leys and Mrs Vann late Gossip late Thomas Worrell for a piece of ground in Belgrave called Knipton Hill Leys and one yard land heretofore sold to Mr Calverwell being a Close of Pasture heretofore called Belgrave Bridge close heretofore Overings Land—Walker pays 5s 9d Mrs Vann 3s 3d ⟨5s 9d purchased by Walker⟩		3	3
Mr David Monk late Mrs Monk of Seagrave late Mr George Chamberlin for a close and Croft there late the land of William Hubbard in fee farm per annum		2	0
(blank) Barsby of Thrussington late Mr Benjamin Storer of Thrussington for one yard land there in fee farm per annum		6	8
William Ward of Houghton for a piece of land late Thomas Roadley's in fee farm per annum		5	0
Henry Peach Esquire late Mr Alderman Peach late William Watts for certain lands leys and Hades in the West Fields of Leicester in fee farm per annum		4	0
Mr George Henton for Sir Thomas Apreece late Schuchburgh Ashby Esquire late Sir Thomas Cave for a messuage or tenement in Hungerton and now or late in the tenure of Thomas Walton in fee farm per annum	1	4	0
George Sheffield of Syston for Syston Mills and a House heretofore sold to Sir Thomas Cave in fee farm per annum deducting 13s for Land Tax	2	13	8

6a Other Rents of Lands and Tenements parcel of the Town Obit Lands of Saint Margarets Guild and parcel of the fee farm lands heretofore demised by Queen Elizabeth to Mr Hawkes and Mr Bates by Indenture expired

The heirs of Mr William Ives for ground late belonging to Houses in the South Gates heretofore Mr Nurse and William Hill's and Francis Cole ruined by the late Wars or heretofore sold to Mr Dannett Abney as follows Withers late Sheffield late Townsend of Aylestone . . . . . . 6 8 Mrs Moore of Leicester deducting 8s for Land Tax 1 12 0	1	18	8

6b   In the Swines Market now called High Street

Mrs Bradley late Mr Fosbrooke late Mr Sismey for a tenement in the Silver Street near the Pump late in the occupation of Mr Robert Dowley now of (blank) Roe, Draper, in fee farm per annum deducting 4s for Land Tax ... 16 4

6c   In or near Belgrave Gate

Mrs Clay Hextall late Mrs Crammant late Mr Newton for a messuage or tenement at the corner of Humberstone Gate in his own occupation in fee farm per annum deducting 4s for Land Tax ... 17 0

Land late Mr Parsons late Mr Joseph Chamberlain and others Mr Chamberlain pays 6s and Sarah Toone 6s in fee farm per annum ... 6 0
⟨6s sold to Toone⟩

Mr Henry Sands late Foulgham (by Fewkes) for a House late in the occupation of William Noon and now of George Noon and (blank) in fee farm per annum deducting 4s for Land Tax ... 16 0

Mr Forrester late Benjamin Liquorish late Smith of Burbage for a House in Belgrave Gate late known by the Sign of the Joseph but now of the Nottingham Arms late in the occupation of John Highton now of Benjamin Johnson's widow in fee farm per annum ... (blank)

(blank) late Thomas Yates late John Yates late Augustine Hefford for a House called the Cock in fee farm per annum ... 6 8

(blank) late Thomas Yates late John Yates for a messuage late in the occupation of Alice Denshire and of another part called the Cock in fee farm per annum sold to John Briggs ... 13 4

John Barlow late Mrs Clarke late John Clarke late Charles Bates for a tenement heretofore in the occupation of Thomas Withers heretofore sold to Robert Roberts in fee farm per annum ... 5 0

6d   St Nicholas' and St Margaret's Parishes

(blank) Swann late Benjamin Cave late Satchell late Alderman Sutton late Joseph Brown and (blank) Flude late William Spencer for Mary Spencer for a messuage or tenement late John Orton's land afterwards Lewin's per annum—Swann late Cave late Satchell pays 7s and Elizabeth Hall late Flude pays 6s ... 13 0 (blank) Carter late Henry Whiteman late Richard Poole late Thomas Nutt late George Carter's heirs for a messuage or tenement in Applegate Street near the West Bridge called the Mitre and Key in the occupation of the said (blank) in fee farm per annum   16   0

Mr James Boulton's widow late John Throsby (Parish Clerk) late Alderman Throsby for a messuage or tenement in High Cross Street heretofore called the Flying Horse in fee farm per annum deducting 6s for Land Tax   1   4   0

7   Other Rents of Lands and Tenements parcel of the Town and Manor of Leicester heretofore amongst other things given and granted unto the said Mayor Bailiffs and Burgesses in fee farm per annum

Mr Carter late Peter Heward late Holmes late of Mr Kirk late John Cartwright for a tenement with the appurtenances in Church Gate   8   0

(blank) Loesby late Stubbs for Mr Lucas late Cobley for a piece of ground in All Saints Parish called the Vine Yard in his occupation in fee farm per annum   4   0

Mr Webster and Mr A. Carr late Johnson 1s 3d each late Seale for part of a piece of ground called the Lion Yard and a messuage or tenement in the occupation of Mr Bradley in fee farm per annum   1   3
   ⟨Websters 1s 3d sold⟩

Joseph Nunneley late Mr S. Bradley late Alderman Gamble for another part of the said Lion Yard and a messuage or tenement in the occupation of Mr Bradley in fee farm per annum   2   6

Mr Kendall late Fosbrooke late Read 30s and Mr Kendall late Barry late A. R. Holmes late Mrs Read late Lieutenant Edmonds late Mr Cave 10s for a House and Barn late Sandy's land in the Saturday Market in their respective occupations   10   0
   ⟨30s sold to (blank)⟩

John Barlow late John Clarke's Widow for a piece of ground in the Church Gate extending from thence to the common oven whereon a House was built by William Cave in fee farm per annum   2   6

Mr William Watts late Robert Hartshorne for a House in Rice's occupation near Frogmore Bridge late a piece of ground in fee farm per annum   (blank)
⟨Supered⟩

Mr William Waring late W. Johnson (by Mr Carter) and Mr Oram late Heston's for a piece of ground in Deadman's Lane   10

8   Other Rents of Corpus Christi Guild in Leicester heretofore in Mr Archer's Collection and now parcel of the lands and Tenements which the Mayor etc. purchased of Queen Elizabeth to them and their successors for ever

John Burrows (Baker) late Neale of Billesdon late Taylor for a messuage or tenement in High Street with the appurtenances in fee farm per annum   13 4

Mr Thomas Gadsby late Phipps (by Mr Lowdham) late John Wildbore of Loseby for a tenement in gallowtree Gate in the occupation of himself and others in fee farm per annum deducting 5s for Land Tax   1 1 8

Mr William Johnson late Marshall late Parkinson late Burgess late also Joseph Simpson for a messuage in Saturday Market now built in fee farm per annum deducting 4s for Land Tax   16 0

(blank) late James Wilby late Larratt for a messuage with the appurtenances (Mr Cramley's) in fee farm per annum deducting 4s for Land Tax   16 0

Messrs Iliffe late Mr Richards for a messuage in Parchment Lane now Swines Market late in the occupation of John Burgess in fee farm per annum   16 0

Mr Henshaw late Josiah Wood of Loughborough as Tenant of the Trust Estate of Joseph Clarke Esquire for certain lands and Pasture grounds in Loughborough aforesaid called Sadler's land for the Trustees of the Hospital at Barrow upon Soar in fee farm per annum   10 0

Whitehead late Neale late Quilter late Harris for Iliffe 4s for several tenements near the East Gates late Smalley for a shop in fee farm per annum   4 0

Webster late King late Reynolds late Hextall for a messuage on the west side of East Gates in his occupation late Hood's in fee farm per annum   12 0

Thomas Webster late Francis Lomas for a piece of ground heretofore a garden in the Town Hall Lane now built upon heretofore Fletcher's land in the occupation of Thomas Webster, Hatter in fee farm per annum	1	0
George Pochin Esquire late Charles William Pochin Esquire of Barkby late Robert James of Houghton for a Croft and Half Yard Land at Barkby late Illson's in fee farm per annum	6	8
The said George Pochin for three quarters of a yard land at Barkby late the land of Thomas Seal in fee farm per annum	6	0
Mrs Smith late Samuel Brooks for a messuage in High Street in the occupation of herself in fee farm per annum	6	0
Mr Perkins of Grantham for certain lands and leys in the Town Fields of Gunnerby in the County of Lincoln in fee farm per annum ⟨Supered⟩	(blank)	
Mr Moore late Day late Samuel Gamble Esquire for a Close near the Cow Drift late Heyrick's land in fee farm per annum	10	0

9a Other Rents of the possession of the late Guild in Leicester parcel of the Town Obit Lands heretofore collected by Mr Tatham

Thomas Robinson late Samuel Robinson late Messrs Mansfield and Miller late Thomas Richards late Goode late Wilcox and heretofore Coates for a messuage or tenement in Applegate Street in fee farm per Annum deducting 4s for Land Tax	16	0
Miss Knight late William Johnson for a messuage or tenement in the same Street late Hursts in the occupation of (blank) Knight and another	9	0
(blank) Hurst (Comb maker) late Bassett late Denshire late Cooper for a messuage or tenement in Applegate Street in the occupation of (blank) in fee farm per annum	8	0
The said Hurst late Cart for Lee for a House in Applegate Street late David Winfield in the occupation of (blank) Chamberlain in fee farm per annum	7	0

The Widow of the late Mr William Hill late Widow Burley 10s and William Burley 4s for a messuage and garden in Applegate Street formerly in the tenure of (blank) Savage in fee farm per annum   14 0

9b   In the South Gates

Hubbard late Mrs Edwyn late Springthorpe's Representatives late Hitchcock for a piece of ground situate in South Gate Street belonging to a House ruined by the late Wars sold to Mrs Hartshorne late Conyers White's occupation and now of John Gibson in fee farm per Annum   10 0

Mr Forrester late Wood for the ground belonging to two tenements now or late in the occupation of (blank) Smith in fee farm per annum
    ⟨Sold⟩

Mr John Marshall late Coates of Stamford late the Executors of late Cobley late Farmer of London for Tenements in Applegate Street late Coates in fee farm per annum   10 0

Mr Thomas Bryan late Stone late Burgess late David Howell for a messuage or tenement in the Cornwall formerly known by the sign of the Queen's Head now built upon in fee farm per annum deducting 5s for Land Tax   1 1 8

Mr Thomas White late William Moore late John Peberdy late Barfoot late Thomas Eames £1 and Alderman Peach late Peach late Watts £1 for a messuage in the Cornwall formerly known by the Sign of the Cinque Foil now new built upon in his own occupation in fee farm per annum deducting 8s for Land Tax   1 12 0

Widow Green late John Clarke for a messuage heretofore known by the Sign of the Buck's Head in her own occupation in fee farm per annum
    ⟨Supered⟩   (blank)

9c   In the Swines Market

Mrs Mansell late James Dowley late John Richards late John Major Esquire for a certain Garden heretofore sold to Michael Whatton of Bushby in fee farm per annum   2 0

9d   In the Belgrave Gate

Richard King late Mr D. Harris late Copson, late Mr Bond, for a messuage or tenement in his occupation late Astle's in fee farm per Annum   16 0

Thomas Peach Esquire late Thomas Lowe late the Widow of Joseph Grocock for a House called the Star Inn in his own occupation late Barry's in fee farm per Annum	13	4
(blank) late Thomas Yates late John Yates and others for two tenements late in the occupation of George Chamberlain and Widow Abney in fee farm per annum	8	0

    N.B. The Tenements in the occupation of (blank) and Copson were the property of the Corporation but have since been resold to Alderman Willey

Mr Noble late Jordan for a tenement and Garden in Belgrave Gate in the occupation of George White in fee farm per annum	6	0
Mr Langdon late Anthony Ward for a House and Garden in the same Street late in the occupation of W. & S. Kelly in fee farm per annum	6	0
(blank) late Thomas Yates late the Executors of John Yates for part of Margaret Fletcher's Land in Belgrave Gate in fee farm per annum	5	0
The heirs of Thomas Palmer for a House and Garden in Church Gate late Mr Inge's in fee farm per annum paid as directed in the next item	5	0
Of them more for an Orchard in Church Gate once Mr Inge's land late Smalley's in fee farm per annum	2	0

    The last two mentioned Rents are paid thus, vizt.

Mr Heward late Holmes late Cartwright .		9
Messrs Dalby & Deakin	1	3
Mr Bass (now Bailey)	1	3
Do.	1	3
Widow Miles late Barrass for Miss Ward .		7½
Joseph Pegg late William Bucknall late Sturgess late Bailey for Frost		7½
Thomas Cartwright late Newbolds for Foulds	1	3
	7	0

9e   In the Sanvey Gate

Mr Robert Clarke late Mrs Gutheridge for a messuage or tenement late in the occupation of William Chamberlain in fee farm per annum deducting 4s for Land Tax	16	0

Richard Dawson for (blank) White for a House & Garden in the occupation of (blank) Dawson in fee farm per annum	8	0
John Johnson late Matthew Johnson late Mrs Barwell for a piece of ground called Saddler's Close in fee farm per annum	5	0

9f   Near St Margaret's Church

Mr Richard Rawson late Reverend Mr Walker late Mr Clayton Apothecary late Mr Cooper for a piece of ground called St Margarets Bed being a Close late the land of James Biggs in fee farm per annum	6

9g   Other part of Wilder's Rent

Mr Moore late Richard Walker, Esquire, for a Close near the Cow Drift in his own occupation in fee farm per annum	13	4
Mr Harrison late Joseph Iliffe late Henry King for Miss Warner of Humberstone for a House and Land there late in the occupation of Dennis Kirk in fee farm per annum 5s		

⟨Sold⟩

Messrs Keen and Taylor late Taylor & Payne late Thomas Ashwell for a messuage or tenement heretofore sold to him and Jane Ward in fee farm per annum deducting 5s for Land Tax	1	1	8
The Poor of Trinity Hospital for a garden and piece of ground near the Butt Close now built upon late in the tenure of Mr Samuel Clarke and others in fee farm per annum		2	0
Mr (blank) late Thomas Yates late the Executors of John Yates for a House and Garden in the Belgrave Gate late the land of Edward Sutton late in the occupation of John Coe and now of (blank) Ash in fee farm per annum		3	4
Joseph Swain late Thomas Barsby (Carpenter) late William Abell late William Barwell's heirs for a tenement with the appurtenances in Sanvy Gate now in the tenure of Nathan Hunt in fee farm per annum		10	0
John Brown late Widow of John Clarke for a messuage or tenement in the Sanvy Gate heretofore Thomas Chattels in the occupation of Richard Harcourt in fee farm per annum		6	8

10 A Rental of the Lands and possessions of and belonging to the College of the Blessed Virgin Mary over against the Castle of Leicester heretofore demised by Queen Elizabeth to Edward Holt Esquire and by Her Majesty granted to the Mayor etc. and their successors (amongst other things) in fee farm per annum

Mr Moore late Mr Day late Samuel Gamble Esquire Ralph Wells for a Close near Aylestone Highway late the land of Mr Robert Heyrick in fee farm per annum — 5 0

The Widow of Joseph Bruce for a messuage or tenement in Soar Lane near the Red cross Street in her own occupation late the lands of John Collison in fee farm per annum — 10 0

Thomas Allsop late Pickard late Hudson Norton late Pochin 1s 3d William Gill late Hunt for Lambert 1s 3d and Bruce late Ward 2s 6d for a tenement in Soar Lane near Red cross Street sold to John Underwood late Thomas Derrick & William Ward's — 2 6

John Hannam late William Barrar late Mr Clayton by Mr Carter late Cooper for a messuage or tenement in Red cross Street and a garden in Chaff Lane adjoining to the House in the occupation of Timothy Atkins called the Old Mitre in fee farm per annum deducting 4s for Land Tax — 16 0

Richard Shipley late Lovett late John Satchell 11s 7d and of Samuel Bennett late Christopher Bennett late Widow of John Brown of Desford 15s 1d for a messuage in Soar Lane near Red cross Street in fee farm per annum late Robert Atkins deducting 5s for Land Tax — 1 1 8

Widow Flewitt late Onesiphoros Coltman late Robert Dugmore for a messuage & Garden in Soar Lane near Red cross Street heretofore sold to John Bonner in fee farm per annum — 12 0

Walter Hall late Mrs Bankart for Mrs Hall .	5	4
William Cooke late Bankart for Dawson . .	5	4
Coltman (sold)	5	4
	16	0

— 10 8

for a piece of ground late Thomas Ward's belonging to a messuage or tenement in the South Gates ruined in the late Wars and for a Croft in fee farm per annum

⟨Cookes 5s 4d sold⟩

(blank) Gee late James Dowley late William Lamb late Mrs Ashby's heirs late Mrs Smalley for a Garden in Sanvy Gate in the occupation of William Sands in fee farm per annum	1	0
Mr Field late Carrick for an Orchard or Garden in Silver Street at Will per annum	2	0
Mr John Moore late Samuel Gamble Esquire for the third part of a close near the Cow Drift in fee farm per annum	4	0
The Poor of Trinity Hospital for part of a Dove cote close beyond the West Bridge in fee farm per annum	1	6
Richard Hashold of Glenfield for a piece of ground then late in the occupation of John Carr in fee farm per annum	(blank)	
Mr Sutton (Coal Merchant) late John Brewin late Tyrringham Palmer for a close near St Margarets Cow Pasture heretofore Bennett's land in the occupation of (blank) in fee farm per annum	3	4
Thomas Mitchell late W. Ruding Esquire for a close in Braunstone Gate late Mr Hunt's land in fee farm per annum	5	0
The Poor of Trinity Hospital for a piece of Meadow ground in the Burgesses meadow called Lady Acre in fee farm per annum	3	4
Joseph Bruce's Widow for a tenement and garden in Soar Lane near Red cross Street in her own occupation on Lease expiring (blank) payable half yearly (sold to Walker)		
Mr Burbidge late Dr Vaughan late Sir Charles Halford for a Garden in Swines Market now High Street late built upon in his own occupation	1	2
Mr Burbidge late Dr Vaughan late the said Sir Charles Halford for a messuage in the same Street heretofore sold to Christian Needham in his own occupation	2	6
(blank) Sly 3s 4d Benjamin Hames late Edward Powers 1s 8d for a Garden in Hot Gate Street alias Thornton Lane late the land of Mr Thomas Pares per annum	5	0
(blank) Hollier late Tebbutt of Bowden Magna for land there now or late in the occupation of John Corrall in fee farm per annum—It is three pieces of meadow called Leicester land	1	0

William Herrick Esquire of Beaumanor late the Reverend
George Coulton late Mr John Herrick of Beaumont Leys
for Lands in Sileby per annum　6d
　　⟨Supered⟩　　　　　　　　　　　　　　　(blank)

The Reverend W. S. Lee late Mr Gulstone late Mr Steadman of Glenfield for land there in fee farm per annum　3d　　(blank)

11　Other Rents of the Town and Manor of Leicester parcel of the
lands and possessions of the Duchy of Lancaster part thereof
being in the County of Leicester

William Smith, Cheesemonger, late Mr Bywater and Mr
Slater 8s 4d each—late Mr Higgs for a messuage or tene-
ment in High Street heretofore Mr John Brooksby late　　8　4
Mr Hood in fee farm per annum

Mrs Edmonds late Mr Dyson for a Horse Malt Mill in
Swines Markct now High Street in fee farm per annum　　1　7　4
deducting 4s for Land Tax

Francis Lomas late Miss Whittle late Abstinence Pougher
for two tenements in Parchment Lane called Swines Market late the land of Mr John Heyrick in fee farm per　　3　4
annum
　　⟨Now Astill 1s 8d Colston 1s 8d⟩

Thomas Coleman for himself & Mr Tilley 13s 2d and
William Bassett late Thomas Gregory 6s and John Hurst
2s 6d for certain ground in the South Gates belonging　　15　8
to two tenements in the occupation of (blank) being the
gift of Mr Hobby
　　⟨Gregory 6s sold⟩

Mr Thomas White late Moore late John Peberdy late
Mr Thomas Eames late Mrs Lee for ground taken from　　5　0
the Sheep Pen

William Clarke late Alderman Oliver for the like　.　.　(blank)
　　⟨Supered⟩

Mr Solomon Bray late Solomon Holmes late Alderman
Hames for the like late Smalley　　　　　　　　　　10　0

Mr Thomas Bryant late Burgess for Do. late Hanwell
paid by Crammant deducting 4s for Land Tax　　　　16　0

Mr Raworth for a piece of ground adjoining to the West
Bridge per annum　　　　　　　　　　　　　　　　2　6

12 Chief Rents belonging to St John's and Saint Leonards to be paid at Michaelmas for the use of the Mayor Bailiffs and Burgesses of the Borough of Leicester

The Wardens of Wigston's Hospital paid by Mr Pares	1	4
The Right Honorable the Earl of Stamford for Thurmaston Mills <Supered>	(blank)	
George Wright Esquire heretofore Sir William Rawlinson late Sir Henry Beaumont for certain lands at Oadby <Supered>	(blank)	
Mr James Norman of Oadby late J. F. Cooper for the Reverend Mr Liptrott for the Vicarage House at Oadby	1	$0\frac{1}{2}$
Mr Robert Clarke late Gutheridge late William Cooke for a House in Sanvy Gate late Webster's Land		9

13   Chief Rents belonging to Corpus Christi Guild

Mr Field late Mr Carrick late Mr Belton late Mr Townsend's Executors for a tenement in Silver Street in his occupation	4	0
Mr Thomas Hollier late John Bullock (by Mr Vassier) late Timothy Atkins late Mr Daniel for a House in Silver Street in the occupation of Vassier and Agar	3	0
Messrs Nutt late Mrs Orme for a messuage or tenement in Gallowtree Gate 2s 2d <Supered>	(blank)	
Mr Higginson for a House in the occupation of Mr Brodribb and Rogers per annum	2	0
Avery Craythorne late William Skelton late Mrs Walker late the widow of Manton Reynolds late Widow Killshall for a piece of ground in Parchment Lanc now called Swines Market late the land of Tobias Heyrick 3d <Sold>		
Mr Pratt late Mr Goode, Hosier, for a messuage or tenement near St Nicholas' Church in his occupation late Britton's Land	1	0
Mr Neale, Pawnbroker, late Stubbs for Slater Mr Brown for a Garden in Deadman's Lane	5	6
Mrs Waring, Shambles Land 10d and Mr Oran 2d for a cottage in Deadman's Lane per annum <Supered Oram's 2d bought>	(blank)	

Mrs Cotchett late John Shipley late Widow Groce for a Garden in Deadman's Lane — 6

Mr William Hardy late Joseph Springthorpe late William Davis for a House in High Cross Street late in the occupation of John Pratt and now of George Smith per annum — 1 0

Mr Westley Oldham late Alderman Oldham for a messuage or tenement in High Street per annum — 14 0

Mr Cotchett late William Hill Esquire for a tenement now divided into two tenements in the occupation of James Wilson & William Collison — 3 0

William Stretton late William Burton late also William Cox for a tenement in High Street in Stretton's occupation — 3 6

The Poor of Trinity Hospital for a Barn called Clarke's Barn — 6

Mr Clement Stretton for a House in Cank Street late in Alderman Bates's occupation — 8½

Mr Birkley late The Reverend T. Burnaby late William Herrick Esquire late Sir John Whatton, Knight, for a close called Shire Hall Orchard in All Saints Parish late in the occupation of James Orton — 6

Mr William Irwin late Edward Marston late Edward Barwell for a messuage or tenement in Humberstone Gate formerly in his own occupation   3s
    〈Sold〉

Mr Willey late Mr James Barston late Mr Bishop, Surgeon, late John Mansfield, Esquire, late Joseph Cooke, Lovell, late Roger Ruding Esquire for a tenement at the corner of Friar Lane lately known by the Sign of the George late in the occupation of Thomas Farmer per annum — 4 0

Mr Woodford for a tenement in High Street late Mark Valentine's — 2 0

Mr Manning late Mr Oldham late Woodford late Arthur Heselridge Esquire for a messuage or tenement in High Cross Street heretofore in the occupation of Mr Mason and others (late Henshaw's land) and now in the occupation of Fowkes — 4 0

James Derbyshire late Thomas Gadsby late Alderman Oliver for a tenement in Gallowtree Gate in his own occupation — 7 0

AA

14   Chief Rents belonging to Saint Margaret Guild

Henry Hitchcock late Westham late Mr Hulse late Cowdall for Walter Ruding Esquire for a piece of ground in Soar Lane called the Moat Yard per annum	6 0
Mr Brydone late Miss Foulgham for a tenement in Belgrave Gate late Sutton's Land	6
Mr Peet of Mountsorrel late Widow Bailey late William Heyrick Esquire for a tenement in Humberstone Gate	6
Mr Cardale for the Leicester Navigation Company late Mr Andrews late Mr Ludlam's for a Close near the Spittle House called the Bailiffs Close per annum	1 0
Mr George Palmer late Joseph Johnson late Edward Johnson for a messuage or tenement near the West Bridge late in the occupation of Weldon Gibbs but now of Samuel Sheen and others	4 0
The Wardens of Wigston's Hospital for a piece of land called the Normandy per annum—paid by Mr Pares	6
Mr William Forrester late Alexander Forrester late George Rayson Pratt for a messuage or tenement in All Saints parish in the occupation of the said Forrester & others 1s 1½d	
⟨sold⟩	
Mr Jackson late Dowley late Joseph Wallin late Mr Pares late Robert Page for a piece of ground taken out of the Pinfold	4
The Poor of Trinity Hospital for a House in the South Gates in the occupation of (blank) late Forster's land	9½
Mr Heyrick for a piece of ground in the Burgesses Meadows late the land of John Guildford	10 0
Samuel Howe late Widow Clarke for Franks late Mrs Davy Widow late Mr Stanley for a tenement in North Gate Street and for two tenements now or late in the tenure of John Harcourt 1s 2d	(blank)
⟨Supered⟩	
Mr Alderman Peach late William Watts late William Ogden for a House in High Street once Otter's Land per annum	3 6
Mr George Palmer late Joseph Johnson late Edward Johnson late Alderman Johnson for a House near the West Bridge called Babington's land in the occupation of (blank)	9

(blank) Porter late Nathan Tuffley late Mr Tebbs of Birstall late Turlington for a House in Birstall late the land of John Raynor now or late in the occupation of the said N. Tuffley	1	0
Mr Higginson for a messuage in the Saturday Market in the several occupations of the said Higginson and Rogers	6	8
Mr T. Mitchell late Walter Ruding Esquire for a close in Braunstone Gate		9
Mr Hutchinson late William Harrison, Blue Boar, late Joshua Howes, late Wigston, late Stevenson, for a House near the South Gates called the Blue Boar late (blank) Budworth's land 9d for two ends 7d and for a shop near the South Gates 5d	1	10
William Burley late John Ryder for a tenement over against All Saints Church late Mr (blank) Rudyards in the occupation of (blank)	2	3
Mr Joseph Ottey late Mr St John late Sir Charles Halford for a messuage in High Street late Bonner's House		6
Nicholson 3d and Dorman 10d for a House in the North Gate Street late Woodlands per annum ⟨3d sold⟩		10
Mr Ottey late Mrs St John late Sir Charles Halford for a House in High Street late Needham & Bailey's land		4
Edward Smith late Mr Mortimer of Narboro' for a House in South Gate Street late Alderman Joseph Taylor	6	8
(blank) Burton late (blank) Springthorpe late Joseph Watson late Sir Charles Halford for a close in High Street near the Horse Malt Mill		6
The Governors of the Leicester Infirmary for St James's Chapel Close in fee farm per annum deducting 5s for Land Tax	1 1	8
Joseph Walker late (blank) Hewins late Nixon late Denshire for a House and Garden in the parish of St Nicholas near the Applegate Street called the Talbot in the occupation of George Taylor in fee farm per annum deducting 4s for Land Tax	16	0

Total of Chief & Fee Farm
Rents   £66 12s 4½d

15 A Rental of Lammas Tithes due yearly to the Mayor Bailiffs and Burgesses for divers Gardens in St Mary's Parish in the possession of the College of Saint Mary against the Castle of Leicester and other acknowledgements etc. which used to be paid but which have for many years been supered

Mr Thomas Coltman late Mrs Wood late Richard Weston for Dove House Close near the Newarke of Leicester late Hickling per annum	1	4
Mr Davies late William Franks Esquire for a close near St James's Chapel Close called Archer's Close	1	4
The Governors of the Infirmary for St James's Chapel Close Tithe	1	0
Messrs H. & T. Wood late Nathan Wright Esquire for the Tithes of Bonningtons Close called Sand Pit Close and Meadow per annum	1	0
Mr Alderman Sutton for a close near Braunstone Gate per annum		6
Mr H. Wood late Nathan Wright Esquire late James Mason for a Close late two Closes called Sand Pit Close and Meadow over against St James's Chapel Close per annum	1	8
Mr Thomas Coleman late Mr Wood late Weston for land near the George once Birstall's land per annum	1	0
Mr Thomas Coleman late Mrs Wood for a Close near St James's Chapel Close late Morton's land per annum		10
Do. late Do. for Seth King's land part of the above Close .		6
Mr Lowdham late Mr Astill for Miss Whiteman's late Mr Iliffe for a Close near Paradise Close		4
Mr Edward Davie late William Franks Esquire for a piece of ground called the Kiln late Cademan's land near St James's Chapel Close per annum		4
Do. for Cademan's land near St James's Chapel Close per annum		10
Mr John Lacey late Mr Joseph Wilkins for an Orchard on the backside of a House late Davis in the South Gates late the land of Hugh Watts Esquire		6
Mr John Moore late Samuel Gamble Esquire for a Close near Aylestone Highway late Mr Heyricks		8
Of him for a Close near the same Highway . . .		4

	£	s
Of him another Close near Archer's Land in St Mary's Parish		10
(blank) late Joseph Tisdale late William Pochin Esquire late Weston for a piece of ground near Saint Mary's Mill Close called the Holmes late Morley's land per Annum late William Simpson, Hosier, deceased	1	8
Nathan Wright Esquire late the heirs of John Farmer, Attorney, for a Close near Aylestone Highway called Sand Pit Close in the occupation of Henry Callis		10
Nathan Wright Esquire late William Wright Esquire for part of the said Close in the occupation of Henry Callis per annum	1	0
Walter Ruding Esquire for a Close in Braunstone Gate called Hunt's land		8
Of him more for a Close called College Close in St Mary's Parish late Hunt's land		4
Mr Edward Harrison late Cart of the Bull Head for a Close late Brookes's Land in St Mary's Parish late Bonnett's Land late Duck Holmes per annum	2	2
Mr William Simpson for a Close called the Tippitts per annum paid by Mrs Brewin	13	4
Thomas Chatwyn for the Tithes of the Newark Mills per annum	2	0
William Wright for a garden or piece of ground in Millstone Lane Armstrong's Land per annum		4
Joseph Bruce for Land in Chaff Lane, Bruce's Land		10
The Widow of Thomas Hall late Francis Ward for a Backside belonging to his house in the South Gate now or late in the occupation of Thomas Ward per annum		6
Foulds late Mr Newton for a House in Thornton Lane late Mr Thompson		4
William Johnson for Paling for Booth's land in Shambles Lane		4
Mr John Jackson for an acknowledgement for an encroachment for putting out two windows from his house in the Cornwall late in Mr Alderman Chambers's occupation per annum	1	1
Mr Thomas Chatwyn for the Tithes of the Newark Mills	16	0
Messrs Johnson & Jordan each one shilling for the Tithes of the Gosling Closes	2	0

Mr (blank) late Alderman Fisher for the Tithes of the North Windmill	2	0
Mr Jordan late Derbyshire late Joseph Orton for the tithes of a piece of grass ground in the Mary Meadow	6	0
Mr Jordan Mr Cooper and Mr Stretton each 7s 4½d for the Tithe of the Beadhouse Meadows	1 9 6	
Mr John Hartshorne for the Tithes of a piece of ground in St Mary's Meadow	(blank)	
Mr Thomas Chatwyn for the Tithes of a piece of ground near the Mill	(blank)	
Mrs Sutton for laying Planks and setting Posts in the River Soar during pleasure	(blank)	

End of Lammas Tithes etc.

16   Freedoms etc.

By Cash received of the undermentioned persons (being Strangers) for the purchase of the Freedom of this Borough, vizt.,

Joseph Burchnall	. . . .	35	0 0
Charles Smith	. . . .	35	0 0
John Hodges	. . . .	35	0 0
John Dove	. . . .	35	0 0

By Cash received of the undermentioned persons on being admitted to their Freedom, vizt.,

William Brumby	. . . .	10	0
William Thurlby	. . . .	10	0
George Evans	. . . .	10	0
James Gray	. . . .	10	0
George Boulter	. . . .	5	0
Thomas Scott	. . . .	10	0
John Haddon	. . . .	10	0
Samuel Allen	. . . .	10	0
Edward Groocock	. . . .	10	0
William Whitehead	. . . .	5	0
Thomas Mitchell	. . . .	10	0
Joseph Clements	. . . .	5	0
George Clements	. . . .	10	0
Joseph Oldershaw	. . . .	5	0
William Chamberlain	. . . .	10	0
William Bevans	. . . .	5	0

James Goodrich	10	0
John Noon	10	0
William Smith	5	0
William Daniel Elliott	5	0
John Palmer	5	0
John Stone	5	0
Francis Burdett	10	0
Alfred Donisthorpe	10	0
James Clarke	5	0
Henry Greenwood	5	0
Henry Forsberry	10	0
John Smith	5	0
William Gilbert	10	0
James Goddard	5	0
George Ludlam	5	0
John Scott	10	0
Thomas Sweet	10	0
Edward Presson	10	0
John Richardson	10	0
Thomas Gamble	10	0
Cornelius Smith	10	0
Thomas Frederick Ross	10	0
William Mann	5	0
George Tow	10	0
John Harrison	5	0
John Ludlam	10	0
Joseph Cowdell	10	0
Robert Feaken	10	0
Rowland Bosworth	5	0
Nicholas Higginson	5	0
Thomas Bull	10	0
John Ball	10	0
Henry Hall	10	0
Hiram Castings	10	0
William Warner	10	0
William Riley	10	0
Theophilus Muston	10	0
William Peake	10	0
Samuel Newton	10	0
John Taylor	5	0
William Johnson	10	0
John Withers	10	0
George Weston	10	0

George Ross	10	0
Edward Turner	10	0
William Carter	5	0
Thomas Gilbert	10	0
Joseph Shepherd Needle	10	0
Samuel Johnson	5	0
Samuel Green	10	0
Robert Robinson	10	0
Edward Shardlow	10	0
Thomas Williamson	10	0
Edward Bennett	10	0
Thomas Elson	10	0
Joseph Bradsworth	10	0
Andrew Ross	10	0
John Sherwood Wheatley	10	0
William Brandreth	10	0
Daniel Bull	5	0
George Keeling	10	0
Robert Barnes	10	0
Thomas Ellis	5	0
John James	5	0
Patrick Johnson	5	0
John Kilborn	10	0
Jonathan Ward	10	0
Charles Poynor	10	0
William Strange	10	0
John Kirk	5	0
John Smith	5	0
Frederick Gill	10	0
John Birch	10	0
John Carr	5	0
Isaac Chatwin	10	0
James Walker	10	0
John Joseph Kinton	5	0
Thomas White	5	0
Samuel Clay	10	0
William Mudford	10	0
John Smith	10	0
Samuel Calvert	10	0
James Calver	5	0
George Calver	10	0
John North	5	0
Samuel North	10	0

William Bentley	10	o
John Warwick	10	o
William Pickering	10	o
John Nicklonson	10	o
Isaac Manship	10	o
John Leach Mitchell	10	o
Lomas Miles	5	o
James Wallin	5	o
George Bunney	10	o
Daniel Warner	5	o
James Jackson	5	o
Thomas Wright	10	o
Henry Goddard	5	o
John Jackson Smith	10	o
William Smith	5	o
John Nicholls	5	o
John Gisborne	5	o
James Noone	5	o
Thomas Noone	10	o
Richard Wilson	10	o
William Lawrence	10	o
Thomas Agar	5	o
Charles Aldridge	10	o
Henry Daft	10	o
William Anderson	10	o
Gowin Scott	10	o
William Holyoak	10	o
Samuel Cox	10	o
Samuel Billson	10	o
Charles Masters	10	o
William Bates	10	o
William Hames	10	o
Charles Guilford	10	o
John Moxon	10	o
Henry Masters	10	o

Total of Freedoms
£198

17   Incidental and Casual Receipts

By Cash received of Messrs Brown and Payne late Chamberlains according to Order of Hall	200	o	o
Mr Harris half year's arrear of Garden rent	1	17	5

Messrs Herbert one year's arrear of rent of Close in South Fields	24	0	0
Mr Pratt one year's arrear of Garden rent . . .	4	19	4
Ackland on account of arrear of Garden Ground . .	5	0	0
Dexter two years arrear of Tithes	6	0	0
Mr Burbidge a year's arrear of Chief rents . . .		8	8
Calow on account of arrears of Chief rents in Mr Brown's year	3	0	0
By the balance of Accounts of Messrs Brown and Payne, late Chamberlains, due to the Corporation (not paid)	(blank)		

[End of Receipts]

[Payments start here]

1   Charitable Gifts

Paid the Gift of Queen Elizabeth to the Head Usher .	10	0	0
Paid the Gift of Sir Ralph Rowlett to the Under Usher .	3	6	8
Paid the Gift of Mr Norris to the Head Usher . .	3	6	8
Paid the Gift of Mr Clarke to the Under Usher . .	1	0	0

Paid the Gift of Mr John Norris out of the Willoughby Lands, vizt.

To Saint Martin's Parish . . .	1	14	4		
Saint Margarets	1	14	4		
Saint Marys	1	14	4		
All Saints	1	7	6	10	0 0
Saint Nicholas		19	6		
Saint Leonards		10	0		
Trinity Hospital	1	13	4		
Saint John's		6	8		

Paid the Gift of Mr John Stanley vizt.

To the Vicar of St Martins . .	1	10	0		
Head Master	1	0	0		
Head Usher		13	4	4	0 0
Under Usher		6	8		
10 Widows or Maids . . .		10	0		

Paid the Gift of Mr William Stanley to the Poor of Trinity Hospital	1	0	0
Paid the Gift of the Earl of Devonshire (part of the Wood and Coal Money)	6	0	0

Paid the Gift of Christopher Tamworth Esquire to the Vicar of St Martins being the clear receipt from land at Whetstone (now reduced to £60 per annum)	60	0	0
Paid the Gift of King Charles the 1st of ever blessed memory part of the Wood and Coal money	52	0	0

Paid the Gift of Mr William Ives, vizt.

To Trinity Hospital . . .	5	12	0		
The new Hospital		8	0		
For 2dy bread for the Parishes 13s 4d				14	0	0
every Friday in Lent . . .	4	0	0		
For eight widows Gowns . . .	4	0	0		

Paid the Gift of Mrs Ives to Trinity Hospital . . .	1	0	0

Paid part of the Gift of Mr Elkington (namely)

To Saint Martins	2	0	0		
Lutterworth (not paid) £2 10s 0d	(blank)			2	10	0
The Town Clerk	10	0			

Paid the Gift of (blank) Poultney Esquire (vizt.)

To Saint Martins Parish . . .	2	4	0		
Saint Margarets	2	4	0		
Saint Mary's	2	4	0	10	0	0
All Saints	1	3	0		
Saint Nicholas		16	0		
Land Tax	1	9	0		

Paid the Poor of Mountsorrel the Gift of Mr Nidd . .	70	0	0
Paid the Gift of Mr Acham in Bread	9	0	0

Paid the Gift of Mr Haines (vizt.)

To the Schoolmaster of Thrussington	6	0	0		
Two Scholars of Lincoln College £6 (not claimed)	(blank)			18	0	0
Three Bibles	1	0	0		
For preaching a Sermon . . .	1	0	0		
Disposed of in wood and coal . .	10	0	0		

Paid the Gift of Mr Botham (vizt.)

To Saint Martins Parish . . .	13	4
Saint Margarets	13	4	2	0	0
Saint Marys	13	4

Paid the Gift of the Earl of Huntingdon to Wigston's Hospital	10	0	0
Acquittance		1	2
Paid the Gift of John Holmes to Trinity Hospital . .	45	0	0
To Saint John's £4 and Bents £2 10s. . . .	6	10	0

Paid the Gift of Mrs Twigden, vizt.
  For 3 Gowns to the Widows of St Johns   1 10 0 ⎫ 2 0 0
  To Do. for Coals .   .   .   .   10 0 ⎭

Nota Bene—The payment to Bents Hospital is omitted here and the accounts of that Charity are to be kept in a separate Book.

Paid the Gift of Mr Moreton out of the Tippetts received ⎫
and paid by the Mayor being disposed of with the Wood ⎬ 3 0 0
and Coal Money ⎭

Paid the Gift of Mrs Ward, vizt. ⎫
  Three Widows of St John's to buy   ⎪
  Gowns .   .   .   .   .   .   1 10 0 ⎪
  Do. for Coals .   .   .   .   10 0 ⎬ 3 0 0
  To 2 Almswomen in Trinity Hospital .   10 0 ⎪
  To the Common Box there .   .   10 0 ⎭

Paid the Gift of William Billers out of the Leroes, vizt., ⎫
  To 2 Widows in Trinity Hospital 1s   ⎪
  each weekly .   .   .   .   .   5 4 0 ⎬ 12 0 0
  To Trinity Hospital for Oatmeal .   5 16 0 ⎪
  For a Gown .   .   .   .   .   1 0 0 ⎭

Paid the Gift of Sir William Courteen and the Gentlemen ⎫
of the Lottery to the different Parishes 2dy Bread ⎬ 4 16 0

Paid the Gift of Mrs Dorothy Baker to the Head and ⎫
Under Ushers ⎬ 1 0 0

Paid the Gift of Mr Julius Bullers to Trinity Hospital .   5 12 0

Paid the Gift of Messrs Bennett & Ward (part of the Wood ⎫
and Coal Money) ⎬ 1 0 0

Paid the Gift of Widow Ossiter Do. .   .   .   6 0 0

Paid the Gift of Mr Hitch to Trinity Hospital .   .   3 0

Paid the Gift of Mr Thomas Gilbert, vizt. ⎫
  To the Head Schoolmaster .   .   3 0 0 ⎬ 5 0 0
  To the Head Usher .   .   .   1 10 0 ⎪
  To the Under Usher .   .   .   10 0 ⎭

Paid the Gift of Mrs Margaret Hobby (vizt.) ⎫
  To the Head Usher .   .   .   12 0 ⎪
  To the Old Hospital .   .   2 6 ⎪
  To the new Do. .   .   .   2 0 ⎬ 1 1 0
  Saint John's .   .   .   .   6 ⎪
  The Poor of Saint Martin's .   .   2 0 ⎪
  Do. of Saint Mary's .   .   .   2 0 ⎭

Paid the Gift of the Countess of Devonshire vizt.

To Saint Martins Parish . . .	9 0	
Saint Margarets	9 0	
Saint Marys	9 0	3 0 0
All Saints	7 0	
Saint Nicholas	6 0	
Saint Leonards	1 0 0	

Paid the Gift of Mrs Haselridge vizt.

To Trinity Hospital . . .	12 0	
Saint John's	7 6	1 1 6
	2 0	

Paid the Gift of Mr William Cooper to St John's Hospital .   2 4 9

Paid the Gift of Thomas Ayre to St John's Hospital.   .   1 0 0

Paid the Gift of Mr John Ludlam to Do.   .   .   .   2 10 0

Paid the Gift of Mr John Wightman to Trinity Hospital .   5 0

Paid the Gift of Mr John Roberts, vizt.

To Trinity Hospital . . .	10 0	
Saint John's	10 0	1 0 0

Paid the Gift of Mr Robert Hall to eight widows of Saint John's Hospital   10 0

Paid the Gift of Mr George Bent to Trinity Hospital   .   5 0

Paid the Gift of Mr William Sutton to St John's Do.   .   2 16 0

Paid the Gift of Do. to Trinity Hospital being the interest of £20   16 0

Paid the Gift of Mr Thomas Topp to Trinity Hospital   .   1 0 0

Paid the Gift of Do. to St John's Hospital   .   .   .   10 0

Paid the Gift of Benjamin Garland to St Martin's Parish .   5 0

Paid the Gift of Alderman Thomas Ludlam, vizt.

For apprenticing a Boy . . .	8 0 0	
For preaching a Sermon for St John's	1 0 0	
For the Nurse of St John's 1s per week	2 12 0	12 0 0
Remainder divided on Sunday after St John's	8 0	

Paid the Gift of Mr Cradock to Trinity Hospital   .   .   4 0 0

Paid the Gift of Mr Andrews to Do. 5 0

Paid the Gift of Mr Blunt on Saint Thomas's Day (vizt.)

For shoes	6 10	0
To be spent	10	0
To the Town Clerk & Macebearer		
2s 6d each	5	0
4 Serjeants at Mace 1s each . .	4	0
Beadle and Cryer 6d each . . .	1	0
Minister of Walton super Wolds .	18	0
Vicar of Saint Margarets . . . 1	0	0
Clerk and Sexton	5	0
The Mayor	5	0
The Spittlehouse Poor . . .	2	0

10 0 0

Paid the Gift of Mr Bent to St John's and Bent's Hospitals

St John's	1 13	4
Bent's	16	8

2 10 0

Gave the Poor of Leicester in Coals . . . .   (blank)

Paid the Poor of St John's Hospital the rent arising from the two tenements in Causeway Lane late occupied by Parrott now in Lease to George Bradley which were built with £50 given by Cammack's Will and £115 arising from the sale of the Hospital Gardens towards building the Town Gaol

18 0 0

Paid the Gift of Miss Mary Cooper (being the interest of £100) to the poor Widows of Saint John's Hospital

5 0 0

Paid the Gift of Mr John Orton Garle (being the interest of £50) to the poor Widows of St John's Hospital

2 10 0

Total of Charities etc.
£454 14s 9d

2   Salaries etc.

Paid Richard Rawson, Esquire his year's Salary as under, vizt.,

Ancient Salary	13	6	8
More out of the rent of the Gosling Closes as allowed by Order of Hall	13	6	8
More being the additional Salary to the Mayor in 1713	20	0	0

	£	s	d
More by Order of Common Hall 1736	40	0	0
More by Order of Common Hall 1769	50	0	0
More by Order of Common Hall 1797	50	0	0
More by Order of Common Hall 1806	50	0	0
More being Coal and Capon Money .	5	11	6
	242	4	10
Paid Edward Goulburn Esquire half a year's Salary as Recorder	52	10	0
Paid John Hildyard, Esquire, Recorder the other half year's Salary due at Michaelmas	26	5	0
Paid the late & present High Bailiffs Salary by Order of common Hall	52	10	0
Paid the late High Bailiff part of the Gratuity during pleasure by Order of Hall up to his decease	12	10	0
Paid the Town Clerk his year's salary due at Michaelmas .	200	0	0
Paid him for the stamp and paper for the Commission for the year	1	10	6
Do. for stamp and paper for the Letter of Attorney . .	1	10	4
The like for the Mayor's Bond	7	0	2
The like for the Chamberlain's Bond	5	0	2

Paid The Reverend Mr Davies, Head Schoolmaster his salary and allowance as under, vizt.

	£	s	d
The Town's free gift during pleasure .	16	0	0
More the Town's annual free gift during pleasure	8	0	0
More the Town's annual free gift during pleasure	3	0	0
More Do. Do.	5	0	0
More by Order of Hall in 17— on condition of his taking Boys free of entrance	5	0	0

N.B. The five foregoing gifts were formerly paid to the Head Master and the Head and Under Usher but by Order of Hall in July 1797 were all directed to be paid to the Reverend Mr Heyrick on his being appointed sole Master and are now paid to Mr Davies

Paid him more the Town's free gift during pleasure by Order of Hall in 1797	30	0	0
More Do. by the like Order being the Rent of a Tenement in Sanvy Gate let to Barrowdale and a Garden let to Widow Abell in Elbow Lane	8	16	6

	75	18	6
Paid the Reverend Mr Erskine his year's salary as Lecturer of this Borough during pleasure	20	0	0
Paid him more by Order of Common Hall as Vicar of Saint Martins	10	0	0
Paid the Reverend Dr Fancourt as Vicar of All Saints during pleasure	10	0	0
Paid him as Vicar of Saint Mary's during pleasure . .	10	0	0
Paid the Reverend Mr Davies as Vicar of St Nicholas the like	10	0	0
Paid the Reverend Mr Irvine as Vicar of St Margarets the like	10	0	0
Paid Miss Valentine a Gratuity during pleasure as Organist of St Margarets	10	0	0
Paid Miss S. Valentine the like as organist of St Martin's .	10	0	0
Paid Mrs Wood late Miss Hewitt the like as Organist of Saint Mary's	10	0	0
Paid the Organist of St George's the like . . .	10	0	0
Paid Miss Morrall during pleasure as Organist of St Nicholas's	10	0	0
Paid the Steward his year's Salary	100	0	0

Paid the Macebearer his year's salary etc. as under, vizt.,

Ancient Salary	7	9	8
More as Inspector of the Corn Market for one year .	2	12	0
More his salary for the like . .	5	0	0
More additional salary ordered by a Common Hall to be paid for rendering his assistance to the Chamberlains	20	0	0
More for 2 Seals		2	0

More by Order of Common Hall in lieu of boarding with the Mayor	40	0	0
More additional salary of Order of Common Hall	20	0	0
	95	3	8
Paid the 4 Serjeants at Mace their Salaries at £20 each .	80	0	0
Paid the Cryer and Beadle their salaries at £20 each. .	40	0	0
Paid the two Bellmen their Salaries at 10 Guineas each .	21	0	0
Paid the 6 Waits their Salary by Order of Hall. . .	30	0	0
Paid the Library Keeper her salary as increased by Order of Hall	5	0	0
Paid the Cryer and Beadle to prevent their going round with their Christmas Box		5	0
Paid them on St Thomas's Day what used to be paid by the Parishes		5	0
Paid for a pair of shoes each for the Cryer and Beadle .	1	2	0
Paid the Mole-catcher a year's salary	1	11	6
Paid Mr Benjamin Sutton as Superintendent of the Market a year's salary due at Michaelmas 1835	126	0	0
Paid Mr Yates a year's salary for superintending the Sheep Markets and Fairs and the New Markets as by Order of Hall	80	0	0

Total Salaries etc.
£1377 6s 8d

3   Miscellaneous

Allowed the Chamberlains for the Auditors' Dinners by Order of Hall	21	0	0
Paid the Bailiffs of the Augmentation for Land Tax to (blank) at Michaelmas & acquittance 7s 4d N.B. This 7s 4d of late has not been demanded.	(blank)		
Paid the Bailiffs of Merton College Oxford two year's Chief Rent issuing and payable out of St John's and St Leonard's in or near the Borough of Leicester		2	6
Paid the Wardens of the Company of Tailors the annual rent of 1s 8d	(blank)		
Paid for tolling the Bell on Michaelmas Day 1s . .	(blank)		

BB

Paid the Halbert men for walking the Fairs and cleaning the Armour on the Fair Days	10	0	
Paid Mr George late Pepys late Lucas a Chief Rent out of the Gainsboro'—Land Tax deducted—late William Morehead Esquire now Philip Hughes Esquire due 10th October	5	18	6
Paid Lady Fitzwilliam's now Earl Pembroke a years fee farm rent out of the South Field Tithes due at Michaelmas—Land Tax deducted	4	7	10
Paid the Clerk of St Mary's for washing the Chancel etc. .		2	6
Paid Thomas Gadsby for winding up the 'Change Clock .	2	2	0
Paid him a bill for repairing Do.	1	10	0
Paid Richard Rawson, Esquire for postage of Letters in his Mayoralty	5	0	0
Paid the Lottery money towards putting out a Boy apprentice	(blank)		
Paid for the Mayor's Standard Newspaper and postages .	9	17	9
Paid for the John Bull Newspaper and delivering . .	1	16	0
Paid for the Herald Newspaper	(blank)		
Paid the Beadle for sweeping after the Fairs . . .	1	12	0
Paid for sweeping Chimnies at the Town Hall and 'Change	2	0	6
Paid for attendance and Weights at the Cheese Fairs in Michaelmas and May	2	18	0
Paid the Grand Jury for 4 Sessions Dinners at £5 15s 6d and additional by Order of Hall at 5 Guineas each Sessions	44	2	0
Do. additional at Mr Serjeant Goulburn's last Sessions .	11	15	6
Paid the Bellmens Christmas Boxes		4	0
Paid the Cryer and Beadle Do.		4	0
Paid for Coal and Kids used at the Town Hall and 'Change	1	0	0
Paid for playing the Engines 4 several times . . .	10	0	0
Paid the annual subscription to the Infirmary . . .	10	10	0
Paid the annual subscription to the Horse Race as increased by Order of Hall	21	0	0
Paid the annual allowance for expences at the Rent Days .	15	15	0
Paid additional expences of Do.	26	0	5

Paid the Cryer for attendance at the Rent Days . .	(blank)		
Paid the Macebearer and Servants for their fees on one newly elected Alderman and the Recorder	16	0	
Paid (blank) Tax for the Corporation Steward to Michaelmas 1835	(blank)		
Paid Messrs Carbonell for a Pipe of Wine . . .	103	1	0
Paid them for a Pipe of Port had in the last Mayoralty .	105	3	0
Paid for Carriage thereof	2	10	4
Paid for lighting Fires etc. and cleaning at the 'Change for one year	7	15	0
Paid for Buns, Biscuits and Ale at the Visitations of the School	1	1	0
Paid the Macebearer what he paid for refreshment at the several Sessions	13	11	5
Paid him for refreshment etc. at the Assizes . . .	3	12	6
Paid him for cleaning and taking care of the Hall and Stoves etc. for one year	10	0	0
Paid him what he paid for cleaning knives etc. . .	4	4	0
Paid for the Insurance of the Houses in the High Cross Street	2	5	0
Paid for Receipt Stamps for the Rent Days . . .	6	5	6
Paid the Parochial Levies assessed upon the Free School for one year	4	12	3
Paid a year's Rent to the Duchy of Lancaster for premises rented on Lease expiring 27th December 1858 & for acquittance	15	1	0
Gave the Waterloo Soldiers and Pensioners in Leicester on the Anniversary of the Battle of Waterloo by Order (blank) at 2s 6d each	(blank)		
Paid Subscription towards lighting the Gas Lamps in the Market Place by Order of Hall	(blank)		
Paid the Gas Company for Gas at the Exchange and Town Hall and for two Street Lamps as per contract up to (blank)	(blank)		
Paid Do. for two other public Lamps for the Season ending May 1835 (the North and High cross Street)	(blank)		
Paid a year's rent to Wigston's Hospital for the new Sheep Market	1	13	8

Paid the Town Servants for attending on the Fair and Market Days to keep the Cattle within the places allotted for them in order to prevent the more public Streets from being incommoded by them	14	18	0
Paid the Lamplighter for lighting and trimming the Corporation Lamps	(blank)		
Paid a year's payment in lieu of Tithes issuing out of the Horsefair Garden to the Prebendary of St Margarets (now Mr Fenwicke) as by St Margaret's award due Michaelmas 1835	1	5	$1\frac{1}{2}$
Paid Guardian Office Insurance of Bull's Head, Swan's Mill and North Mill etc.	22	1	0
Paid one year's rent of Pews at St George's Church to Michaelmas 1835	10	10	0
Paid Mr Hole a year's Interest of £1000 due to him on Mortgage of the Bull's Head	50	0	0
Paid the Reverend Henry Palmer a year's Interest at £4 per Cent of the money borrowed of him on Mortgage	400	0	0
Paid Share of expences of making Culvert in front of the New Market	7	14	0
Paid Mr Bond's fee as Assessor to the Returning Officers at the last Election	10	10	0
Paid the Widow of the late Alderman Edward Marston a Gratuity by Order of Hall	20	0	0
Paid R. Goodacre on account of alterations at the New Market	100	0	0
Paid the Town Clerk's Special Bill for business respecting the Registration etc. under the Reform Act	195	8	10
Paid the Town Clerk's Special Bill in the Action against Taylor, a Beerhousekeeper	132	16	8
Casual Bill	45	17	9

5   Tradesmen's Bills

Paid Mr Yates for Wine	5	7	0
John Jones for Servants Cloaks	1	7	0
H. Wilkinson, Printer	3	15	0
J. Watkinsons, Carpenter	5	12	7
The executors of the late T. Davies	10	14	0

	£	s	d
Mr Yates for Wine	4	7	0
H. Hitchcock for Coals	5	11	0
H. Wilkinson, Printer	7	13	0
C. Collier, Hatter	19	17	0
J. Musson, Glassman	9	19	1
J. P. Clarke for Carpet for Grand Jury Room	2	14	0
W. Jolly, Glassman	4	18	0
W. Parsons & Son, Ironmongers including a Bill against Trinity Hospital of £5 17s 0d	44	16	5
W. Turner, Whitesmith	8	6	3
J. Bowman, Bleacher	3	10	0
Messrs Bosworth and Parr, Drapers	11	2	1
Messrs Jackson & Sons, Drapers	26	12	1
J. Allen for making Town Servants Clothes	4	7	6
Johnson and Son	7	16	0
G. Bellairs	2	16	6
A. Whitewood	18	18	7
Mr Hodges	29	7	6
Part of Grays Bill for Bread	10	10	0
B. S. Chamberlain Printer	47	18	1
Mr Lovells	37	3	2
J. Ottey, Glazier	17	10	3
W. Higginson, Painter	27	18	2
Mrs Swinfen, Glazier	28	19	6
W. Watts	3	14	9
Thomas Higginson, Painter	14	17	0
Thomas Parson for Paint		17	3
H. Hitchcock for Gravel used at the Mill	15	0	0
Messrs Herberts, Bricklayers	33	9	3
Mr Kinton, Ironmonger	15	8	0
W. Barlow for Gravel	15	7	0
J. Swain on account of his Bills	20	0	0
J. Harrison for Timber etc.	33	11	0
Parson and Gill a bill paid by them for advertising from 1830 to 1834	9	8	0
Mr Steads for Wood	6	10	0
Mr N. Stone for valuing Land	5	5	0
Advertising Michaelmas Fair in Stamford and Birmingham Newspapers	1	16	0
J. Mallet, Brazier	17	4	0
Beasley, Bricklayer	12	19	8
J. Measures	2	12	3
Neals, a Carpenter	9	7	9

Mr Cooks		6	2	9
Mr Barston for Coals		2	12	9
Mr James Rawson's		10	3	10
J. Watkinson, Carpenter		24	16	0
Wilson & Co. Ironfounder		73	7	0
T. Hopkins Paviour		36	14	0
Hunter for Books		1	8	0
Parliamentary Vote for 2 years		18	18	0
Town Clerk's General Bill for the year . . .		296	4	4

6   Field Account

Paid Joseph Wain's bills for wood & labour & for repairs
of Fences etc. } 95 9 6

Field Account 105 1 6

7a   Levies and Arrears

Allowed Land Tax on Twigden's Gift 8 0

Land Tax on Houses in South Gate Street . . . 2 9 6

7b   Arrears

As per Account produced 266 7 3

[End of payments]

[Summary]
                    General Statement
                        Receipts

Old Grange South Fields etc.	2160	18	2
Under Charters Grants etc.	1061	15	7
Purchases etc.	892	5	1
Charity Rents etc.	303	3	4
Fee Farm & Chief Rents	66	12	4½
Freedoms	198	0	0
Incidentals	245	5	5
	4927	19	11

                        Payments

Charitable Gifts. 454 14 9

Salaries 1377 6 8

Miscellaneous	.	.	.	.	.	.	.	.	1492	1	6
Tradesmen's Bills	.	.	.	.	.	.	.	1097	0	4
Field expences	.	.	.	.	.	.	.	200	11	0
Levies & arrears	.	.	.	.	.	.	269	4	9

$$4890 \quad 19 \quad 0$$

Receipts	4927	19	11
Payments	4890	19	0
Balance due	37	0	11

10th December 1835
The above Accounts were this day audited by us & allowed & the balance due to the Corporation is £37 0s 11d

(Signed) Isaac Lovell
Thomas Cook
B. Jackson
J. Parsons

SOUTH FIELDS' ENCLOSURE
EXPENSES 1805/7

Money expended in Saint Marys field on the
Enclosure account and Roads & other Works

1805				
9th March	Paid Main & Cox quicking gaps . .		6	0
16th	Paid Main & Co. for removing soil at the Rowdyke near the Turnpike to set the quick	3	0	0
23rd	Paid Cox & Co. for 9 days work fencing gaps 3s	1	7	0
30th	Paid Cox & Co. 8 mens work . .	1	4	0
April 6th	Paid Burdett & Co. for leveling far end of Rowdyke & other Jobs by great	5	3	6
13th	Paid Main & Co. 6½ days Work 3s .		19	6
	Paid Needham 2½ do. 3s . .		7	6
May 4th	Paid Cox 4 days work stoping gaps etc. 3s		12	0
25th	Paid Cox & Co. for weeding quick & drawing thorns in Rails (great Job)	3	0	0
1 June	Paid Main 2 days Counting Rails & Stacking them		6	0
15th	Paid Main 1½ days setting down posts & Rails in the Meadow		4	6
	Paid 14 Mens Work at Gravel Cart against the Infirmary @ 3s	2	2	0
	Paid Bass Two teams & a standing Cart Two days drawing gravel against the Infirmary	3	0	0
	Paid Bateman & Sutton Leveling the ditch adjoining the drift and another piece adjoining Freemens house (by great)	4	15	0

22nd [June]	Paid Robinson & Gadsby 17 days weeding quick at 2s 6d per day	2	2	6
	Paid William Spencer for drawing Wood in field		13	6
	Paid three Men Stacking posts & Rails & other Jobs		9	0
6th July	Paid Main & Co. Leveling Gravel pitt .	2	5	0
	Paid Palmer Surveying Land in the Field		15	0
18th	Paid Mr Alderman Burbidge for 3 fence fleakes		12	0
	Paid Carriage & portage of Letters from Mr Botham		4	9
3rd August	Paid Two men leveling Road & repairing gate in far Meadow		9	6
	Paid Stephenson drawing thorns . .		12	0
10th	Paid Two men Repairing fences . .		6	6
18th	Paid Main & Co. getting Gravel . .	2	16	0
9th September	Paid B. Shenton for several Jobs with Cart and Horse in the Field		14	6
21st	Paid Main 5 days sorting Rails and attending Race Week 3s		15	0
28th	Paid Main & Co. 7 days weeding quick 2s 6d		17	6
	Paid Richard Hughes 9½ days nailing stumps to Rails adjoining Freemens piece 3s 6d	1	13	3
	Paid Thomas Cox 5 days at do. 2s 6d .		12	6
5th October	Paid Hughes 5 days Nailing Stumps 3s 6d		17	6
12th	Paid Cox & Clay 5 days each helping Mr Botham set out the division fences 3s	1	10	0
	Paid Needham & Main 5 days each helping Mr Botham put down stakes 3s	1	10	0

		£	s	d
14th [Oct.]	Paid Hughes for Morticing 350 posts at 1s per Score		17	6
	Paid him for One days work. . .		3	6
16th	Paid postage of a parcel & Letter from Mr Botham		6	8½
	Paid Main & Co. Leveling ditches to set quick, 43½ Acres at 1s 5d per Acre	3	1	7½
2 November	Paid Samuel Ward Looking after field and other Jobs to now	1	3	3
	Paid 6 men 1 day wheeling soil in Meadow		18	0
	Paid Main & Co. 4 days helping Jones .		12	0
	Gave them to drink		4	0
9th	Paid Cox & Co. 16 Mens work scouring drain next freemens pasture 3s	2	8	0
	Paid for a scuttle		1	0
	Paid Main 2 days helping Jones . .		6	0
	Paid Cooper, Ross, Stokes & Mason 4½ days each filling soil in Meadow 2s 6d	2	5	0
	Paid Goodman 1 week wheeling soil in Meadow		14	0
	Paid Timson & Green making pits in Gosling Close		17	0
	Paid them a Job of Cutting & Wheeling in the Meadow	3	3	0
	Paid Cox & 5 other men 1½ day stanking and pudling against River 3s	1	7	0
	Paid Richard Hughes for Morticing 630 posts at 1s 1d per score	1	14	1½
	Paid him for 3 days work 3s 6d . .		10	6
16th	Paid Cox making a Temporary bridge in Meadow		3	0
	Paid Cooper & Ross 4 days each in Meadow removing Soil 2s 6d	1	0	0
	Paid Stokes & Mason 4 days each @ do. .	1	0	0
	Paid Samuel Hextal 5 days loading Wood 2s 6d		12	6

[16 Nov.]	Paid Frank Reynolds 2 days leveling to set quick		5	0
	Paid Stokes 1½ day in Meadow . .		3	9
	Paid a man for carrying quick into the field		2	0
23rd	Paid Main drawing Chains for Mr Botham		3	0
	Paid Samuel Hextal 6 days Careying Wood 2s 6d		15	0
	Paid Carriage of a Letter & Plan from Mr Botham		5	6
	Paid Ben Patrick drawing Chain do. .		1	0
	Paid Carriage of 3 barrows from Shilton .		1	6
30th	Paid Richard Hughes Morticeing 12 score of posts		13	0
	Do. Clevcing 18 posts		1	0
	Paid Samuel Hextal 6 days 2s 6d .		15	0
	Paid Cooper Ross & Morral 3 days each 2s 6d	1	2	6
	Paid Smith scouring ditch . . .		7	6
7th December	Paid Smith & Co. for setting quick & fencing 10½ Acres in Meadow	1	12	6
	Paid Cox & Co. a Job wheeling soil Meadow	1	8	0
	Paid them 25½ days work wheeling soil Leveling etc. 3s	3	16	6
	Paid Samuel Hextal 6 days 2s 6d a Job 5s	1	0	0
14th	Paid Cox & 7 other men 1 week wheeling & different work 3s	7	4	0
	Paid Samuel Hextal 4 days drawing Rails 2s 6d		10	0
21st	Paid Cox & 7 other men 1 week Leveling for quick & wheeling 2s 6d	6	0	0
	Paid Hughes 7 days work felling & Cleveing Wood 3s 6d	1	4	6
	Paid Samuel Hextal 6 days 2s 6d .		15	0

28th [Dec.]	Paid Hughes 2 days fencing 3s 6d .		7	0
	Paid Parsons & Main 5 days each level-ing for quick 2s 6d	1	5	0
	Paid Samuel Hextal 5 days 2s 6d .		12	6
	Gave the Men to drink . . .		1	0

1806

10th January	Paid Samuel Hextal 6 days 2s 6d .		15	0
	Paid Samuel Ward looking after the field from 2 November till now 2s per week	1	0	0
11th	Paid Hughes for Morticeing 21 score of post at 1s per score	1	1	0
18th	Paid Hughes & another man for Mor-ticeing 1155 posts at 1s 1d per Score	3	2	10
	Paid Cooper & 6 other men 1 week each quicking gaps and other Jobs @ 2s 6d	5	5	0
	Paid postage of Letters about Wood .		1	6
25th	Paid Cooper & 6 other men Leveling quicking gaps & other work	5	5	0
	Gave them to drink		2	0
1st February	Paid North for Grubing an Old Hedge up & Leveling to set quick	1	12	0
	Paid him for scouring an Old ditch in the Meadow before quick cou'd be set	1	7	0
	Paid Cox and Main 6 days each odd Jobs 2s 6d	2	5	0
	Paid Hughes 5 days 3s 6d Cleveing Posts		17	6
	Paid Cooper & Two other men 6 days each field work 2s 6d	2	5	0
	Paid John Morral 6 days drawing Rails 2s 6d		15	0
	Paid Bishop Coleorton for 45 thousand of quick at 6s per thousand	13	10	0

[1 Feb.]	Paid Ross & Co. part by the day & part by the Great Leveling a Road through Valentines Brick Kilns	27	6	0
	Paid Timpson & Co. 2 Jobs by the great in Meadow deep cutting & wheeling to fill up Old ditches	29	7	6
	Paid Bullivant & Stanyer for stanking the River in 46 Acre @ 3s 9d per Acre	8	12	6
	Paid them for Work in the Over Meadow part by the day & part by the great	5	15	0
	Paid Cox & Co for cutting a drain across the Freemens pasture and Wheeling into the Old ditches 16 Acres at 10s 6d per Acre	8	8	0
	Paid them for cutting a drain in far Meadow & Wheeling into Old ditch 14 Acres at 17s per Acre	11	18	0
	Paid them for widening another ditch & scouring it	3	12	0
	Paid a man trying for water in Gosling Close		3	0
8th February	Paid John Geary 1 day . . .		2	6
	Paid Needham & 3 other men 6 days each 2s 6d	3	0	0
15th	Paid John Morral 3 days drawing wood 3s		9	0
	Paid Needham & 4 other men 6 days each 2s 9d different Jobs in field	3	6	0
22nd	Paid Needham & 3 other men 6 days fining & quicking Old gaps—and 1 man 4 days 2s 9d each	3	0	6
	Paid Hughes Morticing 19½ score posts @ 1s 1d	1	1	0
	Paid him 1 day & Expences going with me to Rotherby Wood sale		7	6

[22 Feb.]	Paid John Clay 5 days @ 2s 6d letting Water off and other work in Meadows		12	6
	Paid John Morral 4½ days drawing Wood etc. 3s		13	6
1st March	Paid Cox Main & 2 others 6 days each 2s 9d Jobbing & planting young trees	3	6	0
	Paid Clay 3½ days @ 2s 6d Morral 3½ days 3s		17	9
	Paid Warner & Halfpenny for planting quick fenceing it on both sides with posts & rails & backdykeing 177½ Acres @ 5s 3d per Acre	46	11	10½
	Paid them for other Jobs . . .	1	19	6
	Gave them to drink		2	6
8th	Paid Cox & 2 others 6 days each 3s Main 5 days 3s Leveling etc.	3	9	0
	Paid Bullivant & 1 other 5½ days Jobing 2s 6d	1	7	6
	Paid Warner & Halfpenny 1½ day each .		9	0
	Paid Grey 1½ day grubing Hedge . .		3	6
	Paid Morral 4 days 3s . . .		12	0
	Paid Cooper & 2 others leveling against Turnpike 5 days each 3s	2	5	0
15	Paid Cox & 2 others 6 days each 3s and Main 3 days 3s setting trees	3	3	0
	Paid Cooper Ross & Parsons 3 days each against Welford Turnpike Leveling etc. 3s	1	7	0
	Paid Bullivant & his Brother 2 days each 2s 6d		10	0
	Paid John Morral 5 days drawing Rails 3s		15	0
	Another man 4 days do. 2s 9d . .		11	0
22nd	Paid Withers 3 days 2s 6d . . .		7	6
	Paid Gibson for Repairing River bank .	1	7	0
	Paid Cox & 3 other men 6 days each setting Trees & fencing 3s	3	12	0

[22 March]	Paid Hughes for Morticeing 33 Score & 15 posts at 1s 1d . . 1 16 0 30 posts 3 Mortices . . 2 3	1 18	3
	Paid Cooper Ross & Co. for cutting the west side of the New walk hedge and another hedge in the field and scouring the ditch 74 Acres @ 3s	11 2	0
	Paid them for Cutting the Hedge on the East side by the day	4 10	6
	Paid Bullivant & his brother 2 days each 2s 9d	11	0
	Paid John Morral 2 days 3s . .	6	0
29th	Paid Jordan for leveling to set quick .	5	0
	Paid Cox & 5 other men double digging 2550 yards at 4s per hundred—to plant trees	5 2	0
	Paid them for planting the Trees . .	1 16	0
	Paid Cooper & 2 others 3 days each 3s .	1 7	0
	Paid Hughes 5½ days fencing the ends of gates & Quick lines 3s 6d	19	3
	Paid Finney 2 days 3s . . .	6	0
	Paid John Morral 4 days 3s . .	12	0
	Paid Clay 5 days 3s	15	0
5th April	Paid Hughes & Losly—6 days hanging gates and fencing—3s 6d per day	2 2	0
	Paid finney 2 days 3s . . .	6	0
	Paid Cox & 1 other man 6 days each 3s repairing fences	1 16	0
	Paid Main & Needham 6 days each 3s .	1 16	0
	Paid Bullivant for scouring the remainder of the ditch in far Meadow 7½ Acre @ 5s 6d	2 11	3
	Paid Parsons Ross & Cooper 6 days each Cutting hedges & Stoping gaps 3s	2 14	0
	Paid Morral 5 days 3s . . .	15	0
	Paid Clay 3 days 9s Withers 3 days 8s 3d	17	3

12th [April]	Paid Needham Cox & Main 6 days each 3s	2	14	0
	Paid Hughes & Losley 4¾ days work at gates and stiles 3s 6d		19	3
	Paid Losley for Hanging 11 Gates 2s 6d	1	7	6
	Paid Finney 3 days 9s Morral 6 days 18s .	1	7	0
	Paid Morral Laying 3 drains under Gate Ways		3	0
	Paid Cooper Parson & Ross 6 days each setting Trees 3s	2	14	0
	Paid Clay 2 days 6s Withers 2 days 5s 6d .		11	6
	Paid Mr Wright for a pair of gates at the end of the Close near the New Walk end		10	6
19th	Paid Finney 3 days setting quicks 3s .		9	0
	Paid Hughes 4 days 3s 6d Losley 6 days 3s 6d Work at Gates & Fences	1	15	0
	Paid Needham & 3 others 6 days each 3s at drain & Roads	3	12	0
	Paid Raynor 1½ day 3s　.　.　.		4	6
	Paid Parsons Cooper & Ross 6 days each 3s Setting young Trees in Hedgerows	2	14	0
	Paid Clay 6 days 18s. Withers 6 days 2s 9d 16s 6d	1	14	6
	Paid John Morral 6 days 3s　.　.		18	0
26th	Paid Cox & 4 others 6 days each 3s at fences	4	10	0
	Paid Cooper Ross & Parsons 6 days each 3s unbareing for gravel	2	14	0
	A basket for Pump　.　.　.　.		2	0
	Paid Clay 6 days at Hedges 3s　.　.		18	0
	Paid Withers 6 do. at do. 2s 9d　.		16	6
	Paid Ben Shenton for different Jobs in Field with Cart & Horse	1	9	6
	Paid Hughes & Losley 6 days each 3s 6d at Fences	2	2	0

3 May	Paid Cox & 4 others 6 days each 3s at Roads	4	10	0
	Paid Hughes & Losley 5 days each 3s 6d	1	15	0
	Paid them for 39 Acre of fencing @ 6d .		19	6
	Paid Cooper Ross & Needham 5 days each unbareing Gravel 3s	2	5	0
	Paid Ben Shenton drawing Rummel into Mill Lane & Other Jobs		15	6
	Paid a Man Loading Rimmel 1 day .		2	6
10th	Paid Cox & 1 other Man 6 days each 3s scouring ditch & weeding quick	1	16	0
	Paid Moore & Bramley forming Roads 6 days each 3s	1	16	0
	Paid Moore & Bramley Soughing 9 days @ 3s to drink 2s	1	9	0
	Paid Ross Cooper & 3 others 6 days each at Gravel pitt 3s	4	10	0
	Bought a wheel barrow . . .		13	6
	Parsons 6 days at Roads 3s . .		18	0
17th	Paid Hughes & Losley 6 days each at fences 3s 6d	2	2	0
	Paid Cox & 3 other men 2 days each @ Roads 3s	1	4	0
	Paid Main & Parsons 6 days each 3s .	1	16	0
	Paid Cooper & Ross 4 days each at pitt 3s	1	4	0
	Paid William Jee & another man 3 days work each sinking pitt Gosling Close 3s		18	0
23rd	Paid for weeding quicks 1st Race ground piece		5	0
	Paid Measures & another man attending in South field on Sundays to prevent people Riding over the quick Lines		7	6
	Paid Jelly Leveling Rummel in Mill Lane		5	0

[23 May]	Paid Cox & Co. forming 25 Acre of Road at 5s 6d per Acre	6 17 6
	Paid Gilbert for Masons Allowance Ale .	14 0
	Paid Hughes & Losley 6 days each at Fences 3s 6d	2 2 0
	Paid Cooper & Co. forming 17½ Acres of Roads @ 5s 6d per Acre	4 16 3
	Paid Cooper & Ross 2 days each in gravel pit 3s Parsons 6 days 3s	1 10 0
30th	Paid Raynor & 4 others 6 days each at 3s at Gravel pitt	4 10 0
	Paid Hughes 5 days & Losley 6 days 3s 6d @ fences & Gates	1 18 6
	Paid Ross 5 days & Cooper 6 @ 3s Gravel pitt	1 13 0
7th June	Paid Cox & 4 others 5 days each @ 3s do.	3 15 0
	Paid Hughes & Losley 6 days each 3s 6d @ fences & Gates	2 2 0
	Paid Cooper Ross & Parsons 6 days each 3s Roads	2 14 0
14th	Paid Hughes & Losley 6 days each 3s 6d Fences & Gates	2 2 0
	Paid Cox & 4 others at Gravel pitt 3s 1 week	4 10 0
	Paid Main & Needham 6 days each 3s Roads	1 16 0
	Parsons 3 days Roads 3s . . .	9 0
	Paid Withers & Clay for Work at the Fences & different Work	4 13 6
21st	Paid Hughes & Losley at Fences & 6 days each 3s 6d	2 2 0
	Paid them Weeding 43 Acre of quick @ 3d	10 9
	Gave them to drink	2 0
	Paid Cox & 3 others @ Roads 3s 1 week	3 12 0

[21 June]	Paid Cox & Co. forming 25½ of Roads @ 5s 6d	7	0	3
	Paid them pecking in Ruts & Weeding Quick		10	0
	Paid Cooper & 3 others 6 days each 3s at Gravel pitt	3	12	0
28th	Paid Hughes @ fences 6 days 3s 6d .	1	1	0
	Paid Main & 3 others 6 days each at the Gravel pitt 3s	3	12	0
	Paid them forming 4½ Acres of Roads 5s 6d	1	4	9
	Paid them Hoeing Spinney at Turnpike .		12	0
	Paid Cooper & 3 others at Roads 6 days each 3s	3	12	0
	Paid Shenton for Carriage of Rubish into the Mill Lane		2	6
5th July	Paid Hughes 3 days at Gates 3s 6d .		10	6
19th	Paid Cooper Weeding quick & throwing bank down No. 1 (by great)	1	8	0
25th	Paid Mr E. Jones 2 poors Levies for £25 9s 3d @ 20d in the pound	4	4	10½
	Paid Mr Bassett a Road Levy @ 6d as above		12	9
2nd August	Paid 3 women gathering twich 17 days @ 14d		19	10
	Paid Main & Two other men getting out Twich 2 days each 3s		18	0
	Paid for grinding sheers & drink . .		1	6
9th	Paid Ross at twich ground 6 days 3s .		18	0
	Paid 3 women gathering twich 18 days @ 14d	1	1	0
	Paid Cooper 6 days at twich ground & New Walk 3s		18	0
	Paid 2 women gathering twich 9 days 14d		10	6
	Paid Gamble & Co. Leveling Bank in Race ground piece	1	5	0
16th	Paid 5 women 20 days work twich ground @ 14 pence	1	3	4
	Paid Hughes 6 days 3s 6d @ Fences .	1	1	0

		£	s	d
[16 August]	Paid Finney Hughes & Co. from 16 November 1805 to 19th April 1806 For 70½ Acre of Fencing in the Meadows @ 5s 9d . . .	20	5	4½
	9 Acres 5 feet ditch 6s	2	14	0
	17½ Acre of single fencing 3s 4d	2	18	4
	247 Acres & 7 yards 5s 3d	64	18	3
	Hanging 1 gate . .		2	6
	Loss of time Counting Rails		5	0
		91	3	5½
	Paid Gamble & Co. Scouring Main ditch against Newark Mills	1	16	10
23 August	Paid Main & 3 others Scouring the two main ditches each side Freemens Meadow	1	8	0
	Paid Main & 3 others 3 days each @ Roads 3s 6d	2	2	0
	Paid Richard Hughes 6 days @ Fences 3s 6d	1	1	0
	Paid Cox & 4 others unbaring Gravel 1 day each 3s 6d		17	6
30th	Paid Cooper cutting New Walk hedge 4 days 3s		12	0
	Paid 10 men 1 week each @ River 3s 6d	10	10	0
	Paid Ben Shenton 6 nights sitting up to watch @ River		10	6
	Paid Black 3 days Twiching Race ground 2s 2d		6	6
6th September	Paid 10 men 4 days each @ River 3s 6d .	7	0	0
	Paid Main & 3 others 2 days each at Roads 3s 6d	1	8	0
	Hughes 2 days @ Fences 3s 6d . .		7	0
	Paid Raynor watching wood etc @ River		7	0

[6 Sept.]	Paid Cooper 1 week New Walk Hedge 3s		18	0
13th	Paid Raynor & 4 others 6 days each 3s @ Roads		4 10	0
	Paid Hughes @ Fences 1 week @ 3s 6d .		1 1	0
20th	Paid Welton & Bates Attending on Fences at the Race week		1 0	0
	Paid Raynor & 4 others 6 days each @ Roads 3s		4 10	0
27th	Paid do. do.		4 10	0
	Paid them for laying a drain . .		3	0
	Paid Hughes 5 days 3s 6d @ Fences .		17	6
	Paid Bunney going with Mr Custance to shew him the grounds to value Tythe		15	6
4th October	Paid Raynor & 5 other men 6 days each 3s at Roads & Gravel pitt		4 10	0
	Paid Hughes 1 week @ fences 3s 6d .		1 1	0
11th	Paid Raynor 9s 4 other men 1 week @ Roads 3s		4 1	0
	Paid Hughes 1 week @ Fences 3s 6d .		1 1	0
18th	Paid Raynor & 4 others at Gravel pitt and Roads 3s		4 10	0
25th	Paid Raynor & 4 others at Gravel pitt & Roads 3s & Mason 4 days 3s		5 2	0
1st November	Paid Halfpenny scouring a main ditch in Meadow 17 Acres @ 1s 6d per Acre		1 5	6
	Paid Raynor & 4 others 5 days each @ Roads 3s		3 15	0
	Paid Hughes 2 days 3s 6d . . .		7	0
	Paid him Morticeing 88 posts 1s 1d .		4	10
	Paid him do. 117 do. 3 mortices 20d .		9	9
	Paid Parsons Laying drains 3s . .		18	0
	Paid Welton & Bates attending the Fence on the Farmers lees on Sundays 21 days each 2s		4 4	0
8th	Parsons 6 days @ Drains & Roads 3s .		18	0

15th [Nov.]	Paid Richard Hughes 2 weeks Hanging gates and repairing Fences 3s	1	16	0
22	Paid Ross 6 days 2s 6d letting water of Roads etc.		15	0
	Paid for an Ax new stealing . . .		3	0
29th	Paid Hughes 4 days at New Walk & other Fences 3s		12	0
	Parsons & Ross Laying drains & opening ditches—6 days each 2s 6d	1	10	0
	Paid Allam & Murdiff 5½ days making Stanks & a River bank 3s 3d	1	15	9
6th December	Paid them at same work 2 days each 3s 3d		13	0
	Paid Hughes 6 days Felling & Cleveing Wood 3s		18	0
	Paid Parsons & Ross 4 days each @ Roads & drains 2s 6d	1	0	0
13th	Richard Hughes 6 days felling & Cleveing Wood 3s		18	0
	Parsons & Ross 5 days each helping Hughes & other work 2s 6d	1	5	0
	Paid Mr E. Jones a poors Levy @ 20d for No. 1 Race ground	2	2	5
20th	Paid Ross & Parsons 2 days each putting in quick 2s 6d		10	0
27th	Raynor & Needham 2 days each removeing Hovel 2s 6d		10	0
1807				
1 January	Paid Halfpenny 1 day setting quick .		2	6
3rd	Paid Parsons & Ross puting in quick 4 days each 2s 6d	1	0	0
	Paid Cooper 5 days same work 2s 6d .		12	6
	Paid Murdiff & Allum 4½ days each making River bank at the head of the Cistern 3s 3d	1	9	3

[3 Jan.]	Paid Raynor Needham & Main for getting & ridling 190½ yards of Gravel @ 1s 4d per yard	12 14	0
	Paid them for Leveling & Sloping the pitt	5 11	0
10th	Paid Cooper Parsons & Ross 3 days each setting quick 2s 6d	1 2	6
17th	Paid Raynor & Needham for a Job in Collinsons Close Cutting hedge & Wheeling soil into pitt	2 0	0
	Paid Cooper 5 days putting in quick 2s 6d	12	6
	Parsons & Ross 2 days each do. 2s 6d .	10	0
	Examined Thomas Miller	725 14	3

Bills paid for Wood & Fenceing etc in St Marys field & Carriage of Gravel & Woods

No.				
1	Grey for wood	34	4	9
2	Mercer for bricks	6	15	0
3	Mr Stavely surveying	2	2	0
4	Oliver for Carriage	7	3	0
5	Smith Blacksmith		8	2
6	Mortimer for wood	75	9	0
7	Gregory printers		5	6
8	Mr Jackson for thorns	1	15	0
9	Mr Peet wood	68	15	0
10	Black & Smith	409	7	1
11	Rouse Black-smith	1	2	1
12	Simpson & Co Lime	4	3	6
13	Thornton for wood	5	6	8
14	J. Harrison barrows	4	19	0
15	Oliver Carriage	7	10	6
16	Richardson Carpenter . . .	9	18	6
17	Evatt wood	5	8	4
18	Allen Smith wood	2	10	0
19	Stain Blaby wood	3	15	0
20	Mortimer do.	6	0	0
21	Palmer Surveying Land . . .		19	6
22	Cooper wood	11	1	8
23	Henson do.	20	0	0
24	Satchell & Christian fencing . .	177	3	8

25	Oliver Carriages	10	3	6
26	Mortimer for wood	12	14	2
27	Hall for Fencing & Gates . . .	639	14	6
28	Hardy for wood	28	2	6
29	Stephenson Carriage . . .	8	15	0
30	Hardy & Grey wood	92	0	0
31	Baker for quick		14	0
32	Richard Place wood	19	6	3
33	William Place do.	23	0	5
34	John Hardy gates	3	0	0
35	Marston wood	4	17	0
36	Mortimer do.	16	3	9
37	William Hughes do.	130	6	4
38	Astell do.	2	19	7
39	Bray ploughing	8	10	0
40	Mann Carriage		17	6
41	Oliver do.	14	16	6
42	Jones Bricklayer	14	11	5
43	Payne Carpenter		8	10
44	William Johnson quick . . .		18	3
45	Oliver Carriage	24	18	0
46	Horner do.	6	16	6
47	Bray do.	30	0	0
48	Coltman ploughing	16	0	0
49	Mortimer wood	28	19	8
50	Coltman ploughing	20	0	0
51	Hall Ale	4	15	5
52	Shenton slabs	1	10	0
53	Coltman ploughing	17	12	0
54	Richardson on Account . . .	12	7	0
55	Beaty wood	4	10	10
56	Marvin Trees to plant . . .	58	7	6
57	Grey & Matts wood	80	18	6
58	Oliver Carriage	22	18	6
59	James Brown Black-smith . . .	12	7	2
60	Heywood & Cooper in part of their bill } £106 16s 8d	50	0	0
61	Mr Fox tubs for fencing . . .		15	0
62	Henry Mansfield for Carriage & Ale .	16	19	8
		2307	18	2
	Other payments	725	14	3
	Examined Thomas Miller	3033	12	5

Money Received

Of Messrs Mansfield & Co. for Stock sold	1234	5	7
Of do. Borrowed .	800	0	0
Of the Union Canal Company	193	12	6
Of Mr Alderman Clark	89	0	0
Of Mr Heard . .	700	0	0

3016	18	1

ballance to E.P.   16 14 4

Exchange   January 21st 1807

These accounts were thus far examined
& allowed
(Signed)
J. Johnson   Mayor   Thomas Read
Samuel Clarke   John Gregory   W. Firmadge
H. Clark   Thomas Miller

Bills Continued

	Balance due to Edward Parsons brought forward		16	14	4
63	W. Wigston	for Oak wood . .	39	3	9
64	Cooper	Oak posts . .		11	8
65	Warner	Carriage of Gravel etc .	27	6	0
66	Thomas Neal	Ale at Gravel cart .	1	17	7
67	W. Wigston	Oak posts . . .	8	6	0
68	Butcher	repairing pump . .		11	0
69	Thomas Neal	for the use of the yard to lay wood in	2	12	6
70	Joseph Taylor	for Carriage of Gravel Wood etc.	40	2	6
71	William Bradley	for Wood . . .	13	16	3
72	Hardy Grooby	for posts & Rails .	28	6	8
73	Grey & Matts	do. do. . .	34	11	0

74	William Hughes	do. do. . .	9	5	0
75	Thomas Warner	Carriage of Gravel etc	8	8	0
76	Thomas Oliver	do. do. . .	22	10	9
77	John Mortimer	Wood etc. . .	10	1	6
78	Joseph Taylor	Carriage work etc. .	36	0	3
79	Rouse	Blacksmith . .	13	10	0
80	Palmer	Surveying Land .	1	3	6
81	Chamberlin	willow sets & kid-bands		7	10
82	Butcher	for pump work . .	3	0	0
83	do.	for Elm pipes laid in the River	69	18	6
84	Richardson	for Dale planks & other wood do.	91	10	3
60	Cooper & Clarke	for posts & rails part paid before see bill 60	58	0	0
85	Smith	for Ash Rails . .	1	14	7
86	Simpson & Co.	for Lime . . .	4	13	6
87	Hitchcock	for Loss of water while pipes laying in River	9	15	0
88	Shenton	for stones . .		16	0
89	Mr Alderman Burbidge				
		for Repairs of fences .	2	15	2
90	Richard Spencer	for Ale when laying pipes in the River	3	9	11
91	J. Harrison	for Rails & other work	42	7	8
92	Harrison Gardner	for Quick . .	13	14	6
93	Mr Gregory	for Sugar Hogsheads .		12	0
94	Smith	Blacksmith . .		14	2
95	Mr Sarson	Sugar hogsheads .	1	0	0
96	E. Jones	Ale at Gravel cart .		19	3
97	Mr Sarson	Sugar Hogshead .		9	0
98	Nikclinson	for Quick . .	8	8	0

Other Work done in St Marys field and
Corporation Estates.

		£	s	d
24 January	Paid Johnson for 5 thousand of quick 7s	1	15	0
	Do. 1 do. small ash plants . .		3	6
	Paid Barsby & Co. for Cutting & dyking 4½ Acres of hedge		11	3
	Do. 4 Acre at 6s felling Trees & Cutting them up into posts £1	2	4	0
	Paid Cooper 6 days @ 2s 6d putting in quick		15	0
	Do. Raynor & Needham 5 days each puting in quick and other Jobs 2s 6d	1	5	0
31st	Paid Whitmore & Damon 3 days each Morticeing posts etc. 3s 3d		19	6
	Paid Barsby & 2 others 3 days each puting in quick and repairing fences @ 2s 6d	1	2	6
	Paid Parsons & Ross 3 days each puting in quick and repairing fences 2s 6d		15	0
	Paid Ben Shelton fetching pump from Thurmaston		3	0
	Raynor Cooper & Needham 6 days each puting in quick & pumping water out of gravel pitt 2s 6d	2	5	0
7 February	Raynor Cooper and Needham pumping and unbaring gravel 2s 6d per day 3 days each	1	2	6
	Parsons & Ross 6 days each drawing Ash plants and other Jobs 3s	1	16	0
	Whitmore 2 days Morticeing posts 3s 3d		6	6
	West & Barsby 2 days each pointing Rails 3s		12	0
	Paid a man carrying quick . . .			6
14th	Parsons & Ross 6 days each removing posts & Rails and laying a drain 3s	1	16	0
	Paid Allam & Murphy Laying a drain .		5	0
21st	Paid Whitmore 1 day pointing rails .		3	3

[21 Feb.]	Paid for over weight for Slabs . .			6
	Parsons & Ross 6 days each at the fences & Roads 3s	1	16	0
28th	Raynor Cooper & Needham 2 days each pumping water out of gravel pitt 2s 6d		15	0
	Parsons & Ross 6 days each drawing wood and Laying drains in gateways 3s	1	16	0
7 March	Raynor Cooper & Needham for getting and Ridling 162 yards of gravel @ 1s 6d per Yard	12	3	0
	Paid them 1 day each pumping . .		7	6
	Paid Bray & Co. for taking up & replanting a line of quick in the Meadow 23 Acres @ 7s . . . 8 1 0 4 do. 7 0	8	8	0
	Paid Mr Homes a years property tax to Lady day 1807 for the Close the Corporation purchased of Mr William Heyrick		14	0
	Ross & Parsons 6 days each scouring ditch and Loading posts & Rails 3s	1	16	0
	Paid Barsby & others for planting 65 Acre of quick and fenceing both sides with posts & Rails & backdyking 7s	22	15	0
	Paid them for removing & hanging 6 gates	1	5	0
	Paid them 6 days puting in quick & Scouring ditches 3s		18	0
	Gave them to drink		2	0
14th	Paid Bateman & Co. for taking in the Spinney from the Hinckley Road—setting quick fencing it and diging & Leveling the ground & planting it with Ash	18	3	6
	Paid Hughes & Shaw for felling wood and cuting it up Ready for fencing the Spinney	2	8	0

[14 March]	Paid Bray & his brothers setting 12½ Acre of quick next the freemans pasture @ 2s 6d per Acre	1	11	3
	Paid them for trenching 1½ Acre . .		1	6
	Raynor Needham & Cooper 4 days each Leveling pits 2s 6d	1	10	0
	Parsons & Ross 6 days each at different works 3s	1	16	0
	Paid Thomas Howes weeding quick and scouring the ditches upon Everard's Land	2	0	0
21st	Paid Parsons & Ross 6 days each 3s 3 days Jobbing & 3 days planting trees	1	16	0
	Main 3 days at 2s 6d . . .		7	6
	Hows 6 do. 2s 6d . . .		15	0
28th	Main & Ross 6 days each planting willows and pecking in Ruts 3s Parsons 6 days 3s	2	14	0
	Paid Mr Jones a poors Levy for No. 1 @ 20d	2	2	5½
	Do. Church Levy @ 10d . . .	1	1	2½
4 April	Paid Richard Hughes for Choping and Morticeing 220 Oak posts 4 Mortices each 3s per Score	1	13	0
	Paid him 5 days work 3s 6d . .		17	6
	Parsons Main & Ross 5 days each planting willows & Fencing 3s	2	5	0
	Paid Bates & Welton for looking after the field to prevent trespass		5	0
11th	Main & Ross planting willows & other Jobs 6 days each 3s	1	16	0
	Paid Hughes cleaving posts & Rails 6 days 3s 6d	1	1	0
	Paid Bray & Co. for scouring 24 Acres of Main ditch 1s 6d	1	16	0
18th	Paid Ross & Main 6 days each setting quick in the Gosling closes 3s	1	16	0
	Hughes 6 days fencing in Gosling closes 4s	1	4	0
	Parsons 3 days 3s		9	0

22nd [April]	Paid Warner for quick . . .	5	0
25th	Richard Hughes 6 days 4s . . .	1 4	0
	Ross Main & Parsons 6 days each peck- ing Ruts and Leveling gravel pitt 3s	2 14	0
2nd May	Ross & Main getting gravel 6 days each 3s	1 16	0
	Parsons do. 6 3s	18	0
9th	Parsons Main & Ross forming 6½ Acre of Roads 5s 6d	1 15	9
	Paid them 4 days each geting gravel & pecking in Ruts 3s	1 16	0
16th	Ross Main & Parsons 6 days each part at Roads and part weeding spiney 3s	2 14	0
23rd	Paid Ross & Main 5 days each weeding spiney Ailstone Turnpike 3s Parsons 2 days scouring ditch after Flood 3s	1 16	0
30th	Parsons Main & Ross 6 days each weed- ing quick etc. 3s	2 14	0
	Lovett 6 days weeding quick Infirmary close 1s 6d	9	0
	Richardson & Murphey 5 days each at the stanks River 3s 3d	1 12	6
4 June	Paid property tax for No. 1 St Marys field (now Taylor)	8 5	8
5th	Paid Hitchcock for Loss by Land ad- joining the wind mill by the enclosure taking place before the expiration of his Lease	2 12	6
6th	Parsons Main & Ross 6 days each at Gravel pitt 3s	2 14	0
	Richardson & Murphy 3 days each at the River & Stanks 3s 3d	19	6
	Expences going twice to buy wood. .	5	6
13th	Parsons Main & Ross 6 days each @ Gravel pitt and Roads 3s	2 14	0
	Murphy 1½ day at the drain 3s 3d .	4	10½
	Hughes 8 days at the Fences 4s . .	1 12	0

20th [June]	Murphy & Richardson 6 days each repairing the River banks after a Flood 3s 3d	1	19	0
	Paid water men picking up planks after Flood		4	3
	Parsons Main & Ross 6 days each at Roads 3s	2	14	0
	Hughes 3 days repairing fences in the Meadow broke down by floods 4s		12	0
	Murphy & Richardson cleaning out the Cistern at the River & scouring part of the Main ditch	1	11	6
	Hughes 1½ day @ 4s		6	0
4th July	Paid Murphy at Stanks 4 days 3s 3d .		13	0
4 July	Hughes at Fence 2 days 4s . .		8	0
	Lovett weeding spiney Leicester forest .		13	0
11 July	Murphey & Richardson 3 days each @ Stanks 3s 3d		19	6
	Black 1 day crosscuting wood . .		2	6
	Parsons & Ross 4 days each @ Roads 3s .	1	4	0
18th	Hughes 5 days fencing Stanks 4s .	1	0	0
	Murphy & Richardson 6 days each @ Stanks 3s 3d	1	19	0
26th	Hughes fencing stanks 5 days 4s .	1	0	0
	Raynor & 2 other men 2½ days each scouring ditch 3s	1	2	6
	Murphy & Richardson 6 days each at Stanks 3s 3d	1	19	0
	Cooper & Needham cuting the Hedges on both sides the New Walk 57 Acre @ 16d per Acre	3	16	0
	Raking & burning the thorns . .		3	0
1st August	Hughes 6 days at stanks & Cleaving posts 4s	1	4	0
	Murphy & Richardson 6 days each at stanks 3s 3d	1	19	0
	Gave them to drink		2	6

		£	s	d
[1 August]	Paid Needham geting up pebbles in Johnsons garden		5	2
	Lovett 2 days weeding spiny Forest 2s 3d		4	6
8th	Needham pecking in Rutts 2 days 3s .		6	0
15th	Hughes 4 days stoping gaps & Repairing Barn 4s		16	0
22nd	do. sawing wood 1 day 4s Black 1 day 2s 6d		6	6
29th	Cooper & Needham 2 days each @ Roads 3s 6d		14	0
	Black 1 day		2	6
	Murphy & Richardson scouring all the Main ditches	7	0	9
5th September	Black for help		1	0
	Hughes for Cleaving 80 posts & making 4 mortices @ 16d per score		5	4
	Do. for Cleaving 29 score of Rails @ 16d and 8d per score pointing	2	18	0
12th	Hughes 6 days making fence against River 4s	1	4	0
19	Do. 6 days repairing fence of Quilters broke down by flood	1	4	0
	Parsons & Ross 4½ days each at Infirmary quick and Gravel hole 3s	1	7	0
26th	Cooper & Needham 4 days each @ Gravel hole 3s	1	4	0
	Parsons & Ross at Roads 6 days each 3s	1	16	0
	Hughes 6 days @ 3s 6d . . .	1	1	0
3 October	Do. 3 do. 3s 6d . . .		10	6
	Cooper & Needham 6 days each @ Gravel hole 3s	1	16	0
	Parsons & Ross 6 do. do. & Roads 3s	1	16	0
	Murphy & Richardson 2 days each in the Meadow 3s 3d		13	0
17th	Paid Cooper for carriage of bricks . .		2	6
	Murphy & Richardson 1 day each 3s 3d		6	6

[17 Oct.]	Hughes 4½ days Jobbing 3s 6d . .		15	9
	Cooper & Needham 4 days each @ Roads 3s	}	1 4	0
	Hughes falling & Cleaving wood 6 days 3s 6d	}	1 1	0
	Murphy & Richardson Cuting 11 Acre new diking and wheeling at 7s 6d 4 2 6 18½ Old ditch 4s 6d . . 4 3 3	}	8 5	9
	⟨Drains in the Beadhouse Meadow⟩			
	4 days each @ 3s		1 4	0
	Cooper & Needham 4 days each 3s .		1 4	0
31st	Hughes 6 days setting new fences in Beadhouse Meadow 3s 6d	}	1 1	0
7 November	Do. 6 days fencing in the Meadow 3s 6d	}	1 1	0
14th	Hughes 4 do. and ½ at the Fence 3s 6d .		15	9
	Murphy & Richardson 3 days each in field 3s	}	18	0
	Needham & Cooper 2 days each 2s 6d .		10	0
21st	Hughes 6 days at fence side of Welford Road 3s 6d	}	1 1	0
	Murphy & Richardson 4 days each removing Road & Stocking up hedge 3s	}	1 4	0
	Cooper & Needham 2 days each do. 2s 6d	}	10	0
28th	Hughes 6 days at fences & Altering stiles Knighton Road 3s 6d	}	1 1	0
	Murphy & Richardson 4 days each helping hughes @ the fence Roadside 3s	}	1 4	0
5th December	Hughes fencing side of the Road 3s 6d .		1 1	0
	Murphy & Richardson 4 days each backing dyks in the Meadow 3s	}	18	0
12th	Murphy & Richardson 1 day each in Meadow 3s	}	6	0
19th	Hughes 10 days fencing side of the Road 3s 6d	}	1 15	0
	Murphy & Richardson 4 days each Scouring Main ditch 3s	}	1 4	0

DD

24th [Dec.]	Murphy & Richardson 3 days each main dytch 3s		18	0
	2 days Parsons Ross & Morrel filling carts at the Walk 2s 6d		15	0
1808				
2 January	Hughes 7 days fencing 3s 6d . .	1	4	6
	do. pointing 22 Score of Oak Rails @ 9d per Score		16	6
	Parsons Ross & Morrel 5½ days each at Roads 2s 6d	2	1	3
	Murphy & Richardson 3 days each Main dytchs 3s		18	0
9th	Hughes 6 days at Road fence 3s 6d .	1	1	0
	Parsons Ross & Morrel 4½ days each removing soil 2s 6d	1	13	9
16th	Parsons Ross & Morrel 6 days each filling up pitt Road side & Walk 2s 6d	2	5	0
	Ross & Co. for removing Walk side of Welford Road—by great	8	0	0
23rd	Hughes 2 weeks at Road fence 3s 6d .	2	2	0
	Parsons & Ross 6 days each at Road 2s 6d	1	10	0
	Morrel at Road 5 days 2s 6d . .		12	6
30th	Hughes 6 days @ Road fence 3s 6d .	1	1	0
	Parsons Ross & Morrell 6 days each at foot Road 2s 6d	2	15	0
6 February	Paid Brewin weeding Spiney Forrest .	1	8	6
	Hughes 5 days fence Road side 3s 6d .		17	6
	Parsons Ross & Morrel 5 days each Road side 2s 6d	1	17	6
19th	Parsons Needham & Cooper 4 days each grubing hedge 2s 6d	1	10	0
26th	Hughes 7 days 3s 6d Road side .	1	4	6
27th	Murphy & Richardson embanking the River in on the freemens Meadow for the benefit of the Corporation Meadows	1	14	0
	Murphy & Richardson scouring 4 Acre & 8 yards Old dytch 5s 6d	1	3	8
	Paid Bilson 4 poles		2	8

Date	Description	£	s	d
26 March	Parsons Cooper & Needham 1 day each 2s 6d		7	6
	Murphy & Richardson Cuting drain forward in the Beadhouse Meadows 27 Acre @ 2s	2	14	0
	Lovett picking pebbles . . .		8	6
2 April	Parsons Cooper & Needham 3 days each 2s 6d	1	2	6
9th	Murphy & Richardson 3 days each 3s .		18	0
16th	Cooper Needham & Parsons 2½ days each 2s 6d		18	9
	Paid Murphy & Co. for diging the Willow beds 248 Acre @ 1s	12	8	0
	Do. Scouring large dytch 3 Acres 18 yards @ 4s		15	0
	Do. Leveling bank		8	0
23rd	Cooper Needham & Parsons 3 days each 2s 6d	1	2	6
30th	Murphy & Richardson 3 days each setting willows 3s		18	0
7 May	Parsons Needham & Cooper 5 days each setting willows 2s 6d to drink 3s	2	0	6
	Murphy & Richardson 2 days each setting willows 3s		12	0
14th	Do. do. 6 do. 3s . . .	1	16	0
	Cooper Needham & Parsons 6 days each do. 2s 9d	2	9	6
21	Cooper Needham & Parsons 2 days each @ Roads 3s		18	0
	Murphy & Richardson 2 days each scouring Main ditch 3s		12	0
28th	Needham Parsons & Cooper 1 day each hoeing willows 3s		9	0
4 June	Ross 5 days 3s Murphy & Richardson 4 days Hoeing willows 3s	1	19	0
11th	Ross 5 days 3s do. do. 3½ days each do. 3s	1	16	0
	Needham, Cooper & Parsons 3 days each @ Roads 3s	1	7	0

18th [April]	John Harrison 13½ days seting & hoeing willows 3s	2	0	6
	do. 4 days weeding quick round Ash spiny 3s		12	0
	Ross Murphy & Richardson 2 days each willow beds 3s		18	0
	Hughes 6 days fencing 4s . . .	1	4	0
	Cooper Parsons & Needham 5 days each hoeing willows 3s	2	5	0
25th	Paid W. Wigston for weeding the Ash spiney Leicester forest	1	5	0
	Hughes 6 days fencing the willow beds 4s	1	4	0
	Cooper Parsons & Needham 5 days each setting Cabbage plants 3s	2	5	0
2 July	Hughes 6 days fencing willow beds 4s .	1	4	0
	Parsons Cooper & Needham 3 days each setting Cabbage 3s	1	7	0
	Murphy & Richardson 1 do. do. 3s .		6	0
9th	Richard Hughes 3 days @ fence 4s .		12	0
	Parsons Cooper & Needham 5 days each @ Roads 3s	2	5	0
		959	16	7½
	Over Cast in the first Page since the last accounts were examined		10	0
		959	6	7½

Examined John G.

Money Received

1807				
21st January	Of Messrs Mansfield & Co.	150	0	0
10th March	Of do. . . .	100	0	0
23 April	Of do. for Richardson	60	0	0
14th August	Of Mr Ireland then Chamberlin	123	12	7½
	Of Mr Yates do. .	526	4	0

959 16 7½

Over Cast in the first Page since the last accounts were examined   10 0

959 6 7½

Examined John G.

October 18 1808
At a Meeting of the Committee these
accounts were examined & allowed
Samuel Clarke   Mayor
H. Clark
B. Gregory
Thomas Read
John Gregory

SUMMARIES OF ACCOUNTS

EXPLANATION OF THE SUMMARIES AND THE CODE NUMBERS

THE list which follows contains the headings given by the Chamberlains to each section of their accounts. In 1824 there was such a complete alteration of these headings that a fresh list is necessary and this will be found immediately before the Summaries for 1824–35.

Every heading which appears during the period has been assigned a number and, in the summaries which follow, this number appears in the left-hand column. Where the code numbers are not consecutive the missing headings are not used in that year: thus No. 4 in the Receipts, that for the Gosling Closes, does not appear until 1796 when that particular heading was first used by the Chamberlains.

The figures in round brackets in the first column following the code number show how many individual items the Chamberlains received or paid under that heading. The succeeding columns give the amounts collected or spent by the Chamberlains in each year. Continuity from year to year is indicated by an arrow and only when the amount changes is a fresh figure given. Figures are given for all headings in the first year of each summary; where these are italic they indicate that the amount is the same as that for the last year of the previous summary.

The years 1688, 1708, 1729, 1750, 1771, 1792, 1813, and 1835 are in boxes at the top of their columns as a reminder that these years are printed in full in the first portion of the book. In the first portion the code numbers have been placed in bold type against the headings, and are printed in the running head so that reference to any required point can be made easily.

The Chamberlains were elected with the other town officers on 21 September each year, and took office a week later, at Michaelmas. They held office for a whole year and thus the majority of their term falls in the calendar year after their election. However, for clarity, the year at the top of each column is that of the year of election.

A $^+$ indicates that one or more items have been introduced into a heading and a $^-$ that one or more have dropped out to account for a change in the total. A superior figure refers to a note on a change or a comment to be found in the notes following the summaries.

The number of items in some headings fluctuates each year, e.g. Nos. 34, 36, and 37 of the Receipts (Deductions for Taxes, Fines and Miscellaneous Receipts, and Freedoms) or Nos. 4, 6, 7, and 9 of the Payments (Fees and Wages, Accidental Payments, Tradesmen's Bills, and Taxes Allowed). A detailed account of these variations is not possible, but the normal level of items can be gauged from the figures following the code numbers every seventh year.

In some of the headings the items, when added, gave totals including fractions of a penny. As it would have been impossible to include these without confusion, $\frac{1}{4}$d. and $\frac{1}{2}$d. have been neglected and $\frac{3}{4}$d. has been counted as 1d.

Some years end with an attempt made by either the Chamberlains or the Auditors to strike a balance. These often include amounts not in the year's accounts and totals which appear to be adjusted by the auditors. Where these

445

balances occur the year has the note "Summary" printed at the end. After 1824 these are presented more in the form of a balance sheet and are noted as "General Summary".

In the Notes, R.B.L. indicates "Records of the Borough of Leicester Vol. V, Hall Books and Papers 1688–1835".

CODE LISTS FOR 1688–1823

Receipts

1 Rents of Assize and rents-at-will within the Borough.

2 Rents in the Country.
(Amalgamated with heading No. 1 after 1698.)

3 Rents of the Granges with appurtenances and the four yardlands whereof two yardlands called Weightman's land the town purchased in fee-simple and other two called Archers land and half yardland bought by the corporation of Lord Spencer in fee-simple.

4 Gosling Closes.
(First appears in 1796 as a separate heading, previously included in No. 3.)

5 Beadhouse meadows.

6 South Fields.
(First appears in 1777 as a separate heading. From 1796 to 1804 when the South Fields were enclosed it is divided into a. small plots, b. farms. After 1804 it is all one heading.)

7 Saint Mary's Meadow.
(First appears in 1784 as a sub-heading of the South Fields.)

8 Far Meadow.
(First appears in 1784 as a sub-heading of the South Fields.)

9 Halls Grange and Meadows.
(First appears in 1784 as a sub-heading of the South Fields.)

10 Other rents of lands and tenements which the Mayor, Bailiffs and Burgesses hold in fee farm belonging to the Hospital of St John and St Leonard heretofore belonging to the College of the Newarke.
(This main part of the heading is discontinued from 1708 but the sub-headings carry on.)
  a. In the Northgates.
  b. In Senvy Gate.
  c. In Soar Lane or Walker Lane. (First appears in 1696.)
  d. Within the Northgates.
  e. In the Southgates.
  f. In Burgess Meadow.
  g. In the Swines Market. (Later renamed High Street.)
  h. In Parchment Lane. (Discontinued after 1696.)
  i. In the Saturday Market.
  j. In Loseby Lane.
  k. In Gallowtree Gate.
  l. In Gallowtree Gate on the west side.
  m. In Belgrave Gate.
  n. In the Country.

11 a. Other rents, part of the town obiit lands and St Margarets Guild, part of the fee farm rents heretofore demised by Queen Elizabeth to Mr Hawke and Mr Bates.
(This major heading is also sub-headed "In the South Gates" from 1708–29.)
   b. In the Swines Market. (Later renamed High Street.)
   c. In or near Belgrave Gate.
   d. In Senvey Gate. (Discontinued after 1708.)
   e. In Cank Street. (Discontinued after 1801.)
   f. In St Nicholas's and St Mary's Parishes.

12 Other rents etc., parcel of the town and manor of Leicester lately, with others, given to the Mayor, Bailiffs and Burgesses in fee farm for ever.

13 Other rents, part of the Corpus Christi Guild, heretofore in Mr Archer's collection, now part of the lands and tenements which the Mayor, Bailiffs and Burgesses purchased from Queen Elizabeth.

14 a. Other rents, parcel of the Guild called St Margarets Guild and parcel of the town obiit lands heretofore collected by Mr Arthur Tatam.
   b. In the South Gates.
   c. In Gallowtree Gate. (After 1796 this heading is amalgamated with No. 14b.)
   d. In Humberstone Gate. (After 1733 this heading is changed to "In the Swines Market".)
   e. In Belgrave Gate.
   f. In Senvey Gate.
   g. Near St Margarets Church.
   h. Other rents of Mr Wilde's lease.
   i. Other rents parcel of Mr Wilde's second lease.

15 a. Rental of all the lands of the late College of the Blessed Virgin Mary against the Castle demised by Queen Elizabeth to Edward Holt Esq. expired 1606 and regranted to the Mayor, Bailiffs and Burgesses.
   b. Rents payable at the Annunciation belonging to the Newarke. (Amalgamated with No. 15a after 1728.)

16 Receipts for tithes on estates in St Mary's parish payable in kind.
(First appears in 1797 as a section in the middle of No. 15a.)

17 Other rents of the town and manor of Leicester part of the Duchy of Lancaster's possessions in the County of Leicester.

18 The Shambles and Drapery.
(Amalgamated with No. 17 from 1692 until 1703, then with No. 36 until 1706, after which it is moved to No. 10a.)

19 Other new rents received.

20 Rental of the lands purchased by the corporation and other new rents.
(Until 1795 this includes Freake's Grounds as two items, after which they are given a separate heading No. 24.)

21 Rents given to the school and other charitable uses.
(First appears in 1696.)

22 Rents for shops and stalls in the Saturday Market.
(This includes the Glovers', Chandlers', and Mercers' shops, and Shoe-makers' stalls. From 1715–49 they occur under two headings: "Shops in the Saturday Market" and "Stalls and standings in the Saturday Market". In 1749, after the rebuilding of the shambles and stalls, these were leased as one item and occur under No. 10a.)

23 Rent for ground lately built upon taken from the sheep pens.
(First appears in 1749, probably as a result of the rebuilding of the shambles.)

24 Rent for certain grounds near Leicester called Freakes Grounds which were lately two closes but are now divided into smaller plots.
a. In the first close.
b. In the Hill close.
(This first appears in 1796, see No. 20 above, and the two headings are amal-gamated after 1808.)

25 Tack of beasts.
(This heading appears for only a few years, as it is amalgamated with various other headings after 1692 and is discontinued altogether after 1695.)

26 Chapman Guild.
(After 1693 this is amalgamated with No. 27 to form heading No. 36 "Fines and accidental receipts".)

27 The several trades.
(After 1693 this is amalgamated with No. 26 as part of No. 36 "Fines and accidental receipts".)

28 Rent of the Nag's Head Inn and other houses in High Cross Street recently purchased by the corporation.
(This section first appears without a heading in 1809 and continues with additions as other property was bought.)

29 Chief rents belonging to the Hospital of St John the Baptist and St Leonard payable at Michaelmas for the use of the Mayor, Bailiffs and Burgesses.

30 Chief rents belonging to the Corpus Christi Guild.

31 Chief rents belonging to St Margaret's Guild.

32 Chief rents of cocks, capons and hens belonging to the late College of St Mary de Castro payable at Michaelmas.
(Amalgamated with No. 31 after 1695.)

33 Rental of Lammas tithes and herbages due for the land in St Mary's part of the possessions of the College of St Mary de Castro.

34 Deductions for Taxes.
(First appears in 1697. From 1714–28 it follows No. 36 instead of preceding it. Discontinued after 1733.)

35 Rents of the gardens adjoining the New Walk. (Part of the South Fields.)
(First appears in 1817, but items for rents of New Walk gardens are included in No. 36 in 1815 and 1816.)

36 Fines and accidental receipts.
(First appears in 1693. See Nos. 26, 27, and 35 above.)

37 Receipts for Freedoms.
(First appears as a separate heading in 1801. Before 1693 the items in this

section appear in No. 26, but from 1693–1800 they are in No. 36. From 1801–13 the separate heading follows No. 36, thereafter it precedes it.)

Payments

1 Chief rents and other rents paid.
(Discontinued after 1806 when all the chief rents were redeemed.)
2 Paid at the audit held at the Angel in Leicester.
(Discontinued after 1695.)
3 Paid at the audit held at the Horse and Trumpet in Leicester.
(First appears in 1696; from 1772 this heading reads "Formerly held at the Horse and Trumpet". Discontinued after 1806, when these items were redeemed.)
4 Fees and wages.
(This is called "Fees wages and other payments" or "Fines and other payments" after 1708.)
5 Repairs.
6 Accidental payments.
(First appears in 1714 when it replaces No. 5 and also includes some items formerly in No. 4. Amalgamated with No. 4 in 1750.)
7 Tradesmen's Bills.
(First appears in 1732 when it follows No. 6; after 1750, when No. 6 has replaced No. 5 and been absorbed into No. 4, it follows No. 4.)
8 Church, Poor and Highway levies.
(First appears in 1777. It lapses from 1781–5, when it is resumed following No. 9.)
9 Taxes allowed.
(From 1693–9 this is divided into two sections, general and fee farm. After 1772 it appears as "Allowance for the land tax". The amount in the pound varies and the receipts vary with it.)
10 Town Clerk's and Chamberlains' expenses at the audit.
(Discontinued after 1693.)
11 Pious and charitable uses.
(First appears in 1729. Before this these payments form part of a separate group of Pious and Charitable Uses which follows the payments, *q.v.*)

Pious and Charitable Uses

1 Receipts.
(After 1729 this heading is discontinued. It then appears as part of No. 21 in Receipts above.)
2 Payments.
(After 1729 this is included in No. 11 of the Payments above.)

Supers

Arrears
(This group first appears in 1792.)

SUMMARY OF ACCOUNTS 1688–94

RECEIPTS

Code No.	1688	1689	1690	1691	1692	1693	1694
1 (15)	28 16 3						
2 (3)	0 4 4						
3 (9)	164 0 0	167 4 3⁺	169 12 7	175 12 7			
5 (2)	18 0 0				23 15 0⁺	22 10 0	
10a (3)	20 17 4						
b (7)	0 15 8						
d (8)	3 18 4						
e (2)	1 16 0						
f (2)	1 9 4						
g (1)	0 18 0						
h (1)	0 13 4				0 19 4⁺	0 6 0¹	
i (2)	1 4 0						
j (8)	4 14 0				4 8 0⁻		
k (3)	2 3 0						
l (3)	1 14 0					1 10 0²	
m (6)	4 6 4					4 10 4⁺	
n (13)	9 4 4						
11a (6)	5 0 0						
b (1)	1 0 4						
c (8)	7 1 8			6 7 8			
d (3)	1 17 0			2 0 0			
e (1)	0 13 4						
f (2)	1 13 0						
12 (13)	5 15 6						
13 (23)	13 3 0		13 2 0	13 3 0		12 8 7	13 3 0
14a (8)	3 18 0		3 5 0	3 18 0			
b (5)	3 5 0						
c (3)	3 11 8						
d (1)	0 2 0						
e (15)	9 10 2		9 0 2⁻				
f (6)	3 1 0						
g (1)	0 0 6						
h (1)	0 13 4						
i (12)	4 16 4						
15a (38)	32 13 10						
b (8)	4 2 5						
17 (2)	2 10 0				17 10 0³		
18 (1)	15 0 0				17 10 0³		
19 (3)	0 6 8						

RECEIPTS (continued)

Code No.		1688	1689	1690	1691	1692	1693	1694
20	(7)	47 15 0	37 15 0[6]	———	——→	39 15 0+	51 15 0+	40 11 8
22	(47)	13 18 8	13 16 8	14 11 8+	14 9 7	———	———	——→
25	(1)	0 9 2	0 16 4	———	——→	0 17 6[4]	0 8 0[8]	Discontinued
26	(11)	17 15 0	27 0 0+	112 5 0+	18 15 0[5]	40 3 0	[7] amalgamated to form	No. 36 henceforth
27	(2)	1 16 6	2 15 0+	1 12 6	0 16 3	0 15 6		
29	(7)	0 16 9	———	———	———	———	———	——→
30	(36)	4 14 4	———	———	———	———	———	——→
31	(16)	1 3 5	——→	1 3 3	———	———	———	——→
32	(31)	3 2 3	———	———	———	———	———	——→
33	(41)	5 4 8	5 5 8	5 6 6	5 5 8	——→	7 11 1[8]	7 4 8
36	(10)	Starts 1693					60 15 0	157 19 8+
TOTAL		481 4 9	484 18 8	571 1 2	488 11 2	510 3 11	542 10 1	628 19 5

PAYMENTS

Code No.		1688	1689	1690	1691	1692	1693	1694
1	(28)	127 11 4	127 10 0	125 8 10	127 16 4	128 10 4	128 0 4	147 6 8[13]
2	(7)	17 9 10	——→	17 8 4	17 6 4	17 7 4	19 9 4	
4	(184)	318 1 6	416 18 1	250 18 11	425 16 4[9]	299 3 8	244 6 9	477 15 11
5	(53)	38 16 9	33 11 1	31 11 7	75 14 7	62 0 2	32 14 9	45 17 0
9	(47)	18 7 3	57 0 6	66 13 11	72 1 9[10]	85 14 8	a. 81 17 0[11]	67 14 7
							b. 14 16 0	14 3 0
10	(6)	11 11 8	——→	13 6 3+	11 11 8	12 4 0	11 11 8[12]	Not in
TOTAL		531 18 4	664 1 2	505 7 10	730 7 0	605 0 2	532 15 10	752 17 2

PIOUS AND CHARITABLE USES

Code No.		1688	1689	1690	1691	1692	1693	1694
1	(23)	171 4 2	170 10 4	148 8 4−	166 14 2+	155 14 2−	144 0 10−	155 10 10+
2	(29)	192 2 8	192 2 4	Defective	183 2 8	——→	179 2 8	183 2 8

SUPERS

		1688	1689	1690	1691	1692	1693	1694
	(19)	Not in	20 2 0	Not in	3 5 11−	4 3 3	4 19 0	2 11 7

RECEIPTS

Code No.	1695	1696	1697	1698	1699	1700	1701
1 (15)	28 16 3	——————→}		29 0 7[1]	26 0 7[2]	——	
2 (3)	0 4 4	——————→}					
3 (9)	175 12 7	177 12 7+	———————			→}170 15 5[3]	177 12 7
5 (3)	24 10 0	27 10 0	——→	28 10 6[4]	29 10 0	——	
10a (3)	20 17 4	——					
b (7)	0 15 8	0 13 8⁻	——				
c (2)	Starts 1696	0 8 0[5]	——				
d (8)	3 18 4	3 12 4⁻	——				
e (2)	1 16 0	——					
f (2)	1 9 4	——					
g (1)	0 18 0	——→	1 4 0[6]	——			
h (1)	0 6 0	Discontinued[7]					
i (2)	1 4 0	——					
j (7)	4 8 0	4 14 0+	——→	4 8 0⁻	——		
k (3)	2 3 0	——					
l (2)	1 10 0	0 14 0	——→	1 14 0	——		
m (7)	4 10 4	4 18 4	——→	4 6 4	——		
n (13)	9 4 4	——					
11a (6)	5 0 0	7 0 0[8]	——				
b (1)	1 0 4	——					
c (8)	6 7 8	——					
d (3)	2 0 0	——					
e (1)	0 13 4	——					
f (2)	1 13 0	3 3 0[9]	——				
12 (13)	5 15 6	4 5 6⁻	——				
13 (23)	13 3 0	13 13 0[10]	——→	13 18 0[11]	——		
14a (8)	3 18 0	——					
b (5)	3 5 0	——					
c (3)	3 11 8	——					
d (1)	0 2 0	——					
e (14)	9 0 2	——					
f (6)	3 1 0	——					
g (1)	0 0 6	——					
h (1)	0 13 4	——					
i (12)	4 16 4	——					
15a (38)	32 13 10	——					
b (8)	4 2 5	——					
17 (2)}	17 10 0	{ 2 10 0	——————→}			17 10 0	——
18 (1)}		{15 0 0	——————→}				

RECEIPTS (*continued*)

Code No.		1695	1696	1697	1698	1699	1700	1701
9	(3)	*0 6 8*	1 3 4[+]	⟶⟩	0 16 8[−]	⟶		⟶⟩
0	(7)	*40 11 8*	55 3 0[+]	⟶⟩	55 9 8[+]	⟶		⟶⟩
1	(12)	Starts 1696	140 5 0[12]	⟶		⟶⟩	140 15 0[13]	⟶⟩
2	(47)	14 9 8	13 19 8[−]	⟶⟩	13 6 8[−]	⟶		⟶⟩
9	(7)	*0 16 9*	⟶					⟶⟩
0	(36)	*4 14 4*	⟶		[15]⟶⟩	4 10 4	⟶	⟶⟩
1	(16)	*1 3 3*	} 4 5 6	⟶				⟶⟩
2	(31)	*3 2 3[16]*						
3	(41)	8 5 8	5 3 6[−]	⟶		⟶⟩	4 15 6[17]	5 3 6
4	(5)	Starts 1697		8 2 9[18]	Not in	9 6 3[+]	7 1 2[−]	8 18 2
6	(15)	110 12 0[14]	19 8 0	51 18 0	50 14 7	55 9 1	76 1 11	214 13 8[+]
TOTAL		584 12 10	652 11 8	693 4 5	684 18 9	696 15 0	708 7 7	856 1 6

PAYMENTS

Code No.		1695	1696	1697	1698	1699	1700	1701
1	(28)	128 0 4	⟶					⟶⟩
3	(7)	19 9 4[10]	⟶⟩	19 10 10	⟶⟩	12 2 4[20]	17 12 5[+]	19 11 2
4	(157)	358 14 11[21]	267 12 7	404 0 3	348 10 8	230 15 0	281 14 9	438 18 5
5	(20)	10 4 8	31 10 11	32 7 7	62 4 7	8 10 11	70 16 10	39 8 6
9a	(27)	64 13 1	69 15 11	59 5 0	55 9 3	21 11 9[22]	} 53 19 6[23]	75 5 2
b	(47)	10 10 1	13 17 5	12 0 9	11 14 2	11 11 5	Amalgamated	
TOTAL		591 12 5	530 6 6	655 4 9	625 9 10	412 11 9	552 3 10	701 3 7

PIOUS AND CHARITABLE USES

Code No.		1695	1696	1697	1698	1699	1700	1701
1	(23)	152 0 10	158 0 10	⟶				⟶⟩
2	(29)	*183 2 8*	185 2 8	⟶	⟶⟩	180 0 2[−]	⟶	⟶⟩

SUPERS

		1695	1696	1697	1698	1699	1700	1701
	(10)	Defective	12 18 7	Defective	11 18 9	11 3 3	Not in	11 9 7

EE

RECEIPTS

Code No.	1702	1703	1704	1705	1706	1707	1708
1 (18)	26 0 6	27 0 7[1]	Accounts	30 10 7	21 5 7	———	
3 (11)	*177 12 7*	178 12 7[2]	missing	193 12 7[3]	———	⎬ 189 12 6[4]	———
5 (2)	*29 10 0*	———	,,				
10a (3)	*20 17 4*	———⎬	,,	26 17 4[5]	96 17 4[6]	———	
b (6)	*0 13 8*	———	,,				
c (2)	*0 8 0*	———	,,				
d (6)	*3 12 4*	———	,,				
e (2)	*1 16 0*	———	,,				
f (2)	*1 9 4*	———	,,				
g (1)	*1 4 0*	———	,,				
i (2)	*1 4 0*	———	,,				
j (7)	*4 8 0*	———	,,				
k (3)	*2 3 0*	———	,,				
l (3)	*1 14 0*	———	,,				
m (6)	*4 6 4*	———	,,				
n (13)	*9 4 4*	———	,,				
11a (6)	*7 0 0*	———	,,				
b (1)	*1 0 4*	———	,,				
c (8)	*6 7 8*	———	,,			⎬	8 12 8
d (3)	*2 0 0*	———	,,			⎬ Discontinu
e (1)	*0 13 4*	———	,,				
f (3)	*3 3 0*	———	,,				
12 (12)	*4 5 6*	———⎬	,,	5 5 6[7]	———		
13 (24)	*13 18 0*	———	,,				
14a (8)	*3 18 0*	———	,,				
b (5)	*3 5 0*	———	,,				
c (3)	*3 11 8*	———	,,				
d (1)	*0 2 0*	———	,,				
e (15)	*9 0 2*	———⎬	,,	8 13 6[8]	———		
f (6)	*3 1 0*	———	,,				
g (1)	*0 0 6*	———	,,				
h (1)	*0 13 4*	———	,,				
i (12)	*4 16 4*	———	,,				
15a (38)	*32 13 10*	———	,,		———	⎬	33 13 10
b (8)	*4 2 5*		,,	———	⎬	3 9 1[9]	———
17 (3)	*17 10 0*	2 10 0[10]	,,				
19 (4)	*0 16 8*	———	,,				
20 (7)	43 13 4[11]	43 16 8	,,	———		⎬	48 16 8
21 (12)	*140 15 0*	———	,,				

RECEIPTS (*continued*)

YEAR

Code No.	1702	1703	1704	1705	1706	1707	1708
2 (47)	14 6 8$^-$	13 12 8$^-$	Accounts	—————⟩ 15 2 8$^+$		————⟩	15 11 0
9 (7)	0 16 9	—————	missing	——————————————————————⟩			
0 (35)	4 10 4	———	,,	——————————————————————⟩			
1 (47)	4 5 6	———	,,	——————————————————————⟩			
3 (41)	5 3 6	———	,,	————————————⟩ 4 16 10[14]		————⟩	
4 (6)	12 4 0	————⟩	,,	12 12 0	9 8 0	6 18 0$^-$	8 0 6$^+$
6 (14)	449 2 1[12]	124 11 6	,,	206 3 6	152 14 1	413 10 10[13]	48 5 0
TOTAL	1082 19 4	744 18 2		852 1 6	857 13 1	1110 19 9	753 9 9

PAYMENTS

Code No.	1702	1703	1704	1705	1706	1707	1708
1 (28)	128 0 4	127 16 2$^-$	Accounts	128 1 2	128 0 4	————⟩ 127 16 2	
3 (6)	19 11 2	19 11 10	missing	27 2 10$^+$	19 11 10$^-$	——————————⟩	
4 (128)	145 14 10[15] / 626 2 5	147 14 8 / 202 19 1	,,	334 17 5	259 15 8	709 5 4	292 1 3
5 (46)	60 11 11	127 10 9	,,	35 2 3	38 13 10	37 18 6	149 12 9
9 (74)	82 13 10	74 9 11	,,	99 2 9	94 9 4	87 13 2	93 12 2
TOTAL	1062 14 6	700 2 5		624 6 5	540 11 0	982 9 2	682 14 2

PIOUS AND CHARITABLE USES

Code No.	1702	1703	1704	1705	1706	1707	1708
1 (20)	158 0 10	————⟩ Accounts		————————————⟩ 160 0 10			
2 (28)	Not in	193 0 2	missing	179 10 2	————⟩ 188 10 2	————⟩	

SUPERS

Code No.	1702	1703	1704	1705	1706	1707	1708
(13)	Not in	22 19 7	Accounts missing	12 17 3	17 1 6	24 6 6	12 15 3

| | | | | Summary | Summary | Summary[16] | |

RECEIPTS

Code No.		1709	1710	1711	1712	1713	1714	1715
1	(18)	3 15 10	23 5 7[1]	———————————}		3 15 10[2]	23 5 7	24 3 1[3]
3	(11)	307 0 0	308 12 0	307 0 0	——————			———}
5	(3)	28 17 6	————————————————————————————					——}
10a	(4)	96 17 4	————————————————————————————					——}
b	(6)	0 13 8	————————————————————————————					
c	(2)	0 8 0	————————————————————————————					
d	(6)	3 12 4	————————————————————————————					
e	(2)	1 16 0	————————————————————————————				4	
f	(2)	1 9 4	————————————————————————————					
g	(2)	1 4 0	————————————————————————————					
i	(2)	1 4 0	————————————————————————————					
j	(7)	4 8 0	————————————————————————————					
k	(3)	2 3 0	————————————————————————————					
l	(3)	1 14 0	————————————————————————————					
m	(6)	4 6 4	————————————————————————————					
n	(13)	9 4 4	————————————————————————————					
11a	(6)	7 0 0	————————————————————————————					
b	(1)	1 0 4	————————————————————————————					
c	(11)	8 12 8	————————————————————————————					
e	(1)	0 13 4	————————————————————————————					
f	(3)	3 3 0	————————————————————————————					
12	(12)	5 5 6	————————————————————————————					
13	(24)	13 18 0	————————————————————————————					
14a	(8)	3 18 0	————————————————————————————					
b	(5)	3 5 0	————————————————————————————					
c	(3)	3 11 8	————————————————————————————					
d	(1)	0 2 0	————————————————————————————					
e	(13)	8 13 6	————————————————————————————					
f	(6)	3 1 0	————————————————————————————					
g	(1)	0 0 6	————————————————————————————					
h	(1)	0 13 4	————————————————————————————					
i	(12)	4 16 4	————————————————————————————					
15a	(40)	48 10 4+	33 13 10⁻	53 6 6	48 10 4+	48 9 8	48 10 4	————
b	(8)	3 9 1	————————————————————————————					
17	(2)	2 10 0	————————————————————————————					
19	(4)	0 16 8	—————————————————————			———}	1 16 8[5]	0 6 8[6]
20	(7)	88 16 8	73 16 8[7]	88 16 8	————————	———}	59 6 8[8]	————
21	(17)	140 15 0	————————————————————————————————				———}	144 15 0[9]
22	(45)	15 11 0	————————————————————————————			———}	16 8 0	44 11 10[1]

RECEIPTS (*continued*)

de ᵖ.	1709	1710	1711	1712	1713	1714	1715
(7)	*0 16 9*	——————————————————————————————————⟩					
(35)	*4 10 4*	——————————————————————————————————⟩					
(47)	*4 5 6*	——————————————————————————————————⟩					
(38)	*4 16 10*	——————————————————————————————————⟩					
(5)	4 4 0	21 18 8⁺	8 8 0⁻	6 6 0	4 4 0	————————⟩	6 6 0
(13)	226 16 6	141 2 6	318 0 3	335 0 4	226 16 6	304 8 5	210 6 3
TAL	1082 6 6	1005 12 5	1202 0 2	1212 2 1	1082 5 10	1151 15 2	1091 6 4

PAYMENTS

	1709	1710	1711	1712	1713	1714	1715
(27)	*127 16 2*	——————————————————————————————————⟩					
(6)	*19 11 10*	——————————————————————————————————⟩					
(148)	436 13 1	325 0 7	293 18 7	519 19 10	436 3 1	170 3 10	170 5 10
(44)	3 3 4	172 7 9	90 19 2	5 0 5	3 3 4	Henceforth in No. 6	
(141)	Starts 1714					584 5 11[11]	542 10 6
(83)	27 11 4	52 19 7	————————————————————⟩			26 16 9	36 5 5
							40 13 9[12]
TAL	614 15 9	697 15 11	585 5 4	725 7 10	639 14 0	928 14 6	937 3 6

PIOUS AND CHARITABLE USES

	1709	1710	1711	1712	1713	1714	1715
(20)	158 0 10	153 4 10	158 0 10	——————————————————————⟩			
(27)	*188 10 2*	——————————————————————————————————⟩					

SUPERS

	1709	1710	1711	1712	1713	1714	1715
(17)	36 17 0	14 2 10	18 3 10	Not in	36 17 0	13 2 10	18 18 9

| Summary | | Summary | | Summary | | |

RECEIPTS

Code No.	1716	1717	1718	1719	1720	1721	1722
1 (18)	27 5 7[1]				[2]	Accounts	—
3 (10)	306 0 0[3]					missing	—
5 (3)	28 17 6					,,	
10a (4)	96 17 4				}101 17 4[4]	,,	
b (6)	0 13 8				}	,,	1 17 0
c (3)	0 8 0				}	,,	2 17 0
d (6)	3 12 4					,,	—
e (3)	2 9 4					,,	
f (2)	1 9 4					,,	
g (2)	1 4 0					,,	
i (2)	1 4 0					,,	
j (7)	4 8 0				}	,,	12 18 0
k (3)	2 3 0					,,	—
l (3)	1 14 0					,,	
m (6)	4 6 4					,,	
n (13)	9 4 4					,,	
11a (6)	7 0 0	6 10 0[8]				,,	
b (1)	1 0 4					,,	
c (11)	8 12 8	7 18 8[9]			} 11 13 8[10]	,,	
e (1)	0 13 4					,,	
f (3)	3 3 0					,,	
12 (12)	5 5 6					,,	
13 (24)	13 18 0					,,	
14a (8)	3 18 0					,,	
b (5)	3 5 0	4 15 0[11]				,,	
c (3)	3 11 8					,,	
d (1)	0 2 0					,,	
e (13)	8 13 6					,,	
f (6)	3 1 0				}	,,	8 17 8
g (1)	0 0 6					,,	
h (1)	0 13 4					,,	
i (12)	4 16 4					,,	
15a (40)	48 10 4				}	,,	50 0 4
b (8)	3 9 1					,,	
17 (2)	2 10 0				}	,,	7 15 0
19 (3)	0 6 8					,,	
20 (7)	59 6 8					,,	
21 (17)	146 9 2[15]	152 3 4[16]	153 3 4[17]		}155 0 0[18]	,,	153 0 0
22 (61)	53 11 10	53 12 10	55 2 10+			,,	

RECEIPTS (*continued*)

YEAR

de	1716	1717	1718	1719	1720	1721	1722
(7)	0 16 9	———————————————— Accounts					————⟩
(35)	4 10 4	———————————————— missing					————⟩
(47)	4 5 6	———————————————————⟩				,,	4 5 10
(38)	4 16 10	————————⟩ 4 18 10[20] ————⟩				,,	4 19 4[21]
(5)	7 16 6	6 6 0	6 16 6	6 6 0	————⟩	,,	4 4 0
(25)	70 5 8	309 1 4	478 6 1	889 15 6[22]	792 13 10[23]	,,	827 6 9
TAL	966 6 3	1209 12 7	1381 17 10	1792 18 9	1706 8 9		1761 14 6

PAYMENTS

	1716	1717	1718	1719	1720	1721	1722
(27)	127 16 2	———————————————— Accounts					————⟩
(6)	19 11 10	———————————————— missing					————⟩
(28)	171 18 6[24]	177 10 8	————⟩ 207 12 8		206 11 8	,,	————⟩
(112)	307 14 10	274 6 11	227 13 0	669 7 4[25]	221 17 11[26]	,,	432 9 4
(80)	43 11 3	37 10 3	40 13 3	40 3 9	41 1 6[27]	,,	27 10 5
		4 16 4[28]					
AL	670 12 7	641 12 2	593 4 11	1064 11 9	616 19 1		813 19 5

PIOUS AND CHARITABLE USES

	1716	1717	1718	1719	1720	1721	1722
(20)	158 0 10	162 0 6[29]	158 0 10	163 0 10[30]	————⟩ Accounts		163 9 10
(27)	188 9 8[31]	192 10 2[32]	197 19 8[33]	194 9 8	Defective	missing	196 6 4

SUPERS

	1716	1717	1718	1719	1720	1721	1722
(29)	20 17 6	15 8 9	13 18 10	7 13 5	Defective	Accounts missing	9 11 10

Summary		Summary	Summary	Summary	Summary

RECEIPTS

Code No.		1723	1724	1725	1726	1727	1728	1729
1	(18)	27 5 7				[1]——⟩	29 5 7[2]	
3	(10)	306 0 0						
5	(3)	28 17 6			——⟩ 29 17 6[3]			
10a	(5)	107 13 4[4]				⟩122 16 8[5]	123 0 0[6]	121 5 0
b	(6)	1 17 0						
c	(2)	5 12 0						
d	(6)	3 12 4	8 3 4[8]					
e	(2)	2 9 4						
f	(2)	1 9 4						
g	(2)	1 4 0						
i	(2)	1 4 0						
j	(7)	12 18 0						
k	(3)	2 3 0						
l	(3)	1 14 0						
m	(6)	4 6 4						
n	(13)	9 4 4	——⟩ 54 17 6[9]					
11a	(5)	6 10 0						
b	(1)	1 0 4						
c	(11)	11 13 8		—[10]—				⟩ 9 13 8
e	(1)	0 13 4						
f	(3)	3 3 0						
12	(12)	5 5 6						
13	(24)	13 18 0						
14a	(8)	3 18 0				——⟩ 5 18 0[12]		
b	(5)	4 15 0						
c	(3)	3 11 8						
d	(1)	0 2 0						
e	(13)	8 13 6						
f	(6)	8 17 8				——⟩ 8 9 8[13]		
g	(1)	0 0 6						
h	(1)	0 13 4						
i	(12)	4 16 4						
15a	(41)	50 0 4					⟩ 52 16 1[14]	
b	(8)	3 9 1				——⟩ 2 15 9[15]	Amalgamated	
17	(2)	7 15 0						⟩ 5 15
19	(3)	0 6 8						
20	(7)	59 6 8						
21	(18)	162 10 0[16]						
22	(13)	55 2 10[17]	56 12 10	57 2 10 +	58 14 4[18]	43 19 0[19]	45 9 0[20]	46 4

RECEIPTS (*continued*)

Code No.		1723	1724	1725	YEAR 1726	1727	1728	1729
29	(7)	0 16 9	———————————————————————————⟩
30	(35)	4 10 4	———————————————————————————⟩
31	(47)	4 5 10	———————————————————————————⟩
33	(39)	4 17 4[22]	———————————————————————————⟩
34	(9)	4 4 0	——————————⟩		6 6 0	7 7 0	6 9 6	5 7 0
36	(21)	722 15 8	1143 7 4	336 17 2	374 7 2[23]	640 10 8	339 13 6	357 8 7
TOTAL		1675 2 5	2101 15 1	1341 8 1	1383 11 7	1650 2 9	1354 1 5	1365 14 0

PAYMENTS

		1723	1724	1725	1726	1727	1728	1729
1	(7)	127 16 2	124 15 4[24]	——————————————————————————⟩
3	(6)	19 11 0	17 5 4[25]	——————————————————————————⟩
4	(28)	206 11 8	————————⟩	206 13 8[26]	———————————————⟩		207 18 4[27]	207 17 4⁻
6	(104)	351 7 0	955 14 3[28]	674 3 2	446 11 6	769 7 4[29]	403 7 10[30]	341 5 4
9	(74)	27 11 5	21 1 6	27 11 6	41 7 3	52 6 7	37 10 2	36 13 8
11	(30)	Starts 1729						199 2 0
TOTAL		732 17 3	1325 8 1	1050 9 0	836 13 1	1170 8 3	790 17 0	926 19 0

PIOUS AND CHARITABLE USES

		1723	1724	1725	1726	1727		
1	(20)	163 9 10	———————————————————————⟩ Not in				⎫ Discon-	
2	(27)	196 6 4	—————————⟩	196 7 0[32]	196 12 0[33]	199 2 0[34]	————————⟩ ⎬	tinued[31]

SUPERS

	1723	1724	1725	1726	1727	1728	1729
(9)	14 1 11	16 1 11	70 4 11[35]	19 13 9[36]	5 10 3	54 2 2	30 6 11

Summary	Summary	Summary	Summary	Summary	Summary	Summary

RECEIPTS

Code No.	1730	1731	1732	1733	1734	1735	1736
				YEAR			
1 (18)	Accounts	29 5 7	——[1]——⟩		29 5 1	——⟩	29 10 1[2]
3 (10)	missing	306 0 0	—[3]—⟩	310 0 0			⟩
5 (3)	,,	29 17 6					⟩
10a (5)	,,	121 5 0				⟩	123 0 0[4]
b (6)	,,	1 17 0					⟩
c (2)	,,	4 2 0[5]					⟩
d (8)	,,	8 3 4	—⟩	8 2 4[6]	24 2 4	——⟩	27 2 4[7]
e (3)	,,	2 9 4					⟩
f (2)	,,	1 9 4					⟩
g (2)	,,	1 4 0					⟩
i (2)	,,	1 4 0					⟩
j (7)	,,	12 18 0					⟩
k (3)	,,	2 3 0					⟩
l (3)	,,	1 14 0					⟩
m (6)	,,	4 6 4					⟩
n (15)	,,	54 4 4[8]	25 4 4[9]				⟩
11a (5)	,,	6 10 0					⟩
b (1)	,,	1 0 4					⟩
c (11)	,,	9 13 8[10]				⟩	13 3 8[11]
e (1)	,,	0 13 4					⟩
f (3)	,,	3 3 0					⟩
12 (11)	,,	5 5 6					⟩
13 (24)	,,	13 18 0					⟩
14a (9)	,,	5 18 0					⟩
b (5)	,,	4 15 0					⟩
c (3)	,,	3 11 8					⟩
d (1)	,,	0 2 0					⟩
e (13)	,,	8 13 6					⟩
f (5)	,,	6 19 8[12]					⟩
g (1)	,,	0 0 6					⟩
h (1)	,,	0 13 4					⟩
i (12)	,,	4 16 4					⟩
15 (48)	,,	51 16 1[13]				[14]	⟩
17 (4)	,,	5 15 0					⟩
19 (3)	,,	0 6 8					⟩
20 (7)	,,	71 6 8[15]					⟩
21 (18)	,,	161 5 0[16]	—⟩	156 10 0[17]		[18]—⟩	150 10 0[19]
22 (61)	,,	47 19 0[20]	47 9 0[21]	48 11 0[22]	47 14 0[23]	——⟩	49 14 0
29 (7)	,,	0 16 9					⟩

RECEIPTS (*continued*)

Code No.		1730	1731	1732	1733	1734	1735	1736
30	(35)	Accounts	4 10 4	———————————————————— }				
31	(47)	missing	4 5 10	———————————————————— }				
33	(39)	,,	4 17 6	——————[24]——————[25]———— }				
34	(5)	,,	3 8 0	2 5 4	2 4 4	Discontinued		
36	(27)	,,	1184 0 7[26]	729 9 8	549 11 5	689 19 5	662 6 6	596 2 2[27]
Total			2198 4 0	1713 0 5	1533 7 2	1686 13 4	1659 0 5	1597 6 1

PAYMENTS

Code No.		1730	1731	1732	1733	1734	1735	1736
1	(24)	Accounts	124 15 4	——————[28]—————————— }				
3	(4)	missing	17 5 4	———————————————————— }				
4	(30)	,,	197 17 4[29]	——————————— }	198 7 4[30]	248 7 7[31]	———— }	
6	(114)	,,	919 10 0[30]	484 19 3[33]	84 15 7	354 0 4	219 2 9	153 0 8[34]
7	(37)	,,	Starts 1732	302 9 9	273 9 6	192 9 5	263 6 6	116 8 11
9	(71)	,,	24 11 7[35]	15 2 5[36]	23 11 0[37]	33 3 8[38]	33 19 4[39]	33 12 4[40]
11	(30)	,,	197 17 0[41]	199 7 0[42]	——————— }	199 12 6[43]	194 12 6[44]	193 12 6[45]
Total			1481 16 7	1341 16 5	921 1 1	1119 13 11	1101 9 4	887 2 8

SUPERS

		1730	1731	1732	1733	1734	1735	1736
(16)	Accounts missing	37 15 11	24 8 5	22 18 5	15 8 5	27 6 5	50 7 5	

Summary[46] Summary[47] Summary[48] Summary Summary Summary

RECEIPTS

Code No.	1737	1738	1739	1740	1741	1742	1743
1 (18)	24 10 1[1]	—[2]—		Accounts			
3 (10)	309 0 0[3]		⟩	missing	304 0 0[4]		⟩
5 (3)	*29 17 6*			,,		⟩	29 10 0[5]
10a (5)	*123 0 0*			,,		⟩	112 0 0[6]
b (6)	*1 17 0*			,,			⟩
c (2)	*4 2 0*			,,			⟩
d (7)	*27 2 4*		⟩	,,	26 12 4[7]		⟩
e (3)	*2 9 4*			,,			⟩
f (2)	*1 9 4*			,,			⟩
g (2)	*1 4 0*			,,			⟩
i (2)	*1 4 0*			,,			⟩
j (7)	*12 18 0*			,,			⟩
k (3)	*2 3 0*			,,			⟩
l (3)	*1 14 0*			,,			⟩
m (6)	*4 6 4*			,,			⟩
n (14)	*25 4 4*			,,			⟩
11a (5)	*6 10 0*			,,			⟩
b (1)	*1 0 4*			,,			⟩
c (11)	14 3 8			,,			⟩
e (1)	*0 13 4*[8]			,,			⟩
f (3)	*3 3 0*			,,			⟩
12 (12)	*5 5 6*			,,			⟩
13 (24)	*13 18 0*			,,			⟩
14a (9)	*5 18 0*			,,			⟩
b (5)	*4 15 0*			,,			⟩
c (3)	*3 11 8*			,,			⟩
d (1)	*0 2 0*			,,			⟩
e (13)	*8 13 6*			,,			⟩
f (5)	*6 19 8*			,,			⟩
g (1)	*0 0 6*			,,			⟩
h (1)	*0 13 4*			,,			⟩
i (12)	*4 16 4*			,,			⟩
15 (48)	54 12 9[9]	54 11 1		,,			⟩
17 (4)	*5 15 0*			,,			⟩
19 (3)	*0 6 8*			,,			⟩
20 (7)	59 6 8[10]		⟩	,,	58 16 8[11]		⟩
21 (17)	*150 10 0*	149 0 0[12]	147 14 0[13]	,,	154 10 0[14]		⟩
22 (64)	49 14 0[15]		⟩ 41 4 0[16]	,,	47 17 6[17]	46 2 6[18]	52 7 6[19]
29 (7)	*0 16 9*			,,			⟩

RECEIPTS (*continued*)

Code No.		1737	1738	1739	1740	1741	1742	1743
0	(45)	*4 10 4*	———————— Accounts			————————————>		
1	(47)	*4 5 10*	————— [20]—— missing			————————————>		
3	(34)	*4 17 6*	————>		,,	6 13 0[21]	————————>	
6	(16)	684 16 7	318 11 8	289 14 1	,,	428 19 8	572 7 3	763 18 0
TOTAL		1671 19 0	1304 2 5	1265 8 10		1413 19 5	1555 12 0	1742 0 3

PAYMENTS

Code No.		1737	1738	1739	1740	1741	1742	1743
1	(21)	124 5 1	———————— Accounts			————————————>		
3	(4)	*17 5 4*	———————— missing			————————————>		
4	(31)	*248 7 7*	238 7 7[22]	229 7 7[23]	,,	254 7 7[24]	————>	254 8 7[25]
5	(85)	228 8 10[26]	83 16 6	149 14 8	,,	92 6 3	146 0 4	256 8 1
7	(22)	486 17 1	180 2 4	330 17 3[27]	,,	170 7 5[28]	148 0 8	116 0 7
9	(11)	32 13 8[29]	————>	46 14 3	,,	61 7 0[30]	————>	60 0 9[31]
1	(32)	*193 12 6*	————————>		,,	196 8 6[32]	197 4 6[33]	197 9 6[34]
								112 4 1[35]
TOTAL		1331 10 1	870 3 0	1091 16 8		916 7 2	948 10 6	1138 2 0

SUPERS

		1737	1738	1739	1740	1741	1742	1743
	(21)	38 18 1	13 12 1	10 12 9	Accounts missing	12 6 4	12 2 7	12 5 7

		Summary	Summary	Summary		Summary	Summary	Summary

SUMMARY OF ACCOUNTS 1744–50

RECEIPTS

Code No.		1744	1745	1746	1747	1748	1749	1750
1	(17)	24 10 1			→} 19 0 1[1]	Accounts	18 10 1[2]	
3	(10)	304 0 0				missing		
5	(2)	29 10 0				,,		
10a	(4)	112 0 0			→}	,,	167 0 0[3]	147 0 0[4]
b	(6)	1 17 0				,,		
c	(2)	4 2 0				,,		
d	(6)	26 12 4				,,		
e	(3)	2 9 4				,,		
f	(2)	1 9 4				,,		
g	(2)	1 4 0				,,		
i	(2)	1 4 0				,,		
j	(7)	12 18 0				,,		
k	(3)	2 3 0				,,		
l	(3)	1 14 0				,,		
m	(6)	4 6 4				,,		
n	(16)	25 4 4				,,		
11a	(5)	6 10 0				,,		
b	(1)	1 0 4				,,		
c	(11)	14 3 8				,,		
e	(1)	0 13 4				,,		
f	(3)	3 3 0				,,		
12	(12)	4 15 6[5]				,,		
13	(24)	13 18 0			→}	,,	13 19 0[6]	
14a	(9)	5 18 0				,,		
b	(5)	4 15 0				,,		
c	(3)	3 11 8				,,		
d	(1)	0 2 0				,,		
e	(13)	8 13 6				,,		
f	(5)	6 19 8				,,		
g	(1)	0 0 6				,,		
h	(1)	0 13 4				,,		
i	(12)	4 16 4				,,		
15	(47)	52 11 1				,,		
17	(4)	5 15 0				,,		
19	(3)	0 6 8				,,		
20	(6)	58 16 8				,,		
21	(17)	154 10 0		→}157 0 0[7]	159 10 0[8]	,,	→}	159 0 0[9]
22	(78)	52 7 6[10]	54 5 0[11]		→}	,,	2 15 0[12]	
29	(7)	0 16 9				,,		

RECEIPTS (continued)

Code No.	YEAR 1744	1745	1746	1747	1748	1749	1750
0 (35)	4 10 4	———————————————			,,	———————————	}
1 (47)	4 5 10	———————————————			,,	———————————	}
3 (44)	6 13 0	———————————————			,,	———————————	}
6 (39)	734 5 6	749 4 7	726 1 3	798 15 7	,,	565 0 9[13]	474 6 9
TOTAL	1709 15 11	1726 12 6	1705 19 2	1775 14 3		1544 19 8	1433 15 8

PAYMENTS

Code No.	1744	1745	1746	1747	1748	1749	1750
1 (21)	124 5 1	——————————————			Accounts	———————————	}
3 (4)	17 5 4	——————————————			missing	———————————	}
4 (35)	254 7 7[14]	——————————}		254 12 7[15]	,,	254 8 7[16]	} 374 13 5
6 (57)	32 12 1	173 2 0	121 8 6	179 17 8[17]	,,	144 18 10[18]	}
7 (34)	241 19 3	235 10 3	320 19 8	840 0 7	,,	302 13 7	165 11 2
9 (77)	60 9 0	60 13 0	————}	59 19 0[19]	,,	51 12 1[20]	44 3 3
1 (30)	197 9 6	————}	199 19 6[21]	202 9 6[22]	,,	——[23] —}	215 19 6[24]
TOTAL	928 7 10	1062 12 9	1098 18 8	1678 9 9		1097 13 0	941 17 9

SUPERS

	1744	1745	1746	1747	1748	1749	1750
(9)	7 5 7	————}	7 9 4	————}	Accounts missing	2 9 4	2 8 4

Summary Summary Summary Summary   Summary Summary

RECEIPTS

Code No.	1751	1752	1753	1754	1755	1756	1757
1 (17)	18 10 1[1]			[2]			
3 (10)	304 0 0	49 0 0[3]					
5 (2)	29 10 0	291 10 0+					
10a (4)	147 0 0	146 0 0[4]		[5]	148 0 0		
b (6)	1 17 0						
c (2)	4 2 0						
d (6)	26 12 4		10 2 4[6]	17 12 4[7]			
e (3)	2 9 4						
f (2)	1 9 4						
g (2)	1 4 0						
i (2)	1 4 0						
j (7)	12 18 0			13 18 0[8]			
k (3)	2 3 0						
l (3)	1 14 0						
m (6)	4 6 4						
n (14)	25 4 4						
11a (5)	6 10 0						
b (1)	1 0 4						
c (13)	14 3 8						
e (1)	0 13 4						
f (3)	3 3 0						
12 (12)	4 15 6						
13 (25)	13 19 0						
14a (19)	5 18 0						
b (5)	4 15 0						
c (3)	3 11 8						
d (1)	0 2 0						
e (13)	8 13 6						
f (5)	6 19 8	8 8 0[9]					
g (1)	0 0 6						
h (1)	0 13 4						
i (12)	4 16 4						
15 (47)	52 11 1	45 11 1[10]					
17 (4)	5 15 0						
19 (3)	0 6 8						
20 (6)	58 16 8				63 16 8[11]	68 16 8	
21 (17)	159 0 0	158 0 0[12]			154 0 0[13]		146 0 0[1]
23 (4)	2 15 0						
29 (7)	0 16 9						

RECEIPTS (*continued*)

ode No.	1751	1752	1753	1754	1755	1756	1757
) (35)	*4 10 4*						⟩
1 (47)	*4 5 10*						⟩
3 (44)	*6 13 0*	4 13 0[15]					⟩
5 (23)	554 13 11	680 17 2	1003 10 0[16]	882 7 8	363 10 0	462 11 10[17]	646 7 5[18]
TOTAL	1514 2 10	1637 14 5	1943 17 3	1831 4 11	1315 7 3	1419 9 1	1595 4 8

PAYMENTS

	1751	1752	1753	1754	1755	1756	1757
1 (21)	*124 5 1*						⟩
3 (4)	*17 5 4*						⟩
4 (102)	364 14 5[19]	372 6 3[20]	363 1 0	453 5 6	397 5 4	388 1 5	473 15 1
7 (42)	166 9 0	208 17 0	290 1 5[21]	510 14 11[22]	215 17 5	213 0 8	329 13 9
) (75)	44 4 7	35 13 11[23]	29 15 0[24]	— [25]——⟩	42 12 1[26]	56 10 2[27]	——[28]——⟩
1 (39)	*215 19 6*						⟩
TOTAL	932 17 11	974 7 1	1040 7 4	1351 5 4	1013 4 9	1015 2 2	1217 8 11

SUPERS

(11)	2 7 7						⟩

Summary   Summary[29]   Summary   Summary   Summary   Summary   Summary

FF

RECEIPTS

Code No.		1758	1759	1760	1761	1762	1763	1764
1	(16)	Accounts	18 7 7[1]				Accounts	→
3	(3)	missing	56 5 0[2]	61 5 0[3]	→		missing	56 5 0[4]
5	(2)	,,	316 10 0[5]		317 0 0[6]		,,	→
10a	(4)	,,	148 10 0				,,	→
b	(6)	,,	1 17 0				,,	→
c	(2)	,,	4 2 0				,,	→
d	(6)	,,	17 12 4			→	,,	26 12 4[7]
e	(3)	,,	2 9 4				,,	→
f	(2)	,,	1 9 4				,,	→
g	(2)	,,	1 4 0				,,	→
i	(2)	,,	1 4 0				,,	→
j	(7)	,,	13 18 0			→	,,	14 18 0[8]
k	(3)	,,	2 3 0				,,	→
l	(3)	,,	1 14 0				,,	→
m	(6)	,,	4 6 4				,,	→
n	(14)	,,	25 4 4			→	,,	30 14 4[9]
11a	(5)	,,	6 10 0				,,	→
b	(1)	,,	1 0 4				,,	→
c	(13)	,,	14 3 8				,,	→
e	(1)	,,	0 13 4				,,	→
f	(3)	,,	3 3 0				,,	→
12	(12)	,,	4 15 6				,,	→
13	(25)	,,	13 19 0			14 8 0[10]	,,	→
14a	(9)	,,	5 18 0				,,	→
b	(5)	,,	8 5 0[11]		4 11 9[12]	6 8 6[13]	,,	8 5 0[14]
c	(3)	,,	3 11 8				,,	→
d	(1)	,,	0 2 0				,,	→
e	(13)	,,	8 13 8				,,	→
f	(5)	,,	8 8 0				,,	→
g	(1)	,,	0 0 6				,,	→
h	(1)	,,	0 13 4				,,	→
i	(12)	,,	4 16 4				,,	→
15	(46)	,,	45 11 1			→	,,	46 16 1[15]
17	(4)	,,	5 15 0			→	,,	5 10 0[16]
19	(3)	,,	0 6 8				,,	→
20	(6)	,,	68 16 8			69 16 8[17]	,,	70 16 8[18]
22	(16)	,,	151 10 0[19]			152 17 6[20]	,,	156 5 0[21]
23	(5)	,,	2 17 6[22]				,,	→
29	(7)	,,	0 16 9				,,	→

RECEIPTS (*continued*)

YEAR

Code No.	1758	1759	1760	1761	1762	1763	1764
0 (35)	Accounts	4 10 4	————————————————— Accounts				——————>
1 (47)	missing	4 5 10	————————————————— missing				——— ——>
3 (38)	,,	4 13 0	— ——>	4 14 0[23]	——>	,,	4 12 6[24]
6 (21)	,,	318 15 10	556 9 6[25]	450 19 11	586 9 9	,,	344 18 0
TOTAL		1309 8 3	1552 1 11	1443 10 1	1583 13 2		1359 13 11

PAYMENTS

Code No.	1758	1759	1760	1761	1762	1763	1764
1 (21)	Accounts	124 5 1	————————————————— Accounts				——————>
3 (4)	missing	17 5 4	————————————————— missing				——————>
4 (84)	,,	350 15 6	441 3 1	378 16 7	463 0 5	,,	338 17 11
7 (33)	,,	18 9 8	296 1 11	206 16 1	281 9 6	,,	288 16 11
9 (71)	,,	57 17 0	——— —>	54 11 8	53 14 8	,,	53 8 0[26]
1 (39)	,,	215 19 6	—————————————————			,,	——————>
TOTAL		784 12 1	1152 11 11	997 14 3	1155 14 6		1038 12 9

SUPERS

Code No.	1758	1759	1760	1761	1762	1763	1764
(11)	Accounts missing	2 7 7	————————————————>		2 8 4[27]	Accounts missing	2 6 4[28]

	1760	1761	1762	1763	1764
	Summary	Summary	Summary	Summary	Summary

RECEIPTS

Code No.		1765	1766	1767	1768	1769	1770	1771
1	(16)	18 7 7	Accounts					
3	(3)	56 5 0	missing		→}	58 15 0[1]	61 5 0[2]	→}
5	(6)	317 0 0		,,				→}
10a	(4)	148 0 0	155 0 0[3]	,,	157 10 0[4]	143 16 0[5]		→}
b	(6)	1 17 0	2 2 0[6]	,,	4 7 0[7]			→}
c	(2)	4 2 0		,,				→}
d	(6)	14 12 4[8]	15 2 4[9]	,,	52 12 4[10]	42 12 4[11]		→}
e	(3)	2 9 4		,,				→}
f	(2)	1 9 4		,,				→}
g	(2)	1 4 0		,,				→}
i	(2)	1 4 0		,,				→}
j	(7)	14 18 0	→}	,,	13 18 0[12]			→}
k	(3)	2 3 0		,,				→}
l	(3)	1 14 0		,,				→}
m	(6)	4 6 4		,,				→}
n	(14)	36 4 4[13]		,,				→}
11a	(5)	6 10 0		,,				→}
b	(1)	1 0 4		,,				→}
c	(13)	14 3 8		,,				→}
e	(1)	0 13 4		,,				→}
f	(3)	3 3 0		,,				→}
12	(12)	4 15 6		,,				→}
13	(25)	14 8 0		,,				→}
14a	(9)	5 18 0		,,				→}
b	(5)	8 5 0		,,				→}
c	(3)	3 11 8		,,				→}
d	(1)	0 2 0		,,				→}
e	(13)	8 13 6		,,				→}
f	(5)	8 8 0	→}	,,	9 8 0[14]			→}
g	(1)	0 0 6		,,				→}
h	(1)	0 13 4		,,				→}
i	(12)	4 16 4		,,				→}
15	(46)	46 16 1		,,				→}
17	(3)	5 10 0		,,				→}
19	(3)	0 6 8		,,				→}
20	(6)	70 16 8		,,				→}
21	(16)	176 15 0[15]	→}	,,	186 15 0[16]	196 5 0[17]	199 5 0[18]	229 5 0[19]
23	(5)	2 17 6		,,				→}
29	(7)	0 16 9		,,				→}

RECEIPTS (*continued*)

YEAR

ode).	1765	1766	1767	1768	1769	1770	1771
(35)	*4 10 4*	———— Accounts		————————————————————⟩			
(47)	*4 5 10*	———— missing		————————————————————⟩			
(36)	*4 12 6*	———— ,,		————————————————————⟩			
(44)	1718 4 7[20]	737 11 10[21]	,,	360 0 7	304 18 6[22]	289 17 11	311 8 7[23]
TAL	2746 10 4	1773 12 7		1448 6 4	1381 10 3	1371 19 8	1423 10 4

PAYMENTS

	1765	1766	1767	1768	1769	1770	1771
(21)	*124 5 1*	———— Accounts		————————————————————⟩			
(4)	*17 5 4*	———— missing		————————————————————⟩			
(90)	1540 10 5	432 8 1	,,	462 6 8	460 8 9	440 6 6	476 16 8
(50)	178 19 7	621 12 1	,,	336 7 10	237 16 9	225 6 10	499 13 10
(67)	53 4 0[24]	46 11 0[25]	,,	32 17 11[26]	31 1 8[27]	36 5 3[28]	————⟩
(39)	242 14 6[29]	————⟩	,,	304 4 6[30]	313 14 6[31]	316 13 10[32]	—— [33]——⟩
TAL	2156 18 11	1484 16 1		1277 7 4	1184 12 1	1160 2 10	1471 0 0

SUPERS

	1765	1766	1767	1768	1769	1770	1771
(12)	3 1 4	2 6 4	Accounts missing	28 6 3[34]	28 2 11	————————————⟩	

	Summary	Summary		Summary	Summary	Summary	Summary

RECEIPTS

YEAR

Code No.		1772	1773	1774	1775	1776	1777	1778
1	(16)	18 7 7	13 7 7[1]					} 24 7 7[2]
3	(3)	61 5 0						
5	(6)	317 0 0			} 320 10 0[3]	189 0 0[4]	46 0 0[5]	—
6	(29)	Starts 1777					954 1 4	945 7 1[6]
10a	(5)	143 16 0			} 140 0 0[7]	142 10 0[8]		
b	(5)	4 7 0						
c	(2)	4 2 0						
d	(6)	42 12 4						
e	(3)	2 9 4						
f	(2)	1 9 4						
g	(2)	1 4 0						
i	(2)	1 4 0						
j	(7)	13 18 0					[9]	
k	(3)	2 3 0						
l	(3)	1 14 0						
m	(6)	4 6 4						
n	(14)	36 4 4						
11a	(5)	6 10 0						
b	(1)	1 0 4						
c	(13)	14 3 8			} 14 8 8[10]	79 10 8[11]		
e	(1)	0 13 4						
f	(3)	3 3 0						
12	(12)	4 15 6						
13	(25)	14 8 0	[12]	}	13 9 0[13]			
14a	(9)	5 18 0						
b	(5)	8 5 0				} 5 5 0[14]	7 15 0[15]	
c	(3)	3 11 8						
d	(1)	0 2 0						
e	(13)	8 13 6						
f	(5)	9 8 0						
g	(1)	0 0 6						
h	(1)	0 13 4						
i	(12)	4 16 4						
15	(46)	46 16 1	46 15 9[16]		} 54 6 1[17]			
17	(3)	5 10 0						
19	(3)	0 6 8						
20	(6)	70 6 9[18]	71 16 8		} 72 13 8[19]			
21	(16)	229 5 0			} 227 5 0[20]			
23	(5)	2 17 6						

RECEIPTS (continued)

YEAR

Code	1772	1773	1774	1775	1776	1777	1778
(7)	0 16 9	——————————————————————⟩					
(35)	4 10 4	—————————⟩		4 8 4[21]	4 10 4[22]	—————————⟩	
(47)	4 5 10	——————————————————————⟩					
(37)	4 12 6	——————————————————————⟩					
(34)	385 14 10	439 7 2[23]	337 12 10	374 18 3	390 18 7	608 4 5	814 8 7
TOTAL	1497 6 8	1547 8 7	1444 15 3	1488 5 0	1437 9 4	2468 6 6	2676 16 5

PAYMENTS

Code	1772	1773	1774	1775	1776	1777	1778
(21)	124 5 1	——————————————————————⟩					
(4)	17 5 4	——————————————————————⟩					
(99)	454 11 3	459 12 5	476 19 3	565 18 7	489 7 1	470 17 11	515 10 1[24]
(38)	304 6 2	353 19 4	363 4 0	180 11 6	133 10 6	261 6 6	297 5 7
(9)	Starts 1777					48 4 10[25]	61 16 7[26]
(65)	31 1 7	—————————⟩		27 16 10[27]	27 19 2[28]	97 13 10[29]	30 15 7[30]
(40)	316 13 10	—————⟩ 320 18 10[31]		—————⟩	386 0 10[32]	388 0 10[33]	—————⟩
TOTAL	1248 3 3	1302 17 7	1333 14 1	1236 16 2	1178 8 0	1407 14 4	1434 19 1

SUPERS

1772	1773	1774	1775	1776	1777	1778
28 2 11	——————————⟩		30 1 0[34]	——————————⟩		

Code	1772	1773	1774	1775	1776	1777	1778
(12)	Summary	Summary	Summary	Summary	Summary	Summary[35]	Summary[36]

RECEIPTS

Code No.	1779	1780	1781	1782	1783	1784	1785
1 (15)	24 7 7	Accounts					
3 (3)	61 5 0	missing				→	64 5 0[1]
5 (2)	46 0 0	,,	74 8 0[2]	72 18 0[3]	———	→46 0 0[4]	———
6 (29)	947 0 2[5]	,,	540 19 11[6]	557 6 2[7]	549 6 2[8]	509 6 6[9]	507 16 6[10]
7 (6)	Starts 1784					26 11 10	———
8 (4)	Starts 1784					26 9 7	———
9 (4)	Starts 1784					25 8 0	———
10a (5)	142 10 0	,,				→144 5 0[11]	146 0 0[12]
b (5)	4 7 0	,,			→8 7 0[13]		
c (2)	4 2 0	,,			→0 2 0		
d (6)	42 12 4	,,					→40 12 4[14]
e (3)	2 9 4	,,					
f (2)	1 9 4	,,					
g (2)	1 4 0	,,					
i (2)	1 4 0	,,					
j (7)	13 18 0+	,,					
k (3)	2 3 0	,,					
l (3)	1 14 0	,,					
m (6)	4 6 4	,,					
n (4)	36 4 4	,,					
11a (5)	6 10 0	,,					
b (1)	1 0 4	,,					
c (13)	92 0 8	,,					
e (1)	0 13 4[15]	,,					
f (3)	3 3 0	,,					
12 (12)	4 15 6	,,					
13 (25)	13 9 0	,,					
14a (9)	5 18 0	,,					
b (5)	7 15 0	,,					
c (3)	3 11 8	,,					
d (1)	0 2 0	,,					
e (13)	8 13 6	,,					
f (5)	9 8 0	,,					
g (1)	0 0 6	,,					
h (1)	0 13 4	,,					
i (12)	4 16 4	,,					
15 (46)	54 6 1	,,	54 6 3[16]	54 6 1[17]	54 2 9[18]	———[19]———	———[20]———
17 (3)	5 10 0	,,					
19 (3)	0 6 8	,,					

RECEIPTS (*continued*)

Code No.		1779	1780	YEAR 1781	1782	1783	1784	1785
20	(6)	*72 13 8*	Accounts	——————————⟩			89 15 8[21]	————⟩
21	(16)	*227 5 0*	missing	————⟩ 218 5 0[22]		————⟩ 217 5 0[23]		246 10 0[24]
23	(5)	*2 17 6*	,,	———————————————————⟩				
29	(7)	*0 16 9*	,,	———————————————————⟩				
30	(35)	*4 10 4*	,,	———————————————————⟩				
31	(47)	*4 5 10*	,,	———————————————————⟩				
33	(37)	*4 12 6*	,,	————⟩ 4 15 6+	————⟩ 4 15 0[25]		—— [26]——⟩	
36	(30)	1018 16 7	,,	181 15 0	313 3 8	1309 17 3[27]	1395 17 5	1728 14 6
TOTAL		2895 7 6		1680 13 10	1818 1 7	2806 11 10	2922 0 3	3285 7 4

PAYMENTS

		1779	1780	1781	1782	1783	1784	1785
1	(21)	*124 5 1*	Accounts	———————————————————⟩				
3	(4)	*17 5 4*	missing	———————————————————⟩				
4	(99)	548 6 11	,,	728 7 9	657 15 9[28]	676 4 1[29]	641 15 10	794 7 5[30]
7	(38)	238 0 0	,,	367 1 9	580 18 1[31]	351 7 11	197 18 5	559 17 9
8	(8)	62 14 10[32]	,,	64 3 9	Not in[33]	Not in	Not in	2 3 8[34]
9	(62)	25 16 10[35]	,,	25 5 0[36]	28 6 5[37]	80 14 4[38]	28 8 5[39]	80 19 8[40]
11	(49)	417 12 4[41]	,,	400 10 10[42]	379 0 10[43]	391 10 10[44]	————⟩	419 15 10[45]
TOTAL		1434 1 4		1726 19 6	1787 11 6	1641 7 7	1401 3 11	1998 14 9

SUPERS

	1779	1780	1781	
	30 1 0[46]	Accounts missing	——[47]——————[48]——————————⟩	

(7) Summary[49]   Summary   Summary[50]   Summary[51]   Summary[52]   Summary[53]

RECEIPTS

Code No.	1786	1787	1788	1789	1790	1791	1792
1 (15)	24 7 7						
3 (3)	64 5 0						
5 (2)	46 0 0		—⟩ 23 0 0	46 0 0			
6 (14)	507 16 6	508 16 6	215 3 0	508 16 6			—⟩ 507 17 6[1]
7 (6)	26 11 10		—⟩ 13 15 11[2]	26 11 10			
8 (4)	26 9 7	27 9 7+	13 4 9[3]	27 9 7			
9 (4)	25 8 0		—⟩ 12 14 0	25 8 0			
10a (5)	147 10 0[4]	147 0 0[5]	128 10 0[6]	147 0 0			
b (6)	8 7 0			—⟩ 12 7 0[7]	11 17 0[8]	12 7 0	
c (1)	0 2 0						
d (6)	52 12 4[9]		—⟩ 27 12 4[10]	52 12 4			
e (3)	2 9 4						
f (2)	1 9 4						
g (2)	1 4 0						
i (2)	1 4 0						
j (7)	13 18 0		—⟩ 8 8 0[11]	13 18 0			—⟩ 15 3 0[12]
k (3)	2 3 0						
l (3)	1 14 0						
m (6)	4 6 4						
n (14)	36 4 4		—⟩ 22 14 4[13]	36 4 4			
11a (5)	6 10 0						
b (1)	1 0 4						
c (20)	92 0 8		—⟩ 86 0 8[14]	92 0 8			
e (1)	0 13 4						
f (3)	3 3 0						
12 (12)	4 15 6		—⟩ 5 2 3[15]	6 19 0[16]			
13 (24)	13 9 0						—⟩ 14 19 0[17]
14a (9)	5 18 0	3 18 0⁻					
b (5)	7 15 0		—⟩ 5 5 0[18]	7 15 0			
c (3)	3 11 8						
d (1)	0 2 0						
e (13)	8 13 6						
f (5)	9 8 0		—⟩ 8 10 6[19]	9 8 0	13 8 0[20]		
g (1)	0 0 6						
h (1)	0 13 4						
i (12)	4 16 4						
15 (45)	54 2 9		—⟩ 46 15 3[21]	54 2 9			
17 (3)	5 10 0						—⟩ 2 10 0[22]
19 (3)	0 6 8						

RECEIPTS (*continued*)

Code No.		1786	1787	1788	1789	1790	1791	1792
20	(6)	*89 15 8*	——}	46 3 8[23]	89 15 8	92 13 8[24]	———	}
21	(16)	244 10 0[25]	——}	180 12 6[26]	244 10 0	———		}
23	(5)	*2 17 6*	———————————————————					}
29	(7)	*0 16 9*	———————————————————					}
30	(35)	*4 10 4*	———————————————————					}
31	(47)	*4 5 10*	———————————————————					}
33	(37)	4 16 6[27]	——}	4 17 0[28]	4 17 6	4 16 6[29]	———	}
36	(36)	1476 19 7	1558 12 9	1879 19 6[30]	1345 14 4[31]	882 5 8	913 17 4	790 15 2
TOTAL		3045 3 11	3126 7 1	2904 18 4	2919 13 2	2462 11 6	2494 13 2	2370 7 0

PAYMENTS

Code No.		1786	1787	1788	1789	1790	1791	1792
1	(21)	*124 5 1*	———————————————————					}
3	(4)	*17 5 4*	———————————————————					}
4	(62)	656 2 7	695 9 10	693 12 5	1387 1 10[32]	953 9 8	678 11 4	1065 0 10
7	(45)	366 12 1	367 11 5	537 5 7	409 17 1	456 19 3	680 3 7	315 17 11
8	(1)	1 16 0[33]	1 11 4[34]	1 7 4	1 8 0	1 16 0	1 11 4	1 16 0
9	(55)	79 17 2[35]	79 11 4[36]	45 10 7[37]	79 11 4[38]	77 10 11[39]	74 11 6[40]	74 9 4[41]
11	(49)	*419 15 10*	———————————————————					}
TOTAL		1665 14 1	1705 10 2	1839 2 2	2439 4 6	2051 2 1	1996 4 0	2018 10 4

SUPERS

		1786	
	(7)	*30 1 0*	——————————————————— }

ARREARS

			1792
(38)	Starts 1792		163 6 4

	Summary	Summary[42]	Summary[43]	Summary[44]	Summary[45]	Summary

RECEIPTS

Code No.	1793	1794	1795	1796	1797	1798	1799
1 (15)	24 7 7						⟩ 34 7 7[1]
3 (3)	64 5 0			⟩ 33 0 0			⟩
4 (2)	Starts 1796			40 14 0			⟩
5 (2)	46 0 0			⟩ 61 5 5[2]	70 6 11[3]		⟩
6a (14)	507 17 6		⟩ 625 16 9[4]	345 2 0		⟩ 346 3 0[5]	⟩
b (8)	Starts 1796			398 6 0	398 14 0[6]		⟩
7 (6)	26 11 10		⟩ 31 19 11	37 8 0			⟩
8 (4)	27 9 7		⟩ 30 18 3	36 15 0+	35 15 0		⟩
9 (4)	25 8 0			⟩ 29 15 0[7]			⟩
10a (5)	147 0 0			⟩ 147 10 0[8]	150 4 6[9]	148 0 0[10]	153 10 0[11]
b (6)	10 7 0[12]	25 5 0[13]	29 15 0[14]		⟩ 21 12 0[15]	24 10 0[16]	⟩
c (1)	0 2 0						⟩
d (6)	52 12 4						⟩
e (3)	2 9 4						⟩
f (2)	1 9 4						⟩
g (2)	1 4 0						⟩
i (2)	1 4 0						⟩
j (7)	15 3 0			⟩ 16 18 0[17]	18 13 0[18]		⟩
k (3)	2 3 0						⟩
l (3)	1 14 0						⟩
m (6)	4 6 4						⟩
n (14)	36 4 4						⟩
11a (5)	6 10 0						⟩
b (1)	1 0 4						⟩
c (20)	92 0 8	97 7 2[19]	101 11 2[20]		⟩ 103 13 2[21]		⟩
e (1)	0 13 4						⟩
f (3)	3 3 0						⟩
12 (12)	6 19 0						⟩
13 (24)	14 19 0	12 14 0[22]	15 17 0[23]				⟩
14a (8)	3 18 0						⟩
b (5)	7 15 0				11 6 8[24]		⟩
c (3)	3 11 8						⟩
d (1)	0 2 0						⟩
e (13)	8 13 6				⟩ 7 19 6[25]		⟩
f (5)	13 8 0	11 13 0[26]		⟩ 15 13 0[27]			⟩
g (1)	0 0 6						⟩
h (1)	0 13 4						⟩
i (12)	4 16 4						⟩
15 (45)	54 2 9			⟩ 57 5 3[28]	36 1 3[29]		⟩

RECEIPTS (continued)

Code No.		1793	1794	1795	1796	1797	1798	1799
6	(3)	Starts 1797				139 0 8	145 12 6[30]	———>
7	(2)	2 10 0	———					>
9	(3)	0 6 8	———					>
)	(6)	92 13 8	——>	51 2 8[31]	14 1 8	———		>
1	(16)	244 10 0	———	——>	267 0 6[32]	273 0 6[33]	273 19 6[34]	274 18 6[35]
3	(6)	22 17 6[36]	——>	20 14 6[37]	76 8 6[38]	87 14 6[39]	88 2 6[40]	62 14 6[41]
4a	(7)	Starts 1795		39 9 0	78 18 0	———		>
b	(7)	Starts 1795		44 0 6	88 1 0	———		>
)	(7)	0 16 9	———					>
)	(35)	4 10 4	———					>
1	(47)	4 5 10	———					>
3	(34)	4 16 0[42]	57 16 0[43]	——>	57 13 6[44]	114 0 6[45]	——>	114 1 0[46]
5	(23)	663 14 8	512 15 7	2085 11 1[47]	2220 12 1	1276 11 1[48]	1153 9 10	1517 9 0
TOTAL		2261 6 0	2179 11 5	3930 15 5	4357 11 11	3611 4 7	3497 16 8	3852 17 4

PAYMENTS

Code No.		1793	1794	1795	1796	1797	1798	1799
1	(21)	124 5 1	———					>
3	(4)	17 5 4	———					>
4	(98)	878 17 1	1223 12 7	2103 15 11[49]	878 14 5	1591 12 9	1255 12 6[50]	2481 11 10[51]
7	(44)	522 16 11	315 0 5	418 7 2	1987 11 0[52]	240 1 7	506 17 10	717 5 2
8	(1)	1 14 8	3 0 8	1 11 4[53]	3 4 2	3 2 4	3 2 2	3 0 1
9	(57)	76 4 10[54]	75 10 6	78 13 6	76 19 2	77 3 8[55]	77 13 2[56]	37 5 0[57]
	(50)	439 15 10[58]	——>	428 7 6[59]	453 13 10[60]	458 3 10[61]	459 3 10[62]	460 2 10[63]
TOTAL		2060 19 9	2198 10 5	3172 5 10	3541 13 0	2511 14 7	2443 19 11	3840 15 4

SUPERS

		1793	1794	1795	1796	1797	1798	1799
	(7)	30 1 0	30 0 0[64]	———	>	5 12 3[65]	——— [66]—>	

ARREARS

		1793	1794	1795	1796	1797	1798	1799
	(38)	159 11 11	83 19 0	115 3 9	113 12 4	98 9 8	115 6 3	108 9 9

Summary	Summary	Summary	Summary		Summary	Summary

SUMMARY OF ACCOUNTS 1800–6

RECEIPTS

YEAR

Code No.	1800	1801	1802	1803	1804	1805	1806
1 (15)	44 7 7[1]	44 3 9[2]				} 43 13 9[3]	43 12 6⁻
3 (1)	33 0 0						} 51 10 0[4]
4 (2)	40 14 0					} 17 6 0[5]	29 4 0[6]
5 (2)	73 13 7[7]	72 0 3[8]					} 78 15 4[9]
6a (49)	346 3 0				} 493 17 6[10]	} 593 13 7[11]	1208 8 2[12]
b (8)	398 14 0				} 639 12 0		
7 (6)	37 8 0				} 89 6 8	64 0 9	128 1 6
8 (4)	35 19 0				} 83 6 4	47 17 6	95 5 0[13]
9 (4)	29 15 0					} 32 5 0[14]	
10a (5)	151 8 0[15]		} 146 3 0[16]		143 0 0⁻	} 205 10 0[17]	
b (6)	24 10 0	11 17 0⁻				} 0 6 0⁻	
c (1)	0 2 0				} Item sold		
d (6)	52 12 4					} 27 12 4[18]	2 7 10[19]
e (3)	2 9 4	2 0 4⁻					
f (2)	1 9 4						
g (2)	1 4 0	0 18 0⁻					
i (2)	1 4 0						
j (7)	18 13 0	18 3 0⁻				} 16 17 0⁻	8 19 6[20]
k (2)	2 3 0	1 0 0					
l (3)	1 14 0	0 14 0⁻				} 0 10 0	
m (6)	4 6 4	3 14 4⁻					
n (14)	36 4 4	33 14 3⁻			} 50 1 9[21]	36 8 0[22]	44 11 6[23]
11a (5)	6 10 0	4 6 8⁻			} 3 6 8⁻		
b (1)	1 0 4						
c (20)	100 2 5[24]	104 13 0[25]	} 123 12 0[26]		136 11 0[27]	135 15 0⁻	132 12 0⁻
e (1)	0 13 4	Item sold					
f (3)	3 3 0						
12 (12)	6 19 0	1 12 4⁻	8 0 10[28]	1 12 4			
13 (24)	14 5 6[29]	10 8 0⁻	15 18 0[30]	10 8 0		} 10 5 0⁻	9 4 0⁻
14a (8)	3 18 0	3 1 4					
b (8)	11 6 8				} 11 2 8⁻		
d (1)	0 2 0						
e (13)	7 19 6	4 13 4⁻			} 4 1 4		} 3 1 4⁻
f (5)	15 13 0				} 20 13 0[31]		} 16 13 0⁻
g (1)	0 0 6						
h (1)	0 13 4						
i (12)	4 16 4	2 19 8					
15 (39)	36 1 3	31 11 3⁻	31 10 11⁻		} 31 10 8⁻		} 30 18 8[32]
16 (8)	145 12 6				} 147 4 0[33]		202 5 9[34]

RECEIPTS (*continued*)

YEAR

Code No.	1800	1801	1802	1803	1804	1805	1806
(2)	*2 10 0*	2 1 8⁻	————————————————→				
(3)	*0 6 8*	0 5 10⁻	0 3 4⁻	————————————→			
(6)	*14 1 8*	——————————————————————→					15 1 8[35]
(16)	276 13 6[36]	278 18 6[37]	282 18 6[38]	————→ 286 12 9[39]	285 4 0[40]		295 14 0[41]
(5)	76 2 6[42]	60 5 6[43]	60 0 6[44]	53 8 0[45]	53 4 0[46]	58 18 0[47]	68 1 6[48]
a (7)	*78 18 0*	————————————————————→					
b (7)	*88 1 0*	————————————————————→					
(7)	*0 16 9*	0 14 5	————————————————→				
(35)	*4 10 4*	3 13 11⁻	——————————————→				
(47)	*4 5 10*	3 2 1⁻	——————————→ 2 17 9⁻	2 17 6⁻			2 15 0⁻
(39)	*114 1 0*	——————→ 99 19 9[49]	52 18 6[50]	109 3 6[51]	4 16 0[52]	————→	
(19)	1547 16 1[53]	643 17 8[54]	716 6 9	1070 8 4	575 12 7	400 1 1	4294 12 4[55]
(17)	Starts 1801	228 0 0	261 10 0	167 15 0	281 10 0	113 5 0	275 0 0[56]
							6062 4 6[57]
TOTAL	3904 13 10	3173 11 9	3281 0 3	3489 8 7	3685 2 6	2577 7 7	13553 6 3

PAYMENTS

Code No.	1800	1801	1802	1803	1804	1805	1806
(21)	*124 5 1*	——————————————————→ 124 5 4[58]					67 10 2[59]
(4)	*17 5 4*	——————————————————————→					
(115)	2374 8 7[60]	1427 5 2	1549 6 6[61]	1925 6 2[62]	2211 10 0[63]	1670 14 7[64]	10766 11 7[65]
(34)	815 11 11	731 3 10	714 16 4	647 3 4[66]	749 17 9	927 6 4	2006 4 4[67]
(2)	4 18 7	5 0 8	4 3 8	8 5 10	114 16 1[68]	1 18 10[69]	1 1 10
(38)	11 8 6[70]	10 14 10[71]	10 1 10[72]	9 16 10[73]	10 6 10[74]	8 16 0[75]	7 18 0[76]
(50)	*460 2 10*	——————————[77]——→ 479 1 10[78]	492 0 10[79]	498 5 10[80]			509 0 10[81]
TOTAL	3808 0 10	2775 17 9	2880 1 7	3211 4 5	3720 1 11	3243 12 3	13358 6 9

SUPERS

Code No.	1800	1801	1802	1803	1804	1805	1806
(5)	*5 12 3*[82]	——————————————————————————→					

ARREARS

Code No.	1800	1801	1802	1803	1804	1805	1806
(44)	188 3 4	135 1 2	141 19 7	179 17 2	149 8 11[83]	83 3 1	84 13 11

Summary Summary Summary Summary Summary Summary Summary

SUMMARY OF ACCOUNTS 1807–13

RECEIPTS

Code No.		1807	1808	1809	1810	1811	1812	1813
1	(12)	*43 12 6*	43 5 10⁻	————————	——[1]——⟩	41 12 2	————————	——⟩
3	(1)	70 13 6[2]	71 7 0[3]	————⟩	50 13 6[4]	50 0 0	————————	——⟩
4	(2)	41 2 0[5]	————————					——⟩
5	(2)	78 7 9[6]	————————————⟩		96 3 5[7]	115 19 2[8]	————————	——⟩
6	(67)	1363 9 10[9]	1480 4 6[10]	1469 15 6[11]	1448 1 6[12]	1467 0 0[13]	1413 14 3[14]	1453 5 6[15]
7	(7)	*128 1 6*	————————————————					——⟩
8	(7)	*95 5 0*	95 15 0[16]	————————————				——⟩
9	(4)	34 1 6[17]	35 8 0[18]	————⟩	36 6 8[19]	35 8 0[20]	————————	——⟩
10a	(4)	208 0 0[21]	————————————⟩		198 0 0[22]	197 5 0[23]	195 0 0[24]	——⟩
b	(2)	*0 6 0*	————————————————————⟩			0 1 0	————————	——⟩
d	(5)	*2 7 10*	————————————————					——⟩
e	(3)	*2 0 4*	————————————————					——⟩
f	(2)	*1 9 4*	————————————————					——⟩
g	(1)	*0 18 0*	————————————————					——⟩
i	(2)	*1 4 0*	————————————————					——⟩
j	(3)	1 2 0[25]	————————————⟩			0 12 0⁻	————————	——⟩
k	(1)	*1 0 0*	————————————————					——⟩
l	(1)	*0 10 0*	————————————————					——⟩
m	(5)	*3 14 4*	————————————————					——⟩
n	(9)	52 12 7[26]	————————————————					——⟩
11a	(1)	2 6 8⁻	————————————————					——⟩
b	(1)	*1 0 4*	————————————————					——⟩
c	(16)	129 9 0⁻	————————————————					——⟩
f	(3)	*3 3 0*	————————————————					——⟩
12	(8)	1 11 4⁻	————————————⟩			1 10 1⁻	————————	——⟩
13	(16)	*9 4 0*	8 2 4⁻	————————————————————			———⟩	7 18 4[27]
14a	(6)	*3 1 4*	————————————————					——⟩
b	(7)	10 16 8⁻	————————————————————⟩				8 6 8[28]	5 16 8[29]
d	(1)	*0 2 0*	————————————————					——⟩
e	(8)	*3 1 4*	————————————————					——⟩
f	(3)	1 13 0⁻	————————————————					——⟩
g	(1)	*0 0 6*	————————————————					——⟩
h	(1)	*0 13 4*	————————————————					——⟩
i	(12)	2 13 8⁻	————————————————					——⟩
15	(25)	27 8 8⁻	———⟩ 27 7 4⁻	————————————		⟩ 27 6 4⁻	————————	——⟩
16	(15)	*202 5 9*	————————————————					——⟩
17	(2)	*2 1 8*	————————————————					——⟩
19	(1)	*0 3 4*	————————————————					——⟩
20	(1)	13 15 0[30]	————————————————					——⟩

RECEIPTS (*continued*)

Code No.	1807	1808	1809	1810	1811	1812	1813
1 (16)	307 14 0[31]	315 14 0[32]	———	———⟩	321 14 0[33]	327 14 0[34]	344 11 6[35]
3 (12)	91 16 0[36]	107 19 6[37]	99 10 6[38]	95 19 6[39]	103 13 6[40]	77 8 6[41]	106 14 6[42]
4a (7)	*78 18 0*	———⟩	211 19 0[43]	256 19 0[44]	258 19 0[45]	———	———⟩
b (7)	*88 1 0*	———⟩					
8 (4)	Starts 1809		51 0 0[46]	117 0 0[47]	146 5 0[48]	132 0 0[49]	120 0 0[50]
9 (7)	*0 14 5*	———	———⟩	0 15 9[51]	———	———	———⟩
10 (22)	3 4 5⁻	———	———	———	———	2 19 5⁻	———⟩
11 (22)	2 11 0⁻	———	———⟩	2 11 6⁺	———	———	———⟩
13 (39)	*4 16 0*	———⟩	4 15 6⁻	4 16 0	4 15 6	4 16 0	4 15 6
16 (5)	393 2 2	789 1 11	419 11 0[52]	735 0 8	439 2 1	1747 8 4	456 0 0
17 (14)	272 10 0	393 0 0	513 5 0	273 5 0	214 5 0	282 10 0	1130 0 7
						6618 9 6[53]	
TOTAL	3787 15 7	4446 5 2	4273 19 5	4423 7 3	4147 4 4	12049 8 10	5058 1 10

PAYMENTS

Code No.	1807	1808	1809	1810	1811	1812	1813
4 (118)	2290 8 0[54]	2529 4 7[55]	2284 2 1[56]	2934 17 0[57]	2825 7 8[58]	9574 10 11[59]	2967 8 9[60]
7 (44)	1008 2 4	1488 8 3[61]	1215 1 3	962 2 4[62]	747 7 9	1116 12 9	1456 15 4
8 (1)	*1 1 10*	———⟩	0 3 4[63]	0 4 8	Not in	0 4 8	1 6 6
9 (30)	7 14 0⁻	———⟩	7 14 9[64]	8 18 0[65]	9 2 0⁺	8 15 0[66]	———⟩
1 (53)	514 0 10[67]	516 15 7[68]	515 15 7[69]	———	———	———⟩	563 6 6[70]
TOTAL	3821 7 0	4543 4 3	4022 17 0	4421 13 7	4097 13 0	11216 1 11	4997 15 1

SUPERS

Code No.	1807	1808	1809	1810	1811	1812	1813
(7)	*5 12 3*	———	———	———	———	———⟩	7 3 5[71]

ARREARS

Code No.	1807	1808	1809	1810	1811	1812	1813
(38)	103 11 7	92 18 2	97 10 5	112 4 9	132 15 5[72]	82 15 10	67 9 0

	Summary	Summary	Summary[73]	Summary[74]	Summary[75]	Summary	Summary[76]

GG

RECEIPTS

Code No.		1814	1815	1816	1817	1818	1819	1820
1	(8)	*41 12 2*					⟶⟩	42 12 2+
3	(1)	*50 0 0*						⟶⟩
4	(2)	*41 2 0*						⟶⟩
5	(2)	*115 19 2*[1]						⟶⟩
6	(70)	*1453 5 6*	1381 19 0[2]	1400 10 6[3]	1401 13 0[4]	⟶[5]⟶⟩	1326 9 7[6]	1323 14 11[7]
7	(70)	*128 1 6*				⟩ 201 16 6[8]		⟶⟩
8	(7)	*97 19 3*[9]	100 3 6[10]					⟶⟩
9	(3)	*35 8 0*						⟶⟩
10a	(3)	*195 0 0*	275 0 0[11]	285 0 0[12]				⟶⟩
b	(1)	*0 1 0*						⟶⟩
d	(5)	*2 7 10*						⟶⟩
e	(3)	*2 0 4*						⟶⟩
f	(2)	*1 9 4*						⟶⟩
g	(1)	*0 18 0*						⟶⟩
i	(2)	*1 4 0*						⟶⟩
j	(2)	*0 12 0*						⟶⟩
k	(1)	*1 0 0*						⟶⟩
l	(1)	*0 10 0*						⟶⟩
m	(5)	*3 14 4*						⟶⟩
n	(9)	*52 12 7*	51 17 7⁻					⟶⟩
11a	(1)	*2 6 8*						⟶⟩
b	(1)	*1 0 4*						⟶⟩
c	(15)	*116 6 6⁻*		⟩ 139 6 6[13]				⟶⟩
f	(3)	*3 3 0*						⟶⟩
12	(8)	*1 10 1*						⟶⟩
13	(4)	*7 18 4*						⟶⟩
14a	(6)	*3 1 4*					⟩ 2 18 0[14]	⟶⟩
b	(6)	*5 16 8*						⟶⟩
d	(1)	*0 2 0*						⟶⟩
e	(8)	*3 1 4*						⟶⟩
f	(3)	*1 13 0*						⟶⟩
g	(1)	*0 0 6*						⟶⟩
h	(1)	*0 13 4*						⟶⟩
i	(6)	*2 13 8*						⟶⟩
15	(23)	*27 6 4*			⟩ 19 8 10[15]	11 11 4⁻		⟶⟩
16	(15)	*202 5 9*					[16]	⟶⟩
17	(2)	*2 1 8*						⟶⟩
19	(1)	*0 3 4*						⟶⟩
20	(1)	*13 15 0*			⟩ 6 17 6[17] Discontinued			

RECEIPTS (*continued*)

Code No.	1814	1815	1816	1817	1818	1819	1820
21 (16)	361 9 0[18]	356 19 0[19]	352 9 0[20]	332 9 0[21]	312 9 0[22]	————————→	
23 (13)	143 10 6[23]	149 9 6[24]	127 12 0[25]	136 14 6[26]	137 14 6[27]	163 19 0[28]	105 0 6[29]
24 (14)	*258 19 0*	————————————————————→					
28 (7)	132 0 0[30]	——————————————→			127 10 0[31]	130 0 0[32]	————→
29 (5)	*0 15 9*	————————————————————→					
30 (20)	*2 19 5*	————————→		3 2 5+	————————————→		
31 (23)	*2 11 6*	————————————————————→					
33 (39)	*4 16 0*	———— 33 ————————————→					
35 (16)	Starts 1817			63 0 3[34]	69 13 3	76 2 11[35]	263 18 8[36]
36 (5)	373 1 6	400 10 10[37]	265 15 2[38]	879 3 6	890 3 7	916 6 1	481 15 11
37 (20)	274 5 0	332 5 0	273 10 0	156 5 0	246 15 0	185 10 0	340 0 0
TOTAL	4174 3 6	4271 4 7	4079 17 11	4637 14 6	4707 12 7	4706 2 6	4553 4 11

PAYMENTS

Code No.	1814	1815	1816	1817	1818	1819	1820
4 (97)	2470 18 2[39]	2116 5 10[40]	2010 5 9[41]	2374 17 9[42]	2290 2 4[43]	2706 16 10[44]	2691 11 10[45]
7 (48)	1066 0 5	1447 19 1	893 1 7	1067 11 1	1204 13 6	1239 3 5[46]	937 17 8
8 (2)	2 18 0	1 1 10	————————————————→				
9 (31)	8 14 0[47]	10 6 0[48]	9 6 0[49]	9 10 0[50]	9 14 0[51]	————→	9 18 0[52]
11 (55)	573 2 9[53]	570 4 9[54]	566 8 4[55]	587 16 4[56]	582 5 11[57]	583 7 1[58]	579 18 2[59]
TOTAL	4121 13 4	4145 17 6	3480 3 6	4040 17 0	4087 17 7	4540 3 2	4220 7 5

SUPERS

Code No.	1814	1815	1816	1817	1818	1819	1820
(6)	7 3 5[60]	19 3 5[61]	20 10 11[62]	7 3 5	————————————→		

ARREARS

Code No.	1814	1815	1816	1817	1818	1819	1820
(18)	68 3 4	69 19 1	77 7 1	79 16 7	87 18 8	97 16 2	129 5 9[63]

Summary	Summary	Summary	Summary	Summary	Summary	Summary

RECEIPTS

Code No.		YEAR 1821	1822	1823
1	(9)	42 12 2	──────⟩	42 12 11[1]
3	(1)	50 0 0	──────⟩	32 4 10[2]
4	(2)	41 2 0	───────────────|	
5	(2)	115 19 2	─────⟩	111 4 8[3]
6	(70)	1318 18 0[4]	1309 1 11[5]	1284 16 6[6]
7	(7)	201 16 6	───────────────|	
8	(7)	100 3 6	───────────────|	
9	(3)	35 8 0	──────⟩	34 15 0[7]
10a	(3)	130 11 0[8]	150 0 0[9]	─────────|
b	(1)	0 1 0	───────────────|	
d	(5)	2 7 10	──────⟩	2 2 10[10]
e	(3)	2 0 4	───────────────|	
f	(2)	1 9 4	───────────────|	
g	(1)	0 18 0	───────────────|	
i	(2)	1 4 0	───────────────|	
j	(2)	0 12 0	───────────────|	
k	(1)	1 0 0	───────────────|	
l	(1)	0 10 0	───────────────|	
m	(5)	3 14 4	───────────────|	
n	(8)	51 17 7	───────────────|	
11a	(1)	2 6 8	───────────────|	
b	(1)	1 0 4	───────────────|	
c	(16)	139 6 6	───────────────|	
f	(3)	3 3 0	───────────────|	
12	(8)	1 10 1	──────⟩	1 9 1[11]
13	(14)	7 18 4	───────────────|	
14a	(5)	2 18 0	───────────────|	
b	(6)	5 16 8	──────⟩	5 11 8[12]
d	(1)	0 2 0	───────────────|	
e	(8)	3 1 4	───────────────|	
f	(3)	1 13 0	───────────────|	
g	(1)	0 0 6	───────────────|	
h	(1)	0 13 4	───────────────|	
i	(6)	2 13 8	──────⟩	2 8 8[13]
15	(22)	11 11 4	──────⟩	10 18 4[14]
16	(25)	202 4 7[15]	206 13 9[16]	233 1 5[17]
17	(2)	2 1 8	───────────────|	
19	(1)	0 3 4	───────────────|	
21	(15)	312 9 0	307 9 0[18]	303 9 0[19]

RECEIPTS (continued)

de o.	YEAR 1821	1822	1823
(12)	88 5 6[20]	106 8 6[21]	112 7 6[22]
(14)	*258 19 0*	274 10 0[23]	————|
(7)	*130 0 0*	151 0 0[24]	232 0 0[25]
(5)	*0 15 9*	————⟩	0 3 2[26]
(20)	2 3 5	————⟩	2 17 5[27]
(23)	*2 11 6*	————⟩	2 3 10[28]
(39)	*4 16 0*	————|	
(18)	88 9 3[29]	61 2 11[30]	64 13 0[31]
(6)	1094 15 3[32]	1725 14 9[33]	941 13 0
(33)	247 10 0	314 10 0	369 10 0
OTAL	4721 3 9	5455 13 0	4790 5 5

PAYMENTS

(113)	2711 4 0[34]	3251 16 6[35]	2443 15 1
(55)	1474 19 7[36]	1777 6 1	1025 9 2
(2)	1 12 0	1 14 8	1 1 10
(34)	10 4 6[37]	10 4 0[38]	9 18 0[39]
(55)	585 15 7[40]	585 13 9[41]	545 12 5[42]
OTAL	4783 15 8	5626 15 0	4025 16 6

SUPERS

(6)	*7 3 5*	————⟩	5 1 2[43]

ARREARS

21)	106 16 5[44]	75 12 6	Not in

| Summary | Summary | Summary |

The arrangement of the accounts from 1824 to the end of the period is so altered that this new set of headings is inserted.

Receipts

1. Receipts of the Old Grange etc. viz.: South Fields, Burgess Meadows, Beadhouse Meadows, Gosling Closes, etc.
   a. The Newarke Mills and Meadows.   b. Gosling Closes.
   c. Beadhouse Meadows.
   d. In the South Fields which are now enclosed under the Act of 44th Geo. III and divided into small allotments (Except the part over which the race-course runs) and are let upon leases from year to year commencing at Lady Day.
   e. St Mary's Meadow.   f. Far Meadow.
   g. Hall Grange and Meadows. (Also included levy on clay for bricks and kilns of plaster).
   h. Rents of the gardens adjoining the New Walk. (Part of the South Fields.)

2. a. Premises passing under Charters and grants. (This heading includes rent from the Sheep Pens and the North Mills, and receipts from the Saturday Market and the herbage of St Mary's churchyard.)
   b. Receipts for tithes on estates in St Mary's. (The tithes of the Walter Ruding estates are listed separately within this heading.)

3. a. Purchases etc.
   b. Receipts for certain grounds near Leicester called Freake's Grounds which were formerly only 2 closes but which are now divided into smaller closes and let on lease from year to year.
   c. (No separate heading but includes more recently purchased houses such as the Nag's Head Inn, houses in High Cross Street, the Bull's Head Inn, and various stables and shops.)

4. Receipts for the School and Charitable Uses.
   (This includes items formerly entered in other sections.)

(Sections 5–14 all deal with Fee Farm and Chief rents)

5. a. General.   b. Within the North Gates.
   c. In the South Gates.   d. In Burgess Meadow.
   e. In the Swines Market now called High Street.
   f. In the Saturday Market.   g. In Loseby Lane.
   h. In Gallowtree Gate.   i. In Gallowtree Gate on the West side.
   j. In Belgrave Gate.   k. In the Country.

6. a. Other rents of the land and tenements parcel of the town obiit lands of St Margaret's Guild and parcel of the fee farm lands heretofore demised by Queen Elizabeth to Mr Hawkes and Mr Bates by indenture expired.
   b. In the Swines Market now called High Street.
   c. In or near Belgrave Gate.
   d. St Nicholas's and St Margaret's parishes.

7. Other rents of lands and tenements parcel of the town and manor of Leicester

heretofore given and granted to the said Mayor, Bailiffs and Burgesses in fee farm per annum.

8 Other rents of Corpus Christi Guild in Leicester heretofore in Mr Archer's Collection and now parcel of the lands and tenements which the Mayor etc. purchased of Queen Elizabeth to them and their successors for ever.

9 a. Other rents of the possession of the late Guild in Leicester, parcel of the town obiit lands heretofore collected by Mr Tatham.

   b. In the South Gates.   c. In the Swines Market.

   d. In Belgrave Gate.   e. In Sanvey Gate.

   f. Near St Margaret's Church.   g. Other part of Mr Wilder's rent.

10 Rental of lands and possessions belonging to the College of Blessed Virgin Mary over against the Castle of Leicester heretofore demised by Queen Elizabeth to Edward Holt Esq., and by Her Majesty granted to the Mayor etc. and their successors in Fee Farm.

11 Other rents of the town and manor of Leicester parcel of the lands and possessions of the Duchy of Lancaster part thereof being in the County of Leicester.

12 Chief rents belonging to St John's and St Leonard's to be paid for the use of the Mayor Bailiffs and Burgesses of the Borough of Leicester.

13 Chief rents belonging to the Corpus Christi Guild.

14 Chief rents belonging to St Margaret's Guild.

15 Rental of Lammas tithes due yearly to the Mayor, Bailiffs and Burgesses for divers gardens in St Mary's parish in the possession of the College of St Mary over against the Castle of Leicester and of other acknowledgements etc. which were to be paid but which for many years have been supered.
(Items are entered and the amount formerly paid indicated but no totals are taken into the accounts.)

16 Freedoms etc.

17 Incidental and casual receipts.

Payments

 1 Charitable Gifts.

 2 Salaries etc.

 3 Miscellaneous ⎫ The main difference between these two headings is that
                ⎬ No. 3 includes regular payments and No. 4 non-recurrent
 4 Casual   ⎭ items.)

 5 Tradesmen's bills.

 6 South Fields Accounts.
(Money spent in labourers' wages and materials used for fencing, draining, etc., in the South Fields, and repairing occupation roads.)

 7 a. Levies.   b. Arrears.

Where indicated, the payments are followed by a General Statement of Receipts and Payments; totals of the main headings are given, and the final total and balance indicated. A note of when the accounts were audited appears on the same page, signed by the auditors.

SUMMARY OF ACCOUNTS 1824–30

RECEIPTS

Code No.	1824	1825	1826	1827	1828	1829	1830
1a (1)	22 4 10[1]	28 4 10[2]	134 4 10[3]	———	———	———	———
b (2)	41 2 0	———	———	———	———	———	———
c (8)	95 14 8[4]	80 4 8[5]	———	———	———	———	90 7 2[6]
d (63)	1300 4 11	1256 7 8[7]	1271 6 2[8]	1271 18 8[9]	1261 0 9[10]	1276 5 8[11]	1272 18 2[12]
e (11)	201 16 6	———	190 3 0[13]	202 3 0[14]	202 13 3[15]	203 3 6[16]	202 7 0[17]
f (7)	100 3 6	———	———	———	———	———	———
g (6)	171 15 11	271 6 3[18]	190 15 7[19]	162 6 8[20]	154 9 6[21]	92 1 6[22]	100 3 6[23]
h (15)	70 7 3	68 2 11[24]	66 6 5[25]	68 1 4[26]	65 10 7[27]	63 4 11[28]	68 1 4[29]
2a (6)	802 4 11	847 19 2[30]	854 15 2[31]	853 13 3[32]	825 3 6[33]	847 7 9[34]	867 7 2[35]
b (24)	262 4 3	262 3 1[36]	261 17 3[37]	257 13 9[38]	———[39]	———	251 1 11[40]
3a (6)	94 6 0	———	———	———	———	———	———
b (14)	274 10 0	———	274 15 6[41]	276 1 6[42]	277 2 0[43]	262 7 6[44]	242 7 0[45]
c (13)	337 2 6	344 19 4[46]	743 5 0[47]	725 5 5[48]	707 17 3[49]	677 4 7[50]	600 13 4[51]
4 (19)	409 3 4	———	———	———	———	406 3 4[52]	362 3 4[53]
5a (9)	2 4 8	———	———	———	———	———	———
b (4)	0 17 10	———	———	———	———	———	———
c (3)	1 16 4	———	———	———	———	———	———
d (2)	1 9 4	———	———	———	———	———	———
e (1)	0 18 0	———	———	———	———	———	———
f (2)	1 0 0	———	———	———	———	———	———
g (2)	0 12 0	———	———	———	———	———	———
h (1)	0 16 0	———	———	———	———	———	———
i (1)	0 10 0	———	———	———	———	———	———
j (5)	3 10 4	———	———	———	———	———	———
k (7)	4 18 7	———	———	———	———	———	———
6a (1)	1 18 8	———	———	———	———	———	———
b (1)	0 16 4	———	———	———	———	———	———
c (6)	3 4 0	———	———	———	———	———	———
d (3)	2 13 0	———	———	———	———	———	———
7 (7)	1 9 1	———	———	———	———	———	———
8 (13)	6 18 8	———	———	———	———	———	———
9a (5)	2 14 0	———	———	———	———	———	———
b (4)	3 18 8	———	———	———	———	———	———
c (1)	0 2 0	———	———	———	———	———	———
d (8)	3 1 4	———	———	———	———	———	———
e (3)	1 9 0	———	———	———	———	———	———
f (1)	0 0 6	———	———	———	———	———	———
g (7)	3 2 0	———	———	———	———	———	2 17 0
10 (18)	5 7 8	———	———	———	———	———	———

RECEIPTS (continued)

Code No.		1824	1825	1826	1827	1828	1829	1830
11	(8)	4 8 2	——————————————————————————⟩					
12	(3)	0 3 2	0 3 1⁻ ——————————————————⟩					
13	(18)	2 19 8	——————————————⟩ 2 16 8 ——————⟩					
14	(23)	4 6 10	——————————————————————————⟩					
15	(38)	Supered	——————————————————————————⟩					
16	(35)	420 0 0	407 1 0[54]	150 15 0	402 0 0	352 10 0	253 15 0	190 15 0
17	(7)	1057 7 9	1099 5 11	1642 17 1[55]	996 15 3	1101 17 10[56]	1199 14 7	962 17 1
TOTAL		5727 14 2	5854 1 11	6573 6 3	6142 8 11	6132 5 6	6056 5 0	5647 16 1

PAYMENTS

		1824	1825	1826	1827	1828	1829	1830
1	(56)	573 1 1	552 0 5[57]	564 5 9[58]	576 1 0[59]	591 13 0[60]	570 12 5[61]	605 7 3[62]
2	(29)	1327 1 4	1327 2 4[63]	1477 2 4[64]	1477 1 4[65]	1410 8 10[66]	1431 11 8[67]	————⟩
3	(50)	663 10 9	651 15 10	731 2 5	650 6 0	685 15 2 ⎫	1650 2 0	1350 0 8
4	(7)	864 2 6[68]	724 17 11[69]	1516 19 2[70]	1360 16 3[71]	1120 2 9[72] ⎭		
5	(46)	1097 13 8[73]	1034 4 3	1355 16 11	1110 9 0	1103 1 11	1541 8 10	1551 9 7
6	(13)	297 11 5	215 18 6[74]	141 12 1	126 14 9	97 15 6	123 7 0	146 11 0
7a	(3)	3 19 4	4 8 10	4 1 4	2 19 6	3 14 5	3 3 9	4 0 4
b	(18)	11 3 1	58 4 4	25 3 11	21 13 3	11 5 0	16 13 3	23 0 5
TOTAL		4838 3 2	4568 12 5	5816 3 11	5326 1 1	5023 16 7	5336 18 11	5112 0 11

General statement	General statement	General statement	General statement	General statement	General statement	General statement

RECEIPTS

Code No.		1831	1832	1833	1834
1a	(1)	134 5 0	———————————————		
b	(2)	39 16 0[1]	35 5 0[2]	33 0 0[3]	———————
c	(8)	62 9 6[4]	68 15 0[5]	—————————————	
d	(61)	1267 11 8[6]	1242 16 8[7]	1270 10 8[8]	1253 11 2[9]
e	(11)	200 8 6[10]	190 14 6[11]	197 14 6[12]	———————
f	(7)	100 3 6	———————————————		
g	(7)	105 9 9[13]	100 16 0[14]	104 8 4[15]	303 2 2[16]
h	(15)	63 16 2[17]	69 9 0[18]	70 6 10[19]	———————
2a	(5)	854 9 10[20]	761 13 5[21]	850 11 6[22]	818 19 2[23]
b	(28)	249 13 8[24]	246 18 9[25]	242 16 5[26]	———————
3a	(6)	99 6 0[27]	104 6 0[28]	—————————————	
b	(14)	237 15 0[29]	241 10 0[30]	—————————————	
c	(21)	626 11 3[31]	565 1 6[32]	636 12 2[33]	546 9 1[34]
4	(19)	303 3 4[35]	296 4 2[36]	303 3 4[37]	———————
5a	(9)	2 4 8	———————————— [38] ———————		
b	(4)	0 17 10	———————————————————		
c	(3)	1 16 4	———————————————————		
d	(2)	1 9 4	———————————————————		
e	(1)	0 18 0	———————————————————		
f	(2)	1 0 0	———————————————————		
g	(2)	0 12 0	———————————————————		
h	(1)	0 16 0	———————————————————		
i	(1)	0 10 0	———————————————————		
j	(5)	3 10 4	———————————————————		
k	(7)	4 18 7	———————————————————		
6a	(1)	1 18 8	———————————————————		
b	(1)	0 16 4	———————————————————		
c	(6)	3 4 0	———————————————————		
d	(3)	2 13 0	———————————————————		
7	(7)	1 9 1	———————————————————		
8	(13)	6 18 8	———————————————————		
9a	(5)	2 14 0	———————————————————		
b	(4)	3 13 8	———————————————————		
c	(1)	0 2 0	———————————————————		
d	(8)	3 1 4	———————————————————		
e	(3)	1 9 0	———————————————————		
f	(1)	0 0 6	———————————————————		
g	(7)	2 17 0	———————————————————		
10	(18)	5 7 8	———————————————————		

RECEIPTS (*continued*)

Code No.		1831	1832	1833	1834
11	(8)	*4 8 2*	———————————————————————————|		
12	(3)	*0 3 1*	———————————————————————————|		
13	(18)	*2 16 8*	———————————————————————⟩		2 16 2[39]
14	(23)	*4 6 10*	———————————————————————————|		
15	(38)	Supered	———————————————————————————|		
16	(35)	315 0 0	468 15 0	326 5 0	198 0 0
17	(7)	785 11 6[40]	915 19 7	658 10 6	245 5 5
TOTAL		5512 3 5	5609 5 10	5409 11 6	4927 19 10

PAYMENTS

		1831	1832	1833	1834
1	(57)	477 7 1[41]	479 18 6[42]	480 2 11[43]	454 14 9[44]
2	(33)	*1431 11 8*	1448 11 10[45]	1445 16 8[46]	1377 6 8[47]
3	(50)	1602 15 2[48]	1773 5 5[49]	1507 15 9[50]	1492 1 6[51]
5	(2)	1138 18 3[52]	1244 7 11	1125 6 3	1097 0 4
6	(3)	197 17 4	244 19 2	154 3 8	200 11 0
7a	(3)	*4 0 4*	2 18 6	———————⟩	2 17 6
b	(28)	12 15 5	13 13 3	118 8 2	266 7 3[53]
TOTAL		4865 5 3	5207 14 7	4834 11 11	4890 19 0

General statement	General statement	General statement	General statement

NOTES ON SUMMARIES

1688-94

450-1: 1   One tenement sold off.

2   From 1693 onwards, one item in Gallowtree Gate appears to have been moved into the Belgrave Gate section.

3   Nos. 17 and 18 are amalgamated from 1692 on.

4   From 1689 £10 of this is moved into the Charitable Gifts and Uses section.

5   This No. is placed after 27 this year.

6   Part of this No. is entered after 27 this year.

7   A new heading "Fines and Accidental Receipts" replaces Nos. 26 and 27 in position 36 from 1693 on.

8   No. 25 is included in No. 33 from 1693 on.

9   £142 4s. 0d. of this is for new lead pipes for the conduit.

10   Between Nos. 9 and 10 in 1691 is an additional entry of two items dealing with "Interest Money £3 0s. 0d."

11   From 1693–9 this heading is divided into two: (*a*) General; (*b*) Allowance for fee farm rents at 4s. 0d. in the pound.

12   Additional heading after this of six miscellaneous items.

13   Items are in the same order as the previous year but not subdivided. After 1695 the audit would seem to be held at the Horse and Trumpet. The same expenditure as at the Angel formerly is thence incurred under the new heading.

1695-1701

452-3: 1   Nos. 1 and 2 are amalgamated from 1698.

2   The rent of the Sheep pens is reduced from this year.

3   Part payment of one item in this No. is accepted by the Chamberlains.

4   The leasing of the meadows was reorganized this year.

5   New heading "In Soar Lane or Walker's Lane neare the Northgates" comprising two items formerly in Nos. 10b and 10d.

6   Item in Swinesmarket but formerly included in Loseby Lane now added to this No. See corresponding alteration in No. 10j.

7   A sum of 13s. 4d. crossed out with a note in the margin "Not to be in the next rentall". It is discontinued from then on.

8   First item increased by £2.

9   An item of £1 10s. 0d. transferred from No. 12 and for two years, 1697 and 1698, the title of the No. is changed to "In St Nicholas' and St Margaret's parishes".

10   Additional item "Overseers of St Mary's parish for a chamber over the West Gates" 10s. 0d.

11   One item increased by 5s. 0d.

12   From 1696 a new heading "Rents given the Freeschoole and other Charitable uses", normally of 17 items, begins.

13   Increase of 10s. 0d. in rent of Burgess Meadow.

14 Nos. 25, 26, and 27 are now all amalgamated into this heading of "Fines and accidental receipts".

15 Note in margin that 4s. 0d. is not to be included henceforth.

16 Amalgamated with No. 31 from 1696.

17 One item of 8s. 0d. crossed out.

18 From 1697 an item of "Deductions for Taxes" appears. Land tax was usually allowed at the ruling rate.

19 This heading "At the audit held . . . at the Horse and Trumpet" takes the place of the earlier "Paid at the audit held at the Angel" heading.

20 No apparent explanation for the marked decrease.

21 Heading changes this year to "Fees and other payments".

22 This is subdivided for this year into "Taxes at 3s. 0d. per £" (£7 2s. 10d., 37 items) and "Allowed for taxes by Mr Bradley for the first quarterly payments at 2s. 0d. per £" (£14 8s. 11d., 19 items).

23 Nos. 9a and 9b are amalgamated from this year.

pp.
454-5:

1702-8

1 Increased amount for chamber over the East Gates.

2 Increase of £1 in first item.

3 Item for Newarke Mills increased by £15.

4 Item for Newarke Mills reduced by £4.

5 One item increased by £6.

6 Lease of the Shambles (£70) transferred from "Fines and accidental receipts".

7 First item increased by £1.

8 One item of 6s. 8d. struck out and not included in following years.

9 One item reduced by 13s. 4d.

10 Rent for the Shambles and Drapery (£15) crossed out. Mr Pilgrim's rent for the Shambles occurs in "Fines and accidental receipts" from now until 1706 (see note 6).

11 Three items crossed out.

12 One item of £400 is the purchase money from the sale of the Lord's Place in High Street. See R.B.L. no. 132.

13 One item of £200 of White's charity money from Coventry.

14 One item of 6s. 8d. crossed out.

15 Divided into two headings, "Fees and other payments" and "Accidental payments", for 1702–4 only.

16 The summary has final totals which include entries from the "Hospital account book" relating to the setting up of Becket's charity. See R.B.L. nos. 129 and 135.

pp.
456-7:

1709-15

1 First page of accounts this year missing, six items out of a normal 18 are missing.

2 First page of accounts for this year missing (as in note 1).

3 Amount of one item not filled in (usually 2s. 6d.) and rent of Sheep pens and Coker's Kitchen increased by £1.

4 Memo to put an extra item under this heading in the next rental, for "the Swan at the South Gate" 13s. 4d.

5 Rent for shop under the Gainsborough increased by £1.

6 Rent for shop under the Gainsborough crossed out.

7 Reduction because a grazing and not a ploughing rent is charged on one item.

8 Reduction of £30 because a grazing instead of a ploughing rent is charged on Freake's Ground; increase of 10s. 0d. on two smaller items.

9 Increase of £4 for one item.

10 Increase from the rebuilding and re-arrangement of stalls and shops. For details of rebuilding see R.B.L. nos. 270, 272, 275, and 276.

11 This new heading takes in part of No. 4 and all No. 5.

12 An extra page of accounts deals with the expenses of rebuilding in the Saturday Market and includes items for shops taken down, scaffolding etc.

1716-22

pp.
458-9: 1 Increase of £3 on rent of Coker's Kitchen and Sheep pens.

2 An attempt is made here to reference the rental with a series of numbers taking in Nos. 1–15.

3 Decrease of £1 on one item.

4 Extra item of £5 for a windmill rent.

5 First two items both increased from 3s. 4d. to 15s. 0d.

6 Second item increased to £2 15s. 0d. with a note in the margin to "next year charge £5 10s. 0d.".

7 One item increased by £3 10s. 0d. and another by £5.

8 One item of 10s. 0d. crossed out.

9 One item reduced from 15s. 0d. to 1s. 0d.

10 Rent of Richard Scarborough's house increased by £3 10s. 0d. See note 25.

11 First item increased by £1 10s. 0d.

12 Last item changed to "Two new erected houses in the Sanvy Gate" and rent increased from 13s. 4d. to £6 10s. 0d. See note 27.

13 Extra item inserted for the tithes of Housefield Close, part of Dannetts Hall land, £1 10s. 0d.

14 One item added for the use of the chamber over the High Cross, 5s. 0d. and another for the town gaol, £5.

15 One item increased by £1 14s. 2d.

16 One item increased by £4.

17 On the last page under this heading is a detailed note about the payment of Mr Acham's gift. There is another note about the payment of this gift at the end of the Charity Money section in 1724.

18 Rent for land connected with Tamworth's charity increased by £1 16s. 8d.

19 Reduction of £2 as only half a year's rent charged on Burgess Meadow although the rent for the whole year would be increased from £5 to £6.

20 Extra item for "Thomas Wall's windmill" of 2s. 0d.

21 Additional item for putting planks and posts into the river Soar. Note in

pp.
458-9
cont.

the margin against the "Tithe of Gallow Windmill" to leave it out next year.

22 Large amount accounted for by the transfer of £515 11s. 2d. from the last Chamberlains and by allowance of an extra £83 7s. 8d. from the Hospital Account. A further £218 6s. 1d. was received from the Master in Chancery in connection with the case over Sir Thomas White's charity money.

23 A very large number of Freedoms were granted this year which helped to keep the receipts at a high level. They were probably granted for electoral purposes.

24 Below this item and carried over the page are details of an attempt to rectify the accounts, probably inserted by the auditors.

25 £260 paid to the City of Coventry by order of the Court of Chancery. £74 10s. 0d. spent on various bills which come under the heading of Scarborough's House. See R.B.L. nos. 333 and 336.

26 This section is complete but the heading is missed out.

27 Three extra headings at the end of the Payments:
(i) A Particular of the charge of the houses in Loseby Lane built by the Commissioners appointed by the Corporation for their so doing . . . . . . 20 items . . . £177 4s. 4d.
(ii) Expenses for the house in Sanvy Gate by the Commissioners ut supra . . . . . . 15 items . . . £104 11s. 6d.
(iii) Expenses of the house in the North Gate late in the occupation of Ann Morris . . . . . . 15 items . . . £109 4s. 0d.

28 A few miscellaneous items of expenditure included on the last page of the Taxes Allowed; at least one is cut off, so the total is not known.

29 Decrease of one item (? an error in the Chamberlain's copying) and an increase of £4 in rent of land in Leicester Forest.

30 Increase of £5 in rent of land in Leicester Forest.

31 Gift of Mr Hazelrigg reduced by 6d.

32 Page damaged, but total given. Increase of £4 on gift paid from the product of Leicester Forest land.

33 Extra item of £1 from the gift of Mr Thomas Ayre. Increase of £1 in amount from the Leicester Forest land. Comparison with previous year difficult, as 1718 is damaged.

pp.
460-1:

1723-9

1 Half of the first page is missing, but items remaining are the same amounts as in previous years.

2 Rent for the chamber over the East Gates increased by £2 because of the addition of a shop and chamber adjoining.

3 Rent of one meadow increased by £1.

4 Extra item but no amount given.

5 Shambles rent increased by £15 to £85 and first item increased by 3s. 4d.

6 First item increased by 3s. 4d.

7 One item decreased by £1 15s. 0d.

8   The Horsefair Leys split into three items and the rent increased by £4 11s. 0d.

9   Three additional items for Frolesworth and Burbage land (coming to £45 13s. 2d.) purchased the previous year. See note 28.

10   At the bottom of one page of this section is a note, "See Mr Johnson's rentall", and four additional items are given but are not included in the totals at the bottom of the pages. As they do not appear to relate to Belgrave Gate the reason for their inclusion here is not obvious, though a note in 1731 that "These are paid to Mr Mayor" may indicate why the totals are not taken into the accounts. In and after 1771 they are in fact included in the total of No. 11c. They are:

	£	s.	d.
Mr Cooper out of Rawlett's Close the gift of Mrs Twickden	2	0	0
Mr Alcock of Enderby for land there the gift of Mr John Bent to St John's Hospital	30	0	0
Mr Rudings for Duck Holme		13	4
Mr Simpson for Tippets	3	0	0

11   Last item, Scarborough's House, reduced. Noted in the margin "Now set at £3 per annum for 3 years".

12   Extra item of £2 for the Weekday Shambles.

13   A note in the previous year directed that one small item of 8s. 0d. was not to be charged in 1727. The item is in fact entered with another for "Two new erected houses", but the rent for them is not increased.

14   Nos. 15a and 15b are amalgamated from this time.

15   Memo in margin that one item, a house in the Newarke which had been charged at 13s. 4d., had been sold to Baron Carter.

16   An addition of £6 10s. 0d. interest on £130 lent to the parish officers of St Martin. This loan was increased to £300 and the interest to £12 per annum in 1741. In 1755 a third of the loan was repaid and the whole had been paid off by 1757.

17   One item crossed out, two more added.

18   Memo in the margin "To charge Mr Mitchell No. 6 next year in the Shops & No. 7".

19   Fifteen items crossed out and five added.

20   Three items added (£1 5s. 0d.).

21   Marginal note "To be 10s. 0d. only, his shop being pulled down".

22   Item for the tithe of Gallow Windmill (2s. 0d.) left out.

23   Large number of items for Freedoms this year, possibly for electoral purposes.

24   Last three items (£3 0s. 10d.) crossed out.

25   Last two items (£2 6s. 6d.) crossed out.

26   Two shillings charged extra "for seals".

27   Three shillings charged for seals. Beadle's salary increased by £1 6s. 8d.

28   One item of £560 for purchase of the Frolesworth and Burbage estate.

29   Further £200 paid to the heirs of Mr Barwell for the Frolesworth and Burbage estate. On one page twelve items are bracketed together with the note "£72 14s. 4d. being the whole charge of the new building";

pp.
460-1 these items relate to the extension of the town gaol. See R.B.L. no. 449.
cont. 30 The wording "Accidental Payments" is resumed this year. The section had had no heading since 1719.

31 "Pious and Charitable Uses" ceases to form a separate portion of the accounts after 1729. The receipts are included as part of No. 21 in the Receipts, and the payments as part of No. 11 in the Payments portions.

32 8d. added to the gift of Margaret Hobby.

33 One extra item, the gift of Mr Weightman, 5s. 0d.

34 One extra item, the gift of Mr John Ludlam, £2 10s. 0d.

35 A few miscellaneous items not taken into the page totals follow this.

36 Note that the account was not finally settled until 31 May 1734.

pp.
462-3: 1 Note by second item (Rent of Schoolhouse 6d.) "not to be charged this year".

2 Rent of property above and near the East Gates increased by 5s. 0d.

3 Note that the rent of the Newarke Mills is to be increased from £26 to £30 next year.

4 One item increased by £1 15s. 0d.

5 One item reduced to £4.

6 Last item crossed out. Note by another charged at £5 "next year £21".

7 One item increased by £3.

8 Note that land at Burbage was sold to Alderman Hood. See note 26 and note 9.

9 Note by an item of £29 struck out "This sold to Alderman Hood".

10 Rent from land in the Lero (Mr Biller's gift worth £12 per annum) and the application of the £12 are added to the first page of this section but not included in the page totalling.

11 Two additional items, one of £3 10s. 0d., the other not charged.

12 Previous note that one item was to be reduced by £1 10s. 0d. this year.

13 One item reduced by £1.

14 Note by an item of 13s. 4d. "Next year £2".

15 First item (part of Freake's Grounds) increased by £12.

16 Note in previous year that Tamworth's gift to be reduced by £1 5s. 0d.

17 Rent for Ives charity from Swan's Mill (£4 15s. 0d.) struck out.

18 Note that land at Leicester Forest is to be charged at £13 instead of £19 in 1736.

19 Shop previously allowed Mr Noone free charged at £1 10s. 0d.

20 One item reduced by 10s. 0d., stall previously unlet now let at 15s. 0d., three additional stalls let at 10s. 0d. each.

21 Shop No. 8, previously unlet, now let at 15s. 0d. Shop No. 40 "allowed Mr Noone", additional stall let for 5s. 0d. with note "10s. 0d. next year".

22 Two new stalls added.

23 One stall listed as now empty.

24 Note by tithe charge on Paradise Close "to be left out for the future, being exchanged with Mr Bent for other land".

HH

25 Note by tithe charge for Paradise Close that the exchange in note 24 was not effected and the charge is to stand.

26 This includes a payment of £600 by Mr Hood for Burbage land.

27 Apart from the balance of about £500 from the late Chamberlain's Accounts usually included under this heading, there are balances of small sums for four "several late Chamberlains".

28 Three payments in this section have marginal notes "leave this out next year" amounting to 10s. 3d. In the following year this is done, but the payments are added to the end of No. 4.

29 An item of £10 to one of the vicars is unpaid this year.

30 See note 28.

31 Mayor's salary increased to £40 and payment of £10 to one of the vicars resumed.

32 Item of £312 10s. 0d. noted "Mr Edmund Ludlam principal and interest of £300 in full".

33 This heading now divided into two sections, (a) Accidental Payments, (b) Bills Paid. The first section has one item "Paid Mr Mayor and Mr Howkins money laid out about the Bowling Green House". See R.B.L. nos. 492 and 502.

34 Item of £60 10s. 4d. for "Mr Mayor's expences in Solliciting the Parliament about making the river navigable". See R.B.L. no. 531.

35 Heading changed to "allowance of taxes at 1s. 6d. in the pound".

36 Heading "allowance of taxes at 1s. 0d. in the pound".

37 Heading "allowance of taxes at 1s. 6d. in the pound".

38 Heading "allowance of taxes at 2s. 0d. in the pound".

39 Heading "allowance of taxes at 2s. 0d. in the pound".

40 Heading "allowance of taxes at 2s. 0d. in the pound".

41 £1 5s. 0d. less on Tamworth's gift.

42 Two extra gifts totalling £1 10s. 0d.

43 Mr Bent's and Mr Haslerigg's gifts both increased.

44 Gift from Leicester Forest land reduced by £5.

45 Gift from Leicester Forest land reduced by another £1.

46 Note at the end of the summary that the accounts were settled 11 May 1737.

47 Note about settling accounts added on 11 May and 5 September 1737.

48 Note at end of summaries for this and the next two years that the accounts were settled 13 September 1737.

1737-43

1 Rent of Sheep pens reduced by £5.

2 Numbers from "The Old Rentall" indicated by the side of various items in this year's accounts.

3 One item reduced by £1.

4 Part of the Newarke Mills and Meadow reduced by £5.

5 Note that the last item, a windmill near the highway coming from Horse Fair Close, previously charged at 7s. 6d., is to be left out next year, as the

pp.
464-5
cont.

house, watermill, windmill, and holmes are let to John Brookes by lease for £20 per year.

6 £5 rent for the North Mills and a windmill in the tenancy of John Brookes left out, and his rent reduced from £26 to £20, in consideration of his working a bolting mill at his own expense.

7 Note that 10s. 0d. is to be left out from one rent.

8 Rent of two houses reduced.

9 Rent for the herbage of St Mary's churchyard increased from 10s. 0d. to £2. Another item sold off.

10 Note by entry for Freake's Ground "This was £36 a year whilst plowed but the plowing time is expired which reduces the rent to £24".

11 Piece of ground in the Water Laggs previously rented at 10s. 0d. now sold.

12 Land used for the Countess of Devonshire's charity reduced by £1 10s. 0d.

13 Interest on money lent to St Martin's parish reduced by £1 6s. 0d.

14 Interest on money lent to St Martin's parish increased by £6 16s. 0d.

15 Bottom of page missing but apparently same as previous year.

16 Several shops and stalls described as empty.

17 Six shops empty but several rents not charged last year because the tenants had only just taken stalls are now charged.

18 Ten shops and stalls now empty.

19 Four shops empty but eight stalls leased at 10s. 0d. each.

20 Subdivided into "Chief rents belonging to St Margaret's Guild" (16 items, £1 3s. 3d.) and "Chief rents for cocks, capons and hens belonging to the late College of St Mary's Leicester over against the Castle, due and payable at Michaelmas only for ever" (31 items £3 2s. 7d.). Heading from the Old Rental used for this year only.

21 Five extra items but only two charged.

22 Payment of £10 to one of the town vicars not included.

23 Payment of £10 to another of the town vicars left out, Macebearer's salary increased by £1.

24 Macebearer's salary increased by £1, those of Sergeants at Mace by £4.

25 1s. 0d. extra for a seal.

26 Payment of £42 11s. 7d. for "Expences on Account of the severall Treasonable papers Stuck up in Severall parts of the Town by the Whiggs on the First day of February 1737, highly reflecting upon His Majesties Person and Government and the Government of this Corporation, and Defending our Innocence against the Malicious Aspersions therein Charged". See R.B.L. no. 539.

27 This section has a further subdivision this year, "Tradesmen's Bills paid for work etc. at the North Mills", containing fifteen bills amounting to £178 7s. 8d. See R.B.L. nos. 576 and 578.

28 Including four bills under a separate heading for repairs to the Swan's Mill £3 6s. 2d.

29 Heading "allowance of taxes at 2s. 0d. in the pound".

30 Heading "allowance of taxes at 4s. 0d. in the pound", and in 1742–7.

31   Allowance of tax for John Brookes for the North Mill reduced by 18s. 0d.

32   Sutton's gift to St John's Hospital added (£2 16s. 0d.).

33   Sutton's gift increased to £3 12s. 0d.

34   Sutton's gift split into two parts (£2 16s. 0d. to St John's Hospital, 16s. 0d. to Trinity Hospital). Benjamin Garland's gift makes another item.

35   Special heading inserted for "The Account of Expenses in repairing the Church Gate". Among the items are 152 loads of stones (£32 13s. 4d.) and payments for getting 202 loads of gravel; also "for boreing of Gravel and fetching the Machine from Quorndon". See R.B.L. nos. 648, 656, 658, and 661.

1744-50

1   Rent of Sheep pens reduced by £5 to £10.

2   Rent of Sheep pens reduced to £9.

3   Rent for Shambles increases from £85 to £140. The Shambles were rebuilt at the same time as the Gainsborough. See note 7.

4   Rent of Shambles reduced by £20. See R.B.L. nos. 735, 737, 742, and 745.

5   Rent of ground reduced by 10s. 0d. because house pulled down.

6   Extra item after a shop and buildings on the east side of the Round Hill. The occupier to pay another 1s. 0d. "for an acknowledgment for erecting 4 columns upon the Corporation ground belonging to the aforesaid building".

7   Rent of Leicester Forest land increased by £2 10s. 0d.

8   Rent of Leicester Forest land increased by £3 to £18.

9   Rent of Burgess Meadow reduced by 10s. 0d.

10   Same number of shops let, but one increased by 10s. 0d.

11   Additional shop let at £1 12s. 6d.

12   Instead of rents from the Saturday Market shops and stalls, four items, without a heading, for "ground lately built upon taken from the Sheep Pens". In September 1748, Thomas Johnson leased the newly erected Shambles in the Saturday Market, including the stalls, for £140. See note 3 above and R.B.L. nos. 717, 735, 737, 742, and 745.

13   £300 from the executors of Mr Thomas Ludlam who left it for charitable uses; 4 per cent interest to be paid by the Corporation.

14   1s. 0d. less for seals.

15   5s. 0d. extra for seals.

16   4s. 0d. less for seals.

17   Memo at the end of the list of Tradesmen's Bills that "this year the Gainsborough was rebuilt". This accounts for several heavy bills, e.g. £92 2s. 8d. to John Wood stonemason, and £200 16s. 7d. to John Westley builder. In this section of accidental payments is an item for "the inscription on the New Gainsborough" and several payments for stonemason's work. See R.B.L. nos. 710 and 714.

18   Under this heading and the following one are items connected with the case of George Smith (alias Green) *vs.* the Corporation. See R.B.L. nos.

727, 728, 731, and 744. Also several items connected with a petition and Bill for Lighting, Watching, and Cleaning the streets. See R.B.L. no. 732.

19   Augustine Heafford's allowance for taxes cut from £2 4s. 0d. to £1 10s. 0d.

20   Heading "Allowance for taxes 4s. 0d. in the pound for the first half year and . . . 3s. 0d. in the pound for the last half year".

21   Gift from Leicester Forest land increased by £2 10s. 0d.

22   Gift from Leicester Forest land increased by a further £2 10s. 0d.

23   Memo that Mr Topp's charity be included next year (£1 to Trinity Hospital, 10s. 0d. to St John's Hospital).

24   Topp's charity and Mr Ludlam's bequest (£12 per annum) account for increase.

1751-7

1   Half of first page missing, but all other amounts as usual.

2   In this year and subsequent years until 1782–3 items in the receipts are numbered in the margin with numbers "In the Rentall 1652", and under Nos. 11c, 15a, and 31 in this year and the following one the headings used in the 1652 rental are included, but this being a temporary measure the more recent arrangement is retained here.

3   Alterations under this heading and the next are due to a re-arrangement of the South Fields, converting them to grass ground and making three large farms. Riots resulted from the freemen's fear that their common rights would be restricted by this re-arrangement. See R.B.L. nos. 760, 762, 765, 767, 768, 773, 774, 778, 779, 781, 787, 789, 795, 799, and 801.

4   One item reduced from £6 to £5.

5   Marginal note by item for Shambles "Next year charge this to Mr Higginson £122 10s. 0d." (Increase of £2 10s. 0d.)

6   Rent of one item—house, barn, and several leys in the Horse Fair—reduced from £24 to £7 10s. 0d.

7   Rent of item mentioned in note 6 above raised from £7 10s. 0d. to £15.

8   One item increased by £1.

9   One item increased from 6s. 8d. to £1 15s. 0d.

10   £7 for tithe hay in re-arranged South Fields deleted because included in farms' rents. See note 3 above.

11   Rent for Freake's Ground increased from £30 to £35 and marginal note "this to be charged £40 next year".

12   Rent from Burgess Meadow reduced by £1.

13   Interest of £300 lent to St Martin's parish reduced from £12 to £8. Marginal note "part of this £300 is paid in".

14   Last item—£8 interest from loan to St Martin's parish—not entered, because loan repaid. See notes 17 and 18.

15   Six items (£2) relating to re-arranged South Fields land deleted. See note 3 above.

16   Increase of entries due to large number of freemen being enrolled just before 1754 election.

17 Includes £100 from parish officers of St Martin—part of £300 borrowed from Corporation.

18 Includes £100, remaining part of loan to St Martin's parish.

19 This includes an item of 2s. 0d. "Allowed Widow Bothamley when she paid her rent on account of the 11 days being shortened in September last".

20 After this date heading is "Fees and other payments".

21 Several items of expenditure involved in dealing with offenders in South Fields riots. See note 3.

22 Several items of expenditure for proceedings against offenders in South Fields riots. See note 3, including over £160 for Mr Halford, the Solicitor, in law charges.

23 Heading "Allowance of taxes at 3s. 0d. in the Pound for the first halfe year and at 2s. 0d. in the pound for the last halfe year".

24 Heading "Allowance of taxes at 2s. 0d. in the Pound".

25 Heading as previous year. See note 24.

26 Heading "Allowance of taxes, at 2s. 0d. in the Pound for the first half year and 4s. 0d. for the last".

27 Heading "Allowance of taxes at 4s. 0d. in the Pound".

28 Heading "Allowance of taxes at 4s. 0d. in the Pound" from 1757 to 1763.

29 Note at end "Settled March 17th, 1757".

pp.
470-1:

1758-64

1 2s. 6d. formerly paid by vicar of St Martin's for part of the Town Hall "now used with the Viccaridge house" not included this year.

2 Gosling Close let in two parts—the first at £16 5s. 0d., the second at £15 —instead of the whole Close let at £24 as previously. Marginal note of change of tenant and second part to be increased to £20 in following year.

3 See note 2 above.

4 Rent of part of Gosling Close reduced from £20 to £15.

5 Rent of three main farms increased by a total of £25.

6 First two items of meadow amalgamated as one item at £30 instead of £29 10s. 0d.

7 One rent increased from £15 to £24.

8 Last item increased from £7 to £8.

9 Rent of Frolesworth land increased from £16 to £21 10s. 0d.; marginal note that it is to be £27 next year.

10 Rent for chamber over the West Gates increased from 10s. 0d. to 19s. 0d.

11 Rent of one item increased from £2 to £5 10s. 0d.

12 First item £1 16s. 9d. instead of £5 10s. 0d. Note that £3 13s. 6d. to be charged next year.

13 See note 12.

14 First item £5 10s. 0d. instead of £3 13s. 6d. See note 12.

15 Herbage of St Mary's churchyard increased from £2 to £3 5s. 0d.

16 Rent of 5s. 0d. for chamber over High Cross crossed out; in 1758 the High Cross is mentioned as being decayed and the materials from it were sold in 1769. See R.B.L. nos. 834, 941, and 946.

pp.
470-1
cont.

17 Rent of part of Freake's Ground increased from £24 to £25.

18 Rent of part of Freake's Ground increased from £25 to £26.

19 Rent of lands out of which Norris's charity paid increased from £8 to £11, and rent of lands out of which Countess of Devonshire's charity paid increased from £5 to £7 10s. 0d.

20 Rent of land out of which Tamworth's charity paid increased from £7 10s. 0d. to £9 2s. 6d.

21 Rent of land from which Countess of Devonshire's charity paid decreased from £7 10s. 0d. to £6 15s. 0d. Rent of land from which Tamworth's charity paid increased by £4 2s. 6d.

22 Another item—2s. 6d. for piece of ground adjoining West Bridge— added to these.

23 Tithe of Beadhouse Meadow same amount as formerly, but made into one item instead of two. An additional item of 1s. 0d. for setting posts in River Soar.

24 Two items for setting posts in River Soar (totalling 1s. 6d.) deleted.

25 One item of £100 left by Mr Joseph Cradock towards rebuilding of Trinity Hospital. Until such rebuilding undertaken, interest to be paid to the poor of the Hospital.

26 Heading for 1764–5 and 1765–6 "Allowance of Land tax at 4s. 0d. in the Pound". Amount for North Mill increased from £3 5s. 0d. to £3 5s. 6d.; amount for Swan's Mill reduced by 6s. 0d.

27 Same items as before —one increased from 1s. 0d. to 1s. 9d.

28 Same items—that for Swan's Mill reduced from 18s. 0d. to 16s. 0d.

pp.
472-3:

1765-71

1 Half a year's rent of the Newarke Mills on the old lease at the rate of £25 per annum and the other half year at rate of £30 per annum account for increase.

2 Full year's rent of Newarke Mills at rate of £30 per annum accounts for increase. See note 1.

3 Extra item—rent of the Holmes, £6 10s. 0d.—inserted.

4 Additional item included at end of this section, but like two others with it no amount given.

5 Rent of Shambles reduced from £125 to £110; another item increased by £1 6s. 0d.

6 Rent of first item increased from 15s. 0d. to £1.

7 See note 6 above—two items now one, rent £4 instead of £1 15s. 0d.

8 One item normally £24 paid for half year only, so reduction of £12. Marginal note by this payment "to be altered next year".

9 The payment referred to in note 8 is now increased to £50 per annum; only a quarter year's rent due (£12 10s. 0d.), which accounts for increase of 10s. 0d. over last year. Marginal note that £50 be charged for next year.

10 See note 9 above.

11 £40 instead of £50 charged on one item.

12 One item reduced by £1.

13 See 1758–64 note 9.

14 One item increased by £1.

15 Rent of land from which Countess of Devonshire's charity paid decreased by 15s. 0d.; rent of land out of which Tamworth's charity paid increased by £2 15s. 0d. Rent of land from which Nidd's charity paid increased from £32 to £50 10s. 0d.

16 Rent from Leicester Forest land increased from £18 to £28.

17 Rent from Leicester Forest land increased from £28 to £35; rent from Allexton Land (Haine's charity) increased from £19 to £21 10s. 0d., with note that next year to be £24.

18 Rent of land at Bushby from which Nidd's charity paid increased by 10s. 0d. to £51. Rent of land at Allexton from which Haine's charity paid increased by £2 10s. 0d. to £24.

19 Increase over previous year due to: (*a*) rent of land for Nidd's charity increased by £25 to £37; (*b*) rent of land for Norris's gift increased by £5 to £16.

20 Large amount due to £1,287 10s. 0d. received from Mr John Holmes. The Corporation to pay interest to him for life and after his death to pay an annuity of £45 per annum to the poor of Trinity Hospital, £6 10s. 0d. to poor of St John's and the same to Bent's Hospital. See R.B.L. nos. 913 and 915.

21 Increase of entries due to large number of freemen being enrolled just before the 1765 election.

22 Includes a cash item "for Lead at the Cross" (£12 2s. 0d.). See note 16, 1758–64.

23 Between Nos. 33 and 36 occurs a supplementary rental. See transcript of 1771–2 accounts for items and amounts involved.

24 One item—4s. 0d.—left out.

25 Heading "Allowance for Land tax at 3s. 6d. in the pound".

26 Heading "Allowance for Land tax at 3s. 0d. in the pound". One item for £6 16s. 10d. erased.

27 Heading as in note 26. One item increased by 9d., another overcharged by 2s. 0d., and one item £1 19s. 0d. for Forest Closes deleted, with note "not to be charged again, not being paid by the Chamberlains".

28 Heading as in note 25.

29 Tamworth's gift increased by £8 5s. 0d. and Mr Nidd's gift by £18 10s. 0d.

30 Gift from Leicester Forest land increased from £18 to £28, see note 16. In addition gift of Mr John Holmes paid to Trinity Hospital (£45) and to St John's Hospital (£6 10s.). See note 20 for details of founding of Holmes charity.

31 Gift from Leicester Forest land increased from £28 to £35. Mr Haines gift increased from £19 to £21 10s. 0d.

32 Nidd's gift increased by 10s. 0d.; Haine's gift increased by £2 10s. 0d. See note 18. Gift of Mrs Hobby decreased by 8d. to £1 1s. 0d.

33 Heading "Allowance for land tax at 3s. 6d. in the pound". See transcript of 1771–2 accounts for items and amounts involved.

pp.
472-3
cont.

34   In this and subsequent years a note follows the usual Supers that certain Vicarial and Lammas tithes are to be supered, "the same having been agreed to be taken in kind". After deductions for taxes are accounted for the amount of these tithes is added to the usual supers. In this summary this amount is counted as one supered item, because only folio references to amounts are given, not all the individual items. In and after 1794–5 the supered items are indicated in the section for Lammas tithes. See 1793–9 note 65. See R.B.L. nos. 940, 948, and 950.

pp.
474-5

1772-8

1   Item for chamber over East Gates (£5) left out. The town gates were demolished early in 1774. See R.B.L. nos. 990 and 993.

2   Rent of Sheep pens increased by £11 to £20.

3   Rent of Forest Closes increased by £3 10s. 0d. to £12 10s. 0d.

4   One extra item included (£4) and rent of Forest Closes increased by £3 10s. 0d. to £16; the three main South Fields farms and brickyard land are only charged half a year's rent, which reduces them by £139. (Overall reduction is £131 10s. 0d.) Half year only charged because of the proposed enclosure of the South Fields; when the Bill for this failed the fields were re-arranged in a number of small lots. See next year's entry for this heading. See also R.B.L. nos. 1014, 1015, 1021, and 1022.

5   This section now divided into two: (a) Beadhouse Meadows (two items); (b) South Fields (29 items). See note 4 above.

6   Only half a year's rent (£8 14s. 3d.) charged for one item in Gallowfield.

7   One item charged £2 10s. 0d. instead of £6 6s. 0d., and marginal note "half year only at £5".

8   See note 7.

9   Amount is not reduced although one item omitted because the payment for that item was a "damask rose at midsummer".

10   One item in Sanvey Gate increased by 5s. 0d. to £3.

11   Items and amounts mentioned in note 10 for 1723–9 and in note 10 for 1730–6, which were formerly entered under this heading but did not appear to be part of it because amounts were not included in the page totals, are now added in as part of this section.

12   Item for West Gates charged (see note 1 above), but repaid under heading 4 of payments. This item (19s. 0d.) is deleted in subsequent years.

13   See note 12.

14   Rent of first item—house and garden near the South Gates—reduced by £3 to £2 10s. 0d. Probably only part of year charged because of change of tenancy; next year it goes up to £5.

15   See note 14.

16   Item for Easter duties in St Mary's parish reduced by 4d. to 3s. 0d.

17   Easter duties of St Mary's parish 3s. 4d. as usual, not 3s. 0d. as in last two years. Increase from £2 to £9 10s. 0d. on house and garden in St Nicholas's parish.

18   Rent of one item 15s. 1d. instead of £1 5s. 0d., "being half a year and half a quarter due at Michaelmas". Marginal note that £2 5s. 0d. be charged next year.

pp.
474-5 19 Rent for cottage near the Horse Fair increased from £1 5s. 0d. to
cont. £2 2s. 0d.

20 Rent used for Norris's gift £14 instead of £16.

21 One item (2s. 0d.) omitted this year.

22 Item omitted last year included again.

23 Includes £31 17s. 4d. for sale of materials when the town gates were demolished. See note 1. Materials sold for £84 2s. 11d., but demolition expenses and compensation for a house pulled down to "widen the Passage" amount to £52 5s. 7d.

24 Includes an item of £10 17s. 8d. for compilation of a book containing an account of the charities of Leicester with table of when charity money to be paid. (This account is in Leicester Museum Department of Archives. BR III/2/125.)

25 No. 8, Church, Poor, and Highway Levies for St Mary's Fields, starts this year.

26 This section is on a separate page but has no heading this year, although the items are similar to those of the previous year, with the addition of items for South Fields land tax up to Lady Day 1780.

27 Heading as in note 33 for 1765–71. Marginal note by an item for 3s. 0d. that it should be 3s. 6d., and by another for 12s. 9d. that it should be 13s. 9d. This extra 1s. 6d. allowed for in the summary at the end of the accounts.

28 Heading "Allowance for Land tax at 4s. 0d. in the Pound".

29 Heading as in note 28. Back to 65 items and much increased amount because three payments covering the land tax of the South Fields from Michaelmas 1777 to Lady Day 1779 are included.

30 Heading "Allowance of Land tax at 4s. 0d. in the Pound". Item for South Fields land tax is now included under the heading for "Church, Poor and Highway Levies for St. Mary's fields".

31 Two additional items: Mr Cradock's gift to Trinity Hospital (£4 per annum), and Mr Andrew's gift to same (5s. 0d. per annum).

32 Five items previously entered as receipts paid to the Mayor under No. 11c now included both in the rental (see note 11) and in these payments. The total of these five is £65 2s. 0d.

33 Mr Norris's gift increased by £2 to £10.

34 Although several items in Supers crossed out, total amount more because the allowance for taxes (£2 19s. 1d.) in the supered tithes has also been crossed out. See note 34 for 1765–71.

35 Two items of land tax not charged in No. 9 included at end (£4 1s. 0d.).

36 Summary mainly of receipts and payments not included in the main accounts.

pp. **1779-85**

476-7: 1 One item of meadow (£3) transferred from No. 5, and included with the item for the Newark Mills and Meadow in this section. Last year only £1 10s. 0d. charged for this item.

2 Five items of meadow previously under South Fields, now added to Beadhouse Meadows, account for this increase.

3 One rent, which in last year's accounts was described as "not fixed", now only £1 10s. 0d. instead of £3. Note at end of the last five items that next year they must be inserted after the South Fields entries, e.g. as in 1779–80 (see note 2), but this was not done.

4 The five items added under this heading in 1781–2 are now placed after the South Fields section.

5 Two items in Gallowfield (one mentioned in note 5 in 1772–8) now let for £14 17s. 10d., instead of £28 4s. 9d. as last year. Three additional items of meadow let for £15.

6 Reduction partly due to transfer mentioned in note 2, partly to several items being left out; but in some cases rents for items left appear to have been reduced.

7 Extra item—one farmer fined £8 for ploughing; also one item with changed tenant increased from £28 8s. 9d. to £36 15s. 0d.

8 £8 ploughing fine—see note 7 above—included under No. 36.

9 The South Fields are now divided into four headings:

> No. 6. South Fields
> No. 7. St Mary's Meadow
> No. 8. Far Meadow
> No. 9. Hall's Grange and Meadows

In the original accounts items in the first three of the above sections are tabulated to give numbers in "Mr Ashmore's plan", acreage rented, and in which of the three fields—Gallowfield, Middlefield, or Rowdike field—it is situated. Note by one item charged £1 10s. 0d. "not collected this year".

10 One item transferred as in note 1 above accounts for reduced amount. Another item has been transferred from one tenant to another, thus reducing the items but not the amount charged.

11 Rent of North Mill Holmes increased by £1 15s. 0d. to £8 5s. 0d. with marginal note that next year it be £10.

12 Rent of North Mill Holmes increased by £1 15s. 0d. to £10.

13 House formerly listed under Soar Lane and now under this heading accounts for the differences in Nos. 10b and 10c.

14 Rent of Recorder's house reduced this year because of his death; his widow paid £30 instead of the usual £40, and another tenant paid £7 10s. 0d. for a quarter's rent of ground and barns.

15 Two additional items of rents to go towards payment of Mr Blunt's gift and Mr Bent's gift (£12 10s. 0d.).

16 Easter duties of St Mary's parish increased by 2d. to 3s. 6d.

17 Easter duties of St Mary's parish 3s. 4d. instead of 3s. 6d. as last year— see note 16.

18 Item for Easter duties of St Mary's parish left in, but no amount entered.

19 Same as in note 18, with marginal note "not collected this year".

20 Item for Easter duties of St Mary's parish (3s. 4d.) crossed out.

21 Rent for two Freake's Ground Closes increased; one by £13 12s. 0d. to £39 12s. 0d., the other by £3 10s. 0d. to £43 10s. 0d.

22 Rent used for paying Nidd's charity reduced by £9 to £42.

pp.
476-7
cont.

23　See note 33 for 1786–92. Heading now merely "Levies".

24　Rent of land for Norris's gift increased by £1 to £14 again (see note 23); rent of land for Tamworth's gift increased by £28 5s. 0d. to £44 5s. 0d.

25　Item for house adjoining Free School 2s. 6d. instead of 3s. 0d. as previously; this tithe is noted as being either 3s. 0d. or 2s. 6d.

26　Note by charge for the house adjoining the Free School "make this 3s. 0d." The charge is listed as being either 2s. 6d. or 3s. 0d.—for last year and this year 2s. 6d. has been charged.

27　Payments for 79 freedoms included.

28　£14 18s. 6d. paid to officers of St Mary's parish for church, poor, and highways levy.

29　Includes £12 10s. 0d. for Blunt's gift and Bent's gift paid to Chamberlains for 1782–3. See note 43.

30　Included £50 10s. 0d. land tax for St Mary's fields for preceding year, which was omitted from accounts of that year.

31　£51 16s. 9d. paid to land tax collector for South Fields tax.

32　No separate heading, but separate page as in previous year. See note 26 for 1772–8.

33　This section discontinued from this year until 1785–6—the amount is covered by entries under other headings; see notes 28 and 31.

34　No. 8, which up to 1781–2 was inserted in the original accounts after No. 9, now precedes it with heading "Church, Poor and Highway Levies for St Mary's Fields".

35　Heading as in note 30 for 1772–8.

36　Heading as in note 30 for 1772–8.

37　Heading as in note 30 for 1772–8.

38　Heading as in note 30 for 1772–8. Two extra items—one for 8s. 0d., one for land tax of St Mary's fields and meadows (£51 16s. 9d. previously included under No. 8).

39　Notes by several items of increases proposed for next year. Heading as in note 30 for 1772–8.

40　Includes £50 10s. 0d. land tax for St Mary's fields, and increases in several items as proposed in notes inserted last year. Heading "Allowance for land tax at 4s. 0d. in the Pound" for this year and until subsequent ones.

41　Two additional items, Mr Blunt's gift (£10) and Mr Bent's gift to St John's Hospital from houses in Silver Street (£2 10s. 0d.), make up the regular entries. At the end are added on this occasion a note of rents and gifts as paid to Trinity Hospital for the period Michaelmas 1779 to Lady Day 1780. (Total paid £17 1s. 6d.) These payments (which apparently duplicate items in the regular payments) were made when the Duchy of Lancaster reorganized the financial administration of the Hospital early in 1780.

42　See first sentence of note 41 above regarding additional regular entries.

43　Nidd's charity reduced by £9 to £42. A note in this section that Blunt's gift and Mr Bent's gift amounting to £12 10s. 0d. not paid to Chamberlain for this year until after the accounts audited; hence the reduced total of items and amount.

pp.
476-7 44 Items as usual. See note 43.
cont. 45 Tamworth's gift increased by £28 5s. 0d. to £44 5s. 0d.
46 Supers entered as usual but the payments of tithes which from 1768–9 onwards were taken in kind "being refused a suit in the Exchequer has been commenced and the same is now in litigation". See R.B.L. nos. 1153, 1159, 1166, 1181, 1186, and 1200 for settlement of this case.
47 Situation about supered tithes same as in note 46 above.
48 Supers entered as usual, with note about tithes being taken in kind as it was before 46, see above. See also note 34 for 1765–71.
49 Summary contains details of further items supered, amounting to £350 5s. 0d.
50 Various items not received or paid in proper place entered in this summary. Also a detailed note on errors in the accounts entered when they were audited—30 May 1788.
51 Summary followed by auditor's note of corrections made on 30 May 1788.
52 At the back of this volume of accounts are three loose papers with auditor's notes made in 1788 of errors in the 1782–3 accounts and the 1783–4 accounts. Subsequently these have been copied into the volumes concerned; see notes 50 and 51.
53 Includes several payments omitted in the general account.

pp.   **1786-92**

478-9: 1 Acreages that each tenant holds in particular fields not given this year or 1791–2.
2 Only half a year's rent charged for Sheep pens (£10) and ground rents this year account for reduction under Nos. 1, 3, 5, 10a, 10d, 10i, 11c, 14b, 14f, 15a, 20, and 21. Note on the cover of this volume as follows: "Messrs Swinfen and Parsons made the payments for a whole year and received a whole years rent of the Fee farm and Chief rents but of the ground and sheep pens only such as were due at Michaelmas 1789, in consequence of the power of (? an order) made at a Common Hall held on the 23rd February, 1790. 'Ordered that Messrs Swinfen and Parsons the late Chamberlains shall receive only such rents as were due to this Corporation at Michaelmas last in order that the debts which may be owing from the Corporation may be the sooner paid'."
3 See note 2.
4 Rent of tenement in Northgate Street £2 10s. 0d. due to change of tenancy. Marginal note "£2 next year".
5 See note 4.
6 All these items except one—the weekday Shambles—are half year's rent only. See note 2.
7 First item increased by £4 to £8.
8 First item reduced by 10s. 0d. to £7 10s. 0d.
9 Rent of Recorder's house now £50. See note 14 for 1779–85.
10 See note 2.
11 See note 2.

12 One item increased by £1 5s. 0d. to £5 5s. 0d.

13 See note 2.

14 See note 2.

15 Rent of first item increased by £2 3s. 6d. to £3 13s. 6d., but only half a year charged.

16 See note 15.

17 One item increased by £1 10s. 0d. to £2 5s. 0d.; marginal note that it should differ in 1793–4 because this figure is for three-quarters of a year.

18 See note 2.

19 See note 2.

20 Rent of one item increased by £4 to £10.

21 See note 2.

22 Item for town gaol (£3) crossed out with note "Gaol sold".

23 See note 2.

24 One item increased by £2 18s. 0d. to £5.

25 Rent of land for Norris's gift reduced by £2 to £12.

26 See note 2.

27 Tithe for house adjoining Free School increased from 3s. 6d. to 4s. 0d. See note 26 for 1779–85.

28 One extra item (1s. 0d.). Reduction of 6d. because tithe on house adjoining the Free School 3s. 6d. instead of 4s. 0d. (Note says "3s. 6d. or 4s. 0d. varied annually".)

29 Reduction of 1s. 0d. because tithe on house adjoining Free School 3s. 0d. instead of 4s. 0d. (Note says "2s. 6d. or 3s. 0d., varied annually".) See also note 28.

30 Large number of Freedoms accounts for increase; probably enrolled because of 1790 election.

31 Large number of Freedoms, probably because of 1790 election; £256 6s. 3d. of this amount are arrears transferred from 1788–9 accounts.

32 Includes £107 12s. 6d., half the fee of the Mayor's Counsel at the "late contested Election", the other half being paid by Samuel Smith, one of the members. Also includes £15 for the late Town Clerk for "Precedents kept at the 'Change which were destroyed in the late Riots there".

33 No heading. Treated as one item "several Levies for the Church, Poor and Highways, for the Tythes in St Mary's fields and meadows".

34 See note 33. Heading now merely "Levies".

35 Several items crossed out.

36 Two items crossed out (5s. 10d.).

37 Several items, including the land tax for St Mary's fields, paid for half year only. See note 2.

38 One item for 4s. 0d. previously crossed out now included, but another item reduced by 4s. 0d.

39 Several items altered.

40 One item (13s. 0d.) not included because no rent received. Several items reduced in amount without explanation.

41 Various items altered—some rents not paid, so allowance not made. Also an extra item.

pp.
478-9 42 Forming part of the summary are details of bad debts and arrears. Seven
cont. bonds and a promissory note, dated between 1724 and 1753, are considered irrecoverable by the Committee appointed to audit the accounts.
The £120 13s. 0d. which is the amount involved is treated as a payment
so that the true balance of the accounts may be seen; previously these
bad debts had been treated as part of the balance transferred to the new
Chamberlains each year. Similarly the auditors directed that rent arrears
which had accumulated to a total of £256 6s. 3d. should be deducted
from the stated balance to show the cash balance. A detailed statement
of arrears from 1769 onwards is attached to the page following the
summary.

43 Detailed statement of arrears precedes the summary.

44 Several items altered.

45 Statement of arrears as in 1789–90.

pp. **1793-9**

480-1: 1 New lease of Sheep pens from the middle of this year, at £40 per annum
instead of £20; half a year at old rent and half at the new one.

2 First item included at the usual rate for half a year; for the remaining
half year and subsequent year it is split into seven smaller items. Forest
Closes included in this section as usual, but rent increased by £6 4s. 0d.
to £22 4s. 0d.

3 Increase due to full year's rent being charged on the re-arranged plots.

4 Further re-arrangement of the South Fields and Meadows and of
Freake's Grounds took place this year. See R.B.L. nos. 1156, 1158, 1172,
1180, 1183–5, 1189, and 1190. This was done in the middle of a financial
year, so amounts and number of items vary for each half year. The
summary is arranged as before and the new headings not used until the
first full year's operation of the new scheme—1796–7. The number of
items in the first half of the year is the same as indicated from 1792–5;
in the second half as in subsequent years. Many other ground rents were
increased in the first full year of the new scheme; see notes for 1796–7.

5 Item for the Workhouse piece normally included but no amount entered,
now pays £1 1s. 0d.

6 Rent of one farm increased by 8s. 0d.

7 Same items as previously, but three of them increased by a total of
£4 7s. 0d.

8 First item increased by £2 to £3 per annum, but only half a year charged
at the new rate, so increase of 10s. 0d. only.

9 As well as 10s. 0d. increase mentioned in note 8, increase of £2 4s. 6d. on
another item for three quarters of a year.

10 One item reduced by £2 4s. 6d. because let for only half a year.

11 Rent of one house increased by £5 10s. 0d. to £10 10s. 0d.

12 One item of three houses £6 instead of £8 because one house unoccupied.

13 First item increased by £2 2s. 0d. to £8 2s. 0d.; see note 12. Note that in
1794–5 rent to be £12 12s. 0d. per annum. Last item leased to new
tenant and rent increased by £12 16s. 0d. to £16 16s. 0d.

14   See note 13.

15   One rent reduced by £8 3s. 0d. to £8 13s. 0d. because, on failure of previous lease, property relet for part of the year only.

16   Rent mentioned in note 15 increased by £2 18s. 0d. to £11 11s. 0d. because property let for three quarters of a year.

17   Last item let at increased rent for last half of the year. Next year this item to be increased by £3 10s. 0d.

18   See note 17.

19   Three houses in Sanvey Gate, formerly separate items, now all leased to same person, and rent increased by £5 7s. 6d. to £13 2s. 6d. One item (1s. 0d.) unpaid.

20   Item formerly 1s. 0d. (not paid last year, see note 19, above), now £2 2s. 0d., but two years' rent received, so increase of £4 4s. 0d.

21   Additional item (£2 2s. 0d.) for rent of garden given to head schoolmaster.

22   One item untenanted, so decrease of £2 5s. 0d. Next year to be £3 3s. 0d.

23   See note 22 above.

24   Items same as before but no separate heading for No. 14c.

25   One item reduced by 14s. 0d. to 8s. 0d.

26   One house (£1 15s. 0d.) not let this year.

27   Marginal note that two tenements, formerly one house, were unoccupied this year but now let for £4 per annum—so 1796–7 will show an increase of £2 5s. 0d. over the 1793–4 amount.

28   One item let at increased rent for last half of the year. Next year this item to be increased to £15 15s. 0d., £6 5s. 0d. above the 1795–6 figure.

29   In and after 1797–8 eight items are inserted in the middle of this section under a separate heading "Receipts for tithes on estates in Saint Mary's parish payable in kind". This followed the settlement of the Ruding tithe case in 1796, after which the corporation empowered the South Fields Committee to offer landowners leases of the tithes as this extra heading indicates (see R.B.L. no. 1200; also notes 47 and 48). In the first year of the arrangement £5 16s. 4d. of arrears is included in the total under this heading. In the summary this extra heading is treated as No. 16 although in actual fact it is placed in the middle of No. 15.

30   £5 16s. 4d. of arrears included last year now left out, but as one item not charged last year is now charged at £12 8s. 2d., the final total is £6 11s. 10d. more than last year.

31   Freake's Grounds were re-arranged at the same time as the South Fields; see note 4. As this was in the middle of a financial year the amount shown under this heading is the first half year's rent for Freake's Grounds at the old rate plus the other items normally under this heading, which reduced the usual figure by £41 11s. 0d. The second half year's rent is shown under the new heading for Freake's Ground Closes, No. 24.

32   Rent for part of Burgess Meadow increased by £2 18s. 6d. to £4 10s. 0d. Rent of land used to pay Nidd's gift to poor of Mountsorrel increased by £13 12s. 0d. to £55 12s. 0d. Two other items let at increased rent for the last half of the year account for the additional £6.

33 See note 32; the increased rent of the last two items now charged for the whole year, which accounts for the increase of £6.

34 Rent from land for Mr Nidd's gift to poor of Mountsorrel increased by 19s. 0d. to £56 11s. 0d.

35 Rent for Nidd's gift increased by 19s. 0d. to £57 10s. 0d.

36 Additional item for £20 rent for two houses in Causeway Lane belonging to St John's Hospital built with £50 of Mrs Cammack's bequest and £115 from sale of St John's Hospital garden towards rebuilding the town gaol. This item should presumably have been put under No. 21. The rent produced is paid out under Charitable Gifts; see No. 11 under payments.

37 Rent of item mentioned in note 36 reduced by £2 3s. 0d. to £17 17s. 0d.

38 Two additional items in this section of an extra levy for brickmaking in the South Fields; the two brickmakers concerned both paid at the rate of 2s. 0d. per thousand bricks, which accounts for the extra £55 14s. 0d.

39 Additional item of £12 for half year's rent of land in Belgrave Gate recently purchased. Income from levy on brickmaking in South Fields reduced by 14s. 0d.; see note 38.

40 The increase of 8s. 0d. is accounted for by 4,000 more bricks being made in the South Fields this year.

41 Item of £12 for half year's rent of land in Belgrave Gate recently purchased now crossed out. Income from levy on brick made in South Fields reduced by £13 8s. 0d.

42 Tithe for schoolmaster's house either 2s. 6d. or 3s. 0d.—varied annually.

43 Two additional items at end of this section which do not seem to have any connection with tithes. One is the interest on £1,100 stock in 3 per cent Bank Annuities; the other on interest of £400 due on mortgages of the Borough rates. Total increase in income from these is £53. The supered items among these tithe receipts are indicated and are the items mentioned in note 34 for 1765–71.

44 Tithe for schoolmaster's house not received because post was vacant.

45 Item for schoolmaster's house (2s. 6d.) included again; also an extra item of £56 4s. 6d. for a year's interest in the "new" 5 per cent Consolidated Bank Annuities. See note 43.

46 One item increased by 6d.

47 Increased items and amounts due to: (a) large number of Freedoms this year; (b) £1,709 4s. 0d. received as arrears of tithes due after the settlement of the Ruding tithe case. See R.B.L. nos. 1181, 1186, 1187, and 1200.

48 Reminder of arrears of tithes due after the settlement of the Ruding tithe case (£1,000) included in this amount. See note 47.

49 Several big items of expenditure, e.g. £456 10s. 0d., the "remainder" of Mr Lowdham's (Town Solicitor) bill in the Ruding tithe case; and £52 10s. 0d. for a piece of plate given to Mr Lowdham "as a token . . . of his services in the Tythe Cause". Also £400 subscribed by the Corporation to the Government Loyalty loan.

II

50   Includes £62 10s. 0d. for three instalments of income tax.

51   Includes a payment of £843 5s. 0d. towards the redemption of the land tax and one of £320 5s. 0d.—"Mr Serjeant Vaughan's Fee for assisting the Returning officers at the Election in December 1800[!] and his Clerk".

52   Five items which would normally be included under heading No. 4 are put at end of this section and include £600 paid to the Government Loyalty loan and £540 11s. 10d.—the balance of the Chamberlain's Accounts for 1795–6, not received by this year's Chamberlains. Among the normal tradesmen's bills is a payment to Mr Hall of £369 17s. 3d.

53   Additional item—allowance for tithe out of rent of herbage of St Mary's churchyard.

54   Some items altered—extra allowance paid for arrears of rent of previous year.

55   One item of 9s. 0d. halved in 1796–7 because house only occupied for half a year, now charged in full.

56   One item increased by 10d.; an additional item 8s. 8d. for a house purchased by the Corporation.

57   Three items crossed out account for decrease of 14s. 0d. Item for land tax on St Mary's fields is reduced from £50 10s. 0d. to £2 11s. 3d., and for land tax on Freake's Grounds from £7 1s. 8d. to £5 6s. 3d. This reduces the amount paid under this heading by £40 8s. 2d.

58   Additional payment of £20 to St John's Hospital. See note 36.

59   The post of usher of the Free Grammar School vacant this year, and part of the gift to the head usher being withheld, account for decrease of £9 5s. 4d. See R.B.L. nos. 1192, 1198, 1199, 1202, 1209, and 1215. The remaining deficiency of £2 3s. 0d. due to reduced rent from tenements belonging to St John's Hospital.

60   Payments to schoolmaster of £9 4s. 4d. restored (1s. 0d. less than in note 59 above because gift of Mrs Hobby reduced to £1 instead of £1 1s. 0d.). Rent of Leicester Forest land increased by £2 10s. 0d. to £37 10s. 0d.; Mr Nidd's gift increased by £13 12s. 0d. to £55 12s. 0d.

61   Rent of Leicester Forest land increased by £4 10s. 0d. to £42.

62   Gift of Mrs Hobby restored to £1 1s. 0d.—an increase of 1s. 0d.—see note 60; Mr Nidd's gift increased by 19s. 0d. to £56 11s. 0d.

63   Gift of Mr Nidd increased by 19s. 0d. to £57 10s. 0d.

64   One super formerly 1s. 9d. now 9d.

65   Two items (1s. 3d.) deleted. Also part of the section of tithes amounting to £24 6s. 6d., normally supered because of the agreement to take them in kind, is now omitted; see note 34 for 1765–71. The landowners and Corporation agreed on the leasing of the tithes and this is included under heading 16 of Receipts in this year.

66   Between the supers and arrears is a special section giving a list of purchasers of fee farm and chief rents. The persons listed purchased the rents before this year, but as the rents were listed as received in this year's receipts, they have also been included as payments to balance the accounts.

1800-6

482-3: 1 See note 1 for 1793–9.

2 Two items formerly charged 3s. 10d. now sold; the reduction of items and amounts under many of the headings this year is due to the large number of fee farm and chief rents sold in January 1800. See R.B.L. no. 1242.

3 One item of 10s. 0d. "given to St Margaret's Charity School".

4 Half year's rent charged at £33 per annum and half a year at the increased figure of £70.

5 Rent of Gosling Closes reduced because part taken away in enclosure of South Fields. See note 10.

6 Each of the items is charged half year's rent at the old rent and half at an increased rent.

7 Two years' increased rent of £1 13s. 4d. per annum received from the tenant of the Forest Closes by the Corporation who redeemed the land tax on these Closes. See note 51 for 1793–9.

8 See note 7 above.

9 One plot previously charged 15s. 2d. let for only half a year—thereafter "the Corporation took it and it is now planted with willows". Rent of Forest Closes increased by £7 2s. 8d. to £31.

10 The increased and varied amounts shown under Nos. 6a, 6b, 7, 8, and 9 from this year until 1806–7 are due to the re-arrangements and increase in rents involved by the enclosure of the South Fields. The enclosure act was obtained in June 1804, so the 14-year leases held by South Fields tenants from 12 February 1796 were terminated in February 1805. New temporary agreements were then entered into by the tenants, to cover the period from February 1805 until February 1806, when a more permanent arrangement of year-to-year leases was made. By February 1806, the dividing and fencing of the South Fields and Meadows was almost complete. The old system of division into farms and small plots was replaced by 97 small allotments, and in the 1805–6 accounts and subsequent ones, these allotments are numbered in their new order as "on the Plan made on the subdivision of the Fields". These alterations affect the arrangement of the accounts as follows:

1804–5 accounts. Small plots were charged a year's rent under the old agreement and half a year's rent under the new temporary agreement. *Farms and Meadows* were charged half a year's rent under the old agreement and one year's rent under the new temporary agreement.

1805–6 accounts show the new arrangement into small allotments for which half a year's rent is charged under the new permanent arrangement of year-to-year leases, i.e. from Lady Day 1806 to Michaelmas 1806.

1806–7 accounts are the first to show a complete year's rental under the new leases of the 97 plots. Bound into the front of this volume of accounts is a separate accounts book for expenses incurred in enclosing the South Fields. This expenditure account runs from March 1805 to July 1808 and is printed in full on pp. 412–41 of this volume.

11   Although plots are numbered up to 97, 14 of them are in the meadows, so come under Nos. 7 and 8. Under the main South Fields heading, which after enclosure covers Nos. 6a and b (seen note 10), some tenants have two or more plots, which accounts for there being only 65 items. The decreased amounts for this year under Nos. 6a, 6b, 7, 8, and 9 are due to only half a year's rent being charged; see note 10.

12   First full year's rent at final rates after enclosure; an additional item of £39 7s. 6d., as levy for plaster making on Close 34. Two allotments transferred, one to lease of Newark Mills, under No. 3, the other to lease of North Mills, under No. 10a.

13   One item charged £5 18s. 9d. last year when only half a year's rent charged is now only charged £11 7s. 6d. for a full year. Presumably this is a mistake and should be £11 17s. 6d.; the same figure is included in 1807–8 but corrected to £11 17s. 6d. in 1808–9.

14   Rent of one item increased from £7 to £12 per annum: half a year charged at the old rate, half at the new.

15   Rent of house mentioned in note 11 for 1793–9 decreased by £2 2s. 0d. to £8 8s. 0d.

16   One item formerly charged £8 8s. 0d. now £3 3s. 0d., which is rent for part of the year only, as this item was purchased by the tenant.

17   Rent of North Mills increased by £60 to £80; see note 12 above. Rent of North Mill Holmes increased for second half of year accounts for further increase of £2 10s. 0d. (£5 per annum).

18   Only half a year's rent (£25) charged for Bowling Green House because tenant died in the middle of the year.

19   Part of an item formerly charged 4s. 6d. now sold. Bowling Green House, charged £25 last year, "given up" this year on death of Alderman Chambers who had leased it. Note in 1808–9 accounts that house sold to Mr William Heyrick and garden to many different persons.

20   Only half year's rent charged on two items sold in the middle of the year accounts for drop of £7 17s. 6d.

21   Six years' increased rent of £2 14s. 7d. per annum received from the tenant of the Frolesworth land by the Corporation who redeemed the land tax on these closes.

22   See note 21.

23   Rent of Frolesworth land increased by £19 to £46 per annum; half of this year charged at the old rent, half at the new accounts for increases of £9 10s. 0d. Extra rent payable by tenant of this land since the redemption of the land tax by the Corporation ends at Lady Day 1807, so only half a year charged, and the full £2 14s. 7d. is discontinued in subsequent years.

24   One tenant died before rent due, so £3 10s. 9d. less than usual received.

25   One item and part of another, formerly charged £1 12s. 8d., now sold. Increase of £6 3s. 3d. on two other items.

26   A year and a half's rent charged on one item, which is thus increased by £18 19s. 0d. to £64 1s. 0d. Reason for the extra half year charged is not clear.

27   Item mentioned in note 26 now increased by £12 19s. 0d. to £77.

28 Same as last year but £6 8s. 6d. of arrears paid on one of the items sold.

29 One item normally £3 3s. 0d. only £1 11s. 6d. because for half a year only.

30 Same as last year, but £5 10s. 0d. of arrears paid on one of the items sold.

31 Rent of one item increased by £5 to £15.

32 One item and part of another, formerly charged 12s. 0d., now sold.

33 One item formerly included but no amount given is now charged 12s. 0d.; an additional item of 6s. 6d. for the tithes of Hall Meadow also included with an entry of 13s. 0d. for arrears of this item.

34 Three estates subdivided into nine items and most of the tithe charges increased.

35 Only half a year's rent charged for one item reduces total by £2 12s. 6d., but rent for another item increased in second half of year increases total by £3 12s. 6d.

36 Increased rent of £1 15s. 0d. per annum due from tenant of land used for Norris's gift to the Corporation who redeemed the land tax on this land.

37 Rent for Norris's gift increased by £2 5s. 0d. to £16.

38 See note 2.

39 Extra half year's rent of £3 14s. 3d. charged on part of Burgess Meadow, due to re-arrangement of South Fields and Meadows, after enclosure. See note 10.

40 Entry for rent of part of Burgess Meadow omitted, so reduces income by £11 2s. 9d.; further reduction of 6s. 0d. because an item formerly charged 6s. 0d. now sold. Rent of land for Nidd's charity increased by £6 5s. 0d. when rent increased in second part of the year. Rent of land for Haine's charity increased by £4 to £28.

41 Rent for Forest Closes increased by £10 per annum but half year still charged at old rent; rent of land for Nidd's charity charged a full year at the new rent (see note 38 receipts 1799–1806), so overall increase of £11 5s. 0d. Decrease of £1 on rent of Speechley's Close because a small part of it let separately.

42 Increase of £13 8s. 0d. due to 134,000 more bricks being made than previous year.

43 Decrease of £15 17s. 0d. due to 396,200 less bricks being made this year.

44 Although more bricks were made on the small plots in the South Fields this year, no amount is entered for plot 41, giving this reduction of 5s. 0d. An entry for plot 41 is continued, although apparently no bricks were made on it again until 1807–8.

45 66,200 less bricks made this year account for decrease of £6 12s. 6d.

46 Extra item of 5s. 0d. for rent of Soar Lane added on this page. 4,453 less bricks made account for overall decrease of amount.

47 Extra item included for half year's rent of a small piece of ground bought from Mr W. Heyrick, £1 11s. 6d. 41,135 more bricks made account for £4 2s. 6d. extra levied.

48 Two extra items: (*a*) £3 3s. 0d. rent for another part of the land purchased from Heyrick—see note 47, receipts 1799–1806—(also full year's rent of £3 3s. 0d. instead of only half year, charged on other part of this land); (*b*) £9 rent for tenement in Market Place, formerly included in

rent of North Mills. These items give overall increase of £13 14s. 6d., but income from levy on bricks made is reduced by £4 11s. 0d., so actual increase is £9 3s. 6d.

49   One item of income from interest on 3 per cent Consolidated Bank Annuities reduced by £14 1s. 3d., because during the year the capital for this was used to redeem the Land tax.

50   Item mentioned in note 49 above now omitted. The amount is further reduced by only half a year's dividend being received on £1,125 worth of 5 per cent stock.

51   Three and a half years' dividend received on £1,125 stock in new 5 per cent up to 5 January 1806, "soon after which time it was sold out". This increases amount received by £56 5s. 0d. to £84 7s. 6d.

52   The two items added to this section in 1794–5 (see note 43 for 1793–9) now discontinued.

53   Increased number of Freedoms (400), probably due to the election in December 1800, accounts for large total.

54   Receipts from Freedoms, which have previously been included in this section, now follow it with a separate heading—Freedoms.

55   Included is about £2,500 received for several houses in Sanvey Gate and Loseby Lane sold by the Corporation. Other land sold included part of Speechley's Close and land in the Meadows sold to the Union Canal Company. Also £1,234 received from the sale of stock in 5 per cent Consols. This money was raised towards purchasing the land tax and a fee farm rent payable on the Corporation estates, and for the South Fields enclosure expenses. See also note 57, and R.B.L. no. 1616.

56   1807 election accounts for large number of Freedoms.

57   An extra section included this year after Freedoms, for sales of the Horse Fair Garden. This money was used for the same purposes as the amounts mentioned in note 55 above.

58   Two items slightly altered account for increase of 3d.

59   The items normally covered by these headings are included but crossed out. Below them is a note that the £67 10s. 2d. was paid as half year's rent to the Receiver of the Duchy of Lancaster rents for these items, which are various tenements belonging to the Corporation and reserved to the Crown by the original grant from Elizabeth I. These payments are now redeemed by the purchase of the gross rent of £137 13s. 8d. An item under No. 4 gives the payment of £3,410 15s. 6d. to the Duchy for the purchase of these rents.

60   Further £405 4s. 8d. (see note 51 for 1793–9) paid towards redemption of the land tax.

61   Includes a further £265 15s. 5d. paid towards the redemption of the land tax. See notes 51 for 1793–9 and 60 for this period.

62   Includes an item for expenses of Mayor and Town Clerk to London "respecting the Inclosure of the South Fields" (£29 13s. 8d.).

63   Includes a payment of £700 to the Steward, on account of the enclosure.

64   Includes payment of £123 12s. 7d. to the Steward towards enclosure expenses.

65 See note 59 for payment to Duchy of Lancaster. Another payment to account for unusually large expenditure is £3,152 12s. 1d. to the Steward for expenses of subdividing the South Fields on enclosure. A note with this item indicates that details of these expenses are to be found in the Steward's Account, which the South Fields Committee had audited and allowed, and which was to be annexed to this volume and is printed in full on pp. 412–41 of this book. Other large payments this year are £379 to the Recorder, Serjeant Vaughan, for attendance at the 1807 election, and several purchases of land in or near the South Fields for the more convenient arranging of Corporation allotments and roads (about £660).

66 Includes an extra bill of £161 1s. 4d. from the Town Clerk, "arising out of the Inclosure for two years".

67 Includes four bills from William Heyrick, Town Clerk, apart from his normal general bill of £262; they are for extra business arising from Horse Fair Gardens sale (see note 57), from the purchase of the fee farm rent from the Duchy of Lancaster, and from the expenses of leases made on the enclosure. These bills amount to another £561. This section also includes two bills from Alderman Firmadge: for repairs to St Mary's chancel £350; another for planning and selling Horse Fair Garden and the houses there (see note 57), £316.

68 Includes two new items for Poor's Levies on St Mary's field, one at 2s. 0d. in the pound (£52 2s. 2d.), and the other at 2s. 3d. in the pound (£59 11s. 6d.).

69 Two items mentioned in note 68 now omitted.

70 Fifteen items deleted because of the redemption of the land tax, reducing amount by £27 10s. 4d. One item for £1 13s. 10d. added for land in Beadhouse Meadows, "omitted to be redeemed".

71 Two more items deleted, reducing amount allowed by £1 1s. 8d.; another item of 8s. 0d. included, so total reduction is 13s. 8d.

72 Two items deleted, giving reduction of 13s. 0d.

73 Four items amounting to 16s. 0d. omitted, one item of 11s. 0d. added.

74 Increased amount due to payment of arrears.

75 One item for £1 13s. 10d., and 17s. 0d. arrears included last year, now left out. Three additional items amounting to 16s. 0d. included; also 4s. 0d. arrears.

76 Three items amounting to 14s. 0d. omitted, and 4s. 0d. arrears omitted.

77 Although same amounts are paid, several items previously merged are separated. From this year onwards the recipients of the items are also indicated and where payments were made to several institutions and individuals out of one item, the amounts and recipients are given.

78 Income of Mr John Bent's gift to Bent's Hospital increased by £18 19s. 0d. to £64 1s. 0d. See note 26.

79 Income of Mr John Bent's gift to Bent's Hospital increased by £12 19s. 0d. to £77. See note 27.

80 Increased amount (£6 5s. 0d.) paid to Nidd's charity.

81 Gift from Leicester Forest land increased by £5 to £47. Nidd's gift in-

pp.
482-3
cont.

creased by £6 5s. 0d. to £70. Mrs Ward's gift reduced by 10s. 0d. to £2 10s. 0d.

82　Special section between supers and arrears as in previous year. See note 66 for 1793–9.

83　Note opposite page of arrears that after considering the practicability of enforcing payment of arrears the auditors decided that certain arrears (indicated by an asterisk) should be struck out. The total amount of £77 4s. 6d. is thus removed from the arrears to be transferred to the next Chamberlains, so that the amount of arrears transferred is in fact £72 4s. 5d.

pp.

1807-13

484-5:　1　This volume has been severely damaged by damp although most of the amounts are intact in the receipts section.

2　Full increased rent charged, plus 13s. 6d. for half year's rent of small piece of meadow, taken from No. 9.

3　Full year's increased rent charged for item mentioned in note 2.

4　Rent of Newarke Mills reduced by £20 to £50 because tenant died and widow had now taken over lease. Only half year's rent (13s. 6d.) now charged for the other item which in subsequent years is transferred to No. 5—Beadhouse Meadows.

5　Full increased rent charged. See note 6 for 1800–6.

6　Plot mentioned in note 9 for 1800–6 as planted with willows now omitted completely.

7　Rents increased at Lady Day 1811, so half year charged at old rate, half at new, gives increased amount.

8　Full year's increased rents charged and additional item (£2) transferred from No. 3.

9　Increased amount due to some allotments formerly ploughed being converted to grass and charged a higher rent. This changeover occurring in the middle of the year, half these amounts are at the old rate, half at the new, so next year's total will show a further increase. The number of items under this heading varied because leases of the South Fields allotments per person varied, although one person normally rented only one.

10　See note 9.

11　Decrease of £7 5s. 9d.—half a year's rent of plot 58, which was sold in the middle of the year. Also a decrease of £3 3s. 3d. in amount received from levy on kilns of plaster produced out of Close 34.

12　Not an accurate total because of badly damaged pages; see note 1. Several items increased or decreased by small amounts because of alterations to the line of the New Walk, and only half a year's rent charged for one item because plot sold. An additional item of £25 charged for Windmill and Mill Close.

13　Part of the late Windmill Close being included accounts for extra item; see note 57 for removal of windmill.

14　Windmill Close charged £1 7s. 0d. less, part being sold; another plot let to new tenant in the middle of the year has rent increased by £1 1s. 3d. for half the year. The levy on the number of kilns of plaster made from one close is £7 more than last year. These variations give this overall increase of £6 14s. 3d.

15 Increased rent charged on one item for complete year instead of half year (£1 1s. 3d.), but overall total reduced because rent of Windmill Close reduced by £3 10s. 0d. (part being sold) and item for levy on kilns of plaster obtained from South Fields (£18 last year) now moved to heading 23.

16 See note 13 for 1800–6.

17 Full year's rent paid for item mentioned in note 14 for 1800–6 gives increase of £2 10s. 0d., but another item for meadow beyond the Swan's Mill reduced by 13s. 6d. for half the year because a small part of it taken in with No. 3; see note 2. Reduction of another 13s. 6d. in 1808–9 when a full year's rent at the reduced rate is charged.

18 Full year's reduction of rent mentioned in note 17 above accounts for drop of 13s. 6d., but rent of Hall's Grange increased by £2 to £10 per annum.

19 From Lady Day 1811 rent of meadows beyond Swan's Mill increased from £7 10s. 0d. to £13 8s. 0d., so half year charged at old rent, half at new, gives increase of £2 19s. 0d. Extra item (£1 17s. 6d.) for year's rent of the Osier beds. Only part of a year's rent charged for another item (£2 0s. 2d. instead of £5 18s. 0d.) accounts for overall increase of 18s. 8d.

20 Extra item included last year (£1 17s. 6d.) and item only charged for part of last year (£2 0s. 2d.) both omitted, giving decrease of £3 17s. 8d. Full year's rent charged for meadow beyond Swan's Mill, however, gives increase of £2 19s. 0d., so overall decrease is only 18s. 8d.

21 See note 17 for 1800–6.

22 Rent of North Mills reduced by £10 because South Fields windmill which was formerly included in this item removed to Freake's Grounds, and the close in which it stood in the South Fields now "partly cut up for sale".

23 Item formerly charged £3 sold during this year, so only three quarters of a year's rent (£2 5s. 0d.) charged.

24 Item mentioned in note 23 sold accounts for decrease.

25 See note 20 for 1800–6.

26 Full year charged at new rent for Frolesworth land (£46) gives increase of £9 10s. 0d. £1 7s. 3d. extra rent payable by this tenant discontinued (see note 23 for 1800–6), and one item formerly charged 1s. 8d. now sold.

27 One item formerly charged 4s. 0d. now sold.

28 Half year's rent (£2 10s. 0d.) charged for house in Southgate Street sold during the year to the County Justices.

29 One item charged £2 10s. 0d. for half year's rent 1813–14 sold in that year, so no further charges.

30 Two items amalgamated to form one at a rent increased by £1 over last year. Two items formerly charged £2 6s. 8d. now sold.

31 An Orchard in All Saints' parish divided to make two items. The original

rent is increased from £6 to £16 per annum, but half a year charged at the old rent, half at the new, accounts for increase of £5. Half a year's rent (£3) also paid for the additional item. A full year's increased rent is now paid for the Forest Closes, giving a further increase of £5. (See note 41 for 1800–6.) A full year's decrease of £2 on rent of Speechley's Close reduces final total by £1.

32   Full year's increased rent charged on two items for which only half year's rent previously charged. See note 31.

33   Rent of land for Haine's gift increased from £28 to £40. Half year charged at old rent, half at new, accounts for increase.

34   Rent of land for Haine's gift charged a full year at increased rate. See note 33.

35   Rent of land for Tamworth's charity increased during the year by £33 15s. 0d. to £78. Half a year charged at the old figure, half at the new, gives this increase of £16 17s. 6d.

36   Bricks again being made on plot 41 accounts for increase in production, and increased amount of the levy on bricks. See note 44 for 1800–6.

37   Extra amount produced by brick levy accounts for increase.

38   Extra item from one of brickmakers (£7 7s. 0d.) for year's payment towards repairing road to brickyards. Overall decrease because smaller amount produced by brick levy.

39   Item for rent of Soar Lane (5s. 0d.) now deleted. Decrease in number of bricks made accounts for drop of £3 6s. 0d. in money raised by brick levy.

40   Increased total accounted for by extra income from brickmaking levy, because 77,000 more bricks produced this year.

41   One item for repairing roads to brickyards (£7 7s. 0d.) now omitted. Further decrease accounted for by decrease on brickmaking levy, because 189,125 less bricks made.

42   Two extra items included, levy on kilns of plaster, and on plaster stone, produced from South Fields, give increase of £20 8s. 0d. Further increase of £8 18s. 0d. in brick levy, because more bricks produced this year.

43   When the 14-year leases of the plots in the two Freake's Ground Closes expired on Lady Day 1810, the plots were leased on a year-to-year basis in the same way as the South Fields plots. The rents were increased at the same time, so half this year's rent is charged at the old rate, half at the new. The same number of plots were leased but are all listed together, not under the two closes as previously.

44   Full year charged at the new rent. See note 43.

45   Rent of one plot increased by £2 to £27 7s. 0d.

46   An additional section, No. 28, is inserted without heading. It contains four items—rents of an inn and three houses in High Cross Street purchased by the Corporation this year and charged for the half year in which they were in Corporation hands. Another house bought at the same time was unoccupied for this half year.

47   Full year's rent charged for four items mentioned in note 46, but one item reduced by £2; half year's rent charged for house previously unoccupied (£7). A further item at £10 rent is added to these.

48   Increased figure includes £14 5s. 0d. arrears of rent; full year's rent charged on one item gives further increase of £7, and an additional item of £8 is the rent of a shop recently purchased by the Corporation.

49   Total as last year without £14 5s. 0d. arrears.

50   One item normally charged £16 unoccupied three quarters of the year, so only charged £4.

51   First item (1s. 4d.) listed since 1801–2 as sold, now included again.

52   Includes £9 14s. 0d. for 313 square yards of land taken from Freake's Grounds and sold for road widening to the Trustees of the Ashby de la Zouch turnpike, at the rate of £150 per acre.

53   Extra section included as mentioned in note 75 of payments; headed "Received of the following persons the purchase monies, etc., for parts of the South Field etc., sold to them respectively, according to an account rendered by Mr Alderman Firmadge the agent for these sales". The page is divided into columns and gives the names of the purchasers, amount of purchase money, amount received of each for "Curb stone", and amount of interest received of each from the time of taking possession till payment of purchase money, and the total of these amounts.

54   Includes payment of £262 towards pavement of the new street in Horse Fair Garden, and £52 10s. 0d. towards making a street out of High Street into Freeschool Lane. Also £106 10s. 0d. for moving the windmill from the South Fields to Freake's Grounds, and a further £239 16s. 1d. for expenses relating to enclosure of the South Fields.

55   Includes £148 5s. 0d. for work on roads etc. in South Fields; £210 towards celebrating the fiftieth anniversary of the reign of George III; and an allowance of £105 to the last Mayor instead of a pipe of wine.

56   Includes £184 19s. 4d. for work done in South Fields and on occupation roads and altering the New Walk.

57   This volume severely damaged by damp; see note 1, receipts. In this payments section, all the page totals and some of the amounts for individual items are missing. Under No. 4 salary of Town Clerk increased from £5 to £200, although various extra items previously paid to him for special duties, amounting to £18 15s. 6d. are now discontinued. Other large payments are for work in the South Fields—£426 14s. 4d. (in two payments)—and at and near New Walk; £90 for the repaving of Market Street; £79 13s. 6d. for removing the windmill in St Mary's field.

58   Includes payment of £94 6s. 1d. for work done in South Fields and at occupation roads. Also £19 1s. 0d. for carriage of bank tokens from London "at the time of the great scarcity of silver", and a payment of £300 towards poor relief.

59   Unusually high expenditure accounted for by various payments including: £315 Recorder's fee as Counsel for Returning Officers at 1812 General Election; £1,160 repayment of loans; about £3,200 purchase money of houses (which have appeared in the rental since 1809–10); £627 for ground near New Walk, purchased to make new streets; £380 for kerb stones for the new streets "the greater part of which has been or

will be repaid by the purchasers" (see note 53); £74 for work done in the South Fields and on occupation roads.

60   Among payments are following items: £210 to poor of Leicester; £46 for a dinner for officers in the town at the time of a general peace (1814); £107 16s. 8d. for a piece of plate presented to William Heyrick, Town Clerk, on his retirement; £27 8s. 6d. expenses at the illumination of the Exchange on the general peace; and £94 7s. 3d. for work done in the South Fields and on the occupation roads.

61   Includes £274 19s. 9d. to William Bishop for the Corporation Feast in 1807. Also a wine merchant's bill for £124 9s. 8d.

62   Includes Town Clerk's general bill of £187 16s. 1d. and a bill from him for business done in connection with the purchase of houses in South-gate Street, and with the enclosure, a further £133 15s. 6d. See also note 57 for increase in Town Clerk's salary.

63   £1 1s. 10d., the levy formerly paid on Freake's Grounds, now crossed out but item added for Poor's Levies on the Willow Beds (3s. 4d.).

64   Two items of 4s. 0d. each crossed out, but two additional items, one of 4s. 0d., one of 4s. 9d., inserted.

65   Items formerly charged 8s. 9d. now deleted, but other items charged £1 8s. 0d. inserted, giving overall increase of 19s. 3d.

66   An arrear of 8s. 0d. not included this year, but an extra item of 4s. 0d.

67   Charity paid from Leicester Forest land increased by £5.

68   Extra item—gift of Mr John Cooper to St John's Hospital—accounts for increase of £2 4s. 9d. Also gift of Mrs Ward increased by 10s. 0d. to £3.

69   Gift of Earl of Huntingdon to Wigston's Hospital reduced by £1 to £9.

70   Tamworth's gift increased by £16 17s. 6d. to £61 2s. 6d.; extra item for £30 13s. 5d. for gift to the poor in Leicester, in coals.

71   Extra item for £1 11s. 2d. for seven further amounts supered.

72   Auditors' note on page opposite list of arrears that the arrears of rents marked by an asterisk were considered irrecoverable either by lapse of time or because the rents having been sold arrears that accumulated just before the sale could not be claimed: total amount thus lost £63 12s. 0d.

73   Letter from William Firmadge to William Heyrick, Town Clerk, pinned to the summary page. As William Firmadge will be away when the accounts of the Chamberlains are audited, he is sending a note of his receipts and payments during that period. See note 75 for more de-tails.

74   Inserted at end of this volume is a further letter and account from William Firmadge to the auditors, showing money received and paid by him during this year. See note 75.

75   Inserted at end of this volume is another letter and account from William Firmadge, similar to the one mentioned in notes 73 and 74. This account reiterates the other two so that it covers a period from 1810–13. At the end of the receipts section of the next year's accounts (1812–13) is a statement of amounts received for plots sold in the South Fields "accord-ing to an account rendered by Mr Alderman Firmadge, the Agent for these sales". A comparison of the names of purchasers of these plots and

pp.
484-5
cont.

the names listed in William Firmadge's accounts makes it clear that these accounts were connected with sales of South Fields land.

76 Summary includes note of arrears struck out, being considered irrecoverable. This reduces the amount of arrears to be transferred to the next Chamberlains from the figure shown to £53 11s. 8d.

pp.

1814-20

486-7: 1 Since the enclosure of the South Fields space has been left in the margin for the number of the plan of these plots in the Beadhouse Meadows, but nothing has been entered until this year, when these plots are distinguished by letters A to H inclusive and the letters L and N.

2 Seven plots formerly producing £71 6s. 6d. rent sold for building land.

3 Increased rent for race plot during half the year, and an extra item for "land which lay open for sale", give an increase of £24 3s. 6d. This is reduced to an overall increase of £18 11s. 6d. by reductions in the second half of the year of the rents of four plots (parts of two being added to the racecourse), amounting to £5 12s. 0d.

4 Full year's increased rent of race plot (£4 3s. 6d.) and additional item (£3) for rent of small plot open for sale give increase of £7 3s. 6d. Full year's reduced rents on plots 4, 7, 5, and 45 give decrease of £5 12s. 0d., and reduction of 9s. 0d. on plot 8 because part taken into racecourse gives decrease of £6 1s. 0d. Thus overall increase of £1 2s. 6d.

5 Two plots formerly held by one tenant now separated, but same rent charged.

6 Four plots taken from the end of this section and now included under No. 7 give decrease of £73 15s. 0d. Decreases also occur in rents of plots 7, 8, and 11 amounting to £7 0s. 8d., and a plot sold since last year accounts for further decrease of £3. Rents of racecourse plot and plots 24 and 25 (now separate items) are increased by a total of £8 12s. 3d. These re-arrangements give overall decrease of £75 3s. 5d.

7 Full year's increase of rents on plots 24 and 25 gives increase of £2 2s. 3d. Rent of plot 45 is decreased and half year paid at old, half at new, rate gives decrease of £4 16s. 11d., so overall decrease of £2 14s. 8d.

8 Four items transferred from No. 6 (see note 6) account for this increase.

9 Rent of one item (plot 97) increased by £4 9s. 6d. to £23 in middle of the year; half a year charged at the old rent, half at new, accounts for increase of £2 4s. 3d.

10 Full year's increased rent charged for plot 97 (see note 9) gives further increase of £2 4s. 3d.

11 Change of tenant for Saturday Market or Weekday Shambles gives increase of £80 in rent for that item for part of this year; full year's increase of £90 charged next year, making this item £200.

12 See note 11.

13 Rent of Bent's Hospital land in Enderby increased by £23 to £100.

14 One item, "a piece of ground . . . called the Mayors old Hall in Shambles Lane", formerly charged 3s. 4d., now bought by the Corporation.

15 Item formerly charged £15 15s. 0d. sold during this year, but half year's rent charged gives reduction of £7 17s. 6d.

16 Note on opposite page that tithes payable on Walter Ruding's estate (£136) are now payable as ten separate items.

17 The one item left under this heading sold during this year, but half year's rent charged gives this figure. No items in subsequent years.

18 Full year's increased rent charged on land for Tamworth's charity accounts for increase. See note 35 for 1807–13.

19 Rent of land for Norris's gift increased by £4 in the middle of the year, so half paid at old, half at new rent, gives increase of £2. Rent of land for Tamworth's gift and Haine's gift reduced by a total of £13 in the middle of the year, so half paid at old, half at new rent, gives decrease of £6 10s. 0d. These alterations account for the overall decrease of £4 10s. 0d.

20 See note 19. Full year's increased rent charged on land for Norris's gift, and full year's decreased rent charged on land for Tamworth's and Haine's gift, give this overall decrease.

21 Rent of Speechley's Close reduced by half because close sold during year and only half year's rent charged.

22 Speechley's Close, formerly charged £40 (£20 last charged), now sold.

23 No amount received for levy on plaster stone, but increase in number of bricks made (over 250,000 more) accounts for this increased amount.

24 Increased production of bricks and plaster stone gives increase of £11 19s. 0d. this year, but six kilns of plaster less gives decrease of £6, so overall increase is £5 19s. 0d.

25 Decreased production of bricks, plaster, and plaster stone accounts for decreased amount of levies for these products.

26 Item for rent given to St John's Hospital increased by 3s. 0d. to £18. Increased brick production gives further increase of £9 19s. 6d. to brick levy. Amount produced by levy on kilns of plaster reduced by £1. Overall increase of £9 2s. 6d.

27 Item for kilns of plaster and for plaster stone now entered as one item. Slight increase in number of bricks produced accounts for increase.

28 Decrease of £7 in levy on kilns of plaster produced, but increase of £33 4s. 6d. in brick levy.

29 Fall in production of brick and plaster—therefore decrease in amount raised from levy on these products.

30 Item mentioned in note 50 for 1807–13 charged full £16 this year.

31 Rent of house in Highcross Street reduced by £2 to £14 when tenant changed. Half a year paid at the old rate and a quarter at the new account for extra decrease this year.

32 See note 31.

33 Change of headmaster—rent for his house not varied between 2s. 0d. and 2s. 6d. as in previous years.

34 New section inserted with heading "Of following persons for rents of the gardens adjoining the New Walk". Several items occupied for only half the year to be charged in full next year. See notes 37 and 38.

35 Two items which were only charged for half a year and part of a year last year now increased to full year and three quarters of a year, giving an increase of £6 9s. 8d.

36 Two additional items for rent of stables purchased from the Duchy of Lancaster; the large amount is because the rent of these included 11 years of arrears for one item, six and a half years' arrears for the other.

37 Four items included of half year's rent of gardens, part of the South Fields.

38 Twelve items are for rent of gardens adjoining the New Walk,

39 Payments include the following: £86 5s. 1d. for work done in the South Fields and on the occupation roads; £210 subscription to sufferers in the "ever memorable battle of Waterloo"; £14 9s. 0d. for printing a sermon given by Rev. Mr Vaughan.

40 Payments include the following: £66 16s. 4d. for work done in the South Fields and roads; £333 8s. 5d. for Property Tax on Corporation property, up to April 1816, "when it ceased", and money received from Freedoms.

41 Payments include £103 12s. 11d. for work in South Fields and roads, and £40 10s. 0d. for 270 loads of gravel and carriage to the South Fields.

42 Payments include £76 3s. 10d. for work in South Fields and roads, and £8 15s. 0d. to Leicester soldiers and pensioners on the anniversary of the battle of Waterloo. Also £346 16s. 2d. allowed to South Fields tenants, the amount of the poor rates exceeding 8s. 0d. in the pound, i.e. 5s. 0d. in the pound. See R.B.L. no. 1428 for steward's report of tenant's difficulties because of excessive rates and rents.

43 Payments include: £132 5s. 11d. for work in South Fields and on occupation roads; £166 6s. 3d. allowance to South Fields tenants to pay poor rates exceeding 8s. 0d. in the pound—i.e. excess amount of 2s. 3d. in the pound. See note 42.

44 Payments include: £105 subscription to the Fever Institution; £120 towards purchase of old houses at "the bottom of Friar Lane for the improvement of South Gate Street"; £52 10s. 0d. towards the relief of framework-knitters; £337 15s. 4d. allowance to South Fields tenants to pay poor rates exceeding 8s. 0d. in the pound—i.e. excess amount 4s. 9d. in the pound; £44 3s. 0d. for chaise hire and expenses of deputation to London before last election.

45 Payments include: £175 17s. 0d. for piece of plate presented to the Recorder; £100 for relief of framework-knitters; £210 towards building a new church in St Margaret's parish.

46 Includes a bill of £55 14s. 6d. "for repairs of engines". Also £35 9s. 0d. to Samuel Deacon for musical instruments; these would be wind instruments for the Town Waits, recommended to be substituted for the violins they had been using, by an order of Hall for 26 August 1819. See R.B.L. nos. 1443 and 1450.

47 One item for 4s. 0d. omitted, because property this amount allowed on now sold.

48 Additional item of £1 12s. 0d. for two years' allowance of land tax on Nag's Head and houses adjoining.

pp.
486-7 49   One item of 4s. 0d. omitted; additional item mentioned in note 48 only
cont.   16s. 0d. this year, because only one year.

50   Extra item (4s. 0d.) included.

51   Additional item (4s. 0d.) included.

52   Extra item (4s. 0d.).

53   Gift of coals to Leicester poor reduced by £7 1s. 3d. to £23 12s. 2d., and
      Tamworth's gift increased by £16 17s. 6d. to £78, giving overall increase
      of £9 16s. 3d.

54   Tamworth's gift decreased by £4 to £74. Gift of the Earl of Huntingdon
      increased by £1 to £10, and gift of coals to poor of Leicester increased by
      2s. 0d.

55   Tamworth's gift decreased by £4; amount given to poor of Leicester in
      coals increased by 3s. 7d.

56   Gift of Bent's Hospital increased by £23 to £100 and gift to St John's
      Hospital by 3s. 0d. to £18. Gift of coals to Leicester poor decreased by
      £1 15s. 0d., so overall increase of £21 8s. 0d.

57   Gift of coals to poor of Leicester decreased by £5 10s. 5d.

58   Increase of £1 1s. 2d. in allowance of coals to poor of Leicester.

59   Gift of coals to poor of Leicester decreased by £3 8s. 11d.

60   Same amount, but 11 items formerly listed in two groups now separated
      into individual items.

61   Extra item of £12 in addition to usual items is an arrear for a fee farm
      rent which has been supered, as the Corporation has agreed to accept a
      smaller amount than the arrear in full settlement.

62   Two extra items for £13 7s. 6d. in addition to usual items; these are
      arrears supered because they were considered irrecoverable.

63   Note opposite list of arrears that the ones marked with an asterisk,
      amounting to £52 5s. 0d., are to be struck out, being considered irre-
      coverable. Thus the actual amount of arrears transferred to next
      Chamberlains is £77 0s. 9d.

pp.   **1821-3**
488-9: 1   One item formerly charged 6d. marked "supered"; an item of 1s. 9d.
                marked "unpaid".

2   Rent of Newarke Mills reduced, "the Mill being out of repair and useless
     nearly all the year".

3   Rent of five items reduced by a total of £4 14s. 6d.

4   Full year's reduced rent of plot 45, charged this year, gives this reduc-
     tion.

5   Rent of racecourse plot and plots 2 and 3 decreased in the middle of the
     year; half a year charged at the old rent and half at the new in each case
     accounts for decrease of £9 16s. 1d.

6   Various reductions in rent of several plots, the omission of plot 66, and
     plot 45 being unoccupied half the year give decrease of £39 2s. 11d.
     Plots 2 and 3 now let separately account for number of items being same
     as last year. Increase in rent of Windmill Close and half a year's increase
     on plot 38 reduce overall decrease by £14 17s. 6d. to £24 5s. 5d.

pp.
488-9
cont.

7   Rent of Meadows beyond Swan's Mill reduced by 13s. 0d.

8   Rent of North Mills reduced by £54 9s. 0d. to £15 11s. 0d. because they were under repair part of the year. Rent of the Saturday Market reduced by half (£100 instead of £200) because from the middle of this year the Corporation collected the rents of the Market themselves instead of leasing them. Amount of receipts included under heading 36—incidental receipts.

9   Rent of North Mills increased by £119 9s. 0d. to £135 because charged for a full year; item for rent of Saturday Market now entirely omitted because Corporation were managing it themselves, not leasing it to a tenant.

10   Marginal note that item of 5s. 0d. unpaid.

11   One item formerly charged 1s. 0d. now supered.

12   One item formerly charged 5s. 0d. now supered.

13   Marginal note that one item of 5s. 0d. unpaid.

14   One item and part of another (12s. 6d.) unpaid; another item (6d.) supered.

15   See note 16 for 1814–20; tithes payable on Walter Ruding's estate (£136) reduced to £71 4s. 0d. because part of his estate now sold to ten purchasers who each pay their appropriate proportion, totalling £64 18s. 2d. One item for 2s. 6d. is omitted because "now built upon and not tithable" (pencil note in 1819–20 accounts).

16   One item now divided into three and rent increased by £3 2s. 6d.; another item increased by £1 6s. 8d.

17   Four items increased by a total of £32 9s. 10d.; four other items deleted because they have been amalgamated into the above reduce the overall increase by £6 2s. 2d. to £26 7s. 8d.

18   Rent for Norris's gift decreased by £2 to £22, and rent for Haine's gift decreased by £3 to £32.

19   Rent for Norris's gift reduced by £2 to £20, and rent for Tamworth's gift reduced by £2 to £68.

20   Bricks made on one plot which changed tenants this year now charged 2s. 0d. per thousand, the same as those made on the other plot. (From 1812–13 to 1820–1 charged 2s. 6d. per thousand.) This, and the reduction in the number of bricks made, account for decrease of £16 15s. 0d.

21   Rise in production of bricks and kilns of plaster accounts for this increase.

22   One item for £1 supered, and another for 10s. 0d. unpaid. Increase in brick production, however, gives overall increase of £5 19s. 0d.

23   Rent of one plot increased by £15 11s. 0d. to £35, to include rent of the windmill moved from the North Mills to Freake's Ground.

24   Three items (£23) formerly in No. 36 (New Walk gardens) now in No. 27. These, and an item charged for half a year only (£6 instead of £8) when taken over by a new tenant, account for overall increase of £21.

25   Corporation purchased the Bull's Head and a house behind it during this year and this item is now included under this heading; half a year's rent of £75 received for it this year. An item charged for only half a year last year now paying full year's rent makes the further increase of £6.

KK

pp.
488-9 26 Two items formerly charged 12s. 7d. now supered.
cont. 27 2s. 0d. unpaid, and two items formerly charged 3s. 0d. now supered.

28 Two items (6s. 6d.) unpaid; one item formerly 1s. 2d. now supered.

29 One of extra items included last year now divided into two, and an additional item for cropping an untenanted garden. Amount much less because no arrears this year.

30 Amount reduced because items added in 1820–1 now transferred to No. 27 (see note 24), and several items reduced or occupied only part of the year.

31 Items unoccupied or charged only part of last year now paying full rent account for increase.

32 Larger amount because market receipts included; see note 8. An item of £48 11s. 0d. received for willow poles sold.

33 Includes £948 18s. 4d. from market receipts; also £500 borrowed from "the Sale fund".

34 Payments include: £82 3s. 4d. for gas lighting for Town Hall, Exchange, and Free School; £212 13s. 7d. for materials and labour for new market stalls; and £63 for half year's salary of Market Superintendent, appointed when Corporation took over the management of the Market instead of leasing it to a tenant. See note 8.

35 Payments include: £453 10s. 0d. for labourers' wages and other expenses in setting out market stalls, etc.; £263 5s. 0d. to various town officers on swearing in honorary freemen ("630 at 7s. 6d. each"); £15 10s. 0d. for postages of honorary freemen's letters.

36 Includes three bills from the Town Clerk totalling £496 11s. 2d.: a general bill, a bill for costs of action Jones *vs.* Gamble, and a bill for costs in the matter of the Paving and Lighting Bill.

37 Two items increased by 15s. 6d., but another two items in arrears (9s. 0d.), so overall increase of 6s. 6d.

38 One item reduced by 6d., one item of 5s. 0d. still in arrears, as last year.

39 One item of 5s. 0d. still in arrears as in two previous years, and another item (6s. 0d.) deleted.

40 Gift of coals to poor of Leicester increased by £5 17s. 5d.

41 Gift of coals to poor of Leicester decreased by 1s. 10d.

42 Part of Elkington's charity not paid and part of Haine's gift not claimed reduce total by £8 10s. 0d.; only half of Nidd's gift paid, the other half being kept for necessary improvements, gives decreases totalling another £35. An extra £3 7s. 6d. paid to Leicester poor in coals and an extra 1s. 2d. for an acquittance makes overall decrease £40 1s. 4d.

43 Ten items £2 3s. 3d. deleted; one item increased by 1s. 0d.

44 Note opposite this page that one item of £36 to be struck out as irrecoverable, so actual amount of arrears transferred to next Chamberlains is £70 16s. 5d.

pp.   **1824-30**

492-3: 1 This year and subsequent years until 1829 brief index of main headings on page preceding this heading. This amount is "on account of rent", not a full payment because mill under repair.

2 This amount on account of rent because mill under repair most of year.

3 Full rent charged.

4 Only half a year's rent (£15 10s. 0d.) received for some Forest Closes which were sold in middle of the year.

5 Further reduction of £15 10s. 0d. due to sale of Forest Closes. See note 4.

6 Although only half a year's rent (£23 10s. 0d. instead of £47) is charged for first three items, an extra £33 12s. 6d. is included for mowing grass on these meadows.

7 Plots 39, 40, 41, and 42 sold and decreased rents of plots 4, 43, and 45 and of land open for sale gives total reduction of £43 17s. 3d.

8 Rent of four plots increased by a total of £18, but part of plot 50 taken for sale, so rent reduced by £3 1s. 6d., giving overall increase of £14 18s. 6d.

9 Rent of two plots increased and half a year paid at the old rent, half at the new, gives increase of £3 14s. 0d. A further reduction of £3 1s. 6d. on plot 50, part of which was taken for sale last year, gives an overall increase of 12s. 6d.

10 Additional rent on three plots amounts to £3 14s. 0d. Half a year's rent only paid for plot 68 decreases total by £8 4s. 6d. One tenant previously holding five plots became insolvent and paid only a quarter's rent; these plots were let to three other tenants in the second half of the year, so only one quarter's rent, £6 7s. 5d., lost.

11 Rent of eight plots increased by £30 0s. 11d., but rent of six other plots decreased by £14 16s. 0d., so overall increase is £15 4s. 11d.

12 Rent of three plots increased by total of £4 14s. 6d.; rent of three other plots decreased by 12s. 0d., and of Windmill Close by £7 10s. 0d. because mill out of repair. Overall decrease of £4 7s. 6d.

13 Reduction of £11 13s. 6d. in rent of plot 81—the other half year's rent being lost by the insolvency of the tenant, William Chamberlain.

14 Reduction of £11 13s. 6d. in rent of one item last year now made up and increased by 6s. 6d. to £12.

15 One rent increased during second half of year.

16 Full year's increased rent on one item gives this increase.

17 Rent of one item decreased by 16s. 6d. with change of tenant during the year.

18 Increase of £99 10s. 4d. due to increased production of bricks. (Brick levy 2s. 6d. per thousand since 1824; 2s. 0d. before that date.)

19 Reduction of £80 10s. 8d. due to decrease in brick levy because less bricks produced.

20 Reduction of £28 8s. 11d. on levy of bricks and plaster made because less produced.

21 Reduction of £7 17s. 2d. on levy of bricks and plaster made because less produced.

22 Reduction of £55 8s. 0d. on levy of bricks and £7 on plaster levy—"no plaster burn't . . . on account of the falling in of the Pits".

23 Extra item (£6 7s. 6d.) for cropping of meadows beyond the Swans Mill, but tenant of that meadow only charged half year's rent (£6 7s. 6d.), so

total received for these same as usual. Increase of £8 13s. 0d. on brick levy—no plaster burned; see note 22.

24   Two items reduced.

25   Two items reduced by total of £1 16s. 6d.

26   Full year instead of half year's rent paid on one item accounts for increase.

27   Half year's rent (£2 10s. 9d.) of one item lost because tenant insolvent.

28   Half year's rent (£2 5s. 8d.) only paid for one item.

29   Two items formerly let for half year, now let for full year.

30   £25 14s. 3d. more from market receipts; half a year's increase on new buildings at the North Mills (£20).

31   Market receipts increased by £26 16s. 0d., and full year's increased rent of North Mills paid gives further increase of £20. Item for rent of the Sheep pens (£40) taken out of this section reduces overall increase to £6 16s. 0d. Marginal note that rent of Sheep pens kept in hand and included with an item for receipts from the New Market under No. 3c.

32   The fluctuations in this amount in this year and subsequent ones are due to variations in the market receipts, unless otherwise stated.

33   Rent of North Mills reduced because rent of windmill there (£7 10s. 9d.) deducted. Saturday Market receipts down by £20 19s. 9d.

34   Item for North Mills increased by £7 10s. 0d. to £175 because windmill included again, and Saturday Market receipts up by £14 14s. 3d.

35   Saturday Market receipts up by £19 19s. 5d.

36   Small reductions on two items and one item divided into two.

37   One item divided into two but amount reduced by £4 12s. 6d. Three other items increased by £3 16s. 8d., so overall reduction is 15s. 10d.

38   Decrease of £7 13s. 0d. because one item sold to Corporation and one item divided into three and the amount decreased. Three other extra items give increase of £3 19s. 6d., so overall decrease is £3 13s. 6d. Another item also divided into two but amount unchanged.

39   Part of Walter Ruding's estate sold, so this item divided between three owners, who are listed as one item; amounts divided but not increased.

40   This section considerably re-arranged owing to changes of ownership and divided into three main sections with sub-headings "Part of Rudings estate", "Part of Mitchell's tithe and Ruding's", and "Part of Pares' Land".

41   Rent of one close which changed tenants this year increased by 5s. 6d. for half the year.

42   Full year's increased rent paid on one item gives further increase of 5s. 6d. Rent of another close increased, half year paid at new rent, gives increase of £1 0s. 6d.

43   Full year's increased rent paid on one item gives further increase of £1 0s. 6d.

44   One item charged half year's increase of 5s. 6d. Rent of another close reduced by £15 because the windmill on it not occupied.

45   Below the heading is a note: "These closes have been intersected by the Rail Road and the rents and quantities are therefore varied". Half a year

was paid at the old rate for each close, half at the new. In five items the new rent is increased, in seven items decreased, and in one item the same; one item is only part of the year because of tenants' insolvency.

46   Two additional items (£7 16s. 10d.) of garden ground recently purchased. Charged part of year only.

47   Five extra items, mainly land in St Mary's parish, and items added last year now paying a full year's rent increase total by £131 13s. 2d. Receipts from the New Market (now including the Sheep pens—see note 31) give a further increase of £266 12s. 6d.

48   One item omitted and decrease in receipts of New Market and Sheep pens account for decrease of £20 19s. 7d. Increase of £3 on item formerly charged only half a year's rent gives overall decrease of £17 19s. 7d.

49   Additional item of £4 10s. 0d. for three quarters of a year's rent of recently purchased garden in Bowling Green Street. One item reduced by £1 and New Market receipts down by £20 18s. 2d.

50   One item charged a full year's increased rent (£1 10s. 0d. more). Rent of five other items reduced by £17 5s. 0d., and New Market receipts down by £14 17s. 8d.

51   Two items omitted, rent of five others decreased, and drop in receipts for New Market give total decrease of £96 6s. 3d. Three extra items and an increased rent of another reduce this by £19 15s. 0d., giving overall decrease by £76 11s. 3d.

52   Rent for Tamworth's charity reduced by £3 during second half of year.

53   Full year's reduction of rent for Tamworth's charity gives further decrease of £3. Rent for Bent's Hospital from Enderby land decreased by £41 because of insolvency of tenant.

54   Note at end that freemen admitted during late election will be brought into another year's account.

55   Includes £37 9s. 2d. from sale of willow poles, and £100 bequest from Miss Mary Cooper to St John's Hospital.

56   Includes £50 legacy from John Orton Garle to poor of St John's Hospital.

57   £3 10s. 8d. decrease in money given in coals for poor of Leicester. £17 10s. 0d. of Nidd's gift to poor of Mountsorrel retained. This £17 10s. 0d. with £35 retained from same gift in 1823–4 (see note 42 for 1821–3) and about £50 further were to be spent in "material improvements".

58   £5 0s. 4d. more of Nidd's charity paid than last year and Alderman Thomas Ludlam's gift increased by £8. This increase is reduced by the decrease of 15s. 0d. in the gift of coals to Leicester poor. Part of Nidd's charity used for draining and improving the estate as set out in an account opposite the entry for this gift.

59   Nidd's gift restored to original amount (£70), an increase of £12 9s. 8d., but gift of coals to Leicester poor decreased by 14s. 5d.

60   Extra item of £5—gift of Miss Mary Cooper to St John's Hospital. Gift of coals to Leicester poor increased by £10 12s. 0d.

61   £8 of Alderman Thomas Ludlam's gift not paid this year, and gift of coals to poor reduced by £10 0s. 7d.

62 Reductions in Tamworth's gift and Bent's gift amount to £11 3s. 0d. Gift of coals to poor increased by £2 11s. 0d. and a new item for gift of John Orton Garle to St John's Hospital gives an increase of £2 10s. 0d. Another extra item, Haine's charity, gives a further increase of £40 16s. 0d. Although Haine's charity was not a new one, it had not been claimed for many years, so the Corporation had an accumulation of £84 from it. A long note opposite the entry for this gift explains how the money was paid.

63 1s. 0d. more spent on shoes for cryer and beadle.

64 Extra item (£150) for salary of New Market superintendent.

65 Decrease of 1s. 0d. on amount spent on shoes for the cryer and beadle.

66 Extra item for a quarter's superannuation for a former bellman (£12 12s. 6d.), and library keeper's salary increased by 15s. 0d. Salary of superintendent of fairs and New Market reduced by £70.

67 Two items (£12 0s. 4d.) extra for bonds of Mayor and Chamberlains. Superannuation for a former bellman paid for whole year and the library keeper's salary increased, giving further increase of £9 2s. 6d.

68 Includes £150 paid to Town Clerk towards expenses incurred by the "Secret Committee appointed by the Hall respecting the approaching election".

69 Includes £200 paid to Town Clerk by order of the Secret Committee, and £165 11s. 6d. for the prosecution of rioters.

70 Includes £251 10s. 10d. for law bill for opposition to the Corporate Funds bill, and £207 11s. 8d. for law bill for opposition to the petition to Parliament against the Corporation.

71 Includes £126 19s. 4d. for piece of plate for George Harrison (see R.B.L. nos. 1566 and 1572). Also four bills of the Town Clerk on journeys and living expenses in London, concerned with the dispute with Robert Otway Cave, M.P., amounting to £681 6s. 2d.

72 Includes Town Clerk's bill for £150 for setting the Charter House papers and deeds in order and indexing the Hall books; also £250 "on account towards his bill for the Arbitration and other matters in the warfare with Mr Otway Cave".

73 Includes £254 17s. 4d. for Town Clerk's general bill, and £134 8s. 0d. for his special bill for "arranging all the old files and papers in the Town Clerk's chambers".

74 Heading changed to "Field Account".

1831-4

1 One item reduced by £1 6s. 0d.

2 Rent of one item reduced during half the year and full year's reduced rent on other item gives this decrease.

3 Full year's decrease on one item gives this reduction.

4 A re-arrangement of the Beadhouse Meadows appears to have taken place during this year. Most of the plots had new tenants with reduced rents and were renumbered according to "a new plan". An extra item is included with a marginal note that it is inserted with these plots instead

pp.
494-5
cont.

of under No. 1g as formerly. Only half a year's rent is charged for these items, presumably because of the re-arrangement taking place.

5   Items which paid half a year's rent last year now paying full year give increase of £21 10s. 0d. Another item reduced by £3 4s. 6d. and one omitted (£12) reduce overall increase to £6 5s. 6d.

6   Rent of several plots varied (three increased by total of £3 0s. 6d.; three decreased by £8 7s. 0d.). Gives overall decrease of £5 6s. 6d.

7   Rent of several plots varied (two increased by total of £1 9s. 0d.; two decreased and one omitted—giving decrease of £26 4s. 0d.). Gives overall decrease of £24 15s. 0d.

8   Two items reduced by £2 6s. 0d., but full year's increased rent paid on another plot (£30) gives overall increase of £27 14s. 0d.

9   Several plots reduced because parts of them taken for new lunatic asylum give total decrease of £16 19s. 6d.

10   Reductions of two items and increase in one give overall decrease of £1 18s. 6d.

11   Two items reduced by £10 2s. 0d., and another increased by 8s. 0d., give overall reduction of £9 14s. 0d.

12   Full year's rent instead of half year paid on one item accounts for increase.

13   Extra item for cropping meadow now omitted and one item transferred to No. 1c (see note 4) account for decrease of £12 15s. 0d. Increased brick and lime production gives increase of £17 10s. 3d. on the levy for these items, so overall increase of £4 15s. 3d.

14   Although increased brick production gives increase of £3 6s. 3d. in brick levy, no plaster burned this year so overall decrease of £4 13s. 9d.

15   Increased brick production gives this increase of £3 12s. 4d. on brick levy.

16   £198 13s. 10d. extra from brick levy, mainly because two additional entries for the previous year are also included.

17   One item of £4 5s. 2d. unpaid because of tenant's insolvency.

18   Item not paid last year (£4 5s. 2d.) now included again, and another item let for three quarters of year at increased rent give further increase of £1 7s. 8d.

19   One item reduced by £2 2s. 2d. because let for half a year only; another item charged for full year instead of three quarters gives increase of £3.

20   Amount for herbage of St Mary's churchyard (£3 5s. 0d.) omitted and drop of £9 12s. 4d. in the Saturday Market receipts account for decrease.

21   Decrease of £92 16s. 5d. in receipts of Saturday Market.

22   Increase of £88 18s. 1d. in receipts of Saturday Market.

23   Drop of £31 12s. 4d. in Saturday Market receipts.

24   Decrease of £1 8s. 3d. because three items omitted.

25   Four items reduced by total of £2 9s. 11d., and one item of 5s. 0d. omitted.

26   One item previously omitted now charged 16s. 3d., and another item increased by 3s. 2d. Two items omitted give decrease of £5 1s. 9d. Overall decrease of £4 2s. 4d.

27 Rent of one item increased by £5.

28 One item increased by £5.

29 Full year's rent paid at new rates mentioned in note 45 for 1824–30 accounts for further decreases.

30 Full year's increases now charged on one item (£4) and reduction of 5s. 0d. on one item give overall increase of £3 15s. 0d.

31 Rent of six items paid for full year instead of for half year gives increase of £50. Omission of an item, reduction in another, and in receipts from New Market reduce this to overall increase of £25 17s. 11d.

32 Rent of Bull's Head reduced during second half of year by £15, and receipts of New Market down by £46 9s. 9d.

33 Full year's reduced rent of Bull's Head gives further reduction of £15, and an item for 2s. 6d. omitted. Receipts of New Market up by £86 13s. 2d., giving overall increase of £71 10s. 8d.

34 Drop of £90 3s. 1d. in New Market receipts.

35 Rent of Bent's Hospital land at Enderby (£59) omitted.

36 Allowance for wood made to tenant of land for Haine's charity reduces total by £6 19s. 2d.

37 Rent of land for Haine's charity charged in full this year (see note 36) giving this increase.

38 This section of the accounts for this year has been much annotated; in many instances pencil notes have been later rewritten in red ink. The notes were apparently made in 1836 and 1837 by George Bown, the first Borough Accountant to the new Corporation. The content of the notes indicates that many of these fee farm rents had probably not been paid or even demanded for many years, and in some cases the property or its owners could not be traced.

39 6d. omitted from one item.

40 Includes £52 4s. 6d. for old materials in the Knighton Windmill.

41 Payment of Haine's charity omitted (£40 16s. 0d.); payment to Bent's Hospital omitted (£91 17s. 0d.), with note that accounts of this charity to be kept in a separate book; amount given in coals to poor decreased by £3 6s. 4d. This decrease of £135 19s. 4d. is reduced to £127 19s. 4d. by an increase of £8 in Alderman Thomas Ludlam's bequest.

42 Gift to poor of Leicester in coals increased by £2 10s. 7d.

43 Gift of coals to poor increased by 4s. 5d.

44 Gift of coals to poor of Leicester—no amount entered, so decrease of £25 8s. 2d.

45 Two extra items—bond to bankers of £7 0s. 2d. and allowance to organist of St George's church (£10).

46 Decrease of £12 15s. 2d. because three items omitted and another item for superannuation only paid for half a year because the pensioner died. Extra item of £10 for organist of St Nicholas' reduces this decrease to £2 15s. 2d.

47 Reduction in Recorder's salary, death of High Bailiff during the year, and death of a pensioner reduce total by £69. Two items left out last year now included again give overall decrease of £68 10s. 0d.

pp.
494-5
cont.

48   Includes £397 15s. 3d.—the Town Clerk's special bill for "registration etc., under the Reform Act".

49   Includes: £164 18s. 4d. for Town Clerk's special bill for business respecting registration under the Reform Act; £55 to the Recorder for attendances in reference to the Corporation Commissioners; two bills totalling £251 6s. 6d. for journeys to London relating to returns ordered by the House of Commons about Sir Thomas White's trust; £141 19s. 0d. on "other journies to London during 1833".

50   Includes two special bills from Town Clerk, totalling £518 16s. 6d. for business respecting registration under the Reform Act, and the Corporation Commissioners' enquiry.

51   Includes two special bills from Town Clerk, totalling £328 5s. 6d., for business relating to registration under the Reform Act, and in an action against a beerhouse keeper.

52   Includes bill for £3 3s. 0d. for "a new Clarionet for Town Waits", and £4 11s. 0d. for other instruments for Town Waits. Also two bills for advertising Corporation petitions against the Reform Bill in 1831 and 1832, in various newspapers (£38 15s. 7d.).

53   Individual items omitted—a note says "as per account produced".

	Community	*Mayoral*
1688	Thomas Simpson	Joseph Roberts
1689	Francis Churchman	Joseph Wilkins
1690	Samuel Woodland	Richard Townsend
1691	William Harris	Richard Weston
1692	Robert Lord	Thomas Hartshorn
1693	Arthur Noone	Robert Winfield
1694	Thomas Ayre	John Burdett
1695	Nicholas Allsopp	James Annis
1696	John Roberts	William Bent
1697	Richard Foxton	John Ward
1698	Joshua Goodrich	Matthew Fish
1699	George Bent	Thomas Bradley
1700	William Bunney	Edmund Johnson
1701	John Pares	Francis Lewin
1702	Thomas Hemsley	John Smalley
1703	Charles Tuffley	John Cooper
1704	John Denshire	William Goadby
1705	John Pratt	Robert Winfield
1706	Matthew Judd	William Hammond
1707	Roger Lee	William Topp
1708	Edward Palmer	Francis Coltman
1709	Humphrey Chapman	Thomas Ayre
1710	John Newton	John Ayre
1711	Thomas Gamble	Thomas Lambert
1712	Edward Bracebridge	Thomas Ludlam
1713	John Gutheridge	William Page
1714	Richard Jordan	Richard Weightman
1715	Simon Martin	Benjamin Gutheridge
1716	Augustine Heafford	Thomas Orme
1717	Richard Roberts	Robert Reynolds
1718	Henry Smith	John Payne
1719	Samuel Simpson	Edward Howkins
1720	John Earpe	Gabriel Newton
1721	Edward Noone	George Bent
1722	William Lewin	Joseph Bunney
1723	Henry Paine	Richard Goodall
1724	William Cook	Thomas Bass
1725	Thomas Johnson	William Lee
1726	John Willows	William Brushfield

	Community	*Mayoral*
1727	Joshua Goodrich	Edmund Ludlam
1728	John Noone	Edward Bates
1729	John Cartwright	Robert Winfield
1730	William Noone	John Newton
1731	Samuel Miles	Samuel Belton
1732	John Browne	Edmund Johnson
1733	Edward Veasey	Thomas Ludlam
1734	Richard Ogden	Thomas Phipps
1735	Saul Broadhurst	William Helmsley
1736	William Burstall	Joseph Denshire
1737	John Winter	Thomas Topp
1738	Edward Harris	John Smalley
1739	Thomas Davye	Thomas Marten
1740	Robert Lee	Samuel Simpson
1741	Joseph Tayler	Robert Hall
1742	Richard Denshire	William Brabson
1743	Thomas Chapman	Joseph Hall
1744	James Sismey	John Hammond
1745	William Higginson	Robert Belton
1746	Nicholas Throsby	John Westley
1747	Samuel Brown	Samuel Oliver
1748	Henry Gutheridge	Richard Beale
1749	Anthony Ward	John Wigley
1750	Clement Stretton	Joseph Chambers
1751	Joseph Treen	Thomas Thornton
1752	Richard Roberts	John Miles
1753	Hamlet Clark I	John Fisher
1754	John Cartwright	William Orton
1755	William Clarke	Thomas Stretton
1756	John Gamble	Cornelius Norton
1757	John Coxe Brown	William Holmes
1758	John Ward	Samuel Jordan
1759	Thomas Astle	Benjamin Sutton
1760	James Cooper	William Mason
1761	John Cooper	John Poynton
1762	Tyringham Palmer	William Stephens
1763	James Bates	Robert Peach
1764	John Pocklington	Samuel Woodford
1765	Richard Roberts Drake	John Gregory
1766	John Coleman	Joseph Johnson
1767	John Lewin	Henry Watchorn
1768	William Brown	William Simpson

	Community	*Mayoral*
1769	John Hartell	Thomas Phipps
1770	John Clarke	Samuel Topp
1771	William Taylor	Thomas Barwell
1772	Edward Price	William Oldham
1773	James Bishop	James Oldham
1774	Sampson Chapman	John Parsons
1775	William Astle	Hamlet Clark II
1776	Edward Sutton	Robert Dickinson
1777	Thomas Bass Oliver	Joseph Neal
1778	John Eames	Thomas Lockwood
1779	Joseph Burbidge	John Mansfield
1780	Benjamin Gregory	Thomas Anstey
1781	James Willey	Thomas Jeffcutt
1782	William Bellamy	William Bishop
1783	Edward Harris	John Bass Oliver
1784	Abel Webster	William Watts
1785	James Mallett	John Peter Allamand
1786	John Slater	John Saywell
1787	James Cooke	Thomas Peach
1788	Edmund Swinfen	William Parsons
1789	Thomas Chatwyn	Edward Marston
1790	John Freer	Thomas Wright
1791	Thomas Read	Samuel Clark
1792	William Firmadge	Samuel Towndrow
1793	John Stevenson	Mark Oliver
1794	John Reynolds	John Walker
1795	Thomas Copson	David Harris
1796	William Hall	James Cort
1797	Michael Miles	Robert Walker
1798	John Gregory	Charles Sansome
1799	John Jackson	Francis Burgess
1800	Thomas Sutton	Thomas Miller
1801	Robert Johnson	Joseph Dalby
1802	James Mallet, Jr	James Bankart
1803	John Sarson	Isaac Lovell
1804	William Heard	William Sulzer
1805	George Ireland	John Davenport
1806	Thomas Yates	John Adams
1807	Thomas Bryan	Thomas Cook
1808	William Thompson	James Burbidge
1809	Charles Coleman	Thomas Marston
1810	William Hill	Henry Wood, Jr

	Community	*Mayoral*
1811	John Higginson	Mansfield Gregory
1812	James Rawson, Jr	William Forrester
1813	William Howcutt	Richard Warner Wood
1814	John Higginson, Jr	Robert Kinton
1815	Samuel Robinson	Samuel Oliver
1816	John Brown	George Brushfield Hodges
1817	Richard Rawson	Benjamin Jackson
1818	Richard Hunter Bird	John Sargeant
1819	John Bosworth	John D. Jackson
1820	George Bellairs	William Kenworthy Walker
1821	William Hackett	Nicholas Higginson
1822	Samuel Kelly	Willoughby James Bishop
1823	William Wall	Henry Swann
1824	John Oldacre	Thomas Toone
1825	Joseph Fowler Bloomar	George Marston
1826	John Parsons	Joseph Wright
1827	Henry Heighton	William Gregory
1828	Robert Parr	John Moore
1829	Thomas Parsons	Henry Browne
1830	Edward Stavely	Richard Wright
1831	Isaac Abell	Thomas Miller
1832	John George White Young	Edward Rawson
1833	John Garle Brown	Benjamin Payne
1834	Henry Bonnett	Thomas Rawson

INDEX

Abbey, the, 38, 96, 144, 192; stones from, 103
Abbey Gate and Close, 57, 84, 105, 132, 179, 226, 240, 277, 331, 372
Abbey Meadows, race in, 50
Abbott, John, 303, 360; Michael, 135
Abell, Anthony, 23, 81, 130, 177, 224; Isaac, 367, 545; John, 333, 367; Joseph, 98, 126, 146; William, 256, 271, 294, 298, 307, 324, 367, 384; Widow, 315, 346, 367, 404; ——, 307, 369
Ab Kettleby, 225, 275
Abney, Dannett, 11, 32, 33, 50, 69 (Daniel), 90, 117, 139, 163, 185, 209, 233, 261, 282, 313, 339, 377; George, 7, 11, 66, 113, 159, 205; John, 54, 64, 79, 86, 94; Paul, 11, 69, 117, 163, 209, 261, 313; Philip, 5, 37, 50; Widow, 218, 269, 322, 383; ——, 102, 103, 294
Accounts: see under Chamberlains' Accounts
Acham's Gift, Anthony, 60, 85, 107, 133, 151, 180, 197, 227, 250, 278, 296, 332, 354, 372, 399, 498
Ackland, ——, 366, 398
Acquittances, 101
Adams, John, 304, 341, 351, 544; William, 333, 369
Adcock, John, 86; Thomas, 26, 28, 30, 88, 118, 119, 137, 182; William, 4, 63, 110, 156, 201, 253, 301, 374; ——, 143
Address: to Queen Anne, 101; to Prince Regent, 349, 350
Adkinson, Mary, 23
Admiral, the, 224
Advertising, 409; of Address to Prince Regent, 349; of Michaelmas Fair, 409
Agar, Thomas, 397; ——, 279, 335, 388
Alcock, ——, 118, 500
Aldermen, 49, 50; newly elected, 349, 407; see also Mayor and Aldermen
Aldridge, Charles, 397
Ale, 46, 50, 99, 149, 154; at Assizes, 147, 292; at Audit, 44; for Corporation, 43, 47, 48, 49, 50, 51, 100, 148, 193; drawing of, 46, 50, 99, 100; for feasts, 45, 46, 100; for notables, 46, 49, 100; for prisoners, 43; for soldiers, 47, 147; at Visitation of School, 42, 43, 100, 147, 193, 244, 292, 407; for workmen, 51, 52, 54, 422, 428, 429, 430
Alexander, Dr. 327
Allam, ——, 426, 431
Allamand, John Peter, 544
Allchurch, Philip, 169
Allen, J. 409; Robert, 174, 221, 273; Samuel, 394

Allexton: land at, 59, 85, 106, 133, 180, 190, 228, 332, 373, 508; tenant at, 51, 199
All Saints Church, 6, 32, 34, 91, 283, 340, 391; vicar of, 290, 346, 404
All Saints Churchyard, 65, 112, 140, 158, 186, 204, 234, 256, 307, 374
All Saints Parish, 13, 34, 58, 71, 90, 92, 105, 119, 139, 141, 166, 184, 186, 212, 227, 230, 232, 234, 240, 264, 277, 280, 282, 284, 316, 331, 337, 338, 341, 368, 379, 389, 390, 525; gifts to, 353, 354, 356, 398, 399, 401; Officers of, 6, 65, 193
Allsopp, Alsop, Nicholas, 542; Thomas, 63, 110, 156, 201, 218, 253, 301, 325, 373, 385; Widow, 17; ——, 83
Almey, Widow, 124, 171; see also Aumey
Almswomen, Trinity Hospital: gift to, 164, 210, 355, 400
Althorpe, Lord, 277, 331, 372
Anderson, John, vicar of St. Nicholas, 290; William, 143, 397; Widow, 188, 236
Andrews, Rev. Gerrard, 192, 262, 294, 314, 371; Henry, 43; James, 11; William, 127; ——, 45, 50, 210, 232, 241, 246, 248, 262, 282, 338, 352, 390
Andrews' Gift, 297, 356, 401, 510
Angel, the, 9, 31, 67, 89, 115, 137, 161, 183, 206, 231, 280, 337; audit at, 37, 38, 39, 40, 44, 449, 496, 497; dinner at, 44; feast at, 50; meeting at, 44
Angrave, Richard, 351
Anne, Queen: Address to, 101
Annis, Francis, 18, 21, 25, 37, 56, 94, 143, 152, 188; James, 9, 62, 65, 97, 112, 115, 158, 161, 203, 206, 256, 307, 542; Robert, 76, 83, 125, 132, 171, 178; ——, 67, 141
Anstey, 134
Anstey, Thomas, 544
Antill, John, 21
Applegate Street, 16, 33, 34, 74, 75, 91, 122, 123, 140, 169, 185, 186, 201, 211, 215, 216, 222, 233, 234, 253, 264, 267, 268, 273, 283, 301, 316, 320, 321, 327, 340, 341, 374, 379, 381, 382, 391
Apprenticing a boy: gifts for, 101, 291, 348, 356, 401, 406
Apreece, Sir Thomas, 312, 377
Archdeacon Lane, 19, 78, 126, 173, 220, 271, 324
Archer's Close, 35, 92, 141, 187, 235, 284, 341, 392
Archer's Collection, Mr. 14, 72, 120, 166, 213, 265, 317, 380, 447, 491

LL

MM*